Computational and Data Grids:

Principles, Applications, and Design

Nikolaos P. Preve
National Technical University of Athens, Greece

T0338732

Senior Editorial Director:	Kristin Klinger
Director of Book Publications:	Julia Mosemann
Editorial Director:	Lindsay Johnston
Acquisitions Editor:	Erika Carter
Development Editor:	Hannah Ablebeck
Production Editor:	Sean Woznicki
Typesetters:	Adrienne Freeland, Mackenzie Snader
Print Coordinator:	Jamie Snavely
Cover Design:	Nick Newcomer

Published in the United States of America by
Information Science Reference (an imprint of IGI Global)
701 E. Chocolate Avenue
Hershey PA 17033
Tel: 717-533-8845
Fax: 717-533-8661
E-mail: cust@igi-global.com
Web site: http://www.igi-global.com

Library of Congress Cataloging-in-Publication Data

Computational and data grids: principles, applications, and design / Nikolaos Preve, editor.
    p. cm.
  Includes bibliographical references and index.
  Summary: "This book provide relevant theoretical frameworks covering the latest empirical research findings in the area of grid computing, with a critical perspective bridging the gap between academia and the latest achievements of the computer industry"--Provided by publisher.
  ISBN 978-1-61350-113-9 (hardcover) -- ISBN 978-1-61350-114-6 (ebook) -- ISBN 978-1-61350-115-3 (print & perpetual access) 1. Computational grids (Computer systems) 2. Computer networks. I. Preve, Nikolaos, 1979-
  QA76.9.C58C65 2012
  004'.36--dc22
                                        2011009965

British Cataloguing in Publication Data
A Cataloguing in Publication record for this book is available from the British Library.

All work contributed to this book is new, previously-unpublished material. The views expressed in this book are those of the authors, but not necessarily of the publisher.

To Anastasia and Peter, who have always been trying to enlighten the obscure parts of my life by giving me the strength to cope with the difficulties of life

List of Reviewers

Harold Enrique Castro Barrera, *Universidad de los Andes, Colombia*
Edgar Eduardo Rosales Rosero, *Universidad de los Andes, Colombia*
Mario, José Villamizar Cano, *Universidad de los Andes, Colombia*
Mehdi Sheikhalishahi, *Universita' della Calabria Rende, Italy*
Mohamed El-Refaey, *EDC, Egypt*
Bhaskar Prasad Rimal, *Kookmin University, Seoul, Korea*
Florin Pop, *University Politehnica of Bucharest, Romania*
Alexandru Costan, *University Politehnica of Bucharest, Romania*
Roberto Barbera, *University of Catania, Italy*
Cevat Şener, *Middle Eastern Technical University, Turkey*
Philipp M. Glatz, *Graz University of Technology, Austria*
Antonios Gouglidis, *University of Macedonia, Greece*
Axel Tenschert, *High Performance Computing Center Stuttgart, Germany*
Vassiliki Pouli, *National Technical University of Athens, Greece*
Salvatore Distefano, *Università di Messina, Italy*
Francis Xavier Ochieng, *Jomo Kenyatta University of Agriculture and Technology, Kenya*
Mark Anderson, *Edge Hill University, UK*
Bastian Koller, *High Performance Computing Centre Stuttgart, Germany*
Andras Micsik, *MTA SZTAKI, Hungary*

Table of Contents

Section 1
Principles of Grid Infrastructures

Section 2
Grid Network Designs

Giuseppe Andronico, *Italian National Institute of Nuclear Physics, Italy*
Antun Balaž, *Institute of Physics of Belgrade, Serbia*
Tiwonge Msulira Banda, *Ubuntunet Alliance, Malawi*
Roberto Barbera, *Italian National Institute of Nuclear Physics, Italy*
Bruce Becker, *Meraka Institute, South Africa*
Subrata Chattopadhyay, *Centre for Development of Advanced Computing, India*
Gang Chen, *Institute of High Energy Physics, China*
Leandro N. Ciuffo, *Italian National Institute of Nuclear Physics, Italy & RNP, Brazil*
P. S. Dhekne, *Bhabha Atomic Research Centre, India*
Philippe Gavillet, *CETA-CIEMAT, Spain & CERN, Switzerland*
Salma Jalife, *CUDI, Mexico & CLARA, Uruguay*
John Wajanga Aron Kondoro, *Dar Es Salam Institute of Technology, Tanzania*
Simon C. Lin, *ASGC, Taiwan*
Bernard Marie Marechal, *CETA-CIEMAT, Spain & Universidade Federal de Rio de Janeiro, Brazil*
Alberto Masoni, *Italian National Institute of Nuclear Physics, Italy*
Ludek Matyska, *CESNET, Czech Republic*
Redouane Merrouch, *CNRST, Morocco*
Yannis Mitsos, *Greek Research and Technology Network, Greece*
Kai Nan, *Chinese Academy of Sciences, China*
Suhaimi Napis, *Universiti Putra Malaysia, Malaysia*
Salwa Nassar, *ERI, Egypt & NARSS, Egypt*
Marco Paganoni, *University of Milano Bicocca, Italy*
Ognjen Prnjat, *Greek Research and Technology Network, Greece*
Depei Qian, *Beihang University, China*
Sijin Qian, *Peking University, China*
Mario Reale, *GARR, Italy*
Federico Ruggieri, *Italian National Institute of Nuclear Physics, Italy*
Cevat Şener, *Middle Eastern Technical University, Turkey*
Dipak Singh, *ERNET, India*
Yousef Torman, *JUNET, Jordan*
Alex Voss, *University of St. Andrews, UK*
David West, *DANTE, UK*
Colin Wright, *Meraka Institute, South Africa*

Philipp M. Glatz, *Graz University of Technology, Austria*
Reinhold Weiss, *Graz University of Technology, Austria*

Section 3
Applications for Grid Computing

Preface

After a lot of development efforts, computer science led us undoubtedly to technological revolutions which have been characterized by the creation of the Internet that influences the future of this science. The next revolutionary step occurred by the necessity of the creation of a new computer network, when researchers realized that the computer resources are underutilized. Researchers observed that machines spent much time idly waiting for human input increasing their cost through their underutilization. Their efforts concentrated in maximizing the utilization of computational resources, decreasing at the same time the cost of the computers. A vision for a new computer infrastructure was born at Argonne National Laboratory. The fathers of this unforeseen revolution were Foster & Kesselman (1997). They coined a new term about this new infrastructure which changed the way we think about computer science while they aimed to make computational resources available and efficient to everyone, like electricity.

The term *Grid* has defined a new scientific area of computing which combines heterogeneous, geographically dispersed computer resources that are a part of various administrative domains and cooperate in order to reach a common goal. The most significant achievement of this new emerged infrastructure is the resources sharing across various loosely coupled networks. The outcome of resources sharing combination with uniqueness characteristics, such as adaptability, applicability, flexibility, interoperability, usability, and scalability, is a grid network which provides us with vast computational and storage capabilities.

A strong basis of the definition was given by the father of the grid, Foster (2002), who defined a grid network with the following requirements. A grid system should have resources coordination that are not subject to centralized control, the usability of standard, open, general-purpose protocols and interfaces, while it delivers nontrivial Quality-of-Service (QoS). The integration between distributed and heterogeneous resources is achieved through a middleware. The usage of a grid middleware is compulsory because it acts as a mediator layer providing a consistent and homogeneous access to resources managed locally with different syntax and access methods.

Grid systems achieved with great success to integrate, virtualize, and manage resources and services within distributed, heterogeneous, and dynamic Virtual Organizations (VOs). The necessity of grid is obvious in scientific communities which demand to access vast computational resources in order to be able to run high-performance applications. For this reason scientific applications were and are the most important exploiter of grids. However, the continuous increasing demand in specific grid infrastructures from commercial organizations and scientific communities led us to categorize a grid network. There are classes which define a grid network. We have Access Grids, Bio Grids, Computational Grids, Cluster Grids, Campus Grids, Commodity Grids, Data Grids, Knowledge Grids, Science Grids, Sensor Grids, and Tera Grids. Although, a grid network must be evaluated according to the running applications, business value, and scientific results that it delivers, not its architecture (Foster, 2002).

The grid computing is a newly developed technology among similar large-scale computer implementations, such as cloud computing, distributed and parallel computing, Internet, peer-to-peer networks, and virtualization technologies. The benefits of grid technology and its most important achievements are addressed below. These achievements have comprised the basis for next generation computer systems indicating a way for building future network infrastructures.

- A user utilizes a grid infrastructure without having to investigate the underlying architecture while he is able to manage his owned resources
- A grid uses the underutilized processing power, maximizing the available resources of the system and minimizing the execution time of a large job
- Complex resources demanding scientific problems can be solved with parallel CPU and data storage capacities that grid provides
- The computational resources are allocated, aggregated, and collaborated in a grid environment besides its heterogeneity, geographical dispersion, and administrative variety.
- A grid does not share the data between users but it permits common access to them (many-to-many sharing)
- Grid removes the barriers to virtualization technologies expending its capabilities

Nowadays, grids are not a common good for scientific communities only. An increasing interest in this technology has begun from large companies and organizations which focus on grid implementations. This revolution influenced the processor industry which built multithreaded processors based on grid technology assisting to be spread faster. Thus, a need for global standardization occurred ensuring the interoperability of grid infrastructures. After seven years of life the Open Grid Forum (OGF), previously the Global Grid Forum (GGF), is beginning to produce standards that meet the needs of the community and that are being adopted by commercial and open source software providers (Smith et al. 2009). Also, we have to mention some of the most important organizations that made efforts focusing on the development of grid computing with multiple contributions on the field. These are World Wide Web Consortium (W3C), Organization for the Advancement of Structured Information Standards (OASIS), Web Service Interoperability Organization (WS-I), Distributed Management Task Force (DMTF), Internet2, Liberty Alliance, and Enterprise Grid Alliance (EGA).

Grid is a technology that is going to become prominent in the next few years, expecting a wide proliferation in its use. Grid computing infrastructures are already accessible to many users covering their needs in computer resources. Nevertheless, grids will have an ever increasing role comprising a basis in the field of scientific research. It is therefore necessary a thorough understanding of principles, designs, and applications in a grid environment. After so many innovations and achievements in various scientific areas all these years, we are still wondering and carrying opinions and thoughts that computer science is a future science. So, several achievements in computer science such as grid have opened the door for a different future of this scientific area.

BOOK ORGANIZATION

This book is organized into three major sections containing 15 chapters and dealing respectively with principles, designs, and applications of grid computing. A brief description of each chapter follows.

Section 1: Principles include aspects, challenges and trends in grid computing.

Chapter 1 presents a representative set of projects focused on providing solutions for the use of idle computing cycles aiming to provide an overview of the main implementations and research on Desktop Grids and Volunteer Computing Systems (DGVCSs). This chapter also introduces a new taxonomy model dealing with the occurred issues. A discussion aims to the evolution stages, main implementations and research on DGVCSs and through the presented analysis it succeeds in identifying the main characteristics of DGVCSs.

Chapter 2 introduces a new buzzword computing paradigm focusing on the infrastructure. Having the proposed paradigm as a basis, the authors analyze various technologies around it in software and networking domains that are involved in complementing grid and cloud computing. Through the presentation of a new architecture which is mainly inspired by Infrastructure as a Service (IaaS) model to address grid and cloud complementarity approach, they analyze and evaluate current practices and services that are applied in these infrastructures defining new research topics that address this issue.

Chapter 3 extends the discussion through an analysis of the key concepts of Service Oriented Architecture (SOA), grid, and cloud computing demonstrating a tight relation between these concepts in order to develop a highly scalable application system. This chapter also presents a coverage approach for concepts of Web 2.0 related to grid computing and on-demand enterprise model.

Chapter 4 focuses on the resource heterogeneity, the size and number of tasks, the variety of policies, and the high number of constraints which are some of the main characteristics that contribute to this complexity. This chapter presents a holistic approach of the necessity and the requirements of scheduling mechanism in grid systems while it offers a critical analysis of existing methods and algorithms, scheduling policies, fault tolerance in scheduling process, scheduling models and algorithms and optimization techniques for scheduling in grid environments.

Chapter 5 deals with grid infrastructures that produce enormous size of data which should be supported by scalable data storage and management strategies. This chapter addresses the key issues of data handling in grid environments and deals with the upcoming challenges in distributed storage systems. It also presents how existing solutions cope with these high requirements while it indicates their advantages and limitations.

Section 2: Designs focuses on different grid architectures and methodologies for different grid networks.

Chapter 6 introduces the necessity of world standard platforms in order to support e-Science and foster virtual research communities. A description of the developed e-Infrastructure around several countries is follows with an outlook on the very important issue of their long term sustainability.

Chapter 7 focuses on resource aware sensor grid middleware. This chapter investigates misconceptions in design, simulation, test and measurement that need to be overcome or be considered for successful implementations. A framework for design, simulation, and testing is developed in sensor grids. This chapter also presents an approach that implements performance optimizations and resource awareness with a minimum of negative impact from mutual side effects.

Chapter 8 develops an access control model for grid computer environments. The authors analyze the Role Based Access Control (RBAC) and Usage Control ABC (UCON$_{ABC}$) models demonstrating how the theoretical access control models and architectures are implemented into mechanisms. They also provide a comparison between the examined access control models and mechanisms, aiming to expose the different aspects of grid access control.

Chapter 9 examines the challenge of ontology matching in a grid environment in a scalable and high efficient way. An approach for ontology matching based on the requirements of grid architecture is introduced in this chapter while discussing and focusing on related approaches and tools.

Section 3: Applications dealing with emerged issues in the field of various grid implementations.

Chapter 10 faces the issue of security in grid computing introducing an approach to security in grid environments that are built using Service Oriented Architecture (SOA) technologies. This chapter also describes in-depth the security protocols and technologies that have applied on a Web Service (WS) based grid environment.

Chapter 11 proposes a lightweight cryptography algorithm combining the strong and highly secure asymmetric cryptography technique (RSA) with the symmetric cryptography (AES) protecting data and files in a grid environment. In this chapter the authors propose an algorithm named, Secure Storage System (GS^3), and it has been implemented on top of the Grid File Access Library (GFAL) of the gLite middleware in order to provide a file system service with cryptography capability and POSIX interface. A detailed description of GS^3 about its implementation is given based on a well developed evaluation performance.

Chapter 12 extends the usage of grid computing in other scientific fields such as meteorology in order to predict and assess wind and solar resources. This chapter develops an approach based on utilization of remote grid computing essentially undertaking grid computing remotely by accessing the grid computers in host countries with more advanced Information Technology infrastructure.

Chapter 13 describes the implementation of grid services and defines an approach to a development framework which would enable the creation of agile services. The authors present an alternative solution which adopts aspect-oriented programming as a core component in the framework and they achieve to develop agile services in a grid environment focusing on teleworking.

Chapter 14 addresses the requirements of academic end users, the grid paradigm and underlines past developed technologies based on the needs of potential business end users. The authors demonstrate that the trend has changed towards the use of grid technologies within electronic business. This chapter also focuses on the rationale behind the performed developments through the presentation results of the BREIN project. Moreover, a generic solution is presented and it is applied to a variety of distinct application areas.

Chapter 15 presents the potentialities of a new innovative Internet QoS (Quality-of-Service) architecture known as Flow-Aware Networking (FAN). Besides, the QoS provisioning for grid computing, the authors also propose a new promising QoS paradigm as a potential solution to achieve better performance of FAN architecture over DS architecture.

BOOK OBJECTIVE

The vision of grid computing inspired many scientists to get actively involve in the field along these years developing and evolving this emerging technology. This book deals with computational and data grids. The key objective is to provide grid students, practitioners, professionals, professors and researchers with an integral vision of the topic.

The idea of writing this book came up after the increasing success and interest of scientific community on grid computing. So, this book aims to foster awareness of the essential ideas by exploring current and future developments in the grid area. Specifically, this book focuses on these areas that explore new methodologies, developments, deployments, and implementations that cover the latest research findings in the area of grid computing, making this mission even more complex. The book describes the state-of-the-art, innovative theoretical frameworks, advanced and successful implementations as well as the latest research findings in the area of grid computing.

The purpose of this book is to provide the reader with the latest research findings and new presented perspectives which are implemented in various grid implementations around the world. Moreover, it will motivate the reader to follow several different methodologies through the contents. The book delves into details of grids, guiding the reader through a collection of chapters dealing with key topics. By including in our book these characteristics, we target the book to readers who want to go deeper into this scientific field and gear students, practitioners, professionals, professors and researchers who have a basic understanding in grid computing. The reader will also have a working knowledge of how this technology is utilized in computer science and how grid computing is able to support other scientific fields. The presentation of current theories, implementations, applications and their impact on grid computing provide the reader with a strong basis for further exploration in this area. At the same time, the mixed-balanced book structure helps the reader to obtain a holistic approach of today's grid systems around the world.

The value of this book is focused on a compact coverage of grid computing technologies that are important to the reader to know today. It also aims to provide an essential knowledge, comprising the foundations for further development and more in-depth education or specific skills in the scientific area of grid computing. Everyone who reads this book should walk away at least with the terminology and basic background to understand the trends that are currently taking place. This provides the reader with a foundation upon which to build his knowledge. The book may serve both as an introduction and as a technical reference familiarizing the readers with the subject and contributing to new advances in the field.

The book attracted the interest of academia and industry around the world in the area of grid computing. Undergraduate and graduate students, researchers, professors, system designers and programmers, and IT policy makers contributed in this book who are actively involved in the field. The book received 153 full chapter submissions and each submission received two or three blind double-reviews by at least two experts and independent reviewers. As a result, 27 chapter submissions were accepted, with an acceptance rate 17.6%. In this book 15 submissions, out of 27, are included.

REFERENCES

Foster, I. (2002). What is the grid? A three point checklist. *GRIDtoday, 1*(6), 22–25.

Foster, I. & Kesselman, C. (1997). Argonne workshop explores construction of a national computational grid. *Parallel Computing Research Newsletter, 5*(4).

Smith, C., Kielman, T., Newhouse, S., & Humphrey, M. (2009). The HPC basic profile and SAGA: Standardizing compute grid access in the open grid forum. *Concurrency and Computation, 21*(8), 1053–1068. doi:10.1002/cpe.1408

Acknowledgment

This book brought memories in my mind from my early student years in the School of Electrical and Computer Engineering of the National Technical University of Athens when my journey in this science began.

"As you set out for Ithaca, pray that the road is long, full of adventure, full of lore…And if you find her poor, Ithaca will not have fooled you. Wise as you have become, with so much experience, you must already have understood what Ithacas mean." — Constantine P. Cavafy (1911)

A friend of mine recited to me the above poem in a discussion on our future plans in our lives and in this science. A lot of years have passed and a lot of things have changed since then. I have begun my acknowledgment with this poem because I want to address it to the readers of this book who had or still have the same feeling as me.

Every book requires months of preparation, and this book is no exception. The credit for this book goes first and foremost to the authors of each chapter. As editor, I would like to thank them from the bottom of my heart and to express my deepest appreciation to all the authors for their participation in this project, for their excellent contributions and their continuous interest in it. Making this kind of compilation is a huge responsibility which would not have been possible without the efforts and patience of the contributors. This book is a proof that when people work towards a common goal, they cannot be affected by distances, limitations, obstacles, discriminations, circumstances, various situations, different languages and cultures.

I would like to express my appreciation to Jan Travers, Vice President of IGI Global, for the given opportunity. Special thanks also to all the staff at IGI Global for their continuous encouragement and support on this project throughout the whole process, from the inception of the initial idea to the final publication. In particular, to Kristin M. Klinger, Erica Carter, Christine Bufton, and Hannah Abelbeck. So, Christine and Hannah, please accept my warmest compliments for your excellent guidance and professional support. In IGI Global, you prove that you are an excellent publisher who knows about professionalism and cares for its people.

Finally, I would like to express my deepest gratitude to my family for the long evenings and weekends that I spent developing this book and I was not with them.

Nikolaos P. Preve
National Technical University of Athens, Greece

Section 1
Principles of Grid Infrastructures

Chapter 1
Desktop Grids and Volunteer Computing Systems

Harold Enrique Castro Barrera
Universidad de los Andes, Colombia

Edgar Eduardo Rosales Rosero
Universidad de los Andes, Colombia

Mario José Villamizar Cano
Universidad de los Andes, Colombia

ABSTRACT

Desktop Grids and Volunteer Computing Systems (DGVCSs) are approaches of distributed systems aimed at the provision of large scale computing infrastructures to support eScience project, by taking advantage of non-dedicated resources, most of them desktop computers presenting low levels of use. Those computers are available through Internet or Intranet environments, have partial availability, are highly heterogeneous, and are part of independent administrative domains. Currently, the idle computational capabilities of millions of volunteer distributed computing resources are exploited without affecting the quality of service perceived by the end users. This chapter presents a comprehensive state of the art of DGVCSs, providing a global picture of the main solutions and research trends in DGVCSs. It will discuss the evolution of such systems by analyzing representative examples. We identify the main characteristics for DGVCSs, and we introduce a new taxonomy to categorize these projects to make their study easier.

INTRODUCTION

Also known as volunteer computing (Sarmentwa, 2001) or public resources (Anderson, Cobb, Korpela, Lebofsky, & Werthimer, 2002) (SETI@ home, 2010), Desktop Grids and Volunteer Computing Systems (DGVCSs) are approximations of

the distributed computing which seek to maximize the efficient use of partially available computing resources. This includes the non exclusive use of computing resources, while ensuring that interactive users of those shared resources do not perceive any deterioration in the quality of service. Such strategies are intended to provide a computing infrastructure at a large scale, primarily used to support the development of e-science projects,

DOI: 10.4018/978-1-61350-113-9.ch001

without incurring into additional investments for the purchase and maintenance of hardware, physical space and controlled temperature environments of the traditional vertical growth dedicated infrastructures.

DGVCSs focus on the search for an efficient solution to the demand for computing capabilities to large scale, whose provision would be economically unviable through a centralized approach. This solution has focused on leveraging computing infrastructures, characterized by remaining under-utilized and whose capital and operational costs are borne by the users or donor organizations. These features have allowed the deployment of Internet scalable computing infrastructure, composed mainly by economic, heterogeneous, distributed and partially available computers whose added processing power has become in the order of the PetaFLOPS (Floating point Operations per Second) (Anderson & Fedak, 2006).

Taking into account the relevance of DGVCSs, this chapter presents a representative set of projects focused on providing solutions for the use of idle computing cycles. This chapter aims to provide an overview of the main implementations and research on DGVCSs. This discusses their evolution through the analysis of representative projects and proposes a new taxonomy to facilitate their study by identifying the main features available and desirable for DGVCSs. Then, we highlight new issues that should be addressed in future research and finally, we present the conclusions of the chapter.

DGVCSS STATE OF ART

This section provides a description of the most relevant DGVCSs projects, chronologically arranged and categorized by their contribution. We start with the first documented research project on DGVCSs and end with projects still under development.

DGVCSs over LANs

This category represents the origin of DGCVSs and is characterized by the use of pre-existing computational resources with low distribution and heterogeneity, connected by a Local Area Network (LAN). These conditions made experimenting with different strategies to use non dedicated resources easy, particularly by taking advantage of idle computational cycles. Within this category, we highlight two precursor projects: Worm (Shoch & Hupp, 1982) and Condor (Litzkow, Livny, & Mutka, 1988).

Worm Project

The Worm project is considered to be the first-distributed computing project able to use idle computing processing cycles. This project was proposed in 1978 by Xerox Palo Alto Research Center (PARC) and was intended to develop Worm applications, able to span machine boundaries and also replicate themselves in idle machines, moving processes between multiple machines connected over a LAN. Worm included mechanisms for the detection of idle machines and for process replication.

The main contribution of the Worm Project was laying the foundation for the use of not dedicated computing resources by the programming of opportunistic executions during night hours, when most computational resources arranged in Xerox Palo Alto could be considered idle. The test suite was made using an infrastructure with homogeneous characteristics, which included 100 Alto computers, each connected by an Ethernet LAN to file servers, boot servers and name resolution servers. The computational infrastructure used in the experiment is shown in Figure 1 (Adapted from Shoch and Hupp (1982)).

Because of the existence of accessible storage devices through the LAN, as well as dedicated storage servers, the design of the Worm programs originally discarded the possibility of using the

Figure 1. Worm's segment deployment

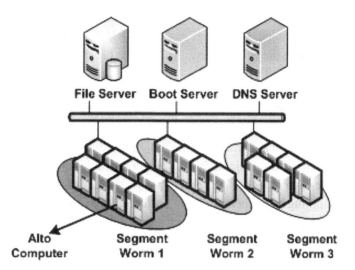

hard disks of the target machines. This character-istic allows diskless computers to be part of a Worm system and eventually leads to the consideration of writing on hard disks of the target machines as an extremely intrusive act.

Idle machine detection was implemented through a simple protocol that included the broadcast of a special package, making the target machines announcing their current status (idle or busy). Idle machines then received a request to boot from the network, loading their assigned Worm segment. A Worm program had several segments, each running on a different machine. The worm segments were able to communicate among themselves, so if a segment fails, they were able to locate another idle machine and run a backup segment there.

Condor Project

In 1988, the University of Wisconsin-Madison began the continuation of the project Remote-Unix (RU) (Livny, 1999) through the development of a specialized load management system for intensive computing tasks named Condor. This High Throughput Computing (HTC) project still remains in force and is aimed at the development,

implementation, deployment, and evaluation mechanisms and policies that support HTC in large sets of distributed computers including the efficient use of idle computing resources (Condor Project, 1993).

Like other batch queuing systems, Condor provides a mechanism to manage a work queue, policy planning, priority schemes, monitoring and resource management. This way, users can send to Condor an individual job or a set of jobs to be scheduled onto the available resources. Condor is responsible for placing the jobs in the work queue, choosing the most suitable resource to run a job based on a planning policy, executing jobs, monitoring their progress and finally informing the user about their completion.

As illustrated in Figure 2 (Adapted from Chapman et al. (2004)), the Condor architecture is based on the master/slave model, where the master component manages the execution of jobs onto a group of slave nodes. In order to better plan the job execution, the master is continuously monitoring its slaves and processing their constant updates, so it knows the current state of the jobs and of the whole cluster. Condor consists of five fundamental demons: Condor_master has as its basic function to simplify management, keeping running every Condor daemon on each machine belonging to the system. Condor_startd is responsible for representing and announcing a machine to the whole system. This includes the publication of the machine's capabilities as well as its usage policies. When Condor_startd is ready to run a job, it invokes Condor_starter, the component responsible for starting a job, monitoring their execution, detecting its completion and transferring the results to the machine that originally sent it. Condor_schedd acts as a manager in the work queue, facilitating handling basic operations such as adding, consulting and deleting jobs. This daemon is complemented by Condor_shadow which processes requests to transfer files, to log progress and to keep statistical reports of finished jobs. Condor_collector is a dynamic database of information about the status of the Condor daemons, resource run locations and resource requests made to the system. Finally, Condor Negotiator is responsible for the system brokerage, including the task of verifying compliance between job requirements and the available machines that make up the system. These last two components run exclusively on the master node.

Single-Purpose DGVCSs over Internet

This category is characterized by the emergence of single-purpose DGVCSs at Internet scale, with the ability to lever pre-existing, highly distributed and heterogeneous computing resources from independent administrative domains. These conditions made the aggregation of processing capabilities easy in the order of petaflops, but imposed restrictions on the size of the messages and files to transfer within the system. This category includes two main projects: GIMPS (Mersenne Research Inc., 2008) and SETI@home (Anderson et al., 2002).

GIMPS

The GIMPS (Great Internet Mersenne Prime Search) project is a distributed computing project dedicated to the search of Mersenne prime numbers, developed by Mersenne Research, Inc. GIMPS is currently licensed under the GNU GPL (General Public License). The project was founded in January 1996 and is considered as the first voluntary computing project in the world, i.e. the first resource donation project at Internet scale. Its main objective is the search for a special type of prime numbers that are especially useful for the development of fast encryption algorithms and for performance tests, such as those used in the manufacture of hardware (especially in processors circuits): the Mersenne primes.

One of the major contributions of GIMPS to the DGVCSs is the use of computing resources through the download and installation of a thin client that allows people to donate idle computing resources for the calculation of Mersennne primes on Windows, Linux, and Mac platforms. This client is developed in the C programming language and runs as a background process in the lowest available priority in the host operating system. Using this configuration ensures a minimal impact on the performance perceived by the owner of the shared resource during its concurrent execution.

The system architecture is based on a client/server model scalable to the Internet. As illustrated in Figure 3 (Adapted from Mersenne Research Inc. (2008)), the GIMPS client communicates with the centralized Prime.net server solely to obtain work and report results. The communication uses HTTP (HyperText Transfer Protocol), making use of lightweight messages, sending an average of a few hundred bytes every week. Such restrictions are justified by the need to operate on a highly distributed environment, whose communication infrastructure must be scalable and efficiently used.

The GIMPS client saves checkpoints every half hour, which makes this period the maximum

Figure 2. Condor architecture

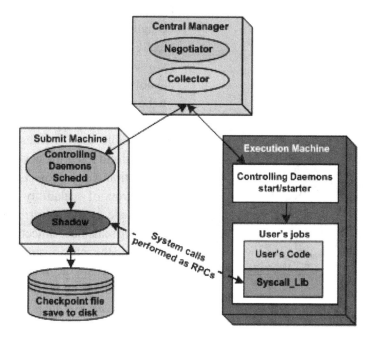

computational time lost unit in case of a failure. Given the distributed approach and the possibility of an unexpected client disconnection, the work distribution process is redundantly using at least two active clients. Although the original client only supports x86 architecture processors, multiple volunteers around the world have developed Mlucas (Mlucas, 2000), the multi-platform version of GIMPS.

SETI@home

The SETI@home project represented the next milestone in the contribution to the DGVCSs by allowing scalable computing of millions of resources in order to solve a single problem: SETI (Search for Extraterrestial Intelligence). The project began in the mid-1999 at the University of California, Berkeley and was credited as the project receiving the greatest computational processing time in history (University of California).

SETI@home focuses on shortwave radio signals processed from space. Such signals are not produced naturally, so a signal whose computational analysis completely dismisses the fact that its source corresponds to some kind of noise, produced by a human source (such as television, radio, satellite, radar, etc. workstations), would be considered as scientific evidence of the existence of extraterrestrial technology, and therefore, extraterrestrial intelligent life (Cullers, Linscott, & Oliver, 1985). A radio signal analysis process needs an enormous amount of computing capabilities to cover a broad spectrum with great sensitivity. In addition, signal analysis can be parallelized and does not require communication between clients, by which SETI@home efficiently uses the public resource computational model on the Internet.

Like GIMPS, SETI@home is based on a lightweight agent developed in the C++ programming language and currently supports nearly all existing operating systems; this was achieved thanks to the collaboration of volunteer developers around the world. SETI@home may run as a screensaver which includes statistical information associated with the opportunistic processing. As

Figure 3. GIMPS deployment

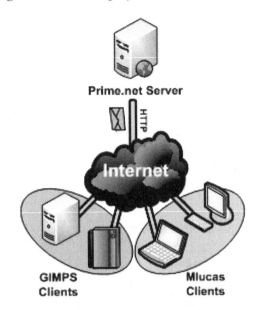

it is shown in Figure 4 (Adapted from Anderson et al. (2002)), the original architecture of SETI@home is an Internet scalable client/server model with direct dependency from a strong centralized server coordinating the work delivery to clients, while receiving their results through small messages communicated over HTTP.

The central server is responsible for a high redundant work distribution (at a double or triple level), not only to deal with unexpected disconnection from clients, but also to double-check the validity of the achieved results. This process allows discarding results produced in compromised machines (because of malicious users or hardware/software issues). Additionally, each client's result is automatically cached in the local hard disk to provide fault tolerance and high efficiency in an environment where clients may be frequently turned off.

One of the major contributions of SETI@home to DGVCSs was the organization of a strategy-award; rewarding the contribution of distinguished participants. This viral marketing strategy is a categorization of participants by the amount of computational processing contributed

to SETI@home, allowing multiple users grouping to enable the competition. This categorization became ranked worldwide, and can be found on the SETI@home official website. It is backed by a set of incentives that includes personalized acknowledgement emails and public recognition on the project's official website. Finally, SETI@home also created a virtual community with configurable user profiles that allows sharing technical and scientific news, forums and general information on the project.

In terms of scalability GIMPS and SETI@home made a major contribution to DGVCSs by proposing scalable architectures at the Internet level, making the setup of computing infrastructures at large scale and the donation of idle computing resources for millions of distributed users around the world easier. Another important contribution is the use of a lightweight, highly portable and easy to install agent, capable of running in a parallel and non-intrusive form, without diminishing the quality of service (QoS) perceived by users. This approach, based on a low-priority background process execution, is continually replicated by implementations that will be studied later.

General Purpose DGVCs over Internet

This category is characterized by the emergence of general purpose DGVCSs at Internet scale. Similar to the previous category, these DGVCSs have the ability to lever pre-existing, highly distributed and heterogeneous infrastructures from independent administrative domains, but here, solutions are not intended to solve a single problem. We include two main projects in this category: Distributed.net (Distributed.Net, 1997) and BOINC (Anderson, 2004).

Distributed.net

Distributed.net is a non-profit organization in charge of a project of the same name, founded

Figure 4. SETI@home deployment

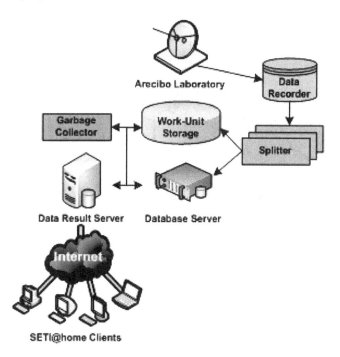

in 1997 under the GNU FPL (Freeware Public Licence). Its greatest contribution to the DGVCSs was proposing the first implementation of a general purpose distributed computing system in the world. The project has been oriented to break encryption algorithms and to search for Optimal Golomb Rulers (OGR)[1], that are especially useful for encoding and combinatorial theories, as well as for the sensor placement for x-ray crystallography and for the study of radio astronomy techniques. Both tasks are characterized by the intensive use of huge processing capabilities and by their natural distribution into non-dependent work units to generate results.

Like GIMPS and SETI@home, Distributed.net is based on the opportunistic execution of a thin client that was developed in the C++ programming language (which currently supports Windows, Linux, Mac, Solaris, and AIX), although the same agent can also run as a Windows service. As illustrated in Figure 5 (Adapted from Distributed. Net (2000)), the system's architecture is based on a three tier client/server model (pyramid architecture) that allows the system to be highly scalable at the Internet level. The Distributed.net client communicates directly with a proxy server which is responsible for assigning the work units obtained from the Bobine centralized server. Once a client has processed a work unit, it delivers its results to its proxy server, which in turn sends them to the main centralized server.

The architecture provides a basic fault tolerance mechanism to allow customers to use round-robin DNS to locate proxy servers, whenever the server originally assigned is no longer available. It considers an optional four layer scheme that uses personalized proxy servers (pproxies) between proxies and clients in order to allow the distribution of work and result reception through firewalls. Communication processes are supported over HTTP and are based on the use of light messages.

Figure 5. Distributed.net deployment architecture

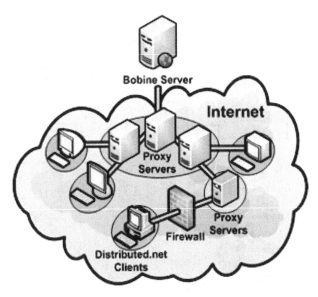

BOINC

The next advantage in this category is represented by BOINC (Berkeley Open Infrastructure for Network Computing) which began in 2002 as an effective response to the shortcomings identified in SETI@home, particularly with regard to improving the security scheme to prevent malicious users, the overall dependency from a central server and the exclusive use of an infrastructure built to solve one single problem. BOINC aims to use computing resources for the development of multipurpose scientific projects, hiding the complexities associated with the creation, operation and maintenance of public-resource computing projects by providing a set of tools for building a secure infrastructure with autonomous domain administrative servers and high scalability on the Internet.

Like GIMPS, Distributed.net and SETI@home, BOINC uses a lightweight agent which runs on every client. However, BOINC's agent contribution differs from all the previous approaches, because the agent is not really responsible for consuming idle computing resources in an opportunistic way, but it acts as a simple interface between the BOINC server and one or more scientific applications running on the client. Thus, the agent consumes a minimum amount of computing resources and provides the scientific application user (through an API developed in C++) with the conditions for using idle computing resources, hiding its complexity. The agent includes a local and a Web management interface for BOINC volunteers, who can set mode and use quota of their computing resource share, verify their participation statistics and select the scientific projects to which they want to contribute their resources as well as the quotas allocated to them. The Web interface allows BOINC client installation and setting preferences on multiple clients bound to a voluntary user account.

Hiding the complexities associated with public computing resources includes the administration of the communications that occur between the clients and the server. This administration makes the development of communication protocols unnecessary for the implementation and execution of scientific applications. BOINC manages the database system interaction layer (MySQL), so that a user project does not require the development of connection or query components on the

Figure 6. BOINC architecture

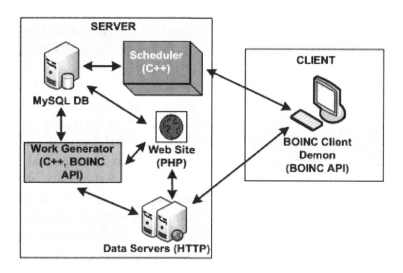

database. BOINC also manages the work distribution and results gathering efficiently and scalable, sometimes with a load of up to 10 million daily requests from its clients (Anderson, Korpela, & Walton, 2005).

As illustrated in Figure 6 (Adapted from Anderson (2004)), BOINC architecture is based on a client/server model Internet scalable, which gives clients the responsibility for requesting work units for scientific applications and for delivering results to the principal server. Work units have metadata about their processing, memory, disk space, software and deadline for result generation requirements.

The BOINC server has a component that maintains and updates the queue with works that will be sent to clients, getting work units from its database. It also has a transition component responsible for control distributed unit life cycle and the collection of results. This same component permanently checks the status of a work unit in order to make the result generation process efficient and to avoid malicious users.

For the latter, two techniques are used: the first is to send calculations with well-known results to a customer and determine the accuracy of the re-

turned calculation; if results are different the client is permanently blocked. The second technique is to make a high distribution of work units: making a redundant distribution, prevents results from a concentration of users, computers with similar hardware or software features, or close geographical regions. At the same time, BOINC implements preference mechanisms in the distribution scheme to send more work units to users categorized as reliable for their collaboration history. BOINC architecture is scalable and modular as it removes the restriction from a centralized server, allowing each of the components to be executed by one or more distributed server instances under the control of each project. This means that the only possible bottleneck in the infrastructure is the MySQL database system manager (Baldassari, Finkel, & Toth, 2006).

The project includes all viral marketing strategies originally implemented in SETI@home, but extends them in a layout for the participation of multiple projects. Additionally, it implements a better security mechanism to protect files containing credits, granted to users for their voluntary contribution of computing resources. BOINC has led the scalable DGVCSs Internet multipurpose approach, allowing the development of multidisciplinary projects, including research on climate prediction, astronomy and high energy physics as well as grid computing projects.

DGVCSs in Grid Computing Environments

This category is characterized by the appearance of DGVCSs specialized in grid computing projects of variable scalability. Similar to the previous category, these DGVCSs have the ability to lever pre-existing public resources. However, projects in this category involve the deployment of middleware and schedulers for work unit processing that requires large computational capacities, particularly large processing capabilities beyond those offered by a single administrative domain. This category includes five projects: Bayanihan Computing.NET (Sarmenta et al., 2002), Condor-G (Frey, Tannenbaum, Foster, Livny, & Tuecke, 2001), OurGrid (Brasileiro & Miranda, 2009), InteGrade (Goldchleger, Kon, Goldman, Finger, & Bezerra, 2004) and UnaGrid (Castro, Rosales, Villamizar, & Jiménez, 2010).

Bayanihan Computing.NET

Bayanihan appeared in 2001 as a generic framework for grid computing based on Microsoft.NET. Bayanihan implements volunteer computing by providing a *PoolService* Web service associated with computers that act as clients and providers (volunteers) of computing resources by using the generic architecture illustrated in Figure 7 (Adapted from Sarmenta et al. (2002)).

The main Web service allows computation clients to create sets of tasks that are sent to volunteers for its implementation and subsequent return of results. The framework allows running applications in the assembler format, such as DLLs (Dynamic Link Library). These files are downloaded by volunteers, implementing basic security mechanisms that are provided by the Microsoft.NET platform. Unlike GIMPS, Distributed. net and SETI@home, Bayanihan allows the execution of general purpose applications.

Web services-based architecture objectives include the provision of simple methods that can be invoked by clients to perform specific functions at the application layer with their own data, as well as the provision of parallel computing for the efficient implementation of intensive computing

Figure 7. Bayanihan computing.NET deployment

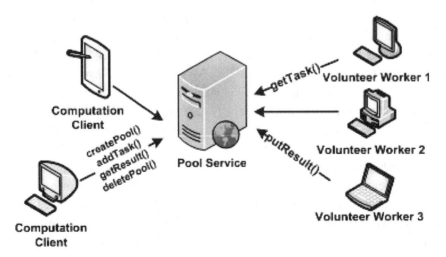

tasks. Its design allows a client to invoke a simple method for performing tasks that are distributed transparently by the framework to several volunteer computing resources to the client.

Web services have a lightweight design so they can be accessed from mobile devices such as PDAs (Personal Digital Assistant) or even mobile phones. Additionally these Web services can be orchestrated, allowing the formation of cluster computing environments or grids of limited scalability. One of the major contributions of Bayanihan is the use of Web services as a platform, representing an alternative to the middleware used by all of its predecessor projects; however, Bayanihan has a coupled architecture which limits its scalability to Internet environments.

Condor-G

The development of Condor as a DGVCS enabled taking advantage of idle computing resources on hundreds of conventional desktop computers within an administrative domain. Due to these benefits, since the year 2000 Condor has been developing a framework to share and lever computing resources among different administrative domains, which has been called Condor-G. Condor-G allows taking full advantage of Condor characteristics, particularly those related to the use of idle resources in an administrative domain, to the availability of tools and mechanisms for resource management and discovery, as well as to the security measures in multi-domain environments provided by Globus, the standard grid middleware. Condor-G combines Globus Toolkit's multi-domain resource management protocols and Condor's intra-domain resource management, allowing users to take advantage of idle computing resources from different administrative domains as if all of these belong to a single domain.

Condor-G can handle thousands of works to be executed on multiple distributed sites, providing features such as monitoring and task management, resource selection, notices, policies, security credentials management, fault tolerance and management of complex dependencies between tasks. Condor-G can be used directly by end users from high level interfaces (brokers) or Web portals. Condor-G is easy to use, users define the tasks to be executed and Condor-G manages all associated aspects to discover and acquire the resources, independent of their physical location; initializing, monitoring and managing the execution on these resources, detecting and acting on failures and notifying users about work completion.

Condor-G fixes various problems encountered in a multi-domain environment by separating three issues focused on the development and adaptation of three main components: access to remote resources, computation management, and remote execution environment. The access issue to remote resources was solved by making different sites to interact using standard protocols; in this case those defined in the Globus Toolkit (GSI, GRAM, GRRP and GASS). Computation management is addressed by implementing a robust and multifunctional agent for computing resource management, which is responsible for resource discovery, for delivery and work management and for fail recovery. The development of this agent took the Condor system as a basis. Finally, remote execution environment is addressed through Condor technology, which allows creating a runtime environment on a remote host. This Condor-G seamlessly uses grid protocols and Condor mechanisms described above, in order to maintain a unified view of the computing status.

Condor-G architecture is illustrated in Figure 8 (Adapted from Frey et al. (2001)). Operation begins when the Condor-G scheduler responds to a request from a user to send work to the grid. Condor-G creates a new GridManager demon responsible for sending and managing these works. A GridManager process manages all works submitted by a user and ends, as soon as they have completed their execution. Each job submission turns into the creation of a Globus JobManager demon. This daemon is connected to the Grid

11

Manager, using GASS for transferring both the binary code and the input files, as well as for providing job's streaming real-time standard error and standard output. Then, the JobManager sends the job for execution by the local scheduler of the remote site. Updates on the status of the job are sent from the JobManager to the GridManager, who updates Condor-G scheduler, where the job status is persistent.

Condor-G implements a new mechanism called GlideIn, with which it is possible to execute jobs by starting a Condor daemon on a remote computer without requiring Condor installation binaries to be in such computers. This allows remote computers to be part of an existing Condor pool because the Condor-G scheduler is informed of these resources' existence. Once the standard Condor demons are started, pending work can be executed by means of GlideIn and the standard Condor mechanisms. Condor provides also the technologies used to implement a sandbox (by catching operating system calls) to safely execute works launched by GlideIn, and so increasing their portability. In Condor, jobs are started by resource owners, while in Condor-G, jobs are automatically started using GRAM dispatch pro-

tocols. This allows Condor-G to dynamically add new resources in a grid environment to an existing resource pool. To prevent the demons started by GlideIn from running while it's not even required, they are turned off when they do not receive jobs after a configurable amount of time. To handle failures on the resources obtained using GlideIn, Condor-G uses standard Condor mechanisms such as forwarding work or work migration.

InteGrade

The next milestone in this category is InteGrade, a GNU LGPL (Lesser General Public License) grid middleware infrastructure, based on the opportunistic use of idle computing resources. The project started in the second half of 2002 as an initiative of the Institute of Mathematics and Statistics of the University of Sao Paulo (EMI-USP), the Department of Informatics of the Pontificia Universidad Católica de Río de Janeiro (PUC-Rio), the Universidad Federal de Goiás (UFG), the Department of Informatics of the Universidad Federal de Maranhão (UFMA) and the Faculty of Computer Science of the Universidad Federal de Mato Grosso do Sul (UFMS) in Brazil. The

Figure 8. Condor-G architecture

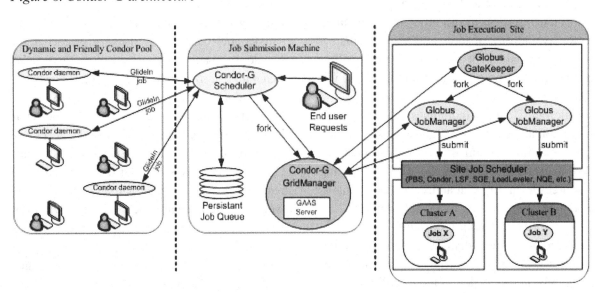

InteGrade architecture is illustrated in Figure 9 (Adapted from Pinheiro, Camargo, Goldchleger, & Kon (2005)).

The main contribution of InteGrade to the DGVCSs is the implementation of a computing-resource usage-pattern analysis-component, capable of collecting statistical data and of probabilistically determining the availability of a machine, as well as the convenience of assigning a specific job to such a machine. This execution evolves in time, because of the permanent data collection, able to determine new prevailing patterns. Based on this component, InteGrade supports sequential, parametric (Parameter Sweep Applications) and parallel (Bulk Synchronous Parallel) applications with communication and synchronization requirements between nodes. To achieve this goal, InteGrade incorporates a component that analyzes the characteristics of the client systems, as well as the network connections between them, making it possible to establish specific parameters for the implementation of work, such as the number of machines, CPU and RAM capacity required, connection speed between nodes, etc. Given the dynamic availability characteristics of opportunistic infrastructures, the BSP parallel application support supposes a best-effort strategy.

In InteGrade, the composition units are clusters, whose hierarchical aggregation allows building a grid composed of both dedicated and partly available resources. InteGrade components are illustrated in Figure 8. The Cluster Manager node is responsible for managing the local cluster, as well as for communicating with other Cluster Manager nodes located on other clusters. The User Node is the component from which a grid user can submit jobs. The Resource Provider Node is a partially available machine that brings a share of their computing to the grid resources, while a Dedicated Node represents a node that has been reserved for the exclusive execution of grid tasks. All architecture roles can overlap, for example, allowing a User Node and a Resource Provider Node to be the same physical machine.

Local Resource Manager (LRM) and Global Resource Manager (GRM) cooperatively managed resources belonging to a cluster. The LRM component runs on each node, collecting its state, such as memory, processor, and network usage data. This information is sent periodically to the GRM using an information update protocol for providing a global state of the grid resources and allowing a better allocation of resources for works execution. The LRM is also responsible for collecting the information associated with the job

Figure 9. InteGrade architecture

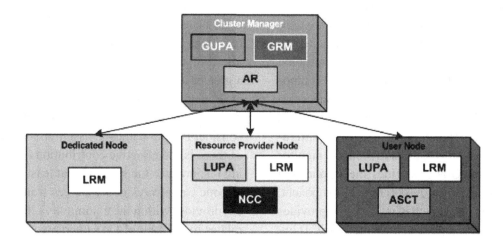

execution status by sending it to the monitoring component. The current implementation of the LRM is done in C++ using O2 (02 project, 2010), while the GRM is implemented in Java, more precisely in JacORB (JacORB, 2004).

Similarly to the LRM and the GRM, the Local Usage Pattern Analyzer (LUPA) and the Global Usage Pattern Analyzer (GUPA) cooperatively manage usage pattern collection within a cluster. The LUPA component runs on each node, collecting local usage pattern by time series analysis (Mitchell, 1997) and regularly sending part of that information, to the GUPA component. Resources selected for their availability information is sent by GUPA to the GRM to allow the final resource allocation. It is important to note that not every data collected by the LRM is sent to the GUPA, because centralizing all the usage pattern information in GUPA, would imply a violation of the shared resources and the owners' privacy. For this reason, LUPA periodically sends only enough data to GUPA, so that the latter segments global requests in accordance with the requirements specified in the job submission data. In this way, each contacted LUPA can answer a request verifying its local data for offering the machine as suitable or unsuitable for the work execution. The distribution of this process also allows objective computing load balancing.

Node Control Center (NCC) enables shared computing resource owners to configure their usage preferences. These settings include periods of time in which they do not want to share their resources, the quotas of computing capacities to share, or special conditions under which a machine can be considered as idle. An additional component called Dynamic Soft Real Time Scheduler (DSRT) (Nahrstedt, Chu, & Narayan, 1998) is implemented for the fulfillment of these configurations. To enable grid users to send and monitor their jobs, InteGrade provides the Application Submission and Control Tool (ASCT) component. The ASCT is implemented in Java, and provides a user-friendly graphical interface: ASCTGui,

designed for users with basic IT knowledge. This application is complemented by ClusterView, a tool for viewing the status of all nodes in a cluster, which includes historical information. Finally, the Application Repository (AR) component provides centralized storage for the binary files of the grid applications.

OurGrid

The following implementation of this category is OurGrid, an Open Source resource sharing system based on a P2P network that makes it easy to share resources equitably to form grid computing infrastructures. In OurGrid each peer represents a whole site in a different administrative domain. Although operational since 2010 (Brasileiro, Duarte, Silva, & Gaudêncio, 2009), the project began in 2004 and was developed at the Department of Systems and Computing at Universidad Federal de Campina Grande in Brazil. OurGrid is currently implemented in the context of the e-science grid facility for Europe and Latin America (EELA-2) project and has two main objectives: the first is to promote the scalable computing resources aggregation to an opportunistic grid infrastructure requiring minimal interaction or negotiation from the resource owner; and the second is the design of an open, extensible and easy to install platform, able to run bag-of-tasks (BoT) applications (Smith & Shrivastava, 1996) (Cirne et al., 2003). OurGrid promotes a culture of resource sharing to ensure a fair access to the grid. The process of sharing resources is based on the principle of donating idle computing cycles in order to have access to a greater amount of computing power provided in cooperation with other participants of the grid.

The OurGrid community participants should consider two fundamental assumptions; the first of these is the effective contribution of computing resources to the system by at least two peers (so one can always get resources from a different provider within the community). The second relates to the lack of QoS guarantees offered to applications deployed on OurGrid. This latter characteristic reduces the complexities associated with traditional grid economy models (Abramson, Buyya, & Giddy, 2002), (Wolski, Plank, Brevik, & Bryan, 2001), prevents negotiations between resource providers and promotes a culture of equitable resources sharing, following a best-effort strategy.

The main components of the OurGrid architecture are illustrated in Figure 10 (Adapted from Brasileiro & Miranda (2009)). OurGrid Worker is an agent that runs on worker nodes and is responsible for implementing a secure environment for running opportunistic grid applications. This agent defines its behavior based on policies set by the resource owner to determine the conditions in which a resource may be considered as idle.

The OurGrid Peer is the component on each site that manages the set of resources available to the grid. This joins the OurGrid community through a discovery service, which notifies other OurGrid Peers of its existence, which also report their presence on the grid to the new peer. OurGrid Peer can be accessed by internal and external OurGrid community users, allowing it to act as a resource provider or consumer. All the OurGrid Peers used a protocol to share resources; this protocol provides messages for the discovery of adequate resources for executing a particular work (by means of broadcast requests), for resource requests, for the acceptance or rejection of work, for job submission, and finally for returning results. Importantly, the mechanisms included in the protocol do not assume an on-demand resource deployment, but it allows their search and dynamic allocation.

OurGrid Broker is responsible for providing user interfaces running applications, as well as for running and managing application scheduling, using the available resources on the grid. Once the OurGrid Broker receives a request for running applications, it contacts the OurGrid Peer (generally in the same site), requesting the number of machines required for carrying out the execution, including parameters such as the operating system, the minimum required memory, etc. When the OurGrid Peer receives a request from the OurGrid Broker, it prioritizes resource search within those currently belonging to its site, and if needed, it is able to contact other Peers OurGrid to request additional resources. As soon as the machines are given to the OurGrid Broker, it is responsible for scheduling tasks and managing its execution.

The main contribution of OurGrid was the incorporation of the concept of Network of Favors (Andrade, Brasileiro, Cirne, & Mowbray, 2007), a partial solution to the problem of non-reciprocal participants in resources sharing system (free-riding peers) (Andrade et al., 2007), which is based on the assumption that an active participant will

Figure 10. OurGrid architecture

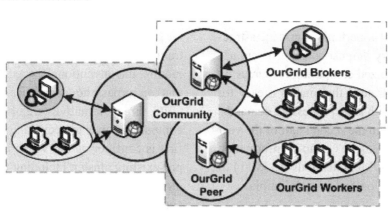

donate their idle computing cycles in reciprocity of a prior grant, marginalizing non-cooperative users through a natural mechanism of symmetry of interests. To do this, each OurGrid Peer locally saved information about participants that have made previous donations, allowing prioritizing requests from participants with greater credit history data. Update of donor user information happens automatically, as soon as they end the job execution. Decisions to provide resources based on donor's information are made independently of any grid economy system or global certificate authority, and local requests receive always a preferential service.

Additionally, and in order to efficiently solve potential security problems associated with the presence of an agent on peer machines, OurGrid uses an approach based on virtual machines, so it can isolate a possible attacker by restricting an execution environment (operating system, libraries, applications) with limited hardware and software resources of the physical machine (those assigned by a type II hypervisor (Xen, 2010)).

OurGrid also provides robust security mechanisms based on private and public keys to certify the authenticity of messages sent using OurGrid protocols. These mechanisms are seeking to prevent denial of service attacks caused by malicious participants. The updated status of the project can be monitored on the official website of the project (OurGrid, 2004).

UnaGrid

UnaGrid is a virtual opportunistic grid infrastructure, whose primary purpose is the efficient use of idle or underutilized computing resources by an opportunistic strategy that makes it easy for grid applications with large processing demands. The project started in the second half of the year 2008 as an initiative of the Group of Information Technology and COMmunications (COMIT) of the Universidad de los Andes in Colombia.

One of the major contributions of UnaGrid to the DGVCSs is the concept of custom virtual cluster (Customized Virtual Cluster - CVC), which refers to a computational infrastructure composed of a set of interconnected, and conventional desktop computers running virtual machines to build a processing grid suitable for grid application deployment. The CVC is based on two basic strategies. The first strategy is the use of virtualization technologies to facilitate encapsulating custom execution environments. This is achieved by making virtual machines to have specific configurations of operating systems, middleware, frameworks, tools and libraries necessary to implement appropriate grid application settings. The second strategy is based on the execution of virtual machines (which make up the custom execution environment), as a low-priority background process. UnaGrid pays special attention to be as non intrusive as possible; the virtual infrastructure deployed may not affect the quality of service perceived by the end user of the shared resource, as the physical machines used are those of traditional computers labs, so end users are not aware of the underlying virtual cluster operations.

As can be seen in Figure 11 (Adapted from Castro et al. (2010)), UnaGrid architecture is based on a master/slave model. Each CVC can be deployed on hundreds of conventional desktop computers which store an image of the virtual machine that implements the slave role, requiring only a single dedicated component for the CVC master role. UnaGrid allows the integration of opportunistic and dedicated infrastructures enabling the participation of opportunistic environments on traditional service grids. Since some applications require unconventional processing capabilities that can surpass the capabilities offered by a single CVC, three alternatives are offered to aggregate computing power to an existing infrastructure: the first is configuring a CVC to be part of another pre-existing cluster, including the allocation of a global master; the second focuses on leveraging computing resource aggregation capabilities offered by some planners such as Condor or SGE (Sun Microsystems Inc., 2005); finally, the third alternative focuses on installing on master nodes a grid middleware component such as Globus Toolkit (Foster & Kesselman, 1998) or gLite (EGEE, 2004).

To control the execution and optimal use of computing resources through CVCs, the schema that has been deployed limits each desktop computer to run a single virtual machine at any time, which is configured to be able to take advantage of the entire computer processing power. CVCs deployment is managed by a Web application called GUMA (Grid Uniandes Management Application), which allows users of research groups to deploy on-demand virtual clusters by specifying the number of computers and the expected virtual machines' run-time. Once a virtual cluster is deployed, users can log into the virtual cluster master node to submit jobs over a secure SSH (Secure SHell) connection.

The GUMA Web portal manages virtual clusters in the administrative domain in which they are deployed by the remote execution of independent instances of the VMware Workstation executing process (one process per desktop computer). Each VMware Workstation process launches its virtual machine, achieving a very efficient overall CVC boot time. GUMA uses a client/server model with authentication, authorization, and privacy

Figure 11. UnaGrid architecture

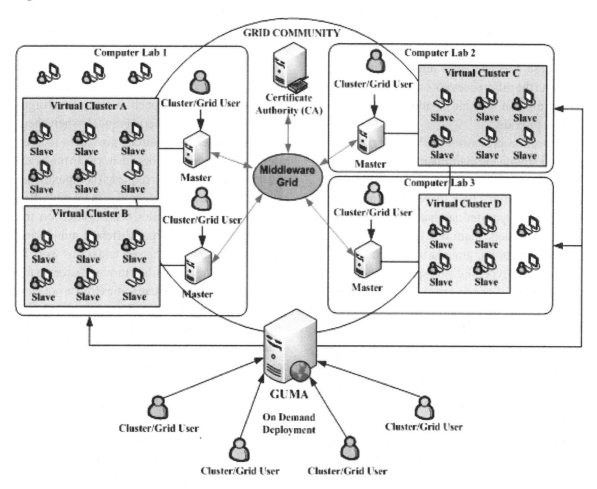

mechanisms, which provide many services to manage the opportunistic grid from thin clients, hiding the complexities associated with the location, distribution and heterogeneity of computing resources, facilitating administrative domain autonomy and providing an intuitive graphical interface to end users. Management services include selection, power up, shutdown and monitoring of physical and virtual machines. End users can also manage their own virtual machines. GUMA is a main contribution of UnaGrid to the DGVCSs, because it gives high usability to an opportunistic system, based on Cloud Computing approaches for deployment and on-demand resource allocation.

DGVCS TAXONOMY

After a careful analysis of these and other DGVCSs projects, we have identified several characteristics which allow us to better study and classify them. These characteristics make it possible to understand the differences not only at a functional level but also on the kind of additional services they may provide.

This section presents a DGVCSs' taxonomy organized around the main characteristics, which differentiate the presented projects: level of scalability, architecture, type of resource provider, scope of the supported applications, supported application models, platforms implementing the DGVCS, portability, granularity for adding resources, license type, ability to specify the desired resources, ease of use and resource usage model (see Figure 12).

Scalability. According to their scalability, DGVCSs can be classified as DGVCSs for Local Area Networks (LAN) or DGVCSs for Internet. DGVCSs for LANs are looking to lever the computational resources in an organization or institution; in this case, the computing resources regularly belong to a single administrative domain, which makes these resource provider systems to have a more stable and reliable connectivity, re-

duces risks associated to security issues and offers a high degree of control over the computing resources that are part of the system. On the other hand, DGVCSs for Internet looks for anonymous geographically distributed computational resources and deals with low-bandwidth communications issues (firewall, NAT, dynamic addressing, etc.), malicious resources and intrusion-related problems, which imply high security risks, unreliable communications and reduced resource availability.

Although DGVCSs for LANs gain some benefits as a greater control over the shared resources as well as an availability and security improvement, they are limited to only use the available resources within an organization or institution. This is why the DGVCSs for the Internet are an option to group computational capabilities to the level of thousands or even millions of computers connected over the Internet; the price to pay: security, reliability and a reduced availability.

Architecture. The different components of a DGVCS are regularly organized using a centralized or distributed approach. A centralized organization uses the client/server model, where there are clients (users), resources providers (shared resources) and servers (coordinators). In this organization client issue work requests (computational jobs) to a server, which receives them and often divided them into smaller tasks. Based on the information gathered from different monitoring services (schedulers), the server assigns work to resource providers, which in turn will execute the jobs using the available capacities (those not used by the resource provider end user). Once a job is finished, the resource provider returns the results to the server which optionally verifies the results before sending them to the client.

Distributed organizations may be classified into two sub categories, those using a peer-to-peer scheme and those using a hierarchical approach. In a peer-to-peer organization, clients and resource providers do exist, but there is not a centralized server. Resource providers have a partial view of

Figure 12. DGVCS taxonomy

the system and manage a distributed scheduling strategy. Clients send work requests to a "close" provider (the master provider for that client), which use the distributed scheduling strategy to assign jobs to other resource providers. Providers executing the jobs eventually return the results to that master provider which verifies them and sends them back to the original requestor client.

In hierarchical DGVCSs, resource providers are organized in such a way that one DGVCS may send a work request to other DGVCSs with available resources. This is done by building a DGVCS hierarchy where high level DGVCSs send jobs to lower-level DGVCSs, when the computational capabilities of the latter are not being fully used. To achieve this, DGVCSs are configured to participate in a hierarchy, connecting every DGVCS to a higher level DGVCS, allowing high-level DGVCSs to see lower DGVCSs as major computing resource providers.

Type of resource provider. Taking into account the way the computers being part of a DGVCS provide their computing resources, DGVCSs can be categorized by the type of resource providers in voluntary and institutional. DGVCSs with voluntary providers get their computing capabilities from computing whose owners/end users decide voluntarily to donate their underutilized computing resources to a DGVCS. DGVCSs with voluntary providers regularly get their resources from Internet users. DGVCSs with institutional providers are those that get computing resources from computers, which are integrated to the system by an institutional system administrator. Often associated to LANs, these DGVCSs take advantage of underutilized computing resources while company staff performs daily activities.

Similar to LAN DGVCSs, institutional DGVCSs have greater control over resource providers, allowing relaxed security policies, as resource providers' end users are normally identified.

Purpose. DGVCSs can also be classified as single-purpose or general purpose DGVCSs. Single-purpose DGVCSs lever their computing capabilities to solve a single specific problem. They are regularly administered by a single organization and are looking to lever the most available resources in environments such as the Internet. General purpose DGVCSs support applications for the resolution of different types of problems; they are regularly administered by several organizations, called virtual organizations, looking to solve different problems through the deployment of multiple applications. General purpose DGVCSs can

be found in both corporate environments and the Internet. In the design of general purpose DGVCSs should be account adequate levels of portability to guarantee the system, can deploy various types of applications, as well as implementing facilities and tools to allow different virtual organizations to manage their applications. These systems must also implement mechanisms to ensure appropriate use of the computing resources, avoiding a single organization to seize all the computing resources that can be levered by the system.

Application model. According to the applications to be executed on them, DGVCSs can be grouped into two main categories: the master/slave model consisting of independent tasks and the parallel programming model which requires communication between processes within a task. In the master/slave model, a master process (server) sends a set of independent tasks to a set of slave processes. The master waits for each slave to execute the job and send back its result. The master receives the results and should have more tasks it assigns a new task to the slave. Tasks running on every slave are totally independent (no communication needed) and can be executed in parallel on different slaves. Execution of a workflow in which each element or workflow task can be run independently also belongs to this category. In this case, it's required the use of a tool that facilitates the synchronization between the different independent tasks of the workflow.

In the parallel programming model, multiple processes cooperate to execute a common task. Such cooperation is achieved by means of communication using different parallel programming paradigms such as MPI (Message Passing Interface), PVM (Parallel Virtual Machine) or BSP (Bulk Synchronous Parallel). In these schemes, a task is carried out through the execution of several processes running on different computers. In such applications, priority should be given to different issues such as synchronization between processes, message passing, remote access to memory, delays in communications, among others. These systems are much more complex than those based on a client/server model because they have to deal with the aforementioned issues on platforms not intended to do so (shared resources, Internet scale, unpredictable availability, etc.)

Platform. Depending on the platform used by resource providers to take advantage of idle computing resources, DGVCSs can be classified into middleware based, Web-based, and virtualization-based.

Middleware based DGVCSs are characterized by the need of installing a specific middleware on the resource providers' operating system. This middleware allows DGVCSs applications to be executed onto the resource provider system. Additionally, it provides management, security, configuration and accounting mechanisms, as well as tools to control the level of intrusion to end users.

In Web-based DGVCSs, applications must be developed in Java and made available as part of a Web page. Resource providers access that Web page through a regular browser and execute the code as an applet. Once executed, task results are typically returned to a server or to a centralized storage system for analysis.

With the rise of virtualization technologies, some DGVCSs use virtual machines to facilitate and expedite the installation, configuration and deployment of the applications required to take advantage of idle processing resources as well as to increase their portability. In these DGVCSs, resource-providers regularly have installed a virtualization tool such as VMware (VMware Inc., 2008), Virtual Box (Sun Microsystems Inc., 2007), KVM (Kernel-based Virtual Machine) (Bellard, 2005), Xen (Barham et al., 2003) or Hyper-V (Microsoft, 2008). Resources are configured, so they implement specific sharing policies and an image of a virtual machine containing all the software (O.S., libraries, middleware and applications) required to execute in the DGVCS context is locally stored. Once configured, the virtual machine runs based on configured parameters and

it begins to form part of the system to execute the different tasks.

Portability. DGVCS portability is related to the deployment capacity on the different operating system resource providers may have. In operating system-dependent DGVCSs, the amount of available resources is limited only to those resources that use the operating system on which the DGVCS software works. On the contrary, DGVCSs that are independent from the operating system, are able to group together more computing resources using one of these strategies: 1) to use a language that is independent from the operating system, such as Java; 2) to create and compile the source code for each of the operating systems on which the DGVCS is expected to work; and 3) to use virtualization tools to allow DGVCS to run on a particular virtualization software, rather than onto a specific operating system.

Granularity of resource aggregation. The achievable DGVCS's computation capacity is based on the amount of resource providers that can be added to the system. Those resource providers offer individual resources (one by one granularity) or cluster resources (an indivisible pool of typically homogeneous resources). On individual aggregation, each computing machine is considered an independent resource provider to build DGVCSs, and tasks are sent to each one of those resource providers. On the other hand, on cluster aggregation, the basic element is a pool of resources; a DGCVS is a set of pools and tasks are sent to those pools. Each pool regularly has a central element that receives the tasks and identifies the computers that are available to run them. Once a task is finished, its results are returned to the pool that originally sent them.

License. Taking into account the type of licensing the DGVCSs can be classified as proprietary or Open Source.

Specification of resources. One of the strategies used in DGVCSs is the possibility to match tasks and resources. It opens two categories, those that allow users the specification of the required resources for the execution of their tasks, and those offering the same type of resources regardless the kind of jobs to be executed. In the first category, the specification is often expressed by a command or a file. When sending a job, the user specifies the required resources and the DGVCS scheduler uses this information to select the resources to be assigned. This ensures a task run at a resource provider that has the required capabilities.

Usability from user perspective. A DGVCS growth can be associated with the facility provided for the installation of the system agents in resource providers; this facility allows that sometimes millions of users can be part of the system. Some agents may require experts in information technology (IT) to perform the deployment and configuration of the agent on resources, limiting the scalability of the system in environments such as the Internet. On the other hand, there exist general public oriented DGVCSs, which don't need any IT knowledge to configure a resource to be part of them. We identify three categories: DGVCSs needing IT staff, DGVCS requiring some IT knowledge, and DGVCS for conventional users.

Resource usage model. Taking into account the form as it is planned and achieved the resource clustering, DGVCSs can be classified into permanent and controlled DGVCSs. In permanent DGVCSs, resources are concurrently shared between DGVCS tasks and end-user tasks. By the correct assignment of priorities, the DGVCS software takes advantage of exclusively idle or underutilized capabilities.

On controlled DGVCSs, resources are used according to a policy defined by resource owners. Several mechanisms are implemented by DGVCS to enforce those policies: to use resources only when the screen saver is activated, to use configuration templates to define conditions to allow resource usage (i.e. based on a processor, RAM or disk activity level), to define time windows (i.e. resource usage is authorized only at nights), to analyze usage patterns, etc.

FUTURE RESEARCH DIRECTIONS

With today's increasing computing capabilities, conventional desktop computers and DGVCSs are attracting a lot of attention. We expect in the years to come to see a new generation of DGVCS to appear, with new tools, frameworks, techniques and mechanisms to improve their utilization. There are several researches being undertaken to improve the benefits of these systems. Below, we present the main trends currently under study to make DGVCS as similar as possible to dedicated infrastructures.

Research on usage patterns and availability (Finger, Bezerra, & Conde, 2010) to take maximum advantage of resources without impacting end-user.

Better support for parallel applications, as well as the development of tools to measure the performance of their execution on DGVCSs (Cáceres, Mongelli, Loureiro, Nishibe, & Song, 2009) (Castro & Costa, 2009) (Goldchleger, Goldman, Hayashida, & Kon, 2005).

New tools and techniques to improve availability and Quality of Service (QoS) provided by DGVCSs. By definition fault tolerance will continuously be the main drawback of these systems, and special attention must be paid to schedulers, so they can manage redundancy as a fundamental mechanism to improve QoS (Anglano & Canonico, 2007) (Abbes, Cérin, & Jemni, 2008).

New tools and middleware development allowing the integration of different DGVCS implementations (Abbes et al., 2008).

Adding Graphic Processing Units (GPUs) to the pool of a DGVCS resources is becoming a standard practice as these processors have unprecendented parallel capabilities, and they have high levels of availability on traditional contexts (Al-Kiswany, Gharaibeh, Santos-Neto, Yuan, & Ripeanu, 2008) (Ino, Kotani, & Hagihara, 2009).

Development of tools to monitor and evaluate the performance of different scheduling strategies. Up to now, tests are conducted using the performance obtained by applications, we lack of benchmarks focus on middleware and DGVCSs themselves (Kokaly, Al-Azzoni, & Down, 2009) (Estrada, Taufer, Reed, & Anderson, 2009).

Processing is the most exploited capability on DGVCSs, and storage is taken for granted most of the time. Taking advantage of the available storage on those same desktops, can open new possibilities for a myriad of applications, not only because of the huge storage capacities widely available, but also because a distributed approach may be more efficient than a centralized storage server (Miller, Butt, & Butler, 2008) (Fedak, He, & Cappello, 2008) (Villamizar & Castro, 2010).

The last important trend in DGVCS is cloud computing. Cloud computing is still a changing paradigm. Their definitions, architectures, models, use cases, database technologies, issues, risks and benefits will be continually redefined in discussions promoted by the public and private sector (Mell & Grance, 2009). Being the latest computing paradigm (Buyya, Yeo, Srikumar, Broberg, & Brandic, 2009), there are no general agreements for its definition (Open Cloud Manifesto, 2009) (Wang et al., 2010), (Maggiani, 2009). In general, cloud computing refers to a novel infrastructure provision system and to development and software platforms that are delivered as a service. This outsourcing integrates features of previous computing paradigms such as: cluster computing (Pfister, 2003), grid computing, global computing (Fedak, Germain, Neri, & Cappello, 2001), Internet Computing (Milenkovic et al., 2003), peer-to-peer (P2P) (Schollmeie, 2002) computing, ubiquitous computing (Weiser, 1993), utility computing (Parkhill, 1996), as well as virtualization technologies. New paradigms and technologies (Weiss, 2007), (Hwang, 2008) have matured to allow cloud computing to differentiate themselves from the earlier resource centralization systems, offering users complex computing infrastructures and services through standard web interfaces.

While the cloud computing large-scale client-server approach represents a contradiction with the voluntary approach of DGVCSs, the characteristics and advantages of this new paradigm promise to overcome the main limitations of DGVCSs. These limitations can be summarized in terms of usability, self-service model, customization of on demand services, scalability and security, resource usage trace ability, monitoring, and delegated administration. The integration of the strengths of cloud computing with the DGVCSs paradigm promises to facilitate the aggregation of computing resources distributed through LAN and Internet networks for the creation of customized development, testing, and production environments that can be deployed, assigned and accessed on-demand, leading to an effective provision of services to suit the dynamic emerging user needs.

One of the more promissory uses of such opportunistic clouds will be the academic context where it will be possible, without important hardware and software investments, to dramatically increase the experimenting environments students are exposed to. Indeed, the development of virtual learning environments and virtual labs will increase students' participation and will promote interdisciplinary work as multiple environments will be easily available for them.

CONCLUSION

This chapter presented a comprehensive state of the art of Desktop Grids and Volunteer Computing Systems (DGVCSs), highlighting the most relevant projects aimed at providing strategies to take advantage of idle computing cycles. The objective of this chapter was to provide a global picture of the main solutions and research trends in DGVCSs. It discussed the evolution of such systems by analyzing representative examples. We identified the main characteristics available and desirable for DGVCSs, and we introduced a new taxonomy to categorize these projects to make their study easier.

DGVCSs have allowed the sharing of distributed computing resources even though those resources are being used for other tasks; in the case of commodity desktops, they are being used for regular end users who should not experiment a significant reduction in the quality of service perceived. This strategy has become of great relevance as it made possible the aggregation of millions of volunteer distributed computing resources, representing an effective solution for the support to different e-science projects, in different areas such as bio-informatics, high energy physics, astronomy, computational chemistry, earth sciences, engineering and others.

Costs reductions and positive experiences around the world, make of DGVCSs a research field with interesting challenges and possibilities. It is expected to see in the next few years new projects and a continuous evolution of most of the projects here presented. Cloud computing is also a major innovation in the computing field, which brings characteristics that can help the popularization of DGVCS in different contexts.

REFERENCES

Abbes, H., Cérin, C., & Jemni, M. (2008). BonjourGrid as a decentralised job scheduler. Proceedings of the *2008 IEEE Asia-Pacific Services Computing Conference*, 89-94. doi:10.1109/APSCC.2008.199

Abramson, D., Buyya, R., & Giddy, J. (2002). A computational economy for grid computing and its implementation in the Nimrod-G resource broker. *Future Generation Computer Systems, 18*(8), 1061-1074. doi:10.1016/S0167-739X(02)00085-7

Al-Kiswany, S., Gharaibeh, A., Santos-Neto, E., Yuan, G., & Ripeanu, M. (2008). StoreGPU: exploiting graphics processing units to accelerate distributed storage systems. *Proceedings of the 17th International Symposium on High Performance Distributed Computing*, 165-174. doi:10.1145/1383422.1383443

Anderson, D. (2004). BOINC: A system for public-resource computing and storage. *Proceedings of the Fifth IEEE/ACM International Workshop on Grid Computing*, 4-10. doi:10.1109/GRID.2004.14

Anderson, D., Cobb, J., Korpela, E., Lebofsky, M., & Werthimer, D. (2002). SETI@home: An experiment in public-resource computing. *Communications of the ACM, 45*(11), 56–61.. doi:10.1145/581571.581573

Anderson, D., & Fedak, G. (2006). The computational and storage potential of volunteer computing. *Proceedings of the Sixth IEEE International Symposium on Cluster Computing and the Grid*, 73-80. doi:10.1109/CCGRID.2006.101

Anderson, D., Korpela, E., & Walton, R. (2005). High-performance task distribution for volunteer computing. *Proceedings of the First International Conference on e-Science and Grid Computing*. doi:10.1109/E-SCIENCE.2005.51

Andrade, N., Brasileiro, F., Cirne, W., & Mowbray, M. (2007). Automatic Grid assembly by promoting collaboration in Peer-to-Peer Grids. *Journal of Parallel and Distributed Computing, 67*(8), 957–966..doi:10.1016/j.jpdc.2007.04.011

Anglano, C., & Canonico, M. (2007). Improving the performance of Fault-Aware scheduling policies for desktop Grids (Be Lazy, Be Cool). *Proceedings of the 16th IEEE International Workshops on Enabling Technologies: Infrastructure for Collaborative Enterprises*, 235-240. doi:10.1109/WETICE.2007.4407160

Baldassari, J., Finkel, D., & Toth, D. (2006). SLINC: A framework for volunteer computing. *Proceedings of the 18th International Conference on Parallel and Distributed Computing and Systems*. doi:10.1.1.121.3363

Barham, P., Dragovic, B., Fraser, K., Hand, S., Harris, T., Ho, A., et al. Warfield, A. (2003). Xen and the art of virtualization. *Proceedings of the Nineteenth ACM Symposium on Operating Systems Principles*, 164-177. doi:10.1145/1165389.945462

Bellard, F. (2005). QEMU, a fast and portable dynamic translator. *Proceedings of the USENIX Annual Technical Conference*, 41-46. Retreived from http://www.usenix.org/ event/ usenix05/ tech/ freenix/ full_papers/ bellard/ bellard.pdf.

Brasileiro, F., Duarte, A., Silva, R., & Gaudêncio, M. (2009). On the co-existence of service and opportunistic Grids. *Proceedings of the 1st EELA-2 Conference*, 51-61. Retrieved from http://www. ciemat.es/ portal.do?TR=A&IDR=1 &identificador=3418

Brasileiro, F., & Miranda, R. (2009). The OurGrid approach for opportunistic grid computing. *Proceedings of the 1st EELA-2 Conference*, 11-19. Retrieved from http://www.ciemat.es/ portal. do?TR=A&IDR=1 &identificador=3418

Buyya, R., Yeo, C. S., Srikumar, V., Broberg, J., & Brandic, I. (2009). Cloud computing and emerging IT platforms: Vision, hype, and reality for delivering computing as the 5th utility. *Future Generation Computer Systems, 25*(6), 599-616. doi:1016/j.future.2008.12.001

Cáceres, E., Mongelli, H., Loureiro, L., Nishibe, C., & Song, S. (2009). Performance results of running parallel applications on the InteGrade. *Concurrency and Computation, 22*(3), 375–393. doi:.doi:10.1002/cpe.1524

Castro, H., Rosales, E., Villamizar, M., & Jiménez, A. (2010). UnaGrid - On demand opportunistic desktop grid. *Proceeding of the 10th IEEE/ACM International Conference on Cluster, Cloud and Grid Computing*, 661-666. doi:10.1109/CCGRID.2010.79

Castro, M., & Costa, F. (2009). MPI support on opportunistic grids based on the InteGrade middleware. *Concurrency and Computation, 22*(3), 343–357. doi:.doi:10.1002/cpe.1479

Chapman, C., Wilson, P., Tannenbaum, T., Farrelee, M., Livny, M., Brodholt, J., & Emmerich, W. (2004). Condor services for the Global Grid: Interoperability between Condor and OGSA. *Proceedings of the UK e-Science All Hands Meeting 2004*. Retrieved from http://www.allhands.org. uk/2004/proceedings/index.html

Cirne, W., Brasileiro, F., Sauve, J., Andrade, N., Paranhos, D., Santos-Neto, E., & Medeiros, R. (2003). Grid computing for Bag-of-Tasks applications. *Proceedings of the 3rd IFIP Conference on E-Commerce, E-Business and EGovernment*. doi:10.1.1.160.236

Condor Project. (1993). *How did the Condor project start?* Retrieved from http://www.cs.wisc. edu/ condor/ background.html

Cullers, D., Linscott, I., & Oliver, B. (1985). Signal processing in SETI. *Communications of the ACM, 28*(11), 1151–1163..doi:10.1145/4547.4549

Distributed.net. (1997). Retrieved from http:// www.distributed.net

Distributed.net. (2000). *Distributed.net FAQ-O-Matic.* Retrieved from http://faq.distributed.net/ cache/ 51.html

EGEE. (2004). *gLite.* Retrieved from http://glite. cern.ch/

Estrada, T., Taufer, M., Reed, K., & Anderson, D. (2009). EmBOINC: An emulator for performance analysis of BOINC projects. *Proceeding of the 23rd IEEE International Parallel & Distributed Processing Symposium*, 1-8. doi:10.1109/IPDPS.2009.5161135

Fedak, G., Germain, C., Neri, V., & Cappello, F. (2001). Xtremweb: A generic global computing system. *Proceedings of the 1st IEEE International Symposium on Cluster Computing and the Grid*, 582-587. doi:10.1109/CCGRID.2001.923246

Fedak, G., He, H., & Cappello, F. (2008). Distributing and managing data on desktop grids with BitDew. *Proceedings of the 3rd International Workshop on Use of P2P, Grid and Agents for the Development of Content*, 63-64. doi:10.1145/1384209.1384221

Finger, M., Bezerra, G., & Conde, D. (2010). Resource use pattern analysis for predicting resource availability in opportunistic grids. *Concurrency and Computation*, 22(3), 295–313. doi:. doi:10.1002/cpe.v22:3

Foster, I., & Kesselman, C. (1998). The Globus project: A status report. *Proceedings of the Seventh Heterogeneous Computing Workshop*, 4-18. doi:10.1109/HCW.1998.666541

Frey, J., Tannenbaum, T., Foster, I., Livny, M., & Tuecke, S. (2001). *Condor-G*: A computation management agent for multi-institutional grids. *Proceedings of the 10th IEEE International Symposium on High Performance Distributed Computing*, 55-63. doi:10.1109/HPDC.2001.945176

Goldchleger, A., Goldman, A., Hayashida, U., & Kon, F. (2005). The implementation of the BSP parallel computing model on the InteGrade Grid Middleware. *Proceedings of the 3rd international workshop on Middleware for grid computing*, 1-6. doi:10.1145/1101499.1101504

Goldchleger, A., Kon, F., Goldman, A., Finger, M., & Bezerra, G. (2004). InteGrade: Object-oriented Grid middleware leveraging the idle computing power of desktop machines. *Concurrency and Computation*, 16(5), 449–459..doi:10.1002/cpe.824

Hwang, K. (2008). Massively distributed systems: From grids and P2P to clouds. *Lecture Notes in Computer Science*, 5036..doi:10.1007/978-3-540-68083-3_1

Ino, F., Kotani, Y., & Hagihara, K. (2009). Harnessing the power of idle GPUs for acceleration of biological sequence alignment. *Proceedings of the 2009 IEEE International Parallel and Distributed Processing Symposium*, 1-8. doi:10.1109/IPDPS.2009.5161091

JacORB. (2004). *The free Java implementation of the OMG's CORBA standard*. Retrieved from http://www.jacorb.org

Kokaly, M., Al-Azzoni, I., & Down, D. (2009). MGST: A framework for performance evaluation of desktop grids. *Proceeding of the 2009 IEEE International Parallel and Distributed Processing Symposium*, 1-8. doi:10.1109/IPDPS.2009.5161133

Litzkow, M., Livny, M., & Mutka, M. (1988). A hunter of idle workstations. *8th International Conference on Distributed Computing Systems*, 104-111. doi:10.1109/DCS.1988.12507

Livny, M. (1999). High-throughput resource management. In Foster, I., & Kesselman, C. (Eds.), *The grid: Blueprint for a new computing infrastructure* (pp. 311–337). Burlington, MA: Morgan Kaufmann.

Maggiani, R. (2009). Cloud computing is changing how we communicate. *Proceedings of the 2009 IEEE International Professional Communication Conference*, 1-4. doi:10.1109/IPCC.2009.5208703

Mell, P., & Grance, T. (2009). *NIST definition of cloud computing*. Retrieved from http://csrc.nist.gov/ groups/ SNS/ cloud-computing/ cloud-def-v15.doc

Mersenne Research, Inc. (2008). *How GIMPS works*. Retrieved from http://www.mersenne.org/ various/ works.php

Microsoft. (2008). *Virtualization with Hyper-V*. Retrieved from http://www.microsoft.com/ windowsserver2008/ en/ us/ hyperv-main.aspx

Milenkovic, M., Robinson, S. H., Knauerhase, R. C., Barkai, D., Garg, S., & Tewari, V. (2003). Toward Internet distributed computing. *IEEE Computer*, *36*(5), 38–46. doi:.doi:10.1109/MC.2003.1198235

Miller, C., Butt, A., & Butler, P. (2008). On utilization of contributory storage in desktop grids. *Proceedings of the 22nd IEEE International Parallel and Distributed Processing Symposium*, 1-12. doi:10.1109/IPDPS.2008.4536246

Mitchell, T. (1997). *Machine Learning* (Series, C. S., Ed.). New York, NY: McGraw-Hill.

Mlucas (2000). *The Mlucas Project*. Retrieved from http://hogranch.com/ mayer/ README.html

Nahrstedt, K., Chu, H., & Narayan, S. (1998). QoS-aware resource management for distributed multimedia applications. *Journal of High-Speed Networking*, *7*, 227–255. Retrieved from http://portal.acm.org/ citation.cfm?id=311277.

Open Cloud Manifesto. (2009). *Open Cloud Manifesto*. Retrieved from http://www.opencloudmanifesto.org/ Open%20Cloud% 20Manifesto.pdf

OurGrid. (2004). *OurGridStatus*. Retrieved from http://www.ourgrid.org

Parkhill, D. (1996). *The challenge of the computer utility*. Boston, USA: Addison-Wesley Publishing Company.

Pfister, G. (2003). Encyclopedia of Computer Science. In Ralston, E. D. A. (Ed.), *Cluster Computing* (pp. 218–221). Chichester, UK: John Wiley and Sons Ltd.

Pinheiro, J., Camargo, R., Goldchleger, A., & Kon, F. (2005). InteGrade: A tool for executing parallel applications on a Grid for opportunistic computing. *Proceedings of the 23th Brazilian Symposium on Computer Networks (SBRC Tools Track)*. Retrieved from http://www.integrade.org.hr/ files/ braga-sbrc05.pdf.

02Project. (2010). *LuaForge*. Retrieved from http://luaforge.net/ projects/ o-two/

Sarmenta, L., Chua, S., Echevarria, P., Mendoza, J., Santos, R., Tan, S., & Lozada, R. (2002). Bayanihan computing. NET: Grid computing with XML Web services. *Proceedings of the 2nd IEEE/ACM International Symposium on Cluster Computing and the Grid*. doi:10.1109/CCGRID.2002.1017182

Sarmenta, L. F. (2001). *Volunteer Computing*. (Doctoral dissertation). Massachusetts Institute of Technology, Massachusetts, USA.

Schollmeie, R. (2002). A definition of peer-to-peer networking for the classification of peer-to-peer architectures and applications. *Proceedings of the 1st International Conference on Peer-to-Peer Computing*, 101-102. doi:10.1109/P2P.2001.990434

SETI@home. (2010). *Official project Website*. Retrieved from http://setiathome.berkeley.edu/

Shoch, J., & Hupp, J. (1982). The "Worm" programs early experience with a distributed computation. *Communications of the ACM*, *25*(3).. doi:10.1145/358453.358455

Smith, J., & Shrivastava, S. (1996). A system for fault-tolerant execution of data and compute intensive programs over a network of workstations. *Lecture Notes in Computer Science*, *1123*, 487–495. doi:.doi:10.1007/3-540-61626-8_66

Sun Microsystems Inc. (2005). *Sun Grid Engine.* Retrieved from http://www.sun.com/ software/ sge/

Sun Microsystems Inc. (2007). *VirtualBox.* Retrieved from http://www.virtualbox.org/

Villamizar, M., & Castro, H. (2010). An Opportunistic Storage System for UnaGrid. *Proceedings of the Latin-American Conference on High Performance Computing (CLCAR 2010)*, Retrieved from http://gppd.inf.ufrgs.br/ clcar2010/

VMware Inc. (2008). *VMware, Inc.* Retrieved from http://www.vmware.com/

Wang, L., Laszewski, G., Younge, A., He, C., Kunze, M., Tao, J., & Fu, C. (2010). Cloud computing: A perspective study. *New Generation Computing, 28*(2), 137–146..doi:10.1007/s00354-008-0081-5

Weiser, M. (1993). Some computer science problems in ubiquitous computing. *Communications of the ACM, 36*(7), 75–84.. doi:10.1145/159544.159617

Weiss, A. (2007). Computing in the clouds. *netWorker, 11*(4), 16–25..doi:10.1145/1327512.1327513

Wolski, R., Plank, J., Brevik, J., & Bryan, T. (2001). Analyzing market-based resource allocation strategies for the computational grid. *International Journal of High Performance Computing Applications, 15*(3)..doi:10.1177/109434200101500305

Xen. (2010). *How are Hypervisors classified?* Retrieved from http://www.xen.org/ files/ Marketing/ HypervisorTypeComparison.pdf

ADDITIONAL READING

Abbes, H., Cérin, C., & Jemni, M. (2008). PastryGrid: Decentralisation of the execution of distributed applications in desktop grid. *Proceedings of the 6th International Workshop on Middleware for Grid Computing.* doi:10.1145/1462704.1462708.

Al-Azzoni, I., & Down, D. (2008). Dynamic scheduling for heterogeneous desktop Grids. Proceedings of the *9th IEEE/ACM International Conference on Grid Computing*, 136-143. doi:10.1109/GRID.2008.4662792

Al-Kiswany, S., Ripeanu, M., Vazhkudai, S., & Gharaibeh, A. (2008). Stdchk: A checkpoint storage system for desktop Grid computing. *Proceedings of the 28th International Conference on Distributed Computing Systems*, 613-624. doi:10.1109/ICDCS.2008.19

Anglano, C., Brevik, J., Canonico, M., Nurmi, D., & Wolski, R. (2006). Fault-aware scheduling for Bag-of-Tasks applications on desktop Grids. *Proceedings of the 7th IEEE/ACM International Conference on Grid Computing*, 56-63. doi:10.1109/ICGRID.2006.310998

Araujo, F., Domingues, P., Kondo, D., & Silva, L. (2008). Using Cliques Of Nodes To Store Desktop Grid Checkpoints. In Springer US, *Grid Computing* (pp. 25-36). doi:10.1007/978-0-387-09457-1_3

Baratloo, A., Karaul, M., Kedem, Z., & Wyckoff, P. (1999). Charlotte: Metacomputing on the Web. *Future Generation Computer Systems, 15*(5), 559-570. doi:10.1016/S0167-739X(99)00009-6

Buyya, R., & Vazhkudai, S. (2001). Compute power market: Towards a market-oriented Grid. *Proceedings of the 1st IEEE/ACM International Symposium on Cluster Computing and the Grid*, 574- 581. doi:10.1109/CCGRID.2001.923245

Byun, E., Choi, S., Kim, H., Hwang, C., & Lee, S. (2008). Advanced job scheduler based on Markov Availability Model and resource selection in desktop Grid computing environment. *Metaheuristics for Scheduling in Distributed Computing Environments, 146*, 153–171..doi:10.1007/978-3-540-69277-5_6

Calder, B., Chien, A., Wang, J., & Yang, D. (2005). The entropia virtual machine for desktop grids. *Proceedings of the 1st ACM/USENIX International Conference on Virtual Execution Environments*, 186-196. doi:10.1145/1064979.1065005

Chakravarti, A., Baumgartner, G., & Lauria, M. (2005). The organic Grid: Self-organizing computation on a peer-to-peer network. *IEEE Transactions on Systems, Man, and Cybernetics. Part A, Systems and Humans, 35*(3), 373–384.. doi:10.1109/TSMCA.2005.846396

Cicotti, P., Taufer, M., & Chien, A. (2005). DGMonitor: A performance monitoring tool for sandbox-based desktop Grid platforms. *The Journal of Supercomputing, 34*(2), 113–133.. doi:10.1007/s11227-005-2336-y

Estrada, T., Taufer, M., & Reed, K. (2009). Modeling job lifespan delays in volunteer computing projects. Proceedings of the *9th IEEE/ACM International Symposium on Cluster Computing and the Grid*, 331-338. doi:10.1109/CCGRID.2009.69

Farkas, Z., Kacsuk, P., & Rubio, M. (2008). Utilizing the EGEE infrastructure for desktop Grids. In Springer US, *Distributed and Parallel Systems* (pp. 27-35). doi:10.1007/978-0-387-79448-8_3

Fedak, G., Germain, C., Néri, V., & Cappello, F. (2001). XtremWeb: A generic global computing system. *Proceedings of the 1st IEEE/ACM International Symposium on Cluster Computing and the Grid*, 582-587. doi:10.1109/CCGRID.2001.923246

Georgakopoulos, K., & Margaritis, K. (2008). Integrating Condor desktop clusters with Grid. In Springer US, *Distributed and Parallel Systems* (pp. 37-42). doi:10.1007/978-0-387-79448-8_4

Georgatos, F., Gkamas, V., Ilias, A., Kouretis, G., & Varvarigos, E. (2010). A Grid-enabled CPU scavenging architecture and a case study of its use in the Greek school. *Journal of Grid Computing, 8*(1), 61–75..doi:10.1007/s10723-009-9143-2

He, H., Fedak, G., Tang, B., & Capello, F. (2009). BLAST application with Data-aware desktop Grid Middleware. *Proceedings of the 9th IEEE/ACM International Symposium on Cluster Computing and the Grid*, 284-291. doi:10.1109/CCGRID.2009.91

Heien, E., Takata, Y., Hagihara, K., & Kornafeld, A. (2009). PyMW - A Python module for desktop grid and volunteer computing. *Proceedings of the 2009 IEEE International Symposium on Parallel & Distributed Processing*, 1-7. doi:10.1109/IPDPS.2009.5161132

Jurkiewicz, J., Nowinski, K., & Bała, P. (2008). Unicore 6 as a platform for desktop Grid. *Proceedings of the International Multiconference on Computer Science and Information Technology, 453-457*..doi:10.1109/IMCSIT.2008.4747282

Kacsuk, P., Kovacs, J., Farkas, Z., Marosi, A., Gombas, G., & Balaton, Z. (2009). SZTAKI desktop Grid (SZDG): A flexible and scalable desktop Grid system. *Journal of Grid Computing, 7*(4), 439–461..doi:10.1007/s10723-009-9139-y

Kane, K., & Dillaway, B. (2008). Cyclotron: A secure, isolated, virtual cycle-scavenging Grid in the enterprise. *Proceedings of the 6th International Workshop on Middleware for Grid Computing*, 1-6. doi:10.1145/1462704.1462706

Kelley, I., & Taylor, I. (2008). Bridging the data management gap between service and desktop Grids. In Springer US, *Distributed and Parallel Systems* (pp. 13-26). doi:10.1007/978-0-387-79448-8_2

Kim, H., Kim, S., Byun, E., Hwang, C., & Choi, J. (2006). Agent-based autonomous scheduling mechanism using availability in desktop Grid systems. *Proceedings of the 15th International Conference Computing*, 174-179. doi:10.1109/CIC.2006.20

Montresor, A., Meling, H., & Babaoglu, O. (2003). Messor: Load-balancing through a swarm of autonomous agents. In Springer Berlin/Heidelberg, *Agents and Peer-to-Peer Computing* (pp. 125-137). doi:10.1007/3-540-45074-2_12

Morrison, J., Kennedy, J., & Power, D. (2001). WebCom: A Web based volunteer computer. *The Journal of Supercomputing, 18*(1), 47–61.. doi:10.1023/A:1008163024500

Neary, M., Phipps, A., Richman, S., & Cappello, P. (2000). Javelin 2.0: Java-based parallel computing on the Internet. In Springer Berlin/Heidelberg, *Euro-Par 2000 Parallel Processing* (pp. 1231-1238). doi:10.1007/3-540-44520-X_174

Noam, N., London, S., Regev, O., & Camiel, N. (1998). Globally distributed computation over the Internet - The POPCORN Project. *Proceedings of the 18th International Conference on Distributed Computing Systems*, 592-601. doi:10.1109/ICDCS.1998.679836

Sarmenta, L. (1998). Bayanihan: Web-based volunteer computing using Java. In Springer Berlin/Heidelberg, *Worldwide Computing and Its Applications - WWCA'98* (pp. 444-461). doi:10.1007/3-540-64216-1_67

Sterritt, R., & Bustard, D. (2003). Towards an autonomic distributed computing environment. *Proceedings of the 14th International Workshop on Database and Expert Systems Applications*, 699-703. doi:10.1109/DEXA.2003.1232102

Uk, B., Taufer, M., Stricker, T., Settanni, G., Cavalli, A., & Caflisch, A. (2003). Combining task- and data parallelism to speed up protein folding on a desktop grid platform. *Proceedings fo the 3rd IEEE/ACM International Symposium on Cluster Computing and the Grid*, 240-247. doi:10.1109/CCGRID.2003.1199374

Wang, J., Sun, A., Lo, Y., & Liu, H. (2006). Programmable GPUs: New general computing resources available for desktop Grids. *Proceedings of the 5th International Conference Grid and Cooperative Computing*, 46-49. doi:10.1109/GCC.2006.76

Zhong, L., Wen, D., Ming, Z., & Peng, Z. (2003). Paradropper: A general-purpose global computing environment built on peer-to-peer overlay network. *Proceedings of the 23rd International Conference on Distributed Computing Systems Workshops*, 954-957. doi:10.1109/ICDCSW.2003.1203674

Zhou, D., & Lo, V. (2004). Cluster computing on the fly: Resource discovery in a cycle sharing peer-to-peer system. *Proceedings of the IEEE International Symposium on Cluster Computing and the Grid*, 66-73). doi:10.1109/CCGrid.2004.1336550

ENDNOTE

[1]   In mathematics, the term "Golomb Ruler" refers to a set of non-negative integers such that no two distinct pairs of numbers from the set have the same difference.

Chapter 2
A Complementary Approach to Grid and Cloud Distributed Computing Paradigms

Mehdi Sheikhalishahi
Universita' della Calabria, Italy

Manoj Devare
Universita' della Calabria, Italy

Lucio Grandinetti
Universita' della Calabria, Italy

Maria Carmen Incutti
Universita' della Calabria, Italy

ABSTRACT

Cloud computing is a new kind of computing model and technology introduced by industry leaders in recent years. Nowadays, it is the center of attention because of various excellent promises. However, it brings some challenges and arguments among computing leaders about the future of computing models and infrastructure. For example, whether it is going to be in place of other technologies in computing like grid or not, is an interesting question. In this chapter, we address this issue by considering the original grid architecture. We show how cloud can be put in the grid architecture to complement it. As a result, we face some shadow challenges to be addressed.

INTRODUCTION

In 1998 and later in 2001, Foster, Kesselman, & Tuecke (2001) introduced Grid Computing as coordinated resource sharing and problem solving in dynamic, multi-institutional Virtual Organiza-tion (VO). Grids have been the center of attention from Science and High Performance Computing (HPC) (Grandinetti, 2008; Gentzsch, Grandinetti & Joubert, 2010) community especially for the distributed and large scale scientific applications and also in collaborative works. A huge number of projects within countries (e.g. National Grid Projects) (TeraGrid, 2010; Italian Grid Infrastruc-

DOI: 10.4018/978-1-61350-113-9.ch002

ture, 2010), continents and companies in various areas were defined around grid during these years. To make grid computing a promising technology, a number of groups and standard bodies such as Open Grid Forum in the industry and science initiated to standardize various components of distributed systems like interfaces and architecture.

For instance, in the Europe, the European Grid Initiative (EGI) (EGI, 2010) is the latest project that represents a new effort to establish a sustainable grid infrastructure in Europe after EGEE-III project. National Grid Initiatives (NGI) (Italian Grid Infrastructure, 2010) within EGI operate the grid infrastructures in each country. In fact, NGI is the main foundations of EGI. In the meantime, a new computing paradigm emerges from commercial sector with focus on Enterprise applications called Cloud Computing (Amazon EC2., 2009). As a matter of fact, some new technologies like virtualization for provisioning of operating system and Web Services were the main foundations behind cloud Computing.

In other words, cloud computing is the next generation IT computing paradigm in which dynamically scalable and often virtualized resources are provided as a service over the Internet. The main concept in cloud is an infrastructure that provides on-demand, instant and also elastic resources or services over the Internet, usually at the scale and reliability of a data center. Cloud platform such as Open Source Nimbus Toolkit (Nimbus, 2010) is one of the first attempts to complement grid and cloud. Nimbus is like Commercial Amazon Elastic Compute Cloud (EC2) (Amazon EC2., 2009) that provides computational capabilities for computing in Enterprise sector; they are often referred as Infrastructure-as-a-Service (IaaS). After the advent of cloud in commercial settings, some interesting new research questions arise like: "Does grid and cloud complement each other?". In addition, the question: "Can IaaS clouds be a good provisioning model for a grid Infrastructure?" is very worthy to be discussed. Again, whether IaaS

clouds can provide enough performance and speed in computation, storage and networking for HPC applications or not, is also an important issue to be examined.

In this chapter, we introduce the new buzzword computing paradigm cloud especially from the infrastructure point of view. After introducing this paradigm, we discuss analytically about various technologies around it in software and networking domains that are involved in complementing grid and cloud. Next, the needs of science to cloud are described, followed by benefits of cloud computing. In next part, the main contribution of this chapter that is grid meets cloud is presented. Then, we analyze and assess current practices and services of cloud in grid. Finally, we define some new research topics that can address this issue.

BACKGROUND

The precise definition of cloud computing varies widely and depends on the context because clouds are not mature enough and they are in the evolution stages. First, we have some explanation about the term cloud. Since the birth of TCP/IP, people have been drawing TCP/IP Network on white boards like cloud metaphor. This metaphor resonates for the same reason the "electron cloud" is a useful metaphor for the behavior of electrons. The cloud represents a black-box, we don't have to know its inner workings, just its behaviors or interfaces are needed by users.

On the other hand, cloud computing is the ability to draw IT resources from an internal, external or third-party source using either Internet-based or local-area infrastructure. The cloud is essentially the Software-as-a-Service (SaaS) model expanded to include hardware-driven functions like storage and processing.

In Information Technology, Software, Platform and Infrastructure are the three main elements that services come from them. Software runs on a Platform and Platform runs on an Infrastructure. Currently, the clouds are trying to cover the three models offering Infrastructure as a Service (IaaS), Platform as a Service (PaaS) and Software as a Service (SaaS).

Science clouds (Science Clouds, 2010) provided by Open Source Nimbus Toolkit and Commercial Amazon Elastic Compute Cloud (EC2) that provide computational capabilities for computing are often referred as IaaS.

PaaS is the purpose of clouds that provide Enterprise-class Web applications on-demand such as Force.com (Salesforce.com, Inc., 2010) or an application development environment and deployment container such as Google's App Engine (2010) without the cost of deploying infrastructure. Finally, clouds that provide services such as Customer Relationship Management (CRM) (CRM at Salesforce.com Inc., 2010), Social Networking (Facebook, 2010), Photo Sharing (Flicker, 2010) termed as SaaS. Amazon's EC2 (2009) offers full virtual machines with GNU/Linux as Operating System (OS) and the opportunity to run any application compatible with the GNU/Linux distribution. Google's App Engine (Google App Engine, 2010) will also let customers run programs in a limited version of Python or Java and use Google's database.

In business scenario, consumers of Commercial Clouds do not own the physical infrastructure, thus they avoid capital expenditure and operational expenses of building and maintaining physical infrastructure by renting compute and storage usage from a third-party provider. They consume resources as a service, paying instead for only the resources they use on a utility computing basis.

In the future, the clients of the cloud will use their cloud-enabled mobile e.g. Android, iPhone or their cloud-enabled Web browsers e.g. Firefox and Google Chrome for application delivery from cloud services (Google App Engine, 2010).

ENABLING TECHNOLOGIES

Some technologies in the Software, Hardware and Network area are going to change the future IT computing infrastructure like clouds or bring new computing paradigm like Client Computing. In the software area, Virtualization Technology and Web Services, in the hardware area, Symmetric MultiProcessing (SMP), multi-core processors, and Non-Uniform Memory Access (NUMA) and in the networking, Security, Virtual Private Network (VPN) and Network Overlay are the most promising and motivating technologies for the future complex computing infrastructure plans. Virtualization Technology provides techniques and conditions to run multiple Virtual Machines (VM) on top of a single physical machine. Implementation of this technology is extremely diverse; different approaches in the virtualization area are represented such as:

Hypervisor or Para-Virtualization (Xen, 2010): Amazon AMI, VMWare, Xen, KVM, VirtualBox Operating System Level Virtualization: OpenVZ, Linux-VServer and Linux Containers (LXC, 2010) in the future Linux Kernel mainstream.

Hardware-assisted virtualization in various colors and flavors: VT-x and NPT extensions on Intel, AMD-V and EPT extensions on AMD.

Briefly speaking, Virtualization Technology is the base of IaaS cloud computing model (Devare, Sheikhalishahi, & Grandinetti, 2009) for the on-demand provision of virtualized resources as a service.

Para-Virtualization provides totally independent and isolated environments with maximum flexibility and security for Virtual Machines (VMs). In addition, they can run any operating system that is suitable for physical hardware and any software on that operating system. For instance, Windows XP, FreeBSD and Fedora Core Linux distribution both can run as two isolated Virtual Machines on top of one physical machine.

In OS Level Virtualization (LXC, 2010), Operating System (kernel) runs multiple isolated instances (called containers or partitions) instead of just one. The OS kernel will run a single OS and provide that OS functionality to each instance. This creates isolated containers on a single physical server and OS instance to utilize hardware, software, data center and management efforts with the best performance and efficiency. In addition to isolation mechanisms, the kernel provides resource management features to limit the impact of one container's activities on the other containers. In other words, VMs on the same physical machine share the same kernel, but they are allowed to run different Operating Systems distributions from only one type such as Linux Distribution.

VT-x and AMD-V are the first generation of hardware-assisted virtualization extensions. Hypervisors use software to trap and simulate certain instructions, memory management and I/O in the host Virtual Machines. These two extensions trapped these instructions in hardware to gain a significant speed improvement. NPT and EPT extensions are the second generation of hardware-assisted virtualization extensions. These two minimize the memory management bottleneck.

Since in OS Level Virtualization all VMs share the same kernel, so processes in containers use the same Operating System's system call interface and do not need to be subject to emulation or run in an intermediate Virtual Machine. Therefore, the performance of OS level implementation is better than Para-Virtualization. Also the performance of Para-Virtualization is close to raw physical performance.

The other important technology that nowadays is the base of many technologies is Web Services. Web Services are Application Programming Interfaces (API) based on the Internet protocols that can be accessed over a network. Often they executed on a remote system hosting the requested service. Interaction between services, resources and agents in a heterogeneous environment that is based on Web Services Technologies would be more interoperable.

Web Services (Web Services, 2010) is defined by the W3C as a software system designed to support interoperable machine-to-machine interaction over a network. It has an interface described in a machine-processable format (specifically WSDL). Other systems interact with the Web service in a manner prescribed by its description using SOAP messages, typically conveyed using HTTP with an XML serialization in conjunction with other Web-related standards.

SMP (the earliest Style of MultiProcessor machine architectures), multi-core, and NUMA are the technologies that put together more than one computing elements such as processor and memory inside one physical system.

SMP and multi-core involve a multiprocessor computer architecture where two or more identical processors are connected to a single shared main memory. Today most common multiprocessor systems use SMP architecture. In multi-core processors, the SMP architecture applies to the cores, treating them as separate processors. In the SMP systems, OS would be able to move tasks between processors to balance the workload efficiently. A single physical processor of multi-core (Intel Corporation, 2010) design type contains the core logic of more than one processor. The multi-core design puts several cores together and packages them as a single physical processor. The main goal is to enable a system to run more tasks simultaneously and thereby achieve greater overall system performance.

In SMP architecture, when several processors attempt to access the same memory performance degrades. NUMA (NUMA, 2010) attempts to address this problem by providing separate memory for each processor. NUMA systems dedicate different memory banks to different processors. Therefore, processors have access to their local memory quickly while it is slower for remote memory. When more than one Virtual Machine run on a multi-core or SMP system simultaneously, each Virtual Machine runs independently of others and also in parallel with the others. In this case, a Multi-processor system like multi-core architectures will have considerably better performance than a uni-processor because different Virtual Machines run on different processors simultaneously. This use-case is the future computing model in clouds, thus multi-core architecture is a perfect hardware technology for cloud computing.

Network security is another enabling-technology for clouds. Clouds as an emerging technology like the other IT infrastructures need special security services. There are four basic security services: authentication and authorization, integrity, confidentiality and non-repudiation. These security services also have to be considered in clouds.

First, authentication and authorization services establish the validity of a transmission, message, and its originator. Second, integrity services address the unauthorized modification of data. To ensure data integrity, a system must be able to detect unauthorized data modification. Confidentiality service restricts access to the content of sensitive data to only those individuals who are authorized. Third, non-repudiation services prevent an individual from denying that previous actions had been performed.

Public Key Infrastructure (PKI) is a scalable and distributed approach to address these security needs. The term PKI is derived from public key cryptography, the technology on which PKI is based. It has unique features that make it invaluable as a basis for security functions in distributed systems. Contemporary clouds are adopting PKI to provide security services.

VPN is a private network that uses a public network, such as the Internet, to connect remote networks (sites or users) together. It uses virtual connections through the public network, instead of using dedicated connections e.g. leased or owned lines to connect private networks, thus resulting in a much lower cost. In addition, VPN provides individuals and remote offices with secure access to their organization's network.

Therefore, VPN makes it easy to build wide-area virtual clusters in case of having firewalls and network address translation within networks. In fact, VPN is an enabling technology for Clouds Federation or Hybrid Clouds. In addition, users can securely access to clouds with the help of VPN technology.

Network Overlay (NetOverlay, 2010) provides facilities to build a network on top of another network, for example, many peer-to-peer (P2P) networks are overlay networks on top of the Internet and dial-up Internet is an overlay upon the telephone network.

Science Clouds: Emergence of Scientific Application Needs

At first we introduce one of the most prominent experiments in the world where the need of having a standard computing infrastructure such as grid arises from. The Large Hadron Collider (LHC) (LHC, 2010) is a gigantic scientific instrument as shown in Figure 1 (particle accelerator) near Geneva, Switzerland. It spans the border between Switzerland and France about 100m underground. Physicists will use the LHC to study the smallest known particles (the fundamental building blocks of all things) and also to recreate the conditions just after the Big Bang. Physicists from around the globe will analyze the particles created in the collisions using special detectors in a number of experiments dedicated to the LHC: ALICE, ATLAS, CMS, LHCb, TOTEM, LHCf. These six experiments at the LHC are all run by the international collaborations, bringing together scientists and individuals from institutes all over the world. In sum, the LHC was built to help scientists to find the answer of a few important unresolved questions in particle physics.

As can be seen nowadays the scientific questions are very complicated, so the technologies in physics and computer science behind them also

Figure 1. ALICE detector (LHC, 2010)

are becoming very complex. In the field of computer science, the computing infrastructure and applications for the scientific problems have to address the challenges of storing the data generated by these instruments and also analyzing these huge amounts of data.

If we research on the Scientific applications, we will find out they are becoming more complicated. They are developed by different groups and individuals, build around various components and technologies and often need a heterogeneous execution environment. More importantly, they may require a custom execution environment, with specific operating system, software libraries, compilers, binaries and so on. Even some scientific applications need to work with a specific version and release of software. In addition, usually these applications process large amounts of input data and produce large amounts of output data and results. This is the result of the complexity of underlying scientific questions to be answered by the scientific application.

STAR (STAR, 2010) is another application in nuclear physics experiment that needs a specific version of operating system and precise specific software environment, libraries, tools and compilers with right configuration to work correctly. Usually, there is no such environment in current grid infrastructure and also it is not easy to be deployed on grid resources immediately. According to Doug Olson: "Even just validating a new platform is a big job even when it all compiles." Also, "STAR is using rarely used features of the language", and "It tends to push the boundaries on what will actually compile". STAR also requires some grid components such as OSG CE as a headnode, OSG WNs as worker nodes with STAR configuration, gridmap files, host certificates, NSF for shared filesystem and PBS as Local Resource Manager to be deployed and configured properly.

Since 2003 a collaboration between two big energy departments, Brookhaven and Argonne National Laboratory (ANL), in the US has been started for building an middleware to facilitate running of STAR application. This collaboration initiated because of the difficulties behind production running of STAR application. The result of this collaboration (Keahey, Figueiredo, Fortes, Freeman, & Tsugawa, 2008) was that STAR scientists with the help of Nimbus Toolkit (developed at ANL) were able to dynamically provision compute resources to build a cluster on TeraPort at ANL and on Amazon's EC2 resources quickly in an order of minutes to run STAR applications at the scale of one hundred nodes.

Benefits of Cloud Computing

Cloud computing now scaling up to massive capacities without having to invest in new infrastructure or license new software. Service consumers use what they need on the Internet and pay only for what they use. The consumer has lower capital expenses, operating expenses and no worry about how the servers and networks are maintained in cloud with location transparency. In this section, we enumerate some applications and benefits of adopting cloud computing.

Server Consolidation

Elasticity: a way to increase capacity or add capabilities on the fly and on-demand without investing in new infrastructure, training new personnel, or licensing new software.

Subscription-Based or Pay-Per-Use Service

Checkpointing: Since virtualization technology encapsulates the OS, it can allow the state of the entire OS to be stored in checkpoints. In the case of a failure, the OS can then be brought back to the state it was in before the failure and continue from there.

Flexibility: Computing resources are utilized with more flexibility. Different OSs/workloads may be run at the same time, and on a SMP/mul-

ticore system, OSs/workloads may be pinned to individual CPUs.

Isolation: Computations running in a hardware virtualized environment do not interfere with one another and they are able to keep their computations secret from the others. Even computations are isolated while running on the same physical resources. In (Kelem & Feiertag, 1991) there are arguments that the isolation provided by a hardware virtualization mechanism can be more easily mathematically abstracted than the isolation provided by a traditional timesharing OS's security model. The sufficiency of the hardware virtualization security model can be evaluated by looking at the isolation at the hardware level. Since hardware virtualization is a simpler mechanism than an OS and has fewer lines of code, its isolation can be more easily proven.

Self/live-migration of workload: A computation running inside an OS (represented by a VM) can be migrated from one node in the virtualized setting to another and keep running. This allows the load on the nodes to be balanced more dynamically. Also, if, for instance, a node is going down for maintenance, its computations may be moved away to other physical nodes non-stop.

New class of sharing: Virtualization provides the sharing of computing resources among several users more dynamically and securely.

Complementary service: Cloud services may be subsequently re-combined as either a complementary resource, for example for backup or disaster recovery scenarios, or used as a standalone platform. In this case, upgrades to OSs and software can be done on virtualized hardware without bringing down the computer. In a transitional phase, both old and upgraded OSs may run simultaneously on the same computer, allowing upgrades without downtime.

Provisioning: One of the interesting aspects of cloud is that by default it incorporates resource provisioning in the preparation process for application execution.

Green IT: Primary use of energy in IT companies is in data centers. Efficient power supply design and evaporative cooling rather than air conditioning are two common ways to reduce the energy consumption. The other interesting method would be to change the infrastructure. One of the other impacts of cloud computing would be on green-IT. Large IT companies are trying to reduce their impact on the environment, and they intend to become carbon neutral and also becoming more environmentally friendly. IT companies will save money as well, in addition to cutting the company's energy consumption.

Clouds Meet Grids

Technically, both cloud computing and grid computing represents the idea of using remote resources. In grid computing, the control over the resources is used stays with the site, reflecting local software and policy choices. The remote user does not have choice what the user like or dislike. Whereas, cloud computing represents a fundamental change of assumption: when a remote user "leases" a resource, the control of that resource is turned over to that user with underlying hypervisor which is isolating the leased resources in secure way. The cloud computing enabling to turn the control of remote resource over to the user makes it possible to equipped flexible grid infrastructure for scientific community. Undoubtedly, clouds and grids are complement to each other to boost the confidence in "On demand" style of resource provision. If the users are systems administrators and integrators, they care how things are maintained in the cloud. They upgrade, install, and virtualize servers and applications. If the users are consumers, they do not care how things are run in the system.

The cloud technology leverages the ideas presented in the grid and utility computing which existed before cloud. As cloud computing paradigm emerges, traditional client-server computing is going to be replaced with Service Oriented Computing promise in Service Oriented Architecture.

After the advent of cloud in commercial settings, some interesting new research questions arise like: "Does grid and cloud complement each other?".

The intelligent answer to this question would be: Yes, grid and cloud complement and meet each other, if from the architectural point of view they be designed to meet. In addition, as part of the complementarity approach, the question: "Can IaaS clouds be a good provisioning model for a grid Infrastructure?" is very worthy to be discussed. Again, whether IaaS clouds can provide enough performance and speed in computation, storage and networking for HPC applications or not, is also an important issue to be examined. This is part of HPC in the Clouds challenge. Despite the pervasiveness of cloud computing in the broader IT industry, the challenges of using this model for high performance computing are unique to the HPC paradigm.

Jha, Merzky, & Fox (2008) have published in Open Grid Forum (OGF) document series, introducing clouds as a replacement for grid. First of all the title of this paper as: "Using Clouds to Provide Grids Higher-Levels of Abstraction and Explicit Support for Usage Modes" is ambiguous. In that paper, there are some vague and false claims about the grid by comparing it with the cloud; we totally disagree with this chapter. For example, better application delivery and usage, complex and detailed abstractions exposure, interoperability and not being successful, clouds are not complementary to grids, clouds are the evolution of grids, grids and clouds: As evolution of clusters are some of the wrong claims discussed in that paper.

The key answer to these claims is as follow. First, grids are under research and development even now; there are various conflicting requirements and goals to be refined and resolved during time; there are diverse set of applications and so on. Second, as technologies evolve and new technologies become available, some obstacles will be removed. For instance, clouds take advantages of new technologies such as virtualization to offer nice features e.g. application interoperability. As we have discussed before, application interoperability is the bonus of virtualization technology. In addition, Foster (2008) replied to these claims by giving some simple examples.

Foster, Zhao, Raicu, & Lu (2008) have compared cloud with grid at 360 degrees angle. To discuss more in detail on grid plus cloud issue, we review the layered grid Architecture here. Foster, Kesselman, & Tuecke (2001) have introduced a grid protocol architecture has been architected to be layered based on the hourglass model. By definition, Fabric, Connectivity, Resource and Collective are the four main layers in the grid architecture as shown in Figure 2.

The Fabric layer represents all resource types such as compute/storage/network resources, codes and catalogs to be shared in a grid infrastructure by grid protocols. Even specific resources like supercomputer, a cluster of compute nodes, a

database or a distributed file system which have their own (vendor) implementation based on their internal can be shared by grid protocols. This layer is implemented by the local and resource/vendor-specific operations and it is not the concern of grid architecture. As it is mentioned in (Foster, Kesselman & Tuecke, 2001), "richer Fabric functionality enables more sophisticated sharing operations", thus virtualized resources with their nice features and operations like creating/building on-demand and dynamic, suspension/resumption capabilities at the virtualization level bring lots of new and interesting operations to the grid infrastructure.

There is no big change in the connectivity layer, since it addresses/defines core communication and security authentication requirements of grid entities. The only requirement in bringing clouds to grids from the communication point of view is the need for a large capacity network infrastructure to make the process of movement of Virtual Machine files faster and reliable. In addition, there are some security challenges that need to be addressed and currently it is under research.

The Resource layer brings the Fabric layer resources into the grid infrastructure, so that they can be operated in the grid level to coordinate single resource sharing relationship. This layer works only with individual resources and invokes the corresponding Fabric layer functions of a resource to manage and control a local resource. Therefore, the management of virtualized resources operations should be added to this layer.

The neck of this hourglass narrowed to incorporate Resource and Connectivity protocols, a few set of core abstractions and protocols.

The Collective Layer is universal or global layer in the grid architecture to coordinate operations on multiple resources. This layer is architected on the neck of hourglass model (Resource and Connectivity), so it can exploit the new functionalities offered by resource layer in adopting cloud model to present new applications and behaviors. For example, by benefiting from suspension/resumption

Figure 2. Grid protocol architecture

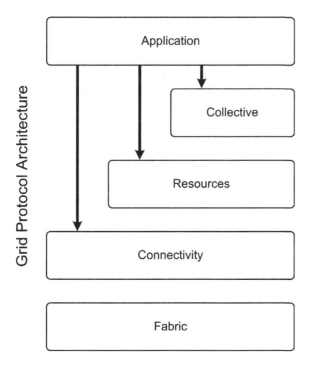

capability of virtualized resources, the Collective layer can provide better co-allocation services, new programming models, etc.

Capabilities in each layer share common characteristics and can build on capabilities and behaviors provided by lower layers, so that all features presented by virtualization and other cloud-related technologies at the fabric and resource layers can be exploited in the collective layer.

The new grid architecture adopting some enabling technologies in cloud presented in Figure 3; this architecture also is a protocol architecture like grid.

With virtualization, virtualized hardware is exposed at the fabric layer, as illustrated in Figure 3. At the fabric layer, the user is allocated virtualized hardware.

In grid, common protocols are designed to address interoperability in the interface level. In the cloud model, the virtualized resource model addresses the other aspects of interoperability issue appear in grid at the Fabric, Resource and Collective layers as well as the final layer, application i.e. VO applications interoperability.

This new architecture is mainly inspired by IaaS model to address grid and cloud complementarity approach. A middleware based on this architecture would be able to provide new services such as federation of resources which are not available currently in the grid and cloud infrastructures.

Current Practices

As we have discussed, IaaS cloud can be embedded into the grid architecture nicely to offer better services and operations in the grid level. There is now growing interest in open source IaaS cloud computing tools like Nimbus and OpenNebula (OpenNebula, 2010) that also provide commercial cloud compatible interfaces. They help organizations to build and customize their own cloud infrastructure.

Nimbus developed within Globus Toolkit community, a de facto standard for grids, so that

Figure 3. Grid architecture adopting IaaS cloud

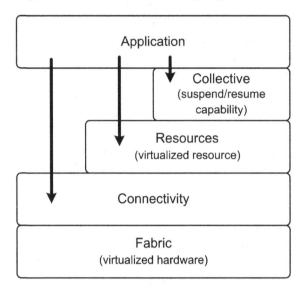

it seems it can bring IaaS cloud into the grid with some straightforward efforts. Also, there are some attempts to use OpenNebula within EGEE Grid.

The current toolkits for cloud computing can be classified in two categories: Local Infrastructure Manager (LIM) and Global Infrastructure Manager (GIM).

Local Infrastructure Manager manages the Local Infrastructure at the scale of an integrated Infrastructure (a data center) that is not geographically distributed while Global Infrastructure Manager controls a geographically distributed Global Infrastructure (a number of data centers).

Nimbus makes it easy for scientific projects to experiment with cloud computing. With the help of Nimbus, scientists can do new jobs in e-Science context:

- Leasing on-demand resources (as VMs) to build turnkey virtual clusters (with Context Broker of Nimbus)
- Finding the right environment in distributed systems
- Deploying network gateways on infrastructures
- Using IaaS features

- Leveraging external Infrastructures with IaaS Gateway

OpenNebula is another Open Source, Interface and Architecture virtual infrastructure manager to create a Virtualization layer between the raw infrastructure and the service layer in the Private and Hybrid Clouds. It responses to the changing demands of a service workload by incorporating external clouds to create a hybrid cloud dynamically with the help of Resources and Services Virtualization without Barriers (RESERVOIR) project (Reservoir, 2010). In addition, OpenNebula can integrate with Nimbus and ElasticHosts cloud providers. Briefly, it supports the following functionalities:

- VM workload management and load balancing
- Server consolidation
- Providing elastic capacity
- Cluster partitioning for different services
- On demand provision of VMs
- Cloud Gateway or Broker

Nimbus and OpenNebula are considered as a Local Infrastructure Manager since they operate at the local level. Thus, from the architecture point of view Nimbus and OpenNebula services appear in the Resource layer.

In addition, multi-cloud feature of Nimbus would allow users to get resources over multiple geographically distributed cloud resource. This feature supports contextualizing across multiple clouds. Also this is true for OpenNebula by its hybrid clouds capability. In this case we can say, Nimbus and OpenNebula are in the class of Global Infrastructure Manager and offer some global services in the Collective layer. Nimbus uses Haizea (Sotomayor, Keahey & Foster, 2008) as its scheduling back-end, thus, Haizea is an LIM's scheduler. Currently, OpenNebula also uses Haizea for its scheduler back-end.

RESERVOIR is a GIM to provide deployment and management of IT services across a number of geographically distributed data centers (federating infrastructures or hybrid clouds) with high quality of service, high productivity, high availability and competitive costs. It is a European Union FP7 funded project to reach the goal of Service-Oriented Computing visionary promise by leveraging Virtualization, Grid Computing and business service management techniques.

The other Open Source cloud middleware tools are Cumulus, EUCALYPTUS, Nimrod, openQRM and Enomaly. EUCALYPTUS (Eucalyptus, 2010) stands for Elastic Utility Computing Architecture for Linking Your Programs to Useful Systems. Its interface is compatible with Amazon's EC2 interface. EUCALYPTUS is implemented using commonly available Linux tools and basic Web Service technologies making it easy to install and maintain. Its functionalities are like Nimbus.

Unlike the Amazon's EC2 service, the Science Clouds like Nimbus do not require users to directly pay for usage. The usage of them is based on asking from the scientist to provide some information about: an email account with the sponsoring institution, web pages, pointers to papers and asking for a short write-up of the scientific project.

FUTURE RESEARCH DIRECTIONS

In this part, we describe some of challenges of incorporating clouds in the grids. Now that we find it useful to embrace the provisioning model of IaaS clouds, it is time to face its challenges. How would be the situation of IaaS cloud provisioning model in the grids?

In this new model, jobs are abstracted by virtual machines; in fact virtual machines are part of jobs. The first difficulty is managing the virtual machines' big files in the preparation phase of provisioning. Since virtual machines encapsulate the operating system, application and data, they would have a very big size at the scale of gigabyte. We should manage to transfer these images to remote grid resources. There are two simple remedy for this challenge: first one is that grid network infrastructure provide enough bandwidth to be able to transfer virtual machine files quickly either by specialized network or by increasing bandwidth, and the second one is pre-deployment approach by replicating and distributing virtual machine files over the grid infrastructure near compute resources; this can be done by VO administrators or Virtual Appliance providers.

The next challenge is regarding resource management and scheduling. Currently in the grids and HPC we have a couple of full-featured local resource management such as Torque, SGE and Condor. They take care of all scheduling and resource management requirements. However, in the new model, IaaS brings new capabilities such as suspension/resumption and at the same time new difficulties such as taking care of virtual machines. Current open source IaaS cloud frameworks provide best-effort scheduling, also Haizea is a research-based IaaS cloud scheduler project providing more features such as supporting advance reservation and deadline driven jobs. Even Nimbus can be integrated by some local resource managers like Torque and SGE to schedule virtual machine deployment requests in batch mode. However, in this model we need something like Metascheduler (GridWay, WMS) in grid to schedule virtual machines at the global level to address co-allocation and co-scheduling requests within this new model considering virtual machine issues. Finally, integration of IaaS cloud tools with grid tools is another challenge. This challenge seems to be easy for Nimbus, since it is developed within Globus Toolkit, and uses GT WSRF services to implement most of the toolkit part, so that integration with GT grid middleware is not hard.

CONCLUSION

In the cloud computing world, IT capabilities are delivered on the fly and on demand through the Internet when the need arises instead of drawing from desktop computers. Currently, more and more enterprises are considering the cloud as a deployment option because the costs of running their own data center are escalating rapidly. For instance, large internet and technological companies including Google, Yahoo! and Amazon are pushing forward their plans to deliver information and software over the net.

There are lots of arguments and analysis comparing cloud computing with grid computing from different points of view. In this chapter, we have investigated this issue by considering grid architecture, and we have concluded that there are some challenges to be addressed when we embrace IaaS cloud model within grid architecture. As a result, we believe clouds are complementary to grid models, this means cloud model will bring new behaviors and functionalities to grid infrastructure.

If we consider the advantages and benefits of cloud computing, we conclude that with the appearance of cloud models, the number of scientific users with different demands and strict software environments will be increased significantly. Moreover, scientific applications will benefit from reliability, accuracy and efficiency of running their computations on Science Clouds (Keahey, Figueiredo, Fortes, Freeman & Tsugawa, 2008). Computation is considered the third mode of science, where the previous modes or paradigms were experimentation/observation and theory. With the introduction of high performance supercomputers, the methods of scientific research could include mathematical models and simulation of phenomenon that are too expensive or beyond our experiment reach. With the advent of cloud computing, a fourth mode of science is on the horizon.

Another set of challenges in the cloud era is doing High Performance Computing in cloud. For instance, if we consider the future of computer systems with many cores, the problem of bringing multiple VMs at the same time on a multi/many-core system becomes critical from the performance and speed point of view. Also, what would be the situation for an extreme-scale computer i.e. a very big supercomputer with one million cores? There are lots of other problems that can be defined for this issue that need to be addressed.

REFERENCES

Amazon EC2. (2009). *Amazon elastic compute cloud official Web site*. Retrieved from http://aws.amazon.com/ ec2

CRM at Salesforce.com, Inc. (2010). *The leader in software-as-a-service (SaaS) official website*. Retrieved from http://www.salesforce.com

Devare, M., Sheikhalishahi, M., & Grandinetti, L. (2009). Virtualization: A foundation for cloud computing. *CiiT International Journal of Networking and Communication Engineering 1*(6), 245-254.

EGI. (2010). *European grid initiative official portal site*. Retrieved from http://www.egi.eu/

Eucalyptus. (2010). *The eucalyptus open-source cloud-computing system project official portal site*. Retrieved from http://eucalyptus.cs.ucsb.edu

Facebook. (2010). *Welcome to Facebook! Official portal site*. Retrieved from http://www.facebook.com

Flicker. (2010). *Welcome to Flickr – Photo sharing official portal site*. Retrieved from http://www.flickr.com/

Foster, I. (2008). *A critique of using clouds to provide grids*. Retrieved from http://ianfoster.typepad.com/ blog/ 2008/ 09/ a-critique-of-u.html

Foster, I., Kesselman, C., & Tuecke, S. (2001). The anatomy of the Grid: Enabling scalable virtual organizations. *The International Journal of Supercomputer Applications, 15*, 200–222. doi:10.1177/109434200101500302

Foster, I., Zhao, Y., Raicu, I., & Lu, S. (2008). Cloud computing and Grid computing 360-degree compared. *In Grid Computing Environments Workshop (GCE '08)* (pp. 1-10).

Gentzsch, W., Grandinetti, L., & Joubert, G. (Eds.). (2010). *High speed and large scale scientific computing. Advances in parallel computing, 18*. Amsterdam, Netherlands: IOS Press.

Google App Engine. (2010). *Google code official portal site*. Retrieved from http://code.google.com/ appengine/

Grandinetti, L. (Ed.). (2008). *High performance computing (HPC) and Grids in action. Advances in Parallel Computing, 16*. Amsterdam, Netherlands: IOS Press. whttp://www.italiangrid.org/

Intel Corporation. (2010). *Intel® Multi-core technology official portal site*. Retrieved from http://www.intel.com/ multi-core/ index.htm

Italian Grid Infrastructure. (2010). *Italian Grid infrastructure official portal site*. Retrieved from.

Jha, S., Merzky, A., & Fox, G. (2008). Using clouds to provide Grids higher-levels of abstraction and explicit support for usage modes. *Concurrency and Computation: Practice & Experience, A Special Issue from the Open Grid Forum, 21*(8), 1087-1108.

Keahey, K., & Figueiredo, R. Fortes, J., Freeman, T., & Tsugawa, M. (2008, October). Science clouds: Early experiences in cloud computing for scientific applications. *In Cloud Computing and Its Application (CCA-08)*, Chicago, IL.

Kelem, N. L., & Feiertag, R. J. (1991, May 20-22). A separation model for virtual machine monitors. In *Proceedings of 1991 IEEE Computer Society Symposium on Security and Privacy*, Oakland, CA (pp. 78-86). Washington, DC: IEEE Computer Society.

LHC. (2010). *CERN - The Large Hadron Collider official portal site*. Retrieved from http://public. web.cern.ch/ public/ en/ LHC/ LHC-en.html

LXC. (2010). *Linux Containers project official portal site*. Retrieved from http://lxc.sourceforge. net/

NetOverlay. (2010). *Network overlay definition*. Retrieved from http://en.wikipedia.org/ wiki/ Overlay_network

Nimbus (2010). *Nimbus project official portal site*. Retrieved from http://www.nimbusproject.org/

NUMA. (2010). *NUMA: Definition and additional resources from ZDNet*. Retrieved from http:// dictionary.zdnet.com/ definition/ NUMA.html

OpenNebula. (2010). *OpenNebula project official portal site*. Retrieved from http://www. opennebula.org

Reservoir (2010). *Reservoir project official portal site*. Retrieved from http://www.reservoir-fp7.eu/

Salesforce.com. Inc. (2010). *What is platform as a service (PaaS) Salesforce.com, Inc. Official Website*. Retrieved from http://www.salesforce. com/ paas/

Science Clouds. (2010). *Science clouds project official portal site*. Retrieved from http://www. sciencecclouds.org/

Sotomayor, B., Keahey, K., & Foster, I. (2008). Combining batch execution and leasing using virtual machines. In *Proceedings of the 17th International Symposium on High Performance Distributed Computing*, Boston, MA (pp. 87-96). Association for Computing Machinery.

STAR. (2010). *The STAR collaboration*. Retrieved from http://www.star.bnl.gov

TeraGrid. (2010). *TeraGrid official portal site*. Retrieved from https://www.teragrid.org/

Web Services. (2010). *Web services architecture*. Retrieved from http://www.w3.org/ TR/ ws-arch/#whatis

Xen (2010). *Xen paravirtualization official portal site*. Retrieved from http://www.xen.org/ about/ paravirtualization.html

Chapter 3
Grid, SOA and Cloud Computing:
On-Demand Computing Models

Mohamed El-Refaey
Middle East Wireless Innovation Center (MEWIC) at Intel Corporation, Egypt

Bhaskar Prasad Rimal
Kookmin University, Korea

ABSTRACT

Service Oriented Architecture (SOA) and Web Services play an invaluable role in grid and cloud computing models and are widely seen as a base for new models of distributed applications and system management tools. SOA, grid and cloud computing models share core and common behavioral features and characteristics by which a synergy is there to develop and implement new services that facilitate the on-demand computing model.

In this chapter we are going to introduce the key concepts of SOA, grid, and cloud computing and the relation between them. This chapter illustrates the paradigm shift in technological services due to the incorporation of these models and how we can combine them to develop a highly scalable application system such as petascale computing. Also there will be coverage for some concepts of Web 2.0 and why it needs grid computing and the on-demand enterprise model. Finally, we will discuss some standardization efforts on these models as a further step in developing interoperable grid systems.

DOI: 10.4018/978-1-61350-113-9.ch003

INTRODUCTION

The furor around Cloud Computing, Grid, and service-oriented paradigm is taking the technology world by storm and is a must for an efficient utilization of computing resources, energy, and capital investment. Service Oriented Architecture (SOA) and Web Services play an invaluable role in grid and cloud computing models, and are widely seen as a base for new models of distributed applications and system management tools. SOA, grid, and cloud computing models share core and common behavioral features and characteristics by which a synergy exists to develop and implement new services that facilitate the on-demand computing model.

A Google trend that is shown in Figure 1 describes the craze of cloud which may even have peaked. Cloud computing has risen from 2007, while grid computing is continuously falling down from 2004 and similarly SOA which is falling down from 2008 onwards.

In this chapter we are going to introduce the key concepts of SOA, grid, and cloud computing and the relation between them. This chapter illustrates the paradigm shift in technological services due to the incorporation of these models and how we can combine them to develop a highly scalable application system such as Petascale computing systems. We will, also, cover some concepts of Web 2.0 technology and why Web 2.0 needs grid computing and the on-demand enterprise model to provide more value.

You will find below some of the key enabling technologies that contribute to the cloud and grid computing which will be identified and covered throughout the chapter:

- Virtualization
- Web Service and SOA
- Workflows and Workflow Orchestration
- Web 2.0
- World-wide Distributed Storage System

Finally, we will discuss some of the standardization efforts on these models as a further step in developing interoperable loosely coupled grid and cloud computing systems. The chapter highlights and sections are illustrated in the mind map shown in Figure 2.

Figure 1. The Google trend of grid computing, SOA, and cloud computing from 2004 to 2010

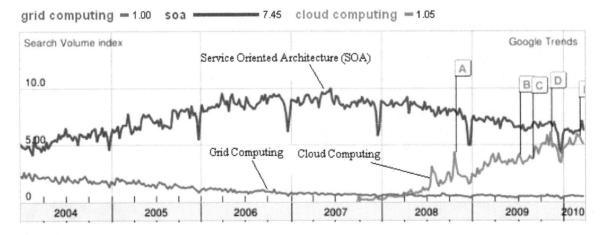

Figure 2. MindMap for the chapter contents

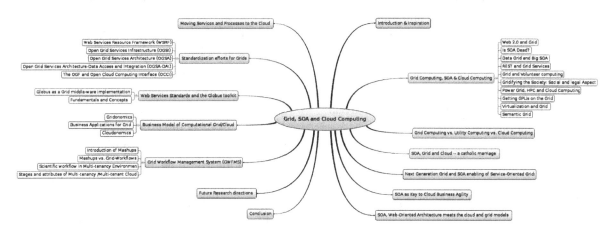

GRID COMPUTING, SOA, AND CLOUD COMPUTING: A PRIMARY INTRODUCTION

Grid Computing

Grid computing is not a new concept, but an old one with new implementation. Grid computing is the next major revolution in information technology after the advent of the internet. The ancestor of the grid computing is Metacomputing (National Center for Supercomputer Applications, 1995). Smarr, and Catlett (1992) coined the term metacomputing around 1987 to describe his concept of a connected, coherent computing environment. The major purpose (Smarr, & Catlett, 1992) of metacomputer was local area metacomputer, user's interfaces that allow for participatory computing and metacomputer out onto Gbit/sec network testbeds.

In 1995, the Information Wide Area Year (I-WAY) experimental project was created evolving the grid technology. Global heterogeneous computing, called "The Grid". During 2000-2005, many grid projects were started such as Next-GRID, Ontogrid, Grid@Asia, DataMiningGrid, CoreGRID, K-Wf grid. The earlier prominent grid effort was SETI@Home which links more than four million computers together into a massive supercomputer. Grid computing is a highly custom endeavor today; with substantial integration effort required to put one into operation; where it is built with toolkits, or leverages which are some of the productized software components. In order to gain the maturity of grid, we need more standardization of a complete solution of application, middleware, and management. Development tools are available such as g-Eclipse, ArguGrid, BERIN, BEinGRID, GridTrust, XtreemOS, and Edutain@Grid.

The basic definition of computational grid had been given by Foster I. and Kesselman C. (1998). A computational grid is a hardware and software infrastructure that provides dependable, consistent, pervasive, and inexpensive access to high-end computational capabilities; enabling co-ordinated resource sharing and problem solving in dynamic, multi-institutional virtual organizations Similarly, Foster, Kesselman, and Tuecke (2001) defined grid as a coordinated resource sharing and problem solving in dynamic, multi-institutional Virtual Organizations (VOs).

The shared resources can be more than just computers. Basically, those resources are storage sensors for experiments at particular sites, application software, databases, instruments, and network capacity. There are many benefits from grid; among them the following important points:

- Exploit underutilized resources
- Resource Balancing
- Virtualized resources across an enterprise
- Enable collaboration for virtual organizations
- Ensured fault tolerance for improved reliability

There are different classifications of grids like:

- Computational Grid: ChinaGrid (Wu et al., 2005), TeraGrid (Catlett, 2002), APACGrid
- Data Grid: LHCGrid (Santelli, & Donno, 2005), GriPhyN, and ASP Grid (NetSolve/GridSolve) (ASP Grid, 2010).
- Knowledge Grid (Italian Knowledge Grid, EU data mining Grid)
- Utility Grid (Gridbus, Data Center)
- HPC Grid (EuroGrid, 2010)
- Green Grid (Dobson et al., 2005; Green Grid New Mexico, 2010; The Green Grid, 2010; Greening Australia, 2010): Many alliances such as Hewlett-Packard, Sun Microsystems, Dell, Microsoft, EMC2, and IBM are heading towards this direction. Green Grid helps to reduce the growing power and cooling demands in enterprise data centers. USA is the leading country in Green Grid; along with others like Japan, UK, Australia, Netherlands, France, India, South Korea.
- Science Grid (Open Science Grid, 2010)
- Enabling Grids for E-sciencE (EGEE, 2010) project, DOE science grid (Department of Energy, 2003), NAREGI (Miura, 2006), BiG Grid (BiG Grid, 2010), Life Science Grid (LSG, 2010)

Service Oriented Architecture

SOA is an architectural approach in which highly independent, loosely-coupled, and component-based software services are made interoperable, and there is now some discussion around a potential synergy between web technologies and SOA. Moreover, SOA is the concepts of services and messages. A service may be defined as a logical manifestation of some physical resources like database, and devices that are exposed to the network. A service is an entity that can send and receive messages. Don Box's four tenets about Service Orientation:

- Boundaries are explicit
- Services are autonomous
- Services share schema and contract, not class (abstractions)
- Service compatibility is determined based on policy

SOA application is a composition of services. Services are the atomic unit of an SOA. Services encapsulate a business process. Service providers register themselves. Service usage involves finding, binding, executing. The basic concept of SOA is shown in Figure 3.

Service Provider: Provides a stateless, location transparent business service.

Service Registry: Allows service consumers to locate service providers that meet required criteria.

Service Consumer: Uses service's providers to complete business processes.

The following are the major benefits of SOA:

- Focus on business domain solutions
- Leverage existing infrastructure
- Agility, loose coupling
- Autonomous service
- Location transparency
- Late binding

Figure 3. SOA basic concept with actors

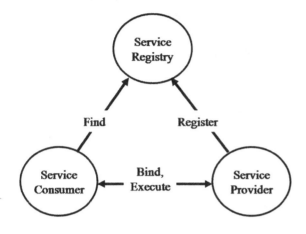

Cloud Computing

Before knowing the history of cloud computing, there is a history of utility computing which is not a new concept, but rather has quite a long history; among its earliest references is:

"If computers of the kind I have advocated become the computers of the future, then computing may someday be organized as a public utility just as the telephone system is a public utility... The computer utility could become the basis of a new and important industry."- John McCarthy, MIT Centennial (1961)

Cloud computing implements the idea of utility computing, which was first suggested by John McCarthy in 1961, where computing is viewed as a public utility, however this idea resurfaced in the new forms as "Cloud Computing". Is cloud computing new? The following data shows the development history of some important technology along cloud computing.

1960 – Supercomputer, SOA (Procedural Programming)
1961 – Utility Computing
1964 – MULTICS (MULTIplexed Information and Computing Service)
1985 – Condor Distributed Batch System

1990 – Linux based parallel computing using commodity hardware
1999 – Seti@Home, Web 2.0
1995 – Grid Computing
1996 – Volunteer Computing
2000 – Representational State Transfer (REST)
2001 – TeraGrid
2003 – Google File System
2004 – Web 2.0 (resurface), Google's MapReduce
2005 – Nutch Distributed File System (NDFS), in 2006, renamed Hadoop Distributed File System
2006 – Amazon EC2 and S3
2007 – Cloud Computing

There is no single canonical definition of cloud computing till now. Many definitions can be found from industry as well as academia. The more important definitions from National Institute of Standards and Technology (NIST), Information Technology Laboratory (Mell, & Grance 2009) have defined Cloud Computing as a model for enabling convenient, on-demand network access to a shared pool of configurable computing resources e.g. networks, servers, storage, applications, and services that can be rapidly provisioned and released with minimal management effort, or service provider's interaction. This cloud model promotes availability and is composed of five essential characteristics. On-demand self-service, broad network access, resource pooling, rapid elasticity, and measured service, three delivery models: Cloud Software as a Service, Cloud Platform as a Service, and Cloud Infrastructure as a Service, and four deployment models: Private Cloud, Community Cloud, Public Cloud, and Hybrid Cloud.

Similarly Foster et al. (2008), defined cloud computing as a large-scale distributed computing paradigm that is driven by economies of scale, in which a pool of abstracted, virtualized, dynamically-scalable, managed computing power, storage, platforms, and services are delivered on demand to external customers over the internet.

Cloud Myths, Hate and Reality

Even though Free Software Foundation guru Stallman R. (Johnson, 2008) primary critics on cloud computing was: *"It is stupidity, it is worst than stupidity, it's a marketing hype campaign. Somebody is saying this is inevitable- and whenever you hear somebody saying that, it's very likely to be a set of businesses' campaigning to make it true."*; but interestingly, the majority of involvement in cloud computing comes from open source community. Similarly, another popular opponent was from Ellison L., the founder of Oracle, who criticized the rash of cloud computing announcements as "fashion-driven" and "complete gibberish"; although Oracle is also doing cloud computing.

Some of the myths behind cloud computing (Cloud Myths Dispelled, 2009).

Myth 1: I am using virtualization/hypervisors in my data center. I am already running a cloud.
Myth 2: Cloud computing is just grid computing by a different name.
Myth 3: Clouds provide infinite scale.
Myth 4: Clouds only provide pay-as-you-go access.

Similarly Gartner (2008) described:

Myth 1: Cloud computing is an architecture, or an infrastructure
Myth 2: Every vendor will have a different Cloud
Myth 3: Software as a Service (SaaS) is the Cloud
Myth 4: Cloud computing is a brand new revolution
Myth 5: All remote computing is cloud computing
Myth 6: The Internet and the Web are the cloud
Myth 7: Everything will be in the cloud
Myth 8: The cloud eliminates private networks

The Dark side of the cloud:

- Separation of developers and Information Technology (IT) professionals
- Migration and reversal (in) abilities
- Risk of hazard dependency
- Building IT masterpiece

Cloud maturity model:

- Consolidation
- Abstraction
- Automation
- Utility
- Market

Focus on the future:

- Innovation
- Conceptualization
- Venture management
- Being process oriented not product driven

Differences between Grid Computing and Cloud Computing

There are several differences between grid and cloud (Keahey et al. 2009; Foster et al., 2008; Myeson, 2009; RightGrid Overview, 2010). However, cloud will not replace grid, but the convergence (grid, HPC, and cloud towards green computing) is needed such as building a strong Infrastructure as a Service (IaaS) (Table 1). As Keahey K. explained as: *"It is more likely that grids will be re-branded, or merge into cloud computing. I think in five years something like 80 to 90 percent of the computation we are doing could be cloud-based."*

WEB 2.0 AND GRID

The termed Web 2.0 is coined by DiNucci (1999) and popularized by O'Relly T. (2005). The features of Web 2.0 are user centric design, interoperable, interactive sharing, and collaboration on World Wide Web. In the context of Web 2.0, Sir Berners-Lee (The inventor of the Web) mentioned that (Laningham, 2006):

Table 1. Comparision between Grid computing and Cloud computing

Grid Computing	Cloud Computing
Requires batch job scheduling, or sophisticated policies for allocation jobs. Globus project is the de facto grid computing standard. Operating cost is expensive. Complex to handle general application, and complex environment. Not always suitable if users are using different OS, or login access. Different computers in the form of one large infrastructure can bind with unused resources to realize a grid computing. Grids provide more domain-specific services. Provisioning resources as utility that can be turned on, or off. Grid is mostly used for High intensive computational requirements.	Cloud does not require large, an upfront investment, and providers are responsible for running and maintaining servers. There is no such single de facto project, even though Amazon EC2 is becoming de facto standards. It seems much less expensive if compared to operating your own data center and running several servers. More flexible and easy to handle application. Users can lease and control the remote resources whenever they want. User need thin clients, grid computing, and utility computing to work with cloud computing Clouds can sit below domain-specific (ex., RightGrid). On-demand resource provisioning. Cloud can be used for High CPU usage, high storage, bandwidth, etc.

"Totally not. Web 1.0 was all about connecting people. It was an interactive space, and I think Web 2.0 is of course a piece of jargon, nobody even knows what it means. If Web 2.0 for you is blogs and wikis, then that is people to people. But that was what the Web was supposed to be all along. And in fact, you know, this 'Web 2.0 means using the standards which have been produced by all these people working on Web 1.0.'"- Laningham S. Postcast (Ed.), IBM developerWorks Interviews: Tim Berners-Lee, August 22, 2006

Even though there are lots of discussion and hype behind Web 2.0, it still does not have the concrete way that is what is it? It's an ongoing research issues. Musser, O'Reilly, and O'Reilly Radar Team. (2006) defined the Web 2.0 is a set of economic, social, and technology trends that collectively form the basis for the next generation of the internet—a more mature, distinctive medium characterized by user participation, openness, and network effects. Behind the huge impact of Web 2.0, Tim O'Reilly mentioned six key ideas on the concept such as:

1. Individual production and user generated content
2. Harness the power of the crowd
3. Data on the epic scale
4. Architecture of participation
5. Network effects
6. Openness

From the technology perspective Web 2.0 uses AJAX (Asynchronous JavaScript, and XML), REST, SOAP, Mashups, and RSS. Table 2 shows some differences between old Web 1.0 and Web 2.0.

The major advantage of Web 2.0 tools is that most of them are free. There is the architecture of participation; this means how I make a site to which people want to contribute. The bloggers write for free. They get as much traffic as the articles and don't cost anything. The supports and documentations are well in Web 2.0. Interestingly, Web 3.0 is the sensor-web, in which we can carry around with us the architecture of participation, which will be automatic and the byproduct of the devices.

Example of Web 2.0 includes web application, hosted services, social-networking, video-sharing site, wikis, Online Surveys, blogs, RSS feeds, Social Bookmarking, Postcasting, mashup, and folksonomies. Some popular Web 2.0 tools are Blogger, Wordpress, Myspace, Google Maps, Youtube, Metacafe, Del.ico.us, dig, Furl, Twitter, Flicker, Facebook, Meetup, Orkut, and LinkedIn. Table 3 List out the top 15 most popular (Top 15

Table 2. Development scenario of Web 2.0

Web 1.0 (1993-2003)	Web 2.0 (2003-present)	Web 3.0 (2010-beyond)
Static	Dynamic	Intelligent
Read	Write and Contribute	Data-driven
Page	Post /record	Personalization
Brochureware	Customization	Natural Language Search
Web browser	Browser, RSS Reader, anything	
Personal web site	Blog	
Client Server	Web Services	
Web Coders	Everyone	
Britannica Online	Wikipedia	
Directories (taxonomy)	Tagging (folksonomy)	
Bookmarking sites	Social bookmarking	
	(web as desktop philosophy)	

Most Popular Web 2.0 Websites, 2010) Web 2.0 websites till Feb 2010.

Some open issues are who owns the messages, how can marketers use this for their advantage, and are masses better than experts. Privacy, reputation, security, data migration, trusted source, search engine optimization are prominent issues on Web 2.0. One considerable problem for intellectual property protection and information overload may start to have a noticeable effect on many people (see Table 4).

Is SOA Dead?

There is hype and discussion these days about the death of SOA, but certainly SOA is struggling to convince companies to invest in BPM, BAM, and ESB in today's economic condition. Manes (2009) argued that SOA is dead, lots of discussion among SOA evangelists is going on, but the question here is the scenario shifting to the newer pastures. One very important thing is that SOA is not just reducing the costs, but it is the process of application re-architect and rede-

sign to shift in the way IT operates. If SOA is an architectural transformation, it should exist with the organizational and cultural transformation of service delivery and Service-Oriented IT (Foody, 2009) otherwise it is dead.

Data Grid and Big SOA

Data Grids are a highly concurrent distributed data structure and management of large amounts of distributed data. They can have over 100 Terabytes of data storage. Oliver (2009) described Data Grid as cache and it is a system of record. Some examples of Data Grid are GiGaSpaces In-Memory Data Grid (GigaSpaces, 2010), Hazelcast In-Memory Data Grid (Hazelcast Software, 2010), Infinispan (JBoss Community, 2010), Java based Data Grid platform, BeSTGRID (BeSTGRID, 2009), and Oracle Coherence (Oracle Coherence, 2010).

Basically, mechanism neutrality, policy neutrality, compatibility with grid infrastructure, and uniformity of information are needed to design Data Grid architecture (Chervenak et al., 2000). There are many approaches to implement SOA;

Table 3. Top 15 Web 2.0 website

YouTube.com	Flickr.com	TypePad.com
Wekipedia.org	WordPress.com	Topix.com
Craigslist.org	IMDB.com	LiveJournal.com
Twitter.com	Dig.com	devianART.com
Photobucket.com	eHow.com	Technorati.com

Table 4. Web 2.0 Vs Grid computing

Web 2.0	Grid Computing
Web 2.0 has a set of major services like GoogleMaps, or Flickr but the world is composing Mashups that make new composite services. End-point standards are set by end-point owners. Many different protocols covering a variety of de-facto standards such as OpenSocial. Admired Web 2.0 technologies are JavaScript, JSON, AJAX PHP, and REST with gadget interface (like Google gadgets). Not so clear that Web 2.0 won't eventually dominate other application areas and with Enterprise 2.0.	Grid computing has a set of major software systems like Condor and Globus and a different world is extending with custom services and linking with workflow. No single grid computing protocol exist. A range of existing protocols, frameworks that are build on internet protocols and services (communication, routing, name resolution). Popular grid technologies are Apache Axis, BPEL WSDL, and SOAP with portlet interfaces. Robustness of grids is demanded by the Enterprise.

they are lying between Big SOA and little SOA. Big SOA is about business alignment. The whole organization, with its business processes and supporting IT systems, is modeled. This is a good approach where all stakeholders can express their concerns and have a shared picture with agreed core principles that helps to set up a coherent roadmap. Little SOA is an architectural style that is needed to build a distributed systems which are loosely coupled components. It does not need the whole organization on board to get started. So, it is a faster approach than Big SOA approach, but it is hard to reuse the services by others. When the approach needs to extend, in this case there may be greater stakeholder difficulties due to lack of governance, overall aims, and agreed principles (see Table 5).

REST and Grid Services

REST stands for Representational State Transfer, an architectural idea and set of principles first introduced by Fielding (2000). It is not a standard, but describes an approach for a client/server, stateless architecture, whose most obvious manifestation is the web, and which provides a simple communications interface using XML and HTTP. Every resource is identified by a URI and the use of HTTP lets you communicate your intentions through GET, POST, PUT, and DELETE command requests. REST is a set of architectural principles which ask the following questions:

- Why is the World Wide Web so prevalent and ubiquitous?
- What makes the Web scale?
- How can I apply the architecture of the Web to my own applications?

Motivation with REST:

- Reduce infrastructure cost
- Make data publishing simple and timely
- Encourage interoperability
- Create a federated business-technical model

RESTful Architectural Principles:

Addressable Resources. Everything on the network should have an ID. With REST over HTTP, every object will have its own specific URI

A Uniform, Constrained Interface. When applying REST over HTTP, stick to the methods provided by the protocol. This means following: the meaning of GET, POST, PUT, and DELETE religiously.

Multiple representations. You interact with services using representations of that service. An

Table 5. Big SOA vs. Little SOA

Big SOA	Little SOA
Top down approach Analyze the business Identify Business areas Map to software	Bottom up approach Autonomous course grained components Message based interactions Run time configuration

object referenced by one URI can have different formats available. Different platforms need different formats. AJAX may need JSON. A Java application may need XML

Communicate statelessly. Stateless applications are easier to scale

Open Grid Service Architecture (OGSA) is the standards on which the service is based. OGSA are the grid services. Grid Service is a kind of transient stateful web service that supports reliable and secure service invocation, lifecycle management, notifications, policy management, credential management, and virtualization. Current version of Globus Tool is based on grid services. The service mechanism in grid: A client sends a service request to a scheduler. In Globus Toolkit 4, GRIS (Grid Resource Information Service) and GIIS (Grid Index Information Service) act as a scheduler. The scheduler goes to find the service provider that can provide the service needed. After negotiation, the URI (Universal Resource Identifier) of that service is returned. The client then invokes the service with input data and other necessary information.

Grid and Volunteer Computing

Volunteer computing emerged as the concept of connecting unused (Volunteer PC) PC over the Internet. Volunteer computing is computing platform that is applicable where we need low financial resources. Volunteer computing uses computers belonging to ordinary people, like you, to create a computing grid that can rival the most powerful supercomputers in the world (Grid Cafe, 2010). With this technology, large scale computational problems are broken up into several small data chunks and send to several volunteer PCs who are simultaneously engaged, after processing it, send back to the central system. Volunteer computing requires a trust between the volunteers and the project managers. The volunteers trust the project to be within legal standards such as security, privacy, and intellectual property laws.

The prominent Volunteer Computing projects include SETI@home, Folding@Home (~200,000 node) (Larson et al., 2002), and Great Internet Mersenne Prime Search (GIMPS) (Great Internet Mersenne Prime Search, 2010). A number of frameworks for volunteer computing have been developed such as Bayanihan (Sarmenta, & Hirano, 1999), Xtremeweb (Cappello et al., 2005), and Entropis (Chien et al., 2003). Among them Berkeley Open Infrastructure for Network Computing (BOINC) which is popular for being comprised of both server and client components (Anderson, 2004). However, BONIC architecture is highly modular and scalable, well suited to large scale projects, and may create complexities and limitation for the researchers who are thinking of small to medium size volunteer computing projects.

Desktop Grid used desktop PCs within an organization; this is slightly similar to volunteer computing, but it has accountability and lacks anonymity, therefore it is significantly different from volunteer computing. In the concept of distributed nature they are same.

Gridifying the Society: Social and Legal Aspects

It is hard to determine exactly when the term Gridifying or Gridification was coined. All users need to gridify their application before it can run on a grid environment. Once gridified, thousands of people will be able to use the same application that is the concept of gridifying the society. The basic steps are:

1. Authentication credentials: consists of a certificate and cryptographic key (private key).
2. Query a catalogue: determine which resources are available and can do the analysis.
3. Submit a job to the grid.
4. Monitor and report progress.

According to Gridify Environment (2010), gridifying a web portal has a capability of administrating users' account and files, applications and services, instantiating and scheduling tasks, submitting and retrieving status query of tasks on different grid infrastructures and middleware. Some examples of gridifying the society are European Space Agency Earth Observation Grid Processing on-Demand (European Space Agency, 2010), BEinGrid (Business Experiments in Grid, 2010), Ionia GlobCover data Distribution Center (European Space Agency, Ionia GlobCover, 2010), GENESI-DR (Ground European Network for Earth Science Interoperations-Digital Repositories, 2010), and GridGrain (Bossa, 2008).

Power Grid, High Performance Computing and Cloud Computing

The application area of grid computing is widening day-by-day and effectively used in scientific research, oil and gas mining, education and banking sectors. Nowadays, grid computing is a powerful and necessary tool for the electrical engineering applications. The power system operation and control involve large data intensive, communication intensive, computation intensive, and time intensive applications. Those requirements can be fulfilled with grid technology, since grid computing is considered as inexpensive comparing to supercomputing. Power system applications developed on the grid computing can provide real time information for the whole system. Grid computing can provide services in power generation, transmission distribution, power utilization, and in its marketing (Irving, Taylor, and Hobson, 2004). Grid can, also, offer efficient and effective services in the power system monitoring and control, scheduling, fault detection, transmission congestion management, regulation, planning, and electricity market analysis such as forecasting. It provides seamless access to the distributed resources, applications, and data as well as security interaction between them. Grid service technology provides a solution for power industry; to develop an open flexible and scalable system for future power system management and control on large number of dispersed sensors and distributed generators.

Traditional High Performance Computing (HPC) (Distributed Computing with MPI) requires very low latency and different interconnect protocols for optimal performance. It requires high-speed parallel file system for optimized I/O performance. HPC uses supercomputers and clusters to perform advanced computation. HPC as a Service (Penguin Computing, 2009) is a computing model where users have on-demand access to dynamically scalable and high-performance clusters optimized for parallel computing including the expertise needed to set up, optimize, and run their applications over the internet. It provides many benefits as follows:

- HPC resources scale with demand and are available with no capital outlay – only the resources used are actually paid for.
- Experts in high-performance computing, help, setup, and optimize the software environment and can help trouble-shoot issues that might occur.
- Computing costs are reduced, particularly where the workflow has spikes in demand.

Walker (2008) had shown a performance gap existing between performing HPC computations on a traditional scientific cluster and on Amazon Elastic Cloud Computing (EC2) (2010) provisioned scientific cluster. This means that cloud service offerings need to upgrade their services in the area of high performance network provisioning. Gavrilvska, et al., (2007) discussed several improvements over the current virtualization architectures to support HPC applications such as HPC hypervisors (sidecore approach that combines VMM componentization with core partitioning and specialization to meet application's performance demands better) and self-virtualized I/O devices.

Therefore, this is a good idea to leverage the concept HPC-Cloud unification that is looked upon as a unification of the traditional HPC environment and the cloud framework. HPC-cloud should embrace Hadoop (2010) (Cloudera (2010) is pursuing a powerful new enterprise data platform built on Apache Hadoop), Map Reduced framework (Dean, & Ghemawat, 2009; Zhao, & Pjesivac-Grbovic 2009), SMP computing, enterprise solution, parallel computing platform, and computing on demand (utility computing). The concept of HPC-cloud unification provides an ability to respond to the data feeds and to customize more computational resources.

There are numerous challenges of HPC-cloud convergence. Some of them are, different interconnect protocol latency requirements, different preferred interconnect protocol, different file system and storage requirement, and complexity of HPC system setup and provisioning.

Getting GPUs on the Grid

Graphics Processing Units (GPUs) (Ownes et al., 2008) is a powerful programmable and highly parallel computing that is increasingly mainstreaming in the general purpose computing applications. Recently, NVIDIA released a new computing architecture, CUDA (Compute Unified Device Architecture, 2010), for its GeForce 8, 9,100, 200-series, Quadro FX, ION, and Tesla GPU products. This new architecture can change, fundamentally, the way in which GPUs are used. GUPs are faster (GeForceFX 5900 observed 20 GFLOPS, 25.3 GB/sec peak, GeForce 6800 Ultra observed 53 GFLOPS, 35.2 GB/sec peak). It is a good concept to introduce the graphical processor units to enhance the performance of cluster computer and supercomputer and grid computing. Berkeley Open Infrastructure for Network Computing (BOINC) is using Nvidia technology in its GPUGRID (GPUGRID.net, 2010), Einstein@home (2010), and SETI@home (2010) projects. The performance of a GeForce GTX 280 GPU running SETI@ is nearly twice as fast as the fastest consumer multicore CPU and almost 10 times faster than an average dual core consumer CPU (Berkeley Open Infrastructure for Network Computing, 2010). This shows that GUP is a well suitable and faster technology for grid projects.

Virtualization and Grid

What is the relation between grid computing and virtualization technology? This is a valid question to be asked since virtualization technology started to be dominant in the enterprises and production systems along with huge benefits and the return of investments for those who adopt their data centers to be virtualized environments.

Virtualization can be considered the most disruptive technology the computation industry has ever faced in a decade, and if adopted and deployed to its full potential, the computer industry's long journey to commodity status could finally be over. Virtualization technology has revolutionized datacenter's technology through a set of techniques and tools that facilitate the provisioning and management of the dynamic datacenter infrastructure. It has become an essential and enabling technology of cloud computing environments. Virtualization can be defined as the abstraction of the four computing resources (storage, processing power, memory, and network or I/O). It is conceptually similar to emulation, where a system pretends to be another system; whereas virtualization is a system pretending to be two, or more of the same system (Chisnall, 2008). As shown in Figure 4, the virtualization layer will partition the physical resource of the underlying physical server into multiple virtual machines with different workloads. The fascinating thing about this virtualization layer, is that it schedules, allocates the physical resource, and makes each virtual machine think that it totally owns the whole underlying hardware's physical resource (Processor, disks, RAM).

Figure 4. Virtualization technology layered architecture

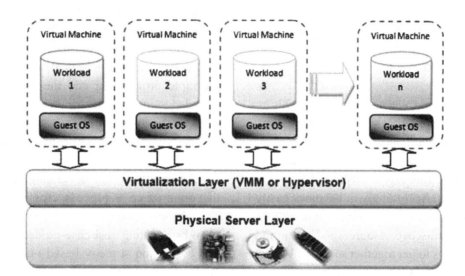

Virtualization, exactly the same as grid, is a trend that's being driven by economics. Rather than having to overprovision on the hardware side to meet peak demands, organizations can use virtualization approaches to get better utilization of existing and underutilized hardware resources. So, both grid and virtualization are heading in the same direction to utilize the computing resources economically.

Virtualization will play an invaluable role in the next generation grids, as it will provide the dynamically provisioned resources that will be needed by the networked grid systems. Grids are considered systems-level virtualizations and, also, the infrastructures for managing workloads and resources (either virtual or physical). In grids, the mission is to execute, optimize, schedule, and manage the resources to help the workloads to work in a better way; and in machine virtualization, the mission is to use, manage, and balance the workloads to utilize the available resources.

From a grid perspective a virtual machine (self-contained operating environment that behaves as if it is a separate computer) can play two different roles:

1. As a resource or container into which any job can be executed.
2. A virtual machine can be considered as a 'workload' that can be scheduled and managed as a job (modulo instantiation).

From this duality of virtual machines that arises from a grid's view, we can see that grids can not only create/use virtual machines, but they can, also, manage them. From all this, we conclude that grids are the key to realizing the full potential of virtualization and vice versa, i.e. exploiting the duality.

In the context of grid computing and SOA, a broader field of application is possible as Freitag et al. (2008) described about how grid computing and SOA can take advantage of resource virtualization by integrating it at different levels of the software stack. Their study has focused on the impact in the area of resource management and on scheduling by supporting virtualization. They proposed to move computing in the grid from a simple job submission towards a more challenging and complex submission of virtual machines. Necessary changes, requirements, and problems at the Grid Middleware and the LRMS level are further discussed. Domination of virtualization technology will affect how we deal with the resources in general; including grids and SOAs.

Semantic Grid

The Semantic Grid (Newhouse et al. 2001) is an approach to grid computing in which information, computing resources, and services are described using the semantic data model. In this model, the data and metadata are expressed through facts, i.e. small sentences. Accordingly, it becomes easily understood by humans. This makes it much easier to automatically discover resources and join up and allows resources to get together to create Virtual Organizations (VOs). The descriptions constitute metadata and are typically represented using the Semantic Web Technology, such as the Resource Description Framework (RDF).

The semantic grid is an extension of the current grid in which information and services are given a well-defined meaning through machine-process-able descriptions which maximize the potential for sharing and reusing it. Figure 5 illustrates the importance of semantic web and semantic grid and the role they play in data and computation versus systems interoperability.

The vision of semantic grid consists of a generically useable e-Research infrastructure, comprised of easily deployed components whose utility transcends their immediate application, providing a high degree of easy-to-use and seamless automation, and in which there are flexible collaborations and computations on a global scale.

This notion of the semantic grid was first articulated in the context of e-Science; observing that such an approach is necessary to achieve a high degree of easy-to-use and seamless automation enabling flexible collaborations and computations on a global scale (De Roure, Jennings, & Shadbolt, 2001). The use of Semantic Web and other knowledge technologies in grid applications is sometimes described as the Knowledge Grid.

Semantic grid extends this by also applying these technologies within the grid middleware.

Worth mentioning, in this context, is the Ontogrid project (Ontogrid, 2010), which aims to produce the technological infrastructure for the rapid prototyping and the development of knowledge-intensive distributed open services for the semantic grid. As designing grid applications, that make use of a semantic grid, requires a new methodology which Ontogrid will develop.

The results aim at developing grid systems that optimize cross-process, cross-company, and cross-industry collaboration; which Ontogrid will show by adopting a use case-guided development and evaluation strategy based on two test case applications of differing, yet stereotypical grid characterization. A principle of Ontogrid is to adopt and influence standards in the semantic grid and the grid computing, in particular the Open Grid Service Architecture.

GRID COMPUTING VS. UTILITY COMPUTING VS. CLOUD COMPUTING

Cloud computing potential and commonality started to be a worth noting phenomena and it is normal to ask, is it really a new concept, is it really an added-value to what we have already, in the distributed computing technology, stack, or is it just new brands to older concepts like utility or grid computing, but with the same identity?!

We shed some lights, in a previous section, on the similarities and differences of these terms' cloud, grid', and now it is the Utility turn to talk about, and see where they complement, where they synergize and where they differ. We will start the discussion with John McCarthy's words about his expectation about computing concepts in the future; McCarthy expected that: "Computation might someday be organized as a public utility"; And his expectations actually came true now, by the emergent of cloud computing and the services it

Figure 5. Scale of data and computation vs. Scale of interoperability

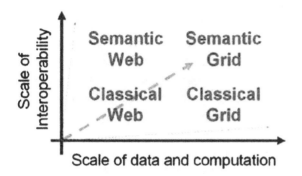

offers with the pay-as-use and on-demand models, it became exactly like a public utility. This means that cloud computing and utility computing are similar in terms of their services' model and the value they offer to their customer's base.

Grid Computing, if we want to give grids a definition, then the best one will be a collection of servers that are clustered together to attack a single problem. For a period of time, the entire resources of the grid are available for an end user to tackle a particularly difficult compute problem. The engineering of such a grid requires complex inter-cluster networking, and, usually, the tuning of a grid is not for the faint of heart.

Cloud Computing has many definitions, National Institute of Standard and Technology (NIST) defines the workable definition for cloud (Mell, & Grance, 2009) computing as a model for enabling ubiquitous, convenient, on-demand network access to a shared pool of configurable computing resources that can be rapidly provisioned and released with minimal management effort, or service provider interaction.

Utility Computing is the packaging of computing resources, such as computation and storage, as a metered service similar to a traditional public utility, such as electricity, water, gas. Utility computing and cloud computing are similar in terms of the customer's value proposition. Both are about a

shared pool of computing resources, where users can get more or less resources on-demand. The critical difference is that a single user at a given point only gets a small portion of the utility, or the cloud (Bunker, & Thomson, 2006). They are fundamentally different in their architecture, though both try to provide similar customer's value. As cloud computing infrastructure is about leveraging commodity hardware, and using the power of software to slice, scale-up, and down the capacity and performance, while delivering a service over public, or private networks. Utility computing focus is on the business model on which providing the computing services are based. In other words, a utility computing service is one in which customers receive computing resources from a service provider and "pay as you benefit," much the same as you do for your public electric, or gas services at home (Carr, 2008).

Amazon Web Services (AWS) (2010), despite a recent outage, is the current poster child for this model, as it provides a variety of services, among them the Elastic Compute Cloud (EC2) (2010) in which customers pay for compute resources by the hour, and Simple Storage Service (S3) for which customers pay based on storage capacity. Other utility services include Sun's Network.com, EMC's recently launched storage cloud service, and those offered by startups such as Joyent and Mosso.

The main benefit of utility computing and cloud computing is better economics. Because you do not have to spend much upfront expenses on hardware before you run your business needs, and your hardware is not fully utilized. So, it will save lots of time and effort getting your infrastructure to just fulfill the business's needs.

One important worth mentioning note is that the challenge facing utility computing is to educate end users and customers about the utility computing service, its value, and benefits. There is a big need for making it widespread amongst people who can consume the service, as it's very hard to sell a service to a client if the client has never heard of it and cannot feel its value.

The differences between utility computing and cloud computing are a fateful issue. Utility computing relates to the business model in which application's infrastructure resources are delivered; while cloud computing relates to the way we design, implement, deploy, and run applications that operate in a virtualized environment and sharing resources that can be dynamically allocated and can be easily scaled up and down according to the needs.

SOA, Grid and Cloud

Noticing the evolution of networking we observe a tight relation between grid, cloud and service-oriented computing paradigms which are based on a life-time partnership. Unless there is a decomposition of underlying services that constitute the architecture of grid and cloud computing services, there will be no elasticity, agility, or flexibility in providing their services in the speed pace they provide right now. As cloud computing architecture and vendors' offerings are mainly based on a loosely-coupled group of web services that represent the main architecture of SOA. The same applies to grid computing and services.

A kind of relation that can stay forever between the three computing models that enables them to flexibly provide on-demand computing capacity and services, and makes grid and cloud computing inseparable from Service-Oriented Architectures (SOA).

NEXT GENERATION GRID AND SOA ENABLING OF SERVICE-ORIENTED GRIDS

Grid applications use the computational as well as storage resources and they are highly diverse in terms of network requirements (low latency and high throughput transfer). However, they need reliable network connectivity and should be available as the Next Generation Network (NGN) applications. There are many scenarios that can combine NGN and grids, or cloud. Some notable features for NGN grid are knowledge discovery Infrastructure, data intelligence, analytics, semantic modeling of data, dynamic resource discovery, ubiquitous computing, global collaboration, integration and convergence of grid and cloud resources, self-healing and autonomous management. European Telecommunications Standards Institute's (ETSI) Technical Committee for grid computing (TC GRID) (European Telecommunications Standards Institute, 2009) proposed the following four scenarios:

1. Grid-enabled NGN application
2. NGN subsystems offering grid services
3. Grid technology for implementing NGN functionality
4. Combining grid and networking resources in a new architecture

Grids to Service-Oriented Knowledge Utilities (SOKU), Next Generation Grid (NGG) Expert Group (Semantic Grid Community Portal, 2006) defined next generation grid as: "Combined with increasingly powerful and ubiquitous network infrastructures, novel service-oriented architectures, and approaches to resource virtualization. Grids will evolve into Service-Oriented Knowledge Utilities (SOKU) capable of delivering knowledge to users and enabling resource sharing, collaboration, and business transactions across individuals and organizations." The overall flow of next generation grid is illustrated in Figure 6.

Many enterprise firms have been investing a remarkable resource into the emerging discipline of Service Computing. The notion of business grid is to provide flexibility and new dimension with the convergence technology of service-oriented architecture from the architectural floor through the infrastructure and on-demand level. Virtualization technology, autonomous, and autonomic initiatives are the fundamentals to achieve the vision of business grid towards the services. To communicate SOA and grid, it requires a common usage of XML-based SOPA/WS. The convergence between grid, web services, and SOA leverages the business potentials. The structural relevancy of grid as an enterprise data bus is shown in Figure 7.

A well architected data layer is at the focal of any SOA system. EDB is an approach that is often used along with the Enterprise Service Bus architecture for virtualizing data access from services. EDB parallels the enterprise service bus. It incorporates a true enterprise data model which can define all enterprise data's entities, attributes and relationships, data dictionary, and naming

standards. Grid as EDB improves scalability, availability, and throughput in SOA concept.

SOA AS KEY TO CLOUD BUSINESS AGILITY

SOA is a popular architectural paradigm to build a software application from a number of loosely coupled and distributed services. This means that the client is independent from the service. An independent service provides flexibility and scalability for evolving applications. SOA is spread through web service approaches. We have some standards such as XML, WSDL, SOAP, and REST to provide interoperable services. SOA enables those standards based interfaces to access data

Figure 6. Next generation grid

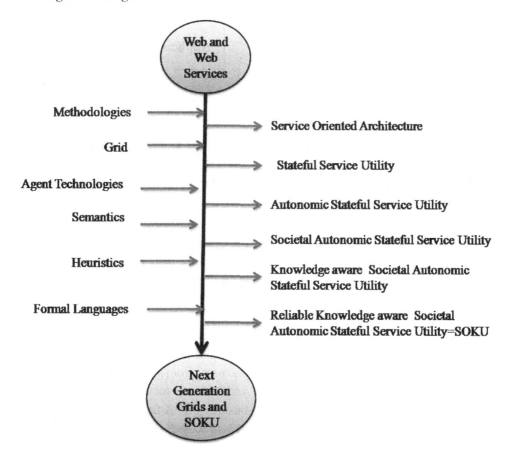

Figure 7. Grid as an enterprise data bus, grid maintains an in-memory copy of the enterprise data

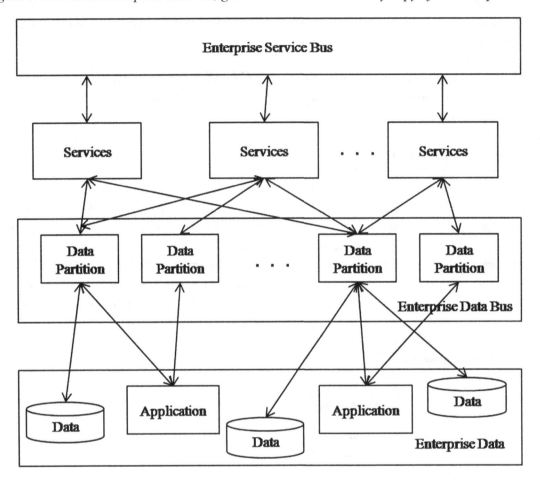

and business logic within the cloud. The users of the cloud do not need to know how cloud works internally, just use services easily. SOA plays a gateway role between cloud users and cloud systems. Amazon web service is an example of a popular web service which is becoming the de facto for cloud computing. The major force behind cloud is the web service by which it is possible to pay as you go. Cloud computing provides a flexible payment model for services (IT resources and availability of resources). Data migration between clouds is the emerging issue for enterprises. SOA may help to make cloud's opaque which can move between clouds

SOA, WEB-ORIENTED ARCHITECTURE MEETS THE CLOUD AND GRID MODELS

Service-oriented architecture is designed to reflect the best practices and business processes of the organization instead of making the business operate according to the rigid structure of a technical environment; and since the devils are usually in the details; SOA abstracts the enterprises from the pluming of the technical details. The same goal for cloud computing is to hide and abstract the end users from getting into these technical details and let them focus on their real core value and business. SOA facilitate the automation of business processes and implement these processes in terms of grid, or cloud models. SOA enables the business process management automation and workflow's management systems as a reality and provides big advantages to the organizations, and can be considered a key enabler to their end value.

MOVING SERVICES AND PROCESSES TO THE CLOUD

Nowadays, we can see most of the data centric applications in the cloud such as CRM, Mail, social network, and data collections analytics. The mathematics software packages Matlab and Mathematica are capable of using cloud computing to perform expensive evaluations. Other desktop applications might benefit from cloud. Data and application migration in cloud means data/application migration between data centers, or different cloud systems. In the current situation, it is not a simple process to move data application between cloud systems. There may be architectural and technical issues such as legacy and target environment, migration framework and approaches, data quality, data loss, availability, governance, security, network bandwidth, scalability, and cost efficiency. They should have re-engineered their architecture. While re-engineering, they should consider a simple mechanism such as moving most of the application into SaaS model and providing maintenance facilities to the external providers. Another mechanism may be developing an automation tools for migrating from on-premise system to cloud hosted application and providing real-time data movement functionality. The following are some mistakes that enterprises can make when moving data into the cloud (Preimesberger, 2004):

- Implementing an Infrastructure that does not fit your cloud needs
- Not verifying, or auditing the security of your cloud- based service provider
- Using Internet bandwidth inefficiently

- Not having backup and disaster recovery plans
- Getting trapped paying hidden fees
- Not knowing where your data is actually kept
- Selecting a vendor on name recognition rather than service quality
- Failure to establish a process to ensure your vendor honors SLAs
- Ignoring cloud management
- Choosing cost over service

STANDARDIZATION EFFORTS FOR GRIDS

There are lots of efforts and development happening in SOA, cloud, and grid computing areas of research; accordingly, standardization is invaluable to ensure the interoperability between different products and implementations. In this section, we will briefly cover the following standardization efforts:

- Web Services Resource Framework (WSRF)
- Open Grid Services Infrastructure (OGSI)
- Open Grid Services Architecture (OGSA)
- Open Grid Services Architecture-Data Access and Integration (OGSA-DAI)
- The OGF and Open Cloud Computing Interface (OCCI)

Web Services Resource Framework (WSRF)

The stateless characteristics of web services (no data persistence between invocations), limits many of the use cases that can be accomplished by web services. Many workaround are there for this limitation, like working with session states through WS-Session, cookies, or let provide the web service the facility to read from a database.

Accordingly, the need for an elegant framework for this web services to become stateful is inevitable and this is the role that Web Services Resource Framework (WSRF) plays over here. It defines conventions for state management; enabling applications to discover and interact with stateful web services in a standard way. The WSRF (Banks, 2006) is a family of OASIS specifications for web services in which IBM and Globus Alliance are considered as main contributors. WSRF provides a set of operations that web services may implement to become stateful. Web service clients communicate with resource's services which allow data to be stored and retrieved. When clients talk to the web service they include the identifier of the specific resource that should be used inside the request; encapsulated within the WS-Addressing endpoint reference. This may be a simple URI address, or it may be complex XML content that helps identify or even fully describe the specific resource in question.

Alongside the notion of an explicit resource reference, it comes with a standardized set of web service operations to get/set resource's properties. These can be used to read and perhaps write resource state, in a manner somewhat similar to having member variables of an object alongside its methods. The primary beneficiary of such a model is the management tools, which can enumerate and view resources, even if they have no other knowledge of them. This is the basis for Web Services Distributed Management (WSDM), a web service standard for managing and monitoring the status of other services.

Open Grid Services Infrastructure (OGSI)

Building on both web services and grid technologies, the Open Grid Services Infrastructure (OGSI) (Tuecke et al., 2007) defines the mechanisms needed to create, manage, and exchange information among entities named Grid Services. A grid service is a web service that conforms to a set of conventions (interfaces and behaviors) that define how a client interacts with a grid service. These conventions, and other OGSI mechanisms associated with grid's service creation and discovery, provide for the controlled, fault-resilient, and secure management of the distributed and often long-lived state that is commonly required in advanced distributed applications.

OGSA does not provide the details of the implementation. It only provides a formal and technical specification needed for the implementation of grid services. It provides a description of Web Service Description Language (WSDL), which defines a grid service. OGSI defines a component model that extends WSDL and XML Schema definition to incorporate the concepts of (Minoli, 2005):

- Stateful web services.
- Extension of web services interfaces.
- Asynchronous notification of state change.
- References to instances of services.
- Collections of service instances, and
- Service state data that augments the constraint capabilities of XML Schema definition.

Figure 8 illustrates a number of concepts surrounding OGSI, and its relation to Web services. The following list describes points of interest related to this model (Joseph, & Fellenstein, 2004).

- Grid services are layered on top of web services.
- Grid services contain application state factors, and provide concepts for exposing the state, which is referred to as the service data element.
- Both grid services and web services communicate with its client by exchanging XML messages.
- Grid services are described using GWSDL, which is an extension of WSDL. GWSDL provides interface inheritance and open port type for exposing the service state in-

Figure 8. Typical web service and grid service layers

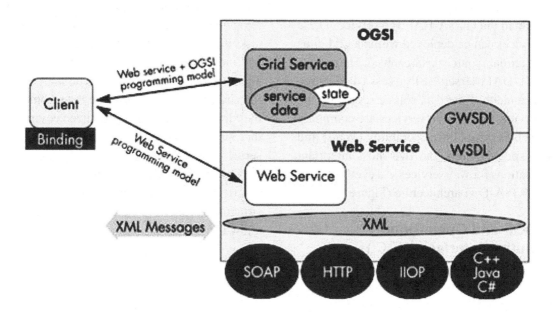

formation-referred to as service data. This is similar to interface properties or attributes commonly found in other distributed description languages.

- The client programming model is the same for both grid service and web service. But grid services provide additional message's exchange patterns such as the handle resolution through OGSI port types.
- The transport bindings are selected by the runtime. Message encoding and decoding is done for the specific binding and high-level transport protocol (SOAP/HTTP).

Open Grid Services Architecture (OGSA)

The Open Grid Services Architecture (OGSA) describes the architecture for a service-oriented grid computing environment for business and scientific use, developed within the Global Grid Forum (GGF). OGSA is based on several other Web service technologies (WSDL and SOAP), but

it aims to be agnostic in relation to the transport-level handling of data.

OGSA seeks to standardize service provided by a grid such as resource discovery, resource management, security, through a standard web service interface. It also defines those features that are not necessarily needed for the implementation of a grid, but, nevertheless, are desirable. OGSA is based on existing web services' specifications and adds features to web services to make it suitable for the grid environment (Foster et al., 2002).

Open Grid Services Architecture-Data Access and Integration (OGSA-DAI)

OGSA-DAI (Karasavvas et al., 2005) is an open source project to develop an effective solution to the challenge of internet-scale data integration and to provide access and integration to distributed data sources using a grid. It is a java-based middleware that produce java web services framework that allows data resources, such as file collections, XML or relational databases, to be accessed, federated, and integrated across the network. These data sources can be queried, updated and transformed via OGSA-DAI web service. These web services can be deployed within a grid, thus making the data sources grid-enabled. The request to OGSA-DAI web service to access a data source is independent of the data source served by the web service. OGSA web services are compliant with Web Services Inter-operability (WS-I) and WSRF specifications, the two most important specifications for web services. An eye-bird view of the OGSA-DAI architecture (Figure 9).

The OGF and Open Cloud Computing Interface (OCCI)

The Open Grid Forum, Open Cloud Computing Interface (OCCI) (2010) working group is aimed to deliver the API specification for the remote management of cloud computing infrastructure, this is to allow the development of the common interoperability tools for common cloud computing tasks that include deployment, autonomic scaling, and monitoring. The API specification is, also, aimed to cover all high level functionality required for virtual machines life-cycle management and their loads running on a virtualized environment that supports dynamic resource allocation and service elasticity.

This move is also targeting the creation of a practical solution to interface with cloud infrastructures exposed as a service (IaaS) and it will allow for:

- Consumers to interact with cloud computing infrastructure on an ad-hoc basis (e.g. deploy, start, stop, and restart).

Figure 9. Virtualization technology layered architecture

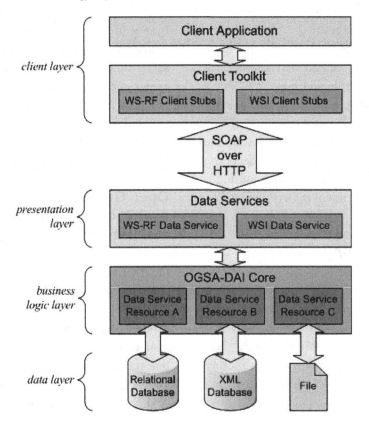

- Integrators to offer advanced management services.
- Aggregators to offer a single common interface to multiple providers.
- Providers to offer a standard interface that is compatible with available tools.
- Vendors of grids/clouds to offer standard interfaces for dynamically scalable service delivery in their products.

WEB SERVICES STANDARDS AND THE GLOBUS TOOLKIT

The Globus Toolkit (GT) (Globus Toolkit, 2010) is an open source software toolkit used for building grids. It is being developed by the Globus Alliance and many others all over the world. A growing number of projects and companies are using the toolkit to unlock the potential of grids for their cause. The Globus Toolkit lets people share computing power, databases, and other tools securely online across corporate, institutional, and geographic boundaries without sacrificing local autonomy. As it illustrated in Figure 10, it includes a bunch of software services and libraries for:

- Resource Monitoring and Management
- Discovery and Management
- Security
- File Management
- Information Infrastructure
- Data Management
- Communication
- Fault Tolerance

It is packaged as a set of components that can be used either independently or together to develop applications. Every organization has unique modes of operation, and collaboration between multiple organizations is hindered by incompatibility of resources such as data archives, computers, and networks. The toolkit was conceived to remove obstacles that prevent seamless collaboration. Its core services, interfaces, and protocols allow users to access remote resources as if they were located within their own machine room, while simultaneously preserving local control over who

Figure 10. Primary GT5 components

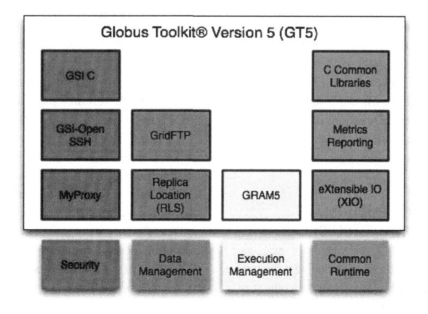

can use resources and when. The current released version is GT5.

Globus Toolkit implements the following standards:

- Open Grid Services Architecture (OGSA)
- Open Grid Services Infrastructure (OGSI)
- Web Services Resource Framework (WSRF)
- Job Submission Description Language (JSDL)
- Distributed Resource Management Application API (DRMAA)
- WS-Management
- WS-Base Notification
- SOAP and WSDL
- Grid Security Infrastructure (GSI)

Foster, Kesselman, and Tuecke (2001) have presented an essential background about GT. The best way to grasp technology is to get your hands dirty with trying it out. For GT installation and how to submit jobs using the toolkit, you can consult the Globus web site (Globus Toolkit, 2010). GT provides a set of components implemented on top of WSRF. It supports the development of new web services using Java, C and Python. Besides the WSRF-based components, GT also includes components that have not been implemented on top of WSRF (such as GridFTP). These components are called pre-WS services. GT offered two ways, client APIs (in different languages) and commands, to access these services. These components realize the functions of security, data management, execution management, information services, and common runtime.

BUSINESS MODEL OF COMPUTATIONAL GRID/CLOUD

In this section, we describe the business integration, influences, and relevancy in the context of grid-cloud resource management and general grid-cloud market. The basic idea of how to design scalable market architectures and pricing model-mechanism is important. There are many simulation tools and software engineering efforts that support the efficient comparative analysis of market-based resource management systems.

Gridonomics

Gridonomics (Grid+Economics) is the broad area that deals with the introduction of economic principles and patters in the field of grid resource management. Gridonomics deals with mechanism design, market design, pricing, optimization of equilibrium theory. Resource estimation, allocation, and pricing are some of the challenges behind Gridonomics. Grid computing has, also, recognized the value of price generation and negotiation for resource allocation and job scheduling; and in general the use of economic models for trading resources and services in increasingly large-scale and complex grid environments.

Basic Terminology

Grid Service and Resource Market: Service Market (Service client-buy services from the service provider) + Resource Market (resource provider).

Resource Market: It is the place where resource providers sell, and service providers buy the resources.

Resource Provider: It provides the sellable resources in the resource market. Resources can be CPU cycle, RAM, bandwidth, or storage.

Service Client: It buys the services at service market from a service provider.

Service Provider: provides the computational resources, network, and storage; and buy resources at resource market from resource provider.

Grid Density: It is the measurement of concentration of grid resources. The high density grid means it is formed by a HPC grid (highly connected core nodes).

There are many grid economics related projects such as GridEcon (2009), SORMA (2009), Gridbus (2009), D-Grid (Neuroth, Kerzel, & Gentzsch, 2007), K-Wf Grid (Truong et al., 2006), GRIA (2010), UniGrids (2010); and many economic approaches in the context of grid such as Buyya et al. (2002) described commodity market model, posted price model, bargaining model, tender/contract model, bid-based proportional resource sharing model, community/coalition/bartering/share holders' model, monopoly/oligopoly model, and auction model. Some examples of grid business models are:

Centralized Grid Economics: The centralized grid economics approached is used in Nimrod/G Resource Broker and G-COMMERCE.

P2P Grid Economics: The computer power market proposes a market-based resource management system for P2P computing. However, their resource traders are based on centralized grid economic based brokers who cannot scale.

Decentralized Grid Economics

Research Grid Business Models: GridASP (2010), GRASP (2010), GRACE (2010), BIG (Weishäupl et al., 2005). These projects promote open value chains for trading services on the grid.

Commercial Business Models: Sun Grid Compute Utility (Sun Grid, 2010), Amazon EC2 (Amazon Web Services, 2010), the Virtual Private Grid (VPG) (Falcon, 2005), and WebEx Connect Application Grid (WebEx Connect, 2006). Both, Sun Utility Grid and Amazon EC2 provide on-demand computing resources, while VPG and WebEx provide on-demand applications.

Business Applications for Grid

Grid could potentially offer tremendous opportunities, the way of developing products, and creating business. The usage of grid is limited, even though it simplifies the resource management. Only smaller number of companies are developing grid related technology; and none of the big enterprises and SMEs are using grid. The potential market sectors for grid are finance, engineering, chemical industry, pharmaceutical industry, automobile industry, and other manufacturing firms.

It can reform the grid business model and economic principles to leverages grid applications in different sectors, such as E-Commerce, E-Governance, E-learning (K12 education, distance learning, open university), Environment and e-Science, telemedicine (virtual doctor, health awareness campaign), Business to Business (B2B), Humanitarian works, Research (Aerospace, Astronomy), Agro-food Business, Travel CRM, Telecommunication, by providing security mechanism, SLA and intelligent negotiations which can support dynamic service and interoperability. Service computing has been transforming the traditional grid computing into business grid that refers to an application of grid computing oriented to service-based enterprise solutions.

To leverage the business application of grid, the way of model should direct towards utility model by providing a virtualized infrastructure that supports transparent, on demand business services as orchestrated concepts. The business paradigm is shifting from corporate to collaboration that can be achieved with global sharing (resource, application, strategies, and policy). Thus, flexible solution architecture, or business grid middleware is needed to reform the traditional grid applications to provide an agile nature of business grid that can meet the technological momentum.

Some EU projects, BEinGRID (Business Experiments in GRID, 2010) (a range of business sectors such as entertainment, financial, industrial, chemical, retail, textiles), XtreemOS (Morin, 2007) (Linux with grid services and support for virtual organizations), and BREIN (Business objective driven REliable and Intelligent Grids for real business, 2010; Oliveros et al., 2008) (academic to critical applications for logistics management at airport, and focused on SMEs). Moreover, Network for Earthquake Engineering

Simulation (NEES, 2010) (infrastructure to couple earthquake engineer with experiment facilities, database), AstroGrid (Walton, Lawrence, & Linde, 2004) (building a Data Grid for UK astronomy), and Access Grid (Ho, Yang, & Chang, 2004) (collection of projectors, cameras, microphones enabling the creation of new tools for collaborative visualization, data-sharing).

Cloudonomics

The big potential draw of cloud computing is massive scalability at low cost. The term Cloudonomics coined by Weinman (2008) AT & T business solution from, means the economy of the cloud, or relevant financial and economic mechanisms that support cloud computing. According to Wienman (2008), there are five questions required to discuss economic / business in the cloud:

- Is demand constant?
- Is the increase predictable?
- Is it possible to manage the demand?
- Where are the users?
- Is the application interactive?

Interactive application is the application of uses (e.g. email document management, CRM) unlike the application running in the background without the user such as calculating charges in telecommunications based on the fundamental benefit of cloud computing (on-demand services, high scalability, and low cost) (Weinman, 2008).

The 10 laws of cloudonomics are:

1. Utility services cost less, even though they cost more.
2. On-demand trumps forecasting.
3. The peak of the sum is never greater than the sum of the peaks.
4. Aggregate demand is smoother than individual.
5. Average unit costs are reduced by distributing fixed costs over more units of output.

6. Superiority in numbers is the most important factor in the result of a combat.
7. Space-time is a continuum.
8. Dispersion is the inverse square of latency.
9. Do not put all your eggs in one basket.
10. An object at rest tends to stay at rest.

Amazon EC2 provides an instance-hour; while Windows Azure lets you just manage the application's instance for billing. This is, fundamentally, the difference between Infrastructure-as-a-Service and Platform-as-a-Service. Currently cloud service pricing structures are based on different factors such as storage capacity and CPU cycles used to monthly traffic allocation. Some service providers have additional charges hidden deep within their Service Level Agreements (SLAs).

Grid Workflow Management System (GWFMS)

In a general perspective, a workflow represents the operational aspects of a work procedure: the structure of tasks, the applications, and humans that perform them. The task is accessed through the order of invocation, synchronization, and the information flow.

The definition of Workflow Management System was given by Hollingsworth (1995), a system that completely defines, manages and executes workflow through the execution of the software whose order of execution is driven by a computer representation of the workflow's logic. Workflow management provides support for the definition, registration, and control of processes. Primarily, workflow engages in computation and data transformation task to perform analysis. Scheduling of tasks executions and data transfers are one of the major challenges in workflow execution. The life cycle of workflow is illustrated in Figure 11. Basically, model the scientific computing application through workflow model and create different workflow instances to execute the workflow.

Mashups vs. Grid-Workflows

A mashup is a website or application that combines content from more than one source into an integrated experience. Content used in mashups is typically sourced from a third party via a public interface or API. Other methods of sourcing content for mashups include, web feeds (e.g. RSS or Atom) and JavaScript. A mashup is the ultimate user-generated content: Users like data source A, data source B, and it puts them together how they like. Figure 12 shows the famous APIs for mashups. GoogleMaps is the most popular one. Similarly, Figure 13 describes the protocol scenario that is used in mashups. REST protocol is famous among other protocols such as SOAP and XML-RPC.

Mashups are the applications that contain a remix of digital data or a combination of different functionality from many sources that can create new innovative services or applications. Different types of mashups are available such as data mashups, and enterprise mashups. OMA (Open Mashup Alliance, 2010) is an initiative work for promoting the enterprise mashups. Google Maps mashup, Yahoo! Pipes mashup (2010), Zillow, and SkiBonk are some of the examples of mashups.

The comparison between them is described in Table 6. Mashups are workflow and vice versa. So, there are, more or less, no architectural differences between grids and Web 2.0; and we can build e-infrastructure or Cyberinfrastructure (e-infrastructure) with either architecture or mix. It should bring Web 2.0 people capabilities to grid (eScience, Enterprise) and use robust grid (motivated by enterprise) technologies in mashups.

Scientific Workflow in Multi-Tenancy Environment

Many workflow management systems for scientific computing have been, already, there in front of research communities such as: Askalon (Trunfioa et al., 2007), D2K (Transforming data2knowledge, 2010), Kepler (Ludäscher et al., 2006), P-Grade (2010), GridAnt (Amin, & Laszewski, 2003), GridNexus (2010), GridServiceBroker (The Cloud Computing and Distributed Systems Laboratory, 2010), Pegasus (Deelman et al., 2007), Teutaa

Figure 11. Life cycle of workflow

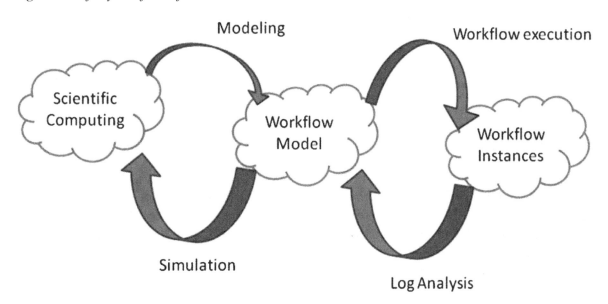

Figure 12. Famous APIs for mashups

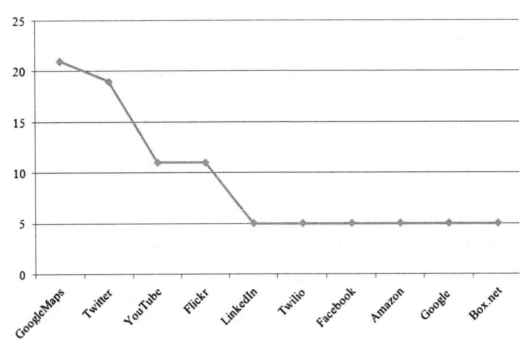

Figure 13. Protocol used by famous APIs for mashups

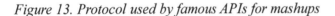

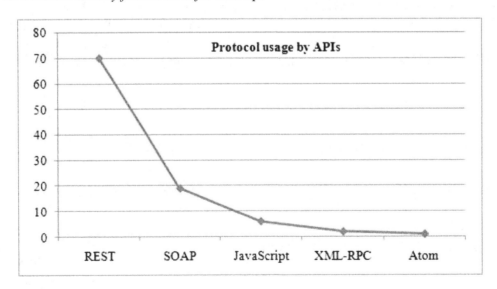

(Performance PROPHET, 2010), Swift (Zhao et al.,2007), and Xbaya (2010). However, processing workflows in a grid is an open issue and imposes many challenges (Yu, & Buyya, 2005). The scheduling of a workflow focuses on mapping and managing the execution of tasks on grid shared resources that are not directly under the control of these workflow systems. Thus, choosing the best strategy for workflow execution in a grid is a challenging research area.

Table 6.Comparison between mashups and grid workflow

	Mashups	**Grid Workflow**
Primary goal	Mashups reuses existing web applications/data as a part of the new application. Easily can develop a web application	It is the way of modeling where data should be processed on grid environment. Easily can develop a grid application
Different from traditional methodology	No need of internal details, just call API	Workflow descriptions independent from actual grid resources or processes
Technology	Calling API, often using JavaScript, AJAX	Mostly XML language
Availability of Graphical tools	Yes (examples are: such as Yahoo! Pipes, Elicit)	Yes (examples are: Triana, Kepler)
Standardization	No any fixed standard. AJAX, REST, and RSS/ATOM feeds are the most popular	Proprietary. WS-BEPL can be used
Application Areas	Business and normal application	Mostly academic research purpose

Multi-Tenant Architecture (MTA), which has a capability for a single instance of hosted application, is used by multiple customers (tenants) simultaneously. MTA allows clients to host multiple clients under one server. Individual tenants are separated by virtual partitions, and each partition stores individual tenant's data, configuration settings, and customized settings. If tenants are hosted on a dedicated and a single server, they will, still, have individual control of configurations and settings.

Multi-Instance Architecture (MIA) by contrast uses one application instance per client. Multi-tenant application must be dynamic in nature or polymorphic, to fulfill individual expectations of various tenants and their users (Salesforce, 2010). MTA is designed to allow tenant-specific configurations at the UI (branding), business rules, business processes, and data model layers. This has to be enabled without changing the code as the same code is shared by all tenants; therefore transforming customization of software into configuration of software. This drives the clear need for metadata driven everything. The other main challenge is able to co-locate (mingle and de-mingle) persistent data of multiple tenants in the same data infrastructure. In other words, the challenge for the multi-tenant application is to behave as if it was fully dedicated to a single tenant, but is actually serving all of them, in parallel,

on the same code base. In MTA, we have to trust in cloud provider service, isolation between costumer's data and virtual machines, and assume that no one can physically access the virtual machine.

The biggest advantage of a MTA for a user is that there is little maintenance effort on the user side as version upgrades are supposed to have no impact on the use of the application. The main advantage of this architecture is:

- Underlying infrastructure is shared; allowing massive economy of scale with optimal repartition of load.
- Because the very costly infrastructure and application development costs are shared, the enterprise grade application can be offered to very small businesses as well.
- Providing adequate levels of security and robustness to the application data.

Multi-Tenancy: Design Criteria

The following are some of the important design criteria for multi-tenancy systems or applications:

Key requirements to build robust multi-tenant SaaS

- Data Access Protection.
- Scalability and Costs.
- Customization and Extensibility.

- High Availability or Business Continuity.

Key components for extensibility to accommodate growth in tenant business model

- Customized predefined fields.
- Customized predefined tables.
- Dynamic fields.

Data should be available at any time

- Real-time replication.
- Incremental backup/restore through WAN.
- Fail-over and dynamic election.
- Partial data and configuration recovery.

Stages and Attributes of Multi-Tenancy/Multi-Tenant Cloud

Multi-tenancy is widely recognized as being the primary method for developing true SaaS systems and is used by most of the SaaS vendors. Vendors using multi-tenancy only have one copy of the system to support, and therefore can execute with maximum velocity and agility. In business applications, multi-tenancy is enabled by a database extensively mechanism, which enables each tenant organization to extend the database, independently of the other tenants. This confers great customizability upon the SaaS application.

Multi-Tenancy Applications often derive further customizability by incorporating workflow facilities which are customizable on a per tenant basis. The workflow facilities enable the system administrators of tenant companies to alter the behavior of the system to suit the tenant organization's business processes. Multiple tenants must not be different companies- they can be different business units or different departments. The key is that there must be a dynamic allocation of resources and scarcity. If all resources are dedicated to one organization and simply switched between applications, it is not cloud computing- it would be simply an infrastructure controlled via API.

There are four common stages (ad-hoc or custom, configurable, multi-tenant, and scalable) (Chong, Carraro, & Wolter 2006) in moving towards an efficient multi-tenancy architecture with user-enabled configuration. There are three attributes of a Single Instance Multi-Tenant Architecture, Scalable, Configurable, and Multi-tenant efficient.

Metadata-Driven Architecture

Multi-tenancy has a capability to run multiple customers (tenants) on a single software instance installed on multiple servers to increase resource utilization by allowing load balancing among tenants that helps to reduce operational complexity and cost. The concept given in (Salesforce, 2010) introduces the concept of meta-data driven architecture for multi-tenant clouds. The overall concept of metadata-driven architecture is shown

Figure 14. Metadata-driven application has clear separation between runtime engine, data, common application metadata, and tenant-specific metadata

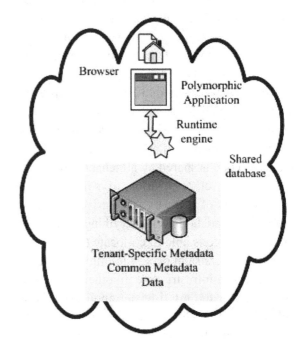

in Figure 14, which has the clear separation between runtime engine, data, common application metadata, and tenant-specific metadata.

Semantic Based Workflow for Multi-Tenant Clouds

Even though there are many semantic based workflows (Berkley et al., 2005; Deelman et al., 2003; Kim, Gil, & Ratnakar, 2006), they cannot meet the concept of multi-tenancy. The reference architecture of semantic based workflow for multi-tenant cloud is shown in Figure 15. The workflow engine manages the total system components such as process instance and definition.

Semantic and semantic Web Ontology Language (OWL) use a pool of resources semantically that are understood and described to enable you to use these resources regardless of that these resources are allocated from multiple tenants and that the Resource Description Framework (RDF) is used to serialize provenance metadata.

Figure 15. Metadata-driven application has clear separation between runtime engine, semantic-based workflow component, data, common application metadata, and tenant-specific metadata

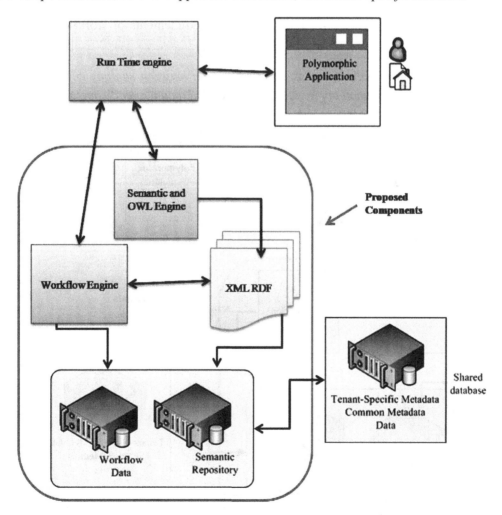

Policy Based Workflow for Multi-Tenant Clouds

Policies can, also, describe much complex requirements of resources and security control. So, it has better flexibility in design time. The reference architecture of policy based workflow is shown in Figure 16, which describes a metadata-driven application that has a clear separation between runtime engine, policy-based workflow component, data, common application metadata, and tenant-specific metadata.

Policy base workflow consists of a centralized policy repository, dynamic policy transformations; and looking up for policies, independent policy engine, and decision-making based on policies. It supports meta-model. GME (Generic Modeling Environment, 2010) or EMF (Eclipse Modeling Framework, 2010) can be used for building the meta-model and concrete model. A centralized policy repository and an independent policy engine to execute policies, make it possible to keep the business rules consistent across the whole enterprise (tenants). Policy includes CPU sharing in virtualization, authorization, Authentication, SLA, dynamic process management (resource allocation), service discovery, and invoke (refinement policies specify the criteria for the selection of the service that is ultimately chosen and invoked to execute the task), configuration/reconfiguration (reconfiguration policies change the structure of the workflow instance by e.g. deleting or adding tasks (tasks can be merged or split). Ouyang (2007) described elements of workflow process meta-

Figure 16. Metadata-driven application has clear separation between runtime engine, policy-based workflow component, data, common application metadata, and tenant-specific metadata

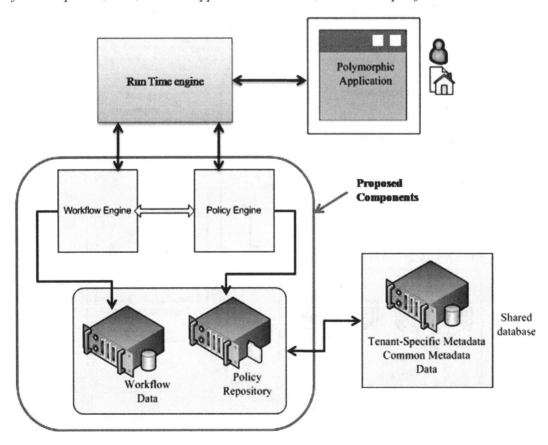

model that contains activities, transaction conditions, tenant model, resource/application/role, and policy control points.

FUTURE RESEARCH DIRECTIONS

The emergence of the service-oriented systems, utility paradigm, and next generation grids is a compelling approach to the future IT architecture. It encompasses several important domains including foundations of service-oriented architecture, grid and cloud computing, business process management. In order to realize the vision, a number of challenging research areas need to be addressed. In this section, we will cover some of these challenges.

Semantic Web and Semantic Grid technologies will take the momentum in the new generation of grid computing research and industry. So, there a big need, in this context, to have a scalable reasoning and formalization methods and heterogeneous and dynamic context semantic descriptions.

Full SOKU (Service Oriented Knowledge Utility) Lifecycle Management (Next Generation Grids Expert Group Report 3, 2006).

European Union has put a report on the Service-Oriented Knowledge Utility (SOKU): Vision and Research Directions 2010 and Beyond (Next Generation Grids Expert Group Report 3, 2006), they clearly signaling their intension to support the research around it, as these are fundamental for wide-scale adoption of grid computing in enterprise applications. SOKU infrastructure will require support for automating the full SOKU lifecycle making use of a semantically rich information representation thereby enabling support for context-awareness and ambient intelligence. In particular, the SOKU lifecycle should enable the following:

On-the-fly service creation and seamless and scalable deployment; enabling large-scale services roll-out and roll-back, dynamic migration, and autonomous reconfiguration - diverse resources ranging from PDAs to supercomputers, from small files to large databases, from small and efficient services to complex, and multidisciplinary applications should be supported.

Robust, efficient, and semantically aware discovery of services based on proven technologies, as well as new approaches proving access to services on-demand particularly interesting issues include versioning support, peer-to-peer approaches, and tight integration with composition functionality.

Composition and composition control of services forming a self-organizing ecology based on semantics - running such virtual organizations will require advanced orchestration and choreography functionality based on the modeling of a number of factors (e.g. enterprise physical/logical organizations, job sequence/data results sequence, dependencies between jobs).

Management of functional, non-functional properties and requirements, which include performance, Quality-of-Service (QoS), dependability, and security aspects in particular, these mechanisms, techniques, and tools must support suitable ways of describing, negotiating, using, proving, and ensuring such properties and/or requirements.

Support for multiple economy models for the grid in particular, such economy models should be able to support reliable and scalable accounting, billing, and secure access to resources and the like.

Adaptability, Dependability, Scalability. It is desirable that a service-oriented approach behind SOKU does not rely on the client-server paradigm of today SOA (identity of a service, its localization on a single server, and/or a centralized service discovery). SOKU should rely on a Next Generation Grid infrastructure that takes the benefit of peer-to-peer systems for a further distribution of functionality such as scheduling, resource discovery, billing, and others. This will ensure that dependability, scalability, and adaptability are intrinsic properties of next-generation architectures.

Increasing the Level of Abstraction. In order to achieve and preserve suitable performance in SOKU, we need to have a common data format that allow data to be smoothly accessed from and exchanged between different remote locations, services, or SOKUs.

Cloud Compliance and Security. A great effort should be exerted on identifying the best practices and implementing process improvements and compliance issues; alongside providing initiatives in for the global cyber-security.

SOA and Enterprise Mashups. Mashups will be the most common form of a user's access to back-end services. The efforts need to be exerted to make services easily and smoothly mashed up to improve business agility and flexibility.

More Synergy between cloud, grid, and SOA. Virtualization echnology is to play an invaluable role in the advance of cloud and grid computing paradigm from different angles (Security, Performance, Scalability, Agility).

Quality Improvements and the trustworthiness of data-flow in the SOAs are eagerly required.

Green IT will get more focus; grid and cloud computing paradigms will play important roles in this area.

CONCLUSION

In short, we have presented the emergence of SOA, cloud, and grid computing; the synergy and tight relation between them all, and highlighted how far the grid and cloud computing became inseparable from virtualization and service-oriented architectures. We have covered some of the major grid and cloud computing efforts around the world and discussed their similarities and differences. We have identified the various challenges facing these technologies and the value they provide in terms of money, flexibility, agility. We also covered some of the standardization efforts happening in these technologies, and gave an overview about the potential areas of research.

A warning should be given, here, to the grid and cloud computing enthusiastic people. Cloud computing and grid are not silver bullets that can take any application and run faster without the need for buying any more machines, or software. Not every application is suitable or enabled to run in the cloud or grid environments.

Some kinds of applications simply cannot be parallelized. For others, it can take a large amount of work to modify them to achieve faster throughput; sometimes it is so difficult for an application that comply to a certain compliance act to be deployed on the cloud for some privacy and security reasons. For all of these reasons, it is important to understand how far the grid and cloud have evolved today and which features are coming tomorrow, or in the far future.

REFERENCES

Amazon Web Services. (2010). *Amazon elastic cloud computing (EC2)*. Retrieved from http://aws.amazon.com/ ec2

Amin, K., & Laszewski, G. V. (2003). *GridAnt: A grid workflow system*. Retrieved March, 2010, from http://www.globus.org/ cog/ projects/ gridant/ gridant-manual.pdf

Anderson, D. P. (2004). BOINC: A system for public-resource computing and storage. In *Proceedings of the 5th IEEE/ACM International Workshop on Grid Computing* (pp. 4-10). IEEE Computer Society.

Australia, G. (2010). Retrieved from http://www.greeningaustralia.org.au/ our-projects/ corporate-responsibility/ greengrid

Banks, T. (2006). *Web Services Resource Framework (WSRF) – primer v1.2*. Retrieved from http://docs.oasis-open.org/ wsrf/ wsrf-primer-1.2-primer-cd-01.pdf

BEinGRID (Business Experiments in GRID). (2010). Retrieved from http://www.beingrid.eu

Berkley, C., Bowers, S., Jones, M. B., Ludäscher, B., Schildhauer, M., & Tao, J. (2005). Incorporating semantics in scientific workflow authoring. In *Proceedings of the 17th International Conference on Scientific and Statistical Database Management* (pp. 75-78). Lawrence Berkeley Laboratory. Berkley, CA, USA.

BeSTGRID. (2009). *Data Grid.* Retrieved September, 2010, from http://www.bestgrid.org/index.php/ Category:Data_Grid

BiG Grid. (2010). Retrieved March, 2010 from http://www.biggrid.nl/ about-big-grid

BONIC. GUU Computing (2010). Retrieved March, 2010 from http://boinc.berkeley.edu/ wiki/ GPU_computing

Bossa, S. (2008). Gridify your spring application with grid gain. *Spring Italian Meeting.* Retrieved from http://www.slideshare.net/ sbtourist/ gridify-your-spring-application -with-grid-gain-spring -italian-meeting-2008

BREIN. (Business objective driven REliable and Intelligent grids for real busiNess) (2010). Retrieved from http://tinyurl.com/y8m5bmk

Bunker, G., & Thomson, D. (2006). *Delivering utility computing.* Hoboken, NJ: John Wiley & Sons.

Business Experiments in Grid (BEinGrid). (2010). Retrieved from http://beingrid.terradue.com

Buyya, R., Abramson, D., Giddy, J., & Stockinger, H. (2002). Economic models for resource management and scheduling in grid computing. *Concurrency and Computation, 14,* 13–15.

Cafe, G. (2010). Retrieved March from http://www.gridcafe.org/ volunteer-computing-.html

Cappello, F., Djilali, S., Fedak, G., Herault, T., Magniette, F., Neri, V., & Lodygensky, O. (2005). Computing on large scale distributed systems: Xtrem Web architecture, programming models, security, tests and convergence with grid. *Journal of Future Generation Computer Science, 21*(3), 417–437. doi:10.1016/j.future.2004.04.011

Carr, N. (2008). *The big switch: Rewiring the world, from Edison to Google.* New York, NY, USA: W. W. Norton & Company.

Catlett, C. (2002). The philosophy of TeraGrid: Building an open, extensible, distributed TeraScale facility. In *Proceedings of the 2nd IEEE/ACM International Symposium on Cluster Computing and the Grid* (p. 8). IEEE Computer Society.

Chervenak, A., Foster, I., Kesselman, C., Salisbury, C., & Tuecke, S. (2000). The data grid: Towards an architecture for the distributed management and analysis of large scientific datasets. *Journal of Network and Computer Applications, 23*(3), 187–200. doi:10.1006/jnca.2000.0110

Chien, A., Calder, B., Elbert, S., & Bhatia, K. (2003). Entropia: Architecture and performance of an enterprise desktop grid system. *Journal of Parallel and Distributed Computing, 63*(5), 597–610. doi:10.1016/S0743-7315(03)00006-6

Chisnall, D. (2008). *The definitive guide to the Xen hypervisor.* Upper Saddle River, NJ: Prentice Hall.

Chong, F., Carraro, G., & Wolter, R. (2006). Multitenant data architecture. *Microsoft Corporation.* Retrieved from http://msdn.microsoft.com/ en-us/ library/aa479086.aspx

Cloud Myths Dispelled. (2009). *Retrieved from* http://www.eucalyptus.com/ resources/ info/ cloud-myths-dispelled

Cloudera. (2010). Retrieved from http://www.cloudera.com

Coherence, O. (2010). Retrieved from http:// www.oracle.com/ technology/ products/ coherence/ index.html

Compute Unified Device Architecture. Nvidia (2010). Retrieved from http://developer.nvidia. com/ object/ cuda.html

Computing, P. (2009). *HPC as a Service*, from Penguin Computing. Retrieved from http://www. penguincomputing.com/ POD/ HPC_as_a_service

De Roure, D., Jennings, N. R., & Shadbolt, N. R. (2001). *Research agenda for the semantic grid: A future e-science infrastructure. UKeS-2002-02.* Technical Report of the National e-Science Centre.

Dean, J., & Ghemawat, S. (2009). MapReduce: Simplified data processing on large clusters. *Communications of the ACM, 51*(1), 107–113. doi:10.1145/1327452.1327492

Deelman, E., Blythe, J., Gil, Y., Kesselman, C., Mehta, G., & Vahi, K. (2003). Mapping abstract complex workflows onto grid environments. *Journal of Grid Computing, 1*(1), 25–39. doi:10.1023/A:1024000426962

Deelman, E., Mehta, G., Singh, G., Mei-Hui, S., & Vahi, K. (2007). *Pegasus: Mapping large-scale workflows to distributed resources. Workflows for e-Science*. Berlin, Germany: Springer.

DiNucci, D. (1999). *Fragmented future*. Retrieved from http://tinyurl.com/ yk345d6

Dobson, J. E., Woodward, J. B., Schwarz, S. A., Marchesini, J. C., Farid, H., & Smith, S. W. (2005). The Dartmouth green grid . In Sunderam, S., Van Albada, G. D., Sloot, M. A. P., & Dongarra, J. J. (Eds.), *Lecture Notes in Computer Science (LNCS)* (*Vol. 3515*, pp. 99–106). Berlin-Heidelberg, Germany: Springer.

Eclipse Modeling Framework (EMF). (2010). Retrieved from http://www.eclipse.org/ modeling/ emf/ ?project=validation

Einstein@Home (2010). *Retrieved March from* http://einstein.phys.uwm.edu

Enabling Grids for E-sciencE. (2010). *Retrieved from* http://www.eu-egee.org

EuroGrid. (2010). *WP4: HPC research GRID*. Retrieved from http://www.eurogrid.org/ wp4.html

European Space Agency. (2010). *Retrieved from* http://gpod.eo.esa.int

European Space Agency. Ionia GlobCover (2010). *Retrieved from* http://ionia1.esrin.esa.int

European Telecommunications Standards Institute (ETSI). (2009). *TR 102 767 V1.1.1: GRID; Grid services and Telecom networks; Architectural options. European Telecommunications Standards Institute*. Sophia-Antipolis, France: ETSI.

Falcon, F. (2005). GRID–A telco perspective: The BT grid strategy. In *Proceedings of the 2nd International Workshop on Grid Economics and Business Models*, Seoul, Korea.

Fielding, R. T. (2000) *Architectural styles and the design of network-based software architectures*. Unpublished doctoral dissertation, University of California, Irvine.

Foody, D. (2009). *Goodbye SOA, we hardly knew you*. Retrieved from http://tinyurl.com/ 9ydlhj

Foster, I., & Kesselman, C. (1998). *The grid: Blueprint for a new computing infrastructure*. Burlington, MA: Morgan Kaufmann Publishers.

Foster, I., Kesselman, C., Nick, J., & Tuecke, S. (2002). *The physiology of the grid: An open grid services architecture for distributed systems integration*. Retrieved from http://www.globus.org/ alliance/ publications/ papers/ ogsa.pdf

Foster, I., Kesselman, C., & Tuecke, S. (2001). The anatomy of the grid: Enabling scalable virtual organizations. *The International Journal of Supercomputer Applications, 15*(3), 200–202. doi:10.1177/109434200101500302

Foster, I., Zhao, Y., Raicu, I., & Shiyong, L. (2008). Cloud computing and grid computing 360- Degree Compared. In *Grid Computing Environments Workshop* (pp. 1-10). IEEE Computer Society.

Freitag, S., Yahyapour, R., Jankowski, G., & Januszewski, R. (2008). *Virtualization management for grids and SOA. CoreGRID. White Paper Number WHP-0005.* Retrieved from http://www.coregrid.net/ mambo/ images/ stories/ WhitePapers/whp-0005.pdf

Gartner (2008). *What is cloud computing? Myths to explore.* Retrieved from http://www.gartner.com/

Gavrilovska, A., Kumar, S., Raj, K., Gupta, V., Nathuji, R., Niranjan, A., & Saraiya, P. (2007). High-performance hypervisor architectures: Virtualization in HPC systems. In *1st Workshop on System-Level Virtualization for High Performance Computing.*

Generic Modeling Environment (GME). (2010). Retrieved from http://www.isis.vanderbilt.edu/ projects/ gme

GENESI-DR. (2010). Retrieved from http://portal.genesi-dr.eu

GigaSpaces. (2010). *XAP in-memory data grid.* Retrieved from http://www.gigaspaces.com/datagrid

Globus Toolkit Homepage. (2010). Retrieved April, 2010, from http://www.globus.org/toolkit

GPUGRID.net. (2010). Retrieved February from http://www.gpugrid.net

GRACE Web site (2010). Retrieved from http://www.gridbus.org/ ecogrid

GRASP Web site (2010). Retrieved from http://eu-grasp.net

Great Internet Mersenne Prime Search (GIMPS). (2010). Retrieved March,2010, from http://www.mersenne.org

Green Grid New Mexico. (2010). Retrieved from http://www.greengridnewmexico.org

GRIA. (2010). Retrieved from http://www.gria.org

Grid, A. S. P. (2010). Retrieved from http://www.aspgrid.com

Grid, S. (2010). Retrieved from http://www.sun.com/software/sge

GridASP Web site (2010). Retrieved from http://www.gridasp.org/en

Gridbus (2009). Retrieved December, 2010, http://www.gridbus.org

GridEcon. (2009). Retrieved November, 2010, from http://www.gridecon.eu

Gridify Environment. (2010). Retrieved from December, 2010, http://www.terradue.com

GridNexus. (2010). Retrieved from http://www.extreme.indiana.edu/ swf-survey/ GridNexus.html

Grids, N. G. (NGG) Expert Group Report 3 (2006). Future for European grids: Grids and service-oriented knowledge utilities. *European Communities.* Retrieved from, ftp://ftp.cordis.europa.eu/ pub/ ist/docs/ grids/ ngg3-report_en.pdf

Hadoop, A. (2010). Retrieved from http://hadoop.apache.org

Hazelcast Software. (2010). *In-Memory Data Grid.* Retrieved from http://www.hazelcast.com

Ho, H. C., Yang, C. T., & Chang, C. C. (2004). Building an e-learning platform by access grid and data grid technologies. In *Proceeding of IEEE International Conference on E-technology, E-commerce and E-service* (pp. 452-455). IEEE Computer Society.

Hollingsworth, D. (1995). Workflow management coalition the workflow reference model. *Document Number TC00-1003 Document Status - Issue 1.1.* Retrieved from http://www.wfmc.org/ standards/ docs/ tc003v11.pdf

Irving, M., Taylor, G., & Hobson, P. (2004). Plug in to grid computing. *IEEE Power and Energy Magazine, 2,* 40–44. doi:10.1109/MPAE.2004.1269616

JBoss Community. (2010). *Infinispan.* Retrieved from http://www.jboss.org/ infinispan

Johnson, B. (2008). *Cloud computing is a trap, warns GNU founder Richard Stallman.* Retrieved March 2010 from http://tinyurl.com/ 4h9o2h

Joseph, J., & Fellenstein, C. (2004). *Grid computing.* IBM Press.

Karasavvas, K., Antonioletti, M., Atkinson, M., Hong, C. N., Sugden, T., & Hume, A. …Palansuriya, C. (2005). Introduction to OGSA-DAI services. *Lecture Notes in Computer Science (LNCS), Vol. 3458.* Berlin-Heidelberg: Springer.

Keahey, K., Tsugawa, M., Matsunaga, A., & Fortes, J. A. B. (2009). Sky computing. *IEEE Internet Computing, 13*(5), 43–51. doi:10.1109/ MIC.2009.94

Kim, J., Gil, Y., & Ratnakar, V. (2006). Semantic metadata generation for large scientific workflows. In *Proceedings of the 5th International Semantic Web Conference* (pp. 357-370). Berlin-Heidelberg, Germany: Springer.

Laningham, S. (2006). *DeveloperWorks interviews: Tim Berners-Lee.* Retrieved from http:// www.ibm.com/ developerworks/ podcast/ dwi/ cm-int082206txt.html

Larson, S. M., Snow, C. D., Shirts, M., & Pande, V. S. (2002). *Folding@Home and Genome@Home: Using distributed computing to tackle previously intractable problems in computational biology. Computational Genomics.* Horizon Press.

Life Science Grid (LSG). (2010). Retrieved March, 2010 from http://www.sara.nl/ projects/ projects_10_eng.html

Lublinsky, B. (2008). *SOA agents: Grid computing meets SOA.* Retrieved from http://www.infoq. com/ articles/ lublinsky-soa-grid

Ludäscher, B., Altintas, I., Berkley, C., Higgins, D., Jaeger, E., & Jones, M. (2006). Scientific workflow management and the Kepler system. *Concurrency and Computation, 18*(10), 1039–1065. doi:10.1002/cpe.994

Manes, A. T. (2009). *SOA is dead: Long live services.* Retrieved from http://tinyurl.com/ 9gdyer

Mell, P., & Grance, T. (2009). *The NIST definition of cloud computing, Ver. 15.* Institute of Standards and Technology (NIST), Information Technology Laboratory. Retrieved from http://csrc.nist.gov/ groups/ SNS/ cloud-computing

Minoli, D. (2005). *A networking approach to grid computing.* Hoboken, NJ: John Wiley & Sons.

Miura, K. (2006). Overview of Japanese science grid project, NAREGI: National Research Grid Initiative. *R & D Project Report, Progress in Informatics, 3,* 67-75. Retrieved March, 2010 from http://www.naregi.org/ index_e.html

Morin, C. (2007). XtreemOS: A grid operating system making your computer ready for participating in virtual organizations. In *Proceedings of the 10th IEEE International Symposium on Object and Component Oriented Real-Time Distributed Computing* (pp. 191-402). IEEE Computer Society.

Musser, J., O'Reilly, T. & O'Reilly Radar Team (2006). *Web 2.0 principles and best practices.* Retrieved from http://oreilly.com/catalog/ web2report/ chapter/ web20_report_excerpt.pdf

Myerson, J. (2009). *Cloud computing versus grid computing.* Retrieved from http://www.ibm.com/ developerworks/ web/ library/ wa-cloudgrid

Network for Earthquake Engineering Simulation (NEES). (2010). Retrieved from https://www.nees.org/ about

Neuroth, H., Kerzel, M., & Gentzsch, W. (Eds.). (2007). *W. German grid initiative D-Grid*. Germany: Universitätsverlag Göttingen.

Newhouse, S., Mayer, A., Furmento, N., McGough, S., Stanton, J., & Darlington, J. (2001). Laying the foundations for the semantic grid. In *Proceedings of AISB Workshop on AI and Grid Computing*. London, UK: London e-Science Centre.

O'Reilly, T. (2005). W*hat is web 2.0*: Design pattern and business models for the next generation of software. Retrieved September 30, 2009, from http://tinyurl.com/ nx36fj

Office of Science U.S. Department of Energy. (2003). *Introduction to the DOE Science Grid*. Retrieved, 2010, from http://doesciencegrid.org/ Grid/ papers

OGSA-DAI. (2010). Retrieved from http:// sourceforge.net/ apps/ trac/ ogsa-dai/ wiki/ User-Documentation

Oliver, B. (2009). *Data grid design patterns*. Retrieved from http://www.infoq.com/ presentations/ Data-Grid-Design-Patterns-Brian-Oliver

Oliveros, E., Munoz, H., Cantelar, D., & Taylor, S. (2008). *BREIN, Towards an Intelligent Grid for Business. Grid Economics and Business Model: Lecture Notes in Computer Science (LNCS 5206)* (pp. 163–172). Berlin-Heidelberg, Germany: Springer.

Ontogrid Project. (2010). Retrieved April, 2010, from http://www.ontogrid.net/ ontogrid/index.html

Open Cloud Computing Interface (OCCI). (2010). Retrieved April, 2010, from http://www.occi-wg.org/ doku.php

Open Mashup Alliance (OMA). (2010). Retrieved from http://www.openmashup.org

Open Science Grid. (2010). [REMOVED HYPER-LINK FIELD]A blueprint for the Open Science Grid. Retrieved from http://osg-docdb.open-sciencegrid.org/ 0000/ 000018/ 009/ OSG%20 Blueprint%20v.14.pdf

Ouyang, S. (2007). Implementation of policy based management in workflow management. [LNCS]. *Lecture Notes in Computer Science, 4402*, 675–666. doi:10.1007/978-3-540-72863-4_67

Owens, J. D., Houston, M., Luebke, D., Green, S., Stone, J. E., & Phillips, J. C. (2008). An introductory paper: GPU computing. [IEEE Computer Society.]. *Proceedings of the IEEE, 96*, 879–899. doi:10.1109/JPROC.2008.917757

P-Grade. (2010). Retrieved from http://www.p-grade.hu/ main.php?m=1

Performance, P. R. O. P. H. E. T. (2010). Retrieved from http://www.par.univie.ac.at/ project/ prophet/ node4.html

Preimesberger, C. (2004). *Top 10 mistakes enterprise can make when moving data into the cloud*. Retrieve March, 2010, from http://www.eweek.com

RightGrid Overview. (2010). Retrieved February, 2010 from http://tinyurl.com/ yeto4bz

Salesforce (2010). *The force.com multitenant architecture*. Retrieved from http://www.salesforce.com/ au/ assets/ pdf/ Force.com_Multitenancy_WP_101508.pdf

Santinelli, R., & Donno, F. (2005). Installing and configuring application software on the LHC computing grid. In *Proceedings of the 1ˢᵗ International Conference on E-science and Grid Computing* (pp. 369-376). IEEE Computer Society.

Sarmenta, L. F. G., & Hirano, S. (1999). Bayanihan: Building and studying Web-based volunteer computing systems using java. *Journal of Future Generation Computer Systems, 15*(5-6), 675–686. doi:10.1016/S0167-739X(99)00018-7

Semantic Grid Community Portal. (2006). *Next generation GRIDs expert group report 3*. Retrieved March, 2010, from http://www.semanticgrid.org/ NGG3

Semantic Grid Vision. (2001). Retrieved, 2010, from http://www.semanticgrid.org/ vision.html

SETI@Home (2010). Retrieved February from http://setiathome.berkeley.edu/ cuda.php

Smarr, L., & Catlett, C. E. (1992). Metacomputing. *Communications of the ACM, 35*(6), 44–52. doi:10.1145/129888.129890

SORMA. (2009). Retrieved November, 2010, from http://www.sorma-project.org

The Cloud Computing and Distributed Systems (CLOUDS) Laboratory. (2010). *University of Melbourne*. Retrieved from http://www.gridbus. org/ broker

The Green Grid. (2010). Retrieved from http:// doe.thegreengrid.org/ joint_projects

The Metacomputing. One from many (1995). *National Center for Supercomputer Applications (NCSA)*. Retrieved from http://archive.ncsa.uiuc. edu/ Cyberia/ MetaComp/ MetaHome.html

Top 15 Most Popular Web 2.0 Websites (2010). Retrieved from http://www.ebizmba.com/ articles/ web-2.0-websites

Transforming data2knowledge (D2K) (2010). Retrieved from http://alg.ncsa.uiuc.edu/ do/tools/ d2k

Trunfioa, P., Talia, D., Papadakis, H., Fragopoulou, P., Mordacchini, M., Pennanen, M., & Haridi, S. (2007). Peer-to-peer resource discovery in grids: Models and systems. *Future Generation Computer Systems, 23*, 864–878. doi:10.1016/j. future.2006.12.003

Truong, H. L., Brunner, P., Fahringer, F., & Nerieri, F. Samborski, R., Balis, B.,…Rozkwitalski, K. (2006). K-WfGrid distributed monitoring and performance analysis services for workflows in the grid. In *Proceedings of 2nd IEEE International Conference on E-science and Grid Computing* (pp. 15). IEEE Computer Society.

Tuecke, S., Czajkowski, K., Foster, I., Frey, J., Graham, S., Kesselman, C.,…Vanderbilt P. (2007). *Open Grid Services Infrastructure (OGSI) v1.0*. Technical report, Global Grid Forum, 2007.

UniGrids. (2010). Retrieved from http://www. unigrids.org

Walker, E. (2008). Benchmarking amazon EC2 for high performance scientific computing. *LOGIN, 33*(5), 18–23.

Walton, N. A., Lawrence, A., & Linde, T. (2004). AstroGrid: Initial deployment of the UK's virtual observatory. *Astronomical Data Analysis Software and Systems XIII ASP Conference Series, vol. 314*. Astronomical Society of the Pacific Conference Series.

WebEx Connect. (2006). *First SaaS platform to deliver mashup business applications for knowledge workers*. Retrieved from http://www.highbeam. com/ doc/ 1G1-151872985.html

Weinman, J. (2008). *The 10 laws of cloudonomics*. Retrieved March, 2010, from http://tinyurl. com/ 5wv9d7

Weishäupl, T., Donno, F., Schikuta, E., Stockinger, H., & Wanek, H. (2005). Business in the grid: The BIG project. In *Proceedings of 2nd International Workshop on Grid Economics and Business Models*, Seoul, Korea. Retrieved from http://www.gridforumkorea.org/ ggf13/ data/ Gecon/ Thomas_Weishaupl.pdf

Wu, Y., Wu, S., Yu, H., & Hu, C. (2005). *Introduction to ChinaGrid support platform. Lecture Notes in Computer Science (LNCS) (Vol. 3759)*. Berlin-Heidelberg, Germany: Springer.

Xbaya (A graphical workflow composer for Web services) (2010). Retrieved from http://www. extreme.indiana.edu/ xgws/ xbaya

Yahoo. Pipes mashup (2010). *Retrieved from* http:// pipes.yahoo.com/ pipes

Yu, J., & Buyya, R. (2005). A taxonomy of scientific workflow systems for grid computing. *SIGMOD Record, 34*(3), 44–49. doi:10.1145/1084805.1084814

Zhao, J., & Pjesivac-Grbovic, J. (2009). MapReduce: The programming model and practice. *SIGMETRICS/Performance '09, Tutorials.* Retrieved from http://static.googleusercontent. com/ external_content/ untrusted_dlcp/ research. google.com/ en// pubs/ archive/ 36249.pdf

Zhao, Y., Hategan, M., Clifford, B., & Foster, I. Von Laszewski, G., Raicu, I.,… Wilde, M. (2007). Swift: Fast, reliable, loosely coupled parallel computation. In *Proceeding of 2007 IEEE Congress on Services* (pp. 199-206). IEEE Computer Society.

Chapter 4
Grid Scheduling:
Methods, Algorithms, and Optimization Techniques

Florin Pop
University Politehnica of Bucharest, Romania

ABSTRACT

This chapter will present the scheduling mechanism in distributed systems with direct application in grids. The resource heterogeneity, the size and number of tasks, the variety of policies, and the high number of constraints are some of the main characteristics that contribute to this complexity. The necessity of scheduling in grid is sustained by the increasing of number of users and applications. The design of scheduling algorithms for a heterogeneous computing system interconnected with an arbitrary communication network is one of the actual concerns in distributed system research. The main concerns presented in the chapter refers to general presentation of scheduling for grid systems, specific requirements of scheduling in grids, critical analysis of existing methods and algorithms for grid schedulers, scheduling policies, fault tolerance in scheduling process in grid environments, scheduling models and algorithms and optimization techniques for grid scheduling.

DOI: 10.4018/978-1-61350-113-9.ch004

INTRODUCTION

Due to grid systems characteristics, the main issue for grid scheduling is to develop a Meta-Scheduling architecture that encompasses heterogeneous and dynamic clusters. This architecture is a decentralized one and represents the solution for the scheduling problem at a global grid level. At this level, the Quality-of-Service (QoS) constraint is very important. The scheduling methods for decentralized heterogeneous environment are based on heuristics that consider complex applications. The tasks that compose these applications can have different dimensions and can be based on diverse data and control patterns.

The specific requirements of scheduling in distributed systems are: the claims of the resource consumers, the restrictions imposed by the resource owners, the need to continuously adapt to changes in the availability of resources, etc. Based on these requirements, a number of challenging issues that must be addressed must be considered: maximization of system throughput, sites' autonomy, scalability, fault-tolerance, and quality of services. On the other hand, the motivation for dynamic scheduling is then presented. The basic idea is to perform task allocation on the fly as the application executes. This is useful when it is difficult, if not impossible, to predict the execution time, the branch selected in a decision, and the number of iterations in a loop. So, dynamic scheduling is usually applied when it is difficult to estimate the cost of applications, or when jobs are coming at unpredictable times. The two major functions used in dynamic task scheduling are described, namely the system state estimation (different from the cost estimation in static scheduling) and the decision making.

A large number of tools are available for local grid scheduling: PBS, Condor, Sun Grid Engine, and LSF. These tools are included in the category of centralized schedulers. Instead, the meta-schedulers are the subject of projects under development, like GridWay (that is an incubator project in Globus) and Globus CSF. There is no meta-scheduler accepted and used on a large scale. A problem that must be solved for this type of scheduling is the scalability. This aspect is more important in the context of heterogeneous systems (that require a simultaneous management of multiple clusters) and of the diversity of middleware tools.

Large distributed systems with many different administrative domains will most likely have different resource utilization policies. Thus it is unlikely that a fixed scheduling policy will suffice for different needs. The system and application oriented policies for dynamic scheduling are important for tasks with dependencies as well. The system oriented policies need monitoring information for applications scheduling and execution in grids. This section will describe the policies which consider Quality-of-Services constrains. QoS is a requirement for many grid applications. QoS might refer to the response time, the necessary memory, etc. It might happen that these requirements are satisfied only by specific resources, so that they only these resources can be assigned for that application. Situations might become more complex when there are more tasks having QoS requirements, and several resources exist which satisfy them. The resource allocation under QoS constrains is another subject for the optimization process. Other type of policy for scheduling in grid computing must also take into account additional issues such as the resource owners' requirements, the need to continuously adapt to changes in the availability of resources, and so on. In these cases, a number of challenging issues need to be addressed: maximization of system throughput and user satisfaction, the sites' autonomy (the grid is composed of resources owned by different users, which retain control over them), and scalability.

The fault tolerance is also important in grid. Two of the problems related to re-scheduling are the high cost and the lack of coping with dependent tasks. For computational intensive tasks, re-scheduling the original schedule can improve the performance. But, re-scheduling is usually costly, especially in Directed Acyclic Graphs (DAGs) where there are extra data dependencies among tasks. Current research on DAG rescheduling leaves a wide open area on optimization for the scheduling algorithms.

In many cases, the data must be transported to the place where tasks will be executed. Consequently, scheduling algorithms should consider not only the task execution time, but also the data transfer time for finding a more realistic mapping of tasks. Only a handful of current research efforts consider the simultaneous optimization of computation and data transfer scheduling.

The optimization techniques for scheduling process in grid are important according with performance assurance. The optimization of scheduling process for grid systems tries to provide better solutions for the selection and allocation of resources to current tasks. The scheduling optimization is very important because the scheduling is a main building block for making grids more available to user communities. The scheduling problem is NP-Complete. Consequently, approximation algorithms are considered, which are expected to quickly offer a solution, even if it is only near-to-optimal. Performance prediction is also used in optimizing the scheduling algorithms. Existing scheduling algorithms only consider an instant value of the performance at the scheduling time, and assume this value remains constant during the task execution. A more accurate model should consider that performance changes during the execution of the application.

Many research activities are being conducted to develop a good scheduling approach for distributed nodes. The activities vary widely in a number of characteristics, e.g. support for heterogeneous resources, objective function(s), scalability, co-scheduling methods, and assumptions about system characteristics. The current research directions are focused on multi-criteria optimization of grid scheduling; approaching complex task dependencies, new scheduling

algorithms for real-time scenarios, backup and recovery from service failures, and optimization of data transfers (provide an optimal solution to the problem of co-scheduling). In compliance with the new techniques in application development, it is more natural to consider schedulers closer to grid applications. They are responsible for the management of tasks, such as allocating resources, managing the tasks for parallel execution, managing of data transfers, and correlating the events. To provide their functions, a scheduler needs information coming from monitoring services available in the platform.

BACKGROUND

The scheduling in grid systems is approached in general using a higher level abstraction for the distributed systems by ignoring infrastructure components such as authentication, authorization, and access control. A very good definition for the distributed system that can be used in this chapter for understanding scheduling problem keys is given by Baker, Buyya & Laforenza (2002). A type of parallel and distributed system that enables the sharing, selection, and aggregation of geographically distributed autonomous and heterogeneous resources dynamically at runtime depending on their availability, capability, performance, cost, and users' quality-of-service requirements (Baker, Buyya & Laforenza, 2002).

More applications are turning to Large Scale Distributed System (LSDS) computing to meet their computational and data storage needs. Single sites are simply no longer efficient for meeting the resource needs of high-end applications, and using distributed resources can give the application many benefits. Effective LSDS computing is possible, however, only if the resources are scheduled well (Roehrig & Ziegler, 2002).

The background for scheduling problems is described by resources environment, task characteristics and assignment policies. It states a general commitment about the resources (represented by processors) and their relation to the tasks: whether there are one or more processors, whether they have identical or uniform speed, whether the environment is a certain shop system and what network topology the processors are connected by. The second one specifies the characteristic of tasks. It is mainly concerned with the admissibility of preemptions, precedence constrains, release times, bounded processing time and deadlines.

According with these aspects about environment and tasks the optimality criteria could be described. These criteria represent the main focus of scheduling policies. First the policies for task processing consider the following aspects: tasks can be processed on any single processor, tasks require fixed numbers of processors, linear speedup, processing times are in the inverse ratio to number of assigned processors, processing times are an arbitrary function of the number of assigned processors, tasks require sub-hypercube of a hypercube network, tasks require sub-meshes of a mesh (array), there is exactly one fixed subgraph specified for each task, or there are sets of possible sub-graphs specified for each task. In the case of communication tasks, the delays are also important. The scheduling policies can consider no communication delays, equals delay or different delays. Another important policy refers to fault tolerance. It considers task duplication that could be allowed or not (Streit, 2002).

In LSDS scheduling process involves three main phases (Schopf, 2004): first, resource discovery, which generates a list of potential resources; second, information gathering about those resources and selection of a best set of resources according with users requirements; third, task execution (system preparation and submission), phase which includes task staging and system cleanup. Because each of the main phases includes some steps, it produces many levels and it's difficult to implement all steps in a real environment (Xhafa & Abraham, 2010).

For a general purpose a scheduling approach should make some assumptions about and have few restrictions to the types of applications that can be executed. Interactive tasks, distributed and parallel applications, as well as non-interactive batch tasks, should all be supported with good performance. This property is a straightforward one, but to some extent difficult to achieve. Because different kinds of tasks have different attributes, their requirements to the scheduler may contradict. For example, a real-time task, requiring short-time response, prefers space-sharing scheduling; a non-interactive batch task, requiring high-throughput, may prefer time-sharing scheduling. To achieve the general purpose, a tradeoff may have to be made. As it is mentioned above, the scheduling method focused on parallel tasks, while providing an acceptable performance to other kinds of tasks (Pop & Cristea, 2009).

Efficiency has two meanings: one is that it should improve the performance of scheduled tasks as much as possible; the other is that the scheduling should incur reasonably low overhead so that it won't counterattack the benefits (Aziz & El-Rewini, 2008).

The fairness refers to sharing resources among users raises new challenges in guaranteeing that each user obtains his/her fair share when demand is heavy. In a distributed system, this problem could be exacerbated such that one user consumes the entire system. There are many mature strategies to achieve fairness on a single node (Hu, M., Guo, W. & Hu, W, 2009).

The dynamics of the scheduling problem means that the allocation algorithms employed to decide where to process a task should respond to load changes, and exploit the full extent of the resources available (Prodan & Fahringer, 2005).

For the transparency of scheduling process the behavior and result of a tasks execution should not be affected by the host(s) on which it executes. In particular, there should be no difference between local and remote execution. No user effort should be required in deciding where to execute a task or in initiating remote execution; a user should not even be aware of remote processing, except maybe better performance. Further, the applications should not be changed greatly. It is undesirable to have to modify the application programs in order to execute them in the system (De Rose et al., 2008).

GENERAL PRESENTATION OF SCHEDULING FOR GRID SYSTEMS

A scheduling model consists of scheduling policy, a program model, a performance model, and a performance measure method. A scheduling model specify the position of scheduler in grid, the scheduler architecture, the communication model between entities involved in scheduling, the process type: static or dynamic, the objective function, the state estimation, and the scheduling policies.

First, a scheduler in grid could work local or global. This is the position of schedulers in grid. The local scheduler uses a single CPU (a single machine) and determines how the tasks are allocated in time and executed on it. It is represented by scheduler from system operating kernel. The global scheduler uses information about system and its components to allocate tasks to multiple resources and try to optimize this process according with specified performance objectives. It is represented by grid scheduler. Next, the scheduler architecture is very important because it split the schedulers in tree classes: centralized, hierarchical and decentralized (Rodero, Guim & Corbalan, 2009).

In the centralized scheduler all tasks are sent to the one entity in the system. This entity is called central server or master or coordination. There is a queue in on this entity for holding all the pending tasks. When a task is submitted to the scheduler, it may not be scheduled at once; it will be put in the queue and waiting for scheduling and resource allocation. The main problem with centralized

scheme is that is not very scalable with increasing number of resources. For example, if a network failure appears and the master is not accessible or responds very slow, the system availability and performance will be affected. As an advantage, the scheduler is able to produce very efficient schedules at local level, because the master has an overview on the available resources and on pending applications (Afrash & Rahmani, 2008). This type of scheduler is recommended for homogenous systems like massive multiprocessors machine or clusters.

The hierarchical scheduler is organized on different levels having a tree structure (Kurowski, 2008): the higher-level components manage direct larger sets of resources and indirect a smaller set of resources using lower-level components. The lower-level components could be local schedulers in clusters that provide to the higher-level components the possibility to schedule a set of task on the managed resources. Hierarchical scheduling, in comparison with the centralized scheduling, addresses the scalability and the problem of single-point-of-failure. Hierarchical scheduling uses some of the advantages of the centralized scheme: higher-level components have a local scheduler and some resources (preferred to be homogenous) managed in a centralized way. One of the issues with the hierarchical scheme is to provide site autonomy.

The decentralized scheduler has multiple components (site) that work independent and collaborate for obtaining the schedule (Lu, 2007). Each site in the grid could be a local scheduler and a computational resource in the same time. The schedule requests could be processed by local scheduler or transferred to other local scheduler where different scheduling policies are possible. In this way, the decentralized scheduler delivers better fault-tolerance and reliability than the centralized scheme, but the lack of a global scheduler, which knows the information of all applications and resources, usually results in low efficiency.

The next attribute for scheduling process is the collaboration mode between involved entities. If a distributed scheduling architecture adopted, the next issue that should be establishes is the working way: cooperatively or independently (non-cooperatively). In the non-cooperative case, individual entities work as autonomous entities and obtain their optimum objects independent of the decision on the rest of system. This model is very good for application-level schedulers in grid which are coupled with an application and optimize their private individual objectives. In the cooperative case, each entity works to a common system-wide goal. The cooperative model requires a communication protocol. An example of cooperative scheduling is presented in (Shan, 2004), where is presented a distributed grid scheduler based on client-server model. The obtained results are compared with centralized scheduling and local scheduling and prove that decentralized cooperative model are more efficient that centralize or non-cooperative scheduler.

Static or dynamic scheduling is used for efficient planning in distributed systems. In the case of static scheduling, information regarding all resources in the grid as well as all the tasks in an application is assumed to be available by the time the application is scheduled. In the static model, every task comprising the task is assigned only once to a resource. For this reason, the assignment of an application to corresponding resources is said to be static. Accordingly, a realistic prediction of the cost of the computation can be made in advance of the actual execution.

By contrast, when talking about dynamic scheduling, the basic idea is to perform task allocation on the fly while other applications are in execution. This is useful in the case where tasks arrive in a real-time mode. Dynamic scheduling is usually applied when it is difficult to estimate the cost of applications, or tasks are coming online dynamically (in this case, it is also called online scheduling). A good example of these scenarios is the task queue management in some meta-computing systems like Condor and Legion. Dynamic task scheduling has two major components: system state estimation (other than cost estimation in static scheduling) and, decision making.

System state estimation involves collecting state information throughout the grid and constructing an estimate. On the basis of the estimate, decisions are made to assign a task to a selected resource. Since the cost for an assignment is not available, a natural way to keep the whole system healthy is by balancing the loads of all resources. The advantage of dynamic load balancing over static scheduling is that the system need not be aware of the run-time behavior of the application before execution. It is particularly useful in a system where the primary performance goal is maximizing resource utilization, rather than minimizing runtime for individual tasks. If a resource is assigned too many tasks, it may invoke a balancing policy to decide whether to transfer some tasks to other resources, and which tasks to transfer.

According to initiation of the balancing process, there are two different approaches: sender-initiated where a node that receives a new task but doesn't want to run the task initiates the task transfer, and receiver-initiated where a node that is willing to receive a new task initiates the process.

In the case that all information regarding the state of resources and the tasks is known, an optimal assignment could be made based on some criterion function, such as minimum make-span and maximum resource utilization. But due to the NP-Complete nature of scheduling algorithms and the difficulty in grid scenarios to make reasonable assumptions which are usually required to prove the optimality of an algorithm, current research, like (Takefusa, 2001), tries to find suboptimal solutions, which can be further divided into the following two general categories: approximate and heuristic algorithms.

The approximate algorithms use formal computational models, but instead of searching the entire solution space for an optimal solution, they are satisfied when a solution that is sufficiently good is found. In the case where a metric is available for evaluating a solution, this technique can be used to decrease the time taken to find an acceptable schedule. The factors which determine whether this approach is worthy of pursuit include: availability of a function to evaluate a solution, the time required to evaluate a solution, the ability to judge the value of an optimal solution according to some metric, availability of a mechanism for intelligently pruning the solution space.

The other branch in the suboptimal category is called heuristic. This branch represents the class of algorithms which make the most realistic assumptions about a priori knowledge concerning process and system loading characteristics. It also represents the solutions to the scheduling problem which cannot give optimal answers but only require the most reasonable amount of cost and other system resources to perform their function. The evaluation of this kind of solution is usually based on experiments in the real world or on simulation. Not restricted by formal assumptions, heuristic algorithms are more adaptive to the grid scenarios where both resources and applications are highly diverse and dynamic, so most of the algorithms to be further discussed are heuristics.

Some of the schedulers provide a rescheduling mechanism, which determines when the current schedule is re-examined and the task executions reordered. The rescheduling taxonomy divides this mechanism in two conceptual mechanisms: periodic/batch and event-driven on line. Periodic or batch mechanism approaches group resource request and system events which are then processed at intervals that may me periodic triggered by certain system events. The other mechanism performs the rescheduling as soon the system receives the resource request.

The scheduling policy can be fixed or extensible. The fixed policies are system oriented or application oriented. The extensible policies are ad-hoc or structured. In a fixed approach, the policy implemented by the resource manager is predetermined. Extensible scheduling policy schemes allow external entities the ability to change the scheduling policy.

Inspired for the real live, there are a few economic models that can be applied in grid systems. The main characters in those models are the producers (resource owners) and the consumers (resource users). The main models are: commodity market (flat or supply-and-demand driven pricing) model, posted price model, bargaining model, tender/contract-net model, auction model, bid-based proportional resource sharing model (Buyya, 2001; Caramia, 2008).

Any parallel application can be modeled by a Directed Acyclic Graph (DAG). Although application loops cannot be explicitly represented by the DAG model, the parallelism in data-flow computations in loops can be exploited to subdivide the loops into a number of tasks by the loop-unraveling technique. The idea is that all iterations of the loop are started or fired together, and operations in various iterations can execute when their input data are ready for access. In addition, for a large class of data-flow computation problems and many numerical algorithms (such as matrix multiplication), there are very few, if any, conditional branches or indeterminism in the program. Thus, the DAG model can be used to accurately represent these applications so that the scheduling techniques can be applied. Furthermore, in many numerical applications, such as Gaussian elimination or Fast Fourier Transform (FFT), the loop bounds are known during compile time. As such, one or more iterations of a loop can be encapsulated in a task and, consequently, be represented by a node in a DAG. The node and edge weights are usually obtained by estimation using profiling information of operations such as numerical operations, memory access operations, and message-passing primitives.

In a general representation, tasks are split into sub-tasks which are split into tasks, the atomic unit of an application. Tasks forming a task contain dependencies if a precedence relation can be established among them. The model applied in this case is a DAG where a node represents a task and a directed arc represents the order of precedence between the nodes it connects.

It is necessary to follow the steps of analyzing the workflow of the application, planning the tasks accordingly, as well as allocating the resources so that the structure of the workflow is respected. An important issue is obtaining the maximum parallelism possible therefore there must be a trade-off between the computational cost and the communication cost.

The DAG scheduling problem is a NP-complete problem. A solution for this problem is a series of heuristics, where tasks are assigned priorities and places in a list ordered by priority. The method through which the tasks are selected to be planned at each step takes into consideration this criterion, thus the task with higher priority receives access to resources before those with a lower priority. The heuristics used vary according to task requirements, structure and complexity of the DAG (Pop, 2008).

Once the priority mechanism is established, it is necessary to take into consideration those tasks that have all dependencies solved (the tasks they depend on have been executed), and minimize the time associated to the critical path. For example, Heterogeneous Earliest Finish Time (HEFT) selects at each step the task with the highest upward rank (the maximum distance from the current node to the finish node given by the computational and communication cost).

Based on these algorithms, the goal is to analyze the performance of the planning criteria and if possible, optimize the task scheduling by combining the best characteristics of a set of algorithms to obtain a hybrid algorithm with better overall results.

There are multiple criteria for algorithm selection. Fist the architecture must be selected: centralized or decentralized architecture. In the case of dependability we could approach an arbitrary graph structure or a restricted graph. Arbitrary

approach is more general. At this level we must describe the communication model and costs. It is possible to consider resources with communication and without communication. The cost, in the case of communication, could be uniform or arbitrary. The fault tolerance is considered, so it is possible to choose for tasks duplication. Then we could have a limited number of resources or a restriction for resources. The last case is a challenge to develop a good scheduling algorithm.

SPECIFIC REQUIREMENTS OF SCHEDULING IN DISTRIBUTED SYSTEMS

A hierarchical taxonomy for scheduling algorithms in parallel and distributed systems was made for the first time by Casavant (1988) (see Figure 1). Scheduling algorithms in grid fall into a subcategory of this taxonomy. This general taxonomy described scheduling models. A part of these models was described in the previous section.

Basically, we have local and global scheduling. A Local scheduler considers a single CPU (a single machine). Global scheduling is dedicated to multiple resources. Scheduling for distributed systems such as the grid is part of the global scheduling class.

For global scheduling there is two way to allocate the resources for tasks: static or dynamic. In the static scheduling model, every task is assigned only once to a resource. A realistic prediction of the cost of the computation can be made before to the actual execution. The static model adopts a global view of tasks and computational costs. One of the major benefits is the simple way of implementation. On the other hand, static strategies cannot be applied in a scenario where tasks appear a-periodically, and the environment undergoes various state changes. Cost estimate does not adapt to situations in which one of the nodes selected to perform a computation fails, becomes isolated from the system due to network

Figure 1. Taxonomy of scheduling algorithms (A hierarchical approach)

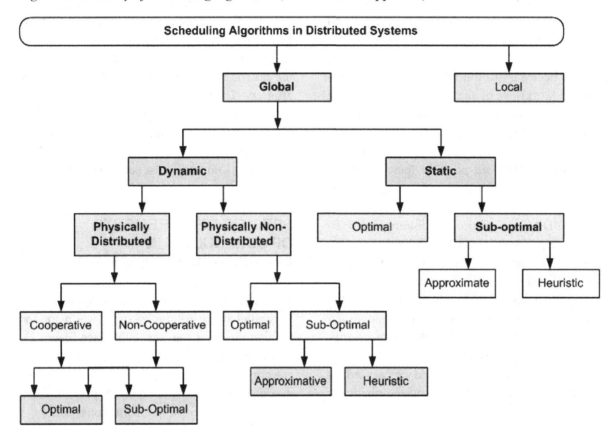

failures, is so heavily loaded with tasks that its response time becomes longer than expected, or a new computing node enters the system. These changes are possible in grids (Braun, 2001). In dynamic scheduling techniques tasks are allocated dynamically at their arrival. Dynamic scheduling is usually applied when it is difficult to estimate the cost of applications, or tasks are coming online dynamically (in this case, it is also called online scheduling). Dynamic task scheduling has two major components: one for system state estimation (other than cost estimation in static scheduling) and one for decision making. System state estimation involves collecting state information through grid monitoring and constructing an estimate. On this basis, decisions are made to assign tasks to selected resources. Since the cost for an assignment is not always available, a natural way to keep the whole system healthy is by balancing the loads of all resources (Takefusa, 2001).

The dynamic scheduling could be done in a physically distributed environment (grids) or in a physically non-distributed system (cluster). Sabin et al (2003) have proposed a centralized scheduler which uses backfill to schedule parallel tasks in multiple heterogeneous sites.

In distributed scheduling (global) the involved nodes could working cooperatively or independently (non-cooperatively). In the non-cooperative scheduling, individual schedulers act alone as autonomous entities and arrive at decisions regarding their own optimum objects independent of the effects of the decision on the rest of system. In cooperative scheduling each grid scheduler has the responsibility to carry out its own portion of the scheduling task (Shan, 2004).

If all information about the state of resources and the tasks is known, an optimal assignment could, considering an objective function. But due to the NP-Complete nature of scheduling algorithms *sub-optimal* algorithms for scheduling represent good solutions (Rewini, 1990).

The sub-optimal algorithm can be further divided into the following two general categories: approximate and heuristic. The approximate algorithms use formal computational models and are satisfied when a solution that is sufficiently good is found. If a metric is available for evaluating a solution, this technique can be used to decrease the time taken to find an acceptable schedule. The heuristic algorithms make the most realistic assumptions about a priori knowledge concerning process and system loading characteristics. The heuristic algorithms are the solutions to the scheduling problem which cannot give optimal answers but require amount of cost and other system resources to perform their function.

The scheduling process, in sub-optimal case, could be conducted by objective functions. Objective functions can be classified into two categories: application-centric and resource-centric (Zhu, 2006) (Figure 2).

Application-centric function in scheduling tries to optimize the performance of each individual application. Most of current grid applications' concerns are about time, for example the makespan, which is the time spent from the beginning of the first task in a task to the end of the last task of the task. On the other hand, the economic cost that an application needs to pay for resources utilization becomes a concern of some of grid users (Buyya, 2001).

Resource-centric function in scheduling tries to optimize the performance of the resources. They are usually related to resource utilization, for example, throughput (ability of a resource to process a certain number of tasks), utilization (which the percentage of time a resource) (Gao, 2005). As economic models are introduced into grid computing, economic profit (which is the economic benefits resource providers can get by attracting grid users to submit applications to their resources) also comes under the purview of resource management policies.

Adaptive Scheduling is used to make scheduling decisions change dynamically according to the previous, current and/or future resource status (Casavant, 1988). In grid, adaptive scheduling could be done considering tree criteria: the heterogeneity of candidate resources, the dynamism of resource performance, and the diversity of applications (see Figure 3).

Relations between tasks divide scheduling algorithms in two classes: independent task scheduling and DAG scheduling (workflow scheduling). Dependency means there are precedence orders existing in tasks, that is, a task cannot start until all its parent are done (see Figure 4).

Some applications involve parallel tasks that access and generate large data sets. Data sets in this scale require specialized storage and management systems and data grid projects are carried out to harness geographically distributed resources for such data-intensive problems by providing remote data set storage, access management, replication services, and data transfer protocols (Allcock, 2005).

Data Scheduling could be done without replication or with replication, ensuring in this case the fault tolerance. If replication is considered, there are possible two cases: decoupled computation (Deelman, 2005) and data scheduling or integrated computation and data scheduling (Ranganathan, 2002).

The grid is a large number of autonomous resources, which could be used concurrently, changing dynamically, interacting with different Virtual Organizations (VOs). In human society and in nature there are systems having the similar characteristics. The Grid Economy approaches and other heuristics inspired by natural phenomena were studied in recent years to address the challenges of grid computing. A short description of these techniques is shown in Figure 6. In "A

Figure 2. Taxonomy of objective functions used by scheduling algorithms

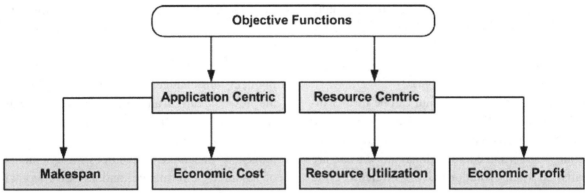

Figure 3. Taxonomy of adaptive scheduling algorithms

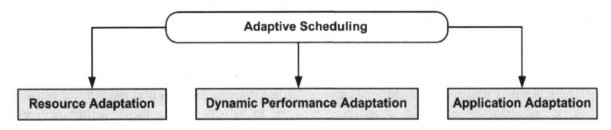

Figure 4. Taxonomy of Task dependency for scheduling algorithms

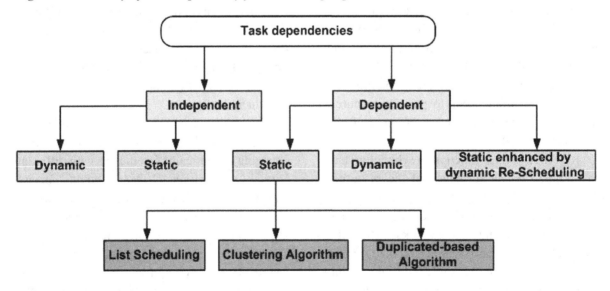

Critical Analysis of Scheduling Algorithms" section these techniques will be presented in details.

Considering scheduling strategies treating performance dynamism, some of the schedulers provide a rescheduling mechanism, which determines when the current schedule is re-examined and the task executions reordered. The rescheduling taxonomy divides this mechanism in two conceptual mechanisms: periodic/batch and event-driven on line. Periodic or batch mechanism approaches group resource request and system events which are then processed at intervals that may me periodic triggered by certain system events. The other mechanism performs the rescheduling as soon the system receives the resource request (Figure 7). The scheduling policy can be fixed or extensible. The fixed policies are system oriented or application oriented. The extensible policies are ad-hoc or structured. In a fixed approach, the policy implemented by the resource manager is predetermined. Extensible scheduling policy schemes allow external entities the ability to change the scheduling policy (Deelman, 2005).

DAG SCHEDULING

Most of the scheduling algorithms are based on the list scheduling technique. These algorithms assign priorities to the tasks and schedule them according to a list priority scheme. A node with higher priority is examined for scheduling before a node with lower priority. This technique is based on the repeated execution of the following two steps for as long as all the tasks of the DAG are mapped:

1. Select the node with higher priority.
2. Assign the selected node to a suitable machine.

Two major attributes frequently used for assigning priorities are the t-level (top level) and the b-level (bottom level). The t-level of a node n_i is the weight of the longest path from a source node to n_i (excluding n_i). The length of a path is computed as the sum of all the node and edge weights along the path. In the computation of the t-level of a node n_i its execution time i is not included. The t-level of n_i identifies the n_i s earliest start time, denoted by TS(n_i), which is determined after n_i is mapped to a machine. It is a dynamic attribute because the weight of an edge may be zeroed when the two incident nodes are mapped to the same processor. Some authors call this attribute ASAP (As Soon As Possible). The procedures to compute the t-level and b-level are in $O(v + e)$ time-complexity. The critical path (CP) of a DAG is the longest path in that graph, i.e. the path whose length is the maximum. There can be more than one CP. The t-level and the b-level are bounded from above by the length of the critical path.

Heterogeneous Earliest-Finish-Time (HEFT). HEFT algorithm is a list heuristic. It selects the task with the highest upward rank at each step. An upward rank is defined as the maximum distance between the current node and the existing node including the both the communication and computation costs. The selected node is assigned to the machine that minimize its earliest finish time with an insertion-based approach which considers the possible insertion of a task in an earliest idle time slot between two already-scheduled tasks on the same resource.

Fast Critical Path (FCP). The purpose of FCT algorithm is to reduce the complexity of the list heuristics while maintaining the scheduling performances. It is possible because most of the list heuristics sort all tasks at the beginning of the scheduling process based on some ranks computed before. The FCT algorithm does not sort all tasks but maintains only a limited number of tasks sorted at a precise time. Instead of considering all processors as possible targets for a given task, the choice is restricted to either the processor from which the last messages to the given task arrives or the processor which becomes idle the earliest.

Figure 5. Taxonomy of algorithms considering data scheduling

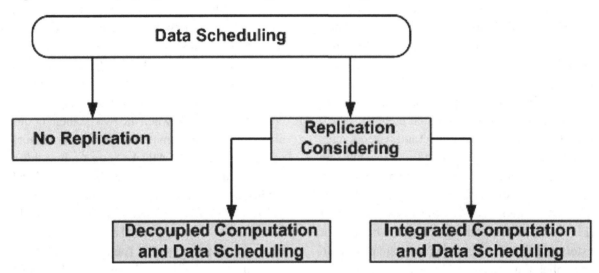

Figure 6. Taxonomy of non-traditional scheduling approaches

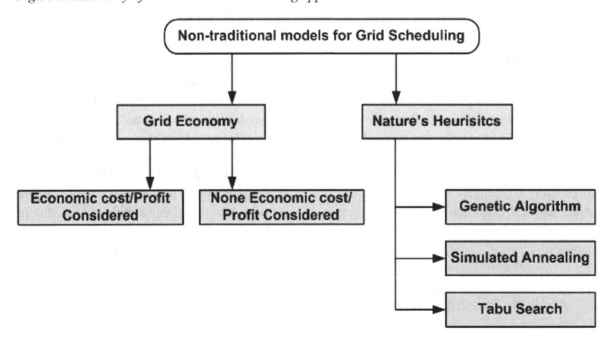

Figure 7. Taxonomy of scheduling strategies treating performance dynamism

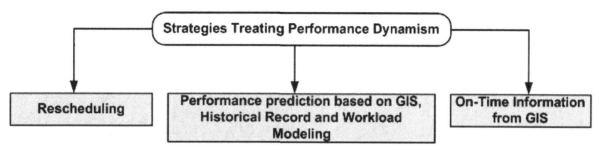

Highest Level First with Estimated Times (HLFET). HLFET is a list scheduling algorithm. It first computes the static b-level for each node and then makes a ready list in descending order of static b-level (ties are broken randomly). Then it repeatedly schedules the first node in the ready list to a processor that allows the earliest start time and updates the list with the new ready nodes. It is a BNP algorithm with $O(v^2)$ time complexity.

A critical issue in list heuristics for DAGs is how to compute a node's rank. In a heterogeneous environment, the execution time of the same task will differ on different resources as well as the communication cost via different network links. So for a particular node, its rank will also be different if it is assigned to different resources. The problem is how to choose the proper value used to make the ordering decision. These values could be the mean value, the median value, the worst value, the best value and so on. But Zhao et al (2003) have shown that different choices can affect the performance of list heuristics such as HEFT dramatically (makespan can change 47.2% for certain graph).

Duplication Based Algorithms. Another way to reduce the makespan is to duplicate tasks on different resources. The main idea behind duplication based scheduling is to use the resource idle time to duplicate predecessor tasks. This may avoid the transfer of results from a predecessor to a successor, thus reducing the communication cost. So duplication can solve the max-min problem. Duplication based algorithms differ according to the task selection strategies for duplication. At the beginning, these kinds of algorithms were used for an unbounded number of identical processors such as distributed memory multiprocessor systems.

Task Duplication-based Scheduling Algorithm (TDS). In the TDS algorithm, for each node in a DAG should be computed the following parameters: earliest start time (*est*), earliest completion time (*ect*), latest allowable start time (*last*), latest allowable completed time (*lact*), and favorite predecessor (*fpred*). The *last* is the latest time when a task should be started; otherwise, successors of this task will be delayed (that is, their *est* will be violated). The favorite predecessors of a node *i* are those which are predecessors of *i* and if *i* is assigned to the same processors on which these nodes are running, *est*(*i*) will be minimized. The level value of a node (which denotes the length of the longest path from that node to an exit node (also known as sink node), ignoring the communicating cost along that path) is used as the priority to determine the processing order of each task. To compute these values, the whole DAG of the job will be traversed, and the complexity needed for this step is $O(e + v)$. Based on these values, task clusters are created iteratively. The clustering step is like a depth-first search from an unassigned node having the lowest level value to an entry node. Once an entry node is reached, a cluster is generated and tasks in the same cluster will be assigned to the same resource. In this step, the last and *lact* values are used to determine whether duplication is needed. For example, if *j*

Figure 8. (a) DAG with communication and computation cost, (b) Lliniar clustering, (c) Nonliniar clustering

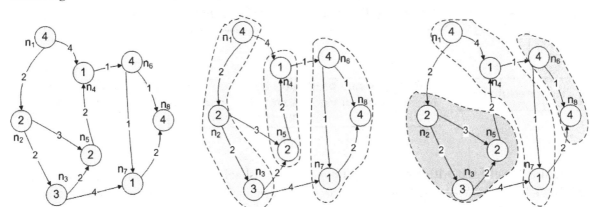

(a)   (b)   (c)

is a favorite predecessor of *i* and (*last*(*i*) - *lact*(*j*)) $< c_{j,i}$, where $c_{j,i}$ is the communication cost between *j* and *i*, *i* will be assigned to the same processor as *j*, and if *j* has be assigned to other processors, it will be duplicated to *i*'s processor. In the clustering step, the DAG is traversed similarly to the depth-first search from the exiting node, and the complexity of this step would be the same as the complexity of a general search algorithm, which is also $O(v + e)$. So the overall complexity is $O(v + e)$. In a dense DAG, the number of edges is proportional to $O(v^2)$, which is the worst case complexity of duplication algorithm. Note, in the clustering step, the number of resources available is always assumed to be smaller than required, that is, the number of resources is unbounded.

Clustering Algorithms. In parallel and distributed systems, clustering is an efficient way to reduce communication delay in DAGs by grouping intensively communicating tasks to the same labeled clusters and then assigning tasks in a cluster to the same resource (Figure 8). In general, clustering algorithms have two phases:

1. The task clustering phase that partitions the original task graph into clusters.
2. A post-clustering phase which can refine the clusters produced in the previous phase and get the final task-to-resource map.

At the beginning of the process, each node in the DAG represents an independent cluster. For each iteration, previous clusters are refined by merging some clusters. Another cluster merging step is needed after clusters are generated, so that the number of clusters generated can be equal to the number of processors. A task cluster could be linear or nonlinear (Muthuvelu et al., 2005).

Linear clustering groups tasks that are sequential in the original DAG, i.e. they belong to a simple directed path. Nonlinear clustering, instead, sequential parallel tasks and can improve the schedule length if communication is slow. So, a tradeoff must be found between parallelization (linear clustering) and offering a sequence (nonlinear clustering).

Dominant Sequence Clustering (DSC). In the DS algorithm the critical path of a cluster is called Dominant Sequence (DS) in order to make the distinction between it and the critical path of a clustered DAG. The critical path of a clustered graph is the longest path in that graph, including both non-zero communication edge cost and task weights in that path. A very important aspect regarding this algorithm is that the makespan in executing a clustered DAG is determined by the Dominant Sequence, not by the critical path of the clustered DAG. In this heuristic, task priorities are dynamically computed as the sum of their *t-level* and *b-level*. While the bottom level is statically computed at the beginning, the top level is computed incrementally during the scheduling process. Tasks are sorted and then scheduled in the order of their priorities so that current node is an unassigned node with highest propriety. Because the entry node has always the longest path to the exit node, clustering begins with the entry node. In each step, the current node is merged with the cluster of one of its predecessors so that the top level value of this node can be minimized. If all possible merging increases the top level value, the current node will remain in its own cluster (Muthuvelu, 2005).

FAULT TOLERANCE IN SCHEDULING PROCESS IN GRID ENVIRONMENTS

When referring to a fault tolerant systems, we refer to a system which supplies a set of services to its clients, according to a well defined contract, in spite of error presence, through detecting, correcting and eliminating errors, while the systems continues to supply an acceptable set of services (Avizienis, 1984). A fault tolerance model highlights possible causes and conditions where errors might appear, with the goal of improving system characteristics do detect and eliminate errors. A grid system is by definition a distributed system, which implies that a fault tolerance model for distributed systems applies to grid systems too. The main classes of errors that might appear in such systems are presented next (Figure 9) (Tudor, 2008).

Network errors. Network errors are environmental errors caused by the communication channel and basically refer to package losses on the transmission path or corrupted incoming packages on the receiving path. These errors can be corrected by the network transmission protocol and in cases where no correction can be applied

the communication path between the two endpoints is considered broken.

Timing errors. Timing errors are errors that can occur either at the beginning of the communication as a result of the impossibility to establish a connection, or during the communication flow when for example the response time of the called exceeds the response time expected by the caller. In case of grid systems which exhibit large and variable communication latencies, such timing conditions add a nondeterministic component to the expected approximate time.

Response errors. Response errors are caused by a service which returns values outside of the expected boundaries by the caller. In such situations, components have to be able to validate a certain response and to appropriately handle the exceptions. A system that is designed as a state machine, can execute uncontrolled transitions in the state space which can be further propagated to other services as a result of the grid service composition.

Byzantine errors. Byzantine errors are arbitrary errors that could appear during the execution of an application. They refer to catastrophic conditions such as crashes and omission errors. A system entering in a Byzantine state has an undefined behavior which might be caused either by the execution impossibility or erroneous execution, or by arbitrary execution outside of the one specified by design.

Physical errors. Physical errors refer to critical conditions of the physical resources such as processor, memory, storage or communication medium. Such errors have to be detected and corresponding resources be declared as nonfunctional.

Life cycle errors. Life cycle errors are particular to components which expose services which can expire at a certain moment. They can apply to component versioning as well. An example of this condition is updating a service while its clients expect that the service is working properly according to its previous specification. Service changes could be both syntactical and structural with different implications on the service callers.

Interaction errors. Interaction errors are caused by incompatibilities at the communication protocol stack level, security, workflows or timing. These are the most common errors in large scale grid systems because all these conditions appear while running the applications and the environmental and interaction states cannot be reproduced during the application testing phases. We expect that for complex grid applications to observe a high probability of interaction error occurrence. Some of these, as for example the ones due to different security levels, could be isolated and eliminated during the testing phases in a high percentage as there is a limited number of calls between virtual organizations.

The main approach to attack fault tolerance is rollback technique, which implies application state logging at a certain time interval and restoring the last stable state in case the application is detected as entering a critical state. The used techniques are either check pointing types where the application state is expected, or logging techniques which implies application message logging and handling. For data grid systems, one of the most common and widespread fault tolerance techniques is provided by replication techniques, at both data provider and computing resources. In the later case, a certain application can be running in parallel on multiple resources and in case of error conditions, computation is continued on the healthy and active resources. Another approach is process migration when the executive state is becoming critical.

One major objective for fault tolerance is to fit in real scenarios in grid computing of communication between these two entities. We have extended our application to a general level in which two scenarios can be perfectly used in task scheduling applications.

Figure 9. A fault tolerant model for the grid

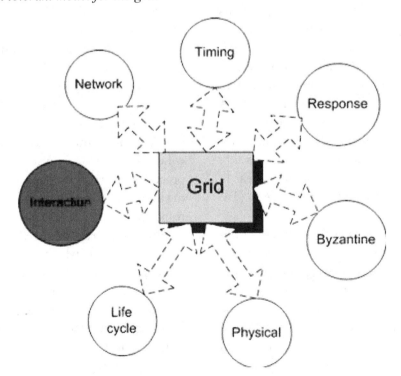

OPTIMIZATION TECHNIQUES FOR GRID SCHEDULING

Optimization methods for decentralized scheduling in grid environment use heuristic (multi-objective) approaches. We present in this section opportunistic load balancing heuristics, methods that are based on minimum execution time, minimum completion time, min-min, max-min, duplex, genetic algorithms, simulating annealing, A^*.

Opportunistic Load Balancing (OLB). The Opportunistic Load Balancing heuristic picks one task arbitrarily from the group of tasks and assigns it to the next machine that is expected to be available. It does not consider the task's expected execution time on that machine, which may lead to very poor maxspan. The advantages of this heuristic are the simplicity and the intention of keeping all the machines as busy as possible. In tasks that come one at a time, rather than in groups of tasks, the Opportunistic Load Balancing heuristic is also named First Come First Served.

Minimum Execution Time (MET). The Minimum Execution Time heuristic assigns each task picked arbitrarily to the machine with the least expected execution time for that task, and is not concerned with the time the machine becomes available. The result can be severe load imbalance across machines, although MET gives each task to its best machine.

Minimum Completion Time (MCT). The Minimum Completion Time heuristic assigns each task, in arbitrary order, to the machine with the minimum expected completion time for that task. The MCT combines the benefits of OLB and MET, and tries to avoid the circumstances in which OLB and MET perform poorly.

Min-Min heuristic begins with the set T of all unmapped tasks. The task with the minimum possible execution time is then assigned on the respective processor, after which the process continues in the same way with the remaining unmapped tasks. The major difference between Min-min and MCT is that Min-min considers all unmapped tasks during each mapping decision and MCT only considers one task at a time. The machine that finishes the earliest is also the machine that executes the task the fastest. The percentage of tasks assigned to their first choice (on the basis of execution time) is likely to be very high, and therefore a smaller maxspan can be obtained.

Max-Min heuristic is very similar to Min-min. The Max-min heuristic also begins with the set T of all unmapped tasks. Then, the set C of minimum completion times is found. The difference from Min-min comes at the next step, when the task with the overall maximum completion time from C is selected and assigned to the corresponding machine. Last, the newly mapped task is removed from C, and the process repeats until C is empty.

Max-min tries to perform tasks with longer execution times first, which usually leads to a better balanced allocation of tasks, and prevents that some processors stay idle for a long time, while others are overloaded.

Duplex heuristic is a combination of the Min-min and Max-min heuristics. The Duplex heuristic performs both of the Min-min and Max-min heuristics and then uses the better solution. Duplex exploits the conditions in which either Min-min or Max-min performs better.

Genetic Algorithms (GA) is technique used for searching large solution spaces. Multiple possible mappings of the meta-task are computed, which are considered chromosomes in the population. Each chromosome has a fitness value, which is the result of an objective function designed in accordance with the performance criteria of the problem (for example makespan). At each iteration, all of the chromosomes in the population are evaluated based on their fitness value, and only the best of them survive in the next population, where new allocations are generated based on crossover and mutation operators. The algorithm usually stops when a predefined number of steps is performed or all chromosomes converge to the same mapping (Figure 10).

Simulated Annealing (SA) is an iterative technique that considers only one possible solution (mapping) for each meta-task at a time. This solution uses the same representation as the chromosome for the GA. SA uses a procedure that probabilistically allows poorer solutions to be accepted to attempt to obtain a better search of the solution space. This probability is based on a system temperature that decreases for each iteration. As the system temperature decreases, poorer solutions are less likely to be accepted. The initial temperature of the system is the maxspan of the initial mapping, which is randomly determined. At each iteration, the mapping is transformed in the same manner as the GA, and the new maxspan is evaluated. If the new maxspan is better (lower), the new mapping replaces the old one (Figure 11).

A* heuristic is a search technique based on a tree, which has been applied in various task allocation problems. The *A** heuristic begins at a root node that is a null solution. As the tree grows, nodes represent partial mappings (a subset of tasks is assigned to machines). With each child added, a new task *T* is mapped. This process continues until a complete mapping is reached.

The scheduling problem in distributed systems considers a set of *n* tasks, $T=\{T_1, T_2, ... T_n\}$, for some finite natural *n*, on a multiple processor system (e.g. grid system) in which each task can be characterized by multiple parameters. For example, $T_i=\{a_i, \tau_i, r_{i...}\}$ where:

a_i is arrival time (the time when the task first becomes runnable),

τ_i is execution time (it can be estimated),

r_i is a rate $0<r_i<1$ (can be a normalized priority), and we can have some other parameters.

As we presented in DAG Scheduling section, the general target architectural/application framework is represented by a graph $G = (V, E, \tau, c)$. The Critical Path (CP) of a set of tasks (graph) is the longest path in that graph, i.e. the path whose length is the maximum. There can be more than one CP. The t-level and the b-level are bounded from above by the length of the critical path. The Dominant Sequence (DS) is the critical path of the scheduled DAG and its weight is called the parallel time. The following formula can be used to determine the parallel time of a scheduled DAG:

$$PT = \max_{n_i \in V} \left\{ t - level(n_i) + b - level(n_i) \right\}$$

(1)

The schedule length (or makespan, or maxspan) can be defined as $\max_i \left\{ C_i \right\}$. The NP-Completeness for scheduling problem is demonstrated in (Sinnen, 2007). One of the objectives of scheduling is to minimize the makespan. For DAG scheduling, the optimization must be done without violating precedence constraints.

If the communication between tasks is considered, there are three models of communication delay:

1. **Intra-task-communication:** communication delays are implicitly hidden in the topology of the multiprocessor tasks,

Figure 10. Genetic algorithms: Functional block diagram

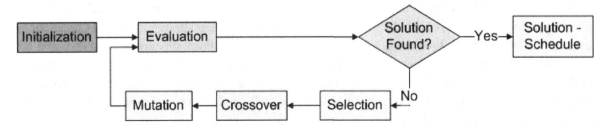

Figure 11. Simulated Annealing

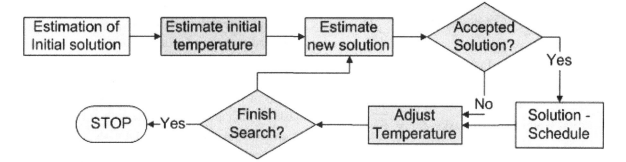

2. **Inter-task-communication:** communication delays occur if depended uni-processor tasks are not processed by the same processor of machine,

3. **Combination of both:** in the case of divisible task scheduling a multiprocessor task can be partitioned into smaller tasks, one partial task is processed by the current processor and the other parts are distributed among the grid processors, phases of inter-task-communication and computation (with intra-task-communication) alternate with each other.

The work done in order to process a task is defined as its running time multiplied by the number of processors assigned to it. Similarly, the work of set of tasks and the work of a schedule are defined. Usually it is assumed that in the case of malleable tasks the work of a task cannot be decreased by spending more processors on it (preservation of work). Similarly the work of a task cannot be decreased by using virtualization.

Efficiency at time t ($Ef(t)$) is the number of active (busy) processors divided by the total number of processors (active + idle).

$$Ef(t) = \frac{\Pr ocBussy(t)}{\Pr ocActive(t) + \Pr ocIdle(t)} \quad (2)$$

Just as qualitative definition, a schedule is considered efficient if the scheduled length is short and the number of processors used is reasonable.

In general we are looking for a feasible solution to scheduling problem. This is a schedule which meets all the requirements and constrains posed by the problem definition. In addition we may define an objective function that has to be optimized.

There are bottleneck objectives (for instance the makespan and the maximum lateness) and sum objectives (the sum of completion times or the number of tardy tasks). The letter ones may also appear in:

Maximum Completion Time (makespan):
$$makespan = C_{max} = \max_i \{C_i\}$$

Mean/Sum of Completion Time: $\bar{C} = \frac{1}{n}\sum_{i=1}^{n} C_i$

Mean / Sum of Weighted Completion Time:

$$\bar{C}_w = \frac{\sum_{i=1}^{n} w_i C_i}{\sum_{i=1}^{n} w_i}$$

Mean / Sum of Flow Time: $\bar{F} = \frac{1}{n}\sum_{i=1}^{n} F_i$

Mean / Sum of Weighted Flow Time:

$$\bar{F}_w = \frac{\sum_{i=1}^{n} w_i F_i}{\sum_{i=1}^{n} w_i}$$

Maximum Lateness: $L_{\max} = \max_i \{L_i\}$

Mean / Sum of Tardiness: $\bar{D} = \dfrac{1}{n}\sum_{i=1}^{n} D_i$

Number of Late Tasks: $\bar{U} = \sum_{i=1}^{n} U_i$

Total Weight of Late Tasks: $\bar{U}_w = \dfrac{\sum_{i=1}^{n} w_i U_i}{\sum_{i=1}^{n} w_i}$

Optimizing a certain sum objective is equivalent to solving the corresponding mean (average) objective since they differ only in a constant factor of n or $\sum_{i=1}^{n} w_i$.

Another important aspect of scheduling optimization considers real-time systems. This type of systems is defined as those systems in which the correctness of the system depends not only on the logical result of computation, but also on the time at which the results are produced. If the timing constraints of the system are not met, system failure is said to have occurred. Hence, it is essential that the timing constraints of the system are guaranteed to be met.

Guaranteeing timing behavior requires that the system be predictable. Predictability means that when a task is activated it should be possible to determine its completion time with certainty. It is also desirable that the system attain a high degree of utilization while satisfying the timing constraints of the system.

It is imperative that the state of the environment, as received by the controlling system, be consistent with the actual state of the environment. Otherwise, the effects of the controlling systems' activities may be disastrous. Therefore, periodic monitoring of the environment as well as timely processing of the sensed information is necessary.

A real-time application is normally composed of multiple tasks with different levels of criticality. Although missing deadlines is not desirable in a real-time system, soft real-time tasks could miss some deadlines and the system could still work correctly. However, missing some deadlines for soft real-time tasks will lead to paying penalties.

Hard real-time tasks cannot miss any deadline; otherwise, undesirable or fatal results will be produced in the system. There exists another group of real-time tasks, namely firm real-time tasks, which are such that the sooner they finish their computations before their deadlines, the more rewards they gain.

For a given set of tasks, the general scheduling problem in real-time systems asks for an order according to which the tasks are to be executed such that various constraints are satisfied. Typically, a task is characterized by its execution time, ready time, deadline, and resource requirements. The execution of a task may or may not be interrupted (preemptive or non-preemptive scheduling). Over the set of tasks, there is a precedence relation which constrains the order of execution. Specially, the execution of a task cannot begin until the execution of all its predecessors (according to the precedence relation) is completed. The system on which the tasks are to be executed is characterized by the amounts of resources available. The following goals should be considered in scheduling a real-time system:

- Meeting the timing constraints of the system
- Preventing simultaneous access to shared resources and devices
- Attaining a high degree of utilization while satisfying the timing constraints of the system; however this is not a primary driver.
- Reducing the cost of context switches caused by preemption
- Reducing the communication cost in real-time distributed systems; we should find the optimal way to decompose the real-time application into smaller portions in order to have the minimum communication cost between mutual portions (each portion is assigned to a computer).

In addition, the following items are desired in advanced real-time systems:

- Considering a combination of hard, firm, and soft real-time activities, which implies the possibility of applying dynamic scheduling policies that respect the optimality criteria.
- Task scheduling for a real-time system whose behavior is dynamically adaptive, reconfigurable, reflexive and intelligent.
- Covering reliability, security, and safety.

Basically, the scheduling problem is to determine a schedule for the execution of the tasks so that they are all completed before the overall deadline.

FUTURE RESEARCH DIRECTIONS

Many models and algorithms for grid scheduling are developed using classic algorithms for traditional systems. Three heuristics are used for scheduling of tasks with precedence orders in heterogeneous parallel and distributed systems: list heuristics, duplicated heuristics and clustering heuristics. Almost all algorithms in the current literature refer to list algorithms. The ideas behind the latter two categories have many advantages in the grid scenario. Since all of these heuristics consider complex application models, where tasks can be fine granular and with data and control dependency, there is great potential for using these heuristics in grid computing.

The dynamism in the grid requires the assumptions approximation algorithms optimizing. To deal with performance variation, resource information and prediction are recently used. As the techniques in this field develop, better performance knowledge prior to the task scheduling stage can be expected. Current scheduling algorithms consider a snapshot value of the prediction when they make the estimate, and assume that value is static during the task execution period. This might be a waste of the prediction efforts which can actually provide continuous variation information about the system. So, heuristics that can exploit multiple stage prediction information should be designed.

Another issue is to reestablish approximating for make-span optimization based on performance predictions. For example, if we know the range of performance fluctuation is bounded, we can find a bound for the ratio of real make-span to optimal finish time accordingly.

The problem with current rescheduling algorithms is high cost and lack of consideration of dependent tasks. For tasks whose make-spans are large, rescheduling for the original static decisions can improve the performance dramatically. However, rescheduling is usually costly, especially in DAGs where there are extra data dependencies among tasks compared to independent applications.

In addition, many other problems also exist, for example when the rescheduling mechanisms should be invoked, what measurable parameters should decide whether a rescheduling is profitable, and where tasks should be migrated. Current research on DAG rescheduling leaves a wide open field for future work.

QoS is the concern of many grid applications. Most current research concentrates on how to guarantee the QoS requirements of the applications like (Vázquez-Poletti, 2007), but few of them study how the QoS requirements affect the resources assignment and then the performance of the other parts of the applications.

Scheduling algorithms in traditional computing paradigms barely consider the data transfer problem during mapping computational tasks, and this neglect will be costly in the grid scenario. Only a handful of current research efforts consider the simultaneous optimization of computation and data transfer scheduling, which brings opportunities for future studies.

Although the grid have the characteristics of heterogeneity and dynamics, these features are not flatly distributed in resources, but are rather distributed hierarchically and locally in many cases, due to the composition of the resources. Current resources are usually distributed in a clustered fashion. Resources in the same cluster usually belong to the same organization and are relatively more homogeneous and less dynamic in a given period.

Inside a cluster, communication cost is usually low and the number of applications running at the same time is usually small. These distribution properties might bring another possibility for new algorithms to deal with the challenges. For example, by taking multiphase or multilevel strategies, a scheduler can first find a coarse scheduling in the global and then a fine schedule in a local cluster.

This type of strategy has the following advantages: At the higher level, where fine resource information is harder to obtain, the global scheduling can use coarse information (such as load balancing, communication delay of WAN links) to provide decentralized load balancing mechanisms. At the lower level, it is easy for local scheduling to utilize more specific information (such as information from a local forecaster) to make adaptive decisions.

In Distributed Systems, various applications, most of them being real-time applications, require dynamic scheduling for optimized assignment of consisting tasks. A number of different scheduling model and algorithms was presented here. The performance metrics can be taken into account in order to design a feasible scheduling algorithm. Those performance metrics can also represent optimization criteria and are based on various constraints such as deadline restrictions, guaranteed completion time, average service time, start and end time, etc. Some of the metrics that can be used to measure the performances of a grid scheduling algorithm are: the global task success rate (percentage of co-allocated tasks that were started successfully before their deadline), the local task kill rate (the percentage of local tasks that have been killed), the total load (the average percentage of busy processors over the entire system), the global load (the percentage of the total computing power that is used for computing the global tasks), the processor wasted time (the percentage of the total computing power that is wasted because of claiming processors before the actual deadlines of tasks), max-span (the total execution time of tasks in the system, and is practically equal to the largest processing time over all processors), average processor utilization (a measure of the average times of utilization of processors, relative to the maximum execution time) and load-balancing (measure of the uniformity of the tasks disposal on the processors, with the purpose to obtain similar execution times on processors, and reduce idle times and overloading).

All this criteria and metrics represent the measure effective computing power that the scheduler has been able to get from the distributed system and managed for tasks execution.

In distributed system middleware a large number of tools is available for scheduling. For cluster scheduling we have PBS, Condor, Sun Grid Engine, and LSF. These tools are included in the centralized scheduling class. Inter-cluster scheduling, known as meta-scheduling are studied, so a number of meta-scheduling research projects are under development, like GridWay (that is an incubator project in Globus), Globus CSF. Still there is no meta-scheduler used on a large scale. A problem that must to be solved for this type of scheduling is scalability. It is an aspect more important in the context of heterogeneous systems and middleware tools.

CONCLUSION

The evolution of distributed systems and specific technologies imposes new scheduling methods, adapted to the user requirements and resource constraints. The optimization of decentralized scheduling in grid environments considers multi-criteria constraints for objective function in scheduling algorithm. The decentralized strategies place the scheduling component on the top of grid architecture in the global grid.

The analysis of algorithms for independent and dependent task scheduling offers a selection base of the best algorithm. A comparative evaluation was performed for different scheduling strategies, using a series of performance metrics and a simulation tool. The grid scheduling algorithms are difficult to implement because the resources are owned by different organizations that have their own policies and charging mechanisms. The complexity of the grid applications increases when the users specify constraints like deadlines and time limitations. The decentralized scheduler adapts to the changes in the system, such as load and resource availability changes, using monitoring information. Also, it ensures the quality of offered services. The communication model based on negotiation offers the possibility to minimize the costs associated to task execution and maximize the provider profits. A genetic scheduling approach, which features a decentralized strategy for the problem of resource allocation, is a key to the optimization of scheduling problem. The comparison of the performance of the decentralized cooperative genetic algorithm was made with three other strategies: opportunistic load balancing, centralized genetic algorithm and decentralized non-cooperative genetic algorithm. It is shown that the algorithm clearly outperforms these methods. Decentralization and cooperation provide significantly better results of load-balancing and average resources utilization increase, as well as of total execution time minimization.

REFERENCES

Afrash, E., & Rahmani, A. M. (2008). A new architecture for better resource management in grid systems. In *Proceedings of the 2008 3rd International Conference on Convergence and Hybrid information Technology, ICCIT* (vol. 2, pp. 194-198). Washington, DC: IEEE Computer Society.

Allcock, W., Bresnahan, J., Kettimuthu, R., Link, M., Dumitrescu, C., Raicu, I., & Foster, I. (2005). The globus striped GridFTP framework and server. In *Proceedings of the 2005 ACM/IEEE Conference on Supercomputing.* Conference on High Performance Networking and Computing. Washington, DC, USA: IEEE Computer Society.

Avizienis, A. (1984). Design diversity: An approach to fault tolerance of design faults. In *Proceedings of the National Computer Conference and Exposition (AFIPS '84)* (pp. 163-171). New York, NY, USA: ACM.

Aziz, A., & El-Rewini, H. (2008). On the use of meta-heuristics to increase the efficiency of online grid workflow scheduling algorithms. *Cluster Computing, 11*(4), 373–390. doi:10.1007/s10586-008-0062-y

Baker, M., Buyya, R., & Laforenza, D. (2002). Grids and grid technologies for wide-area distributed computing. *Software, Practice & Experience, 32*(15), 1437–1466. doi:10.1002/spe.488

Braun, T. D., Siegel, H. J., Beck, N., Bölöni, L. L., Maheswaran, M., Reuther, A. I., & Freund, R. F. (2001). A comparison of 11 static heuristics for mapping a class of independent tasks onto heterogeneous distributed computing systems. *Journal of Parallel and Distributed Computing, 61*(6), 810–837. doi:10.1006/jpdc.2000.1714

Buyya, R., & Vazhkudai, S. (2001). Compute power market: Towards a market-oriented grid. In *Proceedings of the 1st International Symposium on Cluster Computing and the Grid (CCGRID).* Washington, DC, USA: IEEE Computer Society.

Caramia, M., & Giordani, S. (2008). Resource allocation in grid computing: An economic model. *WSEAS Trans. Comp. Res.*, *3*(1), 9–27.

Casavant, T. L., & Kuhl, J. G. (1988). A taxonomy of scheduling in general-purpose distributed computing systems. *IEEE Transactions on Software Engineering*, *14*(2), 141–154. doi:10.1109/32.4634

De Rose, C. A., Ferreto, T., Calheiros, R. N., Cirne, W., Costa, L. B., & Fireman, D. (2008). Allocation strategies for utilization of space-shared resources in bag-of-tasks grids. *Future Generation Computer Systems*, *24*(5), 331–341. doi:10.1016/j.future.2007.05.005

Deelman, E., Singh, G., Su, M., Blythe, J., Gil, Y., & Kesselman, C. (2005). Pegasus: A framework for mapping complex scientific workflows onto distributed systems. *Science Progress*, *13*(3), 219–237.

El-Rewini, H., & Lewis, T. G. (1990). Scheduling parallel program tasks onto arbitrary target machines. *Journal of Parallel and Distributed Computing*, *9*(2), 138–153. doi:10.1016/0743-7315(90)90042-N

Gao, Y., Rong, H., & Huang, J. Z. (2005). Adaptive grid job scheduling with genetic algorithms. *Future Generation Computer Systems*, *21*(1), 151–161. doi:10.1016/j.future.2004.09.033

Hu, M., Guo, W., & Hu, W. (2009). Dynamic scheduling algorithms for large file transfer on multi-user optical grid network based on efficiency and fairness. In *Proceedings of the 2009 5th International Conference on Networking and Services* (pp. 493-498). ICNS. Washington, DC, USA: IEEE Computer Society.

Kurowski, K., Nabrzyski, J., Oleksiak, A., & Węglarz, J. (2008). A multicriteria approach to two-level hierarchy scheduling in grids. *Journal of Scheduling*, *11*(5), 371–379. doi:10.1007/s10951-008-0058-8

Lu, K., Subrata, R., & Zomaya, A. Y. (2007). On the performance-driven load distribution for heterogeneous computational grids. *Journal of Computer and System Sciences*, *73*(8), 1191–1206. doi:10.1016/j.jcss.2007.02.007

Muthuvelu, N., Liu, J., Soe, N. L., Venugopal, S., Sulistio, A., & Buyya, R. (2005). A dynamic job grouping-based scheduling for deploying applications with fine-grained tasks on global grids. In R. Buyya, P. Coddington, P. Montague, R. Safavi-Naini, N. Sheppard, & A. Wendelborn (Eds), *Proceedings of the 2005 Australasian Workshop on Grid Computing and E-Research* (vol. 44). Conferences in Research and Practice in Information Technology Series (vol. 108). Australian Computer Society, Darlinghurst, Australia.

Pop, F., & Cristea, V. (2009). Decentralised meta-scheduling strategy in grid environments. *Int. J. Grid Util. Comput.*, *1*(3), 185–193. doi:10.1504/IJGUC.2009.027646

Pop, F., Dobre, C., & Cristea, V. (2008). Performance analysis of grid DAG scheduling algorithms using MONARC simulation tool. In *Proceedings of the 2008 International Symposium on Parallel and Distributed Computing* (*ISPDC*) (pp. 131-138). Washington, DC, USA: IEEE Computer Society.

Prodan, R., & Fahringer, T. (2005). Dynamic scheduling of scientific workflow applications on the grid: A case study. In L. M. Liebrock (Ed.), *Proceedings of the 2005 ACM Symposium on Applied Computing* (*SAC '05*) (pp. 687-694). New York, NY: ACM.

Ranganathan, K., & Foster, I. (2002). Decoupling computation and data scheduling in distributed data-intensive applications. In *Proceedings of the 11th IEEE international Symposium on High Performance Distributed Computing*. High performance distributed computing. Washington, DC, USA: IEEE Computer Society.

Rodero, I., Guim, F., & Corbalan, J. (2009). Evaluation of coordinated grid scheduling strategies. In *Proceedings of the 11th IEEE international Conference on High Performance Computing and Communications (HPCC)* (pp. 1-10). Washington, DC, USA: IEEE Computer Society.

Roehrig, M. & Ziegler W. (2002). *Grid scheduling dictionary of terms and keywords*. Open Grid forum document, Grid scheduling dictionary working group.

Sabin, G., Kettimuthu, R., Rajan, A., & Sadayappan, P. (2003). Scheduling of parallel jobs in a heterogeneous multi-site environment. []. Berlin-Heidelberg, Germany: Springer.]. *Lecture Notes in Computer Science, 2862*, 87–104. doi:10.1007/10968987_5

Schopf, J. M. (2004). 10 actions when grid scheduling: The user as a grid scheduler . In Nabrzyski, J., Schopf, J. M., & Weglarz, J. (Eds.), *Grid Resource Management: State of the Art and Future Trends* (pp. 15–23). Norwell, MA, USA: Kluwer Academic Publishers.

Shan, H., Oliker, L., Biswas, R., & Smith, W. (2004) Scheduling in heterogeneous grid environments: The effects of data migration. In *Proceedings of International Conference on Advanced Computing and Communication*. Ahmedabad Gujarat, India.

Sinnen, O. (2007). *Task scheduling for parallel systems (Wiley Series on Parallel and Distributed Computing)*. NJ, USA: Wiley-Interscience.

Streit, A. (2002). A self-tuning job scheduler family with dynamic policy switching. In D. G. Feitelson, L. Rudolph, & U. Schwiegelshohn (Eds.), *Revised Papers From the 8th International Workshop on Job Scheduling Strategies For Parallel Processing. Lecture Notes in Computer Science* (vol. 2537, pp. 1-23). Berlin-Heidelberg, Germany: Springer.

Takefusa, A., Matsuoka, S., Casanova, H., & Berman, F. (2001). A study of deadline scheduling for client-server systems on the computational grid. In *Proceedings of the 10th IEEE International Symposium on High Performance Distributed Computing*. High performance distributed computing. Washington, DC, USA: IEEE Computer Society.

Tudor, D., & Cretu, V. (2008). Experiences on grid shared data programming. In *Proceedings of the International Conference on Complex, Intelligent and Software Intensive Systems (CISIS)* (pp. 387-393). Washington, DC, USA: IEEE Computer Society.

Vázquez-Poletti, J. L., Huedo, E., Montero, R. S., & Llorente, I. M. (2007). A comparison between two grid scheduling philosophies: EGEE WMS and Grid Way. *Multiagent Grid Syst., 3*(4), 429–439.

Xhafa, F., & Abraham, A. (2010). Computational models and heuristic methods for grid scheduling problems. *Future Generation Computer Systems, 26*(4), 608–621. doi:10.1016/j.future.2009.11.005

Zhao, H., & Sakellariou, R. (2003). An experimental investigation into the rank function of the heterogeneous earliest finish time scheduling algorithm. In *Proceedings of 9th International Euro-Par Conference*, Klagenfurt, Austria (pp. 189-194). Berlin-Heidelberg, Germany: Springer-Verlag

Zhu, Y., Xiao, L., Xu, Z., & Ni, L. M. (2006). Incentive-based scheduling in grid computing: Research articles. *Concurr. Comput.: Pract. Exper., 14*(18), 1729–1746. doi:10.1002/cpe.1025

Chapter 5
Grid Data Handling

Alexandru Costan
University Politehnica of Bucharest, Romania

ABSTRACT

To accommodate the needs of large-scale distributed systems, scalable data storage and management strategies are required, allowing applications to efficiently cope with continuously growing, highly distributed data. This chapter addresses the key issues of data handling in grid environments focusing on storing, accessing, managing and processing data. We start by providing the background for the data storage issue in grid environments. We outline the main challenges addressed by distributed storage systems: high availability which translates into high resilience and consistency, corruption handling regarding arbitrary faults, fault tolerance, asynchrony, fairness, access control and transparency. The core part of the chapter presents how existing solutions cope with these high requirements. The most important research results are organized along several themes: grid data storage, distributed file systems, data transfer and retrieval and data management. Important characteristics such as performance, efficient use of resources, fault tolerance, security, and others are strongly determined by the adopted system architectures and the technologies behind them. For each topic, we shortly present previous work, describe the most recent achievements, highlight their advantages and limitations, and indicate future research trends in distributed data storage and management.

DOI: 10.4018/978-1-61350-113-9.ch005

INTRODUCTION

During the last years, mainly motivated by the need of applications in eScience where vast amounts of data are generated by specialized instruments and need to be collaboratively accessed, processed and analyzed by a large number of scientists around the world, grid computing has become increasingly popular. The grid embraced the goal of sharing potentially unlimited computing power over the Internet to solve complex problems in a distributed way. A first generation of grids, called computational grids, focused on CPU cycles as resources to be shared. Recent advances in grid computing aim at virtualizing different types of resources (data, instruments, computing nodes, tools) and making them transparently available.

Along with the computational grids, a second generation of grids, namely Data Grids (Chevernak et al. 2000), has emerged as a solution for distributed data storage and management in data-intensive applications. The size of data required by these applications may be up to petabytes. In many applications, Data Grids not only maintain raw data produced by instruments, but need to take into account also aggregations and derivations of these huge size raw data that are periodically generated and potentially concurrently updated by scientists at several sites. Data intensive grids primarily deal with providing services and infrastructure for large scale distributed applications that need to access, transfer and modify massive datasets stored in distributed storage resources. High Energy Physics, governmental and commercial statistics, climate modeling, cosmology, genetics, bio-informatics, etc. are just a few examples of fields routinely generating huge amounts of data. It becomes crucial to efficiently manipulate these data, which must be shared at the global scale.

These data intensive grids combine high-end computing technologies with high-performance networking and wide-area storage management techniques. Many approaches to build highly available and incrementally extendable distributed data storage systems have been proposed. Solutions span from distributed storage repositories to massively parallel and high performance storage systems. A large majority of these aims at a virtualization of the data space allowing users to access data on multiple storage systems, eventually geographically dispersed. While these new technologies reveal huge opportunities for large-scale distributed data storage and management, they also raise important technical challenges, which need to be addressed. The ability to support persistent storage of data on behalf of users, the consistent distribution of up-to-date data, the reliable replication of fast changing datasets or the efficient management of large data transfers are just some of these new challenges.

The objective of this chapter is to give the reader an up-to-date overview of modern data storage and management solutions in grid environments. We discuss the main challenges, and present the most recent research approaches and results adopted in large scale distributed systems, with emphasis on incorporating efficient techniques that increase the reliability and support higher efficiency of the applications running on top of distributed platforms. Future research directions in the area of data storage and processing are highlighted as well.

BACKGROUND

Data intensive environments often deal with applications that produce, store and process data in the range of hundreds of megabytes to petabytes and beyond. The data may be structured or unstructured and organized as collections or datasets that are typically stored on mass storage systems (also called repositories) such as tape libraries or disk arrays. These storage resources are geographically dispersed and usually span over different administrative domains. The data sets are maintained independent of the underlying storage systems and are able to include new sites without major effort. The data collections are further accessed by users from different locations. They may create local copies or replicas of the datasets to reduce latencies involved in wide-area data transfers in order to improve application performance and support eventual failures.

Replica management systems and data replication mechanisms allow users to create, register and manage replicas and enforce consistency. The system may also create replicas on its own using some replication strategies that take into account current and future demand for the datasets, locality of requests, storage capacity of the repositories, scheduling policies and real time monitoring information. A replica catalog contains information about locations of datasets and associated replicas and the additional information associated with these datasets. Users query the catalog using some attributes to conduct operations such as locating the nearest replica of a particular dataset.

In order to enhance the replica retrieval and the consequent processing or to optimize the scheduling decisions and the resource management, data is often annotated with "data about data", namely metadata. That is information describing the datasets and may consist of attributes such as name, time of creation, size on disk and time of last modification. Metadata may also contain specific information relevant to the application context, such as details of the process that produced the data, retrieval time, input and output locations. (Chervenak et al., 2001) makes an important distinction between storage and metadata. While in some cases (i.e. the storage into databases) the combination of metadata and storage into the same abstraction has some advantages, separation of these concepts at the architectural level is however better suited in distributed environments. The authors highlight that this clear separation increases flexibility of the system's implementation while alleviating the impact on others implementations that combine metadata access with storage access.

In the Data Grid context these services are exposed and help users discover, transfer and manipulate large datasets stored in distributed repositories and also, create and manage copies of these datasets. However, a Data Grid may not implement all the previous functionalities. As (Chervenak et al., 2000) observed, at the minimum, a data grid provides two basic functionalities: a high-performance, reliable data transfer mechanism, and a scalable replica discovery and management mechanism. Depending on application requirements, several other services need to be provided. Examples of such services include consistency management for replicas, metadata management, data filtering or aggregation mechanisms. An additional security layer is needed to mediate all operations by handling authentication schemes and enforcing the execution of authorized operations only. In the context of long living experiments with long data life cycles, an important concern is the persistency of the storage process. Data and information associated with data such as metadata, access controls and version changes should be preserved even in the face of platform changes. These requirements lead to the establishment of persistent archival storage (Moore et al., 2005).

Known examples of data grids are the ones built for the LHC (Large Hadron Collider) experiments at CERN, harnessing the processing and the storage power of thousands of resources distributed all over the world in order to cope with the huge data requirements. Custom infrastructures were set up for each experiment: CMS (Compact Muon Solenoid), ATLAS (A Toroidal LHC AppratuS), ALICE (A Large Ion Collider Experiment) and LHCb (LHCbeauty). The ALICE experiment, dedicated to the heavy particles investigation, relies on a complex data infrastructure in order to achieve its physics goals. The ALICE collaboration, consisting of more than 1,000 members from 29 countries and 86 institutes, is strongly dependent on the distributed data and computing environment. The ALICE experiment started running last year and will collect data at a rate of up to four petabytes per year. During its design lifetime of 20 years, ALICE will produce more than 10^9 data files per year, and require tens of thousands of CPUs to process and analyze them. The storage capacities are distributed over more than 80 computing centers worldwide. These resources are heterogeneous in all aspects, from CPU model or storage backend and count to operating system and batch queuing software. The allocated resources should increase over time to match the increase in the data-acquisition rate resulting from changes in experiment parameters, so that a doubling is foreseen in two years, and so on.

Computational and data grids share the general issues and approaches: for instance, the concept of Virtual Organization (VO) grouping the resources and users within a common experiment. In both contexts, the common goal is to make the computing or the storage resources of a Virtual Organization visible and usable as a single entity – any available node can execute jobs and access distributed datasets transparently and independently of the node's location. However, data grids have their distinctive characteristics, which we discuss in the following. Data intensive applications handle *huge datasets* of peta scale, as seen in the previous ALICE experiment example. Therefore an important role is played by the *resource management,* which in the data grids derives into several declinations like minimizing latencies of data transfers, replica management and storage resources administration. The distributed data collections are *shared* within the participants. The concept of data sharing which is the building block of a data grid requires a *unified namespace* in which every data element has a unique logical filename. The logical filename is mapped to one or more physical filenames on various storage resources across the distributed infrastructure. Users might wish to ensure confidentiality of their data or restrict distribution to close collaborators, hence the need for *access control*. Authentication and authorization in data grids involve support for both coarse and fine-grained access restrictions over the shared data collections.

As the usage of the Grid and Cloud approaches extends to more and more application classes, the storage requirements for such large scale systems are becoming increasingly complex due to the rate, scale and variety of data. In this context, storing, accessing and processing very large, structured and unstructured data is of utmost importance. (Venugopal et al. 2000) identified several requirements expected from the infrastructures on which distributed data storage and management systems rely. One important demand is the ability to search the available datasets for the required data and to discover suitable data resources for accessing the data. Usually large-sized datasets need to be transferred between resources, hence another requirement stresses the efficient, fast and reliable movement of data. In a fault tolerant context, data resources need to expose replication capabilities and allow users to manage multiple copies of their data. The systems should further allow the selection of suitable computational resources for processing data on them and manage access permissions for the data. We refine these requirements in the following sections with respect to the particular issues of each topic.

DATA STORAGE

Modern storage facilities are architected to address scientific communities' rapidly advancing needs, while taking advantage of the equally rapid evolution of network technologies in order to provide the most effective solutions with adequate up-to-date performance. As these systems are designed and operated to guarantee full performance to support both large-scale data management and real-time traffic, one of the main concerns are the high demanding requirements expected to be dealt with. We outline in the following the main specific challenges addressed by distributed storage systems.

The *high availability* proves to be the main issue in such environments: the storage should remain available, in a transparent fashion to the users, whenever any single or multiple storage units (disks, servers, tapes, etc.) fail. This translates into *high resilience* levels expected from the storage infrastructure, i.e. the fail of a large number of storage units is tolerated without affecting the overall system's availability and *consistency*. The resilience level is closely coupled to the manner in which the distributed storage system handles corruption of the storage units or even users: this can take various forms ranging from hardware faults, software bugs to malicious intrusions or behavior. The term used in literature for these issues is *arbitrary (or byzantine) faults* and if not treated accordingly, affected systems can deviate from their implemented behavior. Approaches include the use of fault thresholds for long-term storage with service splitting (Chun et al., 2006) and also algorithms that combine strong consistency and liveness guarantees with space-efficiency (Dobre et al., 2008).

However, unless we are dealing with an ideal model, faults cannot be ignored so a reliable system should implement support for *fault tolerance*. To deal with these problems, data should be stored using some redundant techniques, so that any information from a faulty element can be recovered. Fault tolerance is generally addressed in I/O systems using replication, as discussed in the previous section, or RAID (Redundant Array of Inexpensive Disks) based approaches. The latter ones are suitable for storage systems based on commodity disks with higher capacity but lower reliability, leading to more frequent rebuilds and to a higher risk of unrecoverable media errors. RAID systems are generally used for their increased performance due to striping and for the redundancy achieved through mirroring or erasure codes. Still, residing at a single physical location makes them vulnerable in the presence of single points of failures: the disk controller, the network interface, etc. In contrast, high performance storage systems use replication as a reliable fault tolerance technique, distributing

data at several nodes, which can be discovered through the replica catalogs.

Another issue which needs to be addressed by a reliable distributed storage system is *asynchrony*. As users interface with the storage through heterogeneous networks, access delays are likely to incur and difficult to predict. These delays are further increased by storage latency. One approach is to access data in the file system cache or high-speed storage first, and consequently the total I/O workloads can be reduced and performance improved. To achieve these, one needs latency data estimations, which allow users and applications to make better data access decisions based on those retrieval time estimates. Such approaches doubled by efficient concurrency control (Ermolinksiy et al., 2009) improve the overall application performance with more predictable behavior in the presence of asynchrony and even failures.

Fairness is also desirable in such environments, allowing many users to access a storage system in a distributed fashion while conserving efficiency. Solutions make use of local latency estimates at hosts to detect overload or try to limit the host issue queue lengths to provide fairness across hosts (Gulati et al., 2008). Moreover, the system has to take into account the inherent intermittence of the communication and the transient nature of the clients. Access should be allowed in a *transparent* fashion, with the users not being aware of the different locations or the specific devices used to store data and should. They should rather be presented a *uniform view* of data, complemented with *uniform mechanisms* for retrieval. This translates into *neutrality* requirements imposed on mechanisms and policies: it enables their implementation through interfaces that capture and hide the specificities of low-level components and also via high-level procedures. Hence, application specific behaviors are only supported of the higher architectural levels. Such approaches stimulate a wide adoption with the reuse of low-level components, without compromising from the range size of supported applications.

Clearly, compliance with all the above requirements is hard to achieve. There are many tradeoffs: for instance, providing stronger consistency or additional resilience impacts complexity. However, these principles should drive the design of any reliable storage system in order to meet the complex and stringent performance demands of now-days applications.

Storage Systems

Storage systems are responsible with accessing for read/write purposes, creating, deleting, initiating third-party transfers and handling data, which can reside in conventional or high performance parallel file systems, distributed databases or other storage systems. In fact, this approach allows us to broader the common definition of the storage systems, and to further consider the systems implemented by any storage technology, which support the functionalities previously mentioned. Therefore, we are not aiming at direct mapping between storage systems and some low-level storage devices, but rather consider all the technologies able to meet the performance requirements. We detail in the following some of the most important solutions available for large scale distributed environments.

The High Performance Storage System (HPSS 7.1, 2009) is a hierarchical storage system, which manages data over its life cycle; it basically aggregates the capacity and performance of various storage devices into a single virtual file system. The used model keeps active data on highest performing media and inactive data on less effective devices such as tape or low cost, high capacity disks. This model translates into a layered architecture with the local files system on top of the hierarchy, the high speed shared disks and the high capacity shared disks on the intermediate layers and the primary and remote tape libraries on the bottom layer. Transport of data through these layers is automatic and transparent to the client, in such way that the asynchronous migrate and purge allows lower levels to be used as backup

for the higher levels. This hierarchical storage model trades low latencies over high capacities as it puts on top levels the high speed medias. Such systems are then well suited and widely adopted in high performance computing environments and are relatively uncommon in business application where simpler backup and restore strategies are sufficient. HPSS provides long term retention and rapid staging in conjunction with a metadata architecture suitable for medium and coarse-grain file access.

The HPSS components (HPSS Core Server, Metadata DB2 server, HPSS Mover Cluster, Data Disks and Tapes) are connected over a Storage Area Network (Oguchi, 2009). A typical HPSS working scenario involves the following steps: a client issues an access request (read/write) to the Core Server; the Core Server then accesses the metadata information on disk to find location information about the required data and consequently commands Mover to stage file from tape to disk; the Mover stages the file, next the Core Server sends back to the client the lock and the ticket. Now either the client accesses the data directly from the shared disk over the Storage Area Network, or the Mover accesses instead and send the information to the client over his Local Area Network. The storage system is further enhanced with a large set of user and file system interfaces ranging from simple ftp, samba or nfs to higher performance Grid FTP, parallel ftp, client API, local file movers and third party SAN.

HPSS addresses the high availability requirements providing hardware redundancy for the core servers and investing the data movers with the ability to configure redundancy mechanisms. Arguably, the authors consider HPSS as the most scalable disk-and-tape system anywhere. Indeed, its cluster and metadata architecture support horizontal scaling to tens of petabytes and hundreds of millions of files benefiting from gigabytes per second data rates. Extension is achieved easily by adding new heterogeneous components. HPSS is now deployed on several large sites: 3.9 PB of data stored in over 66 million files at National Energy Research Scientific Computing Center (as of January 2009), 11+ PB of data stored at Los Alamos National Laboratory (LANL), 7+ PB of data at Lawrence Livermore National Lab (LNL), 3.6 PB at Stanford Linear Accelerator Center (SLAC), 3 PB at CEA Computer Center in France, etc. (all as of 2007).

Castor CERN Advanced STORage manager (Ponce et al., 2009) is another hierarchical storage management system developed at CERN to address the increased needs of High Energy Physics community for resources able to deal with the data intensive experiments. The system provides a managed storage service for all physics data at CERN, using transparent tape media management, automated disk cache management and a unique global namespace. The goal is to fulfill the Tier-0 and Tier-1 storage requirements for LHC experiments at CERN: this involves support for a Central Data Recording (CDR), data reconstruction and data export to Tier-1 centers.

The Castor architecture (now at version 2) is based on 5 components disposed on three layers: on top of the hierarchy is the Client API, the interface of the storage systems with the users; the intermediate layer consists of the Stager logic and the Central services (e.g. NameServer); the base layer holds the Tape archive subsystem and the Disk cache subsystem. State and handling information are stored in a Relational Database Management System, namely status information about running processes that have stateless components. The Client allows basic interaction with the server in order to get the system's functionalities. To this end, one can either use the command line interfaces for users (supporting stager and RFIO commands) or the Client API written in C to communicate with other third-party applications. The Client interface handles status checks, updates and file retrieval from the tape or disk servers using Rfio, Root, Xrootd and GridFTP.

The Central Services include the DriveQueue-Manager, a daemon for tape queue management,

the VolumeManager, an archive of all tapes available in the libraries, the Castor User Privileges, an authorization daemon providing rights to users and administrators for tape related operations, and the NameServer. The latter is a database implementing a hierarchical view of the name space. It further stores the file location on tertiary storage if the file has been migrated from the disk pool in order to make space for more current files. Files may be segmented or be made up of more than one contiguous chunk of tape media. This allows the use of the full capacity of tape volumes and permits file sizes to be bigger than the physical limit of a single tape volume. Additionally, it provides the ability to create directories and files, change ownership, and stores tape-related information as well.

The Stager acts as a disk pool (a collection of file systems) manager whose functions are to allocate space on disk, to store files, to maintain a catalogue of all the files in its disk pools and to clear out old or least recently used files in these pools when more free space is required. The decisions are taken at the database level (using stored procedures) or by external plugins (schedulers, expert systems); typical decisions include: preparation of migration or recall streams, weighting of file systems used for migration/recall and garbage collection decisions. All these actions are performed by dedicated stateless daemons. These stateless components ensure easy restart and parallelization in the absence of a single point of failure. Moreover, the Stager being split in many independent services makes it fully scalable and able to distinguish between queries, user requests and administrator requests – thus allowing transparent access control. Optimization is achieved by means of minimal footprint of inactive requests: these are not instantiated in terms of processes until they run, but are rather stored in the database and scheduled while waiting for resources.

Current Castor development (Duellmann, 2008) aims at enabling tape aggregation, redundancy and clustering based on name location. The authors also evaluate larger DataBase cluser per VOs and work on increased consistency using the DataBase constraints. The CASTOR storage system is now used by all LHC experiments at CERN and it currently stores more than 23 PB of data in 144 million files, as of March 2010 (CASTOR Website, 2010). However, compared to HPSS, the system offers fewer interfaces, as the CASTOR name space can be viewed and manipulated only through CASTOR client commands and library calls. This approach prevented a wider adoption from the scientific communities.

Enstore (Bakken et al., 2008) is the Fermilab Mass Storage System providing distributed access and management of data stored on tape. Also a hierarchical storage manager, the system supports random access of files, but also streaming, the sequential access of successive files on tape. Its main software components are the pnfs namespace – a virtual file system package maintaining file grouping and structure information via a set of tags, the encp – a program for copying files to and from media libraries, the servers (cofiguration, library managers, movers, logging, accounting, etc.) and the administrations tools. Pnfs provides a hierarchical namespace for Enstore users and also manages the file metadata while Encp is the system's user interface. Scalability and availability are achieved by spreading the server processes across multiple nodes. Access to Enstore is typically granted via dCache caching system using its supported protocols: kerberizedftp, dcap – a native dCache protocol, gridftp, weakftp, http etc. dCache stores users' files on RAID disks pending transfer to Enstore, while files already written to storage media that get downloaded to the dCache from Enstore are stored on ordinary disks. Hence, performance is improved for highly active files by avoiding the need of reading from tape every time a file is needed. The caching system easily scales as nodes are added.

The infrastructure composed by Enstore and dCache provides a data throughput sufficient for transferring data from experiments' data acquisition systems. The system is currently used for local HEP experiments (CDF, D0, minos, mini-boone) generating more than 1 PB data / year and 25 TB/ day peak transfers, also by remote HEP experiments: Tier 1 for CMS generating more than 3.5 PB / year (Oleynik, 2005). Fermilab mass storage system currently stores 10 PB of user data on tape, as of March 2010 (Enstore Website, 2010).

As a conclusion, we observe that there are various solutions to implement reliable distributed storage systems for high performance computing applications, ranging from high performance servers to commodity solutions harnessing available resources. The choice depends on the requirements and the environment of the targeted applications. Lightweight simple solutions often work the best, especially in the case of smaller of highly distributed sites. Wide Area Networks (WAN)-aware architectures should also be considered, as they are best suited for scaling to high performance computing data production requirements.

Storage Resource Management

As seen from the previous section, large data stores use heterogeneous main storage devices along with secondary and possibly tertiary media, as disk or tape systems. All these devices need to be managed and to efficiently interact with the other services (replica management, directory services, scheduling etc.). Hence the manifest need for resource management or brokering. Storage Resource Management (SRM) role is to provide a global view of the storage infrastructure, to monitor the status of all resources, to ensure availability, to implement some level of active management based on the collected information and to optimize the efficiency and speed with which the available storage space is utilized in a Storage Area Network (SAN). In SANs, storage is seen as a server independent logically managed component, rather than an individual entity attached to a server as in the traditional approach; hence, the management of distinct functionality services across IP networks is simplified. Functions of an SRM program include data storage, data collection, data backup, data recovery, SAN performance analysis, storage virtualization, storage provisioning, forecasting of future needs, maintenance of activity logs, user authentication, protection from unauthorized intrusions and management of network expansion.

In recent years, the SRM evolved from simple storage monitoring and reporting tools to advanced frameworks allowing management of the system, the fabric, the application and the storage devices, alerting, trend analysis, reports, backup and recovery of data and even event prediction. This constant evolution was recognized and supported by the Open Grid Forum through creation of a specific working group - the OGF Grid Storage Management Working Group (OGF SRM WG Website, 2010). A complete specification and implementation (Badino et al. 2008) was further developed for the DataGrid. The goal is to implement the required functionality and standardize the interface of SRMs as grid middleware components.

Observing that the concept of a storage resource is flexible, (Shoshani et al., 2002) identifies several types of SRM, according to their targeted media: SRM managing disk caches (referred to as Disk Resource Manager - DRM), SRM managing a tape archiving system (referred to as Tape Resource Manager - TRM) or a combination of both (referred to as a Hierarchical Resource Manager). Moreover, an SRM at a certain site should be able to manage multiple storage resources and handle access and replication across these several storage systems. SRMs should also provide a uniform interface that abstracts from current or future hardware configurations. It is worth mentioning that SRMs do not perform file transfers but rather invoke specific middleware components (such as GridFTP) to perform file transfers, and in general they interact with the mass storage system to perform file archiving and file staging. We detail in the following the main functionalities of the indicated SRM types:

DRM – manages dynamically a single shared disk cache, which can be a single disk, a collection of disks, or a RAID system. Its role is to manage the disk cache based on some client resource management policies set by administrators. It supports cache management policies to minimize repeated file transfers to the disk cache from remote grid sites; these policies are based either on history traces or anticipated requests.

TRM – acts as a middleware interface to systems that manage robotic tapes. Its role is to accept requests for file transfers from clients, queue such requests in case the Mass Storage System (MSS), as HPSS described in the previous sections, is busy or temporarily down, and apply a policy on the use of the MSS resources. As in the case of a DRM, the policy may restrict the number of simultaneous transfer requests by each client, or may give preferential access to clients based on their assigned priority.

HRM – is a TRM that has a staging disk cache for its use, therefore is often viewed as a combination of DRM and TRM. Its role is to use the disk cache for pre-staging files for clients and for sharing files between clients. This functionality proves rather useful taking into account that robotic tape systems are mechanical in nature and they have latency of mounting a tape and seeking the location of a file. Pre-staging masks this latency.

SRM interfaces were developed for all major storage systems (HPSS, CASTOR, Enstore, etc.). Moreover, proprietary SRM solutions exist as stand-alone products, or as part of an integrated program suite. Solutions (HP, 2008; IBM, 2009) vary in the offered components, but most provide a framework for automating the analysis of storage, access, capacity, utilization and availability statistics. Comparing the available SRMs implementations we observe how diverse storage systems can be integrated under uniform metadata and policy driven access mechanisms. Their main advantages include: the streaming model offered to clients - that is, their ability to provide a stream of files to client programs, rather than all the files at once; they also deal transparently with network and storage devices failures. However, best performance is achieved when SRMs are shared by communities of users that are likely to access the same files (as in HPC experiments).

Distributed File Systems

Distributed file systems support the sharing of information in the form of file instances, as basic data units, throughout distributed environments. In an ideal case, the file service would provide transparent access to files stored at remote servers with performance and reliability similar to files stored on local disk. As this is hard to achieve in the context of large scale distributed systems, we review some key requirements needed to be addressed by a well-designed file system able to deal with such challenges. (Coulouris et al., 2005) presented a first set of such requirements. However, these are quite general and usually available for any distributed service. In fact, many of the requirements and issues of the design of distributed services were first observed in the early development of distributed file systems.

Access transparency is a major challenge and clients should be unaware of the distribution of files; they should instead use a single set of operations for data access. Considering that the file service is usually one of the most heavily loaded service in the distributed environment, access should be complemented with *performance* and *scalability*: client programs should continue to perform at required parameters while the load on the service varies or the service is expanded by incremental growth. *Concurrency* control is another issue, not trivial to deal with, in a system which supports frequent concurrent file updates. *File replication* has several benefits: on one hand it enables multiple servers to share the load generated by clients accessing the same set of file, and on the other, it enhance the overall scalability and fault tolerance by allowing clients to use other

servers that hold copies of the targeted file when one has failed.

Recent design advances in distributed file systems considered these requirements and have exploited the increasing capacities of storage systems, higher bandwidth connectivity and new techniques of data organization on disks and tapes to achieve high performance, fault tolerance and scalability. We examine some of these current solutions, dividing them into two main classes: block-based and object-based file systems.

Block-Based File Systems

NFS v4.1 - The Network File System version 4.1 (Shepler et al., 2008) is considered one of the most important technological update and the first performance improvement to NFS in the last years. The IETF working group developing NFS had as goal to exploit the results emerged from file server design over the past decade, such as the use of callbacks and or lease to maintain consistency. The new NFS version keeps all the previous features: simplified error recovery, independence of transport protocols and operating systems for file access, clear design. Unlike earlier versions, however, it now supports recovery from server faults by allowing file systems to be moved to new servers transparently, integrates file locking, has stronger security, enhances scalability by using proxy servers and includes delegation capabilities to enhance client performance for data sharing applications on high-bandwidth networks. Moreover, NFS 4.1 is aware of distributed data using faster and optimized compound RPC calls, discovers the inactive clients through client to server pings, and enforces security with GSS authentication, built in mandatory security on file system level and support for ACLs, thus making it ideal for grid and highly distributed systems.

However, the key component of NFS 4.1 is parallel NFS – pNFS (Pariseau, 2008), which provides parallel I/O to file systems accessible over NFS. This approach, similar to RAID 0 dramatically increases performance by allowing multiple disk drives to serve up data in parallel. pNFS extends the solution to multiple storage devices connected to an NFS client over a network. Aggregation and location transparency are smoothly addressed: the unified namespace used by NFS 4.1 enables the aggregation of large numbers of heterogeneous NFS servers under a single namespace. While NFSv3 servers' access control was limited to groups and users, the newest version includes access control of individual files or applications; file and directory delegations allow greater number of NFS clients to access a single NFS share. As the protocol is able to handle large files and many concurrent users, concerns are raised on the connectivity side, namely if pNFS is can pick up the advantages of high speed networks. To this end (Chai et al., 2007) proved that pNFS handles very well high speed networks such as InfiniBand, and achieves up to 5 times higher throughput compared with using Gigabit Ethernet as the transport. Encouraged by the little overhead added by the pNFS, the authors position it as an efficient parallel solution for cluster storage.

However, a potential drawback could be pNFS requiring users to deal with multiple NFS servers. Depending on how well the NFS vendor integrates these servers, the management overhead may scale with the number of storage devices that are configured for parallel access. It is therefore advised to use tightly integrated servers that provide a true single system image as opposed to a cluster of servers that are merely duct-taped together. Hence pNFS is not yet suited for environments where improved performance for large, sequential files with parallel access is needed. Moreover, since it's a new technology, although the pNFS extension has the support of NAS hardware vendors, it's not yet clear how soon application and operating system vendors will support pNFS.

Grid File Systems. In the context of storing and accessing data at global scale Grid File Sys-

tems prove their utility, as they provide a means to federate a very large number of large-scale distributed storage resources and offer a large storage capacity and a good persistence achieved through file-based storage. Beyond these properties, grid file systems have the important advantage of offering a transparent access to data through the abstraction of a shared file namespace, in contrast to explicit data transfer schemes (e.g. GridFTP-based) currently used on some production grids. Transparent access greatly simplifies data management by applications, which no longer need to explicitly locate and transfer data across various sites, as data can be accessed the same way from anywhere, based on globally shared identifiers. Implementing transparent access at a global scale naturally leads however to a number of challenges related to scalability and performance, as the file system is put under pressure by a very large number of concurrent, largely distributed accesses.

Examples of such file systems include LegionFS (White et al. 2001) and GFarm (Tatebe et al. 2004). The latter, Grid Datafarm (Gfarm), is a distributed file system designed for high-performance data access and reliable file sharing in large scale environments including grids of clusters. To facilitate file sharing, Gfarm manages a global namespace which allows the applications to access files using the same path regardless of file location. It federates available storage spaces of grid nodes to provide a single file system image. Gfarm consists of a set of communicating components, each of which fulfills a particular role. The metadata server stores and manages the namespace hierarchy together with file metadata, user-related metadata, as well as file location information allowing clients to physically locate the files. The file system nodes are responsible for physically storing full Gfarm files on their local storage. In contrast with NFS however, Gfarm does not implement file stripping.

Object-Based File Systems

Recent research (Factor et al. 2005) emphasizes a clear move currently in progress from a block-based interface to a object-based interface in storage architectures, with the goal of enabling scalable, self-managed storage networks by moving low-level functionalities such as space management to storage devices or to storage server, accessed through a standard object interface. This move has a direct impact on the design of today's distributed file systems: object-based file system would then store data rather as objects than as unstructured data blocks. According to the authors, this move may eliminate nearly 90% of management workload which was the major obstacle limiting file systems' scalability and performance. Two approaches exploit this idea.

In the first approach, the data objects are stored and manipulated directly by a new type of storage device called object-based storage device (OSD). This approach requires an evolution of the hardware, in order to allow high-level object operations to be delegated to the storage device. The standard OSD interface was defined in the Storage Networking Industry Association (SNIA) OSD working group. The protocol is embodied over SCSI and defines a new set of SCSI commands. Recently, a second generation of the command set, Object-Based Storage Devices - 2 (OSD-2) has been defined. The distributed file systems taking the OSD approach assume the presence of such an OSD in the near future and currently rely on a software module simulating its behavior. Examples of parallel/distributed file systems following this approach are Lustre (Schwan 2003) and Ceph (Weil et al. 2006). Recently, research efforts (Devulapalli et al. 2007) have explored the feasibility and the possible benefits of integrating OSDs into parallel file systems, such as PVFS (Carns et al. 2000).

The second approach does not rely on the presence of OSDs, but still tries to benefit from an object-based approach to improve performance and scalability: files are structured as a set of objects that are stored on storage servers. Google File System (Ghemawat et al. 2003), and HDFS illustrate this approach.

Hadoop Distributed System. In contrast with the previous examples targeted at high performance infrastructures, we present the Hadoop Distributed File System – HDFS (Wheeler, 2008), an open source file system designed to run on inexpensive commodity hardware. The system organizes files in a hierarchical namespace for storage and retrieval and provides high throughput access to application data. HDFS supports hardware transparency as it runs in user space, as contrasted to the other file systems which are inextricably linked to their operating systems' kernel; therefore HDFS can run on any operating system supported by Java. HDFS implements replication mechanisms for data across multiple machines in a cluster. This scheme provides not only fault tolerance, but also the potential for extremely high capacity storage given that the overall capacity will be based on all usable space of all disks across all machines. HDFS also assumes that the data will be written only once and is able to gain extra performance by optimizing for subsequent reads while disallowing subsequent writes.

Hadoop's file system architecture is built around a master / slave model with a single NameNode (plus a seconday NameNode for checkpointing), as a master server that manages the file system namespace and regulates access to files by clients, and a number of DataNodes, usually one per node in the cluster, which manage storage attached to the nodes that they run on. DataNode are thus responsible for low-level operations including block creation, deletion, reads and writes. A NameNode keeps track of which DataNodes have which blocks of data and uses this information to manage the hierarchy of the overall file system. Being open source, HDFS is widely adopted and due to the use of commodity components is actively developed in business environments also. Yahoo! is the greatest contributor and the largest user (4000 nodes and 16 PB of raw disk capacity) but is also deployed at Google, Facebook, ImageShack, Last.fm.

Amazon Simple Storage Service (S3). In the context of the emerging Cloud Computing paradigm Amazon S3 (Amazon S3 Website) 2010 is the storage solution on which Amazon EC2 (Elastic Computing) cloud service relies for providing basic data management services. It is fast, reliable, scalable and inexpensive data storage infrastructure, to which access is given using a web service for storing any amount of data. Data is stored across the system in containers named buckets, where each bucket may contain multiple objects. The S3 framework was designed with simplicity in mind, to handle objects that may reach sizes in the order of GB: the user can write, read, and delete objects simply identified by a unique key. The access interface is based on well-established standards such as SOAP. Careful consideration was invested into using decentralized techniques and designing operations in such way as to minimize the need for concurrency control. A fault-tolerant layer enables operations to continue with minimal interruption. This allows S3 to be highly scalable. On the downside however, simplicity comes at a cost: S3 provides limited support for concurrent accesses to a single object.

Although the details of S3's design are not made public by Amazon, the system is widely used in several distributed collaborations and applications like SlideShare, Twitter and SmugMug. Moreover, Apache Hadoop file systems can be hosted on S3, as its requirements of a file system are met by S3. As a result, Hadoop can be used to run MapReduce algorithms on EC2 servers, reading data and writing results back to S3.

Studies show more than 80% (Grimes 2008) of data globally in circulation is unstructured. Furthermore, data sizes increase at a dramatic level. Large repositories for data analysis programs, data streams generated and updated by continuously running applications, data archives are just a few examples of contexts where unstructured data that

easily reaches the order of TBs. Unstructured data are often stored as a binary large object (blob) within a database or a file. However, these approaches can hardly cope with blobs which grow to huge sizes. To address this issue, specialized abstractions like MapReduce propose high-level data processing frameworks intended to hide the details of parallelization from the user. Such platforms are implemented on top of huge object storage and target high performance by optimizing the parallel execution of the computation. This leads to heavy access concurrency to the blobs, thus the need for the storage layer to offer support in this sense. As in the previous paragraphs, parallel and distributed file systems also consider using objects for low-level storage. In other scenarios, huge blobs need to be used concurrently at the highest level layers of applications directly: e.g. high-energy physics applications. Motivated by these remarks and beyond the above developments in the area of parallel and distributed file systems, we present some other recent efforts that rely on objects for large-scale data management, without exposing a file system interface.

BlobSeer (Nicolae et al. 2008) addresses the problem of storing and efficiently accessing very large, unstructured data objects, in a distributed environment. The blob management service was specifically designed to deal with large-scale distributed applications, which need to store massive data objects and to efficiently access (read, update) them at a fine grain. In this context, the system is be able to support a large number of blobs, each of which might reach a size in the order of TB. BlobSeer employs a powerful concurrency management scheme enabling a large number of clients to efficiently read and update the same blob simultaneously in a lock-free manner. To cope with very large data blobs, BlobSeer uses striping: each blob is cut into fixed-size pages, which are distributed across the local storage of a large number of grid nodes, acting as providers of storage space. This fragmentation allows both to store huge data blocks and to avoid contention for disjoint accesses to pages.

A metadata scheme facilitates access to a range (offset, size) for any existing version of a blob snapshot, by associating such a range with the physical nodes where the corresponding pages are located. Metadata are organized as a segment-tree like structure and are scattered across the system using a Distributed Hash Table (DHT). Distributing data and metadata is the key choice of the BlobSeer design: it enables high performance through parallel, direct access I/O paths, as demonstrated in (Nicolae et al. 2008). Further, BlobSeer provides concurrent clients with efficient fine-grained access to blobs, without locking. Using a consistent versioning scheme, concurrent writes to the same page can proceed in parallel on multiple versions of that page. Versioning further allows dealing with mutable data by enabling access to multiple versions of the same blob within the same computation and allowing clients to roll back data changes when desired.

To illustrate BlobSeer's performance and prove file systems' convergence in large scale distributed environments, the authors recently investigated integration capabilities of their approach with other object based file systems. Therefore they substituted the original data storage layer of Hadoop with a new, concurrency-optimized storage layer based on BlobSeer. By using BlobSeer instead of its default storage layer, Hadoop significantly improves its sustained throughput in scenarios that exhibit highly concurrent accesses to shared files. The authors report on extensive experimentation both with synthetic microbenchmarks and real Map-Reduce applications. The results illustrate the benefits of this approach over the original HDFS-based implementation of Hadoop. Moreover, in this setting additional features are supported such as efficient concurrent appends, concurrent writes at random offsets and versioning. These features could be leveraged to extend or improve functionalities in future versions of Hadoop or other Map-Reduce frameworks.

We note however some aspects which still need consideration, BlobSeer being a project under current development. Fault tolerance, which becomes critical in grid environments, is only partially addressed. The authors currently leverage some fault-tolerance mechanisms provided by the DHT on which the implementation of some of the composing entities relies, like the metadata provider and the provider manager. This enhances the availability of metadata thanks to the underlying replication used by the DHT. However, the versioning manager, though under heavy load, is still a single point of failure, similarly to the *namenode* in HDFS. Besides, data is statically replicated using a replication factor indicated by users at blob create time. A dynamic scheme, adapting the replication factor based on real-time observations could be envisioned. Also, when exposing this interface in a cloud context, some security policies should also be considered in order to self-protect the system from malicious clients.

We conclude this section observing that file systems and their mass or commodity storage systems integration are still under continuous efforts of research and development. Solutions exist and range from high performance proprietary file systems to low-cost hardware based, open source projects. In order to achieve better integration however, there is a constant need for joint work between storage and software providers.

DATA MOVEMENT AND RETRIEVAL

Applications and distributed mass storage systems apply several techniques for maximizing the retrieval data rate achieved across WANs, SANs and LANs. Both hardware and software optimization mechanisms are exploited for this purpose. Multithreaded parallel streaming has been proven as a good and inexpensive way for aggregating I/O. Other enhancement techniques such as buffering, pre-fetching, and proper cache replacement policies are considered very supportive in improving applications' performance. However, pre-fetching and cache management are considered to be application- dependant features (Malluhi et al., 2002), therefore an optimal pre-fetching algorithm for one application may be the worst for another one with different data type and/ or access patterns.

Another observation that may be speculated is that in high performance computing environments applications usually require access to only subsets of the distributed datasets since handling the whole dataset at once, if possible, considerably degrades the performance of the client machines. One aiming at designing a reliable retrieval system should then consider that users needn't spend long time waiting for retrieving the whole dataset, if only partial data is needed at any time. Therefore, mass storage system should provide clients with data retrieval APIs that allow partial data transfers. Some storage systems have provided low-level block accesses, which resulted in reducing the startup time required by the applications. Other systems just stripe the dataset into several blocks that are equal to the number of data nodes used in distributing the data object (Chen et al. 2002, Ye et al. 2006). This restriction limits the use of the storage system to file transfer since handling large data chunks may not be useful. It may also result in long network latencies and degrades the positive threads overlapping.

Data Transfer

Much of data storage and retrieval systems' performance is in conjunction with their data movement capabilities. The tiered data distribution model of today's intensive computing applications involves dissemination of data from the production sites to the storage and processing sites across a highly geographical distributed hierarchy of tiers. In order to harness all the advantages of the always rapidly advancing network technologies (among the latest we note GigaByte, InfiniBand and optical networks), applications must rely on robust and efficient data transfer protocols. As we will see in this section, this proves to be a non-trivial task.

Indeed, recent experiences with grids and High Energy Physics experiments at CERN revealed numerous issues related to data transport across widely heterogeneous networks. For instance, much effort is spent on bulk transfers (Paisley et al., 2006), which originated from a historical view of the WAN and can affect the QoS delivered to other users of the network. Solutions to this problem vary from identifying the applications that produce the bulk traffic (usually at bounded set: SRMs, GridFTP) using detection methods based on application signatures (which proves however difficult to achieve in real-time) to using large relatively cheap network capacities for bulk transfers. Other issues comes from the observation that although some file systems (as Hadoop) rely on the paradigm that "moving computation is cheaper than moving data", that is not generally true in supercomputing applications. Hence a manifest's need for significant storage resources near the computing elements. Moreover, data transport in these environments cannot capitalize on opportunistic resources and movement of data can result in large wasted network bandwidth unless much of the data is reused. Missing files problems require significant bookkeeping efforts; large jobs startups delays are frequent until all of the required data arrives; the transport proves sometimes unstable, with high latencies and un-predictable for real-time access. In this section we concentrate on the high-level data transfer solutions, examining how they cope with the above challenges and studying their compliance with the distributed systems' general requirements.

The Grid File Transfer Protocol – GridFTP (Allcock et al., 2003) is a set of extensions to the FTP that define a general-purpose mechanism for secure, reliable, high-performance data transfer. The protocol is part of the Globus Toolkit 4 (Foster, 2005) and enables efficient data transfer between end-systems by employing techniques like multiple TCP streams per transfer, striped transfers from a set of hosts to another set of hosts, and partial file transfers. GridFTP is based on TCP but it further allows multiple TCP streams creation between the source and the destination in order to offset the network congestion and improve throughput. GridFTP was early adopted by large communities and deployed with much enthusiasm as it is basically the first transfer protocol to address the specific HPC needs. The protocol is thus continuously updated, many interfaces with storage and retrieval systems are developed, and various extensions are built to address specific applications. An example is the Globus Striped GridFTP framework (Allcock et al., 2005), a set of client and server libraries designed to support the construction of data-intensive tools and applications. The GridFTP server proved faster than other FTP servers in both single-process and striped configurations, achieving high speeds both in memory-to-memory and disk-to-disk transfers. Moreover the server can easily scale and supports thousands concurrent clients without excessive load. The authors argue that this combination of performance and modular structure make the Globus GridFTP framework both a foundation on which to build tools and applications, and a testbed for the study of innovative data management techniques and network protocols.

However, currently GridFTP does not incorporate optimizations which affect network routing or take into account any network parallelism. Hence, there is still place for improvement. (Khanna et al., 2008a) explored the use of two key optimizations, namely, multi-hop path splitting and multi-pathing and proposed optimization algorithms which can exploit these optimizations to maximize file transfer throughput. These optimizations were implemented using GridFTP as the underlying protocol and the authors observed that the proposed solutions yield significant performance improvements for communication patterns like 1-to-all broadcast, all-to-1 gather, data redistribution. In contrast, for scenarios involving data replication, no significant improvement was observed.

Another concern in GridFTP is the heterogeneous nature of the environment and dynamic availability of shared resources, which need to be considered at the time of the data transfers. (Khanna et al., 2008b) proposes a solution that takes into account the dynamically changing network bandwidth. To this end the authors develop an algorithm that dynamically schedules a batch of data transfer requests with the goal of minimizing the overall transfer time. The proposed algorithm performs simultaneous transfer of chunks of files from multiple file replicas, if the replicas exist; the dynamicity of the bandwidth is considered when adaptively selecting replicas to transfer different chunks of the same file by taking. GridFTP is the underlying mechanism for data transfers and the history traces from previous GridFTP transfers are sued to make new estimations on network bandwidth and resource availability.

(Kourtellis et al., 2008) makes a detailed workload analysis of the performance and reliability of the GridFTP, based on traces of reported data from different distributed installed components. The authors focus on three aspects: quantification of the volume of data transferred during the monitored interval (1.5 years) and characterization of user behavior; understanding of how tuning capabilities are used; finally, the quantification of the user base as recorded in the database and the prediction of usage trends. The analysis revealed a small use of the tuning parameters (i.e. users tend not to set the buffer size explicitly leaving it to the OS) and also confirmed the large adoption of GridFTP both in terms of IPs (users) / domains (Virtual Organizations) and volume transferred.

Fast Data Transfer (FDT Website, 2010) is a new application for efficient data transfers, capable of reading and writing at disk speed over Wide Area Networks (WAN), with standard TCP. FDT is developed within the MonALISA monitoring framework (presented in the next Chapter) to support efficient large scale data transfers and also to help in the active monitoring of the available bandwidth between sites. FDT can be used as an independent application but it can also be controlled and managed by the MonALISA system to provide effective data transfer services. The application is based on an asynchronous, flexible multithreaded system and is using the capabilities of the Java NIO libraries. Its main features include: streaming datasets (lists of files) continuously, using a managed pool of buffers through one or more TCP sockets, the use of independent threads to read and write on each physical device, data transfers in parallel on multiple TCP streams, when necessary, the use of appropriate-sized buffers for disk I/O and for the network, restoring the files from buffers asynchronously and resuming file transfer sessions without loss, when needed.

FDT can be used to stream a large set of files across the network, so that a large dataset composed of thousands of files can be sent or received at full speed, without the network transfer restarting between files. The FDT architecture allows to plug-in external security APIs and to use them for client authentication and authorization. Currently FDT supports several security schemes like IP filtering, SSH, GSI-SSH, Globus-GSI, and SSL. The application enjoys a wide adoption as it very easy to use and portable, being written in Java. Performance evaluation showed very good results both in memory-to-memory tests (achieving 9.4 Gb/s throughput over 10 Gb links) and in disk-to-disk tests conducted over the USLHCNet network. In the last scenario, FDT proved capable to transfer data over WAN at the limit of the disks IO rate showing rates decreasing in time as the write speed on normal disks decreased (as the disks were filled).

REPLICATION

Large scale distributed systems are hardly ever "perfect". Due to their complexity, it is extremely difficult to produce flawless designed distributed systems. Fault tolerance is the ability of a large-scale distributed system to perform its function correctly even in the presence of faults occurring in various components. Traditional approaches for high availability (high resilience to faults occurrences) are based on the combination of redundancy and 24/7 operations support, which often prove prohibitive expensive. The characteristics of large-scale distributed systems make fault tolerance a difficult problem from several points of view. A first aspect is the geographical distribution of resources and users that implies frequent remote operations and data transfers. These lead to a decrease in the system's capability to detect faults, to manage correct group communications and consensus. Another problem is the volatility of the resources, which are usually available only for limited periods of time. The system must ensure the correct and complete execution of the applications even in the situations when the resources are introduced and removed dynamically, or when they are damaged. Solving all these issues still represents a research domain.

One widely used technique to guarantee the availability and dependability of large-scale distributed systems in the presence of faults is replication. Replication implies the use of more services or components performing the same function. Whenever a replicated entity encounters a failure (a crash is the most commonly used scenario, but some replication solutions are even adapted to deal with Byzantine failures) another replica is switched on and takes its place. Data replication is a reliability improvement technique used in many types of distributed systems. By replicating the data over multiple nodes, the system can support the failure of some of these nodes, without losing its ability to function correctly. Moreover, data replication is employed for load balancing reasons. Instead of overwhelming a single node with many data access requests, the requests can be evenly distributed to all the nodes containing replicas of the requested data. In a typical distributed environment that collects or monitors data, useful data may be spread across multiple distributed nodes, but users or applications may wish to access that data from a central location (data repository). A common way to ensure centralized access to distributed data is by means of maintaining replicas of data objects of interest at a central location. However, when data collections are large or volatile, keeping replicas consistent with remote master copies poses a significant challenge due to the large communication cost incurred

By means of performance enhancement, replication is used for storing data that is likely to be reused and avoid latencies of fetching it form the originating resources or for workload sharing between servers in the same cluster (domain). However, there are limits to the effectiveness of replication as a performance-enhancement technique, especially in environments with frequent updates of data, where overhead is incurred from protocols designed to ensure that clients receive up to date data. Data replication also enables increased availability when used at a number of failure-independent servers. Still, highly available data does not necessarily mean strictly correct data. Correctness concerns the freshness of the data supplied to users and the effects of users' operations on data. Other common requirements imposed to data replication are consistency, that is the compliance between (possibly conflicting) operations upon a set of replicated data and its correctness specifications, and also transparency, namely, clients should not be aware of the existence of several copies of data.

Since replication implies that identical data copies exist, replicas need to be uniquely identified through logical and physical filenames. Moreover, there is a manifest need for a service responsible with naming and locating replicas. (Allcock et al., 2002) identified the major components of a high performance data replication system and their basic functionalities:

Replica Management – the service should create new copies of a complete or partial collection of files, register the copies with a naming and location directory service, allow users and application to query the directory to find all the existing copies of a particular file or collection of files;

Replica Catalog – stores naming and location information about the registered data; provide mappings between logical names for files or collections and one or more copies of those objects on physical storage systems; the authors proposed a set of three types of entries for data registration within the catalog: logical collections (user defined group of files, suitable for handling large amounts of data and having the advantage of reducing both catalog entries and the number of catalog manipulation operations), locations (mappings between logical collections and their particular physical instances), and logical files (optional entry suitable for individual files).

The presented prototypes were implemented within the Globus Toolkit (GT) and continuously evolved along with GT new releases. In the current GT version 4.2 the replica management service is implemented by the Data Replication Service – DRS (Chervenak et al., 2008). DRS allows user to identify files, replicate and transfer them and across the network and to register them into the Replica Location Service. Throughout the replication operations, the service maintains state about each file, including which operations on the file have succeeded or failed. The DRS is implemented as a Web Service and it thus exposes the previous functionality through a WS-Resource ("Replicator"), which represents the current state of the requested replication activity. This allows users to query or subscribe to various Resource Properties in order to monitor the state of the resource and control the replication request's behavior.

The Replica Catalog was initially implemented as a simple, centralized service based on LDAP technology. This approach however revealed some serious limitations when deployed in production hence it was updated to the Replication Location Service – RLS (Chervenak et al., 2004). RLS provides a mechanism for registering the existence of replicas and discovering them. It consists of two types of services, a catalog service and an index service. The Local Replica Catalog (LRC) maintains a catalog of replica information in the form of mappings from logical names for data items to target names. These target names may represent physical locations of data items, or an entry in the RLS may map to another level of logical naming for the data item. The other component, the Replica Location Index (RLI) aggregates and answers queries about mappings held in one or more LRCs. An RLI server contains a set of mappings from logical names to LRCs. In a typical use case scenario the LRC sends an index of its contents to its associated RLI service as well as multiple remote RLI services at collaborating sites. Clients interested in a particular logical name will first query a RLI service to find the LRC services, then they will query one or more LRC services to find the target names (which may correspond to storage location URLs).

Besides the Globus solutions, there is a continuous research effort in enhancing replication mechanisms with features compliant with the requirements indicated at the beginning of this section. One concern is related to the selection of the best candidate site where replicas should be placed. (Rahman et al. 2007) uses a multi-objective model to tackle this problem. The multi-objective model considers the objectives of p-median and p-center models simultaneously to select the candidate sites that will host replicas. The objective of the p-median model is to find the locations of p possible candidate replication sites by optimizing total (or average) response time; where the p-center model finds p candidate sites by optimizing maximum response time. In addition, observing that candidate sites currently holding replicas may not be the best sites to fetch replica on subsequent requests due to dynamic latencies, the authors propose a dynamic replica maintenance algorithm that re-allocates to new candidate sites if a performance metric degrades significantly over last time periods.

(Ramabhadran et al., 2008) studies the problem of guaranteeing data durability in distributed storage systems based on replication. This proves to be difficult because the data lifetimes may be several orders of magnitude larger than the lifetimes of individual storage units, and the system may have little or no control over the participation of these storage units in the system. The authors use a model-based approach to develop engineering principles for designing automated replication and repair mechanisms to implement durability in such systems. In (Duminuco et al., 2007) it is discussed the moment when data should be replicated. Since node failures can be either transient or permanent, deciding when to generate the replicas is not trivial. In addition, failure behavior in terms of the rate of permanent and transient failures may vary over time. The authors propose a new technique to deal with these issues, combining advantages from both reactive approaches (in which new redundant fragments are created as soon as failure is detected) and proactive approaches (which create new fragments at a fixed rate depending on the knowledge of failure behavior). The proposed solution is based on an ongoing estimation of the failure behavior that is obtained using a model that consists of a network of queues; hence the solution combines adaptiveness of reactive systems with smooth bandwidth usage of proactive systems.

The current replication techniques can be classified in two classes: active and passive replication. In case of active replication, each request is processed by all replicas. The technique ensures a fast reaction to failures. However, active replication uses processing resources heavily and requires the processing of requests to be deterministic. This is a very strong limitation since, in a distributed application, there are many potential sources of non-determinism. With passive replication (also called primary-backup), only one replica (primary) processes the request, and sends update messages to the other replicas (backups). The technique uses fewer resources than active replication does, without the requirement of operation determinism. On the other hand, the replicated service usually has a slow reaction to failures. For instance, when the primary crashes, the failure must be detected by the other replicas, and the request may have to be reprocessed by a new primary. This may result in a significantly higher response time for the request being processed. An alternative approach to replication combines the power of these two classes. The new class, called semi-passive replication (Defago et al. 2002), retains the essential characteristics of passive replication while avoiding the necessity to force the crash of suspected processes.

Zyzzyva (Kotla et al. 2004) is a Byzantine Fault Tolerance protocol that uses speculation to reduce the cost and simplify the design of the state machine replication. In Zyzzyva, replicas respond to a client's request by optimistically adopting the order proposed by the primary. This approach has the advantage of reduced the time needed for the client to receive a response. However, replicas can become temporarily inconsistent with one another, but clients detect inconsistencies, help correct replicas converge on a single total ordering of requests, and only rely on responses that are consistent with this total order. This approach allows Zyzzyva to reduce replication overheads to near their theoretical minima.

Due to the overhead incurred, in many real-world environments exact replica consistency is not maintained. Some form of inexact, or approximate, replication is typically used instead. Approximate replication (Olston 2003) is often performed by refreshing replicas periodically. Periodic refreshing allows communication cost to be controlled, but it does not always make good use of communication resources: in between refreshes some remote master copies may change significantly, leaving replicas excessively out of date and inaccurate, and meanwhile resources may be wasted refreshing replicas of other master copies that remain nearly unchanged. There is a fundamental and unavoidable tradeoff between precision and performance: when data changes rapidly, good performance can only be achieved by sacrificing replica precision and, conversely, obtaining high precision tends to degrade performance. Two natural and complementary methods for working with the precision-performance tradeoff are proposed to achieve efficient communication resource utilization for replica synchronization: maximize replica precision in the presence of constraints on communication cost and minimize communication cost in the presence of constraints on replica precision. In (Tang et al. 2007, Liu et al. 2006) other optimal replica placement strategies for different types of distributed systems (e.g. data grids) are presented.

Several replication solutions exist for commodity hardware. Clustered-JDBC (Cecchet et al. 2004) is an open-source middleware solution for database clustering. C-JDBC offers various load balancers according to the degree of replication the user wants. Full replication is easy to handle. It does not require request parsing since every database backend can handle any query. Database updates, however, need to be sent to all nodes, and performance suffers from the need to broadcast updates when the number of backends increases. To address this problem, C-JDBC provides partial replication in which the user can define database replication on a per-table basis. Load balancers supporting partial replication must parse the incoming queries and need to know the database schema of each backend. Postgres-R (Postgres Website 2010) is designed to run on shared-nothing clusters with a low latency interconnect. It provides conflict-free (eager), multi-master replication on the basis of binary changeset replication. The main component of Postgres-R is the replication manager, a separate process added to Postgres which mainly coordinates messages. It arranges and maintains the connection to the group communication system, to the backends which process local transactions as well as to the helper backends which process remote transactions. Slony-I (Slony-I Website

2010) is an asynchronous replicator of a single master database to multiple replicas, which in turn may have cascaded replicas. Cascading replicas over a WAN minimizes bandwidth, enabling better scalability and also enables read-only (for example, reporting) applications to take advantage of replicas. PGCluster (PGCluster Website 2010) is the synchronous replication system of the multi-master composition for PostgreSQL. It consists of three kinds of servers, a load balancer, Cluster DB, and a replication server with two functions: load sharing function and a high availability.

Some of the presented replication models for commodity hardware introduce a relatively large overhead while processing the queries. For example, Postgres-R uses changesets to replicate the databases. The replication manager sends the received requests to a replica which inserts them into a database, then send to the replication manager the changes made by the previous queries, the replication manager broadcasts the changeset to all replicas and finally it uses two-phase-commit protocol for committing. Hence, this solution introduces a relatively large delay, even if the replicas are completely synchronous. Finally, some of these models are experimental software (e.g. Postgres-r) and are used mostly in scientific experiments (C-JDBC).

FUTURE RESEARCH DIRECTIONS

We discuss several trends that will drive innovation within data storage and management technologies in large scale distributed systems. One important direction in the current context will focus on enhancing collaboration between participating partners in the large scale data grids. Although these grids are built around the concept of Virtual Organization, which emphasizes on sharing resources, current technologies do not provide much of the capabilities required for enabling collaboration between participants. For instance, the tree structure on which replication

mechanisms often rely inhibits direct copying of data between participants that reside on different tree sides. Hence, replication systems will need to consider some new approaches that rely on peer-to-peer links between different branches for increased collaboration.

With the emergence of the workflow paradigm, data management in grids will include this approach based on service composition. Workflow management systems allow the users to develop complex applications at a higher level, by orchestrating functional components and specifying the dependencies among them without handling the implementation details. This approach is similar to the users' goals when handling huge amounts of data in large scale collaborations. Scientific applications will benefit from the new emerging workflow technologies to achieve their performance requirements. To this end, we observe that data has a central role in all the phases of the workflow lifecycle. During workflow creation, appropriate input data and workflow components need to be discovered. During workflow mapping and execution data need to be staged-in and staged-out of the computational resources. As data are produced, they need to be archived with enough metadata and provenance information so that they can be interpreted and shared among collaborators. Thus, from the point of view of data, the workflow lifecycle includes the following transformations which map to the general data handlings steps in grids: data discovery, setting up the data processing pipeline, generation of derived data, archiving of derived data and its provenance. However, service composition also requires selecting the right services with the required QoS parameters. This impacts both replication and resource allocation and leads to diversification of objective functions and strategies from the current static methods.

Another future trend in data handling is the convergence between Grid and Cloud approached for data storage and management. Data Grids and Cloud Data Management share similar objectives. However, the development of the grid and of the cloud have only been loosely coupled for several reasons. First, they both focused on specific user communities: scientific communities in case of the grid as opposed to commercial customers in case of the cloud. Second, both environments have different origins: the main driver for the grid has been the High Energy Physics community while the proliferation of the cloud has been dominated by large providers of IT services that already had the necessary computing re- sources (data centers) in place and were heading towards a more optimal utilization of their capacities. Third, grid computing is better suited for organizations with large amounts of data being requested by a small number of users (or few but large allocation requests), whereas cloud computing is better suited to environments where there are a large number of users requesting small amounts of data (or many but small allocation requests). Therefore, despite the initial separation between Data Grids and Cloud Data Management, the requirements both environments need to address more and more converge.

We argue that in the current context the difference between the two paradigms only seems to be a naming one: although fundamentally different, they are still faced with the same issues related to data handling: transparency, fault tolerance, scalability, access control. All these issues have different semantics and suffer specific derivations within each paradigm; however they solutions to address them are similar. Therefore we anticipate a convergence of the technologies involved in data handling within both approaches.

CONCLUSION

In this chapter, we have studied several aspects related to data storage, retrieval and management in large scale distributed systems. We examined the architectures, strategies and practices that are currently followed in this domain. We further stressed some of the shortcomings and identified gaps in the current architectures and systems. As more and more application classes and services start using the grid and cloud paradigms in order to achieve their high requirements, the demand for adequate, scalable data storage and management strategies is ever higher. One important requirement in this context is the ability to efficiently cope with accesses to continuously growing data, while supporting a highly concurrent, highly distributed environment.

We observed that current scientific data grids mostly follow the hierarchical or the federated models of organization with the data sources that are few and well established on top of the hierarchy. These data sources are generally mass storage systems from which data is transferred out as files, large objects or datasets to other repositories. The requirement to transfer large datasets has led to the development of high-speed, low latency transfer protocols exploiting parallelism and the advances in networking technologies. Currently, massive datasets are being replicated mostly statically by project administrators in specific locations. However, intelligent and dynamic replication strategies still need to be implemented in production data intensive grids. These represent some of the directions that can be followed in the future by researchers in this area, along with required advances in terms of scalability, interoperability and data maintainability

REFERENCES

Allcock, B., Bester, J., Bresnahan, J., Chervenak, A. L., Foster, I., & Kesselman, C. (2002). Data management and transfer in high-performance computational grid environments. *Parallel Computing, 28*(5), 749–771. doi:10.1016/S0167-8191(02)00094-7

Allcock, W. (2003). *GridFTP: Protocol Extensions to FTP for the Grid*. Argonne National Laboratory.

Allcock, W., Bresnahan, J., Kettimuthu, R., & Link, M. (2005). The Globus Striped GridFTP Framework and Server. In: *Proceedings of the 2005 ACM/IEEE Conference on Supercomputing. Conference on High Performance Networking and Computing.* IEEE Computer Society, Washington, USA. Amazon S3 Website. Retrieved on March 30, 2010 from http://aws.amazon.com/ s3.

Badino, P., Barring, O., Baud, J. P., Donno, F., Perelmutov, T., Petravick, D., et al. (2008). The storage resource manager interface specification version 2.2. Retrieved from March 30, 2010 from: http://sdm.lbl.gov/ srm-wg/ doc/ SRM.v2.2.html

Bakken J., Berman, E., Huang, C. H., Moibenko, A., Petravick, D., Rechenmacher, R., & K. Ruthmansdorfer. (2008). Enstore Technical Design Document, *Joint Projects Document JP0026.*

Carns, P., Ligon, W., Ross, R., & Thakur, R. (2000). PVFS: A parallel file system for linux clusters. In: *Proceedings of the 4th Annual Linux Show-case and Conference* (pp. 317–327), Atlanta, GA, USA. Castor Wesite, Retrieved on March 30, 2010 from: http://castor.web.cern.ch/ castor/

Cecchet, E., Marguerite, J., & Zwaenepole, W. (2004). C-JDBC: flexible database clustering middleware. *In Proceedings of the Annual Conference on USENIX Annual Technical Conference* Berkeley, CA, 26-26.

Chai, L., Ouyang, X., Noronha, R., & Panda, D. K. (2007). pNFS/PVFS2 over InfiniBand: Early experiences. In: *Proceedings of the 2nd International Workshop on Petascale Data Storage: Held in Conjunction with Supercomputing '07* PDSW '07. ACM, New York, NY, (pp. 5-11).

Chen, J., Akers, W., Chen, Y., & Watson, W., III. (2002). Java parallel secure stream for grid computing. In: *Proceedings of the 6th Joint Conference on Information Sciences*. NC, USA.

Chervenak, A., Foster, I., Kesselman, C., Salisbury, C., & Tuecke, S. (2000). The data grid: Towards architecture for the distributed management and analysis of large scientific datasets. *Journal of Network and Computer Applications, 23*(3), 187–200. doi:10.1006/jnca.2000.0110

Chervenak, A., Schuler, R., Kesselman, C., Koranda, S., & Moe, B. (2008). Wide area data replication for scientific collaborations. *Int. J. High Perform. Comput. Netw., 5*(3), 124–134. doi:10.1504/IJHPCN.2008.020857

Chervenak, A. L., Palavalli, N., Bharathi, S., Kesselman, C., & Schwartzkopf, R. (2004). Performance and Scalability of a Replica Location Service. In: *Proceedings of the 13th IEEE international Symposium on High Performance Distributed* Computing (pp. 182-191). IEEE Computer Society, Washington, DC.

Chun, B., Dabek, F., Haeberlen, A., Sit, E., Weatherspoon, H., Kaashoek, M. F., et al. (2006). Efficient replica maintenance for distributed storage systems. In: *Proceedings of the 3rd Conference on Networked Systems Design & Implementation - Vol. 3* (pp. 4-4) (San Jose, CA. USENIX Association, Berkeley, CA. Defago, X., Schiper, A. (2002). Specification of replication techniques, semi-passive replication, and lazy consensus. *Report for School of Knowledge Science*, Japan Advanced Institute of Science and Technology.

Devulapalli, A., Dalessandro, D., Wyckoff, P., Ali, N., & Sadayappan, P. (2007). Integrating parallel file systems with object-based storage devices. In *SC '07: Proceedings of the 2007 ACM/IEEE conference on Supercomputing* (pp. 1–10), New York, NY, USA

Dobre, D., Majuntke, M., & Suri, N. (2008). Low-latency access to robust amnesic storage. In *Proceedings of the 2nd Workshop on Large-Scale Distributed Systems and Middleware LADIS '08, Vol. 341.* (pp. 1-3) ACM, New York, NY.

Duellmann, D. (2008). *CERN storage update, HEPiX Fall 2008.* Taipei, Taiwan: Academia Sinica.

Duminuco, A., Biersack, E., & En-Najjary, T. (2007). Proactive replication in distributed storage systems using machine availability estimation. In *Proceedings of the 2007 ACM CoNEXT Conference.* CoNEXT '07 (pp. 1-12). ACM, New York, NY. Enstore Website, Retrieved on March 30, 2010 from: http://www-isd.fnal.gov/ enstore/

Ermolinskiy, A., Moon, D., Chun, B., & Shenker, S. (2009). Minuet: Rethinking concurrency control in storage area networks. In: *Proceedings of the 7th Conference on File and Storage Technologies* (pp. 311-324). Seltzer, M., & Wheeler, R. (Eds.) USENIX Association, Berkeley, CA.

Factor, M., Meth, K., Naor, D., Rodeh, O., & Satran, J. (2005). Object storage: The future building block for storage systems. *In Local to Global Data Interoperability - Challenges and Technologies,* 119–123. FDT Website, Retrieved on March 30, 2010 from: http://monalisa.cern.ch/ FDT/

Foster, I. (2005) Globus toolkit version 4: Software for service-oriented systems. *In NPC, ser. Lecture Notes in Computer Science,* (pp. 2-13). Jin, H., Reed, D. A. & Jiang, W. (Eds.) Vol. 3779. Springer.

Grimes, S. (2008). *Unstructured data and the 80 percent rule.* Carabridge Bridgepoints.

Gulati, A., & Ahmad, I. (2008). Towards distributed storage resource management using flow control. In *SIGOPS Oper. Syst. Rev. 42*(6), 10-16.

HP. Storage Essentials – Delivering on the promise of Storage Automation. (June 2008). Retrieved on March 31, 2010 from: http://www.hp.com/ go/ storageessentials

HPSS 7.1 High Performance Storage System User Guide, Release 7.1. (February 2009). Retrieved on March 31, 2010 from: http://www.hpss-collaboration.org/ hpss/ users/ docs/ AdobePDF/ 7.1/ users_guide.pdf

IBM. Release notes - Tivoli Storage Manager Server Version 6.1. (2009). Retrieved on March 31, 2010 from: http://publib.boulder.ibm.com/ infocenter/ tsminfo/v6/

Khanna, G., Catalyurek, U., Kurc, T., Kettimuthu, R., Sadayappan, P., Foster, I., & Saltz, J. (2008). Using overlays for efficient data transfer over shared wide-area networks. In: *Proceedings of the 2008 ACM/IEEE Conference on Supercomputing. Conference on High Performance Networking and Computing* (pp. 1-12). IEEE Press, Piscataway, NJ.

Khanna, G., Catalyurek, U., Kurc, T., Kettimuthu, R., Sadayappan, P., & Saltz, J. (2008). A Dynamic Scheduling Approach for Coordinated Wide-Area Data Transfers using GridFTP. In *Proceedings of the 22nd IEEE International Parallel and Distributed Processing Symposium.*

Kotla, R., & Dahlin, M. (2004). High throughput Byzantine fault tolerance. In *Intl. Conf. on Dependable Systems and Networks* (pp 575). IEEE Computer Society.

Kourtellis, N., Prieto, L., Iamnitchi, A., Zarrate, G., & Fraser, D. (2008). Data transfers in the grid: workload analysis of globus GridFTP (2008). In *Proceedings of the 2008 International Workshop on Data-Aware Distributed Computing.* DADC '08 (pp. 29-38). ACM, New York, NY.

Liu, P., & Wu, J. (2006). Optimal Replica Placement Strategy for Hierarchical Data Grid Systems. In: *Proc. of the 6th IEEE Intl. Symp. on Cluster Computing and the Grid (CCGrid)* (pp. 417-420).

Malluhi, Q., & Zeyad, A. (2002). DTViewer: A High Performance Distributed Terrain Image Viewer with Reliable Data Delivery. In *Proceedings of the 2nd International Workshop on Intelligent Multimedia Computing and Networking.*

Moore, R., Rajasekar, A., & Wan, M. (2005). Data grids, digital libraries and persistent archives: An integrated approach to publishing, sharing and archiving datas. In: *Proceedings of the IEEE (Special Issue on Grid Computing) Vol. 93*(3).

Nicolae, B., Antoniu, G., & Bougé, L. (2008). *Distributed management of massive data: An efficient fine-grain data access scheme* (pp. 532–543). In VECPAR.

OGF SRM WG Website. Retrieved on March 31, 2010 from: http://sdm.lbl.gov/ srm-wg/

Oguchi, M. (2009). Research works on cluster computing and storage area network. In *Proceedings of the 3rd International Conference on Ubiquitous information Management and Communication* ICUIMC '09 (pp. 366-375). ACM, New York, NY.

Oleynik, G. (2005). Fermilab Mass Storage System, Retrieved March 31, 2010 from: http://storageconference.org/ 2005/ presentations/ oleynik.ppt

Olston, C. (2003). Approximate Replication. *Doctoral Thesis. UMI Order Number: AAI3090652.*, Stanford University.

Paisley, J., & Sventek, J. (2006) Real-time detection of grid bulk transfer traffic. In*: The Tenth IEEE/IFIP Network Operations and Management Symposium 2006* (NOMS 2006), Vancouver, British Columbia, Canada.

Pariseau, B. (2008) What is parallel NFS and will it assist storage virtualization? Retrieved on March 31, 2010 from: http://searchstorage.techtarget.com.au/ articles/ 26445-What-is-Parallel-NFS-and-will-it -assist-storage-virtualisation-

PgCluster Website. (2010). Retrieved on March 30, 2010 from http://pgcluster.projects.postgresql.org/

Ponce, S. (2009) CASTOR developments: status and plans, *Castor External Operation Meeting.*

Postgres-R Website. (2010). Retrieved on March 30, 2010 from http://www.postgres-r.org/ documentation/

Rahman, R. M., Barker, K., & Alhajj, R. (2007). Study of Different Replica Placement and Maintenance Strategies in Data Grid. In *Proceedings of the 7th IEEE International Symposium on Cluster Computing and the Grid* (May 14 - 17, 2007). CCGRID (pp. 171-178). IEEE Computer Society, Washington, DC.

Ramabhadran, S., & Pasquale, J. (2008). Durability of replicated distributed storage systems. In: *Proceedings of the 2008 ACM SIGMETRICS International Conference on Measurement and Modeling of Computer Systems.* SIGMETRICS (pp. 447-448). ACM, New York, NY.

Schwan, P. (2003). Lustre: Building a file system for 1000-node clusters. In: *Proceedings of the linux symposium.*

Shepler, S., Eisler, M., & Noveck, D. (2008) NFS Version 4 Minor Version 1, December 2008, Retrieved on March 31, 2010 from: http://www.ietf.org/ internet-drafts/ draft-ietf-nfsv4-minorversion1-29.txt

Slony-I Replicator Website. (2010). Retrieved on March 30, 2010 from http://www.onlamp.com/ pub/ a/ onlamp/ 2004/ 11/ 18/ slony.html

Tang, X., & Chanson, S. (2007). Optimal Replica Placement under TTL-Based Consistency . *IEEE Transactions on Parallel and Distributed Systems*, *18*(3), 351–363. doi:10.1109/TPDS.2007.47

Tatebe, O., & Sekiguchi, S. (2004). Gfarm v2: A grid file system that supports high-performance distributed and parallel data computing. In *Proceedings of the 2004 Computing in High Energy and Nuclear Physics.*

Venugopal, S., Buyya, R., & Ramamohanarao, K. (2006). A taxonomy of Data Grids for distributed data sharing, management, and processing. *ACM Computing Surveys, 38*(1). doi:10.1145/1132952.1132955

Weil, S., Brandt, S., Miller, E., Long, D., & Maltzahn, C. (2006). Ceph: a scalable, high-performance distributed file system. In *OSDI '06: Proceedings of the 7th symposium on Operating systems design and implementation* (pp. 307–320). Berkeley, CA, USA.

Wheeler, T. (2008) Exploring Scalable Data Processing with Apache Hadoop, November 2008, Retrieved on March 31, 2010 from: http://jnb.ociweb.com/ jnb/ jnbNov2008.html

White, B., Walker, M., Humphrey, M., & Grimshaw, A. (2001). LegionFS: A secure and scalable file system supporting cross-domain high-performance applications. In *Proc. ACM/ IEEE Conf. on Supercomputing*, New York, NY, USA, ACM Press.

Ye, W., & Ning, G. (2006). An approach for robust distributed data retrieval in data intensive grid environments. In *Proceedings of 1st International Symposium in Pervasive Computing and Applications* (pp. 194-199). IEEE Computer Society.

ADDITIONAL READING

Ahmad, I., & Majumdar, S. (2008). Performance of resource management algorithms for Processable Bulk Data Transfer" Tasks in Grid Environments. In *Proceedings of the 7th International Workshop on Software and Performance*. WOSP '08 (pp. 177-188). ACM, New York, NY.

Ahmed, M. U., Zaheer, R. A., & Qadir, M. A. (2005). Intelligent cache management for data grid. In *Proceedings of the 2005 Australasian Workshop on Grid Computing and E-Research*: Vol. 44. (pp. 5-12). Australian Computer Society.

Chervenak, A. L., Schuler, R., Ripeanu, M., Ali Amer, M., Bharathi, S., & Foster, I. (2009). The Globus Replica Location Service: Design and Experience. *Parallel and Distributed Systems . IEEE Transactions on, 20*(9), 1260–1272.

De Camargo, R. Y., & Kon, F. (2006). Distributed data storage for opportunistic grids. In: *Proceedings of the 3rd international Middleware Doctoral Symposium*. MDS '06, *Vol. 185*. ACM, New York, NY.

Deng, Y., & Wang, F. (2007). Opportunities and challenges of storage grid enabled by grid service. *SIGOPS Oper. Syst. Rev., 41*(4), 79–82. doi:10.1145/1278901.1278915

Doraimani, S., & Iamnitchi, A. (2008). File grouping for scientific data management: lessons from experimenting with real traces. In: *Proceedings of the 17th International Symposium on High Performance Distributed Computing*. HPDC '08. (pp. 153-164). ACM, New York, NY.

Garrison, J. A., & Reddy, A. L. (2009). Umbrella file system: Storage management across heterogeneous devices. *Trans. Storage, 5*(1), 1–24. doi:10.1145/1502777.1502780

Hameurlain, A. (2008). Mobile agent-based data management in grid systems. In: *Proceedings of the 10th international Conference on information integration and Web-Based Applications & Services*. (pp. 2-2). Kotsis, G., Taniar, D., Pardede, E. & Khalil, I. (Eds.) iiWAS '08. ACM, New York, NY.

Hameurlain, A., El Morvan, F., & Samad, M. (2008). Large scale data management in grid systems: A survey. In Information and Communication Technologies: From Theory to Applications. ICTTA 2008. In: *Proceedings of the 3rd International Conference*. IEEE Computer Society.

Hildebrand, D., & Honeyman, P. (2007). Direct-pNFS: scalable, transparent, and versatile access to parallel file systems. In: *Proceedings of the 16th international Symposium on High Performance Distributed Computing*. HPDC '07 (pp. 199-208). ACM, New York, NY.

Jagatheesan, A., Moore, R., Paton, N. W., & Watson, P. (2003). Grid data management systems & services. In: *Proceedings of the 29th international Conference on Very Large Data Bases - Vol. 29.* Freytag, J. C., Lockemann, P. C., Abiteboul, S., Carey, M. J., Selinger, P. G., & Heuer, A. (Eds.) Very Large Data Bases. VLDB Endowment, 1150-1150.

Jagatheesan, A., & Rajasekar, A. (2003). Data grid management systems. In: *Proceedings of the 2003 ACM SIGMOD international Conference on Management of Data* (San Diego, California, June 09 - 12, 2003). SIGMOD '03. ACM, New York, NY, 683-683.

Li, M., Shu, J., & Zheng, W. (2009). GRID codes: Strip-based erasure codes with high fault tolerance for storage systems. *Trans. Storage, 4*(4), 1–22. doi:10.1145/1480439.1480444

Moore, R. W., Rajasekar, A., & Wan, M. (2005). Data grids, digital libraries, and persistent archives: An integrated approach to sharing, publishing, and archiving data. *Proceedings of the IEEE, 93,* 578–588. doi:10.1109/JPROC.2004.842761

Plale, B., Gannon, D., Alameda, J., Wilhelmson, B., Hampton, S., Rossi, A., & Droegemeier, K. (2005). Active management of scientific data. *Internet Computing, IEEE, 9,* 27–34. doi:10.1109/MIC.2005.4

Ranaldo, N., & Zimeo, E. (2009). Time and Cost-Driven Scheduling of Data Parallel Tasks in Grid Workflows. *Systems Journal, IEEE., 3*(1), 104–120. doi:10.1109/JSYST.2008.2011299

Scholl, T., Bauer, B., Müller, J., Gufler, B., Reiser, A., & Kemper, A. (2009). Workload-aware data partitioning in community-driven data grids. In *Proceedings of the 12th International Conference on Extending Database Technology: Advances in Database Technology.* Kersten, M., Novikov, B., Teubner, J., Polutin, V. & Manegold, S. (Eds.) *EDBT '09: Vol. 360* (pp. 36-47). ACM, New York, NY.

Scholl, T., & Kemper, A. (2008). Community-driven data grids. *Proc. VLDB Endow: Vol. 1.* (pp. 1672-1677).

Stewart, G. A., Cameron, D., Cowan, G. A., & McCance, G. (2007). Storage and data management in EGEE. In *Proceedings of the 5th Australasian Symposium on ACSW Frontiers: Vol. 68* (pp. 69-77). Brankovic, L., Coddington, P., Roddick, J. F., Steketee, C., Warren, J. R. & Wendelborn, A. (Eds.) ACM International Conference Proceeding Series, Vol. 249. Australian Computer Society, Darlinghurst, Australia.

Stockinger, H., Samar, A., Holtman, K., Allcock, B., Foster, I., & Tierney, B. (2001). File and object replication in data grids. In *Proceedings of the 10th IEEE international Symposium on High Performance Distributed Computing.* High Performance Distributed Computing (pp. 76). IEEE Computer Society, Washington, DC.

Stoica, R., Frank, M., Neufeld, N., & Smith, A. C. (2008). Data Handling and Transfer in the LHCb Experiment. *Nuclear Science . IEEE Transactions on, 55*(1), 272–277.

Thompson, C. W. (2006). Toward a grid-based DBMS. *Internet Computing, IEEE, 10*(3), 87–90. doi:10.1109/MIC.2006.68

Vazhkudai, S. S., Ma, X., Freeh, V. W., Strickland, J. W., Tammineedi, N., Simon, T., & Scott, S. L. (2006). Constructing collaborative desktop storage caches for large scientific datasets. *Trans. Storage, 2*(3), 221–254. doi:10.1145/1168910.1168911

Voicu, L. C., & Schuldt, H. (2009). How replicated data management in the cloud can benefit from a data grid protocol: the Re:GRIDiT Approach. In *Proceeding of the 1st International Workshop on Cloud Data Management* (Hong Kong, China, November 02 - 02, 2009). CloudDB '09. (pp. 45-48). ACM: New York, NY.

Wen, Z., Junwei, C., Yisheng, Z., Lianchen, L., & Cheng, W. (2008). An integrated resource management and scheduling system for grid data streaming applications. In *Proceedings of the 9th IEEE/ACM International Conference on Grid Computing* (September 29 - October 01, 2008). International Conference on Grid Computing. (pp. 258-265). IEEE Computer Society, Washington, DC.

Zhao, M., & Figueiredo, R. J. (2007). A user-level secure grid file system. In *Proceedings of the ACM/IEEE Conference on Supercomputing* (Reno, Nevada, November 10 - 16, 2007). SC '07. (pp. 1-11). ACM, New York, NY.

Section 2
Grid Network Designs

Chapter 6
E–Infrastructures for International Cooperation

Giuseppe Andronico
Italian National Institute of Nuclear Physics, Italy

Antun Balaž
Institute of Physics of Belgrade, Serbia

Tiwonge Msulira Banda
Ubuntunet Alliance, Malawi

Roberto Barbera
Italian National Institute of Nuclear Physics, Italy

Bruce Becker
Meraka Institute, South Africa

Subrata Chattopadhyay
Centre for Development of Advanced Computing, India

Gang Chen
Institute of High Energy Physics, China

Leandro N. Ciuffo
Italian National Institute of Nuclear Physics, Italy & RNP, Brazil

P. S. Dhekne
Bhabha Atomic Research Centre, India

Philippe Gavillet
CETA-CIEMAT, Spain & CERN, Switzerland

Salma Jalife
CUDI, Mexico & CLARA, Uruguay

John Wajanga Aron Kondoro
Dar Es Salam Institute of Technology, Tanzania

Simon C. Lin
ASGC, Taiwan

Bernard Marie Marechal
CETA-CIEMAT, Spain & Universidade Federal de Rio de Janeiro, Brazil

Alberto Masoni
Italian National Institute of Nuclear Physics, Italy

Ludek Matyska
CESNET, Czech Republic

Redouane Merrouch
CNRST, Morocco

Yannis Mitsos
Greek Research and Technology Network, Greece

Kai Nan
Chinese Academy of Sciences, China

Suhaimi Napis
Universiti Putra Malaysia, Malaysia

Salwa Nassar
ERI, Egypt & NARSS, Egypt

Marco Paganoni
University of Milano Bicocca, Italy

Ognjen Prnjat
Greek Research and Technology Network, Greece

Depei Qian
Beihang University, China

Sijin Qian
Peking University, China

Mario Reale
GARR, Italy

Federico Ruggieri
Italian National Institute of Nuclear Physics, Italy

Cevat Şener
Middle Eastern Technical University, Turkey

Dipak Singh
ERNET, India

Yousef Torman
JUNET, Jordan

Alex Voss
University of St. Andrews, UK

David West
DANTE, UK

Colin Wright
Meraka Institute, South Africa

DOI: 10.4018/978-1-61350-113-9.ch006

ABSTRACT

E-infrastructures are becoming in Europe and in other regions of the world standard platforms to support e-Science and foster virtual research communities. This chapter provides the reader with a comprehensive view of the developments of e-Infrastructures in China, India, Asia-Pacific, Mediterranean, Middle-East, Sub-Saharan Africa, South-East Europe and Latin America and with an outlook on the very important issue of their long term sustainability.

INTRODUCTION: SOME OF THE WORLD "DIVIDES"

Almost 250 years after the publication of the illuministic and equalitarian theories of J. Rousseau, today's world still suffers from a very uneven distribution of opportunities. Figures 1, 2 and 3 show, respectively, the world maps of growth competitiveness, education attainment, and digital inclusion (Maplecroft, 2008).

Looking at the maps above, two considerations can be highlighted:

First, there is a considerably strong correlation among the three quantities reported: thus several factors contribute in parallel to keep increasing the gap between more advanced and less advanced countries, inducing endemic problems like large-scale immigration, under-development, alienation, and poverty. Along the same reasoning, fighting against more than one problem simultaneously could then help to alleviate the others. As reported by the Education and Training Task Force (ETTF) of the e-Infrastructure Reflection Group (e-IRG ETTF, 2008), country studies carried out both by the Organisation for Economic Co-operation and Development (OECD) and the World Bank have confirmed an obvious correlation between investment in education and quality of life and GDP.

Second, there are several centres of excellence and "hot-spots" in many of the countries suffering from the above mentioned "divides" and there is a need for cooperation actions aiming at improving their scientific competitiveness.

In this chapter we will demonstrate how the adoption of e-Infrastructures can effectively foster scientific cooperation between several more-developed and less-developed regions of the world, thus reducing endemic problems such as the "digital divide" and the "brain drain".

THE EUROPEAN AND THE GLOBAL RESEARCH AREAS

At the onset of the 21st century, the way scientific research is carried out in many parts of the world is rapidly evolving to what is nowadays referred to as e-Science, i.e. a scientific method which foresees the adoption of cutting-edge digital platforms known as e-Infrastructures throughout the process from the idea to the production of the scientific result. The e-Science vision is depicted in Figure 4.

Scientific instruments are becoming increasingly complex and produce huge amounts of data which are in the order of a large fraction of the whole quantity of information produced by all human beings by all means. These data are often relative to inter/multi-disciplinary analyses and have to be analyzed by ever-increasing communities of scientists and researchers, called Virtual Organisations (VOs), whose members are distributed all over the world and belong to different geographical, administrative, scientific, and cultural domains. The emerging computing model which is being developed since a decade or so is what is called "The Grid", i.e. a large number of computing and storage devices, linked among them by high-bandwidth networks, on which a special software called middleware (intermediate between the hardware and the operating system and the codes of the applications) is installed,

Figure 1. Geographical distribution of growth competitiveness in the world

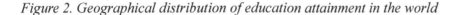

Figure 2. Geographical distribution of education attainment in the world

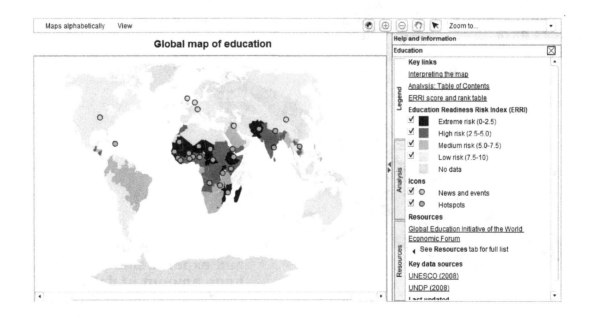

Figure 3. Geographical distribution of digital inclusion in the world

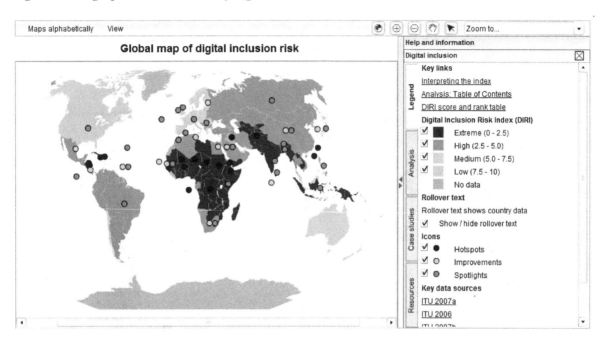

Figure 4. The vision of e-Science

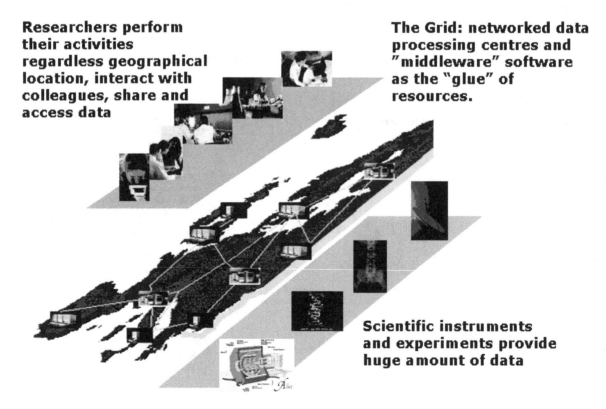

Figure 5. E-Infrastructure model of the European Research Area

allowing the resources to behave as a single huge distributed computer which dissolves in the fabric of the Internet and can be accessed ubiquitously through virtual services and high-level user interfaces. The grid and the underlying network constitute the e-Infrastructure (Figure 5).

The European Commission (EC) is heavily investing through its Framework Programmes in e-Infrastructures and this platform is by now considered as one of the key enablers of the European Research Area (ERA). In fact, at the top of the three-layers model of an e-Infrastructure there is the most important "network": the human collaboration among scientific communities of researchers that work together on unprecedented complex multi-disciplinary problems whose solu-

tions are highly beneficial for the society and the progress at large.

The European Research Education Network, which connects about 3900 Institutions in more than 40 countries in the continent, and support the work of more than 30 millions of students, teachers, and researchers, is realized in the context of the GÉANT, GÉANT2 (GÉANT2, 2009), and GN3 (GN3, 2010) projects, coordinated by DANTE (DANTE, 2010). The pan-European Grid is realized by flagship projects like the EGEE (EGEE, 2010) series, for High Throughput Computing (HTC) applications, and DEISA (DEISA, 2010) and PRACE (PRACE, 2010), for the High Performance Computing (HPC) ones.

In order to bridge the digital divide between Europe and other less developed regions of the world, over the past 6 years the European network and the European Grid have been expanded well outside the borders of the "old continent" in the context of several successful EC co-funded projects that have been complemented by other national/regional initiatives. The current "landscape" consists of: ALICE (ALICE, 2008) and ALICE2 (ALICE2, 2010) (network projects for Latin America), EUMEDCONNECT (EUMEDCONNECT, 2008) and EUMEDCONNECT2 (EUMEDCONNECT2, 2010) (network projects for the Mediterranean and the Middle-Eastern region), GÉANT2-ERNET (GÉANT2-ERNET, 2006) (network collaboration for India), ORIENT (ORIENT, 2009) (network project for China), SANREN (SANREN, 2010) (the South African National Research and Education Network), SEEREN, SEEREN2 (SEEREN2, 2008), SEE-FIRE (SEE-FIRE, 2006), and SEE-LIGHT (network projects for the South-Eastern European region), TEIN2 (TEIN2, 2008) and TEIN3 (TEIN3, 2010) (network projects for the Asia-Pacific region), the Ubuntunet Alliance (Ubuntunet, 2010) (an international initiative aiming to create a Regional Research and Education Network in Sub-Saharan Africa), EELA (EELA, 2007) and EELA-2 (EELA-2, 2010) (Grid projects for Latin America), EUAsiaGrid (EUAsiaGrid, 2010) (Grid project for the Asia-Pacific region), EUChinaGRID (EUChinaGRID, 2008) (Grid project for China), EU-IndiaGrid and EU-IndiaGrid2 (EU-IndiaGrid2, 2010) (Grid projects for India), EUMEDGRID (EUMEDGRID, 2008) and EUMEDGRID-Support (EUMEDGRID-Support, 2010) (Grid projects for the Mediterranean and the Middle-Eastern region), SAGRID (SAGRID, 2010) (the South African National Grid Initiative), and SEE-GRID (SEE-GRID, 2006), SEE-GRID2 (SEE-GRID2, 2008), and SEE-GRID-SCI (SEE-GRID-SCI, 2010) (Grid projects for the South-Eastern European region).

All together, the above mentioned projects/initiatives have created the global network and the global grid depicted in Figures 6 and 7.

All projects share the same work plan whose virtuous cycle is depicted, in a graphical way, in Figure 8.

In the following sections of this chapter we will describe all the regional e-Infrastructures cited above and, for each of them, we will show the network layer, the grid layer and the applications deployed and running underlining how the three actors enable the virtuous cycle depicted in Figure 8.

E-INFRASTRUCTURES IN THE ASIA-PACIFIC REGION

Network

Network provision in the Asia-Pacific region has long been an issue for e-Infrastructure development as it has been characterised by extreme heterogeneity, lack of connectivity and single points of failure in the links to other regions such as the US and Europe. Through the efforts of the Asia-Pacific Advanced Network (APAN, 2010) organisation and the TEIN3 (TEIN3, 2010) project, these issues are presently being addressed and the

countries in the region are now benefitting from an increasingly mature high performance network for research and education, similar to those in other regions. The third generation of the Trans-Eurasia Information Network (TEIN3) provides today a dedicated high-capacity Internet network for research and education communities across Asia-Pacific. It currently connects 11 countries in the region (Australia, China, Indonesia, Japan, Korea, Laos, Malaysia, Philippines, Singapore, Thailand and Vietnam) and provides direct connectivity to Europe's GÉANT2 network (Figure 9).

International cooperation coordinated through APAN is beginning to address network weaknesses such as bottlenecks and network disruptions such as those caused by the typhoon Morak. In that case, ASGCnet (the Taiwanese Research and Education Network) provided TEIN and APAN with a backup route to Europe during the network outage affecting them.

The recent incorporation of APAN as a legal entity based in Hong Kong will further help to strengthen the organisational arrangements and structures at the policy level to improve network provision in the region. The APAN organisation is based on the principle of national representation, with only one Primary Member from each country. Currently, there are 15 Primary Members forming a Council, the highest governing body of APAN. The governance structure of APAN follows the principles of subsidiarity as it allows individual members to operate largely under their own rules according to the policies and funding principles of their countries but benefitting from the international collaboration and coordination provided through APAN. This arrangement aims to overcome the significant differences in the socio-economic and political characteristics of countries in the region. For the sake of completeness, Figure 10 shows the Asia-Pacific backbone topology by funding source.

Figure 6. The global network

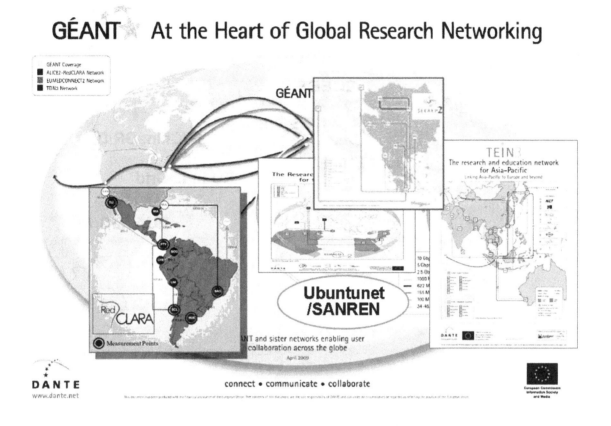

Grid

The development of grid infrastructures in the Asia-Pacific region has been driven by the participation in the CERN Large Hadron Collider (LHC, 2010) experiments as well as a number of applications of specific interest such as biomedical research, engineering applications and disaster mitigation. The EUAsiaGrid project (EUAsiaGrid, 2010), co-funded by the European Commission in the context of its Seventh Framework Program, has played a crucial role in building the capacity currently available in a number of countries such as Malaysia, Indonesia, the Philippines, Thailand and Vietnam. This infrastructure ensures that local support and key services such as user interface

nodes, compute and storage elements can be taken for granted by researchers and that the core of a sustainable e-Infrastructure in the region is put in place.

While a number of countries in the Asia-Pacific region have significant investments in e-Infrastructures for research, the level of funding is still very heterogeneous and only a few countries have National Grid Initiatives (NGIs) that provide the necessary coordination at the national level to leverage the capability of grids to provide persistent and sustainable e-Infrastructures that can be taken for granted by researchers and that enable them to focus on their substantive research. Until recently, most grid-related initiatives were based at individual institutions that sought to build up

Figure 7. The global grid

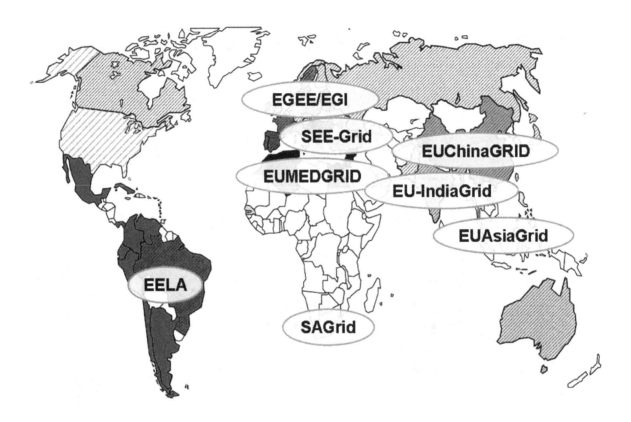

capacity to support specific research projects and application areas. As a consequence, many resource providers ended up trying to support installations with different middleware stacks, stretching their resources. Clearly, a coordinated approach to the development of a persistent and sustainable e-Infrastructure would not only maximise the return on investment by enabling a wider range of researchers to benefit from the resources but would also help resource providers cope with the heterogeneity and continuous evolution of grid technologies.

Through the coordination and support provided by EUAsiaGrid, much needed local capacity has been developed, both in terms of resources available as part of the world-wide EGEE infrastructure and in terms of the supporting human infrastructure that is needed to carry on their ongoing operation and effective exploitation by researchers. To minimize barriers to access the grid infrastructure, the EUAsiaGrid project also created and maintained a catch-all, application neutral, Virtual Organisation called EUAsia. Furthermore, several Certification Authorities (CAs) approved by the International Grid Trust Federation (IGTF, 2010) already operate in the region, with the Academia Sinica Grid Computing one (ASGCCA, 2010) serving as a catch-all CA and taking care of users of those countries that do not yet have their national CA. Any researcher

Figure 8. The virtuous cycle of regional grid projects

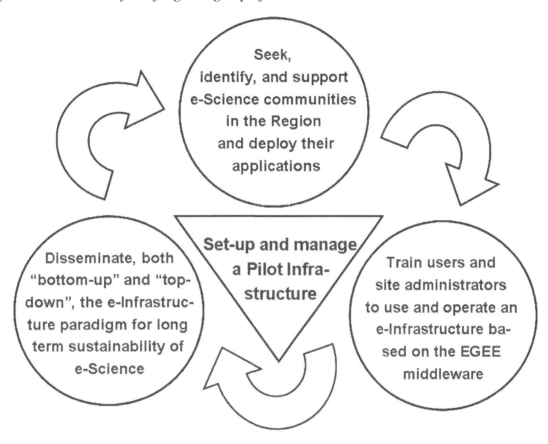

from the region interested in trying the grid for his/her research can get a certificate through a nearby Registration Authority and immediately subscribe to the EUAsia VO. Although application neutral, nodes serving this VO have installed many application packages to be easily available. Also, each partner has set up a user interface to provide local access to the grid.

The EUAsiaGrid project will come to an end in June 2010 but the EUAsiaGrid Consortium has agreed to keep open, on a best effort basis, the existing infrastructure (Figure 11) and a Memorandum of Understanding is being approved and signed by the following partners:

- Academia Sinica, Taipei, Taiwan;
- Advanced Science and Technology Institute, Quezon Cirty, Phylippines;
- CESNET, Czech Republic;
- Hydro and Agro-Informatics Institute, Bangkok, Thailand;
- Institut de la Francophonie pour l'Informatique, Hanoi, Vietnam;
- Istituto Nazionale di Fisica Nucleare, Italy;
- Institut Teknologi Bandung, Bandung, Indonesia;
- National University of Singapore, Singapore;
- Universiti Putra Malaysia, Selangor, Malaysia.

Figure 9. Topology map of the TEIN3 network

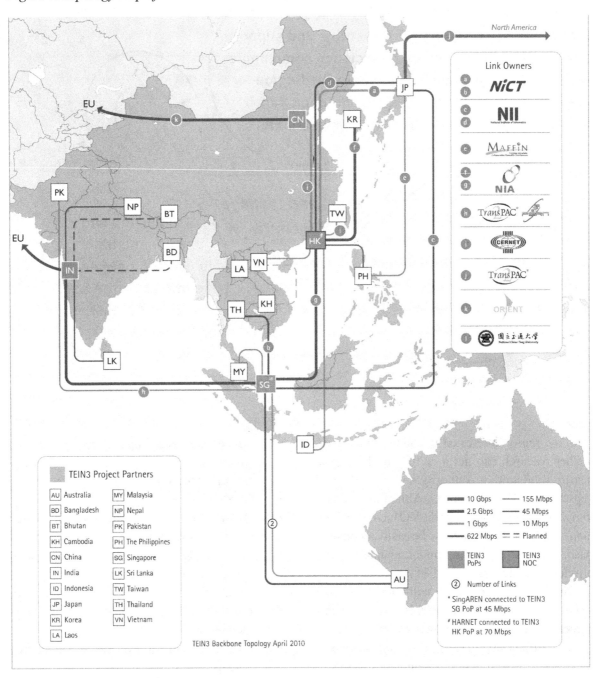

Figure 10. Asia-Pacific backbone topology by funding source

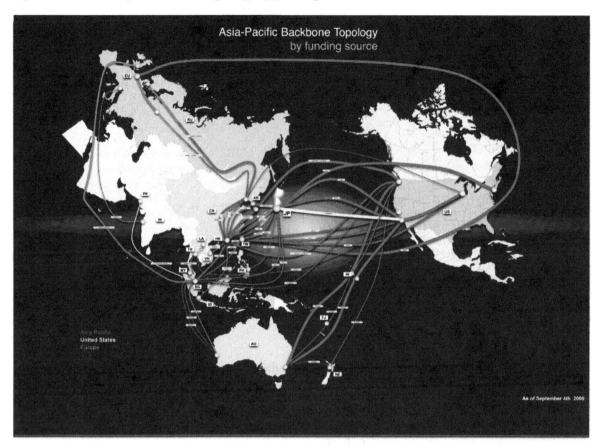

Applications

TEIN3 offers Asia-Pacific a gateway for global collaboration, enabling over 45 million users from 8,000 universities and research centres across the region to participate in joint projects (TEIN3 Applications, 2010) with their peers in Europe and other parts of the world.

The EUAsiaGrid project has also helped to identify application areas with either extensive researchers community in the region or that deal with subjects of specific interest for the Asia-Pacific region. While many such areas overlap with other regions, use of grid for disaster mitigation, life sciences, early stages of new drug discovery and cultural heritage are the most prominent new areas with the highest potential impact on society. The region faces many natural disasters, ranging from typhoons and resulting floods and landslides up to earthquakes, volcanic eruptions, and resulting tsunamis. All these disasters are usually not constrained locally and their effect spans many countries. grids, with their distributed nature, are thus ideal platforms to support region wide collaboration as well as collaboration between the region and Europe. Already started international collaborations use the grid as a computing tool for complex simulation, the most prominent example being the use of grids for earthquake simulations, where ASGC joined efforts with several other institutes in the region to build new models and develop new methods that are best suited for the distributed grid infrastructures. Also, similarly to what is happening

Figure 11. Map of the EUAsiaGrid project grid infrastructure (source: Google Maps)

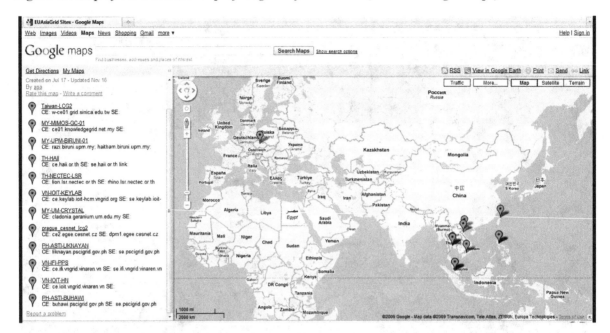

in Latin America, more and more institutions are adopting the WRF4G software (WRF4G, 2010) to model climate change and do weather forecast. On the other hand, grids are started to be used to support data gathering and fast processing from various sensors (weather and seismic stations, ocean probes for tsunami detection, etc.). This way, the adoption of grid technology is fostering the needed international collaboration for disaster prediction and mitigation.

Several data challenges have been run in the region to help the *in silico* screening of the potential drug precursors. People in the region suffer from many diseases that are either rare or neglected in the developed world, hence not in the primary focus of the pharmaceutical companies. Joining forces, with extensive use of grid infrastructures, to help with early stages of drug discovery against these diseases marks a dawn of a new era for millions of people currently without a proper cure.

The region is rich on culture, but its protection is rather weak. Digitization and use of grid technologies to process, store and publish this rich

cultural heritage at least in the digital form could keep the region richness also for future generations. Although in just early stages, this novel use of grids could have the broadest societal impact world-wide.

E-INFRASTRUCTURES IN CHINA

Network

The Chinese network for education and research is made of two infrastructures: CSTNET (CSTNET, 2010) and CERNET (CERNET, 2010). CSTNET, the China Science and Technology Network (Figure 12), is the final phase of almost eleven years long activities in developing network connections among Chinese Academy of Science's (CAS) institutes from all over China.

CSTNET is a nationwide network for the scientific and technical communities, relevant government departments and hi-tech enterprises, providing services such as network access, host trusteeship, virtual host and domain name registration. CSTNET is becoming one of the top large-scale networks in China and is playing a key role in the development of China Internet Industry.

It is made of a backbone at 10 Gb/s, Metropolitan Area Network (MAN) links at 1 Gb/s and Wide Area Network (WAN) links at 155 Mb/s – 2.5 Gb/s. The network interconnects 12 sub centres that cover more than 20 Chinese provinces, linking more than 100 research institutes of CAS and many other scientific and technical communities in the country for a total of more than 1 million end users. CERNET, the China Education and Research Network, is a network connecting hundreds of Universities in more than 20 Chinese towns (Figure 13).

The development of CERNET started in 1994 as the first IPv4 nation-wide Internet backbone. Since 2003 CERNET is evolving in to CERNET2, the largest next-generation Internet backbone which is the core network of the China Next-Generation Internet (CNGI) demonstration project, a nation-wide, and world's largest, academic network based on a native IPv6 backbone. When fully completed, CERNET2 will connect all key research universities distributed in 20 cities around China at speeds comprised between 2.5 and 10 Gb/s and it will provide IPv6 connectivity to more than 200 universities, other research institutions and R&D organizations.

The basic connection between China and the rest of the world is ensured by means of three international connections: ORIENT (ORIENT, 2009), TEIN3 (TEIN3, 2010), and GLORIAD .

ORIENT (Figure 14) is a collaborative ICT project aiming to connect the research and education networks of China and Europe. Jointly funded by China and the European Commission, the project has procured and currently operates a high capacity data-communication link between the pan-European GÉANT2 backbone network and Chinese research and education networks.

The ORIENT project, working with TEIN2 has successfully procured a 2.5 Gb/s link on the shortest-possible trans-Siberian route. In fact, ORIENT is the single largest circuit using this important east-west communications route. After a period of testing and optimisation, the circuit was brought into full production service in January 2007.

TEIN3 (Figure 9 above), the third generation of the Trans-Eurasia Information Network, provides a dedicated high-capacity Internet network for research and education communities across Asia-Pacific. TEIN3 already connects researchers and academics in China, India, Indonesia, Japan, Korea, Laos, Malaysia, Nepal, Pakistan, the Philippines, Singapore, Sri Lanka, Taiwan, Thailand, Vietnam and Australia, Bangladesh, Bhutan and Cambodia are in the process of getting connected, bringing to 19 the total number of partners involved in the project.

GLORIAD (Figure 15) is built on a fibre-optic ring of networks around the northern hemisphere of Earth, providing scientists, educators and students with advanced networking tools that improve communications and data exchange, enabling active, daily collaboration on common problems.

With GLORIAD, the scientific community can move unprecedented volumes of valuable data effortlessly, stream video and communicate through quality audio- and video-conferencing. GLORIAD exists today due to the shared commitment of the US, Russia, China, Korea, Canada, the Netherlands and the five Nordic countries of Denmark, Finland, Iceland, Norway and Sweden, to promote increased engagement and cooperation between their countries, beginning with their scientists, educators and young people. The benefits of this advanced network are shared with Science & Education (S&E) communities throughout Europe, Asia and the Americas.

Figure 12. Topology map of the CSTNET network

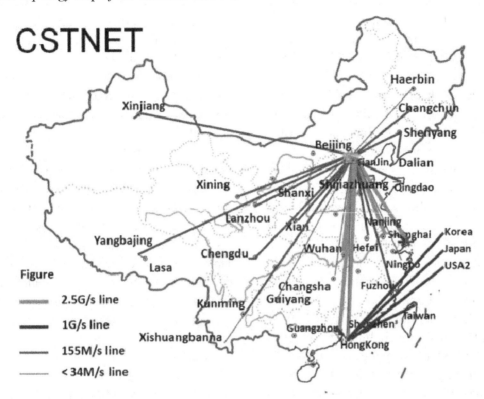

Grid

China has developed both grid middleware and nation-wide e-Infrastructures. The most relevant are:

CNGrid (Figure 16), the China National Grid Project, is supported by the "High Performance Computer and its Kernel Software" project which, in turn, is a key project belonging to the National High-Tech R&D Program. The CNGrid is a test bed for the new generation of information infrastructure by integrating high performance computing and process transaction capacity. It efficiently supports various applications including scientific research, resource and environment research, advanced manufacturing and information service by sharing resources, collaborating and service mechanism. It also propels the progress of national e-Infrastructure and related industry through technology innovation. It is based on

a middleware developed in China named GOS (Wang, 2010);

ChinaGrid (Figure 16), the China Education and Research Grid, is an important project funded by Chinese Ministry of Education and aims at constructing a public service system. It is also supported by the National High Technology Research and Development Program of China in the context of the "863 Program". The goal of ChinaGrid is to integrate heterogeneous mass resources distributed in the China Education and Research Network (CERNET), share those resources in the CERNET environment effectively, avoiding the resource islands, provide useful services, and finally form the public platform for research and education in China;

CROWN Grid is a test-bed to facilitate scientific activities in different disciplines, based on the Globus Toolkit middleware. It was formerly developed at the Beihang University and then

Figure 13. Topology map of the CERNET network

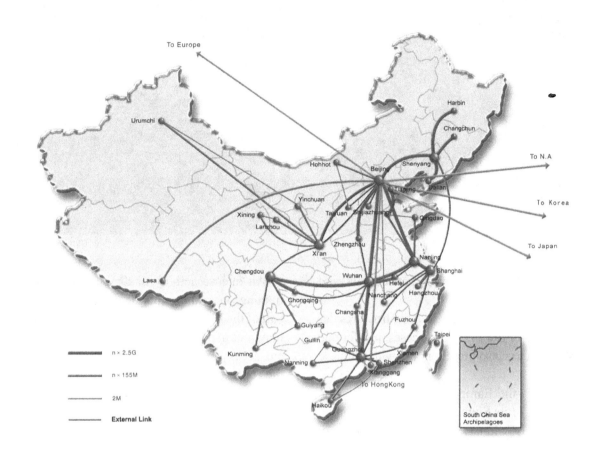

Figure 14. Pictorial map of the ORIENT network

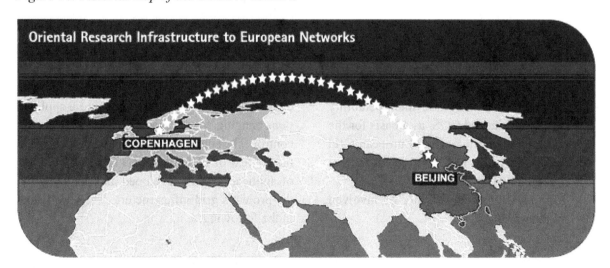

Figure 15. Topology map of the GLORIAD network

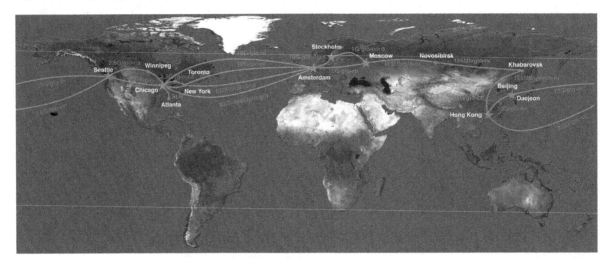

became matter of cooperation between UK and China.

A lot of other smaller grid infrastructures deployed just for few or, in some cases, just for one application are also present in the wide Chinese scenario.

In 2005, the European Commission, in the framework of its Sixth Framework Programme, funded the EUChinaGRID Project that ran from the 1st of January 2006 to the 31st of March 2008. The project aimed to foster a wider cooperation between Europe and China in the field of e-Infrastructures.

In detail, the main goals of the project were:

- To build a common grid test-bed between China and Europe (Figure 17);
- To support a set of applications which were selected as demonstrators;
- To study the middleware interoperability between gLite and GOS, as a basis for the real interconnection of the European Grid operated by the EGEE project and that managed by CNGrid;
- To study IPv6 compatibility of involved middleware.

An intense activity of dissemination of and training on grid computing paradigm was also part of the EUChinaGRID work plan and several hundreds of people were inducted to install, operate, access and use the grid services deployed in the context of the project.

The project showed the feasibility and interest of such a common infrastructure. A gateway to connect gLite- and GOS-based infrastructures was developed and the IPv6 study produced a simple code checker to verify basic IPv6 compliance and a report was prepared on components of several middleware. This activity opened the way for a serious route to interoperation between European and Chinese e-Infrastructures.

Applications

The different e-Infrastructure present in China are exploited by a large number of Chinese applications ranging from aeronautic design to forest control. The scientific domains were selected in the context of EUChinaGRID and a handful set of application was developed and deployed on the project's grid infrastructure. They are listed in the following:

Figure 16. Map of the CNGrid and ChinaGrid infrastructures

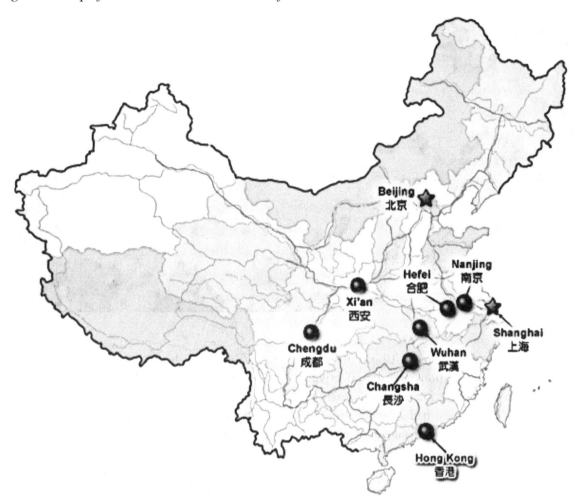

High Energy Physics: the ATLAS and CMS software simulating and analysing the data taken by the corresponding detectors installed at the CERN Large Hadron Collider. In the lifetime of the project three sites were deployed from people participating to these collaborations and the teams located at these sites were able to join the world-wide grid activities of the two large experiments.

Astroparticle Physics: the data mover of the ARGO experiment. ARGO is a cosmic ray observatory placed in Yangbajing (Tibet) and handled from a collaboration between Italian and Chinese scientists. The biggest problem of the collaboration was to transfer the acquired data from Yangbajing to Beijing and to Bologna in Italy, where the data

have to be analysed. With the support of EUChinaGRID, the ARGO collaboration was provided with a fast link between Yangbajing and Beijing, while the connection with Bologna was obtained by means of the ORIENT link with GÉANT. Specific services were developed and deployed on the project's grid infrastructure to automate the data transfer from the observatory to the analysis sites and to execute the required analysis tools.

Biology: *in silico* creation of new kinds of proteins. A collaboration among scientists coming from Italy, Poland and China computationally explored new proteins and studied their properties relevant for the creation of new compounds and drugs.

Figure 17. Map of the EUChinaGRID infrastructure

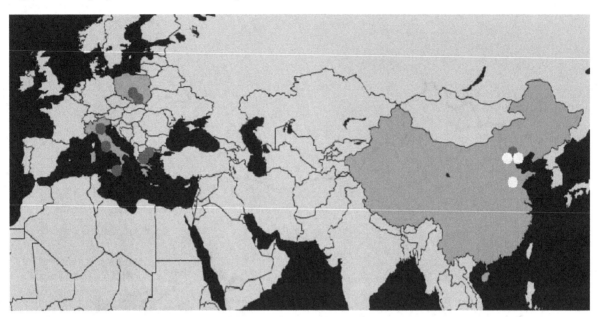

The successes obtained by EUChinaGRID in supporting these applications and the effective dissemination raises the interest in accessing and using the shared test-bed of other groups from Earth observation, health care and cultural heritage.

E-INFRASTRUCTURES IN INDIA

Network

In the last few years, the connectivity developments in India have been enormous, both at National and International level. In October 2006, as part of the EU-India co-operation program in ICT, for the first time the GÉANT-ERNET (GÉANT2-ERNET, 2006) link was established to promote collaborative research between European and India with a link at 45 Mb/s. At present, the TEIN3 link interconnects the GÉANT network with India at 2.5 Gb/s.

The most prominent landmarks in the connectivity area since 2006 have been:

- The establishment of the 45 Mb/s ERNET-GÉANT link and routing of regional WLCG (WLCG, 2010) data to CERN and subsequently the EU-IndiaGrid traffic to EGEE in 2006;

- The upgrade of the GÉANT-ERNET link from 45 Mb/s to 100 Mb/s in 2008 and then to 175 Mb/s in 2009 and the upgrade of domestic bandwidth for the Indian organisations participating to WLCG;

- The establishment of a dedicated 1 Gb/s TIFR-CERN link for LHC research in 2008 and peering with GÉANT in 2009;

- The establishment of the National Knowledge Network (NKN) in April 2009;

- The TEIN3 link at 2.5 Gb/s connecting India to GÉANT since February 2010;

- The approval, by the Government of India, of the full National Knowledge Network Plan, in March 2010, with a total budget of about 1 billion euro.

The office of Principal Scientific Adviser to the Government of India and the National Knowledge Commission (NKC, 2010) have recently recommended the creation of the National Knowledge Network (NKN) as absolutely necessary for India's development. The objective of the National Knowledge Network is to bring together all the stakeholders in Science, Technology, Higher Education, Research & Development, and Governance with speeds in the order of 10's of Gb/s coupled with extremely low latencies. NKN will interconnect all institutions engaged in research, higher education and scientific development in the country, over a period of time. It would enable use of specialized applications, which allow sharing of high-performance computing facilities, e-libraries, virtual classrooms, and very large databases.

In the initial phase of NKN, 15 core locations and about 57 institutes covering leading national R&D labs and educational institutes, have been connected at varying bandwidths of 100 to 1000 Mb/s (Figure 18).

NKN has been proposed as national program and the network will be sustained through continuous government funding. In its final phase, around 5,000 leading national academic and research institutes are going to be connected by NKN. On March 2010, the Government of India approved the full National Knowledge Network Plan with a total budget of about 1 billion euro.

NKN with its multi-gigabit, low-latency, optical fibre based backbone is acting as national transport for all existing networks. The Indian National Grid Initiative GARUDA (GARUDA, 2010) is based on NKN. The regional WLCG in India is going to be migrated to NKN. NKN will provide transport to ERNET (ERNET, 2010) (the Indian National Research and Education Network) replacing its existing backbone. The main design consideration for NKN is to create an infrastructure that can scale and adapt to future requirements.

The project's ultimate aim is to unite stakeholders in science, technology, higher education, R&D and e-governance. The NKN is expected to foster collaboration and the creation of new national intellectual assets, enabling the sharing of high-performance computing facilities, e-libraries,

virtual classrooms, and more. The NKN will also provide access to global content on emerging technologies, thus allowing close coordination among different institutions across nations. NKN will be used for the following major applications.

Education: Education is going to be a major application to be deployed over NKN. E-Learning services, Digital Libraries, Data Centres, Compute Servers, Secure monitoring systems, Information search services, voice and video conferencing across educational institutions are waiting for larges scale deployment. Besides, high-degree molecule decomposition, polymer synthesis simulations, aerodynamic and thermo-dynamic modeling are all waiting for the appropriate environment. All these applications not only require very high bandwidth, but also require real-time guarantees that the required bandwidth will indeed be available on-demand. In fact, the applications envisaged are more appropriate for India, more than any other country in the world. All of them have a direct impact on the quality of life and the quality of education in our country. Countrywide virtual classrooms alone will justify any amount of bandwidth and any amount of investment.

Health care and related sciences have experienced exponential development of knowledge and it is almost impossible for any medical library to store such huge knowledge database, which is constantly updated. The NKN will be able to address this concern as well. Also the proposed network would facilitate in reducing the differences among different medical institutions in infrastructure, teaching material, and quality of knowledge, skill and teachers. NKN will thus foster knowledge sharing and collaborative research. Besides, NKN will enable applications in the domain of telemedicine leading to better quality of life. Cardiac care, eye care, cancer care are a few applications that touch human lives.

Agriculture would be a major thrust area in the field of content creation. The content would include research on horticulture, livestock, fisheries, biochemistry, agronomy, environmental science,

Figure 18. Topology map of the NKN network

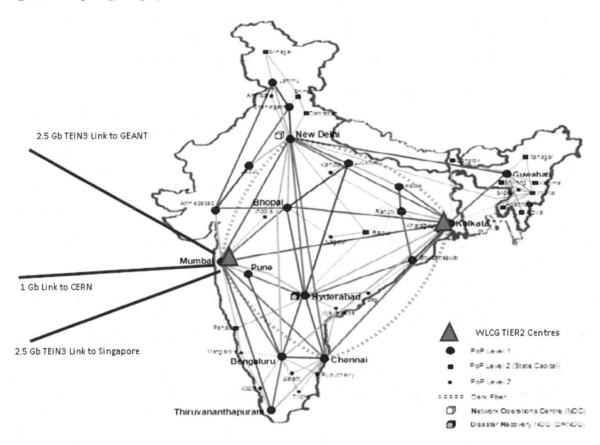

microbiology, seed research and genetics. The content shared on the proposed network would also include the agricultural statistical research, remote sensing, GIS5, production & area study and estimation.

Global R&D Applications: Today, unlike in the past, the research and development activities are not limited to few developed countries. India has been playing an increasingly important role in the global scenario and has actively contributed in development of new technologies. NKN would provide access to global content on emerging technologies, would allow close coordination among different institutions across nations. Therefore, NKN will help promote further research in specialized areas like bio-informatics, grid computing, genetics, etc.

In the design philosophy of NKN, high speed connectivity to global research networks have also been envisaged. To provide high-speed connectivity to users of NKN, a TEIN3 Point of Presence (PoP) has been co-located at the ERNET PoP in Mumbai and it is acting as hub for connecting research networks in South Asia, except Pakistan. From Mumbai, two high speed links at 2.5 Gb/s each have been commissioned to Europe and Singapore and are now operational providing direct connectivity both to GEANT and the TEIN3 PoP in Singapore. India is now acting as a hub for connectivity between Europe and the Asia-Pacific countries. The European Commission is partly funding the connectivity under TEIN3. At present, the TEIN3 PoP is located inside the

C-DAC campus in Mumbai. In the long run, it will be relocated at the NKN PoP, still in Mumbai.

Grid

In India, two main Grid Initiatives have been taken at governmental level: Regional WLCG set up by the Department of Atomic Energy (DAE), in coordination with the Department of Science & Technology (DST), and the GARUDA National Grid Initiative. The EU-IndiaGrid project, operating within the Sixth Framework Program of the European Commission, has played a bridging role between European and Indian grid infrastructures and its successor, EU-IndiaGrid2 (EU-IndiaGrid2, 2010), aims at increasing the cooperation between European and Indian e-Infrastructures capitalizing on the EU-IndiaGrid achievements.

The Worldwide LHC Computing Grid in India

The Large Hadron Collider (LHC, 2010), built at CERN near Geneva, is the largest scientific instrument on the planet and it just started its data-taking phase. In full operation, it will produce roughly 15 million gigabytes of data annually, which thousands of scientists around the world will access and analyse. The mission of the Worldwide LHC Computing Grid (WLCG, 2010) project is to build and maintain a data storage and analysis infrastructure for the entire high-energy physics community that will use the LHC. The Indian Department of Atomic Energy (DAE) is actively participating to the scientific program taking active part in CMS (CMS, 2010) and ALICE (ALICE Experiment, 2010) experiments, devoted to find answers to the most fundamental questions at the foundations of matter constituents. The data from the LHC experiments will be distributed around the globe, according to a four-tiered model. Within this model, to support researchers with required

infrastructure, India has also setup regional Tier-2 centres connected to CERN. In India there are two Tier2 centres: one for CMS at TIFR in Mumbai and one for ALICE at Saha-VECC in Kolkata. These centres provide access to CMS and ALICE users working from Tier-3 centres at Universities and national labs and LCG Data Grid services for analysis. TIFR is presently connected to CERN at 1 Gb/s and very soon it will exploit the 2.5 Gb/s TEIN3 link. Now TIFR and VECC are also being connected through NKN at 1 Gb/s.

Specific activities are also ongoing in the area of Grid Middleware Software development, devoted to ensuring grid enabling of IT systems. These activities cover the area of Grid Fabric management, Grid Data management, Data Security, Grid workload scheduling and monitoring services, fault tolerant systems, etc. DAE developed number of grid based Tools in the area of Fabric management, AFS file system, Grid View and Data Management, which are being deployed by CERN in their LHC grid operations since September 2002. So far, the number of software tools and packages such as a correlation engine, grid operations monitoring, problem-tracking system, Pool Database Backend Prototype, Scientific Library Evaluation and Development of Routines, AliEn Storage System and Andrews File System, were developed by DAE team members under a Computing Software agreement. Currently, BARC engineers are working on the enhancement of the Grid View software tool.

GARUDA: The National Grid Initiative of India

GARUDA (GARUDA, 2010) is a collaboration of scientific and technological researchers for a nation wide grid comprising computational nodes, mass storage systems and scientific instruments. It aims to provide the technological advances required to enable data and compute intensive science for the 21st century.

C-DAC, one of EU-IndiaGrid's main partners, ensures progressive evolution and durable integration as manager of the Indian National Grid Initiative and, from the start of its activity, the EU-IndiaGrid project established an excellent collaboration with GARUDA. The map of GARUDA sites is shown in Figure 19.

GARUDA has transitioned form the Proof of Concept phase to the Foundation Phase in April 2008 and currently is in its third phase: Grid Technology Services for Operational Garuda. This phase has been approved and funded for three years until July 2012.Some of the envisaged deliverables of this phase include:

- Delivering Service based grid with tools to support ease of use;
- On-demand provisioning of resources;
- Ensure QOS and end-to-end reliability for applications;
- Open and standards based implementation;
- Supports Inter-operability across grids;
- Deploy select identified application as service for end user consumption.

The GARUDA project coordinator, CDAC, established in November 2008 an IGTF recognized Certification Authority (IGCA, 2010) which allows access to worldwide grids for Indian Researchers.

GARUDA aims at strengthening and advancing scientific and technological excellence in the area of grid and peer-to-peer technologies. It will also create the foundation for the next generation grids by addressing long term research issues in the strategic areas of: knowledge and data management, programming models, architectures, grid management and monitoring, problem solving environments, tools and grid services.

The EU-IndiaGrid & EU-IndiaGrid2 Projects

EU-IndiaGrid and EU-IndiaGrid2 are part of a group of projects, funded within the Sixth and Seventh Framework Programs for Research and Scientific Development of the European Commission, which aim at integrating the European grid infrastructure with other regions in order to create one broad resource for scientists working on existing or future collaboration.

The EU-IndiaGrid project ran from 2006 to 2009. The leading responsibilities of the EU-IndiaGrid Indian partners and the project bridging role between European and Indian e-Infrastructures gave to EU-IndiaGrid project the opportunity to be at the core of the impressive developments in India in the e-Infrastructures domain and to effectively contribute at improving cooperation between Europe and India in this area. In all these activities, the role and the contribution of EU-IndiaGrid partners, as well as the bridging role of the EU-IndiaGrid project, was particularly relevant and obtained full recognition at the highest level by representatives of the Indian Government and of the European Commission so contributing at supporting the improvement of the e-Infrastructures capabilities. Its successor EU-IndiaGrid2 (EU-IndiaGrid2, 2010) will run from January 2010 to December 2011 and capitalizes on the EU-IndiaGrid achievements by acting as a bridge across European and Indian e-infrastructure to ensure sustainable scientific, educational and technological collaboration.

The project launch, on January 11th 2010, occurred in the same week of the EU-India Thematic Workshop on Research Infrastructures, one of the agreed bilateral actions under the overall ambit of India – European Union Science & Technology Cooperation. The Workshop, where the EU-IndiaGrid2 project actively contributed, underlined the role of e-Infrastructure to favor Euro-India Science and Technology cooperation and the role of agreement where the project ac-

Figure 19. Map of the GARUDA infrastructure

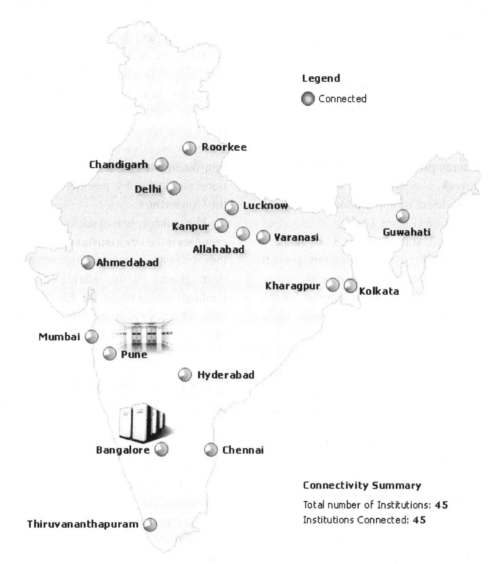

tively contributed. The EU-IndiaGrid contribution in the Euro-India e-Infrastructures cooperation's scenario and the perspectives for EU-IndiaGrid2 can be well resumed in the words of Dr. Chidambaram, Principal Scientific Advisor to the Govt. of India, who gave the opening speech both at EU-India Thematic Workshop on Research Infrastructures and at the EU-IndiaGrid2 project launch: *"I am happy to learn about the second phase EU-IndiaGrid2 project – Sustainable e-Infrastructures across Europe and India. The first phase has benefited immensely a variety of scientific disciplines including biology, earth science and the Indian collaboration for the Large Hadron Collider (LHC). The successful working of the initial phase of multi-gigabit National Knowledge Network, Indian Certification Authority, and participation in Trans-Eurasia Information Network (TEIN3) phase 3 are some of the important building blocks for supporting virtual research communities in India and their collaboration work with other countries."*

Applications

The EU-IndiaGrid e-Infrastructure successfully supported a set of applications which, with effective deployment and increasing usage of the Grid service, achieved a set of relevant results in the domains of High-Energy Physics, Biology, Material Science, Earth and Atmospheric Science. According to the vision discussed above, e-Infrastructures provide a core of services, including network, computing and storage for the benefit of a wide set of applications optimizing resource utilisation (Figure 20).

EU-IndiaGrid2, started on the 1st of January 2010, will capitalise on the previous project achievement and of its involvement in the major Indian grid initiatives providing support for the following application areas: Climate change, High Energy Physics, Biology and Material Science.

Climate change is a worldwide concern and climate change studies are among the priorities in European and Indian research programs. In particular climate change is one of the flagship activities within the NKN program. EU-IndiaGrid2 aims to support climate change modelling studies on European and Indian e-Infrastructures thanks to the involvement of premier research groups with leading international reputations and a solid collaboration basis enhanced and strengthened in the course of EU-IndiaGrid. A dedicated conference to e-Infrastructures for climate change, involving worldwide actors in this domain is within the project activity program.

High Energy Physics through the Large Hadron Collider (LHC) program represents one of the unique science and research facilities to share between India and Europe in the field of Scientific Research in general and in the ICT domain in particular. The Indian partners in the project represent both the ALICE and the CMS communities actively engaged in the LHC program. The role of the EU-IndiaGrid project in this specific activity has been widely recognised within the European Commission and the Indian

Government and EU-IndiaGrid2 will continue its action in sustaining this community.

Biology and Material Science: these broad areas require computational tools and techniques spawning different disciplines: they will challenge the project in setting up and providing cross disciplinary research services. The successful work of its predecessor EU-IndiaGrid, performed in these areas, allowed the establishment and the reinforcement of relevant EU-Indian collaborations supported by premier Institutions within the Consortium.

The enlargement of such significant user communities is the key to sustainability since motivate the e-Infrastructures existence and then drive their development. EU-IndiaGrid2 will sustain a set of applications strategic for EU-Indian collaboration, which can exploit the possibilities offered by network and grid infrastructures.

E-INFRASTRUCTURES IN LATIN AMERICA

Network

CLARA (CLARA, 2010) (Cooperación Latino Americana de Redes Avanzadas) is the legal entity responsible for the implementation and management of the network infrastructure that interconnects the Latin American NRENs: the RedCLARA. The RedCLARA backbone (Figure 21), composed of 9 nodes, interconnects 12 Latin American NRENs: RNP (Brazil), InnovaRed (Argentina), REUNA (Chile), RENATA (Colombia), CEDIA (Ecuador), RAICES (El Salvador), RAGIE (Guatemala), CUDI (Mexico), RedCyT (Panama), RAAP (Perú), RAU2 (Uruguay) and REACCIUN (Venezuela).

The RedCLARA backbone is also connected to the pan-European network GÉANT, as well as to other international research networks.

CLARA was created in June 2003, as a membership association for national NRENs in Latin

Figure 20. Schematic view of the scientific domains supported by the EU-IndiaGrid e-Infrastructure

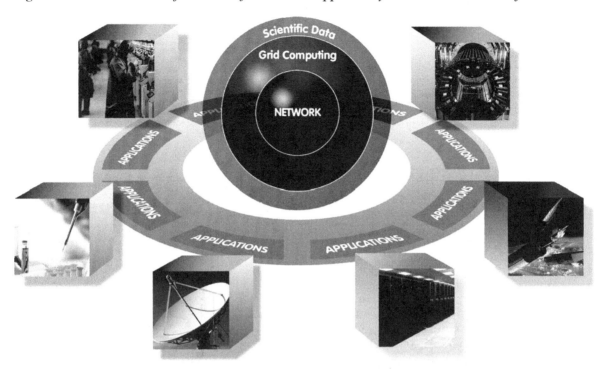

America. The European Commission EuropeAid project ALICE (ALICE, 2008), within the @LIS programme, was jointly executed between 2003 and 2008 by 4 European NRENs (from France, Italy, Portugal and Spain) and the Latin American NRENs members of CLARA, with the coordination of DANTE (DANTE, 2010), afterwards assisted by CLARA itself. The principal deliverable of ALICE was the RedCLARA network, inaugurated in September 2004. The ALICE project was in large part financed by the European Commission, with contributions from the Latin American NRENs. After ALICE termination, in March 2008, the network continued to be maintained by Latin American contributions.

In 2008, a new project, ALICE2 (ALICE2, 2010), was approved by the European Commission and will receive funding until 2012. It has as principal aim to build a robust and modern regional network, which will be financially sustainable after its end. The project, which began in November 2008, is coordinated by CLARA which

is seeking to acquire long-term access to telecommunications infrastructure, such as optical fiber and wavelengths, which can be used to provide scalable network capacity with low maintenance cost. The resulting network is expected to display large increases in bandwidth, compared with the present capacity. The first results of this new approach became available in the "Southern Cone" countries in 2009, where international links of 10 Gb/s were made available. Additionally, the ALICE2 roadmap includes the improvement of network connectivity of the individual Latin American NRENs through sharing the new telecommunications infrastructure.

In the second quarter of 2009, CLARA, InnovaRed, RNP, the AugerAccess (AugerAccess, 2009) project and Silica Networks enabled provisioning of RedCLARA's first 10 Gb/s "lambda", between Buenos Aires and Santiago of Chile. The joint infrastructure provided access to the Pierre Auger Southern Cosmic Ray Observatory (Pierre Auger, 2010) in Malargüe, Argentina.

Figure 21. Topology map of the RedCLARA backbone network

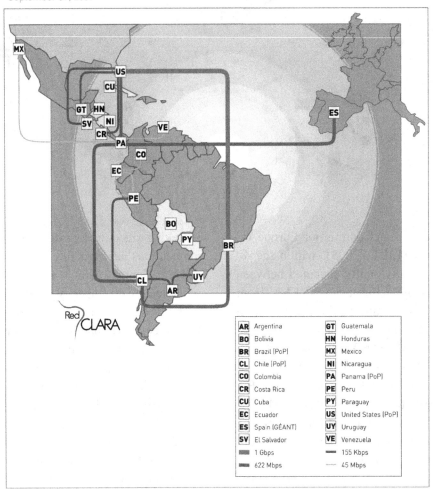

Complementary to the investments in ALICE2, Brazil will also invest up to US$ 10,000,000 in three years to fund connections between Mercosur (Mercosur, 2010) countries, which will form part of RedCLARA. This investment is complementary to ALICE2 and will be used as a contribution to counterpart funding of this project. In this context, a joint Brazil-Argentina project is under study with engineering and management under CLARA responsibility, to be operational by 2010 and connecting Buenos Aires, Rosario, Uruguaiana, Porto Alegre, and Sao Paulo. For the connection Brazil–Uruguay opportunities of acquiring optical fibre are under investigation. There are also discussions under way for a Brazil–Paraguay connection, using fibre on energy transmission lines from the Itaipu Binational hydroelectric scheme.

Plans in the remainder of the region are less well-defined, but follow the same strategy of seeking strategic partners with their own optical fibre. In many countries, the most likely candidates are electrical companies which can install optical cables along their high-voltage transmission lines. Many of these countries have agreements with their neighbours which have led to cross-border integration of electrical transmission networks, and also, as a consequence, of optical fibre networks.

In México, the local NREN CUDI is currently negotiating the creation of a new high capacity network based on optical fibres belonging to electrical companies. This network will provide 10 Gb/s links to 9 cities as well as cross border links to the neighbour countries of the US (three 10 Gb/s links) and Guatemala (a single 2.5 Gb/s link).

In Central America, since 2001, an ambitious plan for regional development, known as the Proyecto Mesoamérica, formerly Plan Puebla-Panamá (Plan Puebla-Panamá, 2010), is being carried out by the contiguous set of countries from México to Colombia with financial support from the Inter-American Development Bank (IADB) and the Central American Bank for Economic Integration (CABEI). Amongst the projects being carried out are SIEPAC (System for Electrical Interconnection of Central American countries) and AMI (Mesoamerican Information Highway), and these are expected to be completed during the lifetime of the ALICE2 project, permitting a terrestrial fibre link between Mexico and Panama (to the Colombian border).

Similar integration is going on in the northern Andean region of South America, where the Colombian electrical company ISA (Interconexiones Elétricas S.A.) is a leading player in initiatives to build transmission lines interconnecting the power grids of several countries (Colombia, Venezuela, Ecuador, Peru, Bolivia). Internexa, a telecommunications company of the ISA group, now acts as a player in the international telecommunications market and has provided connectivity for RedCLARA between Colombia, Ecuador and Peru since 2008.

Thus, there are reasonable expectations within the near future of continuous high-capacity terrestrial connections between Latin American countries from Mexico as far south as Bolivia, and also within the Southern Cone countries (Argentina, Brazil, Chile, Paraguay and Uruguay). In order to complete the North-South connectivity, there remains the gap along the Pacific coast between southern Peru and central Chile where only conventional telecommunications companies are present. This is the area of the Atacama Desert, home to several large-scale astrophysics observatories, such as Atacama Large Millimeter/submillimeter Array (ALMA), European Southern Observatory (ESO) and Cerro Tololo Inter-American Observatory (CTIO). These sites are of great interest to the international scientific community and it is expected that this will provide the necessary impetus to establish high-capacity connectivity to the international research networks, both northward, towards the terrestrial links to Central and North America, and also southward, towards to the "Southern Cone" interconnections and their submarine cable links to the US and Europe, through the provision of fibres to Peru and central Chile, in partnership with RedCLARA.

Finally, it should be emphasized that the upgrades planned in RedCLARA through the introduction of high-capacity terrestrial fibre links will also benefit the NRENs, who will be able to share the same fibre links in order to improve internal connectivity in the countries traversed by the international links. This process has already begun in Argentina, where InnovaRed is building out a new 10 Gb/s backbone network in partnership with RedCLARA (and others). This is expected to serve as the new paradigm for NREN deployment in the foreseeable future.

Grid

The EELA-2 Project (EELA2, 2010) (E-science grid facility for Europe and Latin America) is by far the most inclusive initiative that has gone on in Latin America in the area of distributed computing infrastructures. EELA-2, ended on the 31st of March 2010, aimed at building a high capacity, production-quality, scalable grid to answer the needs of a wide spectrum of applications from European-Latin American scientific collaborations.

Its focus was on:

- Offering a complete set of versatile services fulfilling Applications requirements;
- Ensuring the long-term sustainability of the e-Infrastructure beyond the term of the project.

Such an ambitious project would not have been possible without the prior existence of a consolidated e-Infrastructure, set up with the early intention to build a sustainable grid platform. This was the objective of the EELA first-phase (EELA, 2008) project that provided its users with a stable and well supported grid which proved, over 2006-2007, that the deployment of an European-Latin American e-Infrastructure was not only viable but also responding to the real needs of a significant part of the Scientific Community.

By the end of the project, the EELA-2 Consortium encompassed 78 Institutions from 16 countries, 5 from Europe (France, Ireland, Italy, Portugal and Spain) and 11 from Latin America (Argentina, Brazil, Chile, Colombia, Cuba, Ecuador, Mexico, Panama, Peru, Uruguay and Venezuela).

The EELA-2 infrastructure, shown in Figure 22, consists of 29 Resource Centres for a total of 8,000 CPU cores and 200 TB of storage.

Applications

The EELA project and its successor EELA-2 deployed a very strong dissemination plan to promote grid computing within new institutions and scientific communities in several Latin American countries. As a result, most of the institutions participating in the consortium proposed an application to be ported to the grid infrastructure of the project.

Overall, 61 applications from 8 different scientific domains (Bioinformatics, Civil Protection, Computer Science and Mathematics, Earth Science, Engineering, Fusion, High Energy Physics, and Life Sciences) were supported by the project during its lifetime.

At the end of EELA-2 (31st of March 2010), 53 applications (out of the 61 supported in total) were completely deployed and interfaced with the grid middleware (Table 1). Besides these, several Resource Centres also supported the applications of the 5 Virtual Organizations related to well known High Energy Physics experiments such as ALICE (ALICE Experiment, 2010), ATLAS (ATLAS, 2010), CMS (CMS, 2010), LHCb (LHCb, 2010), and the Pierre Auger Observatory (Pierre Auger, 2010).

Based on the experience acquired supporting the aforementioned applications, it can be said

Figure 22. Map of the EELA-2 infrastructure (source: Google Maps)

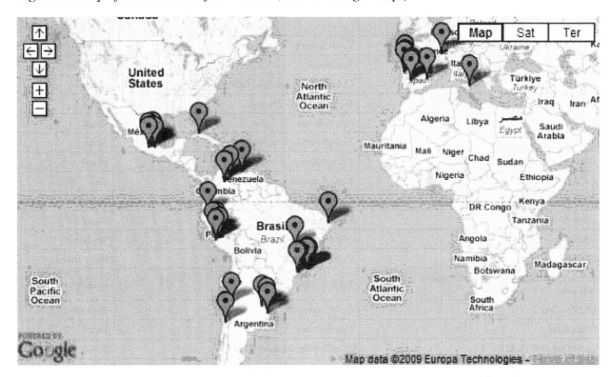

that grid users in Latin America may be broadly divided into three groups: (i) those participating in collaborative experiments which requires High Throughput Computing (HTC) across many computing and storage clusters; (ii) those that have true computational and storage demands that cannot be handled by their local resources in a reasonable time - these users require to access extra resources belonging to others only for the purpose of attending the excess in their workload; and (iii) those with modest computational needs that could be easily handled by a local cluster or storage server. In this case, the affiliation of these groups with a large grid project might allow them to overcome the digital divide just by granting access to extra computing resources.

Such a diversity of users is one of the consequences of the grid expansion across many institutions/countries facing different maturity levels of IT infrastructures, network connections and e-science awareness. This is also reflected on

the application's profile. On one hand, EELA-2 supports applications that runs thousands of parallel jobs per week each one lasting for many hours and handling gigabytes of data, but on the other hand there is also "bag-of-task" applications that runs one single job on an occasional basis and consumes a very few computing resources.

The complete list of applications supported by EELA-2, as well as their descriptions and references, can be inspected at (EELA-2 applications, 2010).

E-INFRASTRUCTURES IN THE MEDITERRANEAN AND THE MIDDLE-EAST

Network

The EUMEDCONNECT (EUMEDCONNECT, 2008) project, co-funded by the European Com-

Table 1. Applications fully deployed on the EELA-2 e-Infrastructure

Application	Scientific Domain	Country
AERMOD	Earth Sciences	Cuba
AeroVANT	Engineering	Argentina
Aiuri	Computer Science and Mathematics	Brazil
BiG (Blast)	Bioinformatics/Genomics	Spain
BioMD	Life Sciences	Brazil
bioNMF	Bioinformatics/Genomics	Spain
BRAMS	Earth Sciences	Brazil
C/CATT-BRAMS	Earth Sciences	Chile / Brazil
CAM	Earth Sciences	Spain
CardioGrid Portal	Life Sciences	Argentina
CATIVIC	Life Sciences (Chemistry)	Venezuela
Cinefilia	Computer Science and Mathematics	Italy / Brazil
CIS - Classification of Satellite Images with neural networks	Earth Sciences	Ecuador
CROSS-Fire	Civil Protection	Portugal
DicomGrid	Life Sciences	Brazil
Dist-SOM-PORTRAIT	Bioinformatics/Genomics	Brazil
DistBlast	Bioinformatics/Genomics	Brazil
DKEsG	Fusion	Spain
DRI/Mammogrid	Life Sciences (e-Health)	Spain
eIMRT	Life Sciences (e-Health)	Spain
FAFNER2	Fusion	Spain
fMRI	Life Sciences (e-Health)	Portugal
G-HMMER	Bioinformatics/Genomics	Colombia
G-InterProScan	Bioinformatics/Genomics	Colombia
GAMOS	Life Sciences	Spain
gCSMT	Earth Sciences	France
GenecodisGrid	Bioinformatics/Genomics	Spain
GrEMBOSS	Bioinformatics/Genomics	Mexico
Grid Bio Portal	Bioinformatics/Genomics	Spain
GRIP - Grid Image Processing for Biomedical Diagnosis	Life Sciences	Chile
GROMACS	Life Sciences (Chemistry)	Brazil
gRREEMM	Engineering	Cuba
gSATyrus	Computer Science and Mathematics	Brazil
Heart Simulator	Life Sciences	Brazil
HeMoLab	Life Sciences	Brazil
Industry@Grid	Engineering	Brazil
Integra-EPI	Life Sciences	Brazil
InvCell	Life Sciences	Brazil
InvTissue	Life Sciences	Brazil

continued on following page

Table 1. Continued

Application	Scientific Domain	Country
LEMDistFE	Engineering	Mexico
MAVs-Study	Engineering	Argentina
META-Dock	Bioinformatics/Genomics	Mexico
Phylogenetics	Life Sciences	Spain
PhyloGrid	Life Sciences	Spain
PILP	Computer Science and Mathematics	Portugal
Portal de Porticos	Engineering	Venezuela
ProtozoaDB	Life Sciences	Brazil
PSAUPMP	Engineering	Mexico
SATCA	Earth Sciences	Mexico
Seismic Sensor	Earth Sciences	Mexico
SEMUM3D	Earth Sciences	France
WAM	Earth Sciences	Ireland
WRF	Earth Sciences	Spain

mission in the context of its Sixth Framework Program, has played a pioneeristic role in the promotion of Communication Networks, as fundamental components of e-Infrastructures in the Mediterranean. This activity is currently being coordinated with two main initiatives: the EUMEDCONNECT2 (EUMEDCONNECT2, 2010) project and the recently launched Arab Scientific Research and Education Network (ASREN) initiative.

EUMEDCONNECT2, a follow-up of EUMEDCONNECT, is co-funded by the European Commission in the context of its Seventh Framework Program and aims to sustain and upgrade the high-capacity IP-based data-communications network serving the research and education communities in seven countries across the southern Mediterranean, enabling them to participate in collaborative projects. Offering a direct link to GÉANT, its pan-European counterpart, EUMEDCONNECT2 allows approximately 2 million users in around 700 institutions across North Africa and the Middle East to collaborate with their peers at more than 3,000 research and education establishments in Europe. EUMEDCONNECT2, whose topology map is shown in

Figure 23, acts as a real gateway to global research collaboration.

The Arab Mediterranean countries participating in the EUMEDCONNECT project series (Morocco, Algeria, Egypt, Palestine, Jordan and Syria) have signed the "Rome Declaration" in September 2006. These countries stated that they will support the establishment of National Research & Education Networks (NREN) in their countries, lead the efforts to further develop this regional network, and also conduct the proper promotion among these countries to use this research infrastructure. These countries are currently working to establish a legal organisation called ASREN which will focus on raising the necessary funds to build the regional network and to promote the use of networks and e-Infrastructures in research and education.

Grid

Co-funded by the European Commission within the Sixth Framework Programme, the EUMEDGRID (EUMEDGRID, 2008) has run in parallel but in conjunction with EUMEDCONNECT project and has supported the development

Figure 23. Topology map of the EUMEDCONNECT2 network

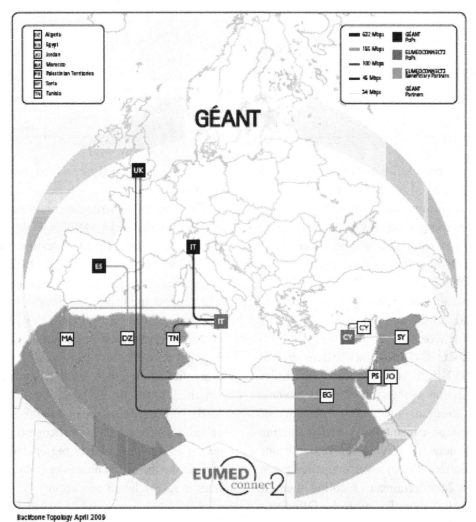

Backbone Topology April 2009

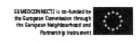

of a grid infrastructure in the Mediterranean area. EUMEDGRID also promoted the porting of new applications on the grid platform, thus allowing Mediterranean scientists to collaborate more closely with their European colleagues. EUMEDGRID has disseminated grid awareness and competences across the Mediterranean and, in parallel, identified new research groups to be involved in the project, helping them to exploit grids' enormous potential to improve their own research activities.

The implementation and coordination of a grid infrastructure at a national (or wider) level can be regarded as an opportunity to optimize the usage of existing, limited storage and computing resources and to enhance their accessibility by all research groups. This is particularly relevant for the non-EU countries involved in the project.

Sustaining the European and Mediterranean Countries

Many research fields have indeed very demanding needs in terms of computing power and storage capacity, which are normally provided by large computing systems or supercomputing centres. Furthermore, sophisticated instruments may be needed to perform specific studies. Such resources pose different challenges to developing economies: they are expensive, they need to be geographically located in a specific place and they cannot attract a critical mass of users because they are usually very specific and are relevant only for small communities of researchers scattered across the country/region. This is the case even in some strategic domains such as water management, climate change, biodiversity and biomedical activities on neglected or emerging diseases. Thus, a significant part of researchers is forced to emigrate to more developed countries to be able to continue their scientific careers. However, thanks to the creation of global virtual research communities and distributed e-Infrastructure environments, all these drawbacks can be overcome: through an appropriate access policy, different user groups can use resources wherever dispersed, according to their availability. Furthermore, geographically distributed communities working on the same problem can collaborate in real time thus optimizing not only hardware and software resources but also human effort and brainware.

The EUMEDGRID project was conceived in this perspective and has set up a pilot grid infrastructure for research in the Mediterranean region which is interoperable and compatible with that of the EGEE project and related initiatives. The EUMEDGRID's vision focused on improving both the technological level and the know-how of networking and computing professionals across the Mediterranean thus fostering the introduction of an effective Mediterranean Grid infrastructure for the benefits of e-Science.

The EUMEDGRID achievements can be categorised into two main areas:

1. The creation of a *human network* in e-Science across the Mediterranean.
2. The implementation of a pilot grid infrastructure, with *gridified* applications, in the area.

Impact of EUMEDGRID

Cooperation among all the participants has been demonstrated by the enthusiastic participation to common workshops and meetings organized during the lifetime of EUMEDGRID and the success obtained fostering the creation of National Grid Initiatives and national Certification Authorities (CAs) officially recognized by IGTF. Impressive results were also obtained in the events of knowledge dissemination on grid technology and services. A large community, including system administrators, researchers, and final users, was involved with good results in terms of number of participants (more than 700 individuals) and feedback obtained through dedicated questionnaires.

The promotion of National Grid Initiatives carried out in all non-EGEE Partner Countries registered a good level of success with programmes already operational in Algeria, Egypt, Morocco and Tunisia and well advanced plans in Jordan and Syria. The national impact and policy level awareness in some of these countries has led to an initial financial support of the initiatives.

The project has been very active in promoting the creation of national Certification Authorities which issue digital certificates necessary to allow secure grid access to the users. The process is completed in Morocco, the first African Country to become member of EUGridPMA (EUGridPMA, 2010), the international organisation to coordinate the trust fabric for e-Science grid authentication in Europe, and well advanced in the other countries. In the meanwhile, a temporary catch-all CA was set-up at INFN in order to fulfil the needs of EUMEDGRID users not having a Certification Authority in their countries (see Figure 24).

A pilot grid infrastructure, composed to date of 25 sites in 13 countries, was set up during the time span of EUMEDGRID.

Besides its scientific mission, EUMEDGRID had also a significant socio-economic impact in the beneficiary countries. Fostering grid awareness and the growth of new competences in EU Neighbours' scientific communities is a concrete initiative towards bridging the digital divide and the development of a peaceful and effective collaboration among all partners.

e-Infrastructures also contribute to mitigate the so-called "brain-drain" allowing brilliant minds in the area to stay in their regions and contribute significantly to cutting edge scientific activities, concretely enlarging the European Research Area (ERA). Research and Education Networks and grids are fundamental infrastructures that will allow non-EU researchers to carry out high quality work in their home laboratories without the need to migrate in more advanced countries.

An extended Mediterranean Research Area could thus be seen as a first step towards the realisation of more politically ambitious plans of open market, open transportation infrastructures, free circulation of citizens, etc.

Finally, the EUMEDGRID Consortium has agreed before coming to an end to keep open, on a best effort basis, the existing Infrastructure and a formal agreement has been approved and signed by the following partners:

- Centre de Recherche sul l'Information Scientifique et Technique (CERIST), Algeria.
- Centre de Calcul Khawarezmi (CKK), Tunisia.
- Centre National pour la Recherche Scientifique et Technique (CNRST), Morocco.
- Consortium GARR (GARR), Italy.
- Cyprus Research and Academic Network (CYNET), Cyprus.
- Egyptian Universities Network (EUN), Egypt.
- Electronic Research Institute (ERI), Egypt.
- Greek Research and Technology Networks S.A. (GRNET), Greece.
- Higher Institute of Applied Sciences and Technology (HIAST), Syrian Arab Republic;.
- Jordanian University Network (JUNET), Jordan.
- Istituto Nazionale di Fisica Nucleare (INFN), Italy.
- Tubitak Ulusal Akademik ag ve Bilgi Merkezi (TUBITAK ULAKBIM), Turkey.
- Universita ta Malta (UoM), Malta.

EUMEDGRID-Support

EUMEDGRID finished in 2008 but the new project EUMEDGRID-Support (EUMEDGRID-Support, 2010), co-funded by the European Commission,

Figure 24. EUMEDGRID partners operating grid sites

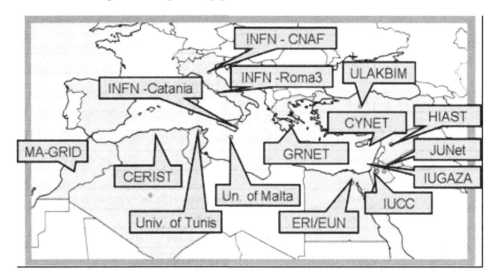

has recently started on the 1ˢᵗ of January 2010 and will continue until the 31ˢᵗ of December 2001. EUMEDGRID-Support obviously builds on EUMEDGRID outcomes and aims at:

Pushing for a consolidation of the existing EUMEDGRID infrastructure and for the development of sustainable e-Infrastructures in the Mediterranean region in a broad, general, meaning.

Promoting the completion of the process of creation of Certification Authorities in the Mediterranean Countries.

Exploiting the maximum level of synergy with other initiatives and projects and specifically cooperate with the EPIKH (EPIKH, 2010) project for advanced knowledge dissemination actions.

Applications

Several applications have been deployed on the EUMEDGRID infrastructure spanning different fields of interest: High Energy Physics, Biology and Biomedicine, Hydrology, Archaeology, Seismology and Volcanology. New communities and applications of regional interest were also discovered during the lifetime of the project by means of a survey based on a web questionnaire.

The list of EUMEDGRID applications is reported in Table 2.

Several of the applications reported in Table 2 were *gridified* during a dedicated event: the first EUMEDGRID School for Application Porting (EGSAP-1, 2007) that was held in Cairo on the 17ᵗʰ – 28ᵗʰ of April 2007. Conceived as a full immersion experience for selected new communities of regional interest, the school was the first event of this type in the Mediterranean region deemed of paramount importance for the uptake of new applications on the regional pilot infrastructure. EGSAP-1 was accordingly one of the largest dissemination efforts in the whole lifetime of the project, involving personnel from the beneficiary countries and instrumental for the involvement of new communities in the project activities. It provided them with the knowledge needed to build upon the e-Infrastructure and deploying their own applications. All selected applications were ported to the EUMEDGRID e-Infrastructure and several of them were even integrated in the GENIUS (GENIUS, 2010) web portal.

Table 2. Applications deployed on the EUMEDGRID e-Infrastructure

Application	Country	Institute
ARCHAEOGRID	Italy	University of Florence
CODESA-3D	Italy - Tunisia	CRS4
GROGET	Morocco	Faculté des Sciences de Meknes
HERO	Egypt	Helwan University
HuM2S	Turkey	Bogazici Univerisy
JP2_GRID	Tunisia	ESSTT
MINSP	Syria	HIAST
PAREL	Tunisia	ESSTT
SACATRIGA	Morocco	UAE/FST Laboratory of Radiation & Nuclear Systems
SimCommsys	Malta	University of Malta
Grid Taxation	Greece	University of Macedonia
McStas	Italy	University of Roma TRE
An evolutionary model with Turing machines	Italy	University of Roma TRE
ASTRA	Swiss/Italy	CERN, INFN, Conservatorio di Salerno

E-INFRASTRUCTURES IN SOUTH-EAST EUROPE

Network

In the past 6 years, a number of targeted initiatives funded by the European Commission via its RTD programmes, as well as national and regional funding sources, have contributed to bridging the digital divide in the South-Eastern European (SEE) region.

The SEEREN and SEEREN2 (SEEREN2, 2008) (South-East European Research and Education Networking initiatives) projects have established the SEE segment of the pan-European GÉANT network and successfully connected the research and scientific communities in the region. Most of the countries in the region are now part of GÉANT. Currently, the SEE-LIGHT project is working towards establishing a dark-fibre backbone that will interconnect most national Research and Education networks in the region. The dark fibre backbone is funded by Hellenic Plan for the Economic Reconstruction of the Balkans

(HiPERB). The topology of available fibres at the study/analysis stage is show in Figure 25.

Grid

The SEE-GRID (SEEGRID, 2006) and SEE-GRID2 (SEE-GRID2, 2008) (South-East European GRid e-Infrastructure Development) projects have established a strong human network in the area of scientific computing and have set up a powerful regional grid infrastructure, and attracted a number of applications from diverse fields from countries throughout South-East Europe. The current SEE-GRID-SCI (SEE-GRID-SCI, 2010) project, ending in April 2010, empowers the regional user communities from fields of meteorology, seismology and environmental protection in common use and sharing of the regional e-Infrastructure. Current dedicated resources for these 3 major VOs are in the order of 2000 CPU cores and 300 TB of storage, spread over more than 40 grid sites (Figure 26).

The joint regional operations consist of maintaining deployed core services for SEEGRID

Figure 25. Topology map of the SEE-LIGHT network

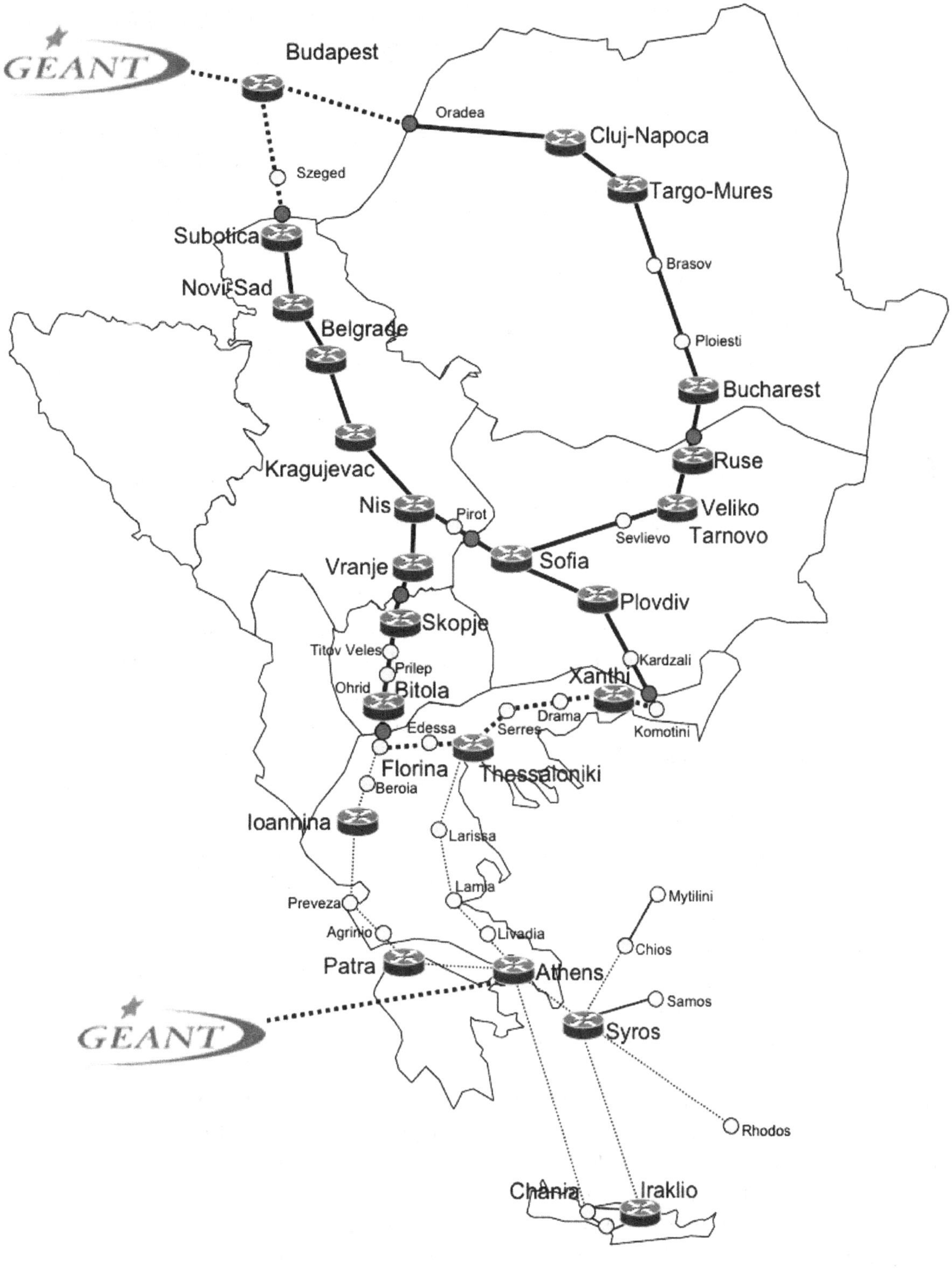

Figure 26. Map of the SEE-GRID-SCI infrastructure

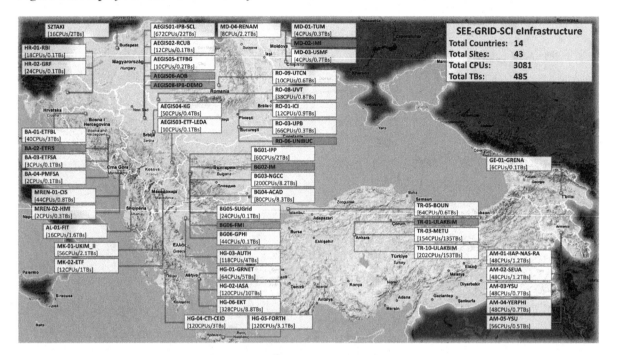

Virtual Organisation and three discipline-specific VOs, as well as core services for the ops.vo.egee-see.org VO used for testing of the infrastructure. A set of operational and monitoring tools is maintained and used to manage and assess the status of the infrastructure. In this way, operations are distributed and countries which are not part of pan-European EGEE infrastructure are effectively supported.

The grid initiatives are coordinated by the Greek Research & Technology Network (GRNET, 2010) and the wider consortium, which is in long-term formalised via a Memorandum of Understanding for a multi-national Joint Research Unit, consists of representatives from National Grid Initiatives of Bulgaria (IPP), Romania (ICI), Turkey (ULAKBIM), Albania (UoPT), Bosnia-Herzegovina (UoBL), FYR of Macedonia (UKIM), Serbia (UOB), Montenegro (UOM), Moldova (RENAM), Armenia (IIAP NAS RA), Georgia (GRENA) and Azerbaijan (Institute of Physics).

The wider SEE region can be considered as a model region that has achieved European e-Infrastructures full integration, apart from network aspects where the non-GÉANT countries such as Albania, Bosnia-Herzegovina and Caucasus still require specific funding actions for network links.

The High Performance Computing initiatives in SEE are starting in different countries separately, with an upcoming HP-SEE project to coordinate them at a regional level.

Applications

The regional user communities from fields of meteorology, seismology and environmental protection are currently the ones most strongly supported in the current SEE-GRID-SCI project. The previous two phases of the project (SEEGRID and SEE-GRID2) supported a very diverse variety of scientific fields, consisting of around 30 applications from high-energy physics, biomedicine and life sciences, astrophysics, computer science, electronics, metallurgy, etc. The current support

Figure 27. World map of the scientific divide

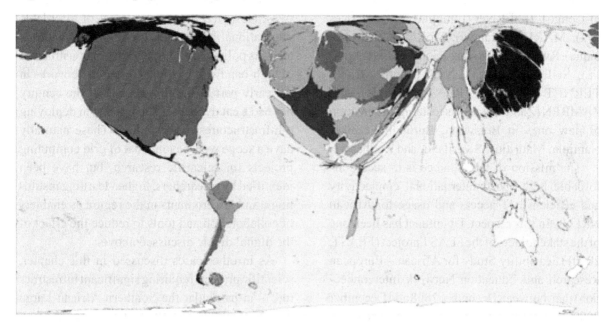

focus is on: Seismology VO, which has six applications ranging from Seismic Data Service to Earthquake Location Finding, from Numerical Modelling of Mantle Convection to Seismic Risk Assessment; Meteorology VO, with two comprehensive applications, following an innovative approach to weather forecasting that uses a multitude of weather models and bases the final forecast on an ensemble of weather model outputs, while the other problem attacked is the reproduction/ forecasting of the airflow over complex terrain; Environmental (Protection) VO, which supports eight applications focusing on environmental protection/response and environment-oriented satellite image processing (SEE-GRID-SCI user communities, 2010).

E-INFRASTRUCTURES IN SUB-SAHARAN AFRICA

Network

With few exceptions, African universities and research centres lack access to dedicated global research and education resources because they are not connected to the global infrastructure consisting of dedicated high capacity regional networks. The consequence is that research and higher education requiring such access can currently not be conducted in Africa and the continent is not well represented in the global research community. This is witnessed by the world map of scientific divide (Figure 27) where territory size shows the proportion of all scientific papers (published in 2001) written by authors living there (Worldmapper, 2010).

An important bottleneck is the lack of direct peering with other research and higher education networks. This bottleneck can be removed only by creating dedicated National Research and Education Networks (NRENs) connecting research and tertiary education institutions in each African country to a Regional Research and Education Network (RREN) interconnected to the peer infrastructures on other continents. In this context, a pioneering and very important role has been played by the Ubuntunet Alliance (Ubuntunet, 2010). Incorporated in 2006, Ubuntunet gathers the following 12 NRENs in Eastern and

Southern Africa: Eb@le (Democratic Republic of Congo), EthERNet (Ethiopia), KENET (Kenya), MAREN (Malawi), MoRENet (Mozambique), RwEdNet (Rwanda), SomaliREN (Somalia), SUIN (Sudan), TENET (South Africa), TERNET (Tanzania), RENU (Uganda), and ZAMREN (Zambia) and it is fostering the creation of new ones in Botswana, Burundi, Lesotho, Namibia, Mauritius, Swaziland, and Zimbabwe.

The mission of the Alliance is to secure affordable high speed international connectivity and efficient ICT access and usage for African NRENs. In this respect, Ubuntunet has been one of the stakeholders of the FEAST project (FEAST, 2010) (Feasibility Study for African – European Research and Education Network Interconnection) that, between December 2008 and December 2009, has studied the feasibility of connecting African NRENs to the GÉANT network and has documented the relevant issues in the region inhibiting these enabling technologies. In its final study (FEAST final report, 2010), FEAST has identified the opportunities available in Sub-Saharan Africa in terms of new intercontinental submarine cables with abundant capacity (Figure 28) and emerging regional and national terrestrial fibre optic backbones.

FEAST has also paved the way for the creation of the AfricaConnect consortim that should take care, under the coordination of DANTE, of the creation, in the next 3-4 years, of a RREN in Sub-Saharan Africa at a total cost of 15 M€, 80% funded by the European Commission and the rest co-funded by the beneficiary countries.

Grid

Notwithstanding the large dissemination activities of strategic projects, such as IST-Africa (IST-Africa, 2010), EuroAfrica-ICT (EuroAfrica-ICT, 2010), and eI-Africa (eI-Africa, 2010), co-funded by the European Commission in the context of its Sixth and Seventh Framework Programs, the Sub-Saharan region of Africa has seen the least

amount of activity in distributed computing initiatives. However, the recent advent of affordable international bandwidth, the reform of national telcoms policies and the subsequent construction of high-bandwidth national research networks in the early part of the first decade of the century has had a catalytic effect on interest in deploying e-Infrastructures in the region. These naturally have a scope well-beyond that of grid computing projects for scientific research, but have been identified by researchers, higher-learning institutions, and governments in the region as enablers of collaboration and tools to reduce the effect of the digital divide discussed above.

As in other cases discussed in this chapter, scientific projects requiring significant infrastructure – in particular the Southern African Large Telescope (SALT, 2010) and the Karoo Array Telescope (KAT, 2010) – were great stimuli of the interest in deploying networks and grids in the region. The remote location of the scientific equipment and the wide geographic separation of the members of the collaborations using it were prime motivators, for example, for the development of the South African NREN. Data sharing considerations were long a concern, too, for the South African participation to two experiments of the Large Hadron Collider. Two groups of research centres participate to the ALICE and ATLAS experiment, respectively, and the hub of medical and fundamental nuclear physics research undertaken at the iThemba Laboratories was one of the original drivers for experimenting with a national data and compute grid.

South Africa is the only country in the Sub-Saharan region with a dedicated activity to coordinate distributed computing, which started with two projects centrally funded by Department of Science and Technology. These were the national research and education network (SANREN, 2010) and the Centre for High-Performance Computing (CHPC, 2010), which was inaugurated in 2006. The plan for a high-speed network connecting the country's universities and national laboratories

Figure 28. Map of the submarine cables currently available around Africa

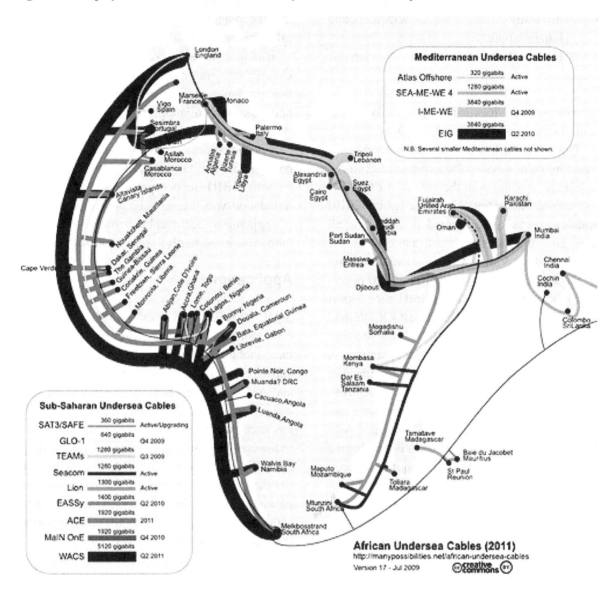

generated interest in the creation of a federated distributed computing infrastructure based on the grid paradigm. The creation of a Joint Research Unit in mid-2008 was the start of this project, which aimed to integrate existing computing clusters and storage distributed in the institutes into a national grid computing platform.

The South African National Grid (SAGRID, 2010) by the start of 2010 consisted of a federation of seven institutes taking part in grid operations and belonging to the SAGrid JRU:

- Meraka Institute (Cyberinfrastructure Programme, Pretoria)
- University of Cape Town, including the UCT-CERN Research Centre
- University of the Free State (Bloemfontein)
- University of Pretoria (Pretoria)
- North-West University (Potchefstroom)

- University of Johannesburg (Johannesburg)
- University of the Witwatersrand (Johannesburg)
- iThemba Laboratory for the Accelerator-Based Sciences (Faure)

with open activities under way for futher inclusion of other universities in the country.

The development of the national grid was based in many ways on the experience acquired in Europe, starting with the model of EGEE-III and regional activities. The gLite (gLite, 2010) middleware stack was adopted as standard at all sites, ensuring that the infrastructure would be easily used by Virtual Organisations operating on the EGEE resources. Integration into operational tools such as the Global Grid User Support (GGUS), Grid Operations Database (GOCDB) and monitoring tools such as the Real Time Monitor (RTM) and GSTAT ensure that the operations in South Africa are performed in a compatible manner to that of the other international infrastructures.

Grid computing services and identity management are most often secured and managed with X.509-standard digital certificates issued from a trusted Certificate Authority. A major obstacle in the Sub-Saharan region was the lack of a CA accredited by IGTF. Since there is indeed no region of the IGTF responsible for Sub-Saharan Africa, the nearest Policy Management Authority (PMA) is that responsible for Europe and the Near East: EUGridPMA. A proposal to accredit a new CA for South Africa, the SAGrid CA (SAGrid CA, 2010), was accepted by EUGridPMA in 2009 and full accreditation is expected in early 2011. To avoid delays, the INFN CA (INFN CA, 2010) has assigned Registration Authorities in several South African institutes which are able to issue digital certificates for individuals and services locally.

The grid infrastructure in South Africa makes of course use of the high-bandwidth SANReN network and aims to integrate the distributed computing resources attached to it providing their users with a powerful platform for collaboration and scientific research. This platform, due to its

interoperability and operation as a single unit, can be considered as an extension of international infrastructures elsewhere, and access and usage of it is to a large degree location-independent. Coordinated training and development events both in South Africa and the broader region, undertaken in collaboration with the GILDA t-Infrastructure (GILDA, 2010) have expanded the base of competent site administrators and users, in concert with similar activities undertaken by the EUMEDGRID-Support project (see above). This foundation work is essential in developing the base of applications, technical experts and eventually (and most importantly) users in the region.

Applications

South Africa stands apart from the rest of the continent with a substantial research infrastructure, including e-Infrastructure. South African participation to the LHC experiments ALICE and ATLAS – both heavily dependent on grid computing – since 2004 and 2009, respectively, has accelerated usage of distributed computing in the country. The EGEE Virtual Organisations BIOMED and e-NMR have also been enabled on the sites belonging to the SAGrid infrastructure, providing access to researchers in these domains to these applications, while contributing resources from South Africa.

Other domains, notably astronomy, biodiversity and bio-informatics, have also had a long interest in distributed data and computing activities in a grid paradigm. The recent existence of the national grid infrastructure described above has greatly accelerated these and with participation to projects such as EPIKH (EPIKH, 2010) this usage is expanding to many other domains. The dedicated application porting schools run by South African and other partners in EPIKH have seen several new applications being ported to the grid, in research domains such as:

- Detector design and simulation
- Gene sequencing

- Molecular dynamics
- Distributed data management for the Southern African Large Telescope
- Computer science and genetic programming
- Human language technologies

Trans-national research and collaboration has traditionally not been very common in the region, resulting in exacerbating the so-called "digital divide" and "brain drain" effects. In recognition of this certain projects have been identified and funded to stimulate these kinds of e-Science activities which would make use of e-Infrastructure in the region. Two of these will be mentioned here: ERINA4Africa (ERINA4Africa, 2010) and the HP/UNESCO project "Piloting Solutions for Reversing Brain Drain into Brain Gain for Africa" (HP/UNESCO, 2009).

ERINA4Africa (Exploiting Research Infrastructure PotentiAl for boosting research and innovation in Africa) is an project co-funded by the European Commission under the "Research Infrastructures" program to extend the lessons learned during the ERINA study (ERINA study, 2008)) in Europe, and provide African and European policy makers with an analysis of scenarios for exploiting e-Infrastructures. ERINA4Africa also makes use of the results of the FEAST project and its identified "lighthouse demonstrators". These are applications and research activities identified as having a high chance of success given access to advanced e-Infrastructures, especially high-bandwidth networks and compute grids. Examples of these, from the FEAST final study, are:

Collection of DNA from malaria patients at the University College of Medicine in Blantyre, Malawi, to be analysed in collaboration with the University of Liverpool, UK.

The High-Performance Liquid Chromatography (HPLC) laboratory at Makerere University (Uganda) and Muhimbili University of Health and Allied Sciences (MUHAS) in Dar-es-Salaam (Tanzania), in collaboration with the Karolinska Institute in Stockholm, Sweden.

Notably, the UbuntuNet Alliance is a partner in both the FEAST and ERINA4Africa projects, providing a hub of coordination in the region from their base in Malawi together with work done by other non-network specific infrastructure projects in South Africa, such as SAGrid.

The HP/UNESCO project aims to address the "digital divide" and "brain drain" issues by providing resources and training to selected research projects throughout the African continent, with many of them in the Sub-Saharan region. The ultimate goal is to re-establish links between researchers who have stayed in their native countries and those that have left, connecting scientists to international colleagues, research networks and funding opportunities. Faculties and students at beneficiary universities will also be able to work on major collaborative research projects with other institutions around the world. The beneficiaries of the project are institutes from Burkina Faso, Cameroon, Ethiopia, Ghana, Ivory Coast, Kenya, Senegal, and Uganda whose research projects, based on High Performance and Grid Computing, are selected by an advisory panel. Together with GILDA and SAGrid, training is being provided to these beneficiaries on the usage and potential of Grid applications, as well as the deployment of new sites in their countries. So far, almost 200 scientists and technicians have been trained.

FUTURE PERSPECTIVES AND LONG-TERM SUSTAINABILITY

The large uptake, in several regions of the world, of the e-Infrastructure paradigm for e-Science by virtual research communities belonging to many diverse scientific domains makes their long term sustainability a crucial issue.

Sustainability is, in a general sense, the capacity to maintain a certain process or state indefinitely. The term has its roots in ecology as the ability of an ecosystem to maintain ecological processes, functions, biodiversity, and productivity into the future. Sustainable development is a pattern of resource use that aim to meet human needs while preserving the environment so that these needs can be met not only in the present, but in the indefinite future.

World's sustainable development is based on three fundamental pillars (Figure 29):

1. Social development: also known as social change, refers to:
   a. Change in social structure: the nature, the social institutions, the social behaviour or the social relations of a society, community of people, and so on.
   b. Any event or action that affects a group of individuals that have shared values or characteristics.
2. Environmental protection: is the process of making sure current processes of interaction with the environment are pursued with the idea of keeping the environment as pristine as naturally possible.
3. Economic development: is made of three building blocks, i.e. information, integration, and participation.

As shown in Figure 29, (i) A system that meets conditions 1. & 2. is defined as bearable; (ii) A system which meets conditions 1. & 3. is defined as "equitable"; and (iii) A system which meets conditions 2. and 3. is defined as "viable". Only systems that meet all of the three conditions are sustainable. Grid-based e-Infrastructures can effectively be compared to the real world if one makes the following fundamental analogy: *Grids are complex "ecosystems" of services "sold" and "bought" by virtual communities.* This analogy allows to make the correspondences between the real world's and the e-Infrastructures' pillars of sustainable development shown in Table 3.

By the same analogy, the pillars of e-Infrastructures' sustainable development can then be depicted as shown in Figure 30.

One of the conditions for the real word's sustainable development is the occurrence of a social change (also referred to as social development). By the same analogy stated above, this means that an e-Infrastructure can be sustainable only if a change occurs in the way we consider and support Virtual Organisations of users. Any model of long-term sustainable e-Infrastructures should then put the user at the centre and be scalable and dependable.

E-Infrastructure Sustainability in Europe

The model and structure of a sustainable Europe-wide e-Infrastructure have been the focuses of the European Grid Initiative Design Study (EGI_DS, 2009) project that ran from the 1st of September 2007 to the 31st of December 2009. The ultimate goal of EGI_DS was indeed the conceptual setup and operation of a new organizational model of a sustainable pan-European grid infrastructure. One of the major outcomes of EGI_DS was the EGI Blueprint (EGI Blueprint, 2008) which describes the proposal developed by the project to establish a sustainable grid infrastructure for science in Europe in place by the end of EGEE in April 2010. The Blueprint is based on the vision of a large pan-European distributed computing and data grid infrastructure responding to the needs and requirements of the research community in

Table 3. Correspondences between real world's and e-Infrastructures' pillars of sustainable development

Real world	e-Infrastructures
Social development	Virtual Organisations
Environmental protection	Resource Centres + Service Providers = National Grid Initiatives
Economic development	Middleware services, Application support, and Training

Figure 29. The pillars of world's sustainable development

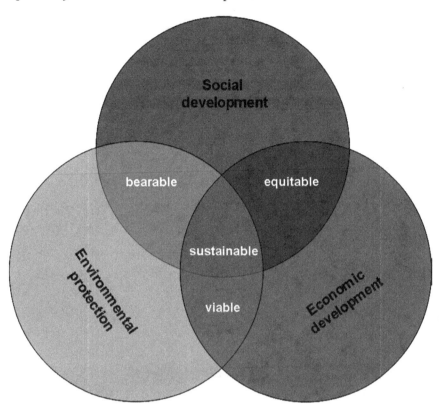

the European Research Area (ERA, 2010) (ERA) as described in the EGI Vision Document (EGI Vision, 2007) that sets the following objectives for the European Grid Initiative:

- Ensure the long-term sustainability of the European e-infrastructure.
- Coordinate the integration and interaction between National Grid Infrastructures.
- Operate the European level of the production grid infrastructure for a wide range of scientific disciplines to link National Grid Infrastructures.
- Provide global services and support that complement and/or coordinate national services (Authentication, VO-support, security, etc).
- Coordinate middleware development and standardization to enhance the infrastructure by soliciting targeted developments

from leading EU and National Grid middleware development projects.

- Advise National and European Funding Agencies in establishing their programmes for future software developments based on agreed user needs and development standards.
- Integrate, test, validate and package software from leading grid middleware development projects and make it widely available.
- Provide documentation and training material for the middleware and operations. (NGIs may wish to make the material available in turn in their local language).
- Take into account developments made by national e-science projects which were aimed at supporting diverse communities.
- Link the European infrastructure with similar infrastructures elsewhere.

Figure 30. The pillars of e-Infrastructures sustainable development

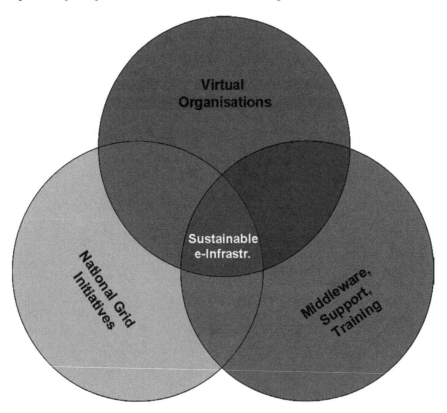

- Promote grid interface standards based on practical experience gained from grid operations and middleware integration activities, in consultation with relevant standards organizations.
- Collaborate closely with industry as technology and service providers, as well as grid users, to promote the rapid and successful uptake of grid technology ·by European industry.

The ideas of the EGI Blueprint have been further expanded in the last year and have finally brought to the creation of the legal entity EGI.eu (EGI, 2010) which has been incorporated in the Netherlands in February 2010. EGI.eu will run the continental e-Infrastructure with funds coming both from the European Commission (through the project EGI-InSpire) and the National Grid

Initiatives of the various member countries. In more detail, EGI.eu will:

- Ensure the long-term sustainability of the European e-Infrastructure.
- Coordinate the integration and interaction between National Grid Infrastructures.
- Operate the European level of the production grid infrastructure for a wide range of scientific disciplines.

It is worth noting that basically all the countries involved in the grid projects addressing the South-Eastern European area are now members of EGI.eu.

E-Infrastructure Sustainability in India

The Commitment of Indian Government and its scientific community towards e-Infrastructures marked the beginning of 2010 with three major events:

1. The Government approval for the establishment of the National Knowledge Network (already operational in its initial phase).
2. The entering of GARUDA National Grid Initiative in its full operational phase (phase 3) and its NKN based high speed connectivity.
3. The deployment of the TEIN3 high speed links with Europe and South East Asia.

These landmarks represent at the same time the result of the impressive evolution in e-Infrastructures in the last few years in India and the foundations for a sustainable approach in the next future.

NKN will enable scientists, researches and students from diverse spheres across the country to work together for advancing human development in critical and emerging areas. Health, Education, grid Computing, Agriculture and e-Governance are the main applications identified for implementation and delivery on NKN. Combined with the interconnection at high speed towards Europe and South East Asia, thanks to TEIN3 and with the support to GARUDA connectivity, NKN will provide the necessary e-Infrastructure services for the benefit of outstanding applications, in a national and international framework, motivating the investment and supporting its long term sustainability.

E-Infrastructure Sustainability in the Mediterranean

The new EUMEDGRID-Support (EUMEDGRID-Support, 2010) project will be instrumental to support long term sustainability of e-Infrastructures in the Mediterranean area. EUMEDGRID-Support will run from January 2010 to December 2011 and builds on the successful outcomes of the EUMEDGRID (EUMEDGRID, 2008) project.

The work already done in the EUMEDGRID project led to a pilot Grid Infrastructure which covers almost all the Mediterranean Area. EUMEDGRID-Support will start from there and make a further step to push towards a larger production quality e-Infrastructure and the adoption of more sustainable organisational models for the provision of services. To maximise impact, EUMEDGRID-Support adopts a two-fold approach:

1. **Bottom-up:** serving to raise awareness among researchers, students and technical personnel who can greatly benefit from using e-Infrastructures in their work.
2. **Top-down:** bringing into sharp relief the need for a policy framework developed with funding bodies highlighting the value-add and need for e-Infrastructures to empower researchers and advance the frontiers of scientific research.

There is no need for e-Infrastructures without a user community correspondingly exploiting them. The project has taken the important responsibility to support existing user's applications and assist new applications that will run on the Mediterranean e-Infrastructure. This activity is also committed to study and deliver a strategy for the long-term sustainability of the support system that will be put in place during the project lifetime. These goals will be achieved through:

- Supporting the applications of relevance in the region.
- Identifying new relevant applications.
- Creating a two-tier Competence Centre that will support application porting.

E-Infrastructure Sustainability in Latin America

Long term sustainability of e-Infrastructure has been one of the main concerns of the EELA-2

(EELA-2, 2010) project. During its course, EELA-2 has developed the model of a dependable Latin American Grid Initiative (EELA-2 DSA1.3, 2008). The LGI model defines precisely the long-term objectives at each level, Institution (Resource Centres - RC), Country (National Grid Initiatives – NGI or Equivalent Domestic Grid Structures - EDGS) and Continent (Latin American Grid Initiative - LGI), of the e-Infrastructure.

The roles envisaged for the different components of the e-Infrastructure are the following:

1. Institution Level - Resource Centres (RC):
    ○   Get all RC Services fully operational at all GISELA sites.
    ○   Responsibility: The Institution housing the RC. Indeed the RC is a self-contained and self-governed grid environment, providing all services required to its proper operation independently from any other infrastructure.
2. Country Level - Grid Operation Centre (GOC):
    ○   Implement all GOC Services at the country level.
    ○   Responsibility: The JRU and later the NGI / EDGS governance when created.
3. Continent Level - Grid Support Centre (GSC) & Network Support Centre (NSC):
    ○   Implement all GSC and NSC Services at the Latin America level.
    ○   Provide a catch-all GOC for a duration depending on the NGI / EDGS creation and estimated to last about 2 years.
    ○   Responsibility: The LGI governance.

The GISELA Project

During EELA-2, the LGI model presented above has been discussed with and approved by CLARA. It will be implemented in the course of the GISELA (Grid Initiatives for e-Science virtual communities in Europe and Latin America) project that has been selected for funding in the context of the European Commission's call FP7-INFRASTRUCTURES-2010-2 and will start in Fall 2010. According to the GISELA work plan, CLARA will take the responsibility of the operation of LGI and will integrate network and grid coordination.

Between the end of EELA-2 and the start of GISELA, the Latin American Grid Infrastructure will be operated by the IGALC (Iniviativa de Grid de America Latina y Caribe) Regional Operation Centre (IGALC, 2010) whose support has been secured by means of a Memorandum of Understanding signed by the EELA-2 members.

No web site is on-line yet for GISELA but its coordinator Bernard Marechal (co-author of this chapter and reachable at marechal@if.ufrj.br) can be considered as the official contact.

E-Infrastructure Sustainability in Asia-Pacific

The EUAsiaGrid project has developed a roadmap (EUAsiaGrid roadmap, 2010) to outline the pathway towards the persistent and sustainable infrastructure of the future, integrated with the European Grid Initiative and other Regional Grid Initiatives such as the Latin American Grid Initiative.

Based on the experience with creating regional grid infrastructures in Europe and in Latin America and building on the experience with existing regional collaborations at the network level such as APAN, the EUAsiaGrid roadmap foresees, as first step, the establishment of the Asia Pacific Grid Initiative (APGI) to provide international coordination and collaboration within the region. This is especially important as there are no political structures in the region providing the same level of coordination provided by the European Commission. APAN has been successfully established in the area of networking to provide international coordination based on national networking initiatives and efforts like PRAGMA (PRAGMA, 2002) witness that there is sustained interest in the use of grid technologies for research.

This demonstrates that there is potential within the region to develop a persistent sustainable e-Infrastructure based on national initiatives and funding with the APGI providing the necessary international collaboration platform and coordination mechanisms that will ensure that the societal benefits are maximised. As National Grid Initiatives are not yet established in many countries and international collaboration is very fragmented, it is not possible to simply suggest a straightforward adoption of a model such as the one provided by the EGI Blueprint. Instead, the EUAsiaGrid roadmap proposes to start with the development of the AGPI as an umbrella organisation for different collaborations of individual institutions. Over time, these collaborations will give rise to the development of coalitions of institutions collaborating at the national level, based on local institutes that have already proved their willingness to foster the e-Science approach through their active involvement, for example within EU-funded research projects. In order for the APGI to be scalable and sustainable, these coalitions will need to evolve into fully-fledged National Grid Initiatives (NGI) with the necessary funding and societal mandate.

At the international level, the roadmap proposes the creation of the APGI as a lose federation of institutions agreeing to a set of general operating principles and procedures that ensure a sufficient degree of coordination and collaboration between individual institutions and coalitions while leaving them free to establish the internal governance mechanisms and operating principles that they require. To distinguish these initial arrangements from the model that the roadmap ultimately aims to establish – the APGI as an incorporated international organisation based on the representation of National Grid Initiatives – in the roadmap they call it the Asia-Pacific Grid

Initiative Union (APGI-U). It will play the role of a forum for the exchange of expertise in the development of sustainable e-Infrastructures and through its standard operating principles and procedures will foster an increasing alignment of initiatives at the national level with the emerging Asia-Pacific e-Infrastructure, laying the foundations for a transition towards a model based on formal representation by National Grid Initiatives and the establishment of APGI as an incorporated international organisation comparable to the EGI. eu organisation in Europe.

At the operational level, APGI-U will build on the existing infrastructure established through the EGEE Asia Federation and the EUAsiaGrid project, leveraging existing arrangements such as the Asia-Pacific Grid Policy Management Authority (APGridPMA, 2010) for the governance of Certification Authorities and the Asia-Pacific Regional Operating Centre (APROC, 2010) for operational support and monitoring of the e-Infrastructure. APGI-U will also work closely with other projects and initiatives within the region, such as APAN at the network level and PRAGMA, to exchange expertise about evolving Grid technologies.

The EUAsiaGrid roadmap outlines a model for the gradual establishment of the necessary national and international structures required to continue to build and to sustain an Asia-Pacific e-Infrastructure for research. Starting from a flexible model based on the federation of individual contributing institutions, the model contains the necessary elements that will ensure that the structure can evolve over time to accommodate a larger number of participating resource providers and users by introducing National Grid Initiatives as important entities that can coordinate activities at a national level, allowing the national coordination of funding arrangements and policy making while reaping the benefits gained by increased international collaboration.

The first steps to establish the APGI-U have already been taken with the help of the EUAsiaGrid project and as part of the preparation of the EGI-InSPIRE and CHAIN project (see below) proposals. APGI-U is being formed based on the experiences made in the contexts of APAN and PRAGMA and will collaborate closely with these initiatives, enabled by overlapping memberships. The standard operating principles and procedures that are part of this roadmap have been developed based on prior experience and with a view to ensuring openness while providing enough structure to ensure that the aim of establishing a persistent and sustainable e-Infrastructure can be achieved and that a reliable and predictable process is put in place that will encourage participation by all stakeholders, potential resource providers, funders and researchers alike.

The CHAIN Project

In the framework of the European Commission's call FP7-INFRASTRUCTURES-2010-2, opened in July 2009 and closed in November 2009, the CHAIN[1] (Co-ordination and Harmonisation of Advanced eINfrastructures) proposal was submitted and got approved. It is expected to start on the 1st of December 2010 and will last for a period of two years.

CHAIN ultimate goal is to coordinate and leverage the efforts made and the results achieved over the past six years by the European Commission co-funded projects aiming at creating e-Infrastructures in different regions of the world. CHAIN will define and implement the vision of a harmonised and optimised interaction model for e-Infrastructures and specifically grid interfaces between Europe and the rest of the world. The project will elaborate a strategy, define the instruments and deploy them in order to ensure coordination and interoperation of the European Grid Infrastructures with other external e-Infrastructures.

The CHAIN consortium, consisting of leading organisations in Europe, Africa (both the Mediterranean and the Sub-Saharan part), Asia

(China, India and the Asia-Pacific region), and Latin America, will ensure global coverage, European leadership, and most efficient leveraging of results with respect to preceding regional initiatives. First, the project will define and deploy a coherent operational and organisational model, where a number of EU countries/regions will act, in collaboration with EGI.eu, as bridges/gateways to other Regions/Continents. Further, the project will validate this model by supporting the extension and consolidation of worldwide virtual communities, which increasingly require distributed facilities (large instruments, distributed data and databases, digital repositories, etc.) across the regions for trans-continental research.

Finally, the project will act as a worldwide policy-watch and coordination instrument, by exploring and proposing concrete steps for the coordination with other initiatives and studying the evolution of e-Infrastructures.

CONCLUSION

E-Infrastructures based on large-bandwidth dedicated wide area networks and on geographically distributed computing and storage resources, are becoming paradigmatic platforms to enable e-Science and e-Research by those virtual research communities known as Virtual Organisations. Thanks to dedicated projects co-funded by the European Commission, in the context of its Framework Programmes, network and grid infrastructures are becoming global and are providing their users with cutting edge High Throughput and High Performance Computing services operated around the clock. In this chapter a comprehensive view of the developments carried out in China, India, Asia-Pacific, Mediterranean, Middle-East, Sub-Saharan Africa, South-East Europe and Latin America has been provided, together with an outlook on the crucial issue of long term sustainability.

REFERENCES

ALICE2. (n. d.). Retrieved from http://alice2.rcdclara.net

ALICE. (n. d.). Retrieved from http://alice.dante.net

APAN. (n. d.). Retrieved from http://www.apan.net

APGridPMA. (n. d.). Retrieved from http://www.apgridpma.org

APROC. (n. d.). Retrieved from http://aproc.twgrid.org

ASGCCA. (n. d.). Retrieved from: http://www.twgrid.org/ en/ index.php?option=com_ content &task=view&id=27&Itemid=153

ATLAS. (n. d.). Retrieved from http://www.cern.ch/atlas

AugerAccess. (n. d.). Retrieved from http://www.augeraccess.net

Blueprint, E. G. I. (n. d.). Retrieved from http://www.eu-egi.eu/ fileadmin/ public/ EGI_DS_D5_3_V300b.pdf

CERNET. (n. d.). Retrieved from http://www.edu.cn/ english_1369 / index.shtml

CHPC. (n. d.). Retrieved from http://www.chpc.ac.za

CLARA. (n. d.). Retrieved from http://www.redclara.net/ index.php?lang=en

CMS. (n. d.). Retrieved from http://www.cern.ch/ cms

CSTNET. (n. d.). Retrieved from http://www.cstnet.net.cn/ english / index.htm

DANTE. (n. d.). Retrieved from http://www.dante.net

DEISA. (n. d.). Retrieved from http://www.deisa.org

e-IRG ETTF (n. d.). Retrieved from:

EELA. (n. d.). Retrieved from http://www.eu-eela.org/ first-phase.php

EELA-2. (n. d.). Retrieved from http://www.eu-eela.eu

EELA-2 applications (n. d.). Retrieved from http://applications.eu-eela.eu

EELA-2 DSA1.3 (n. d.). Retrieved from:

EGEE. (n. d.). Retrieved from http://www.eu-egee.org

EGI. (n. d.). Retrieved from http://www.egi.eu

EGI_DS (n. d.). Retrieved from http://www.eu-egi.eu

EGSAP-1. (n. d.). Retrieved from http://www2.eumedgrid.eu/ egsap-1

eI-Africa (n. d.). Retrieved from http://www.ei-africa.eu

EPIKH. (n. d.). Retrieved from http://www.epikh.eu

ERA. (n. d.). Retrieved from http://ec.europa.eu/ research/era

ERINA4Africa (n. d.). Retrieved from http://www.erina4africa.eu

ERINA study. (n. d.). Retrieved from http://www.erina4africa.eu/ docs/ ERINA-Dissemination-Report.pdf/ at_download/file

ERNET. (n. d.). Retrieved from http://www.eis.ernet.in

EU-IndiaGrid2 (n. d.). Retrieved from http://www.euindiagrid.eu

EUAsiaGrid. (n. d.). Retrieved from http://www.euasiagrid.eu

EUAsiaGrid road map (n. d.). Retrieved from http://www.euasiagrid.eu/ roadmap

EUChinaGRID. (n. d.). Retrieved from http://www.euchinagrid.eu

EUGridPMA. (n. d.). Retrieved from http://www.eugridpma.org

EUMEDCONNECT2. (n. d.). Retrieved from http://www.eumedconnect2.net

EUMEDCONNECT. (n. d.). Retrieved from http://www.eumedconnect.net

EUMEDGRID. (n. d.). Retrieved from http://www2.eumedgrid.eu

EUMEDGRID-Support. (n. d.). Retrieved from http://www.eumedgrid.eu

EuroAfrica-ICT. (n. d.). Retrieved from http://www.euroafrica-ict.org

Experiment, A. L. I. C. E. (n. d.). Retrieved from http://www.cern.ch/alice

FEAST. (n. d.). Retrieved from http://www.feast-project.eu

FEAST final report (n. d.). Retrieved from http://www.feast-project.org/documents/FEAST-Final-Report-2010-03-22.pdf

GN3. (n. d.). Retrieved from http://www.geant.net

GARUDA. (n. d.). Retrieved from http://www.garudaindia.in

GÉANT2. (n. d.). Retrieved from http://www.geant2.net

GÉANT2-ERNET. (n. d.). Retrieved from http://global.dante.net/ server/ show/ nav.1416

GENIUS. (n. d.). Retrieved from https://genius.ct.infn.it

GILDA. (n. d.). Retrieved from https://gilda.ct.infn.it

gLite (n. d.). Retrieved from http://www.glite.org

GRNET. (n. d.). Retrieved from http://www.grnet.gr

HP/UNESCO. (n. d.). Retrieved from http://www.unesco.org/ en/ higher-education/ reform/ brain-gain-initiative

http://documents.eu-eela.org/ getfile.py?docid=1099&name= EELA-2-DSA1.3-v1.11&format=pdf&version=1

http://www.e-irg.eu/images/stories/ publ/ task_force_reports/ ettf_long_report_final_july08.pdf

IGALC. (n. d.). Retrieved from http://www.igalc.org

IGCA. (n. d.). Retrieved from http://ca.garudaindia.in

IGTF. (n. d.). Retrieved from http://www.igtf.net

INFN CA. (n. d.). Retrieved from http://security.fi.infn.it/CA/en

IST-Africa. (n. d.). Retrieved ftom http://www.ist-africa.org

KAT. (n. d.). Retrieved from http://www.kat.ac.za

LHC. (n. d.). Retrieved from http://www.cern.ch/lhc

LHCb. (n. d.). Retrieved from http://www.cern.ch/lhcb

Maplecroft (n. d.). Retrieved from http://maplecroft.org

Mercosur (n. d.). Retrieved from http://www.mercosur.int

NKC. (n. d.). Retrieved from http://www.knowledgecommission.gov.in

(n. d.). *Orient (Paris)*. Retrieved from http://global.dante.net/ server/ show/ nav.1418.

Pan Puebla- Panamá. (n. d.). Retrieved from http://www.planpuebla-panama.org

Pierre Auger. (n. d.). Retrieved from http://www.auger.org

PRACE. (n. d.). Retrieved from http://www.prace-project.eu

PRAGMA. (n. d.). Retrieved from http://pragma. sdsc.edu

SAGRID. (n. d.). Retrieved from http://www. sagrid.ac.za

SAGrid CA. (n. d.). Retrieved from http://www. sagrid.ac.za / index.php/ ca.html

SALT. (n. d.). Retrieved from http://www.salt. ac.za

SANREN. (n. d.). Retrieved from http://www. meraka.org.za/ sanren.htm

SEE-FIRE. (n. d.). Retrieved from http://www. seefire.org

SEE-GRID2. (n. d.). Retrieved from http://www. see-grid.eu

SEE-GRID. (n. d.). Retrieved from http://www. see-grid.org

SEE-GRID-SCI. (n. d.). Retrieved from www. see-grid-sci.eu

SEE-GRID-SCI user communities (n. d.). Retrieved from: http://www.see-grid-sci.eu/ user_communities/ index.php?language=en

SEEREN2. (n. d.). Retrieved from http:/www. seeren.org

TEIN2. (n. d.). Retrieved from http://www.tein2. net

TEIN3. (n. d.). Retrieved from http://www.tein3. net

TEIN3. (n. d.). Retrieved Applications, from http:// www.tein3.net/ server/ show/ nav.2201

Ubuntunet (n. d.). Retrieved from http://www. ubuntunet.net

Vision, E. G. I. (n. d.). Retrieved from http://www. eu-egi.eu/ vision.pdf

Wang, Y., Cheng, Y., & Chen, G. (2010). Interoperability between GOS and gLite. In S. C. Lin & E. Yen (Eds.), *Production grids in Asia: Applications, developments and global ties* (pp. 155-173). Springer, US: Business Media, LLC 2010.

WLCG. (n. d.). Retrieved from http://www.cern. ch/lcg

Worldmapper (n. d.). Retrieved from http://www. worldmapper.org/ display.php?selected=205

WRF4G (n. d.). Retrieved from http://www.meteo. unican.es/ software/ wrf4g

ENDNOTE

[1]   No web site is on-line yet for CHAIN but its coordinator Federico Ruggieri (co-author of this chapter and reachable at federico. ruggieri@roma3.infn.it) can be considered as the official contact.

Chapter 7

Architecturing Resource Aware Sensor Grid Middleware:
Avoiding Common Errors in Design, Simulation, Test and Measurement

Philipp M. Glatz
Graz University of Technology, Austria

Reinhold Weiss
Graz University of Technology, Austria

ABSTRACT

Resource aware sensor grid middleware is subject to optimization of services and performance on one side and has to deal with non-functional requirements and hardware constraints on the other side. Implementing different applications and systems on different types of hardware and architectures demands for sophisticated techniques for modeling and testing. This chapter highlights common misconceptions in design, simulation, test and measurement that need to be overcome or at least be considered for successfully building a system. Rules of thumb are given for how to design sensor grids such that they can easily be simulated and tested. Errors that are to be expected are highlighted. Several practical issues will be discussed using real world examples. A sensor grid utilizing network coding and duty cycling services serves as an example as well as a multi-application middleware and a localization system. The approach shows how to implement performance optimizations and resource awareness with a minimum of negative impact from mutual side effects. This type of view on system development of sensor grids has not been looked at before in detail. Therefore the reader will get valuable insights to state of the art and novel techniques of networking and energy management for sensor grids, power profile optimization, simulation and measurement and on how to translate designs from one stage to another.

DOI: 10.4018/978-1-61350-113-9.ch007

INTRODUCING THE COMBINATION OF GRID MIDDLEWARE AND WIRELESS SENSOR NETWORKS FOR PERVASIVE SERVICES

Computing anything, anywhere at any time as envisioned by Weiser (1991) gives a good specification for what is targeted by ambient computing technologies. The challenge when setting up such ubiquitous systems is twofold. First, functional constraints need to be satisfied for providing services at a given Quality-of-Service (QoS) or for achieving a given end-user performance in terms of throughput or sampling rate. Second, a suitable technology needs to be selected and integrated for setting up the system satisfying non-functional constraints like ambient integration or low power operation.

For achieving a cost efficient solution one needs to apply suitable modeling techniques, simulation environments and pre-deployment characterization using modeling, simulation and testbeds for the chosen technology. Yick et al. (2008) and Akyildiz et al. (2002) have presented surveys on Wireless Sensor Network (WSN) technology. Using WSNs as an enabling technology for Pervasive Computing, services can be provided by means of sensor grids (Lim H.B. et al., 2005). Tham and Buyya (2005) give an example of a hierarchically organized sensor grid using Mica2 motes. These motes have been introduced by Hill and Culler (2001) and will serve as target technology in this chapter as well. Though novel platforms have been introduced like TelosB and others Mica2 motes provide a valid platform for planning and implementing development and deployment techniques and different kind of optimization. An example for how to implement the technique called low power listening on the different platforms has been shown by Moon et al. (2007).

Similar to the twofold structure of the challenge, the approach presented in this chapter will take two perspectives as well. On one side, functional constraints for sensor grid services will be discussed. A middleware layer will be presented considering two often used communication paradigms. It will be designed and optimized suitable for worst case assumptions in the middleware, the networking and the Media Access Control (MAC) layer. Functionality will be tested using modeling and simulation-based approaches.

On the other side WSN hardware will be discussed. Its implications for the maximum end-user performance that can be achieved will be related to the MAC layer and Power State Models (PSM) as well as higher level protocols' impact on the energy balance. Instead of only running simulations, the main aspect will be on how measurement systems and testbeds can be set up.

Chapter Objectives

Both ways mentioned need to be combined for arriving at a complete analysis of a sensor grid prior to deployment. Apart from introducing and discussing novel and state of the art solutions for different levels of abstraction a main focus will be given on modeling, simulation, measurement and test errors. Functional and non-functional properties of the system may experience different kinds of errors. We give a novel description of how to avoid or at least recognize these errors and compare different errors' impacts.

Especially for WSNs the modeling of the wireless channel is a tough challenge. Usually, accurate characterization of wireless scenarios can only be done using in-network measures when the system has been deployed. We will introduce and discuss means of modeling scale dependent issues in laboratory sized environment and discuss its implications on errors when profiling testbeds compared to online characterization of deployments. Figure 1 gives an overview of different levels of abstraction that are used in the chapter. Environmental conditions will be considered as far as energy harvesting is considered. Power supply issues are the main issue then as are how the energy reservoirs are impacted by power dissipa-

Figure 1. During the different phases of development the design has to be validated at different levels of abstraction. Modeling, simulation, measurement and profiling in testbeds will be considered. The maximum end-user performance that can be achieved depends on different levels of abstraction of the network stack. A cross-layer perspective will be taken in that interaction among different levels of abstraction will be considered.

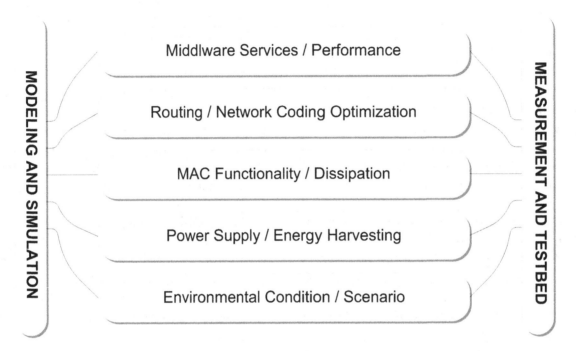

tion given some MAC order, routing functionality and middleware services which will be simulated and measured.

Chapter Organization

Related work overviews state of the art methods and technologies for setting up mesh structured sensor grids briefly. Optimization issues for hardware components and software implementations will be discussed and simulation and measurement environments will be overviewed as well. Next, the design and implementation tradeoffs will be discussed. Results will then compare different optimizations' benefit to inaccuracies that may result from modeling, simulation, measurement and test errors. These aspects will be discussed on a per topic basis, because it is assumed to be more convenient for the reader to have a brief introduction to the different topics as it is needed instead of summing up everything at once. Finally, we conclude giving guidelines for which aspects are the most valuable ones when being given decent consideration.

RELATED WORK FOR LOW POWER WIRELESS SENSOR NETWORKS

First, Energy Harvesting Systems (EHSs) for WSNs will be explained. Networking protocols based upon state of the art MAC protocols are explained. Network Coding will serve as an example for optimization at the networking layer given mesh structured WSNs. Simulation environments and measurement setups are discussed as well as other work discussing errors in simulation and measurement frameworks as well.

Energy Harvestings Systems for Wireless Sensor Networks

EHSs are the state of the art enabling technology for long lived WSNs. Furthermore, recent developments for energy management for advanced resource awareness are based upon properties and effects of using EHSs.

Different EHSs for WSNs have been presented. A well-known example is Heliomote (Lin et al. 2005) which attaches solar cells to Mica2 motes. Based upon such platforms the term energy neutral operation has been introduced by Kansal et al. (2004) and has been refined in Kansal et al. (2007). The idea is to estimate future EHD power profiles based on past modeling periods. As soon as the variation of these values stays below a certain value compared to estimated values the estimation process of the average energy that is to be expected per modeling period is stopped. From that point in time the system can continue operation in energy neutral mode. Despite the fact that these enabling results for EHSs may allow for long-lived operation, this type of EHS-enhanced WSNs is not yet error free.

Coarse grain models for energy storage architectures, harvesting devices, converter circuitry and other hardware related issues are already available in literature, though we are still missing an unified approach for optimizations of existing architectures. But, what is more impacting usability of such systems is that the community still lacks a pool of protocols for actually dealing with the different situations that the system might transit into.

Energy neutral operation can only continue to deliver a given end-user performance if EHS protocol overhead – especially for synchronization – does not demand for too much additional energy to be used and especially if environmental conditions do not change too fast. Glatz et al. (2008) give an example that common harvesting theory cannot cope with. If conditions change too fast the network may become unstable due to leaving the duty cycle operating point that has been calculated for energy neutral operation (Kansal et al., 2004). So, thresholds are introduced when an EHS double layer capacitor (DLC) approaches the limits of its operating range. Glatz, Hörmann, Steger and Weiss (2010) give insights into EHS efficiency on a more fine grained level. Especially for EHS with DLCs it holds that the system's efficiency increases when being operated on a higher values of its energy storage.

While there is no suitable approach yet for giving applicable bounds of environmental or other conditions, there are still other aspects from where we can start from. So we start introducing a special sort of networking optimization applicable to EHS-enhanced WSNs such that it is even applicable to further extend the view from only energy conservation to energy management given the constraint that EHS technology is being used. As we have no complete bounds for exactness or reliability for EHSs, what we can do is to describe the optimization exploiting the context set up by EHS-enhanced WSNs. Describing the optimization itself as well as the ways for how to simulate it will allow us to at least give estimates on how exact a simulation or measurement can be which will allow to further develop the issue throughout this chapter.

Network Coding for Energy Conservation Management in Sensor Communication

As the enabling technologies of EHSs and state of the art motes have been introduced the next level of abstraction according to Figure 1 must be the MAC layer. The latest version of TinyOS2 when writing this chapter is capable of power aware communication in that a low power listening technique can be supported (Moon et al. 2007). Given such an approach the ratio of average power dissipation for sending a message compared to listening to the message can be estimated to be approximately 2. Measurements that have been used by Glatz et al. (2009) validate this assumption. The first step of modeling worst case conditions on the MAC layer for setting up a cross layer view based upon that starts here as well.

The LINDONCS approach by Glatz and Weiss (2009) allows switching on and off a network coding approach that has initially been introduced by Ahlswede et al. (2000). Following this approach, for communication middleware, network coding may be treated as a service that can be switched on and off as a service that is being requested. One way of doing so might be to use a high level state machine which offers network coding as one of its services. It might be used to improve dependability. Another way would be to have network coding implemented on sensor nodes as a means of energy usage optimization as mentioned by Glatz, Hein and Weiss (2009). The grid structure used in that approach will serve as an example for sensor grid architecture. This approach that will serve as an example here can also be used to have energy management implemented upon it as presented by Glatz, Loinig, Steger and Weiss (2010).

Wireless Sensor Networks Simulation, Testbeds and Measurement Experiences

There are prominent examples for WSN deployments failing due to false assumption being made ahead of the deployment. The most well-known example may be the Great Duck Island Experience as reported by Mainwaring et al. (2002). As of 2010 novel sniffing techniques for debugging WSNs start deserving more and more interest as mentioned by Kay Römer in his keynote speech at PerCom 2010. Many different approaches for modeling, sniffing and debugging in the context of BTNode style of motes (Beutel et al. 2004) are under active development.

Other teams are currently dealing with the issue as well. Especially the group related to the PowerBench setup (Haratcherev et al. 2008) gives insights to what can be gained in terms of visibil-

ity when using real world testbeds. Based upon that Glatz, Hörmann and Weiss (2010) discuss the accuracy that is possible with measurement based approaches compared to simulation based ones. Apart from power state models the invaluable information of EHS efficiency models is discussed for different operating points as well. The main outcome is that for EHS-enhanced WSNs it must not only be considered to draining different motes' energy reservoirs such that they all run out of energy nearly at the same. Also for all other operating points of the energy reservoir the efficiency varies that drastically – it doubles for the EHS presented by Glatz et al. (2008) – such that it may impose severe constraints on the maximum end-user performance that can be achieved if not being considered carefully.

The two most commonly used tools for profiling WSN motes' power dissipation ahead from deploying it may be AEON based on Avrora by Landsiedel et al. (2005) and PowerTOSSIM based on TOSSIM or PowerTOSSIM-Z for version 2 of TinyOS as presented by Perla et al. (2008). The problem with these simulation-based approaches is that though they have accuracy usually below 20% for the overall energy consumption of the motes and below maybe 5% for shorter parts they still do not capture the dynamic behavior well. Unfortunately, short term variation in the power profile may completely render power profiles useless just because the hardware components may behave differently due to peaky power profiles that are not considered when averaging over time.

ESTIMATING AND PROFILING POWER-AWARE SENSOR GRID PROTOCOLS

Related work has shown several examples of different hardware and software platforms for WSNs and means of modeling, developing and testing them. Furthermore different experiences show lessons that have to be learned with their outcomes considered when rolling out WSN applications. Related work has been discussed that is concerned with important steps when developing and profiling energy conservation optimization measures.

For explaining what can be expected from applying optimization measures for energy conservation compared to how much different errors impact profiling of these measures the concept splits in two parts.

First, we will define a setup of a WSN middleware for mesh structured sensor grids. State of the art networking methods will be discussed for low power WSNs with energy management. Next, we discuss a methodology for modeling, simulating, estimating and measuring. A detailed step-by-step analysis will be given for translating an application design to a running deployed system. A multi-application middleware and a localization system – both implemented on Mica2

WNSs – serve as real world examples as well for keeping the approach from being academic. Figure 2 gives an overview of different issues that will be considered when translating an application design to a deployed system. At different stages of development different errors in terms of traced functionality of power profiles have to be considered.

We set up a concept for guiding developers through the process of finding which parts of the problem should be considered based on their impact. For the example at hand - a sensor grid middleware with network coding - we will consider the following issues: The networking itself and how messages are being forwarded, the optimization that is possible with applying network coding, the errors that are to be expected from simulation and testbed experience and ways for applying a robust development method.

Figure 2. We start with the application design phase. Along the way that makes us arriving at a running application that has been deployed different phases of development may introduce logical and profiling errors. That is what will be neatly narrowed down in this chapter.

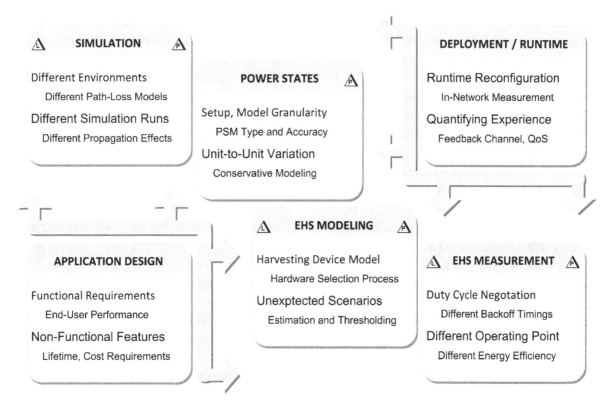

Figure 3. For mesh structured WSNs the energy for up to 50% percent of inner nodes' messages' transmissions can be conserved with network coding compared to routing

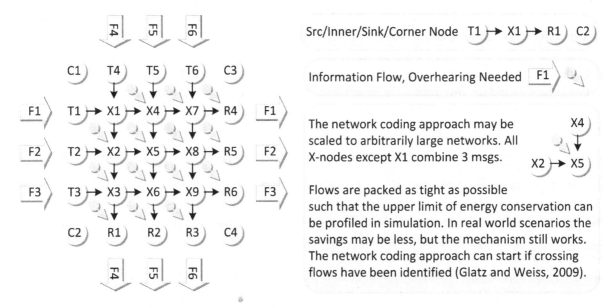

Networking in Mesh Structured Sensor Grids

We set up a 10x10 mesh structured WSN using Mica2 motes similar to the structures introduced by Glatz, Hein and Weiss (2009). Figure 3 depicts the topology, possible flows of information and the information that is needed for coding information flows in the network. Transmitter nodes T1-T6 send information flows F1-F6 to sink nodes R1-R6. All inner nodes Xk of the network need to send two messages if routing is used but only need to send one message if XOR-coding is applied to all three incoming messages except for X1 where only two messages need to be combined. R1-R6 can combine three incoming messages using XOR-coding as well for arriving at the messages initially injected into the network.

From an analytic point of view one could evaluate the performance of network coding compared to routing using the lifetime of the grid before batteries need to be replaced. A common criterion is to check the number of messages that need to be sent as the radio module is considered the most energy hungry component of a mote

most of the time (Rincón et al., 2007). Plotting the energy that is conserved due to the reduced number of messages to be sent averaged over the network for differently sized networks, one arrives at the results plotted in Figure 4.

The problem with that type of modeling is that we do not consider what happens if single nodes run out of energy. Taking EHSs into account – which serves as a basis for the energy management scheme presented by Glatz, Loinig, Steger and Weiss (2009) – different nodes will be supplied and drained differently. Shutting off a single node due to energy shortage influences neighbouring nodes as well. First, the node cannot participate in message transmission any more. For routing as well as for network coding all messages of one session that are to be sent along a route using that node might be dropped. Next, energy management schemes or other types of higher level protocols including energy harvesting duty cycling might get stalled.

For considering these effects as well we need to analyze how the spatio-temporal variation of mote's residual energy is affected. For doing so we apply an analytic model and combine it with

Figure 4. For differently sized quadratic grid networks we plot the gain from network coding over routing as the ratio of messages that need to be sent when injecting flows of information as shown in Figure 3. The gain converges at 2 as expected

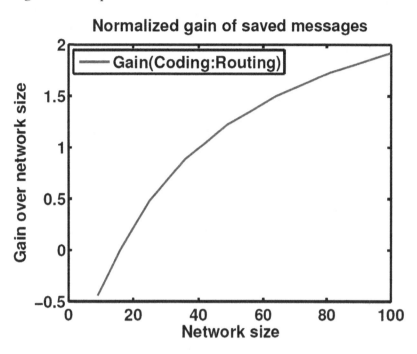

measurement results from Mica2 motes using low power listening to arrive at a ratio of sending cost to receiving cost of approximately 2. While this factor is technology and protocol dependent it suits well to characterize state of the art WSN technology and MAC protocols. For test purposes we have set up a simplified 10x10 network with a grid structure as introduced in Figure 5. It is simplified in that only 4 flows are injected in only two sessions and no network coding is used yet. This allows concentrating on other issues in more detail. The MAC order is assigned statically such that each node is assigned a MAC slot in each time slot. So, all nodes can transmit virtually collision free without the need for difficult synchronization protocols. While allowing full overhearing, where each node's radio may impact each other node's radio, degrades performance per energy spent, it opens possibilities for validating performance results with translating them from simulations to testbeds. MAC slots are ordered starting with the lower right corner node C4, continuing right

receiver nodes, the upper right corner node C3 and all other columns bottom up and from right to left. Motes are numbered the other way round starting the upper left corner node C1, left sending nodes, C2, the leftmost upper sending node and continuing columns top down from left to right. Following this definition and starting with node identifier 1 we define source nodes 3, 6, 21 and 51 and sink nodes 93, 96, 30 and 60. This setup suffices to set up routes during a flooding phase that do not intersect for parallel information flows. Flooding is being initiated from sink nodes and all flooding messages are broadcasted to neighboring nodes in an up to 8 nodes neighborhood from a logical point of view.

Arriving at the simplified model, we have more room to consider effects that are hard to track with more detailed scenarios. Therefore, we include the initialization phase and a power model as well. While the TOSSIM simulation environment by Levis et al. (2003) provides full and fast functional simulation we annotate events for the most

Figure 5. The variance of the EHS-enhanced mote's energy balance is plotted differentially for the DLCs residual energy according to the power model which has been annotated for the TOSSIM simulation environment. Residual energy is plotted for different motes of a 10x10 grid over time where TOSSIM events serve as a timeline. The initial depression of residual energy comes from flooding the network from the sink nodes 30, 60, 93 and 96. After that the surface starts to increase due to power from EHDs with another short depression for sending 2 sessions of 4 messages each.

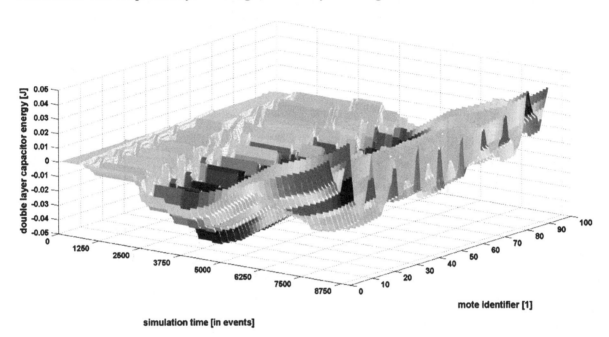

important components impacting a node's power dissipation profile. According to Mica2 hardware measurements using the setup provided by Glatz, Hörmann, Steger and Weiss (2010) we annotate 1.88 mJ for sending and 0.94 mJ for listening to an incoming message that are removed from the simulated energy level. Assuming small scale EHDs we add 2mW on average.

One of the main issues when comparing different approaches is to provide conditions that stress both - routing and network coding - equally strong. One issue has already been discussed that makes comparisons among approaches that complicated. It is packet loss. Packets that are not acknowledged by overhearing forwarding of unique identifiers marking messages are resent. The maximum number of resends is limited by 5. In Figure 5 the change of residual energy for all

motes is plotted according to a TOSSIM simulation that is annotated with the power model. All nodes at the perimeter of the network remain at the positive side of the energy balance. They receive less impact from overhearing in up to 8 node neighborhoods. The residual energy depression for transceiver nodes in the network becomes perfectly flat if flows are packed tightly as shown in Figure 3 if network coding is applied. In other words the messaging workload can perfectly be balanced among nodes given that no messages need to be resent. Further experiments that incorporate the effects of accessing persistent memory as well have been implemented, but results are not considered here. Though they provide the basis for the energy management approach by Glatz, Loinig, Steger and Weiss (2010), they do not further provide to the issues targeted by this chapter.

Preparing Realistic Simulation Scenarios and Resulting Trade Offs

While introducing the simplified model in the previous section some assumption have been made that make life easier when it comes to translating simulation results to hardware testbeds. We have allowed for full overhearing for being able to run the same software in simulations and directly on hardware as well which is invaluable for realistic testing. It has also been mentioned that for being able to do that the price we pay is that we do not measure the exact power profile, but we at least we know exactly what we measure. That is what will be explained in this section. We start with the system setup and will then present as special situation where one can clearly see the differences that comes from sending or listening to single messages. For the sending cost we will consider a setup-specific question while listening cost will be related to that by exploring a technology dependent factor. The factor has been profiled on real hardware to be in the range of 2.1 to 2.3 for reasonable modes of low power listening as long as single messages are considered with the additional power for transitioning the radio module to receiving or sending averaged over time.

Starting with the setup of testing the multi-application middleware, Figure 6 shows a setup that has been chosen for profiling the congestion characteristics of the middleware. Such structures can be used to support an aspect of grids that has not been considered for sensor grids before. Handling several applications in grid systems at the same time is called virtual organization as introduced by Thonhauser et al. (2010). The idea is to allow switching back and forth between different types of behavior of grid nodes. It is similar with the multi-application middleware for WSNs. Different routing behavior can be achieved by different needs that are posed by different applications. Different

sensing can be accomplished and applications may even decide to yield control to other motes as well. Due to the fact that the development is in its early stages of being characterized it has not been set up with the same structure as the network coding approach that has been presented. Instead, we present a setup that can be used for bandwidth and delay characterization of a network. Future use for implementing sensor grids based on that architecture will obviously be possible similar to what is proposed in terms of virtual organizations.

Again these experiments have been run using full adjacency matrices as far as the physical channel has been concerned. The middleware has been configured to allow full communication as well, but the applications create different logical channels. In the 8-node setup – which is 7 nodes and a sniffing base station – Flows F1 and F2 are injected at T1 and the applications that reside on the motes are configured such, that F1 is routed T1-X1-X3-R1 and back via the same path again. The 6-node setup is configured such that R5 sends back the flow via B2. These two choices have been considered for being able to compare the effect of sending back an acknowledgement (ACK) via the same channel compared to the cost of all nodes overhearing each other for reasons explained before. It turns out that the setup does not improve in terms of the data rates that are still acceptable before packet loss starts to increase though nodes B1 and B2 are selected as the logical back channel while the delay does not change significantly as well. This holds for both sides of the routes where different routes are used by applications with different message buffer size. X2, X4 and X6 have a buffer size of only 2 while all other nodes are using a message buffer with 10 elements. What can be observed is that there are strange effects in the experiment due to other reasons.

Figure 6. The multi-application middleware has been simulated using Avrora with AEON (Landsiedel et al. 2005) and has been implemented on Mica2 motes. Motes have been profiled using an accurate measurement setup as well. Running different experiments in parallel leads to overhearing which allows gathering insights into errors of estimating and measuring power dissipation and networking protocols.

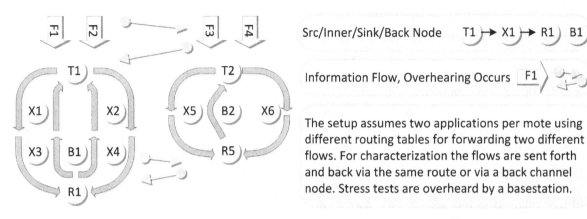

Src/Inner/Sink/Back Node   T1 ➤ X1 ➤ R1) B1)

Information Flow, Overhearing Occurs   F1)

The setup assumes two applications per mote using different routing tables for forwarding two different flows. For characterization the flows are sent forth and back via the same route or via a back channel node. Stress tests are overheard by a basestation.

A Power Profile Analysis of the Multi-Application Middleware

Two laboratories have been used in parallel for profiling the middleware in terms of throughput and delay and in terms of power dissipation. Putting lots of effort into designing and characterizing robust middleware, test and measurement design and making simulation and measurement comparable, we finally missed to have all motes switched off and locked away that have not been expected to be included in a given set of experiments. Tracking down some strange behavior that occurred from time to time we have found out that conditions may exist where communication between motes situated in the two different labs is possible. A NACK-based protocol has been implemented that resends messages if it does not hear messages that it has sent being forwarded further on. From time to time messages did not get resent despite the fact that there was no designated receiver that could have signaled an ACK. For this special case, when motes from the other laboratory got overheard by transmitting nodes that have been connected to the National Instruments setup by Glatz et al. (2010), will be used for depicting the difference in actually dissipated power if a single message need not be transmitted

Wireless Sensor Network Power State Models Looked at in Detail

Figure 7 shows the Mica2 power profile and the digital debug output that marks time stamps when applications pass their messages to the middleware. So, switches from 0 to 1 and 3 to 2 indicate that application 1 has sent a message and switches from 1 to 3 and 3 to 2 indicate that application 2 has sent a message. The overall trace has lasted for 60 seconds where the power profile has been sampled with 100 kS with a National Instruments PXI-6221 data acquisition card.

In Table 1 we provide characteristics of different parts of the power profile using their mean dissipation, the standard deviation, absolute error and relative error. First, the 3 seconds subsequence of the overall 59.5 seconds shows the same behavior as the full length trace. For depicting the difference of having a resend or not, suitable parts of the trace are chosen. As the power trace shows quite some variation as can be seen in Figure 8 we have chosen specific bounds for all parts to keep them comparable. Figure 8 depicts the traces that have been used for profiling the power dissipation of the radio send operation. Two peaks of the scheduler timer that fires periodically every 5 ms are chosen. In case the sub-

Figure 7. The multi-application middleware sends counter values and resends messages once if no ACK is received. In the sending period between 1.0 and 1.5 seconds the applications send their messages to the middleware layer which can be seen by toggling the LSB at the digital debug output for application 1 and LSB+1 for application 2. In that special interval no resending occurs though resends would be expected.

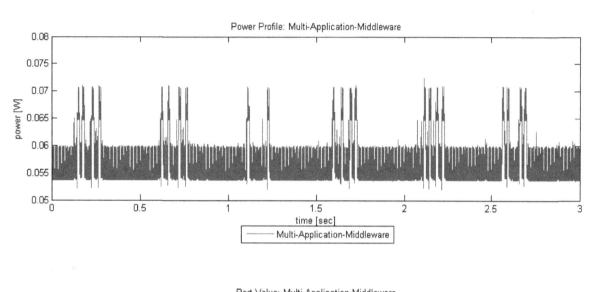

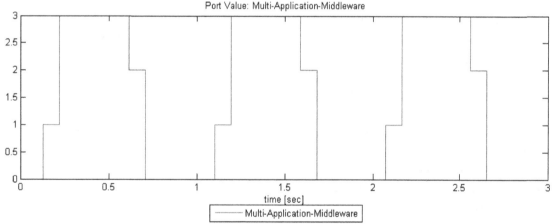

sequence that is chosen for evaluation may be chosen arbitrarily short anywhere in the trace, the error can obviously rise above 5mW or 50% of the average additional power dissipation that occurs when the radio is switched to sending mode. Furthermore, Figure 8 shows that both plots match very well and it looks like the only difference in the two power traces is the offset that is due to transmission power dissipation. So, the circuitry of the radio, that is switched on additionally in this case, seems to have no further side effects. Though, respecting the periodicity is still important as mentioned before. The approach presented by Glatz et al. (2010) allows for applying frequency analysis for automated selection of suitable subsequences. Table 2 summarizes measurements of a null program, different programs activating LEDs and programs firing timer events

Table 1. The 3 seconds block starts after 10 seconds of the full program. The first messages' power profiles are averaged over 500 ms. The first two radio activations, marked by the debug transition 0 to 1, is a subsequence of these 500 ms. The first block of 2 activations without resend after 1 second is profiled as well as is the subsequence of the first single radio activation. Finally, a two scheduler switch length has been profiled where the radio is active but not sending and full activation of the radio is profiled as well. The latter two traces can be found in Figure 8.

Program Part	Mean Power	Std. Dev.	Length	Abs. Error	Rel. Error
Full Program	56.089 mW	3.588 mW	59500 ms	1.236 mW	2.20%
3 Second Segment	56.089 mW	3.588 mW	3000 ms	1.236 mW	2.20%
1. 4 Msg Block	56.200 mW	3.713 mW	500 ms	1.238 mW	2.20%
1. 2 Msg Subblock	58.572 mW	4.958 mW	92.6 ms	1.287 mW	2.20%
1. 2 Msg Block	55.505 mW	2.879 mW	500 ms	1.224 mW	2.21%
1. 1 Msg Subblock	56.686 mW	4.083 mW	92.8 ms	1.248 mW	2.20%
No Radio Send	54.744 mW	1.382 mW	9.7 ms	1.208 mW	2.21%
Full Radio Send	65.806 mW	1.223 mW	9.7 ms	1.436 mW	2.18%

at variable frequencies. The empty TinyOS2 program has been measured and its power dissipation is subtracted from all other measurements. The different LEDs on the Mica2 mote consume a variable and significant amount of power compared to approximately 11 mW that can be calculated from Table 1 for starting the send process.

Another aspect that is considered by Table 2 is the superposition of different power states. First of all it has to be kept in mind that superposition can only be applied if startup times or other timing issues do not interact with each other. Consider the example of two components sharing the same bus system where one cannot start and stop both components at the same time if they need to be under permanent control via the same bus system. For that reason we have chosen non-interacting components: timer and LEDs. The combined and averaged power consumption of toggling the red LED every time a 10 ms timer generates an event is compared to 50% the power dissipation of the LED plus the timer. The last line in Table 2 shows that the error is tolerable, especially compared to unit variation among different motes it is quite small.

Another effect that has its results presented in Table 2 is scaling the timeline. Frequency analysis has been applied similar to what is shown in Figure 8 for accurate results. The average additional power dissipation of the timer decreases monotonically with increased time periods as expected, but it is nonlinearly depending on the period length. This effect occurs due to finite range of registers being used for counting ticks until the timer has to be fired in software. Visual inspection of traces for 500 ms and 1000 ms periods shows additional events in between the events that are signaled to the application.

Apart from actual values that have been traced we have experienced that a lot of debugging capabilities lies within visual inspection of power profiles as has also been mentioned by Haratcherev, Halkes, Parker, Visser and Langendoen (2008). Figure 9 provides an example for the combination of register access, interrupt handling and forwarding through software layers which makes up the significant parts of a timer. Timers are needed for switching state machines, switching hardware and software components, generation of time stamps and for synchronization – they are virtually used everywhere. Fortunately, timers

Figure 8. Zooming into the power trace reveals the timed scheduler behavior for a typical low behavior at 1.00206 seconds of Figure 7 and the lower plot shows the behavior when sending at 1.01179 seconds of Figure 7. Approximately every 5 ms it checks if there is a task pending that has to be dealt with.

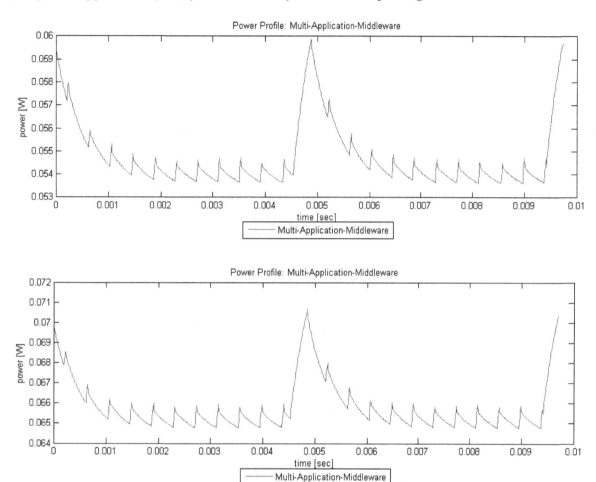

have a very characteristic profile as can be seen in the plot. Though the different motes result in different traces, they all share the same structure. Therefore they are good candidates for automated recognition, especially as timers are usually used before other hardware components are switched on which leads to transitioning into another power state. Furthermore, we have already seen that scheduler events, task switches, a running radio module and a transmitting radio module can be identified directly as well. Therefore, future directions might be to use this knowledge for including

automated recognition of power state transitions from power profiles.

Another important factor for sensor grids is the transmission power. Throughout this article we have suggested using full transmission power for sending messages via the radio. We will now present results on power dissipation for sending differently sized messages at different transmission power. Table 3 gives an overview of profiles that have been traced for sending messages every 250 ms.

Table 2. Different programs running on a Mica2 mote have been profiled using a measurement setup based upon a National Instruments data acquisition card NI PXI-6221 DAQ

Program	Mote1	Mote2	Mote3	Mote4
Empty TinyOS2	9.189 mW	9.219 mW	9.222 mW	9.146 mW
Green LED	6.758 mW	6.695 mW	6.726 mW	6.671 mW
Red LED	7.525 mW	7.586 mW	7.580 mW	7.565 mW
Yellow LED	6.965 mW	7.062 mW	6.924 mW	6.878 mW
Timer 1 ms	3.422 mW	3.288 mW	3.391 mW	3.264 mW
Timer 10 ms	0.919 mW	0.883 mW	0.899 mW	0.853 mW
Timer 50 ms	0.255 mW	0.248 mW	0.249 mW	0.239 mW
Timer 100 ms	0.124 mW	0.121 mW	0.117 mW	0.115 mW
Timer 500 ms	0.056 mW	0.056 mW	0.054 mW	0.054 mW
Timer 1000 ms	0.042 mW	0.044 mW	0.039 mW	0.042 mW
Red LED + 10 ms	3.715 mW	3.742 mW	3.742 mW	3.734 mW
Superpostion Error	0.048 mW	0.051 mW	0.048 mW	0.049 mW

First, Table 3 shows that mote 2 seems to have its radio hardware altered somehow. Furthermore, we do not get significant results for differently sized messages. Using batteries for supplying the motes for these experiments may have influenced the setup's accuracy, but we conclude, that the additional power dissipation or longer messages using the networking implementation as of Tinyos 2.1 does not significantly impact power dissipation on average. So, especially if network coding or other message-size related optimizations are being applied, we conclude that the maximum message size that is supported by the network stack in use should be selected. Spending only a very small fraction of time and power dissipation for sending longer messages we can conserve energy and make networking more reliable by reducing the pressure on MAC protocols. Splitting up a given payload among a little more messages is far less efficient and reliable than sending a little longer payload.

Furthermore, Table 3 shows that increasing radio sending power does not increase power dissipation too much for Mica2 motes. So it is a similar situation as with message length. Invest-ing a little more power dissipation on average pays off for more robust transmissions and ease of networking. This is obvious when comparing Table 3 entries for increased transmission power with what can be conserved from saving a full message in Table 1.

As a last component the sounder will be characterized and then be profiled when being used as a component for ranging in a localization system based on acoustic ranging.

Table 4 lists sensorboard measurements for using the sounder. Though the sounder is suitable for building Time-Difference-of-Arrival (TDoA) measurement based indoor localization systems it consumes power in the order of power that is dissipated by the CPU alone. While the CPU is the last component that has not been considered in detail so far, we will only give a short example. Different low power modes are not explicitly considered by this work. Their characterization can be neglected compared to operational modes. The only thing that has to be considered here are the possible wake up events and hardware wake up time.

Figure 9. Four different motes have been profiled running a timer fired periodically every 50 ms. All four motes' power profiles have been traced and are plotted above.

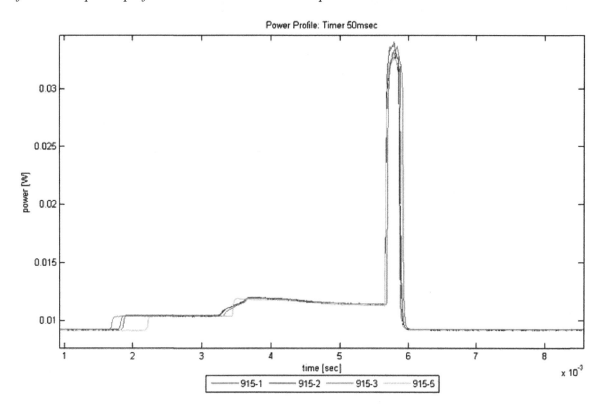

Table 3. Different programs running on a Mica2 mote has been profiled using a measurement setup based upon a National Instruments data acquisition card NI PXI-6221 DAQ

Program	Mote1	Mote2	Mote3	Mote4
1 Byte	46.719 mW	44.914 mW	46.209 mW	45.681 mW
2 Bytes	46.606 mW	44.651 mW	45.985 mW	45.704 mW
5 Bytes	46.565 mW	45.038 mW	45.949 mW	45.488 mW
10 Bytes	46.822 mW	44.924 mW	45.976 mW	45.554 mW
25 Bytes	46.729 mW	44.487 mW	46.195 mW	46.206 mW
10 Bytes -20 dBm	45.385 mW	43.990 mW	44.792 mW	44.250 mW
10 Bytes -10 dBm	45.639 mW	44.140 mW	44.794 mW	44.320 mW
10 Bytes 0 dBm	45.517 mW	44.113 mW	44.935 mW	44.974 mW
10 Bytes 1 dBm	45.751 mW	44.239 mW	45.180 mW	44.751 mW
10 Bytes 2 dBm	45.357 mW	44.182 mW	45.212 mW	44.815 mW
10 Bytes 10 dBm	47.445 mW	44.510 mW	46.611 mW	46.409 mW

Table 4. Three different Mica2 sensor boards have been profiled. Sounder measurements are named with the period length first and then the sounder active period length. Both values are given in microseconds. Mote1 has been used for the sounder measurements not subtracting the null program here.

Program	Mote1	Mote2	Mote3	Mote4
SB1 Null	9.132 mW	9.163 mW	9.168 mW	9.095 mW
SB2 Null	9.131 mW	9.159 mW	9.163 mW	9.093 mW
SB3 Null	9.132 mW	9.162 mW	9.163 mW	9.092 mW
Sounder Programs	SB1	SB2	SB3	Mean
Snd 100-10 ms	10.315 mW	10.284 mW	10.299 mW	10.300
Snd 100-50 ms	14.396 mW	14.246 mW	14.353 mW	14.332 mW
Snd 1000-10 ms	9.303 mW	9.305 mW	9.305 mW	9.304 mW
Snd 1000 50 ms	9.703 mW	9.716 mW	9.728 mW	9.716 mW
Snd 1000 100 ms	10.157 mW	10.177 mW	10.147 mW	10.160 mW

On the CPU Load when Performing Calculations in a Localization System

For computing the position on a mote from an over determined system the least squares solution can be calculated making use of a technique called Singular Value Decomposition (SVD). Figure 10 shows the power profile of a mote calculating SVD and sending a chirp signal from the sounder after sending a beacon for allowing to perform TDoA measurements at the receiver.

Simulation and Testbed Accuracy and Different EHSs and their Efficiencies

From a hardware technology point of view all results presented so far have been traced using Mica2 motes. This section will extend the view to EHSs as well. They usually have an energy measurement system on board or may even be such a system and have sensory hardware and a radio module as well. So, they may primarily be measurement devices and secondly be wireless sensors as well.

The measurements may be based on counting energy packets or from integrating a shunt based power measurement over time. An energy packet counting approach has been implemented by the EHS by Glatz et al. (2008) which can be seen in Figure 11 including results from an EHS efficiency model measurement setup as well. Furthermore, an EHS using shunt-based measurement approaches is depicted in Figure 12 including a plot for its dynamic range and accuracy of the shunt-based measurement approach. The second approach called RiverMote – due to the fact that it is tailored towards in-river water level measurements – is built around the same microprocessor as the TelosB architecture.

Though the measurement results using a cheap approach – in terms of money and power – are less accurate than what can be measured with the other EHS, it is much more efficient. Still, the accuracy is in the range of what can be simulated with state of the art power profiling tools in terms of power dissipation. Furthermore, the results from the efficiency measurements from Figure 11 show that output efficiency alone drops to half the value at the lower threshold (approximately 60% of what can be stored in the DLC) compared the upper threshold with a full DLC. Both systems are utilizing photovoltaic cells as energy harvesting devices, and DLCs as energy storage. Additionally, both systems are of approximately the

Figure 10. Computational resources are scarce as well. Therefore the computationally demanding parts of applications like the SVD calculation when performing localization significantly contribute to the power dissipation profile. The upper plot shows the SVD calculation. The lower plot compares the impact of message transmission and acoustic pulse generation.

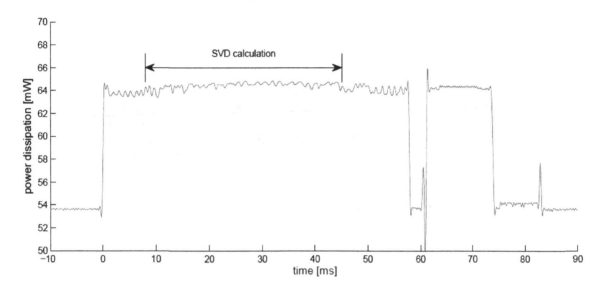

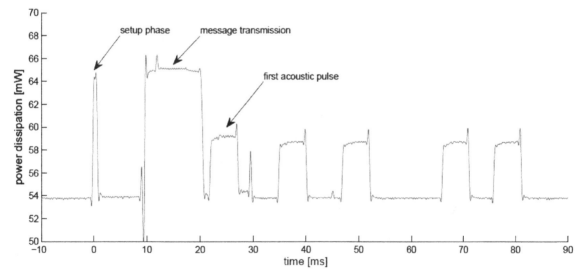

same price if both the EHS and the mote are being considered. So, we can compare both approaches easily. The RiverMote design results in an overall input to output efficiency that will always be above 60%. This is the final example of showing that the tradeoff between using low-power or low-cost hardware, simulation and testbed setups may lead to significantly different results. In this hardware related example it suffices to have quite low accuracy due to the fact that the information is available at runtime and other components are efficient enough.

Figure 11. The EHS presented by Glatz et al. 2008 and the measurement of the EHS efficiency model with a laboratory power supply attached with the measurement setup as presented by Glatz, Hörmann, Steger and Weiss (2010)

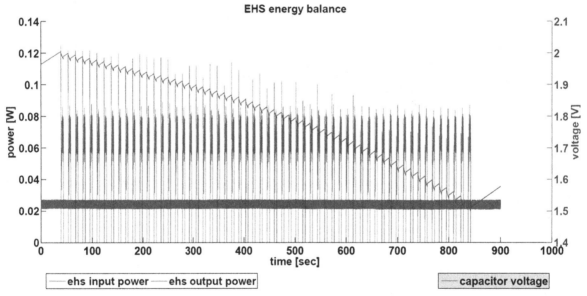

FUTURE RESEARCH DIRECTIONS

Ongoing work at the department dealing with the EHSs and the measurement setup is concerned with further automating the measurement setup and working towards providing a validation suite for power profiling simulation. A first step into that direction is being taken by the presentation of the TOSPIE2 (Tiny Operating System Plug-In for

Energy Estimation) approach by Glatz, Steger, & Weiss (2010). The Eclipse plug-in operates a power state model database, allows for automated hardware and software measurement runs and evaluation and can annotate the information gathered back into the system. Different research groups around the world are currently dealing with that issue of interconnecting and therefore validating measurement and simulation based approaches.

Figure 12. RiverMote is shown without the top of its water-tight housing. The lower plot shows test measurements that have been profiled from different RiverMote's input power measurement circuitry. The accuracy varies among different motes, but it stays below the accuracy of typical simulation-based approaches for regions that significantly contribute to the overall motes' energy consumption.

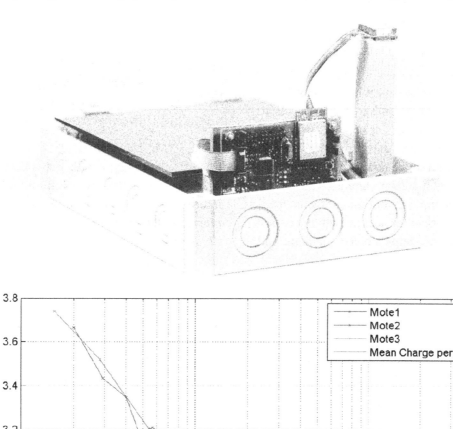

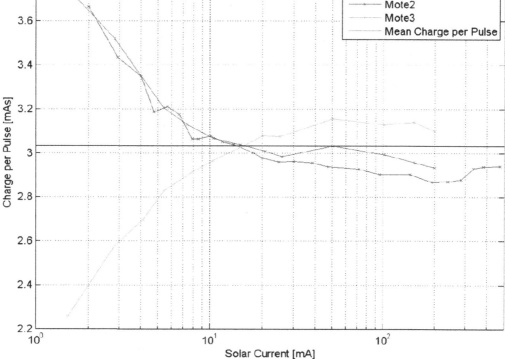

CONCLUSION

This chapter has presented the different steps that have to be taken when designing and running wireless sensor networks. Energy harvesting systems and mote hardware have been profiled accurately in terms of power dissipation and energy conservation characteristics.

The often neglected problem of translating a model from simulation-based approaches to hardware measurements has been discussed and a methodology has been outlined for how to deal with that issue given the task of implementing a network stack optimization. Here, network coding serves as an example for outlining of what measures are appropriate for dealing with the issue.

Other hardware-implemented methods and applications have been profiled as well with their pitfalls explained for keeping the approach from being academic. A novel multi-application middleware and an acoustic range-based localization system have served as an example. This way the reader has been guided through state of the art approaches for designing WSN hardware, dealing with channel access, networking in sensor grids and their middleware aspects as well as application development issues.

REFERENCES

Ahlswede, R., Cai, N., Li, S.-Y., & Yeung, R. (2000). Network information flow. *IEEE Transactions on Information Theory, 46*(4), 1204–1216. doi:10.1109/18.850663

Akyildiz, I. F., Su, W., Sankarasubramaniam, Y., & Cayici, E. (2002). Wireless sensor networks: A survey. *Elsevier Computer Networks, 38*(4), 343–422. doi:10.1016/S1389-1286(01)00302-4

Beutel, J., Kasten, O., Mattern, F., Römer, K., Siegmund, F., & Thiele, L. (2004). Prototyping wireless sensor network applications with BT-Nodes. In *Proceedings of the 1st European Workshop on Wireless Sensor Networks (EWSN'04)*, Berlin, Germany.

Glatz, P. M. (2010). *A scalable middleware with energy management for environmentally powered sensor networks* (unpublished doctoral dissertation). Graz University of Technology, Austria.

Glatz, P. M., Hein, K. B., & Weiss, R. (2009). Energy conservation with network coding for wireless sensor networks with multiple crossed information flows. In: *Proceedings of the 10th International Symposium on Pervasive Systems, Algorithms and Networks (I-SPAN'09)*, Kaohsiung, Taiwan.

Glatz, P. M., Hoermann, L. B., Steger, C., & Weiss, R. (2010). A system for accurate characterization of wireless sensor networks with power states and energy harvesting system efficiency. In *Proceedings of the 6th IEEE International Workshop on Sensor Networks and Systems for Pervasive Computing (PerSeNS'10)*. Mannheim, Germany.

Glatz, P. M., Loinig, J., Steger, C., & Weiss, R. (2009). A first step towards energy management for network coding in wireless sensor networks. In *Proceedings of the 9th IEEE Malaysia International Conference on Communications (MICC'09)*, Kuala Lumpur, Malaysia.

Glatz, P. M., Meyer, P., Janek, A., Trathnigg, T., Steger, C., & Weiss, R. (2008). A measurement platform for energy harvesting and software characterization in WSNs. In *Proceedings of the IFIP/IEEE Wireless Days Conference*, Dubai, UAE.

Glatz, P. M., Steger, C., & Weiss, R. (2010). Poster Abstract: TOSPIE2: Tiny operating system plug-in for energy estimation. In *Proceedings of the 9th ACM/IEEE International Conference on Information Processing in Sensor Networks (IPSN'10)*, Stockholm, Sweden.

Glatz, P. M., & Weiss, R. (2009). LINDONCS: Localized in-network detection of network coding structures in wireless sensor networks. In *Proceedings of the 4th ACM International Workshop on Performance Monitoring, Measurement and Evaluation of Heterogeneous Wireless and Wired Networks (PM2HW2N'09)*, Teneriffa, Canary Islands, Spain.

Haratcherev, I., Halkes, G., Parker, T., Visser, O., & Langendoen, K. (2008). PowerBench: A scalable testbed infrastructure for benchmarking power consumption. In *Proceedings of the International Workshop on Sensor Network Engineering*, Santorini Island, Greece.

Hill, J., & Culler, D. (2001). *A wireless embedded sensor architecture for system level optimization.* Technical Report. U. C. Berkeley.

Kansal, A., Hsu, J., Zahedi, S., & Srivastava, M. (2007). Power management in energy harvesting sensor networks. *ACM Transactions on Embedded Computing Systems*, 6(4), 32. doi:10.1145/1274858.1274870

Kansal, A., Potter, D., & Srivastava, M. (2004). Performance aware tasking for environmentally powered sensor networks. *SIGMETRICS Performance Evaluation Review*, 32(1), 223–234. doi:10.1145/1012888.1005714

Landsiedel, O., Wehrle, K., & Gotz, S. (2005). Accurate prediction of power consumption in sensor networks. In *Proceedings of the 2nd IEEE Workshop on Embedded Networked Sensors.* Sydney, Australia.

Levis, P., Lee, N., Welsh, M., & Culler, D. (2003). TOSSIM: Accurate and scalable simulation of entire TinyOS applications. In *Proceedings of the 1st International Conference on Embedded Networked Sensor Systems (SenSys'03)*, Los Angeles, CA.

Lim, H. B., Teo, Y. M., Mukherjee, P., Lam, V. T., Wong, W. F., & See, S. (2005). Sensor grid: Integration of wireless sensor networks and the grid. In *Proceedings of the Annual IEEE Conference on Local Computer Networks (LCN'05)*, Sydney, Australia.

Lin, K., Yu, J., Hsu, J., Zahedi, S., Lee, D., & Friedmann, J. …Srivastava M. (2005). Poster Abstract: Heliomote: Enabling long – Lived sensor networks through solar energy harvesting. In *Proceedings of the 3rd International Conference on Embedded Networked Sensor Systems (SenSys'05)*, San Diego, CA.

Mainwaring, A., Culler, D., Polastre, J., Szewczyk, R., & Anderson, J. (2002). Wireless sensor networks for habitat monitoring. In *Proceedings of the 1st International Workshop on Wireless Sensor Networks and Applications (WSNA'05)*, Atlanta, Georgia, USA.

Moon, S., Kim, T., & Cha, H. (2007). Enabling low power listening on IEEE 802.15.4-based sensor nodes. In *Proceedings of the IEEE Wireless Communications and Networking Conference (WCNC'10)*, Hong Kong, China.

Perla, E., Catháin, A. Ó., Carbajo, R. S., Huggard, M., & Goldrick, C. (2008). PowerTOSSIM z: Realistic energy modelling for wireless sensor network environments. In *Proceedings of the 3rd ACM Workshop on Performance Monitoring and Measurement of Heterogeneous Wireless and Wired Networks (PM2HW2N'08)*, Vancouver, Canada.

Rincón, F. J., Susu, A. E., Sánchez-Élez, M., Atienza, D., & Micheli, G. (2007). A simulation model for wireless sensor networks based on TOSSIM. In *Proceedings of the 22nd Conference on Design of Circuits and Integrated Systems (DCIS'07)*, Barcelona, Spain.

Tham, C., & Buyya, R. (2005). *SensorGrid: Integrating sensor networks and grid computing. CSI Communications, Special Issue on Grid Computing.* Computer Society of India.

Thonhauser, M., Kreiner, C., & Leitner, A. (2010). A model-based architecture supporting virtual organizations in pervasive systems. In *Proceedings of the 15th IEEE International Conference on Engineering of Complex Computer Systems* (ICECCS'10) (pages 22-26). IEEE Computer Society.

Weiser, M. (1991). The computer for the 21st century. *Scientific American, 265*(3), 94–101. doi:10.1038/scientificamerican0991-94

Yick, J., Mukherjee, B., & Ghosal, B. (2008). Wireless sensor networks survey. *Elsevier Computer Networks, 52*(12), 2292–2330. doi:10.1016/j.comnet.2008.04.002

Chapter 8
Grid Access Control Models and Architectures

Antonios Gouglidis
University of Macedonia, Greece

Ioannis Mavridis
University of Macedonia, Greece

ABSTRACT

In recent years, grid computing has become the focal point of science and enterprise computer environments. Access control in grid computing systems is an active research area given the challenges and complex applications. First, a number of concepts and terminology related to the area of grid access control are provided. Next, an analysis of the Role Based Access Control (RBAC) and Usage Control ABC (UCON$_{ABC}$) models is given, due to their adaption from the grid computing systems. Additionally, a presentation of well known grid access control architectures illustrates how the theoretical access control models are implemented into mechanisms. In a comparative review of the examined access control models and mechanisms, their pros and cons are exposed. Apart from the mapping of the access control area in grid computer systems, the given comparison renders valuable information for further advancement of current approaches.

INTRODUCTION

The grid is an emergent technology that can be defined as a system able to share resources and provide problem solving in a coordinated manner within dynamic, multi-institutional virtual organizations (Foster, Kesselman, & Tuecke, 2001).

This definition depends mostly on the sharing of resources and the collaboration of individual users or groups within the same or among different virtual organizations, in a service oriented approach. The grid's unique characteristics, such as its highly distributed nature and the heterogeneity of its resources, require the revision of a number of security concepts.

DOI: 10.4018/978-1-61350-113-9.ch008

Trust, authentication, authorization and access control are some of the security concepts met in grid systems, as these are identified in the existing literature (Gouglidis & Mavridis, 2009). In this chapter, we will further examine the latter of the aforementioned. Access control is of vital importance in a grid environment since it is concerned with allowing a user to access a number of grid resources. An extensive research has been done in the area of access control in collaborative systems (Tolone, Ahn, Pai, & Hong, 2005; Zhang, Nakae, Covington, & Sandhu, 2008). Nonetheless, further examination is demanded. This is mainly due to the partially or weak fulfillment of the access control requirements in grid systems.

The aim of this chapter is to provide the reader with a comprehensive report on the access control models and architectures currently used in grid computing systems. The value of this chapter is the mapping of the grid access control area, so as to assess the applicability of access control solutions in modern grid applications. Along with the identification of a number of core grid access control requirements, a comparative review of access control models and mechanisms determines their pros and cons. The results from the comparison greatly value the applicability and appropriateness of both models and architectures in being used in grid systems.

The structure of the remainder of this chapter is as follows. The next section provides a prerequisite terminology used in access control, in the context of grid systems. Furthermore, a number of grid access control requirements are presented. An analysis of the Role Based Access Control and the Usage Control models follows. In addition, an examination in regard to the implementation of the theoretical access control models into mechanisms is displayed. A complementary discussion section provides a comparative review of all the examined access control models and mechanisms, respectively. Finally, we present our concluding remarks along with some future thoughts.

BACKGROUND

This section introduces the basic concepts and terminology, related to grid systems and access control. A presentation of the access control process and the identification of core grid access control requirements follow.

Terminology and Access Control Concepts

As mentioned in the definition of the grid, terms such as users, resources and services play an important role. To this effect, we explicitly set the following definitions, mainly based on (Benantar, 2005; Chakrabarti, 2007; Ferraiolo, Kuhn, & Chandramouli, 2003; Foster & Tuecke, 2005; Ravi S. Sandhu, 1994).

A *service* is an implementation of well defined functions that are able to interact with other functions. The Service Oriented Architecture (SOA) is comprised of a set of services that can be realized by technologies such as the web services.

A *domain* can be defined as a protected computer environment, consisted of users and resources under an access control policy. The collaboration which can be established among domains leads to the formation of a virtual organization.

A *user* in a grid environment can be a set of user identifiers or a set of invoked services that can perform on request one or more operations on a set of resources. Furthermore, we identify two types of users. These are the resource requestor and the resource provider. The former type of user acts like a resource access or usage requestor, and the latter type of user acts like a provider of its own sharable resources. All users are restricted by the policies enforced in their participating domains and virtual organization.

A *resource* in a grid environment can be any sharable hardware or software asset in a domain and upon which an operation can be performed.

Access control's role is to control and limit the actions or operations in the grid system that are

Figure 1. Conceptual categorization layer

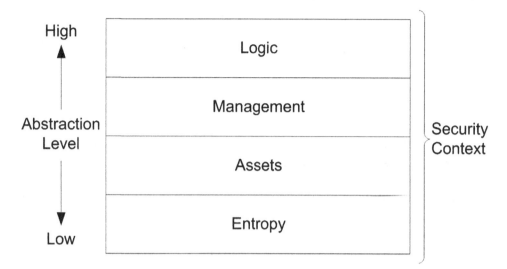

performed by a user on a set of resources. In brief, it enforces the access control policy of the system, and at the same time it prevents the access policy from subversion. Access control in the literature is also referred to as access authorization or simply authorization.

A grid *access control policy* can be defined as a grid security requirement that specifies how a user may access a specific resource and when. Such a policy can be enforced in a grid system through an *access control mechanism.* The latter is responsible for granting or denying a user access upon a resource. Finally, an *access control model* can be defined as an abstract container of a collection of access control mechanism implementations, which is capable of preserving support for the reasoning of the system policies through a conceptual framework. The access control model bridges the existing abstraction gap between the mechanism and the policy in a system.

Grid Access Control Requirements

The identification and definition of grid access control requirements, namely the access control policy, greatly amplifies the design of a model and the implementation of a mechanism regard-

ing access control. In order to appoint the core access control requirements we use the conceptual categorization for grid systems proposed in (Gouglidis & Mavridis, 2010). Figure 1 depicts the four layers of the conceptual categorization. A set of core requirements for access control systems that are considered important for the grid environment, follows. These requirements may vary depending on the use cases that need to be supported by a specific system.

In the initial layer of entropy, we identify two basic requirements. The first is that access control should be enforced among all the collaborative domains. Thus, interoperability among domains should be supported within and among virtual organizations. Although each domain has its own access control system, in order for them to successfully collaborate, a unified access control system should be provided. The second requirement refers to the number of the participating domains or users that can change during the time span of the collaboration. In more detail, during the collaboration it is possible for new domains or users to join, and existing ones to quit. The access control system should be able to be monitored continually and handle such modifications in the structure of the virtual organization.

Regarding the layer of assets, we identify a dyadic nature regarding the access and sharing of an asset. More specifically, we recognize that the fine-grained sharing of any resource in a grid system includes a resource requestor and a provider. When user requests access to an asset, access must be granted only if the requestor is a legitimate user and also authorized to access the specified asset. Additionally, resource providers should be able to define quality factors on their shareable resources. The quality factors concern the level of resource usage and can also be characterized as obligations that must be met from a provider when granting access to a resource requestor. For instance, quality factors could apply for setting disk quotas, memory or CPU utilization levels and so on and so forth.

In the management layer, we define a list of requirements that refer to the management of the policies of the individual domains, as well as the virtual organization itself. A first requirement is that each administrative user of a domain should administer the local policies of the domain. Additionally, administrators should run the policies in the collaboration that refer to resources of the administrator's domain. Furthermore, it must be guaranteed that no conflicts should exist among the policies of the individual domains at the level of the virtual organization, where policies are joined. Last but not least, the process of identifying policy violations should be automated, both in intra-domain and inter-domain collaborations.

At the logic layer, we identify the enforcement of the autonomy and security principle (Shafiq, Joshi, Bertino, & Ghafoor, 2005). The autonomy principle refers to the permission of an access under secure interoperation, if it is also permitted within the individual domain. The security principle pertains to the denial of an access under secure interoperation, if it is also denied within the individual domain. Furthermore, the principle of containment (Ravi Sandhu, 2008) that subsumes the principles of the separation of duties, least privilege and so forth, should be supported in

each and among domains. The latter requirement greatly enhances the adoption of grid technologies in business organizations, where the existence of conflict of interest policies is presumed.

Access Control Enforcement

In this section, a brief presentation of the reference monitor concept is given. This is mainly done because the application of the reference monitor concept is known to achieve high assurance access control mechanisms. Furthermore, it provides guidelines for the design and implementation of secure computer systems (Ferraiolo, Kuhn, et al., 2003).

The process of access control in any computer system guarantees that any access to the resources of the system conforms to its access control policy. The application of the abstract concept of the reference monitor is capable of providing the requirements that are posed from the access control process. As it can be also seen in Figure 2, the reference monitor operates as an access mediator between the subject's access requests and the system's objects. The accesses comply with the system's security policy. The reference monitor can be informed for the security policy of the computer system from an access control database. Moreover, all the security relevant transactions are kept into an audit file for security and traceability reasons.

The architecture of the reference monitor is the result of the application of three key implementation principles. These principles are the completeness, isolation and verifiability. Completeness requires from the reference monitor to invoke all the subject's references to an object and also to constitute it impossible to bypass it. The isolation principle assures that the reference monitor must be tamper-proof. This means that it must be impossible for an attacker to penetrate the reference monitor in a malicious way. Lastly, the verifiability principle appertains to the checking and validation of the system's security design

Figure 2. The reference monitor

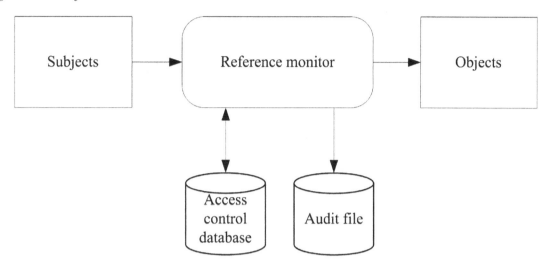

through the use of software and system engineering techniques.

Nonetheless, the aforementioned reference monitor principles seem to be insufficient, especially in enterprise environments. This is mostly because the main objective of the reference monitor is the enforcement of each system's policy. Yet, it does not interfere with the articulation of a system's security policies. Thus, the principles of flexibility, manageability and scalability are introduced. The first principle assures that the access control policy of an enterprise can be enforced by the existing security system. The next refers to the ease of policy management and the latter requires from the security system to cope with the fluctuations in the number of the participating users and resources in a computer system.

The concept of reference monitor in open systems has been standardized with the X.812 access control framework (ITU-T, 1995). In brief, the main functions in X.812 are the Access Control Decision Function (ADF) and the Access Control Enforcement Function (AEF). The former component is responsible for the making of access control decisions. The decisions are made based on information applied by the access control policy rules, the context in which the access request is

made, and the Access Control Decision Information (ADI). ADI is a portion in the Access Control Information (ACI) function, which includes any information used for access control purposes, including contextual information. Lastly, the AEF is responsible for the enforcement of the decision taken from the ADF. Figure 3 illustrates the fundamental access control functions in X.812.

ACCESS CONTROL MODELS

During the last decades various access control policies have been introduced, namely the Mandatory Access Control policies (MAC), the Discretionary Access Control policies (DAC) and the Role Based Access Control policies (RBAC). Each one of them serves specific security requirements in different working environments. As mentioned in the definition of the access control policy, a number of access control models are required and were developed in order for the policies to be represented by formal methods. Research on the MAC, DAC and RBAC has proven that an access control model, which can express the role based access control policies is also capable of enforcing both MAC and DAC policies (Ferraiolo,

Figure 3. Fundamental access control functions in X.812

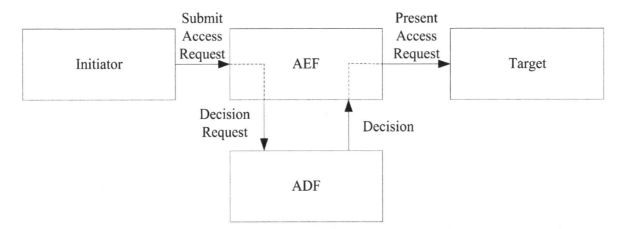

Kuhn, et al., 2003). It is noteworthy that an attempt started along with the advancement of RBAC for the design of a series of Attribute Based Access Control models (ABAC). The ABAC model was mainly introduced to overcome a number of RBAC's shortcomings (Yuan & Tong, 2005) and has also been proven capable of enforcing MAC, DAC and RBAC policies (Park & Sandhu, 2004). For the aforementioned reasons, we will present the standard for the role based access control (American National Standard Institute, 2004), and Usage Control (Park & Sandhu, 2004; R. Sandhu & Park, 2003; Zhang, et al., 2008) in the rest of this section. Both RBAC's and UCON's characteristics are able to tackle the complexity posed from grid systems at a satisfactory level.

Role Based Access Control (RBAC)

The RBAC access control model has received considerable attention from researchers, mainly due to its abstraction and generalization. It is abstract because it includes only properties that are relevant to security, and it is general since it supports various designs that can all be interpreted as valid ones. More of RBAC's virtues are the support of a significant number of principles, namely the least privilege, separation of administrative functions and separation of duties (Sandhu, Coyne,

Feinstein, & Youman, 1996). Following in the section, RBAC's standard model will be put forward. This model consists of four different components and each one of them assigns to RBAC a number of functionalities. These components are the core RBAC, the hierarchical RBAC, the static separation of duty relations and the dynamic separation of duty relations.

As it is illustrated in Figure 4, the core RBAC model is composed of five static elements. These elements are the users, roles, and permissions, with the latter being composed of operations applied on objects. The relationship among the elements of the core model is straightforward. Roles are assigned to users and permissions are assigned to roles. The type of relation between users and roles and between roles and permissions is many-to-many. This means that one user can be assigned many roles and that many users can be assigned one role. The same applies for the role to permission assignment as well. Declaration of negative permissions is not supported in RBAC. This indirect assignment of users to permissions greatly enhances the administration in RBAC. Revocation of assignments can also be easily done. Moreover, we identify two distinct phases in RBAC. The first is the design and the second the run-time phase. During the design phase, a system administrator can define a number of as-

Figure 4. The core RBAC model

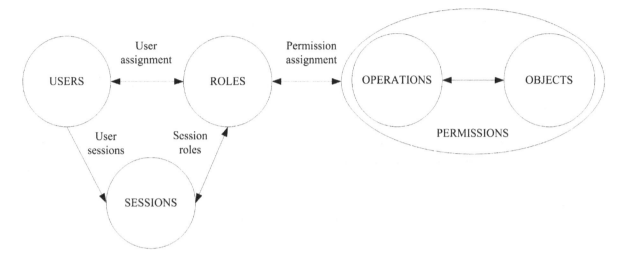

signments between the elements in the computer system. At the run-time phase, the assignments in the system are enforced by the model as it is specified by the security policy of the system, which was prescribed during the design phase.

The run-time phase that was previously mentioned can be supported in RBAC through the concept of the session. The latter distinguishes RBAC from other group based mechanisms and adds great features and functionality to the RBAC model. During a session, roles for a subset of users are allowed to be activated. This means that a user could be assigned various roles during the design phase, but these roles do not need to be activated always or simultaneously, preserving at the same time the principle of least privilege. Without the support of the notion of sessions this would not be possible to achieve. It is also feasible to enforce a number of constraints during a session. We will further discuss the support of constraints in RBAC latter in this section. However, although the sessions strengthen RBAC, there has been an argument concerning the existence of sessions that proposes their replacement from a separate component in the core RBAC model (Li, Byun, & Bertino, 2007). The argument continues regarding the number of activated roles

during a session. It is proposed that it should be possible for core RBAC to further support the activation of single roles during a session, as a requirement of some systems.

The hierarchical RBAC provides the model with a great enhancement in regard to the administration of its policies. Role inheritance provides more flexibility in the management of the policies in an organization. Permissions that are assigned to a role can easily be inherited to another role, without the need to reassign the same permissions to the latter role, too. For instance, let's assume two roles R1 and R2 and two permission sets P_{R1} = (P1, P2) and P_{R2} = (P3, P4), which are initially assigned to roles R1 and R2, respectively. If role R1 inherits role R2, it means that all of R2's permissions are available via R1. The available permissions to role R1 are expressed by the union of permissions on sets P_{R1} and P_{R2}. When hierarchies are represented in graphs, the immediate inheritance relation is shown as $\rightarrow$. The head of the arrow or the arc defines both the permissions and user membership inheritance. For the previously mentioned example, we have R1 $\rightarrow$ R2. User membership refers to the assignment of users to roles in a hierarchy. In such a case, users are authorized to access all the permissions assigned to roles either directly or via inheritance relationships. Yet, another functionality that is provided in the hierarchical RBAC is the support of both general and limited role hierarchies. General hierarchies comprise the most common cases in role inheritance, and they are depicted as partial order sets. However, in more restrictive environments there might be the requirement for the support of limited hierarchies. This involves usually the existence of either a single immediate ascendant or descendant role in the hierarchy tree structure.

Another virtue of RBAC is the support of constraints. The two components that can enforce constraints are the static and dynamic separation of duty relationships. The main objective in both types of constraints is to preserve the security of the system and prevent it from being compromised. Usually they are used to deliver business requirements to the security system that incorporates an enterprise's logic. Static separation of duty relationships copes with the enforcement of conflict of interest policies. For example, let R1 and R2 be two conflicting roles, and user U1 assigned to role R1. By enforcing a static separation of duty constraint between roles R1 and R2, RBAC prohibits the assignment of user U1 with role R2, since the two roles are conflicting. These types of constraints are defined and enforced in RBAC during the design phase. In the presence of a role hierarchy, the static separation of duties constrains are enforced in the same way for all the directly assigned and inherited roles. Dynamic separation of duty relationships handles conflict of interest policies in the context of a session. In this case, the user is actively logged into the system and a set of the user's assigned roles is activated. These constraints are described during the design time, as it happens with the static separation of duty relationships. However, they are applied during the run-time, in the context of a session, and they prevent the simultaneous activation of two or more conflicting roles. In case of role hierarchies, the same as in static separation of duty relationships

applies with the difference that they are enforced only on the activated user's roles.

Lastly, one of its greatest virtues is the role based administration of RBAC. It can be said that RBAC is divided into user space and administrator space. The former includes user and the latter administrative roles, permissions and operations, respectively. Once again, the principle of least privileged is maintained. In the literature various models have been proposed, each one providing a different approach in the role based administration of RBAC (Crampton, 2002; Ferraiolo, Chandramouli, Ahn, & Gavrila, 2003; Oh & Sandhu, 2002; R. Sandhu, Bhamidipati, & Munawer, 1999).

Usage Control (UCON)

ABAC has lately gained a lot of attention due to the development of internet based distributed systems. However, in contrast to RBAC, attribute based access control has not been standardized yet. The latter type of access control models can provide access decisions on resources based on the requestor's owned attributes. The advantage of this approach is that it is possible to provide access to users in a collaborative environment without the need for them to be known by the resource a priori. In this section, we will present in brief the UCON$_{ABC}$ model (Park & Sandhu, 2004) as a representative attribute based access control model, which is based on a modern conceptual framework. The UCON conceptual framework encompasses traditional access control, trust management and digital rights management for the protection of digital resources. Nonetheless, functionalities such as administration and delegation are still absent.

UCON has introduced a number of novelties compared to both RBAC and other ABAC models, like its support for mutable attributes and continuity of access decision. Research has also been done regarding its usage in collaborative systems (Zhang, et al., 2008). Figure 5 illustrates the UCON$_{ABC}$ model, which consists of eight components, viz. subjects, subject attributes, objects, object attributes, rights, authorizations, obligations and conditions. The notion of subjects and objects as well as the association with their attributes is straightforward. A subject can be an entity in a system and its definition, as well as its representation, is given by a number of properties or capabilities in the associated subject's attributes. For instance, role hierarchies similar to RBAC can be formed through the use of subject attributes. In regard to objects, they also represent a set of entities in a system. Each object can be associated with object attributes. Subjects can hold rights on objects. Through these rights, a subject can be granted access or usage of an object. This type of attributes can serve, for example, in the classification of the associated objects, by representing classes, security labels and so on and so forth. It is worth mentioning that both subject and object attributes can be mutable. This means that the values of the attributes can be modified as a result of access. When an attribute is characterized as immutable, its value can be modified only by an administrative action and not by its user's activity.

Up to now, a presentation of the most common components of the $UCON_{ABC}$ model was given. However, its novelties in access control are accrued mostly from the rest of its components. The rights component represents a number of privileges that can be held and exercised from a subject to an object. In a similar way to RBAC's roles, the UCON conceptual framework supports hierarchies among rights. It is also notable that rights are not set a priori, but they are determined during the access. The access decision is given from a usage function by considering the following factors of subject and object attributes, authorizations, obligations and conditions. Authorizations in UCON are functional predicates, whose evaluation is used for taking decisions, namely if access to a subject is granted to an object. In a same manner with the usage function, the evaluation of the authorizations is based on subject and object attributes, requested rights and a set of authorization

rules. Authorizations can be characterized as pre-authorizations or ongoing-authorizations. The pre prefix refers timely before the requested right and the ongoing prefix during the time span of access.

Furthermore, obligations in UCON are used to capture the requirements that must be met from a subject requesting the usage of an object. They are also expressed as functional predicates and, as already mentioned, they are used in the evaluation of access both in the usage function as well as with authorizations. Obligations are also divided into pre-obligations and ongoing-obligations. The former is used usually for the retrieval of history information and the latter to check if the requested requirement is fulfilled during the time span of access. Last but not least, conditions in UCON are used to capture factors that are accrued from the environment of the system. The semantic differential between conditions and other variables, namely authorization and obligation, is that the former cannot be mutable, since there is no direct semantic association with subjects.

GRID ACCESS CONTROL MECHANISMS

As mentioned above, the terms of authorization and access control are used interchangeably. Nonetheless, the former definition is most commonly used in grid systems. In this section, we will further analyze some of the access control mechanisms implemented in existing grid middleware. A clustering of a number of implemented authorization infrastructures by the capabilities they support is provided in (Schlager, Sojer, Muschall, & Pernul, 2006). The access control architecture used in the majority of them is based on an attribute based approach. The main components in this architecture are the Attribute Authority (AA), the Policy Enforcement Point (PEP), the Policy Decision Point (PDP), and the Policy Authority (PA). This architecture is based on the access control framework recommended in

Figure 5. The UCON$_{ABC}$ model

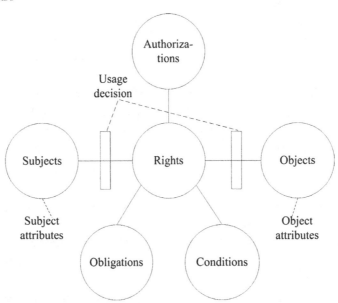

(ITU-T, 1995). In X.812 the policy enforcement and decision point are referred to as Access control Enforcement Functions (AEF) and Access control Decision Function (ADF), respectively.

The AA is responsible for the generation and management of the subject, object and environment attributes. It is also responsible for the association of attributes with their owning elements as well as the provision and discovery of the attributes. The policy enforcement point requests and enforces access decisions coming from the policy decision point, which have to do with subject to object authorizations. The policy decision point is responsible for evaluating the system's policies and for decision taking. The decision for the granting or denial of access is passed to the policy enforcement point. Lastly, the policy authority is responsible for the creation and management of the authorization policies.

Furthermore, the grid authorization systems are also characterized by the way the authorization of a user to a resource is achieved (Chakrabarti, 2007). There are two different models used in the currently implemented grid authorizations systems. These are the push and the pull models.

Most systems support either the former or the latter model. However, there are grid authorization systems that support both of them. In the push model, a certificate generator usually creates certificates based on the user's credentials. Each one of the certificates is pushed on an access controller so as to grant or deny access to the resource, based on the validity of the certificate. On the contrary, when the pull model is used by the authorization system, a minimum number of user credentials is provided to the access controller. In turn, it is the controller's responsibility to check the validity of the user based on the policies of the system. The push model is considered to be more scalable than the pull model. Nonetheless, the push model lacks usability, something in which the pull model is better, since users do not have to obtain the certificate from the certificate generator. Moreover, the responsibility of granting access to a user is passed to the access controller.

Last but not least, the grid authorization systems can be categorized as virtual organization level systems and resource level systems (Chakrabarti, 2007). The former refers to systems where a centralized authorization system handles the provision of credentials to the users, in order for them to access the resources. In opposition to the virtual organization level, systems that allow the users to access the resources based on the credentials presented by the users are characterized as resource level ones. It is worth mentioning that as noted in (Chakrabarti, 2007) the virtual organization and the resource level authorization systems cope with different aspects of the grid authorization. The first category of systems provides a consolidated authorization service for the Virtual Organization and the second category of systems implement the decision to authorize resource access. As a consequence, they complement each other and can provide a holistic authorization solution if combined.

Community Authorization Service (CAS)

The Community Authorization Service (CAS) (Pearlman, Welch, Foster, Kesselman, & Tuecke, 2002) is a virtual organization level authorization service developed by the Globus team. Its main objective is to cope with the flexibility, scalability and policy hierarchy issues, which primarily exist in Grid Security Infrastructure (GSI) and GridMap, since the latter provides only a one-to-one mapping between global user names and local ones. CAS is capable of allowing the resource owners to grant access on portions of their resources to the virtual organization by letting the community determine who can use this allocation. CAS manages to overcome the limitations existing in GridMap by introducing a CAS server that operates as a trusted intermediary between the users of the virtual organization and the resources. The CAS server is capable of managing all the policies that control the access to the resources of a community. It contains information about the users, resources, certificate attributes, servers as well as policy statements. According to CAS, a user has to contact the CAS server at any request to access a resource in a community. This requires

from the user to be authenticated by providing the user's own proxy credential. The identity and the rights that the user holds in the virtual organizations are established by using its local database. In turn, the server issues a signed policy assertion with the user's identity and rights in the target virtual organization. The policy assertion is then embedded in a new proxy certificate generated by the CAS client. The new proxy certificate is used on the resource of the virtual organization to authenticate the user and to grant access to the resource based on the embedded policy assertion. The certificates that are used in CAS are X.509 extensions. The proxy credentials that authenticate the user on the CAS server have much longer span of life that the proxy certificates.

Virtual Organization Membership Service (VOMS)

The Virtual Organization Membership Service (VOMS) (Alfieri et al., 2003) is also a virtual organization level authorization service developed for the European Data Grid (EDG) that solves the same problems as CAS does but in EDG. The VOMS system operates as a front-end on top of a database and it consists of four components, viz. the user server, user client, administration server and administration client. The user server receives requests from a client and returns information regarding the user. The user client contacts the server by presenting the certificate of a user or proxy to the latter and receives a list of groups, roles and capabilities of the user. The administration server is responsible for accepting the client's request and updating the database. Lastly, the administration client is used by the administrators of the virtual organization for administrative issues like the addition of new users, the creation of new groups and so on and so forth. According to VOMS, a bidirectional authentication of the server and the client occurs. During the authentication process, a safe communication channel is instantiated between them. In turn, the client can send a request to the server. When the server receives the request from the client, the request is checked for its integrity and if no problem exists, the server sends a pseudo-certificate to the user. The client also checks the pseudo-certificate for its integrity. The user can now create a proxy certificate based on the received pseudo-certificate and present it to the resources to gain access on them. A user in VOMS is allowed to be a member of many virtual organizations and also to receive credentials from multiple VOMS systems.

GridMap

GridMap is the simplest and most widely used resource level authorization service. It is rather static and lacks scalability. GridMap is implemented as a file, which holds a list of authenticated distinguished names of the grid users and their mapping with the equivalent account names of the local users. The policies that describe the access restrictions are kept in each local resource. The access control is also left to the local systems, so when a user requests access to a resource, the decision to grant or deny the access permission is based on the information present in the local access control mechanism and the local GridMap file.

Akenti

Akenti (Thompson, Essiari, & Mudumbai, 2003) is a resource level authorization system that was created to cope with environments that consist of highly distributed resources and their use by multiple stakeholders. A stakeholder is defined as someone who controls access on a resource. Akenti consists of a resource gateway that operates as a policy enforcement point and of resources, which are accessed via the resource gateway. It makes use of X.509 certificates for the authentication of the users who request access to a resource. The communication between the user and the resource gateway is accomplished through secure SSL/TLS channels. When a user requests access to a

resource, access is determined by the combined policy on the resource. These policies can be created by different and unrelated stakeholders and are expressed with signed certificates. The resource gateway can ask from the Akenti server the privileges that a user has on a resource. The Akenti server operates as a policy decision point. In turn, the server retrieves all the relevant certificates, checks their validity and sends a response back to the resource gateway. The latter enforces the operation indicated by the policy decision point. This architecture gives Akenti the ability to restrict access to resources based on predefined access control policies, without requiring the existence of a central administrative authority.

Privilege and Role Management Infrastructure Standards Validation Project (PERMIS)

PERMIS is a role based X.509 privilege management infrastructure and resource level authorization system (D. Chadwick, 2005; D. W. Chadwick, Otenko, & Ball, 2003) that supports the hierarchical RBAC model. The main components that constitute PERMIS are the PERMIS authorization enforcement point, the authorization decision point, the authorization policy and the privilege allocator. The first two components are responsible for the user authentication and decision making, respectively. The authorization decision point can retrieve policies and attribute certificates from LDAP servers and base its decision on the retrieved information. The descriptions of the policies are specified by the authorization policy. The content of the policies specifies who has access on which resource and under what conditions. The privilege allocator is responsible for the allocation of privileges to the users. The privileges are attribute certificates that include role to user associations. Additionally, a delegation issuing service provides the users with the ability to delegate a subset of their privileges to another user of their domain. When a user requests use of a resource, the authorization enforcement point authenticates the user. In turn, the enforcement point passes the user's distinguished name to the decision point. The latter retrieves information relevant to the user from an LDAP server. After performing the validation of the policies, the roles that are embedded in the attribute certificates are transferred as an object to the user. The user is authenticated in every attempt to access a resource. This results in the transfer of the object, which keeps the roles of the user embedded, from the enforcement to the decision point, so as to grant or deny access.

Usage Based Authorization Framework

An attempt to apply a usage based authorization framework in grid systems is presented in (Zhang, Nakae, Covington, & Sandhu, 2006). Subject and object attributes are used for the definition of usage control policies, and conditions provide context based authorization for the support of ad-hoc collaborations. Continuity of decision and mutable attributes are also supported. Yet, obligations are not supported. In the current state, the management of attributes is centralized. Nonetheless, in case of a distributed attribute repository, a lot of complexity is added, since the system must keep all the multiple copies of the attributes consistent. The main components of the framework's architecture include a policy decision point and a policy enforcement point. The attributes and the identity certificates of users can be stored in attribute and identity authorities, respectively. When access is requested, the decision point makes the control decision based on the collected attributes and is enforced by the enforcement point. A notable feature is its support of a hybrid model that uses both the pull and push models to cope with the different types of attributes. Immutable attributes in the usage based authorization framework are pushed to the policy decision point by the requesting subject. On the contrary, when it comes to immutable attributes, they are pulled from the attribute repositories.

DISCUSSION

In this section, the access control models and architectures described in this chapter are compared. The comparison is attempted with respect to the conceptual categorization for grid systems, proposed in (Gouglidis & Mavridis, 2010) with a view to specify a number of deficiencies in the examined models and architectures. The criteria used throughout the comparison are based on the requirements that were defined and the evaluation is based on the level of fulfillment of the requirements by the access control models and architectures, respectively.

Comparing the Access Control Models

Table 1 illustrates the evaluation of the RBAC and UCON$_{ABC}$ models with respect to the entropy, assets, management and logic layers of the conceptual categorization. Concerning the entropy layer, the requirements that were defined, demand both the support of access control among different domains and the dynamic joining of new ones. The proposed standard RBAC model, as already seen, handles better centralized architectures and is rather weak in inter-domain collaborations. Such functionality is absent from the standard model. However, research in (Shafiq, et al., 2005) has proven that RBAC can also be applied in multi-domain environments where distributed multiple organizations inter-operate. Yet, RBAC requires that all user domains must be known a priori, in order to access an object. On the contrary, the UCON$_{ABC}$ model, due to its support of attributes, can cope better with highly distributed environments. Furthermore, one of UCON's features is that it is possible to provide access to users in a collaborative environment without the need for them to be known by the resource a priori.

In regard to the layer of assets, we mentioned that fine-grained access to resources should be supported. Additionally it should support obligations from the side of the resource provider. RBAC usually provides more course-grained access control to resources in contrast to $UCON_{ABC}$. Research has also been done in RBAC to extend it and to support finer-grained access control through the use of context (Tolone, et al., 2005). Obligations are supported in $UCON_{ABC}$, but not in the notion demanded by the requirements. The notion of obligations is completely absent in RBAC.

RBAC supports improved administrative capabilities on the level of a domain in comparison to $UCON_{ABC}$. In more detail, RBAC can also provide management in a role-based fashion (Ferraiolo, Kuhn, et al., 2003). However, a number of issues arise when it comes to inter-domain management of policies, and solutions are provided in existing literature (Shafiq, et al., 2005). In contrast to RBAC, $UCON_{ABC}$ lacks administration.

Finally, the fulfillment of requirements in the logic layer is fairly the same in both access control models. Nonetheless, RBAC supports the principles of separation of duties and least privilege better.

Comparing the Access Control Mechanisms

Table 2 depicts the evaluation of the access control mechanisms with respect to the entropy, assets, management and logic layers of the conceptual categorization, while Table 3 illustrates a summary of the comparison. Besides the specified requirements, in our evaluation, we consider a list of extra parameters as stated in (Chakrabarti, 2007). This is due to the adaption of an attributed based approach with strong resemblance by the authorization systems, thus making their evaluation more difficult.

The parameters of interoperability, user and mechanism scalability were taken into account in the layer of entropy. Besides the GridMap authorization system, the rest of them handle interoperability well. This is mainly due to the support of standard protocols, namely the SAML and XACML. The support of attributes helps in the fulfillment of the requirements we have defined for the entropy layer. User scalability is affected by two factors. These are the authorization model in use and the type of policy management. Usually systems that support a push based model and a centralized management of policies are less complex. In overall, GridMap exhibits the worst performance in the entropy layer, while CAS, VOMS, PERMIS and Usage based authorization the best.

Regarding the evaluation of the authorization systems for the layer of assets, we examined their ability to permit multiple users to control access on the same resource. As depicted in Table 2, VOMS and PERMIS are able to support multiple stakeholders on a resource. In regard to the parameter of obligations, only the Usage based authorization system supports it. Yet, obligations are from the side of the user and not from the resource provider.

The evaluation of the management of policies is based on multiple parameters, namely the administrative overhead, revocation of attributes, decentralized management, ease of management and automation. As we already mentioned, ABAC approaches lack management. Nevertheless, they provide support of decentralized management and require low administrative overhead in most implementations. Automation of procedures is absent or weakly supported. Lastly, revocation of privileges is present mostly in resource level solutions, and encounter problems in the rest of them.

The principles defined as requirements in the logic layer, in conjunction with the usability of the system, serves as evaluation parameters for the last layer. The principles of autonomy and security are fairly supported by all the examined systems. Nonetheless, the principle of containment

Table 1. Comparisons between the different access control models

Access control models	Conceptual categorization layers			
	Entropy	**Assets**	**Management**	**Logic**
RBAC	Low / Medium	Low / Medium	Medium / High	Medium
UCON$_{ABC}$	High	Medium	Low	Medium

Table 2. Comparisons among the different access control mechanisms

Access control mechanisms	Conceptual categorization layers													
	Entropy			Assets		Management					Logic			
	Iteroperability	User scalability	Mechanism scalability	Multiple stakeholders	Obligations	Revocation	Administrative overhead	Decentralized management	Ease of management	Automation	Usability	Autonomy	Security	Containment
CAS	+	+	+	-	-	-	+	-	O	-	-	O	O	-
VOMS	+	+	+	+	-	-	+	-	O	-	-	O	O	O
GridMap	-	O	-	-	-	O	-	+	O	-	+	O	O	-
Akenti	O	O	-	+	-	+	+	+	O	O	+	O	O	-
PERMIS	+	+	+	-	-	+	+	+	O	O	+	O	O	+
Usage based authorization	+	+	+	-	O	+	+	-	-	O	+	O	O	+

+: Parameter is supported. -: Parameter is not supported. O: Partially or weak support of the parameter.

is present in PERMIS and Usage based authorization, due to the support of RBAC. Lastly, the usability of a system is affected from either the push or pull model in use.

CONCLUSION

This chapter introduced and explained in detail the problem of access control in grid computer environments, including associated concepts and requirements. Access control models and authorization systems in the grid context are of vital importance due to their distributed nature. This is why we outlined two of the most prominent access control models for collaborative systems. Through the synopsis of both the RBAC and UCON$_{ABC}$ models, we identified their unique and of primal importance characteristics. In addition, a summary of well known grid authorization

Table 3. Summary of the comparisons among the different access control mechanisms

Access control mechanisms	Conceptual categorization layers			
	Entropy	Assets	Management	Logic
CAS	High	Low	Low	Low
VOMS	High	Medium	Low	Low
GridMap	Medium	Low	Low	Low / Medium
Akenti	Medium / High	Medium	Medium	Low / Medium
PERMIS	High	Low	Medium	Medium
Usage based authorization	High	Medium	Low / Medium	Medium

system was given. This helped clarifying how the theoretical access control models are turned into access control mechanisms for the grid systems. A first comparison of the RBAC with the $UCON_{ABC}$ model has shown that neither of them can tackle the difficulties raised from the defined grid access control requirements flawlessly. Based on the results of the foregoing comparison, it was expected for the grid authorization mechanisms to have the same level of applicability in grid environments. Indeed, the hypothesis has proven right, indicating that the examined mechanisms cannot handle well the defined requirements and parameters in all the layers of the conceptual categorization. Based on the results stemmed from our research, we believe that the design and implementation of proper access control models for the grid systems is needed. Current access control models are not specifically designed to tackle the requirements of grid systems. By applying the conceptual categorization for the grid systems, we illustrated how to identify a list of core requirements and how to use it as a comparison tool. In result, we expect the applied methodology to serve as a foundation for defining access control requirements in grid computing systems and moreover, to result in improved or new access control models and mechanisms.

REFERENCES

Alfieri, R., Cecchini, R., Ciaschini, V., dell'Agnello, L., Frohner, A., & Gianoli, A. ...Spataro, F. (2003). *VOMS, an authorization system for virtual organizations* (pp. 33-40). Paper presented at the European Across Grids Conference.

American National Standard Institute. I. (2004). Role based access control, *ANSI INCITS 359-2004* (p. 56).

Benantar, M. (2005). *Access control systems: Security, identity management and trust models.* New York, NY: Springer-Verlag.

Chadwick, D. (2005). Authorisation in grid computing. *Information Security Technical Report, 10*(1), 33–40. doi:10.1016/j.istr.2004.11.004

Chadwick, D. W., Otenko, A., & Ball, E. (2003). Role-based access control with X.509 attribute certificates. *IEEE Internet Computing, 7*(2), 62–69. doi:10.1109/MIC.2003.1189190

Chakrabarti, A. (2007). *Grid computing security.* New York, NY: Springer-Verlag.

Crampton, J. (2002). *Administrative scope and role hierarchy operations.* Paper presented at the Proceedings of the 7th ACM Symposium on Access Control Models and Technologies.

Ferraiolo, D. F., Chandramouli, R., Ahn, G.-J., & Gavrila, S. I. (2003). *The role control center: Features and case studies*. Paper presented at the Proceedings of the 8th ACM symposium on Access control models and technologies.

Ferraiolo, D. F., Kuhn, D. R., & Chandramouli, R. (2003). *Role-based access control*. London, UK-Boston, MA: Artech House, Inc.

Foster, I., Kesselman, C., & Tuecke, S. (2001). The anatomy of the grid: Enabling scalable virtual organizations. *International Jounral of Supercomputer Applications, 15*(3).

Foster, I., & Tuecke, S. (2005). Describing the elephant: The different faces of IT as service. *Queue, 3*(6), 26–29. doi:10.1145/1080862.1080874

Gouglidis, A., & Mavridis, I. (2009). A foundation for defining security requirements in grid computing. *Informatics, Panhellenic Conference on,* 180-184.

Gouglidis, A., & Mavridis, I. (2010). *On the definition of access control requirements for grid and cloud computing systems networks for grid applications* (*Vol. 25*, pp. 19–26). Berlin, Heidelberg: Springer.

ITU-T. (1995). *X.812 recommendation: Data networks and open system communications security - Information Technology – Open systems interconnection – Security frameworks for open systems: Access control framework* (p. 44). ITU.

Li, N., Byun, J.-W., & Bertino, E. (2007). A critique of the ANSI standard on role-based access control. *IEEE Security and Privacy, 5*(6), 41–49. doi:10.1109/MSP.2007.158

Oh, S., & Sandhu, R. (2002). *A model for role administration using organization structure*. Paper presented at the Proceedings of the 7th ACM Symposium on Access Control Models and Technologies.

Park, J., & Sandhu, R. (2004). The UCON ABC usage control model. *ACM Transactions on Information and System Security, 7*(1), 128–174. doi:10.1145/984334.984339

Pearlman, L., Welch, V., Foster, I., Kesselman, C., & Tuecke, S. (2002). *A community authorization service for group collaboration*. Paper presented at the Proceedings of the 3rd International Workshop on Policies for Distributed Systems and Networks (POLICY'02).

Sandhu, R. S., & Bhamidipati, V. (2008). *The ASCAA principles for next-generation role-based access control*. Paper presented at the Proc. 3rd International Conference on Availability, Reliability and Security (ARES), Barcelona, Spain.

Sandhu, R. S., Bhamidipati, V., & Munawer, Q. (1999). The ARBAC97 model for role-based administration of roles. *ACM Transactions on Information and System Security, 2*(1), 105–135. doi:10.1145/300830.300839

Sandhu, R. S., Coyne, E. J., Feinstein, H. L., & Youman, C. E. (1996). Role-based access control models. *IEEE Computer, 29*(2), 38–47.

Sandhu, R. S., & Park, J. (2003). *Usage control: A vision for next generation access control computer network security* (*Vol. 2776*, pp. 17–31). Berlin, Heidelberg: Springer.

Sandhu, R. S., & Samarati, P. (1994). Access Control: Principles and Practice. *IEEE Communications Magazine, 32*(9), 40–49. doi:10.1109/35.312842

Schlager, C., Sojer, M., Muschall, B., & Pernul, G. (2006). *Attribute-based authentication and authorisation infrastructures for e-commerce providers: E-Commerce and Web Technologies, 4082* (pp. 132–141). Berlin, Heidelberg: Springer.

Shafiq, B., Joshi, J. B. D., Bertino, E., & Ghafoor, A. (2005). Secure interoperation in a multidomain environment employing RBAC policies. *IEEE Transactions on Knowledge and Data Engineering*, *17*(11), 1557–1577. doi:10.1109/TKDE.2005.185

Thompson, M. R., Essiari, A., & Mudumbai, S. (2003). Certificate-based authorization policy in a PKI environment. *ACM Transactions on Information and System Security*, *6*(4), 566–588. doi:10.1145/950191.950196

Tolone, W., Ahn, G. J., Pai, T., & Hong, S.-P. (2005). Access control in collaborative systems. *ACM Computing Surveys*, *37*(1), 29–41. doi:10.1145/1057977.1057979

Yuan, E., & Tong, J. (2005). *Attributed based access control (ABAC) for Web services*. Paper presented at the Proceedings of the IEEE International Conference on Web Services.

Zhang, X., Nakae, M., Covington, M. J., & Sandhu, R. (2006). *A usage-based authorization framework for collaborative computing systems*. Paper presented at the Proceedings of the 11th ACM Symposium on Access Control Models and Technologies.

Zhang, X., Nakae, M., Covington, M. J., & Sandhu, R. (2008). Toward a usage-based security framework for collaborative computing systems. *ACM Transactions on Information and System Security*, *11*(1), 1–36. doi:10.1145/1330295.1330298

Chapter 9
Grid Computing for Ontology Matching

Axel Tenschert
High Performance Computing Center Stuttgart (HLRS), Germany

ABSTRACT

This chapter is examines the challenge of ontology matching in a grid environment in a scalable and high efficient way. For this, ontology matching approaches as well as grid computing are considered with the aim to present an approach for ontology matching on various resources. Hence, related approaches and tools are presented and discussed in order to provide an adequate background. Through this, a distributed ontology matching as it is required for ontology matching in a distributed environment such as the grid becomes usable. However, a novel ontology matching approach which meets the requirements of a grid architecture is considered in this chapter.

INTRODUCTION

Nowadays, lots of different ontologies as well as tools and frameworks that support matching are available. However, the amount of available semantic data structures is significantly growing. This issue faces the challenge of ontology matching in a scalable way considering large scale ontologies. For this, a strategy for handling big data sizes in an efficient way is required. Further,

DOI: 10.4018/978-1-61350-113-9.ch009

the field of bioinformatics is a beneficial use case because of the amount of available domain ontologies such as from the official NCBO BioPortal website (The National Center for Biomedical Ontology, 2009) and the need to examine several ontologies to solve a specific question.

The complexity of matching large-scale ontologies and ontology matching in urgent computing use cases entails the problem of matching in a scalable way. Hence, distribution techniques such as grid computing are used to increase scalability by executing it by the use of distributed heterogeneous computing resources. Hence, the aim of this work is to support ontology matching strategies with a grid architecture to provide required computing resources for compute resource intensive and urgent computing use cases. The ontologies that are considered for this work are mostly OWL ontologies.

Furthermore, the LarKC project (The LarKC project, 2010) in which new techniques for processing large datasets are developed for the usage of concrete use cases such as "Semantic Integration for Early Clinical Development" or "Carcinogenesis Reference Production" is a beneficial basis for this work. Within LarKC project ontologies are used as well and new techniques usage of large-scale data sets are developed and used for real time applications such as an urban city use case that requires continuously semantic data with the aim to analyze such data in a time-saving way. For use cases as they are mentioned above, sophisticated techniques are required to run several processes at same time in a distributed fashion as it is done in the grid. At this, the new idea is to set one ontology from a given set as the priority ontology which is enhanced by matching the concepts of the priority ontology with the concepts of other selected ontologies from a given set.

This work supports an adequate matching procedure as well as a mapping of similar concepts or properties of the ontologies in a grid. For this, the first step is to define an adequate architecture which meets the requirements of ontology matching in a grid. After the matching is executed the ontology parts and the matching results are merged together in the priority ontology with the aim to extend this ontology. However, the matching strategy will be aligned to the grid architecture. The presented idea for matching ontologies in a grid environment is an effective method to solve the challenge of matching in a scalable, robust and time-saving way. Further, it is of interest to examine the principles and design issues for this topic.

Currently, lots of ontology matching strategies have been published so far. Hence, a clear distinction between this work and current approaches is required. This work aims to map concepts, properties as well as relations between entities of several ontologies in a semi-automatic manner by considering well known developments in this field and extension of these approaches. Further, the ontology matching is supported by a distributed architecture in order to use several compute resources. Beyond the distribution of ontology matching processes, ontologies are selected with the aim to enhance one ontology to a priority ontology of a given set. In order to achieve an adequate mapping of similarities for the enhanced priority ontology similarity values for entity pairs within the matched ontologies are calculated. However, the calculation of similarity values for entity pairs encounters the problem of evaluating one measurement out of lots of values such as similarity of properties or relations and relevance to neighboring entity pairs and much more.

Further, as mentioned the matching of large data sets requires a high amount of compute resources as well. For this, processing algorithms at same time on several nodes (e.g. cluster architecture) is a beneficial solution. However, this raises the challenge of distributing the jobs in a high effective way as well as aligning algorithms to avoid latencies or conflicts. Therefore, two main issues are considered in this work: (i) Ontology matching based on similarity values, and (ii) Distributed ontology matching on several resources by usage of a grid architecture.

RESEARCH BACKGROUND

At present the number of different semantic information is growing significantly because of a huge amount of different available resources. This trend raises the problem of managing required information in order to increase heterogeneity among this data. This challenge is crucial for ontology matching to ensure a merging of different information from disparate ontologies with varying structures. Further, the use of various ontologies has the problem of dealing with similar as well as competing ontologies with different sets of terms, classifications or schemas. Hence, the interoperability of disparate ontologies has to be solved. For this, ontology matching methods have to be improved and adjusted to a specific use case scenario with the aim to increase data heterogeneity.

The heterogeneity problem is present even if two ontologies with disparate structures contain similar elements and attributes. In this particular case when correspondences between both ontologies are available the correspondences have to be exposed and in case of merging elements and attributes of both ontologies, the correspondences have to be allocated to a matching entity or attribute. Euzenat and Shvaiko (Euzenat & Shvaiko, 2007) are describing the data heterogeneity problem in the field of ontology matching by presenting two XML files that are used as ontologies. Both files have a different but similar content but the structure is different. When thinking of ontologies with disparate structures, as an example we can think of the two XML files with a disparate structure but similar concepts and features, the matching by considering the structure should be considered. In this case the question is now, how to handle the different structure and match the similar entities of both XML files? From this question the next question is derived, how to handle this issue for ontologies with even different format?

Lots of strategies are available for ontology matching but the challenge of increasing heterogeneity within ontologies with different structures is still an important research question. This issue is also presented by Euzenat & Shvaiko (2008) by pointing out the issues to be solved when matching ontologies with different structures. However, the problem of automatically or semi-automatically management of heterogeneity among several data

structures within ontologies is a broad research field also for future research.

Current approaches consider aspects such as measurement a grade of similarity or using specific rules for automatically or semi-automatically ontology matching. However, if there is an automatically generated measurement which describes the similarity between concepts there is always the problem of trust. Only if there is a 100 percent matching or a 0 percent matching full confidence is ensured. Through this, there are only very few or even not a single full-confidence matching between a selection of entities taken from selected ontologies. Nevertheless, a matching that ensures a high grade of confidence is required in cases where lots of information sources are considered.

Furthermore, the measurement of similarities is used to merge concepts, features and new relations from a selected ontology to a priority ontology. If the similarity grade reaches a certain level of similarity the merge is performed. Nevertheless, if a new concept or relation is added to the priority ontology this has to be integrated and connected to other concepts in the priority ontology as well.

However, a probability value has to be generated which identifies the grade of similarity with the aim to merge only matching results with a high similarity grade. This merge enhances the selected priority ontology.

When thinking matching ontologies, we have to think of the problem of matching similar concepts with different features or meanings as well. This problem might be solved through the additional matching of features of the targeted concepts. Furthermore, matching the features might also support the decision if a concept should be added to another concept in the priority ontology.

This work targets the combination of matching strategies for generating measurements which expresses the grade of similarity between concepts in different ontologies and an adequate management of handling uncertainties of matching results in order to provide an automatic / semi-automatic merge between different but similar ontologies.

For this ontology matching in a distributed environment such as the grid is a promising solution for handling huge amounts of data within the ontologies as well as a high number of ontologies. Furthermore, established approaches in this field are considered. Bloehdorn et al. (Bloehdorn, Haase, Huang, Sure, Volker, van Harmelen & Studer, 2009) have indentified an ontology matching process divided into five steps and a number of iterations depending on the number of new proposed alignments. For the described process input is required in terms of two or more selected ontologies in order to generate one output ontology that includes the proposed alignments. Additionally, a user is enabled to enter already established matches manually. Bloehdorn et al. are identifying the whole process as a matching process but the steps for comparing the alignments are defined as mapping. The five mapping steps are as follows:

Feature Engineering. Relevant features of the ontology set are selected.

Search Step Selection. A defined search space of matches is derived.

Similarity Computation. Probability values within the matches are defined.

Similarity Aggregation. Several probability values of one match (e.g. similarity between properties, relations, etc.) are aggregated to one.

Interpretation. In the final interpretation step the produced similarity steps are used to derive matches between entities.

However, the similarity of one entity pair influences the neighboring pairs as well. Hence, within the iteration the probability values of the neighbors are considered. When the last proposed new alignment is calculated the iteration terminates. Further, several algorithms processing the iterations for the ontology matching process are executed at same time. Nevertheless, a previous selection phase for receiving relevant domain ontologies is not considered within this five step model. Therefore an additional previous step should be included as well. The previous step is used for identification of relevant ontologies for the further matching of the ontologies from the given set. This pervious step is an identification phase that might be supported by a domain expert.

When thinking of distribution techniques MapReduce (Hadoop MapReduce, 2009) is taken into account as well. MapReduce is based on Apache Hadoop (The Apache Hadoop project, 2009), an open-source software project for reliable, scalable and distributed computing. Hence, the MapReduce framework is developed for processing vast amounts of data on several nodes of a cluster in parallel. The advantage of MapReduce is the support of ontology matching in a cluster environment on several nodes within this cluster. This approach ensures that required compute resources are available even for large datasets. However, this approach is limited to the available compute resources within the cluster. This is a relevant issue when thinking of a small cluster with restricted compute resources. For this purpose a grid architecture that allocates compute resources from several clusters or servers seems to be beneficial. Urbani et al. (Urbani, Kotoulas, Oren, & van Harmelen, 2009) have analyzed the problem of scalable and distributed reasoning by usage of MapReduce. Within their work they have addressed the challenge of partitioning reasoning in a scalable way. The advantage for reasoning in a parallel way is the possibility to scale in two dimensions, the hardware performance of each node and the number of available nodes in the cluster. Urbani et al. have proposed an approach for reasoning of very large amounts of data. This approach has outperformed other common published approaches within their specific test conditions. Through this, MapReduce seems to be an approach that should be considered for further research as well. However, within the LarKC project MapReduce is used and analyzed as well and therefore, for future research the results of the LarKC project should be considered as well.

However, other common approaches for reasoning such as Falcon-AO (The Falcon-AO infrastructure, 2008) or DBpedia (The DBpedia project 2010) have been published. Hu et. al (Hu, Cheng, Zheng, Zhong & Qu, 2006) are presenting Falcon-AO as a significant component of Falcon for automatic ontology alignment. Within Falcon-AO Hu et al. are describing the PBM component that is used for partition of ontologies. This technique is required to manage large-scale ontologies. The Falcon-AO tool is used for partition and alignment of ontologies. The partition of ontologies allows the matching of several parts of an ontology at same time. This strategy is beneficial when thinking of distribution of several matching jobs.

DBpedia is a community effort for extracting structured information from Wikipedia with the aim to make them available in the web. Within DBpedia several projects are available such as DBpedia Ontology, a cross-domain ontology that covers classes and properties for describing the Wikipedia content in a structured way.

However, the OntoGrid project (The OntoGrid project, 2007) has to be considered as well. OntoGrid has developed various grid compliant ontology services for matching ontologies in the semantic grid. Thus, an environment for processing semantic knowledge in the grid is enabled which can be used for further developments. Within the OntoGrid project ontology services within a grid environment are considered as well. Therefore, the OntoGrid results are useful in order to use such ontology services as a useful basis for an ontology matching approach within a grid environment. The described approaches are addressing the challenge of reasoning at same time as well as handling large data sets. Hence, they are considered for defining an effective approach for distributed ontology matching.

ONTOLOGY MATCHING IN A GRID ENVIRONMENT

Issues, Controversies and Problems

Beyond current approaches and solutions the research field of ontology matching is of great interest, especially when thinking of large datasets. For this, an algorithm for resource effective ontology matching and sufficient compute resources is required. Both issues are relevant aspects that are envisaged by ontology matching in a grid environment. Through this, it becomes possible to allocate required compute resources by usage of a grid architecture that addresses several compute jobs on various available compute resources. These compute resources are nodes in a cluster or several servers in a Virtual Organization (VO). Hence, on the one hand the challenge is to allocate the required compute resources for matching large scale ontologies and on the other hand the challenge is to execute several matching jobs in a resource efficient and scalable way. For this, ontology matching at same time is an encouraging approach. However, in order to avoid latencies, overlaps and matching conflicts an adequate management for processing matching jobs at same time as well as a beneficial ontology matching are required.

The main issues regarding this work are summarized in the following:

- A grid architecture for managing various compute resources (e.g. maybe in a VO) is required
- The job execution of several matching processes at same time has to be managed
- A resource effective and scalable strategy for matching ontologies is required

Within this work the three mentioned points are considered in order to solve the problem of matching ontologies in a high efficient and scalable way. Referring to previous work approaches for ontology matching at same time on several resources are available. Within a former publication we have pointed out different workflows for parallelization of processes (Tenschert, Assel, Cheptsov & Gallizo, 2009). These workflows are listed in the following:

- Single Code Multiple Data (SCMD workflow)
- Multiple Code Single Data (MCSD workflow without conveyer dependencies)
- Multiple Code Multiple Data (MCMD workflow)

These workflows are highly beneficial for parallel execution and should be considered. Nevertheless, the first step is the development of a grid architecture in order to provide the required compute resources for executing the matching jobs at same time. When this is done, a concept for managing several jobs at same time is required. When thinking of the selected ontologies, it is obvious that there are relations between the matched entities. These relations have to be considered within a matching. Beyond the compute resource allocation, the handling of several jobs on different resources goes hand in hand with the development of a beneficial ontology matching strategy. Regarding the ontology matching strategy it is a challenge to be aware of the relations between entities within the matched ontologies and match such entities at same time. The neighboring entities should be considered within a matching process in order to include the relations for generating a more precise matching result. However, of the neighboring entities are matched at same time and change within the entities and their relations take place based on the matching results the matching result for the other neighbored entities is influenced as well. This issue has to be considered within an ontology matching at same time.

Solutions and Recommendations

The matching of ontologies assumes a selection of relevant ontologies before processing the matching. This is previous step is the identification of ontologies. Further, the selection of relevant ontologies is a basis for ontology matching and extraction of new semantic knowledge structures. The following figure presents a generic sequence diagram for ontology matching.

A matching stack includes a selection of relevant ontologies for further matching. The ontology stack is enhanced by identification of ontologies that are adequate for the specific needs of a use case. When the set of ontologies is identifies the next step is to select entities from the ontologies out of the ontology stack in order to process a matching, the execution of the jobs for ontology matching. Thereafter, the matching results are stored and rated. The ranking of the matching results is required for making statements about the usability of the matching results. The useful matching results, that have a good ranking, are send back to the ontology stack in order to extend one priority ontology from the ontology stack. Trough this, it becomes possible to enlarge one identified ontology from the ontology stack with further knowledge structures. However, the presented ontology matching sequence is a step by step sequence that does not include ontology matching at same time on various compute resources. For this, the presented generic sequence diagram has to be extended with the ability to process ontology matching jobs at same time. Furthermore, the presented generic sequence presents ontology matching but it does not present the management of parallel ontology matching jobs. Therefore, the following figure presents an enhanced sequence for ontology matching at same time.

When extending the ontology matching sequence the next step is to identify the processes that are executed at same time. For this, Figure 2 exposes the parallel execution and an additional

Figure 1. Generic ontology matching

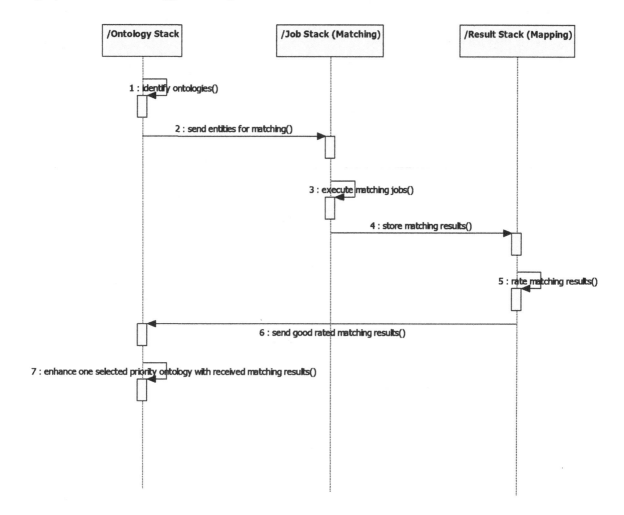

step is identified. The additional step is the last one in this sequence, it validates if further matching processes are initiated or if the matching processes will terminate. However, the only process that will not be executed with other processes at same time is the identification phase for creating a set of adequate ontologies. The identification of relevant ontologies is a phase that takes place before the matching is initiated.

Regarding the ontology matching processes that takes place after the identification phase it has to be considered that these processes will take place at same time. More detailed this means that several entities taken from ontologies out of the ontology stack are matched at same time. Though, a management of these matching processes at same time is highly required in order to avoid latencies in case that the matching processes are finished at different times. Further, the matching results are stored and rated within the result stack. Afterwards, the good matching results are send back to the ontology stack with the aim to enhance one selected priority ontology. After this, new matching processes are initiated or the ontology matching processes are terminating. Nevertheless, the mentioned processes are executed at same time but they are determined at different times and therefore the matching of new matching

Figure 2. Ontology matching at same time

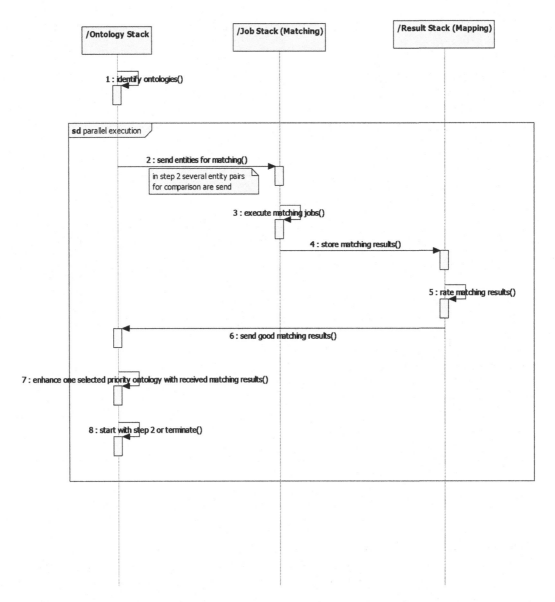

processes is initiated at various times as well. Furthermore, within the matching of entities that takes place in parallel but at different, overlapping and various times the enhancement of the priority ontology take place. This approach implies a parallel matching of several entities at different times with a priority ontology that is changing during the matching. However, this approach results in a matching strategy that assumes a so-phisticated entity matching sequence that considers the dependency of the time when the selected entities are matched because of changes in the priority ontology during the matching phase. Though, another approach is to store the matching results in the result stack and enhance the priority ontology after all matching processes are terminated.

This strategy avoids the problem of receiving different matching results in case that entity pairs are matched at different times when different changes were made in the priority ontology. However, this strategy implies the problem that in case that several ontologies are compared with the priority ontology it is possible that for one entity from the priority ontology several similar matching results for the one entity or several disparate matching results for the one entity are available. Therefore, another strategy is to match the entity pairs as already described but just selecting one ontology and the priority ontology. When these matching processes are terminated and the priority ontology in enhanced with the results the next entities from another ontology taken from the set are matched with the entities from the priority ontology. Nevertheless, this strategy expects that the sequence for selecting ontologies from the set is relevant as well because of the fact that the priority ontologies changes with every ontology matching iteration and therefore the matching results are different as well.

Beyond the described ontology matching within a distributed environment, the ontology matching approach has to be considered as well. The usage of similarity values for ontology matching increases the accuracy of matching strategies. This approach is envisaged within this work. When thinking of Bloehdorn et al. the calculation of the similarity values (Similarity Computation) is the third step of the ontology matching process. Therefore, we have to take look at the two steps before, the "Feature Engineering" and the "Search Step Selection". Within the first step a user has to define relevant features for the matching. The relevancy of features regarding a matching depends on the research question as well as the topic of the ontologies. Further, a set of ontologies needs to be defined by a domain expert as well. Through this, the topic and the amount of data that is considered within the matching are specified precisely. However, as mentioned before, a previous step should be the identification of relevant ontologies in order to create a stack including domain ontologies that meets the requirements of a specific use case. Regarding this work OWL ontologies from the biomedical research field are considered.

The "Search Step Selection" defines the search space of all entities that are considered for the matching. The search space affects the accuracy of matching results as well. A wider range of the search space might lead to a better analysis of neighboring entities that influences the current entity pair. However, this may lead to an amount of data that becomes hard to compute in an efficient and scalable way. However, as mentioned before, a previous step should be the identification of relevant ontologies in order to create a stack including domain ontologies that meets the requirements of a specific use case. Regarding this work OWL ontologies from the biomedical research field are considered.

Figure 3 describes the prerequisites for calculating the similarity value. First of all, a set of ontologies is identified to provide the matching process with the required input data. Afterwards, an entity pair is selected and a selection of relevant features for the matching are determined. The next step is to define the range of the search space.

The similarity value of an entity pair consists of several aspects, such as the similarity of concepts, features of concepts, the taxonomy and the relations to other entities within the defines search space. Especially, when thinking of the relations between entities in an ontology it becomes obvious that related entities (neighboring entities) have to be considered as well. At this, the search space describes the range of neighboring entities that are considered. However, an issue for further research is an algorithm for calculating the similarity values for entities out of a set of similarity values, namely of the concepts, features of the concepts, the taxonomy and the relations between entities.

Figure 3. Similarity measurement calculation prerequisites

To summarize the main issues for measuring the similarity value (*SimV*) between two selected entities we identify the following relevant similarity values that are required in order to calculate one value (*SimV*).

- The grade of selected concepts - *SimC*
- The features of and between the concepts - *SimF*
- The taxonomy - *SimT*
- The relations of the entities – *SimR*

Hence, *SimV* consists of *SimC*, *SimF*, *SimT* and *SimR*. The challenge for creating *SimV* is to measure the similarities in an adequate manner, generating one similarity out of the identified similarities as well as considering the search space of the matches. Furthermore, the usability of the matching results depends as well on the identification of relevant ontologies.

Beyond the described iteration, including the calculation preparation and the calculation of the similarity value, it has to be considered that several iterations will take place. Lots of these iterations are processed at same time. Therefore, a solution for distributing the iterations on several resources is required. For this work, an algorithm for distribution of ontology matching process iterations on several resources is required.

When thinking of the presented approaches for distribution of ontology matching strategies and the matching strategy considering similarity values with the aim to enhance the grade of trustiness for the matching results, it is obvious to combine both strategies. Through this, the accuracy of the enhancement of one selected priority ontology is improved as well as the usage of several compute resources in a scalable, robust and effective way. The similarity value ensures a precision of the matching result which allows a mapping of entities within the priority ontology that is provides new knowledge structures for the priority ontology. Further, the combination with an adequate distribution technique supports the selection of lots of large scale ontologies. Through this, a domain expert is enabled to select all relevant ontologies in the ontology stack and initialize the matching process without considering a bad performance of the matching processes. This approach for ontology matching in a distributed environment by using similarity values for the matching results in order to enhance one selected priority ontology offers a strategy to manage high effective ontology matching.

FUTURE RESEARCH DIRECTIONS

When thinking of future research directions the topic of matching ontologies in a grid environment becomes more and more a highly important topic. The growing amount of available information and semantic data faces the challenge of handling large data sets in a scalable manner. For this, a framework for usage of several compute resources as it is provided in a grid architecture is a solution for this challenge. Further, managing ontology matching by involving similarity values is ensures the grade of convenience regarding the matches of several entities.

The management of extremely large-datasets becomes more and more relevant and therefore, algorithms for allocation of compute resources with the aim to distribute matching processes on these resources, is a research question for the future as well. Therefore, current research approaches in the field of ontology matching and semantic data management consider more and more distributed architectures in order to solve the challenge of ontology matching with extremely large data sets. Even in the research field of urgent computing, a good performance is highly required.

Furthermore, the data heterogeneity problem is a challenge for further research as well. Within the high amount of available data it has to be ensured that the data structures are usable even if they are structured in a different way or if the data is stored in another format. The current trend for storing semantic data follows not a single data format but lots of different structures and formats. Further, when thinking of ontologies it has to be considered that the definition of an ontology is very broad. Even a text including information that are related to each other can be defined as an ontology. Hence, the data heterogeneity problem for ontologies includes as well the problem of defining which types of ontologies to use for a matching that is performed in an automatic or semi-automatic way by usage of an adequate ontology matching approach.

The current trend of grid architectures is highly important when thinking of distributed computer resources and Virtual Organizations (VOs). Beyond grid computing, current research trends in the field of distributed architectures consider approaches for cloud computing as well. This new paradigm should be considered within future technologies as well.

CONCLUSION

The presented approach for ontology matching in a grid environment supports a highly efficient and scalable execution of processes. Through this, large amounts of data as well as a time urgent execution of processes are provided in a compute resource efficient way. In addition to that, the usage of similarity values increases the grade of quality of the ontology matching processes. Furthermore, the combination of an ontology matching strategy that is based on measurement of similarities between entities and a grid environment is a promising approach for matching very large data sets and urgent computing cases that require a very fast ontology matching approach.

Hence, this approach is a basis for further work done in the field of ontology matching on distributed compute resources. The usage of a distributed architecture such as a grid enables the usage of several compute resources and therefore maintenance required resources even for very large data sets. Through this, various resources are accessible for distributing compute jobs for ontology matching in a scalable way on several compute resources. The usage of distributed compute resources combined with an effective matching strategy for several ontologies ensures a matching in a time saving way even for large-scale ontologies.

REFERENCES

Bloehdorn, S., Haase, P., Huang, Zh., Sure, Y., Volker, J., van Harmelen, F., & Studer, R. (2009). Ontology management . In Davies, J., Grobelnik, M., & Mladenic, D. (Eds.), *Semantic knowledge management* (pp. 3–20). Berlin-Heidelberg, Germany: Springer-Verlag. doi:10.1007/978-3-540-88845-1_2

Euzenat, J., & Shvaiko, P. (2007). *Ontology matching*. Berlin-Heidelberg, Germany: Springer-Verlag.

Hadoop MapReduce. (2007). Retrieved on July 18, 2009, from the *Hadoop MapReduce* website: http://hadoop.apache.org/ mapreduce/

Hu, W., Cheng, G., Zheng, D., Zhong, X., & Qu, Y. (2006). The results of Falcon-AO. In *Proceedings of Ontology Alignment Evaluation Initiative*.

Shvaiko, P., & Euzenat, J. (2008). 10 challenges for ontology matching. In *Proceedings of the International Conference on Ontologies, DataBases, and Applications of Semantics*.

Tenschert, A., Assel, M., Cheptsov, A., & Gallizo, G. (2009). Parallelization and distribution techniques for ontology matching in urban computing environments. In *Proceedings of the 4th International Workshop on Ontology Matching of the International Semantic Web Conference*.

The Apache Hadoop project. (2007). Retrieved on July 16, 2009, from *The Apache Hadoop* website: http://hadoop.apache.org/

The DBpedia project. (2010). Retrieved on March 12, 2010, from the *DBpedia* website: http://db-pedia.org/About

The Falcon-AO infrastructure (2001-2007). Retrieved July 10, 2008, from the *Falcon-AO* website: http://iws.seu.edu.cn/ projects/ matching/

The LarKC project. (2008, April 1). Retrieved March, 2010 from official *LarKC project* website: http://www.larkc.eu/

The National Center for Biomedical Ontology. (2009). *The National Center for Biomedical Ontology.* Retrieved February 3, 2009, from: http://bioportal.bioontology.org/

The OntoGrid project. (2007). Retrieved 2007, from official website: http://www.oeg-upm.net/

Urbani, J., Kotoulas, S., Oren, E., & van Harmelen, F. (2009). Scalable distributed reasoning using MapReduce. In *Proceedings of 8th International Semantic Web Conference* (pp. 634-649).

ADDITIONAL READING

Ontology Matching. (2000). Retrieved March 9, 2010 from *The Ontology Matching* website: http://www.ontologymatching.org/

The Ontology Alignment Evaluation Initiative. (2004). Retrieved June 22, 2009 from *The Ontology Alignment Evaluation* website: http://oaei.ontologymatching.org/

The Ontology Engineering Group. (1991). Retrieved 2010 from *The Ontology Engineering Group* website: http://www.oeg-upm.net/

The Semantic Web. (1994). Retrieved September 27, 2009 from *The Semantic Web* website: http://semanticweb.org/

KEY TERMS AND DEFINITIONS

Distributed Computing: The distribution of processes among several compute resources.

Grid Computing: A distributed computing architecture consisting of loosely coupled compute resources.

Ontology Matching: The comparison of concepts, features of the concepts and relations of entities with two or more ontologies.

Ontology Merging: The enhancement of a selected ontology with concepts, features and relations from another ontology.

Section 3
Applications for Grid Computing

Chapter 10
Security Standards and Issues for Grid Computing

Athanasios Moralis
National Technical University of Athens, Greece

Vassiliki Pouli
National Technical University of Athens, Greece

Mary Grammatikou
National Technical University of Athens, Greece

Dimitrios Kalogeras
National Technical University of Athens, Greece

Vasilis Maglaris
National Technical University of Athens, Greece

ABSTRACT

Security in grid environments that are built using Service Oriented Architecture (SOA) technologies is a great challenge. On one hand, the great diversity in security technologies, mechanisms and protocols that each organization follows and on the other hand, the different goals and policies that these organizations adopt, comprise a complex security environment. Authenticating and authorizing users and services, identity management in a multi-organizational scenario and secure communication define the main context of the problem. In this chapter, we provide an overview of the security protocols and technologies that can be applied on a Web Service (WS) based grid environment.

INTRODUCTION

A Grid is a large-scale generalized network system that offers computing resources across multiple organizations and administrative domains. For the transport of the data across the grid nodes and the

DOI: 10.4018/978-1-61350-113-9.ch010

interaction of the users with the grid resources, mechanisms should be utilized to assure those. The Web Services (WSs) based on the Service Oriented Architecture (SOA) provide this.

SOA provides the basic paradigm for building software applications that can be applied in today's complex and heterogeneous environments. SOA is the first integration and architectural framework that uses services available in the web and promotes loose coupling between software components, thus resulting in reusable components. SOA uses as basic building blocks the services. A service is an implementation of a well-defined business functionality. Following this strict approach, this kind of services can then be consumed by clients in different applications or by business processes. SOA in general does not impose any style of services. However, the de-facto standard is using WS Architecture to realize a SOA architecture. WSs are based on various eXtensible Markup Language (XML) standards such as Simple Object Access Protocol (SOAP), Universal Description, Discovery and Integration (UDDI), Web Services Description Language (WSDL) and designed to support interoperable machine-to-machine interaction over a network.

The wide acceptance that WSs meet is largely due to the need of integration heterogeneous applications across different systems belonging to different organizations across the Internet. WS Technologies enable more dynamic, loosely-coupled and synchronous or asynchronous interactions between both inter-domain and intra-domain applications. WSs expose in a standardized way to external clients the application's interface, with the use of WSDL, hiding in most cases the application's internal complexity. As they are often used over the Internet, for mission-critical transactions with the possibility of dynamic, short-term relationships, security is a major concern. This elevates the value of securing them against a wide range of attacks, both internal and external. The main security issues that have to be addressed are authentication, authorization, confidentiality, data integrity, non-repudiation, single sign on, delegation, trust and identity mapping.

To meet these security requirements, some WS compatible mechanisms have been defined, i.e. WS Security Specifications (Rosenberg & Remy, 2004), that apply at the message level and provide ways to transfer security tokens and credentials

thus generally achieving end-to-end (from client to service) security functionality.

Specific consortiums have been constituted to address and provide standards for these kinds of WS related issues (Singhal, 2007). Major standardization initiatives, among them, are the World Wide Web Consortium (W3C) and the Organization for the Advancement of Structured Information Standards (OASIS). These organizations try to standardize WS specifications (including WS Security Specifications) and provide a common and global framework so that organizations and applications can interoperate in heterogeneous environments. Principal developers of the WS Security (O'Neill, 2003) standards are the IBM, Microsoft, VeriSign that have submitted the WS Security Specification to OASIS and it was approved.

The rest of the chapter is organized as follows. In the following section we provide the basic background, covering the WSs Security (WSS) standard. The next section describes the additional standards that complement the WSS, along with related issues that each standard may have. The two last sections provide the future directions while they conclude the chapter.

BACKGROUND

Traditionally, communications have been protected at the network layer by adopting technologies such as the Secure Socket Layer (SSL) or the Transport Layer Security (TLS) (Dierks & Rescorla, 2006) and the Internet Protocol Security (IPSec) (Kend & Atkinson, 1998).

SSL/TLS is a connection oriented protocol that offers several security features including authentication, data integrity and data confidentiality. SSL/TLS enables point-to-point secure sessions. Similarly, IPSec is a network layer standard for transport security that provides secure sessions with host authentication, data integrity and data confidentiality. Both of these technologies are point-to-point, meaning that if the content of a packet needs to be processed in an intermediary node, the SSL/TLS/IPSec connection must terminate on that node; another SSL/TLS/IPSec connection is necessary to be established in order to achieve client-to-server secure communication. In simple cases where no intermediaries are involved, the secure tunnel through which traffic is secured is adequate. In the scenarios where either a SOAP request needs to traverse multiple intermediaries (e.g. firewalls and proxies) or asynchronous communications are involved, these technologies do not provide the required functionality of end-to-end secure communications. Enforcement of the security at the message level (SOAP message) is required to offer that.

Other case where end-to-end secure communication is essential is when the WSs based applications require a high level of granularity. Specifically, they need to maintain secure context and control it according to their security policies. Also some information inside the message should be displayed in clear so that it can be accessible by those recipients of the message that need to process the information.

WS-Security (Nadalin et al., 2006a) offers this end-to-end functionality as it allows secure SOAP exchanges. It provides a set of SOAP extensions that can be used to implement message integrity, confidentiality and authentication. The main features follow:

- Multiple Security Token Formats. Those tokens bare the authentication information needed for authentication to a service.
- Multiple Trust Domains.
- Multiple Signature Formats.
- Multiple Encryption Technologies.
- End-to-end message content security and not just transport level security.

WS-Security specification is organized in parts, the Core and the Profiles. The Core specification defines an abstract security model to offer confi-

dentiality and integrity and authorize the SOAP messages using signatures and security tokens. Message protection is achieved by encryption of the body, or parts of the SOAP message, whereas, integrity and message origin is verified by signatures either on the header or the body or any combination of them. The specification defines how the various security tokens are included in the message, but not how they are issued, acquired, renewed or validated by the participating parties. These are implementation details and can vary among different security mechanisms and systems.

All the security related information targeted to a specific recipient is included in the <wss: security> security header block that is attached within the SOAP header. If the message is targeted to more than one recipient then more than one header blocks may exist. Inside the security header various items (tokens) can be attached (Table 1):

When sending a SOAP message protected by WS-Security a security header as described earlier needs to be attached. It should contain a security token or a security token reference. Then depending on the actions chosen, a signature can also be included and the under encryption elements are substituted by their ciphertext.

Except from the core specification, there are additional documents that define the WS-Security using X.509 certificates (Nadalin et al., 2006b), Kerberos tokens (Nadalin et al., 2006c; Monzillo et al., 2006). Kerberos Token specification and SAML (Security Assertion Markup Language, 2010) assertions were released in version 1.1 of the WS-Security Specification. These documents are actually extensions of the core specification intended to meet the specific requirements of each security mechanism.

Conceptually, the WS-Security standard specifies an abstraction layer on top of any organization's particular application security technology (PKI, Kerberos, etc.) that allows such dissimilar infrastructures to participate in a common trust relationship.

Table 1. WS-Security tokens (WSS Core)

Token	Description
Username Token	Optionally included, it provides a username.
Binary Security Tokens	They are non XML binary tokens, like X.509 certificates or Kerberos tickets.
XML Tokens:	They are used for xml based security tokens
EncryptedData Tokens	For encrypting other tokens (when needed) using an embedded encryption key or a reference to a separate encryption key.
SecurityTokenReference Elements	Provide a reference to the token or other mechanism that should be used for retrieving the key of encryption or signature. It includes Direct Reference that directly reference tokens using URI, Key Identifier that specify the token or an embedded reference.
Signatures	Demonstrate the knowledge of a key associated with an accompanying token. A signature token that contains an xml signature may be attached in the security header.
XML Encryption Reference List	Lists all the encrypted <xenc: EncryptedData> that are the encrypted elements within the SOAP envelope.

However, WS-Security cannot provide the required functionality in a grid environment alone, where heterogeneous organizations operate. In this environment each organization has its own distinct security architecture and technology, following its own access policy and its user and system identities as provided by its own Identity Providers. Identity Providers are entities that issue credentials to individual end users and also verify that the issued credentials are valid. Various WS related security specifications such as WS-Federation, WS-Trust and others offer a solution to the above problem. In the next chapter, we give an overview of these specifications.

WEB SERVICE SECURITY RELATED PROTOCOLS

XML Encryption

XML Encryption provides rules for encrypting and decrypting XML Documents with the help of security tokens (certificates, Kerberos tickets) and representing them, in the end, as XML encrypted documents. The encryption can be enforced either to the whole XML Document or to parts of it. The standard has been proposed by the W3C XML Encryption Working Group (Imamura, Dillaway & Simon, 2002).

XML Encryption often referred as XML-Enc allows each party, when exchanging XML Documents, to maintain secure and insecure states of information even in the same document. In addition, XML-Enc provides the means to handle both XML and non-XML data. Specifically it can be used for encrypting:

- The complete XML document.
- An XML element.
- The content of an XML element.
- Non-XML data (Arbitrary Data) within an XML document.

Keys for encryption/decryption can either be asymmetric or symmetric, following the mechanisms of public key and secret key cryptography respectively. Numerous cryptographic algorithms are supported by the standard (i.e. tiple-DES, AES-128, RSA-1.5, Diffie Hellman, SHA1). However by following the syntax and the recommendations of the standard, user specified algorithms can also be supported.

In practice, by applying XML Encryption to an element or to a whole XML document, an XML Encrypted Element is produced in its place. This element includes the cipher text (encrypted data) and optionally includes the encryption method used to encrypt the element, the information about the retrieval of the cryptographic key and the encryption properties that are used during the encryption and are essential for the decryption procedure e.g. date/time stamp.

XML-Enc, being an XML standard, provides document-based security. Consequently, it is utilized by WS-Security in order to provide encryption of the elements of a SOAP message thus offering a solution to the problem of message confidentiality. In Table 2, an example of XML encryption of an element is given.

XML Digital Signature

XML Digital Signature specification (Bartel et al., 2008) defines XML signatures processing rules and syntax. An XML Signature can be applied to any digital content including an XML document such as a SOAP message. Signatures are related to digital content through the use of Unique Resource Identifier - URI. An XML document can contain more than one XML signatures. XML Digital Signatures, when used in communication, can offer message authentication, integrity and non-repudiation ensuring that the message is not altered during transfer. Although the term signature refers to Public Key Cryptography, XML signature can also use Symmetric Cryptography. In this case, the signature is named Authentication Codes.

In general, a digital signature of a data object is produced by digesting it and encrypting the resulting value using either symmetric or asymmetric cryptography. XML Signatures follow this rule and conform to the XML standard. As so, a XML Signature is represented as a Signature element. The standard suggests as digesting algorithm the SHA-1 and discourages the use of MD5 algorithm.

A typical XML Signature according to the specification is accompanied by:

- The SignedInfo, that includes the canonicalization algorithm, the signature algorithm and number of references.

Table 2. An example of an XML encrypted document

Initial XML Document	`<?xml version='1.0'?>`
	`<Payment xmlns='http://example.org/creditCardPayment'>`
	`<Name>Name Surname</Name>`
	`<Number>3112 4581 0007 0036</Number>`
	`<Issuer>Example Bank</Issuer>`
	`<Expiration>06/10</Expiration>`
	`</CreditCard>`
	`</PaymentInfo>`

Produced XML Document by encrypting the contents of the <Number> element of the Credit Card	`<?xml version='1.0'?>`
	`<Payment xmlns='http://example.org/creditCardPayment'>`
	`<Name>Name Surname</Name>`
	`<Number>`
	`<EncryptedData xmlns='http://www.w3.org/2001/04/xmlenc#'`
	`Type='http://www.w3.org/2001/04/xmlenc#Content'>`
	`<EncryptionMethod`
	`Algorithm='http://www.w3.org/2001/04/xmlenc#tripledes-cbc'/>`
	`<CipherData> <CipherValue2FsdGVkX1/qO5W2aRUUjmy7MxtgiA+sIZy</CipherValue>`
	`</CipherData>`
	`</EncryptedData>`
	`</Number>`
	`<Issuer>Example Bank</Issuer>`
	`<Expiration>06/10</Expiration>`
	`</CreditCard>`
	`</PaymentInfo>`

- The SignatureValue, that contains the actual value of the signature.
- The optional Keyinfo element that enables a recipient to obtain the credentials needed to validate the signature.
- The optional Object element that specifies the encoding and the MIME type, used for informational purposes.

The XML Signature specification, by design, does not mandate use of a particular trust policy. The signer of a document is not required to include any key information but may include an element that specifies the key itself, a key name, X.509 certificate, a PGP key identifier etc. Alternatively, a link may be provided to a location where the full information may be found. The information provided by the signer may therefore be insufficient by itself to perform cryptographic verification and decide whether to trust the signing key, or the information may not be in a format the client can use. (Nadalin et al., 2006a)

Both the XML Digital Signature and the XML Encryption standards present performance limitations due to the canonicalization that they perform before signing/encrypting the SOAP messages (Zhang, 2007). These standards are used in WS Security specification to provide: (a) Message protection by encrypting the body or parts of it and (b) Message integrity by signing parts or the whole SOAP message. The encryption/signature can be achieved by the use of various credentials/security tokens such as X.509 certificates or Kerberos tickets as defined by the WSS X.509 Token Profile and Kerberos Token Profile respectively. The last specifications define how the various security tokens are included in the message but not how they are acquired. These are implementation details and depend on the underlying security system. A performance comparison of the X.509 and Kerberos Token Profiles is presented from Moralis et al. (2007).

XKMS (XML Key Management System)

XKMS (Ford et al., 2001) is a specification that hides the complexity of the underlying Public Key Infrastructure (PKI) mechanisms by exposing PKI as a WS, thus allowing delegation of trustworthy decisions to one or more WSs, the XKMS services. It was produced by the W3C XML Key Management Working Group that has now been issued as a W3C Recommendation in two parts: (i) The main XML Key Management Specification (XKMS 2.0) document, and (ii) the companion XML Key Management Specification (XKMS 2.0) Bindings. XKMS hides the infrastructure detail from a simple client and provides PKI key management support to applications utilizing XML. In particular, it is a goal of XML key management to support the requirements of XML Encryption, XML Digital Signature, and to be consistent with the Security Assertion Markup Language (SAML).

XKMS can be classified into two services:

1. X-KISS (XML Key Information Service Specification): A protocol for delegating part or all of the tasks required to process the XML XKMS service.
2. X-KRSS (XML Key Registration Service Specification): A protocol for registering and subsequently managing the public user key information.

The common XML vocabulary used to describe authentication, authorization, and profile information in XML documents makes XKMS services completely platform, vendor and transport-protocol independent.

In more detail, the XML Key Information Service Specification (X-KISS) defines a protocol to support the delegation of the key information processing associated with an XML signature from an application to a service, thus minimizing the complexity of applications using XML Signature. When a client of the XKMS service is becoming trusted the application is relieved from the complexity and syntax of the underlying PKI used to establish trust relationships, which may be based upon a different specification such as X.509/PKIX, SPKI or PGP.

The XML Key Registration Service Specification (X-KRSS) describes a protocol for registration and subsequent management of public key information. The X-KRSS defines a protocol for a web service that accepts registration of public key information. Once registered, the public key may be used in conjunction with other web services including X-KISS. A client of a conforming service may request that the registration service binds information to a public key. The information bound may include a name, an identifier or extended attributes defined by the implementation. The key pair to which the information is bound may be generated in advance by the client or by a request generated by the service. The Registration protocol may also be used for subsequent management operations including recovery of the private key and reissue or revocation of the key binding. The protocol provides for authentication of the applicant and, in the case that the key pair is generated by the client, Proof of Possession (POP) of the private key. A means of communicating the private key to the client is provided in the case that the private key is generated by the registration service.

Both protocols X-KISS and X-KRSS are defined in terms of structures expressed in the XML Schema Language, protocols employing the Simple Object Access Protocol (SOAP) and relationships among messages defined by the WSs Definition Language (WSDL).

SAML (Security Assertion Markup Language)

The Security Assertion Markup Language (SAML, 2010) provides the means for exchange of security information (assertions) across organizational boundaries (security domains) and describes the rules for access control, authentication and authorization purposes. It is a product of the OASIS Security Services Committee. The security information is expressed in the form of assertions that concern subjects (entities which have an identity in a security domain). Assertions can provide information about authenticating or/and authorizing the subject or attributes of it.

- The SAML V2.0 consists of three groups of specifications (Table 3) that define different aspects:
- The SAML Core, that defines the semantics of the SAML assertions and protocols for exchanging.
- The bindings that dictate how the requests and responses are expressed through standard messaging and communication protocols.
- The profiles that describe how SAML is executed in a specific domain, by using a combination of assertions, protocols and bindings.

In general the specification adopts standard XML technologies: XML for the exchanged messages, XML schemas for describing the assertions and protocols, XML encryption for protecting names, assertions etc, XML signatures for authenticating the exchanged messages, and http and/or SOAP as communication protocols.

Apart from the profiles defined in SAML v2.0, third party profiles have also been proposed, such as SAML 2.0 Profile of XACML (eXtensible Access Control Markup Language) v2.0 (Moses, 2005), Liberty Identity Federation Framework (ID-FF, 2010) and the OASIS WS Security, the SAML Token Profile 1.1 (Monzillo et al., 2006). The latter is of great significance in SOA environments as it enables the provision and administration of authentication and authorization across multiple systems and security domains. The goal of this WSS specification is to define the use of

Table 3. SAML V2.0 assertions, protocols, bindings, profiles

Assertions	Protocols	Bindings	Profiles
Authentication statements Attribute statements Authorization decision statements	Assertion Query and Request Protocol Authentication Request Protocol Artifact Resolution Protocol Name Identifier Management Protocol Single Logout Protocol Name Identifier Mapping Protocol	SAML SOAP Binding (based on SOAP 1.1) Reverse SOAP (PAOS) Binding HTTP Redirect (GET) Binding HTTP POST Binding HTTP Artifact Binding SAML URI Binding	SSO Profiles Web Browser SSO Profile Enhanced Client or Proxy (ECP) Profile Identity Provider Discovery Profile Single Logout Profile Name Identifier Management Profile Artifact Resolution Profile Assertion Query/Request Profile Name Identifier Mapping Profile SAML Attribute Profiles

SAML v1.1 and v2.0 assertions in the context of WSS. Specifically it describes how:

- SAML assertions are carried in and referenced from WS-Security headers.
- SAML assertions are used with XML signature to bind the subjects and statements of the assertions to the SOAP message.

It does not indicate how the service provider will acquire these assertions but only how they will be attached to the SOAP message. SAML can by itself provide the inter-domain authentication and authorization in a federation. The authorization is performed by checking against the local rules at the Service Provider the assertion (role) that the Identity Provider (IdP) has provided. However, some issues, such as the access policy of the Service Providers, the different security architectures and the different tokens required for authentication and trust relationship, are not covered by SAML.

WS-Policy

WS-Policy (Vedamuthu et al., 2007) is a W3C recommendation since September 2007. It defines how a WS can publish its security policy along with its interface specification as part of a WSDL document. A policy is actually a collection of policy alternatives, which are a collection of one or more policy assertions. The alternatives are not ordered, thus there is no sense of preference between the alternatives. The WS-Policy specification describes the capabilities and constraints of the policies i.e. required security tokens, supported encryption algorithms, privacy rules, transport protocol, privacy policies, authentication schemes, Quality-of-Service (QoS) characteristics on intermediaries and endpoints. It is also designed to work with the other Web service components e.g. WSDL service descriptions and UDDI registries. Nevertheless it does not specify how the policies are discovered or attached to the WS.

Other specifications such as the WS-Policy-Attachment (Vedatmuthu et al., 2007) can define that. A user wishing to interact with the service can examine its published policy and gather the needed credentials to call it. Typically the service provider exposes the policy under which the requestor can interact with the service. When the service receives the client request it examines if it satisfies the policy assertions and it acts accordingly.

An example of a policy expression as described in the specification (Vedamuthu et al., 2007) is shown in Box 1.

where the policy expression (<wsp:Policy ...>) contains a collection (<wsp:ExactlyOne>) of policy alternatives (<wsp:All>) each one containing a collection of policy assertions (<Assertion ...>).

Box 1. Policy expressions example

```
<wsp:Policy ... >
<wsp:ExactlyOne>
          (<wsp:All> (<Assertion  ...> ... </Assertion >)* </wsp:All>)*
</wsp:ExactlyOne>
</wsp:Policy>
```

WS-SecureConversation

WS-SecureConversation is a WSs specification, created by IBM and others, that works in conjunction with WS-Security, WS-Trust and WS-Policy to allow sharing of security contexts. While WS-Security provides mechanisms for securing a single message in a one-way message exchange, in cases where multiple messages are exchanged then it is more effective to establish some form of context via a security session between the service provider and the requestor in order to reduce the burden of securing each message in isolation. Thus the WS-SecureConversation specification defines extensions to the basic mechanisms of WS-Security in order to allow security context establishment and session key derivation in the multiple message exchanges. In this way, contexts can be established and more session keys or new key material can be exchanged. The quicker and more effective submission of messages increases the overall performance and security of the subsequent exchanges. The WS-SecureConversation accomplishes that by defining Security Context Tokens to offer mutually authenticated security contexts between the service requestor and the WS and vice versa. The security context is defined as a new WS-Security token type that is obtained using a binding of WS-Trust. Although WS-SecureConversation defines a binding for WS-Trust, it is not a goal of the specification to define how trust is established or determined. Its primary goals are:

- To define how security contexts are established.
- To describe how security contexts are amended and finally.
- To specify how derived keys are computed and passed to the message.

WS-SecureConversation specification introduces a security context and its usage. As such, WS-SecureConversation by itself does not provide a complete security solution. WS-SecureConversation is a building block that is used in conjunction with other WS and application-specific protocols (for example, WS-Security) to accommodate a wide variety of security models and technologies that can be used within the SOAP model.

WS-Trust

WS-Trust (Nadalin et al., 2007) is an OASIS standard since March 2007 and describes a framework for trust models that enables WSs to securely interoperate. More specifically, in order to secure a communication between two parties, the two parties must exchange security credentials (either directly or indirectly). However, each party needs to determine if they can trust the asserted credentials of the other party.

The goal of WS-Trust is to enable the exchange and brokering of these security credentials (e.g. UsernameToken, SAML Token etc.) thus offering the applications a more effective way to construct trusted message exchanges. Based on the core security mechanisms of WS-Security the WS-Trust defines additional primitives and extensions for security token exchange to enable the issuance and dissemination of credentials within different trust domains. Using these extensions, applications can engage in secure communication designed to work with the general Web services framework, including WSDL service descriptions, UDDI business services and binding templates, and SOAP messages.

WS-Trust also addresses the issue of trust interoperability between the multiple formats of security tokens that might be used in a WS-Security protected message because even if a given security token's format is acceptable to a recipient of a WS-Security-protected SOAP message, simple interoperability at the syntax level is no guarantee that the recipient will be able to trust the token. For instance, a SOAP Service supporting Kerberos tokens would not be able to accept Kerberos tickets from arbitrary Kerberos Key Distribution Centers the service would not have the necessary trust (in the form of shared symmetric keys) with these KDCs to decrypt and verify such tickets.

Whenever communicating parties need to accomplish trust among them, the WS-Trust specification provides a protocol agnostic means to issue, renew, and validate security tokens and ways to establish, assess and broker trust relationships. It intentionally does not describe explicit fixed security protocols because its scope is to provide a flexible set of mechanisms and services that can be used in conjunction with a range of security protocols such as WS-SecureConversation, WS-Security and others. Moreover, the specification does not deal with issues like password authentication, token revocation, management of trust policies, how to establish a security context or even derive the security keys from the tokens. On the contrary it deals with matters like how to request and obtain the security tokens and how to establish, manage and assess trust relationships. For this purpose, it specifies various characteristics of the requested token in the request. Some of them are the validity period or lifetime for the token and also information concerning the key

length, the key types and the token issuer. The security token service typically indicates in the response the characteristics of the returned token. It should be mentioned that efforts must be applied to ensure that the specific security profiles and message exchanges constructed using the WS-Trust specification are not vulnerable to attacks (or at least that the attacks are understood).

The WS-Trust accomplishes all the above, by defining a service model, the Security Token Service (STS) and a simple request/response protocol for requesting/issuing/validating the security tokens which are described by WS-Policy and used by WS-Security. The STS acts as an Identity Provider and its primary purpose is to issue identity security tokens containing claims for the identity requestor. In this security token exchange, a client asks for the security token to be exchanged by sending a RequestSecurityToken (RST) to the STS. The STS responds back with a RequestSecurityTokenResponse (RSTR) containing the new token. This request/response exchange addresses some issues that concern the format, the trust and the namespace of the messages and arise when the SOAP messages are only WS-Security protected.

In order to clarify the use of WS-Trust (Figure 1) an example is given where a client identified by its X.509 certificate initiates a secured call to a WS that understands only SAML authentication assertions but the client is not aware of it. In this case:

- The client sends the SOAP message with the X.509 token contained inside the request.
- The WS understands only SAML assertions, thus it has a WS Handler that catches the SOAP request and creates a WS-Trust request to the STS asking for the mapping of the client's X.509 token to a SAML assertion.
- The STS, which is responsible for the mapping, returns a WS-Trust response to the

Figure 1. Example of the use of WS-Trust

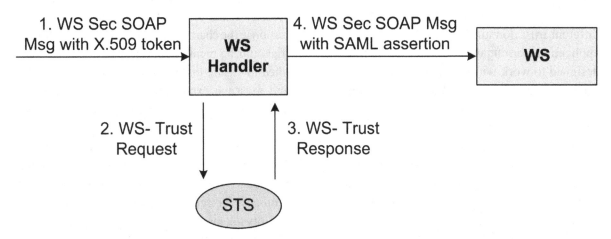

WS-Handler containing a SAML assertion for the client.

- The WS-Handler forwards the client's SOAP message with the SAML assertions instead of the initial X.509 token to the plain WS for its further processing.

Special cases of token exchange are the token issuance and token validation. Token validation is the case where a client sends a request containing a token to an STS and asks from the STS to validate it. Token issuance is the case where a client presents a claim to an STS in order to authenticate him and asks for the issuance of a security token in order to access services.

The token exchange, issuance, and validation functions are analogous to the ones existing in current security technologies. In X.509 scenarios a user, after providing his supporting evidence of who he is, asks from a Trusted Certification Authority to issue a certificate for him. The Authority after verifying his identity, issues the certificate. Likewise, in Kerberos scenarios, a client, after authenticating to the Key Distribution Center, is granted a Ticket Granting Ticket which will be used to request service tickets.

For the X.509 world, a proposal for XML-based token issuance and token validation already exists, namely, the X-KRSS and X-KISS components of the XML Key Management Specification (XKMS) currently being standardized under the W3C. It remains to be seen how WS-Trust and XKMS will compete, cooperate, or coexist in this area.

WS-Federation

WS-Federation (Lockhart et al., 2006) is an Identity Federation specification, developed by BEA Systems, BMC Software, CA, Inc., IBM, Layer 7 Technologies, Microsoft, Novell, and VeriSign. It defines how to construct federated trust relationships between various organizational entities e.g. between a Kerberos and a PKI domain that have established relationships for securely sharing resources. This means that a resource provider in the one domain can authorize access to his resources to a principal that provides claims asserted by an Identity Provider belonging to another domain. This can be achieved because the Resource and Identity providers have established a federation context between them and have agreed on the claims, assertions and mechanisms required for the secure access to the resources. The Resource

Providers in each domain, after establishing the federation context, expose the configuration information (federation metadata) in order to make their services and how they can be accessed known.

To accomplish an easier cross-realm communication required in a grid environment the WS-Federation has defined its mechanisms for identity brokering, attribute discovery and retrieval, authentication and authorization assertions and secure claim exchange across the domains as extensions to the WS-Security, WS-Policy, WS-SecureConversation specifications. This enables the protocol to accomplish federation in a heterogeneous environment through mapping of identities and credentials realized by proxies or other trusted intermediaries. Moreover, based on the RST/RSTR protocol of the WS-Trust STS model, WS-Federation enhances the interoperability between the applications as it allows for a general token type to be transmitted and does not restrict the user to a specific security token format.

By extending the STS model, various Federation Services such as Authentication, Authorization, Privacy, Attribute and Pseudonym Services can be developed. More specifically, in the Authentication Service the WS-Trust specification defines a parameter (AuthenticationType) to specify the authentication type and the assurance levels required in the RST/RTSR message exchange. In the Authorization Service, the specification provides a common model for the authorization services to interact and communicate their authorization decisions to each other. The Privacy Service is responsible for expressing the privacy requirements of the user and the service respectively. The Attribute Service can provide additional information/claims for a principal if required by a service. Finally the Pseudonym Service can provide various pseudonyms to a principal whenever it wants to access different resources but is concerned about the risks of identity fraud.

A Computing Grid Scenario Using WS-Security, WS-Policy, WS-Trust and WS-Federation

In this section, we shall describe how WS-Security, WS-Policy, WS Trust and WS-Federation could be utilized in a grid environment. We assume the grid uses a modern approach following the Open Grid Services Architecture (OGSA) (Foster et al., 2005) (Foster et al., 2002). The OGSA dictates an architecture that follows Web Services concepts and technologies. Globus Toolkit (Globus, 2010) since version 3 is build upon the OGSA principles. Such OGSA grid use cases have been proposed and demonstrated in great extend (Foster et al., 2004).

Following the grid paradigm we assume a multi-organization, dynamic environment as described in (Nagaratnam et al., 2002). In such an environment, it is unreal to have a single security technology, common protocols, policies and identity management governing the grid environment. Thus, the integration of different security technologies (e.g. Kerberos and PKI), the exchange of messages using WS, the protocol mapping, the trust relationships and trust establishment are considered a major driving force.

A grid environment is in practice a federated environment, which is defined by a group of self-governed organizations that have defined a mutual arrangement to share and consume resources in a secure way. The participating organizations have also agreed on the exchange rules of data and services. By following a SOA architecture, the secure inter-exchange of information and invocation of services among different organizations poses a significant challenge. The WS technologies presented above provide a solution.

WS-Security provides the secure exchange of messages by authenticating and authorizing the requests. These requests can be either between services or between users and services. Services could be Storage Elements, Computing Elements or Resource Brokers in a Computational Grid.

Because of the Grid Security Infrastructure (GSI) utilized, WSS Certificate Token Profile is used to attach the certificates within a SOAP message. The WSS Certificate Token Profile dictates that a certificate is used as a Binary Token or as a Security Token reference when it comprises a reference to a certificate. By the use of WS-Security, public key cryptography is utilized.

In the scenarios where a large number of messages need to be exchanged between specific services within a small time frame, WS-SecureConversation could be used. WS-SecureConversation establishes a secure session, thus negates the overhead of asymmetric cryptography. Asymmetric cyptography is used in the first message and for the subsequent messages in the whole session duration, symmetric cryptography is utilized. This improves the overall performance.

WS-Security and WS-SecureConversation solve problems regarding the secure message exchange. Messages are encrypted using XML-Encryption and/or signed using XML-Signatures. However this does not solve the problem of inter domain communication. If the request arrives from a different organization, the federated nature requires each service to expose, in addition to the WSDL, its security policy (required security tokens, supported encryption algorithms, privacy rules) using the WS-Policy, prior to invocation of a Service Provider. Additionally to the WS-Policy, when the request to the service provider originates outside the organization, WS-Trust and WS-Federation may be used. In this case, a trusted third party is required within the federation. Using WS-Trust's STS, this can be achieved.

However, the federated nature of a grid environment can pose restrictions on how the user data is treated and the definition of privacy rules could be a requirement. So, additional services that the WS-Federation provides, such as authorization, authentication types, attribute services, pseudonym services, and privacy along with the federation metadata, enrich the overall Grid Security functionality and provide the required solution.

FUTURE RESEARCH DIRECTIONS

Although all of WS-Security related standards, described in this chapter, have been defined and some of them implemented by various vendors, still there are some issues that need to be solved. Some of them are identified below:

Services do not advertise their authorization requirements thus the requestor cannot know what CA authority is trusted by the service and where to obtain the credentials from in order to access it.

Due to the heterogeneity of the worldwide systems and the various entities that need to have access to the distributed resources a global mapping mechanism has to be developed for the effective access control of the attributes/roles among the various systems. Although hardcoded solutions exist there is no standardized way to achieve this mapping.

Guides for auditing information technologies do not consider WSS yet. An audit process should be developed that will allow for audit control in case of security events. Thus full knowledge of the system interaction with the users will be available for further analysis or future reference (Gutierrez et al., 2004).

In the case of XKMS, although it offers a trustworthy service over the PKI some issues still remain unsolved: When a validation is done, it must be done according to a set of rules. These rules depend upon the application. In particular some root keys may be adequate for an application, but not for another. Trust elements cannot be uniform and cannot be left open to the validate server.

CONCLUSION

Summarizing, in today's heterogeneous environments where access to distributed and differently administered resources is required, security is a major challenge that needs to be addressed. To access resources and achieve interconnection in this heterogeneous environment we use WSs and we describe the security related specifications defined to try and solve the problems of trust, non-repudiation, authentication, authorization and the issues that still remain to be solved.

REFERENCES

Bartel, M., Boyer, J., Fox, B., LaMacchia, B., & Simon, E. (2008). XML signature syntax and processing (2nd Edition). *W3C Recommendation.* Retrieved December 20, 2008, from http://www. w3.org/ TR/ xmldsig-core

Dierks, T., & Rescorla, E. (2006). The transport layer security (TLS) protocol version 1.1 (RFC 4346). *IETF RFC.* Retrieved from: http://www. ietf.org/ rfc/ rfc4346.txt

Ford, W., Hallam-Baker, P., Fox, B., Dillaway, B., LaMacchia, B., Epstein, J., & Lapp, J. (2001). XML Key Management Specification (XKMS). Retrieved March 30, 2001, from http://www. w3.org/ TR/ xkms

Foster, I., Gannon, D., Kishimoto, H., & Von Reich, J. J. (2004). Open grid services architecture use cases. *OpenGridForum.* Retrieved from http://www.gridforum.org/ documents/ GWD-I-E/ GFD-I.029v2.pdf

Foster, I., Kesselman, C., Nick, J., & Tuecke, S. (2002). The physiology of the grid: An open grid services architecture for distributed systems integration. *Open Grid Service Infrastructure WG, Global Grid Forum.* Retrieved June 22, 2002, from http://www.globus.org/ alliance/ publications/ papers/ ogsa.pdf

Foster, I., Kishimoto, H., Savva, A., Berry, D., Djaoui, A., & Grimshaw, A. …Von Reich, J. J. (2005). The open grid services architecture, version 1.0. *OpenGridForum.* Retrieved January 29, 2005, from http://www.gridforum.org/ documents/ GFD.30.pdf

Globus Toolkit. (2010). Retrieved from http:// www.globus.org/toolkit

Goodner, M., Hondo, M., Nadalin, A., McIntosh, M., & Schmidt, D. (2007). *Understanding WS-Federation.* Retrieved January 10, 2009, from http:// download.boulder.ibm.com/ ibmdl/ pub/ software/ dw/ specs/ ws-fed/ WS-FederationSpec05282007. pdf?S _TACT=105AGX04&S_CMP=LP

Gutierrez, C., Fernandez-Medina, E., & Piattini, M. (2004). A survey of WSs security . In Laganà, A., Gavrilova, M. L., Kumar, V., Mun, Y., Tan, C. J. K., & Gervasi, O. (Eds.), *Computational science and its applications-ICCSA 2004* (pp. 968–977). Berlin-Heidelberg, Germany: Springer. doi:10.1007/978-3-540-24707-4_109

Imamura, T., Dillaway, B., & Simon, E. (2002). XML encryption syntax and processing. *W3C recommendation.* Retrieved December 20, 2008, from http://www.w3.org/ TR/ xmlenc-core

Kent, S., & Atkinson, R. (1998). IPSec, security architecture for the Internet protocol (RFC 2401). *IETF RFC.* Retrieved from http://www.ietf.org/ rfc/ rfc2401.txt

Liberty Identity Federation Framework (ID-FF). (2010). *Web wervices and service-oriented architectures.* Retrieved January 5, 2009, from http:// www.service-architecture.com/ web-services/ articles/ identity_federation_framework_id-ff.html

Lockhart, H., Andersen, S., Bohren, J., Sverdlov, Y., Hondo, M., & Maruyama, H. …Prafullchandra, H. (2006). *Web services federation language (WS-Federation), version 1.1.* Retrieved November 6, 2008, from http://specs.xmlsoap.org/ ws/ 2006/ 12/ federation/ ws-federation.pdf

Monzillo, R., Kaler, C., Nadalin, A., & Hallem-Baker, P. (2006). Web services security-SAML token profile 1.1. *OASIS Standard Specification.* Retrieved January 2, 2009, from http://www.oasis-open.org/ committees/ download.php/ 16768/ wss-v1.1-spec-os-SAML TokenProfile.pdf

Moralis, A., Pouli, V., Grammatikou, M., Papavassiliou, S., & Maglaris, V. (2007, June). *Performance comparison of WSs security: Kerberos token profile against X.509 token profile.* Paper presented at the 3rd International Conference on Networking and Services (ICNS '07), Athens, Greece.

Moses, T. (2005). eXtensible Access Control Markup Language (XACML) version 2.0. *OASIS Standard Specification.* Retrieved January 5, 2009, from http://www.oasis-open.org/ committees/ tc_home.php?wg_abbrev=xacml

Nadalin, A., Goodner, M., Gudgin, M., Barbir, A., & Granqvist, H. (2007). WS-Trust 1.3. *OASIS standard.* Retrieved January 10, 2009 from http:// docs.oasis-open.org/ ws-sx/ ws-trust/ 200512/ ws-trust-1.3-os.html

Nadalin, A., Goodner, M., Gudgin, M., Barbir, A., & Granvist, H. (2008). WS-SecureConverasation 1.4. *OASIS standard.* Retrieved January 9, 2009, from http://docs.oasis-open.org/ ws-sx/ ws-secureconversation/200512

Nadalin, A., Kaler, C., Monzillo, R., & Hallam-Baker, P. (2006a). WS-Security X509 token profile 1.1. *OASIS standard specification.* Retrieved January 2, 2009, from http://www.oasis-open. org/ committees/ download.php/ 16785/ wss-v1.1-spec-os-x509TokenProfile.pdf

Nadalin, A., Kaler, C., Monzillo, R., & Hallam-Baker, P. (2006b). Web services security: SOAP message security 1.1. *OASIS standard specification.* Retrieved January 2, 2009, from http:// www.oasis-open.org/ committees/ download.php/ 16790/ wss-v1.1-spec-os-SOAPMessageSecurity. pdf

Nadalin, A., Kaler, C., Monzillo, R., & Hallam-Baker, P. (2006c). WS-Security Kerberos token profile 1.1. *OASIS standard specification.* Retrieved January 2, 2009, from http://www.oasis-open.org/ committees/ download.php/ 16788/ wss-v1.1-spec-os-KerberosTokenProfile.pdf

Nagaratnam, N., Janson, P., Dayka, J., Nadalin, A., Siebenlist, F., Wech, V., & Tuecke, S. (2002). *The security architecture for open grid services.* Retrieved January 7, 2009, from http://www. cs.virginia.edu/~humphrey/ ogsa-sec-wg/OGSA-SecArch-v1-07192002.pdf

O'Neill, M. (2003). We know Web services need security, but what type? *Web Services Journal, 3*(3), 18–27.

Rosenberg, J., & Remy, D. (2004). *Securing WSs with WS-security: Demystifying WS-security, WS-policy, SAML, XML, signature and XML encryption.* Indiana, USA: Sams.

Security Assertion Markup Language (SAML) Specifications. (2010). Retrieved from http:// saml.xml.org/ saml-specifications

Singhal, A., Winograd, T., & Scarfone, K. (2007). Guide to secure Web services. *National Institute of Standards and Technology (NIST) Special Publication 800-95,* 1-128. Retrieved September 18, 2008, from http://csrc.nist.gov/ publications/ nistpubs/ 800-95/ SP800-95.pdf

Vedamuthu, A. S., Orchard, D., Hirsch, F., Hondo, M., Yendluri, P., Boubez, T., & Yalcinalp, U. (2007). Web services policy 1.5 - Framework. *W3C Recommendation 04 September 2007.* Retrieved December 16, 2008, from http://www.w3.org/ TR/ ws-policy

Vedamuthu, A. S., Orchard, D., Hirsch, F., Hondo, M., Yendluri, P., Boubez, T., & Yalcinalp, U. (2007). Web services policy 1.5 - Attachment. *W3C Recommendation.* Retrieved January 9, 2009, from http://www.w3.org/ TR/ ws-policy-attach

Zhang, J. (2007). Position paper for W3C workshop on next steps for XML signature and XML encryption. Retrieved October 14, 2008, from http://www.w3.org/2007/ xmlsec/ws/ papers/ 06-zhang-ximpleware

ADDITIONAL READING

Alonso, G., Casati, F., Kuno, H., & Machiraju, V. (2003). *Web services: Concepts, architectures and applications*. Berlin-Heidelberg, Germany: Springer.

Amoroso, E. (1994). *Fundamentals of computer security technology*. Upper Saddle River, NJ: Prentice Hall.

Carroll, J. M. (1987). *Computer security* (2nd ed.). Stoneham, MA: Butterworth Publishers.

Douranee, B. (2002). *XML security*. New York, NY: McGraw-Hill Osborne Media.

Endrei, M., Ang, J., Arsanjani, A., Chua, S., Comte, P., Krogdahl, P.,…Newling, T. (2004). *Patterns: Service-oriented architecture and Web services*. IBM Redbooks.

Hartman, B., Flinn, J. D., & Beznosov, K. (2003). *Mastering Web services security*. Wiley Publishing Inc.

Hatala, M., Eap, T., & Shah, A. (2005). Federated security: Lightweight security infrastructure for object repositories and Web services. In *Proceedings of Next Generation Web Services Practices (NWESP '05)* (pp. 287-298). IEEE CS Press.

Hollar, R., & Murphy, R. (2005). *Enterprise Web services security*. Charles River Media/Thomson.

Janakiraman, M., Hankison, W., Hiotis, A., Janakiramam, M., Prasad, V. D., Trivedi, R., & Whitney (2002). *Professional Web services security*. Wrox Press Ltd.

Kaufman, C., Perlman, R., & Speciner, M. (1995). *Network security: Private communications in a public*. Upper Saddle River, NJ: Prentice Hall.

Kleijnen, S., & Raju, S. (2003). An open Web services architecture. *ACM Queue; Tomorrow's Computing Today, 1*(1), 38–46. doi:10.1145/637958.637961

Lesk, M., Styltz, M. R., & Trope, R. L. (2007). Providing Web service security in a federated environment. *IEEE Security and Privacy, 5*(1), 73–75. doi:10.1109/MSP.2007.16

McGraw, G., & Felten, E. W. (1997). *Java security: Hostile applets, holes, and antidotes*. New York, USA: Wiley Computer Publishing.

Newcomer, E., & Lomow, G. (2004). *Understanding SOA with Web services*. USA: Addison Wesley, Professional.

Niles, D. E. III, & Niles, K. (2002). *Secure XML: The new syntax for signatures and encryption*. USA: Addison-Wesley Professional.

Pfleeger, C. P. (1996). *Security in computing (2nd)*. Englewood Cliffs, NJ, USA: Prentice Hall.

Potts, S., & Kopak, M. (2003). *Teach yourself Web services in 24 hours*. Sams Publishing.

Ray, E. T. (2001). *Learning XML*. Sebastopol, CA: O'Reilly and Associates.

Stallings, W. (1995). *Network and Internetwork security: Principles and practice*. Englewood Cliffs, NJ: Prentice Hall.

Thomas, E. (2005). *Service-Oriented Architecture (SOA): Concepts, technology, and design*. Englewood Cliffs, NJ: Prentice Hall, PTR.

Wiehler, G. (2004). *Mobility, security and Web services: Technologies and service-oriented architectures for a new era of IT solutions*. Wiley-VCH/Siemens.

Zimmerman, O., Tomlinson, R. M., & Peuser, S. (2005). *Perspectives on Web services: Applying SOAP, WSDL and UDDI to real-world projects*. Springer Professional Computing.

KEY TERMS AND DEFINITIONS

WS-Federation: Federation standard for Web Services.

WS-Policy: Policy standard for Web Services.

WS-SecureConversation: Secure Conversation standard for Web Services.

WS-Security: Security standard for Web Services.

WS-Trust: Trust standard for Web Services.

Chapter 11
Information Security in Data and Storage Grids through GS³

Vincenzo Daniele Cunsolo
Università di Messina, Italy

Salvatore Distefano
Università di Messina, Italy

Antonio Puliafito
Università di Messina, Italy

Marco Scarpa
Università di Messina, Italy

ABSTRACT

In grid computing infrastructures, the data storage subsystem is physically distributed among several nodes and logically shared among several users. This highlights the necessity of: (i) Availability for authorized users only, (ii) Confidentiality, and (iii) Integrity of information and data: in one term security.

In this work we face the problem of data security in grid, by proposing a lightweight cryptography algorithm combining the strong and highly secure asymmetric cryptography technique (RSA) with the symmetric cryptography (Advanced Encryption Standard, AES). The proposed algorithm, we named Grid Secure Storage System (GS³), has been implemented on top of the Grid File Access Library (GFAL) of the gLite middleware, in order to provide a file system service with cryptography capability and POSIX interface. The choice of implementing GS³ as a file system allows to protect also the file system structure, and moreover to overcome the well-known problem of file rewriting in gLite/GFAL environments. This chapter describes and details both the GS³ algorithm and its implementation, also evaluating the performance of such implementation and discussing the obtained results.

DOI: 10.4018/978-1-61350-113-9.ch011

INTRODUCTION

The actual Information Technology (IT) trend definitely brings towards network-distributed paradigms of computing. Among them, the grid is one of the most widely spread. Its success is due to the fact that it manages and makes available large quantities/amounts of computing and storage resources for allocating and elaborating data as required by users' computation workflows. The management of such resources is transparent to the user that only has to specify his /her requirements in terms of resources. Then, the grid system manager automatically determines where the process is executed and which resources have to be allocated to it (Foster, & Kesselman, 1998). Sharing data in distributed multi-user environments triggers problems of security concerning data confidentiality and integrity. Grid middlewares usually provide resources management's capabilities, ensuring security on accessing services and on communicating data, but they often lacks of data protection from direct malicious accesses, at system level. In other words, the fact that data are disseminated and stored in remote distributed machines, directly accessible from their administrators, constitutes the main risk for data security in grid environment. Security problems, such as insider abuse/attack, identity thefts and/or account hijacking, are often not adequately covered in grid context. It is therefore mandatory to introduce an adequate data protection mechanism, which denies data intelligibility to unauthorized users, also if they are (local) system administrators.

The problem of a secure storage access has been mainly faced in literature as definition of access rights (Junrang et al., 2004), in particular addressing problems of data sharing, whilst the coding of the data is demanded to the user, since no automatic mechanism to access to a secure storage space in a transparent way has been defined.

Scardaci, & Scuderi, (2007) proposed a technique for securing data disseminated over grid gLite (gLite, 2010) environment based on symmetric cryptography (Advanced Encryption Standard, AES). The key security is entrusted to a unique keystore server that stores it, to which all the data access requests must be notified in order to decrypt the data. This algorithm implements a spatial security policy: the security lies in physically hiding and securing the keystore server, and the access to the keystore is physically restricted and monitored in order to protect from malicious users, external attacks and insider abuses. Seitz, Pierson, & Brunie (2003) studied in depth the problem of data access, and propose a solution based on symmetric keys. In order to prevent non-authorized accesses to the symmetric key the authors propose to subdivide it on different servers. A similar technique has been specified by Shamir (1979), used in PERROQUET (Blanchet, Mollon, & Deleage, 2006) to modify the PARROT middleware (Thain, & Livny, 2005) by adding an encrypted file manager. The main contribution of such work is that, by applying the proposed algorithm, the (AES) symmetric key, split in N parts, can be recomposed if and only if all the N parts are available. HYDRA (2010) implements a data sharing service in gLite 3.0 medical environments, securing data by using the symmetric cryptography and splitting the keys among three keystore servers (Montagnat et al., 2006).

All the proposals above mentioned are based on symmetric cryptography. Most of them implement keys splitting algorithms. The underlying idea of the key splitting approach is that at least a subset of the systems (key servers) over which the keys are distributed will be trustworthy. However this approach is weak from three points of views: the security, since the list of servers with key parts must be adequately secured, the system administrators can always access the keys and it is really hard to achieve trustworthy on remote and distributed nodes for users; the reliability/availability, since if one of the server storing a part of the key is unavailable, the data cannot be accessed; the performance, since there is an initial overhead to rebuild a key, depending on the number of parts in which the key is split. A solution for improving reliability/availability is to replicate the key servers, but this contrasts with security challenges.

The goal of our work is to provide a mechanism capable to store data in grid environment in a secure way, the Grid Secure Storage System (GS^3). In order to do that, we propose to combine both the symmetric and the asymmetric cryptography. Therefore, the main contribution of the work is the specification of a lightweight and effective technique for secure data storage in grid environment that conjugates the high security goal with performance issues, as also Tu et al. (2009) have suggested. The GS^3 technique we propose, it has been really implemented into the gLite middleware in order to demonstrate the feasibility of the approach, supported by the encouraging results obtained through the GS^3 performance evaluation. Other interesting contributions of GS^3 to the state of the art are the organization of the grid data into a file system, the protection of both data/files and of the file system structure, and the introduction of the capability of file rewriting in gLite storage systems, not actually implemented.

The rest of the chapter is organized as follows. After a short introduction of background concepts in the section below, we describe the GS^3 algorithm and its implementation into the gLite middleware. Then the results obtained by evaluating our implementation are discussed. A discussion on benefits and drawbacks of the GS^3 technique is developed in following section, and the final section proposes some final remarks and possible future work.

BACKROUND

The grid is a distributed architecture of protocols, which allows to use a set of computational and storage resources scattered across the world as a single system (Foster, & Kesselman, 1998; Foster, 2002). The collection of software resources, services,

API, primitives, commands, tools, protocols and interfaces for managing grid computing environments are usually grouped altogether into unique middlewares. Several different grid middlewares have been implemented, both commercial and freeware. Among them, Globus (Globus Toolkit, 2010) is one of the most widely spread. Other well-known, open, grid middlewares are Condor (Thain, Tannenbaum, & Livny, 2002), BOINC (Anderson, 2004) and gLite (gLite, 2010), this latter developed starting from Globus protocols and services.

In a loose sense, the term grid means a specific computing infrastructure designed to aggregate a set of resources. Grids can be broadly categorized by resource, scale and service. A resource driven taxonomy classifies a grid by considering the type of resources the grid share, identifying four classes:

- Computational Grids: If the primarily shared resources are the CPU.
- Data Grids: When the main goal is to share data resources, such as the results of experiments, among users.
- Storage Grids: Designed to provide users with access to an enormous amount of storage space.
- Equipment Grids: That can also be set up to share access to physical resources (astronomical telescopes, satellites, etc.).

However, some grids may fall into more than one of such categories. Grids can also be classified by how they geographically distribute their resources:

- Internet-scale Grids can potentially include anyone with access to the internet.
- Virtual Organization (VO) scale grid contains several academic or corporate entities.
- A Local Grid is entirely contained within one organization.

In each of these cases, the companies have access to their own clusters for processing tasks. From a user perspective, the important thing about a grid is the services it provides. A Data Grid gives access to specific data resources, such as results from a large physics experiment. At the moment, the most prevalent types of service offered by grids are forms of graphical rendering, scientific simulations and web applications.

Realizing the full promise of the grid requires solutions to fundamental issues such as authentication, authorization, resource discovery, resource access, and most notably, incompatibility of resources and policies for managing them. A wide variety of projects and products offer services intended to address these issues. The Globus Toolkit (2010) is an open-source software that simplifies collaboration across dynamic, multi-institutional VOs. The toolkit includes software services and libraries for resource monitoring, resource discovery and management, security, information infrastructure, data and file management, communication, fault detection, and portability. It is packaged as a set of components that can be used either independently or together to develop applications. The Globus Toolkit was conceived to remove obstacles that prevent seamless collaboration. Its core services, interfaces and protocols allow users to access remote resources as if they were located within their own machine room while simultaneously preserving local control over who can use resources and when.

The Globus Toolkit has grown through an open-source strategy similar to the Linux operating systems, and distinct from proprietary attempts at resource-sharing software. Another middleware for grid environment management is gLite (gLite, 2010). Since our work has been implemented starting from the gLite middleware, we mainly focus this background section to such middleware.

The Middleware: gLite

GLite (2010) is a middleware software for managing grid computing infrastructures, developed by CERN with the aim of implementing a highly distributed, powerful and flexible computing and storage platform for the Large Hadron Collider (LHC) (2010) (see Figure 1).

Services in gLite comprise security, monitoring, job and data management, developed by following a Service-Oriented Architecture (SOA):

- **Job.** The job management service is hierarchically implemented and split among Computing Elements (CE) and Worker Nodes (WN). The CE collect the jobs submitted to the grid-gLite infrastructure into specific queues and then dispatch such jobs to WN that process them.
- **Security.** Based on the Globus Security Infrastructure (GSI, 2010), that uses X.509 (Tuecke et al., 2004) certificates for implementing credentials delegation mechanisms to authenticate the user (Single Sign-On). The grid resources are grouped in VOs and there is a Virtual Organization Management System (VOMS) (Alfieri et al., 2003) to ensure security policy in a distributed environment that covers different hardware resources localized on different sites.
- **Data.** Information is located on storage resources called Storage Element (SE), which manage disk pools and hardware needed to store data.

All the grid resources are managed by the Resource Broker (RB) in a centralized way: all the job execution requests income to it that looks for the resources necessary for processing such jobs (resources discovery), allocates them and transfers the job context to the corresponding

Figure 1. gLite grid infrastructure

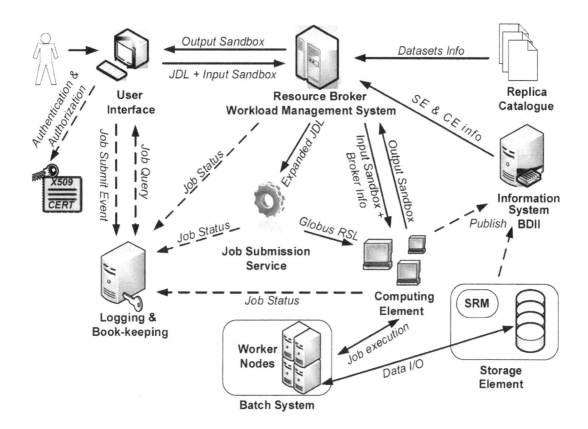

resources. The access point of gLite services is the User Interface (UI), a collection of utilities for interacting with the grid-gLite infrastructure.

Grid File Access Library

Grid storage interactions today require the use of several existing software components: the replica catalog services to locate valid replicas of files; the Storage Resource Manager (SRM) software to ensure that files exist on disk (they are recalled from mass storage if necessary) or space is allocated on disk for new files (they are possibly migrated to mass storage later). SRM also ensures a mechanism to access files from the storage system on the worker node.

The Grid File Access Library (GFAL) (Scardaci, 2007) hides these interactions implementing a Posix interface for the I/O operations. The currently supported protocols are: file for "nfs-like" local access, dcap, gsidcap and kdcap (dCache access protocol) and rfio (CASTOR access protocol). The function names are obtained by prepending *"gfal_"* to the Posix names, for example: gfal_open, gfal_read, gfal_close, and so on. The argument lists and the values returned by the functions are identical to the Posix ones. GFAL accepts the following file naming conventions: Logical File Name (LFN), Grid Unique IDentifier (GUID), storage file replica (SURL) or a transport file name (TURL).

Universally Unique IDentifier

The Universally Unique IDentifier (UUID) is a distributed mechanism of identification, formally specified by Leach, Mealling, & Salz (2005), that guarantees unique identifiers without a centralized registration process or coordination. It is widely used in software engineering. A UUID is essentially a 16-byte (128-bit) number. In its canonical form, a UUID consists of 32 hexadecimal digits, displayed in 5 groups separated by hyphens, for a total of 36 characters.

In grid contexts UUID are sometimes identified as GUID acronym that stands for Globally Unique IDentifier or Grid Unique IDentifier. In the EDG Replica Manager and the Globus Replica Location Service the GUID is essential to map between the Replica Metadata Catalog (holding the Logical File Name) and the Local Replica Catalog (holding the Storage URLs). In the more modern LCG File Catalogs, LCG File Catalog and FiReMan, it is not necessary for the user to know the GUID as the tables holding Logical File Name and Storage URL are held in the same database.

Cryptography

With regard to data security, we select to implement in GS^3 a cryptography technique. There are two basic types of cryptography systems: Symmetric (also known as conventional or secret key), and Asymmetric (public key). Symmetric ciphers require both the sender and the recipient to have the same key. This key is used by the sender to encrypt the data, and again by the recipient to decrypt the data. The most widely used symmetric cryptography algorithm is the Advanced Encryption Standard (AES) (Federal Information 197, 2001), also known as Rijndael. With asymmetric ciphers each user has a pair of keys: a Public Key and a Private Key. Messages encrypted with one key can only be decrypted by the other key. The public key can be published, while the private key is kept secret. One of the most interesting asymmetric cryptography algorithm is RSA (Rivest, Shamir, & Adelman, 1978).

Asymmetric ciphers are much slower, and their key sizes must be much larger than those used with symmetric cipher. At the moment, to break both the AES and the RSA algorithms only the brute force attack is effective, but it requires great power computing and long elaboration time to obtain the key, especially in the latter case. An interesting technique that combines and synthesizes the high security of asymmetric cryptography algorithms with the efficiency of the symmetric approach is PGP (Pretty Good Privacy) (Garfinkel, 1994). In PGP data are encrypted by using a symmetric cryptography. Then, in order to secure the symmetric key, an asymmetric cryptography algorithm is applied. An algorithm similar to PGP has been developed by GNU in the open source project GPG (GNU Privacy Guard, 2010).

GS^3: THE GRID SECURE STORAGE SYSTEM

The main goal of this work is to achieve data security in storage grids specifically conceived for providing users with access to an enormous amount of storage space. In such context, data confidentiality and integrity must be pursued avoiding both outsider and, in particular, insider attacks: no one except the user/owner can access data, including system administrators.

In order to achieve data security, the best solution is the cryptography. As discussed in the introductory section, till now, the most successfully approach adopted for solving the problem is the symmetric cryptography due to its performance against the asymmetric one. The best approach is therefore to encrypt data by exploiting a symmetric cryptography algorithm, moving the problem of security towards a problem of symmetric key (DataKey) securing-hiding, as also stated by the Kerckhoffs' principle (Kerckhoffs, 1883).

With regard to the key securing-hiding problem, the key splitting algorithm is a solution that partially achieves security issues, as discussed in the introductory section. Vulnerabilities such as insider abuses, account-hijacking and/or identity thefts are not adequately covered by such approach, since administrators can access the key components/splits. A more effective solution is required. For this reason, in order to secure-hide the DataKey we propose to encrypt this by the user public key, exploiting an asymmetric encryption algorithm. In this way only the user-owner of data can access them. In this section, we provide a logical description of the GS³ approach. In the following subsections we will describe the security algorithm while we will provide details about the architecture that puts into practice such algorithm.

Logic Security Architecture

GS³ combines both symmetric and asymmetric cryptography into a hierarchical approach, ensuring high security. A logic architecture of such approach is depicted in Figure 2. An authorized user, authenticated by his/her own X509 certifi-

cate through the user interface, contacts the grid storage system where his/her data are located. Data in the grid storage are encrypted by a symmetric cryptography algorithm whose symmetric DataKey *(K)* is also stored in the grid storage, in its turn encrypted by the user/owner public key K_{PUB}, obtaining the encrypted DataKey $K_{PUB}(K)$. In this way, only the user that has the matching private key K_{PRIV} can decrypt the symmetric DataKey and therefore the encrypted data. The encrypted DataKey $K_{PUB}(K)$ is stored together the data in order to allow the user-owner to access data from any node of the grid infrastructure. A user needs the smartcard containing the private key. In order to implement data sharing, the DataKey *K* is saved into the grid storage, replicated into as many copies as the users authorized to access data. In this way, as shown in Figure 2, a copy of DataKey encrypted by the ith authorized user public key $K^i_{PUB}(K^i_{PUB}(K))$ must be stored into the grid storage in order that the user can access the data.

Notice that, in the proposed algorithm, the decryption is exclusively performed into the authorized users' node where the corresponding X509 certificate is hosted, and the decrypted

Figure 2. GS³ logic security architecture

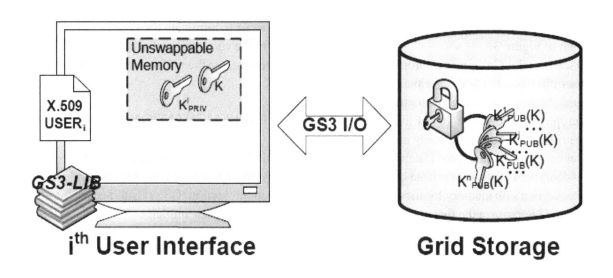

symmetric key, the data and all the other information concerning these latter are kept into unswappable memory locations of such node to avoid malicious accesses. In this way the highest layer of security is achieved and ensured: data and keys are always encrypted when they are far from the user, both in the remote storage and in transfers; they are in clear only when reach the trust user host, always and exclusively kept in the user space unswappable memory.

Algorithm

From an algorithmic point of view, the security logic architecture just described can be decomposed into two steps: (i) the symmetric DataKey K is encrypted through the user public key K_{PUB}, and it is written in the grid storage; then (ii) K is ready to be used for data encryption. The algorithm implementing this mechanism can be better rationalized in three phases: Initialization, Data I/0, and Finalization/Termination, detailed in the following subsections.

Initialization

The first phase of the GS³ algorithm is devoted to the initial setting of the distributed environment. The step by step algorithm describing the initialization phase is reported in form of activity diagram in Figure 3.

Once a user logs in the grid environment trough the user interface, the GS³ algorithm requests to the grid storage system the symmetric DataKey K encrypted by the public key of the user K_{PUB}. If the grid storage has been already initialized, its answer contains the encrypted DataKey $K_{PUB}(K)$, that is decrypted by the user private key K_{PRIV} and then saved in a safe memory location of the user interface. Otherwise, a the first access to the grid storage, a DataKey K must be created by the user interface side of the algorithm and therefore encrypted and sent to the other side.

Data I/O

GS³ organizes the data stored in the grid storage through a file system structured in directories. The data are managed and accessed by well-known primitives such as open, close, read, write, delete, list, rename, etc. In Figure 4, the algorithms implementing read, write and generic operations (delete, rename, list, etc) are represented by activity diagrams. In particular the read algorithm of Figure 4(a) implies the decryption of data received by the grid storage, while the write algorithm of Figure 4(b) requires the encryption of data before they are sent to the storage system. A generic operation instead only sends a command or a signal, as shown in Figure 4(c).

Termination

The termination phase algorithm is described by the activity diagram of Figure 5. Before the user logouts the grid, it is necessary to remove the symmetric Datakey and the other reserved information from the user interface memory.

But, since a user could still have one or more data I/O operations active/alive, it is possible he/she wants to know the status of such operations, and therefore asks to the grid storage system about that. Then, evaluating the obtained answer he/she can choose to terminate the current session or to wait for the completion of some of them. Finally the user logouts the grid.

GS³ IMPLEMENTATION OVER GLITE

The idea of combining symmetric and asymmetric cryptography in the data security algorithm detailed in section GS³ (Grid Secure Storage System), has been implemented as a service in the gLite grid middleware. In order to describe such implementation, in the following subsection we will introduce constraints and requirements motivating the implementation choices, and then

Figure 3. GS³ initialization phase algorithm

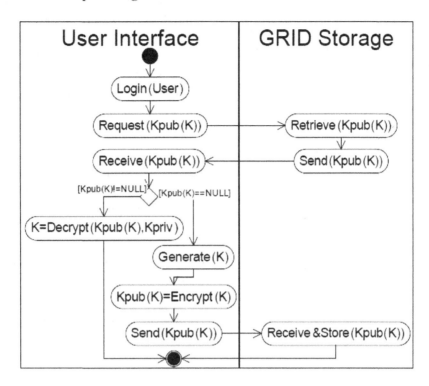

Figure 4. GS³ data I/O primitives algorithm: (a) read, (b) write, (c) generic ops

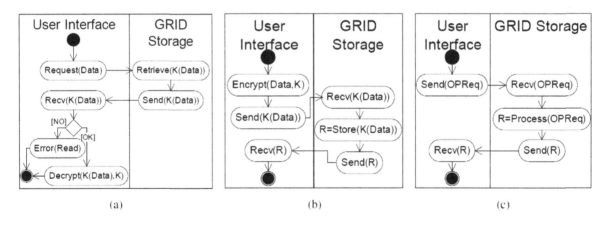

we will detail the storage architecture and the designed library.

Requirements and Specifications

Since the GS³ implementation must be integrated in the gLite environment which uses its own stor-

age libraries (GFAL), the best solution available to simplify the use of the grid secure storage and to better integrate such implementation into the gLite middleware is to base on GFAL. In order to ensure high security it is also necessary that the secure storage service must be available in

Figure 5. GS³ termination phase algorithm

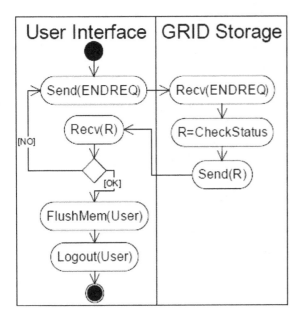

interactive mode from the UI that exclusively performs data decryption.

In such implementation, we choose the AES (Federal Information 197, 2001) algorithm for symmetric encryptions, and the Public Key Infrastructure (PKI) (Rivest, Shamir, & Adelman, 1978) for asymmetric cryptography. Moreover, for the sake of simplicity and portability towards other paradigms a POSIX interface has been implemented.

Storage Architecture

The architecture implementing the GS³ algorithm in the gLite middleware, satisfying the requirements and specifications above described, is depicted in Figure 6(a). Thus, GS is implemented as a layer working on top of GFAL, providing a file service with security/cryptography capability by means of POSIX interface.

The GS³ storage service creates a virtual file system structuring the data in files, directories and subdirectories without any restrictions on

levels and number of files per directory. Since we build this architecture on top of GFAL, in GS all data objects are seen as files stored on the SE, accessible by users through the GFAL interface (LFN, SRM, GUID, etc). Thanks to the storage architecture and the internal organization, this GS³ implementation provides all the benefits of a file system. One of the most interesting is the capability of file modification and/or rewriting, operation not implemented by the GFAL library. GFAL only allows to create/write new files, without any possibilities of modifying those after creation.

A GS³ file can be entirely stored in the SE in one chunk with variable length or it can be split into two or more blocks with fixed, user defined length, specified in the GS³ setup configuration, as reported in Figure 6(b). To avoid conflicts among file names, we univocally identify each chunk of data stored on the SE by a UUID identifier. The file index shown in Figure 6(b) (GS³FI), maps a file to the corresponding blocks in the SE. Such file index is encrypted through the symmetric DataKey and is kept in UI unswappable memory locations. In this way the user operates on a virtual file system whose logic structure usually does not correspond with its physical structure in the SE, since each file can be split into many blocks stored in the SE as files. But the main goal of file indexing is the optimization of the file I/O operations, since it reduces the data access time. Moreover, since the GS³ file rewriting and modification on the SE has to be implemented through GFAL primitives, these operations are performed by deleting the file and rewriting its modified version; splitting a GS³ file into several chunks/blocks files in the SE is the only feasible way to reach the goal. The file system is created and stored on the SE when the GS³ initialization is performed. Each file referring to data stored on the SE is encrypted by a symmetric DataKey stored on the same SE and encrypted by the user public key.

Figure 6. GS³ gLite implementation: (a) architecture, (b) file system

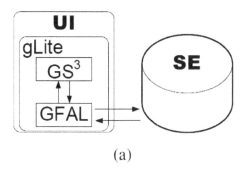

(a)

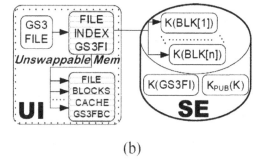

(b)

In order to optimize the file I/O operations performance, a local cache of encrypted blocks/chunks (GS³FBC) is held in the UI unswappable memory. All the operations involving blocks/chunks already loaded in the UI cache are performed locally, varying the content of such blocks/chunks. When a file is closed, the blocks stored in cache are updated to the SE. A specific GS³ primitive (gs3_flush) has been specified to force the flushing of data from the UI cache to the SE storage. This remarkably speeds-up the performance of the storage system, reducing the number of accesses to the SE. Problems of cache coherence may arise if there are more than one simultaneously active access on the grid storage working on the same data. At the moment, we apply a relaxed consistency protocol allowing to have different copies of the same data on local caches.

GS³ Interface Library and API

Since the library commands implement a POSIX.1 interface, the access to a file on the virtual encrypted file system is similar to the access to a local file. GS³ specifies the same library functions set of GFAL: in the former case the functions are prefixed by "gs3_*" while in the latter case by "gfal_*". The main difference between GS³ and a POSIX interface is constituted by the initialization and the termination phases as described in section "Algorithm". In the following we specify

the GS³ primitives starting from the same phases characterization identified above.

Initialization

The initialization phase is the most important phase of the GS³ gLite implementation. In this phase the library context is initialized with the user preferences set on environment variables: GS3_PATH (URL base where the data files are stored), GS3_PUBKEY (user's public key used to encrypt), GS3_PRVKEY (user's private key used to encrypt).

A user needing to access the SE must invoke the gs3_init function in order to read from storage space the symmetric DataKey K encrypted by the user public key K_{PUB}. As shown in Figure 7 and also introduced in subsection "Initialazation", two cases distinguish the first from successive accesses. In the first initialization phase, gs3_init generates the symmetric key K as sequence of random numbers, returned by an OPENSSL function. In the following accesses gs3_init loads K and the file index GS3FI from the storage elements. The algorithms in both cases are similar: firstly the *UI* checks the presence of the encrypted key $K_{PUB}(K)$ in the SE by a gfal_stat, then, in case it does not exist, a new key is created (Figure 7a) and sent to the SE, otherwise the key and the file index are loaded in the *UI* by two consecutive gfal_read operations (Figure 7b) The encrypted

Figure 7. gs3_init() Library Initialization: (a) first, (b) following uses

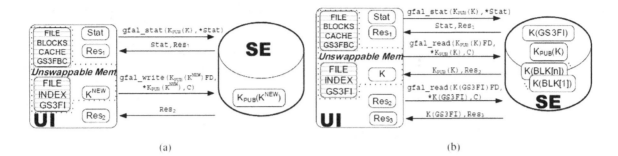

(a)　　　　　　　　　　　　　　　　(b)

Datakey $K_{PUB}(K)$ is therefore decrypted by the user private key and placed into an unswappable memory location of the *UI* to avoid malicious accesses.

Data I/O

GS3 data I/O operations are implemented through I/O POSIX primitives such as: open, read/write and close. Files are always encrypted in memory; the encryption is performed at runtime. To improve the GS3 performance and the usability of its library the accessed files' chunks are locally buffered into a cache in the *UI* until the corresponding files are closed. At file closing, the *UI* cache is synchronized with *SE*.

More specifically, the gs3_read(int fd, void *buf, int c) primitive reads c bytes of data of the file referred by the fd file descriptor placing that in the local *UI* buffer buf. As it is illustrated in Figure 7(a), by using the file index and the input parameters, the corresponding SE blocks descriptor set ($BLKD_1$) is obtained. The blocks not present in the cache, identified by the set $BLKD_2 \subseteq BLKD_1$, are loaded from the SE by a gfal_read call. Such data, with the data loaded from cache, are placed in the output buffer, and the *file blocks cache* is updated with the data just loaded from the SE. The sets $BLKD_1$ and $BLKD_2$ correspond to the vectors $BLKD_1$ [] and $BLKD_2$ [] of Figure 8(a).

The gs3_write(int fd, const void *buf, int c) is an operation entirely performed locally to the

UI, as shown in Figure 8(b). The data blocks to modify in the SE are temporarily saved into the file blocks cache. When the file is closed, renamed, moved, deleted, the flush of the cache is forced, or the gLite GS3 session is terminated, the data in cache are synchronized with the corresponding one in the SE.

gs3_<op>(int fd, <par>) is a generic data I/O operation mapped into the corresponding GFAL operation gfal_<op>(int fd, <par>). When a gs3_<op>(int fd, <par>) modifies the file system structure (delete, rename, move, mkdir, etc) it is necessary to update the file index in the SE.

Termination

The main goal of the termination operation is the synchronization of data between the UI cache and the SE. This is implemented by the gs3_finalize() function, a simplified version of which is detailed in Figure 9. It describes two separated gfal_write operations into the SE: the first writes all data of the *UI* file blocks cache (GS3FBC), the other writes the *UI* file index (GS3FI).

This sequence implements a gs3_flush function, called each time a file is closed, deleted, renamed, etc. Moreover, this is a simplified version of gs3_flush, since the GFAL libraries do not implement the rewriting capability: a file can be written only when created. Thus, if a file already exists in the SE, GFAL does not allow to modify it. In order to implement this capability in GS3,

Figure 8. GS³ data I/O primitives: (a) gs3_read, (b) gs3_write, (c) gs3_<op>

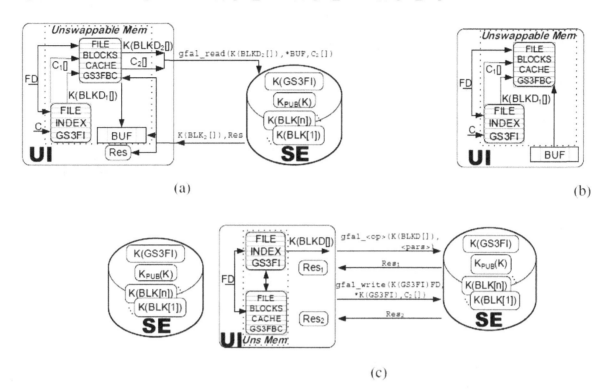

(a)

(b)

(c)

using the GFAL library, it is necessary to bypass the problem of rewriting by deleting and creating a new file each time the file is modified. This mechanism is a little bit complex and hard to depict, so we only show a simplified version in Figure 9. However, the rewriting algorithm has been entirely implemented in the GS³ library.

PERFORMANCE

Tests to evaluate the performance of the GS³ have been executed (Figure 10). In such tests a file has been created/written and then we have performed read and delete operation over it. The tests have been performed by varying the file size from 2^8 to 2^{17} bytes, doubling its size in each experiment. Therefore in total we made 10 different tests. By these, we evaluate the performance of the GS³ primitives.

The behavior of GS³ has been compared with that of the GFAL, and of an enhanced version of GFAL in which we added only the encryption feature, we call it CGFAL. In order to provide a complete picture of the GS³ performance we have made the same measures on the local file system (LOCAL).

In the tests, we have evaluated the performance of operations directly performed into the SE by considering the different environments. This could be considered as the worst case for GS³, in which the operation is directly synchronized with the SE, without taking into account the cache. As performance metric we consider the elaboration time, i.e. the time elapsed from the operation's launching until the results are fed back to the user. In order to provide significant measures, we have repeated each test 1000 times, and calculated the average of the results thus obtained.

Figure 9. gs3_finalize primitive implementation

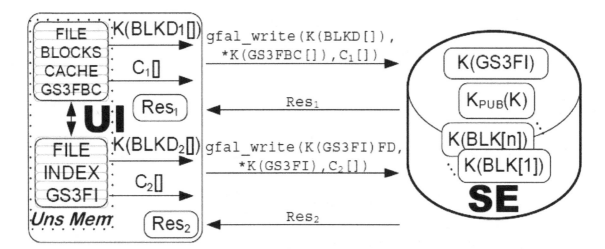

Write

The results obtained by evaluating the elaboration time of the create/write calls are reported in Figure 10(a). Such results show similar trends for all the considered environment. As can be easily expected, the elaboration times of write operations from UI to SE are affected by the file size since it hardly affect the data transferring and storing. By comparing the results of the different libraries, we can observe that, without considering the impact of cache, GS[3] is considerably slower than GFAL, CGFAL and obviously than LOCAL calls.

This is due to the fact that, each time a GS[3] write into the SE is performed, it is also necessary to update the SE file index, and therefore two consecutive gfal_write are needed, as shown in Figure 9. But, as we can note by observing the performance of the encrypted CGFAL and the GFAL ones, the time spent to access the communication network is orders of magnitude greater than the computational time spent for encrypting data. This justifies the performance gap among GS[3] and the others: in the former case two network storage accesses are required; the first for storing data, the second for storing the file index, while in the other cases only one access is needed.

This is the cost of rewriting: to implement such important feature, GS[3] introduces the file splitting and therefore the file index table.

Read

The performance obtained by the read tests are showed in Figure 10(b). Similarly to the write operation, the elaboration time trends increase by increasing the data size due to the role of the interposed network. But, in this case, the results of the worst case gs3_read elaboration are comparable to the gfal_read ones and also to those obtained by the CGFAL. This is due to the fact that in read operations we don't have to update the file index, and the computational overhead is mainly due to the encryption. The trends also confirm that the time spent in encryption tasks is negligible with regards the time spent in communication.

Delete

Figure 10(c) reports the results obtained by the evaluating delete operations. Obviously, the performance of delete operations do not vary with file size, since only a signal, few bytes, are sent. As in the write case, also in this case there is a great

Figure 10. Performance of GS³ operations against GFAL: (a) write, (b) read, (c) delete

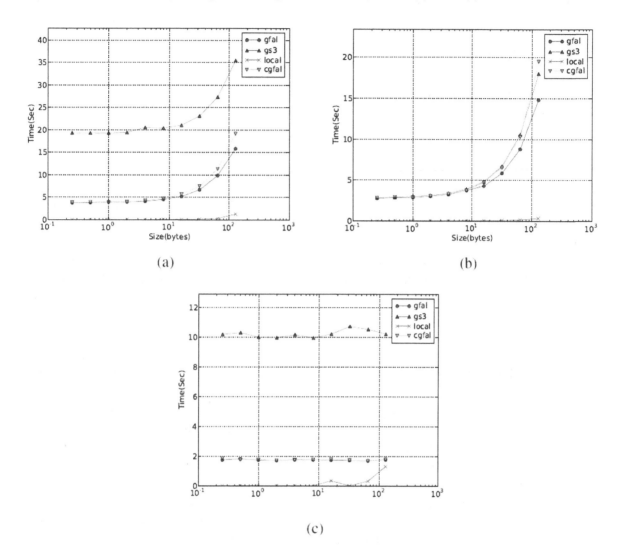

(a)

(b)

(c)

gap between the GS³ performance and the others, due to similar motivations: a GS³ file deletion, as shown in Figure 8(c) needs to update the SE file index after removing the file from the SE. This introduces a further gfal_write operation of such file index, increasing the overall elaboration time of the GS³ file deletion. It can be also noticed that, the performance of delete operation do not vary with file size.

DISCUSSION

The proposed GS³ approach and the implementation were based on the main idea of providing a secure file system instead of secure files, by combining both asymmetric (RSA) and symmetric (AES) cryptography. However, this approach has several advantages:

- **Security** - encrypting the symmetric DataKey by the user public key ensures that data and DataKey are exclusively accessible by only and exclusively the authorized user-owner.

- **Security Level -** both data, files and the file system structure are encrypted.
- **Library Interface API -** a complete set of library functions is available, introducing new capabilities (files' modification, rewriting, renaming, etc), and optimizing the existing one with the aim of security.
- **Performance -** the GS³ architecture is designed for satisfying specific performance requirements (file indexing, local file cache, etc).
- **Dependability and Fault Tolerance -** since the DataKey is not split among different nodes, it is possible to implement dependable and fault tolerant storage systems.

The proposed approach experiences also the following drawbacks:

- **Security -** no one can access the access the contents of GS³ files, but site administrators can anyway physically erase them.
- **Overhead -** to maintain a local file system structure has the disadvantage that each time a file is closed, renamed, delete, etc, the structure of the storage system must be updated, introducing an extra remote write operation.
- **Consistency problems -** the presence of a cache can introduce problems of data consistency in case of different contemporary accesses and modifications to the same files.

Anyway, such disadvantages do not affect or compromise the validity of the approach that provides a significant contribution to the related state of the art briefly introduced in the introductory section, highlighted by the points in favor.

Moreover, they constitute materials for future work on GS³, as presented below.

CONCLUSION

In this work we described the Grid Secure Storage System (GS³), a secure (encrypted) storage system for storage grids. It has been implemented and integrated into the gLite middleware. In this chapter we detail both the GS³ security algorithm and its implementation. The security algorithm is based on the idea of combining symmetric and asymmetric cryptography. The symmetric cryptography is directly applied to data, generating encrypted stored data. The symmetric key decrypting such encrypted data is in its turn encrypted by the user-owner public key (asymmetric cryptography) and stored into the grid remote storage system. Decryption is performed by the user interface node, and both the key and the data are allocated into unswappable memory locations of such node. In this way the data can be accessed exclusively by the data owner. In order to share such data with other users it is necessary to store in the grid storage copies of the DataKey encrypted by such users private keys.

The strength point of the GS³ implementation into the gLite middleware is the definition of a specific secure file system on top of the GFAL library. This choice allows to protect both data/files and also their structure, the whole file system. Moreover, the gLite GS³ implementation introduces a new capability: the file modification and rewriting. This implementation has been evaluated, in particular with regards the three main operations: read, write and delete. The tests are performed by considering the worst case, in which the GS³ always operates directly to the SE, comparing GS³ to other libraries (GFAL, CGFAL, LOCAL) The results obtained shown higher elaboration times of GS³ than the others in write and delete operations, due to the file index writing for each of these operations, while in read operations they are very close to the GFAL and CGFAL ones. A deeper investigation on the GS^3 performance by also considering the impact of cache is one of the imminent/short term development. Other interesting points to further investigate are: security improvements, cache coherence, data sharing, fault tolerance, Quality-of-Service (QoS), system optimization and jobs batch.

ACKNOWLEDGMENT

This work makes use of results produced by the PI2S2 Project managed by the Consorzio CO-META, a project co-funded by the Italian Ministry of University and Research (MIUR) within the Piano Operativo Nazionale "Ricerca Scientifica, Sviluppo Tecnologico, Alta Formazione" (PON 2000-2006). More information is available at http://www.pi2s2.it and http://www.consorzio-cometa.it

REFERENCES

Alfieri, R., Cecchini, R., Ciaschini, V., Frohner, A., Gianoli, A., Lorentey, K., & Spataro, F. (2003). VOMS, an authorization system for virtual organizations. In *Proceedings of the 1ˢᵗ European Across Grids Conference* (pp. 33-40).

Anderson, D. P. (2004). BOINC: A system for public-resource computing and storage. In *Proceedings of the 5ᵗʰ IEEE/ACM International Workshop on Grid Computing* (pp. 4-10). Washington, DC., USA: IEEE Computer Society.

Blanchet, C., Mollon, R., & Deleage, G. (2006). Building an encrypted file system on the EGEE grid: Application to protein sequence analysis. In *Proceedings of the 1ˢᵗ International Conference on Availability, Reliability and Security* (pp. 965–973). Washington, DC., USA: IEEE Computer Society.

Federal Information 197 (2001). *Advanced Encryption Standard (AES)*. Processing standard publication.

Foster, I. (2002). What is the grid? - A three point checklist. *GRID today 1*(6), 22-25.

Foster, I., & Kesselman, C. (1998). *The grid: Blueprint for a new computing infrastructure*. Waltham, MA, USA: Morgan Kaufmann Publishers.

Garfinkel, S. (1994). *PGP: Pretty good privacy*. Sebastopol, CA, USA: O'Reilly Media.

gLite (2010). Retrieved from http://glite.web.cern.ch/ glite

Globus Security Infrastructure (GSI). (2010). Retrieved from http://www.globus.org/ Security

Globus Toolkit. (2010). Retrieved from http://www.globus.org

HYDRA Project. (2010). Retrieved from https://twiki.cern.ch/ twiki/ bin/ view/ EGEE/ DMEncryptedStorage

Junrang, L., Zhaohui, W., Jianhua, Y., & Mingwang, X. (2004). A secure model for network-attached storage on the grid. In *Proceedings of the 2004 IEEE International Conference on Services Computing* (pp. 604-608). Washington, DC., USA: IEEE Computer Society.

Kerckhoffs, A. (1883). La cryptographie militaire. *Journal des sciences militaires IX*, 5-83.

Large Hadron Collider (LHC). (2010). Retrieved from http://public.web.cern.ch/ public/en/ lhc/ lhc-en.html

Leach, P., Mealling, M., & Salz, R. (2005). A universally unique identifier (UUID) URN namespace. *Network Working Group RFC 4122*. Retrieved from http://www.ietf.org/ rfc/ rfc4122.txt =0pt

Montagnat, J., Jouvenot, D., Pera, C., Frohner, A., Kunszt, P. Z., & Koblitz, B. ...Loomis, C. (2006). Implementation of a medical data manager on top of glite services. *EGEE Technical Report.* Retrieved from http://cdsweb.cern.ch/record/ 941801/ files/ egee-tr-2006-002.pdf

Privacy Guard, G. N. U. (2010). *GnuPG: Documentation Sources.* Retrieved from http://www. gnupg.org/ documentation

Rivest, R. L., Shamir, A., & Adelman, L. M. (1978). A method for obtaning digital signatures and public-key cryptosystems. *Communications of the ACM, 21*(2), 120–126. doi:10.1145/359340.359342

Scardaci, D. (2007). *GFAL Java API.* Retrieved from https://grid.ct.infn.it/ twiki/ bin/ view/ GILDA/ APIGFAL

Scardaci, D., & Scuderi, G. (2007). A secure storage service for the glite middleware. In *Proceedings of International Symposium on Information Assurance and Security* (pp. 261-266). Washington, DC., USA: IEEE Computer Society.

Seitz, L., Pierson, M. J., & Brunie, L. (2003). Key management for encrypted data storage in distributed systems. In *Proceedings of the 2nd IEEE Security in Storage Workshop* (pp. 20-30). Washington, DC., USA: IEEE Computer Society.

Shamir, A. (1979). How to share a secret. *Communications of the ACM, 22*(11), 612–613. doi:10.1145/359168.359176

Thain, D., & Livny, M. (2005). Parrot: An application environment for data-intensive computing. *Scalable Computing: Practice and Experience, 6*(3), 9–18.

Thain, D., Tannenbaum, T., & Livny, M. (2002). Condor and the grid . In Berman, F., Fox, G., & Hey, T. (Eds.), *Grid computing: Making the global infrastructure a reality* (pp. 299–355). Hoboken, NJ, USA: John Wiley & Sons.

Tu, M., Li, P., Yen, I. L., Thuraisingham, B., & Khan, L. (2009). Secure data objects replication in data grid. *IEEE Transactions on Dependable and Secure Computing, 7*(1), 50–64.

Tuecke, S., Welch, V., Engert, D., Pearlman, L., & Thompson, M. (2004). Internet x.509 Public Key Infrastructure (PKI) proxy certificate profile. *Network Working Group RFC 3820.* Retrieved from http://www.ietf.org/ rfc/ rfc3820.txt =0pt

Chapter 12

Application of Grid Computing for Meteorological Assessment of Wind and Solar Resources in Sub-Saharan African Countries

Francis Xavier Ochieng
Jomo Kenyatta University of Agriculture and Technology (JKUAT), Kenya

ABSTRACT

Developing countries especially those in sub-Saharan Africa face a major challenge in meteorological prediction and numerical assessment of wind and solar resources. This is mainly attributed to lack of expertise and requisite equipment. A proven approach is the utilization of remote grid computing essentially undertaking grid computing remotely by accessing the grid computers in host countries with more advanced Information Technology infrastructure. This chapter details the utilisation of a Numerical Mesoscale model with a horizontal resolution of 1 km in assessing wind resources in Kenya. The presented country in Sub-Saharan Africa uses a large-scale High-Performance Computer (HPC) that combines heterogeneous computing resources in Germany. The same model can be used for assessment of solar resources.

DOI: 10.4018/978-1-61350-113-9.ch012

INTRODUCTION

German Grid Initiative (D-Grid)

The D-Grid Initiative (German Grid Initiative) (Neuroth, Kerzel, & Gentzsch, 2007) provides a grid computing infrastructure that helps in establishing the concept of e-Science in three main areas, namely Grid computing, Knowledge management and e-Learning. Started in September, 2005, the initiative consists of the following 6 community projects, an integration project and several Partner projects as shown in Table 1.

The D-Grid Integration project essentially seeks to be the grid resource and service provider for the science community in Germany. Thus it deals with D-Grid base software, deployment and operation of the D-Grid infrastructure, networks and security and lastly manages the D-Grid project office. It thus manages all the developments from different community projects in one common D-Grid Platform.

Of particular interest to the development of renewable energies in Sub-Saharan Africa is the WISENT project. This e-Science project investigates the influence of weather and climate on transformation, transport and utilisation of Energy. It integrates the cooperation of scientific organizations that use grid technologies in the field of energy meteorology.

WISENT

WISENT (Wissensnetz Energiemeteorologie) utilizes grid resources to develop forecast methods capable of determining the level of power generation in near real-time in order to control power plants for optimal energy production. This helps ameliorate the challenge of determination of the availability of renewable energy sources like wind and solar, due to their fluctuations as a result of meteorological factors. The main project partners in this project are the German Aerospace Centre (DLR), University of Oldenburg, OFFIS, and Meteocontrol GmBH. Their expertise and roles in the WISENT project is shown in Figure 1.

The need for grid computing in energy meteorology is to help overcome the challenges like accessing distributed data, exchanging large heterogeneous data sets, archiving data and speeding up applications. The grid allows running of more complex models and large data set processing, hence improving forecast methods and optimal micrositing of power plants.

ACCESS PORTAL TO THE D-GRID

The WISENT High-Performance Computing Cluster (HPCC)

In a bid to enhance the use of simulation models for purposes of improving forecast methods and optimal micrositing of power plants, the WISENT project received from the D-GRID, grid middleware (Globus Toolkit, UNICORE, gLite, etc) which were installed and configured in a High-Performance Computing Cluster (HPCC). The aim was to allow the utilisation of resources within the D-GRID infrastructure. In the year 2008, the cluster system was expanded further with other Master nodes as well as implementation of a RAID-System. Additionally a Mesoscale Model, the Weather Research and Forecasting (WRF) model was installed. This model is the one to be used in simulations of solar and wind resources.

Table 1. Main projects within the German grid initiative

Community Projects	Partner Projects
AstroGrid-D, C3-Grid, GDI-Grid, HEP-Grid, InGrid, MediGRID, SuGi, TextGrid	WISENT

Figure 1. Project partners and their expertise

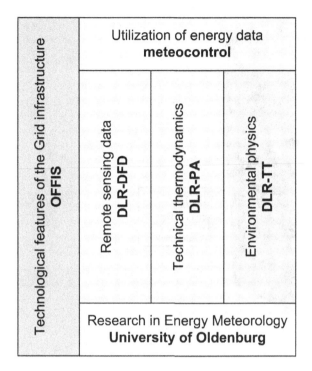

Hardware Configuration and Cluster Access

The Cluster System is composed 45 computing nodes with a total of 94 AMD 2.2 GHz Dual-Core Opteron Processors and 8 or 16 GB central hard drive per node. Thus for calculations a total of 188 computing nodes are available (Figure 2).

Of the total computing nodes, 24 of them are interconnected with Infinibad, due to its low Latency as compared to the Gigabit-Ethernet. In addition there are 2 Master nodes with a storage facility in a RAID system with 16 Terabyte (13 TB Net) Hard Drive Capacity available. Using Linux SSH protocol one can gain access to the WRF calculating portal in the D-GRID initiative by use of the protocol *ssh –X username@ srvgrid01.offis.uni-oldenburg.de*.

WRF: A MODEL APPLICABLE IN GRID COMPUTING

About Weather Research and Forecasting

The Weather Research and Forecasting (WRF) model is a next generation Mesoscale numerical weather prediction system for use in operational forecasts as well as other atmospheric research needs. It is a portable and flexible state-of-the-art atmospheric simulation system that is efficient and portable on available parallel computing platforms. It features multiple dynamical cores, a 3-dimensional variations (3DVAR) data assimilation system, and a software architecture allowing for computational parallelism and system extensibility. WRF is suitable for a broad spectrum of applications across scales ranging from meters to thousands of kilometres.

Its ability to allow for computational parallelism is what makes WRF very attractive for application in grid computing environments. It consists of 4 main parts i.e. the WRF Preprocessing System (WPS), WRF-Var, ARW solver and postprocessing and visualization tools. The workflow and the inteconnection of these parts is shown in Figure 3 below (NCAR, 2010).

Deployment / Execution of WRF in WISENT

To achieve deployment, the WRF model code is downloaded and compiled to form the models executables. This then allows the compilation of different variants of WRF with totally different compilers and compilation options. Figure 4 shows the workflow deployed in Wisent for executing WRF model on the D-GRID infrastructure.

Figure 2. WISENT High-Performance Computing Cluster (WISENT, 2010)

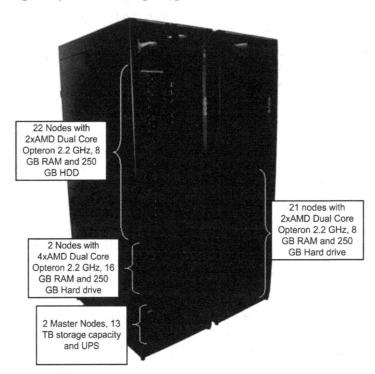

22 Nodes with
2xAMD Dual Core
Opteron 2.2 GHz, 8
GB RAM and 250
GB HDD

21 nodes with
2xAMD Dual Core
Opteron 2.2 GHz, 8
GB RAM and 250
GB Hard drive

2 Nodes with
4xAMD Dual Core
Opteron 2.2 GHz, 16
GB RAM and 250
GB Hard drive

2 Master Nodes, 13
TB storage capacity
and UPS

WRF Variants Compiled on the WISENT D-GRID

Table 2 shows the compiled variants available on WISENT D-GRID. An option also exists to configure and compile custom made WRF variations.

GRID COMPUTING IN SUB-SAHARAN AFRICA

In Sub-Saharan Africa, excluding South Africa and Northern Africa, the concept of grid computing is almost non-existence; there is virtually no existing grid computing infrastructure. However, the downward trends in prices of hardware applicable to grid computing, it is expected that more resources and efforts will be channelled towards this direction.

Nevertheless due to the need of forecasting of the solar and wind resources in this region which is quite amenable to grid computing, the need for utilising grid computing facilities located in other continents is the key. For this to occur, certain expertise and technical resources will be required from both the host country and the end user. An example of using the WISENT D-GRID in Germany and a home user in Kenya is analyzed to assess these requirements.

Technical Resources Required from both the Host (Germany) and User (Kenya) of the Grid Computing Resources

Varied technical resources and expertise are required from both the host and end user.

The Transmission Mode

The user compiles and configures the WRF model variant to be used, thereafter, the model is

Figure 3. WRF modelling system flow chart

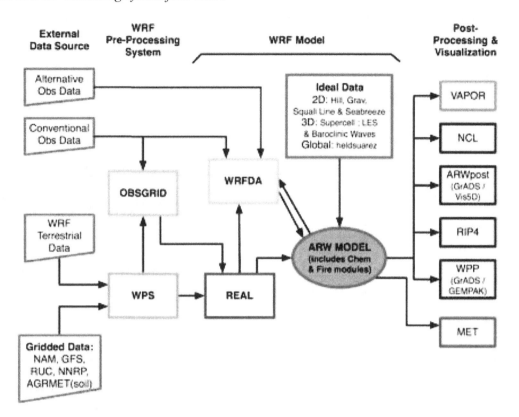

configured and run in a distributed fashion in the varied processors. Important in this approach is that a maximum of 8 processors should be used per run. A higher number has proved to lead to the model exploding or giving uncertain results due to the high finite division of the iterations to the processors.

Before sending the run command, one has the option to choose on which band the simulation is to be done i.e. whether on infiband or the others. Further, a check can be done to find out which processors/nodes are free (Figure 5) (WISENT, 2010).

From Figure 5 it is seen that out of the total 44 nodes, only about 3 nodes (12 processors) are free. Sending a run command at this time for a work that utilised more than 4 processors, will mean that your work will be queued, since some of the idle processors are dedicated to either post

processing or for quick test or pilot runs. The master node cluster on the extreme left with about 8 nodes, is not used for simulation processing.

Challenges that a User May Experience when Utilizes this Approach

To allow for ease in configuring the simulation and giving the run command, a user interface within WRF exists. However, the interface lacks in the data transmission of the results from the cluster to the client end user. For this purpose, a special data transfer interface called the GridFTP was developed.

The GridFTP protocol supports the efficient transfer of large amounts of data between conforming servers deployed as part of a scientific grid infrastructure. These servers may be either a part

Figure 4. Execution of WRF on the D-GRID infrastructure

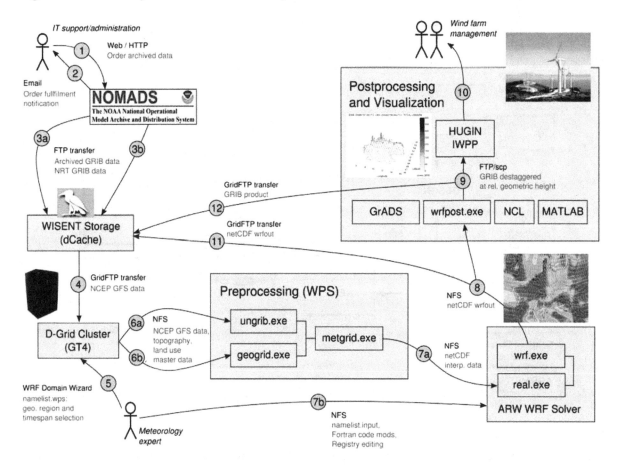

of execution sites to which user jobs are submitted, or they may provide access dedicated storage elements with substantial disk or tape capacity for archiving grid users' data. For example, the GridFTP server shipped in the popular Globus Toolkit middleware belongs to the former, and the GridFTP Door of the dCache middleware to the latter category (Ploski, 2010).

The major challenge users especially from Africa may experience is the configuring and utilization of the model. In addition due to the high costs of obtaining a dedicated internet connection, only organisations can afford this type of internet connection. The need for a high speed dedicated internet connection is based on the fact that a huge amount of data is generated by the model runs, and need to be transferred to the client. In case the simulation is seen to generate less data sizes

(less than 100 MB), due to choice of a smaller domain size during model configuration, then a lower speed and shared internet connection can be recommended for the client. Nevertheless, on the host side, a physical presence is required for one to obtain a grid licence in order to use the GridFTP interface. Thus, for most users, a SCP approach may need to be used.

CONCLUSION

The utilization of grid computing in economies of Sub-Saharan African has huge impacts especially in areas like:

- Disaster management
- Early warning system

Table 2. WRF Variants compiled on WiSENT D-GRID

Variant Name	Compiler	Description
01_serial_nn	pgi6.2	PC Linux x86_64 (IA64 and AMD Opteron), PGI compiler 5.2 or higher (Single-Threaded, No Nesting)
02_rsl_serial_yn	pgi6.2	PC Linux x86_64 (IA64 and AMD Opteron), PGI compiler 5.2 or higher (Single-Threaded, RSL, Allows Nesting)
03_openmp_yn	pgi6.2	PC Linux x86_64 (IA64 and Opteron), PGI compiler SM-Parallel (OpenMP, allows nesting using RSL without MPI). Note: this configuration did not exist in arch/configure.defaults. It was created by adapting an existing OpenMP configuration.
04_rsl_mpich_yn	pgi6.2	PC Linux x86_64 (IA64 and AMD Opteron), PGI 5.2 or higher, DM-Parallel (RSL, MPICH, Allows nesting)
05_rsl_lite_mpich_yn	pgi6.2	PC Linux x86_64 (IA64 and AMD Opteron), PGI 5.2 or higher, DM-Parallel (RSL_LITE, MPICH, Allows nesting, No P-LBCs)
19_rsl_osu_yn	pgi6.2	PC Linux x86_64 (IA64 and AMD Opteron), PGI 5.2 or higher, DM-Parallel (RSL, MVAPICH, Allows nesting). Compiled against mvapich-0.9.7-mlx2.2.0 from PGI 6.2-5. Using InfiniBand drivers distributed in ofed-1.1.
20_rsl_lite_osu_yn	pgi6.2	PC Linux x86_64 (IA64 and AMD Opteron), PGI 5.2 or higher, DM-Parallel (RSL_LITE, MPICH, Allows nesting, No P-LBCs). Compiled against mvapich-0.9.7-mlx2.2.0 from PGI 6.2-5. Using InfiniBand drivers distributed in ofed-1.1.
21_rsl_lite_osu_yn_openmp	pgi6.2	PC Linux x86_64 (IA64 and AMD Opteron), PGI 5.2 or higher, DM-Parallel (OpenMP, RSL_LITE, MPICH, Allows nesting, No P-LBCs). Compiled against mvapich-0.9.7-mlx2.2.0 from PGI 6.2-5. Using InfiniBand drivers distributed in ofed-1.1.
22_rsl_osu_yn_openmp	pgi6.2	PC Linux x86_64 (IA64 and AMD Opteron), PGI 5.2 or higher, DM-Parallel (OpenMP, RSL, MPICH, Allows nesting). Compiled against mvapich-0.9.7-mlx2.2.0 from PGI 6.2-5. Using InfiniBand drivers distributed in ofed-1.1.
24_rsl_mpich_yn_infinipath	pgi6.2	PC Linux x86_64 (IA64 and AMD Opteron), PGI 5.2 or higher, DM-Parallel (RSL, MVAPICH, Allows nesting). Compiled against MPI and InfiniPath drivers from the following RPMs: mpi-libs-2.0-1377.734_fc3_psc.i386 infinipath-kernel-2.0-1377.734_fc3_psc.x86_64 infinipath-libs-2.0-1377.734_fc3_psc.i386 infinipath-2.0-1377.734_fc3_psc.x86_64 infinipath-devel-2.0-1377.734_fc3_psc.noarch
25_rsl_osu_yn	pgi5.2	PC Linux x86_64 (IA64 and AMD Opteron), PGI 5.2 or higher, DM-Parallel (RSL, MPICH, Allows nesting). Compiled with MVAPICH 0.9.5.
30_rsl_lite_mpich_yn	g95-0.91	PC Linux x86_64 (IA64 and AMD Opteron), g95 compiler DM-Parallel (RSL_LITE, MPICH, Allows nesting)
32_rsl_openmpi_yn	pgi7.1	RSL variant compiled with openmpi_pgcc-1.2.4-1 on Scientific Linux 2.6.9-67.0.4.EL.cernsmp
33_rsl_openmpi_yn	pgi6.2	RSL variant compiled with openmpi-1.2.4 on SLES SP1 x86_64
96_rsl_serial_yn_gfortran	gfortran4.1.0	PC Linux x86_64 (IA64 and Opteron), GNU Fortran compiler (Single-threaded, RSL, Allows nesting). Note: this configuration does not exist in arch/configure.defaults and was created from scratch. See also https://bi.offis.de/wisent/tiki-index.php?page=WRF-gFortran

- Weather prediction and analysis
- Changes in land use
- Resource assessment of Solar and Wind resource
- Prediction of solar and wind resources

By enhancing the use of grid computing, the economies of Sub-Saharan African countries will be greatly impacted mainly due to disaster risk reduction measures in early warning and weather

Table 3. Technical resources and expertise for using grid computing resource

	Kenya (End-User)	**Germany (Host)**
Connectivity Technology	Cheapest approach is to use WiMax Technology, Costs € 62 / month	Most of the hosts are already on T1 lines.
Connectivity Speeds	265 kbits / sec (32 kB / sec) during the day and 1Mbit/ sec (128 KB/Sec) during the night	Much higher than the T1 line of about 1.544 Mbits/sec (193 KB/sec) upstream & Downstream
Dedication	Connection is dedicated, not shared	Connection is shared
Ease of Use	Through SSH protocol	Through SSH protocol
Analysis and Processing Technology	At least a Core 2 Duo computer with minimum 2.2 Ghz processor. An external hard drive for data storage is necessary	See 2.2 and 3.3

Figure 5. Status of nodes

Cluster status: 168 CPU cores busy on 44 nodes. No queued jobs.

prediction aspects and also enhancing of energy security through resource assessment.

REFERENCES

German Federal Ministry of Education and Research. (2008). *D-GRID WISENT*. Retrieved May 13, 2010, from https://bi.offis.de/wisent/ tiki-download_file.php?fileId=352

Hasselbring. W., Heinemann, D., & Ploski. J. (2008). WISENT: Grid technology for energy meteorology. *In D-GRID Newsletter #2, Q2/2008*, 1-12. Retrieved on May 13, 2010, from http:// www.d-grid.de/ fileadmin/ rundbrief/ D-Grid-Newsletter-2008-Q2-en.pdf

National Centre for Atmospheric Research (NCAR). (2010). *User's guide for the advanced research WRF (ARW) modeling system version 3.2*. Retrieved on May 14, 2010, from http://www. mmm.ucar.edu/ wrf/ users/ docs/user_guide_V3/ ARWUsersGuideV3.pdf

Neuroth, H., Kerzel, M., & Gentzsch, W. (Eds.). (2007). *German grid initiative D-Grid.* Universitaetsverlag Goettingen Publications. Retrieved on May 14, 2010, from http://webdoc.sub.gwdg. de/ univerlag/2007/ D-Grid_en.pdf

Ploski, J. (2010). *GridFTP-client arbeitspaket 3.2.* Retrieved on June 1, 2010, from http:// bi.offis.de/gridftp/ downloads/ GridFTP_Client_User_Guide.pdf

Ploski, J. (2010). *WRF Benchmarks in WISENT.* Retrieved on May 15, 2010, from https:// srvgrid01.offis.uni-oldenburg.de/ wrf-benchmark/ benchmarks.pl

WISENT. (2010). *High performance computing cluster.* Retrieved on May 14, 2010, from https:// srvgrid01.offis.uni-oldenburg.de/ maui/status.pl

Chapter 13
Adaptive Grid Services

Mark Anderson
Edge Hill University, UK

Laeeq Ahmed
University of Engineering & Technology Peshawar, Pakistan

Mandeep Joshi
Liverpool Hope University, UK

Sujan Kansakar
Liverpool Hope University, UK

ABSTRACT

The chapter aims to explore the implementation of grid services and defines a theoretical approach to a development framework which would enable the creation of agile services. At present, services are written with specific goals in mind which may support the majority of users of the service. However if the requirements of the users change, or there exist users who require a slightly alternative form of the service, then either multiple services must be orchestrated to provide the required functionality to the users, or a new service must be implemented to address any gaps in functionality. An alternative solution is presented in the chapter which adopts aspect-oriented programming as a core component in the framework. By utilizing this paradigm, it becomes possible to develop services that are agile; capable of combining the capabilities required to support requests being submitted to the grid node dependent upon individual needs. To facilitate this mechanism, a pool of service components must be created from which the weaving component of the framework can select, via semantic discovery, the most appropriate.

INTRODUCTION

Teleworking is a phenomenon by which employees are given freedom to work from any location and at any time by using Information and Communication Technology (ICT). With its undoubted advantages, teleworking has found itself a niche market in a fast moving and dynamic e-business. In the United Kingdom, British Telecom reckons that there are about two million people working at home and that more than a quarter of them are teleworkers (iVillage, unknown). The model commonly adopted is for employees to work in virtual offices, forming virtual communities, and collaborating

DOI: 10.4018/978-1-61350-113-9.ch013

through distributed toolsets. Research in the field considers the support of teleworking through the development of software or middleware solutions on a distributed system (Dangelmaier et al., 1997; Sugawara et al., 2003).

The field of teleworking is one which can be closely linked to the development of virtual environments. The aim of these environments is to create widely distributed applications to support the communication and collaboration of workers in a Virtual Office or Virtual Community. In this chapter, the similarities between these fields and the potential offered by grid computing are explored. We also examine some of the potential limitations in the way that grid services are currently developed, and propose an alternative strategy making use of Aspect Oriented Programming (AOP) to enable the creation of fully dynamic services to support the needs of an agile user base.

Whilst the development of distributed systems has evolved rapidly over recent years (Coulouris et al., 2005), there remain limitations related to individual nodes in a system. These relate to the hardware being used such as the processors and hard disks (Abbas, 2004). Following recent work in the field which explores the use of Web Services to support teleworking (Braun & Schill, 2002), a potential solution to these limitations for teleworking appears to lie in grid computing. There appears to be much in common with the field of grid computing which itself aims to support distributed resources and users in Virtual Organisations (VOs) through a service-oriented architecture.

The objectives of this chapter are to explore the limitations in Service-Oriented Architectures (SOA). Specifically, the chapter will focus on the creation of dynamic services to support users in Virtual Organizations (VOs) who may be highly diverse in their needs. The key aspects to be considered include the identification of suitable service components to form the functionality of the service, and also the construction of a service using those identified components.

BACKGROUND

Teleworking and Grid Computing

The field of grid computing has been evolving over the past decade or so, having been derived from the notion of electricity grids; that is, on-demand facilities that are distributed and adaptable to the user needs. Two key areas in which grid computing can be closely aligned with concepts derived for teleworking are

The dynamic nature of a grid means that services and resources can be added or removed as required. This aligns well with the agile and dynamic nature of a teleworking environment.

The notion of Virtual Organizations which relate physically disparate resources and users together and involves issues of trust, authorization and authentication to be successfully implemented. The relationship with teleworking lies in the concept of forming a community that will logically join geographically separated resources.

The technology currently employed to implement grid-based solutions is now mature. Open Grid Services Architecture (OGSA) uses a common representation for storage and computational resources, networks, programs, and so on (Joseph & Fellenstein, 2004). All are treated as *services*—network-enabled entities providing facilities through the exchange of messages (Foster et al., 2002a). Grid toolkits based on OGSA, such as Globus (Globus Alliance, 2005), are aligned with web service standards. In particular, this features the embodiment of the Web Services Resources Framework (WSRF) (Globus Alliance, 2005; (Sotomayor & Childers, 2006). As such, these toolkits offer an ideal opportunity in which to develop teleworking tools using an architecture which offers a stable framework to support a SOA based on a computing grid. Indeed, a proposed architecture for using a SOA based on Web Services to support teleworking has identified a number of categories where teleworking could be facilitated (Braun & Schill, 2002). The natural extension from the use of Web Services to Grid Services ensures that perceived benefits can be retained with the added features available in Grid Services to further augment a virtual teleworking environment.

Developing Grid Applications

The common development cycle for a grid service using Globus is a five stage process (Sotomayor, 2005):

1. Define the service interface
2. Implement the service in Java
3. Create the service deployment descriptor
4. Generate a grid archive file for the service
5. Deploy the service into a container

The implementation of the service is typically coded in Java, an object-oriented and platform independent programming language (Flanagan, 1999). Therefore, a service should be designed using Object Oriented (OO) methodologies. Whilst the issues around OO Programming have been well documented (Scholtz et al., 1993), there remain inherent problems with OO methodologies which may be present in the design and implementation of grid services. Critically, it can also be noted that this development cycle is largely static in that an iteration of the cycle develops a single fully-featured service. Implementing additional features requires a further iteration in development.

Overcoming Issues in Object-Oriented Methodologies

When a problem is solved using Object Oriented (OO) models, the work performed to solve the problem isn't easily reused across objects due to confinements in OO models to a particular problem domain. Furthermore, there may be requirements that extend over all the objects within a domain which require code to be developed for solving that problem repeatedly for each object

affected (Kiselev, 2002). Whilst it appears that OOP has the characteristic of modularization, it is good at modularising core concerns but not all that good when it comes to modularising the crosscutting concerns.

For example, consider a travel agency employing teleworking services which develops and deals with a portfolio of holidays. The travel agent application, employing travelling representatives, is a typical example of SOA used by the customers to book holidays, arrange trips, and so on (Navarro et al., 2006). In the design of the services to support teleworking within the company there could be two distinct hierarchies supporting the marketing and the sales of the holiday products (Figure 1).

The services could be management services to track the marketing of new destinations, or to identify sales issues. OOP would require inheritance to be used to enable sub-classes to inherit behaviours or properties from their parent class. However, the system analysts/developers would need to know all these concerns in advance of the system design (Laddad, 2003). In real world scenarios many of these concerns might not be known, possibly until quite late in the development process.

It is important to note here that there are behaviours added that have no relation with the original object's domain. The design operation has nothing to do with how communication takes place, how operations are protected using security mechanisms or how workflow of the service tasks is managed. The case is similar for each service, regardless of the hierarchy in which that service exists. So communication, security and other behaviours are the concerns that are independent of the object problem domain and this independence makes these concerns crosscutting.

Aspect Oriented Programming (AOP) is used to solve these problems by separating the crosscutting business concerns from the original problem domain (Laddad, 2003). OOP solves common concerns by capturing common features on top of a class hierarchy. Conversely, AOP attempts to

Figure 1. Service hierarchy

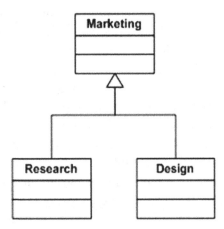

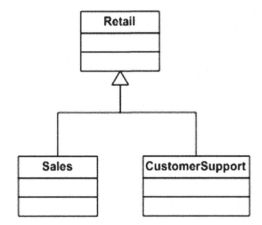

modularise common features in a software layer that spreads across classes regardless of domain, thus increasing modularity of the software. Using AOP, programmers can *dynamically* change a static OO model and create a system that can grow to meet any new requirements that arise. The aspects can be kept in a single location rather than code being spread across an OO model. In this way, AOP can address normal OO complexities resulting in a more modularised architecture for the resultant code.

An Aspect-Oriented Grid Approach

Applying AOP to the design and implementation of grid services for teleworking can bring great benefits to the development of services to support communities of remote users. These benefits can be seen as being:

- **Simplification.** Only components specific to a service will need to be analyzed and implemented.
- **Reusability.** Modularity is increased through the use of aspects which can be woven in where required.
- **Extensibility.** Services can easily be modified or extended by changing the aspects.

All services using that aspect will adopt the modification.

To make use of these benefits, a new architecture has been designed to support the implementation of Aspect Oriented Grid Programming (AOGP) (Figure 2). The grid resource allocation process is adapted to enable the modification of services by the discovery and weaving of aspects into a service if a match for a client's requirement cannot be found. The notion of incorporating AOP into grid application development promotes the concept of agile grid applications, allowing grid services to adapt to the client demands.

The goal is to create a framework for an adaptive environment to support teleworking through the adoption of emergent technologies, such as grid computing and Aspect-Oriented Programming (AOP). The remainder of this chapter will consider the concept of dynamically weaving cross-cutting concerns at both the service and the client side of a grid application, and the mechanism used to identify relevant aspects. In order to achieve this aim, there are two key aspects which must be considered in relation to the framework. The first relates to mechanisms which support dynamic weaving. The second considers how aspects can be successfully selected for weaving from an available pool.

Figure 2. High-level view of proposed architecture

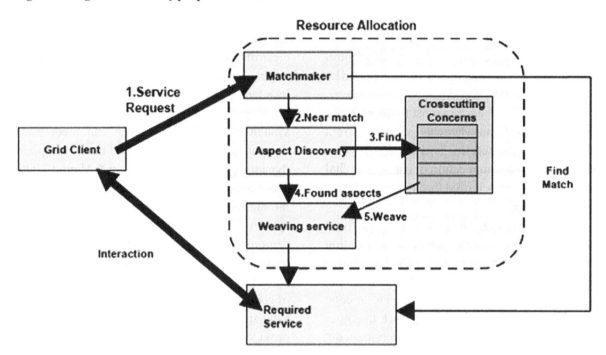

DYNAMIC SEARCHABLE SERVICES

Issue 1: A Dynamic Grid

A system is said to be dynamic if it provides support for changing its organization as a concurrent activity to the application providing services. A system is said to support dynamic applications if the organization or functionality of applications based on the system can be changed without the application being interrupted (Chitchyan & Sommerville, 2004).

A grid system can be determined as a dynamic system as it provides support for changing its organizations as a concurrent activity to the application providing services; e.g. in a VO, its organization can be changed at any time as users can join or leave the group at anytime. However, the current approach for service development and deployment in a grid environment is highly static, as demonstrated earlier, and can lead to unmanageable applications. The composition of

grid services to provide a dynamic adaptation at runtime is still an open issue. At the deployment level, a computing grid which supports dynamic applications is much desired by companies adopting teleworking as a working model.

As an example for this notion, we return to the travel agent application that was developed by Navarro et al (2006). The example can be extended to illustrate how a travelling salesman who is teleworking with a travel agent application can benefit from a grid with support for dynamic applications and demonstrates why crosscutting concerns are an issue for such an application.

In this scenario, the application needs to enable flight booking and support hotel booking at the destination city for a corresponding period based on the flights booked. In a real life situation, this is an excellent example where a grid can be implemented as different part of the service composition is decentralized with each node dealing with a particular subset of the business process at different locations crossing organizational boundaries but within the grid. The nodes communicate directly with each other to transfer data and control instead of relying on a central coordinator. This concept of distribution and non central administrator behaviour is very well supported by virtual organization in grid computing. However, this distributed architecture must frequently, and dynamically, accommodate changes to the current workflow of grid service. Two examples where this dynamic accommodation of changes is vital and which can be achieved through dynamic application support are:

Error handling: Hotel booking and flight booking sub processes of the agent application are generally provided by two different services at different locations. If one of the process results in a failure, the system should be able to cope with the failure either by rolling back the other process or by finding the alternative service node. So a failure situation may require the termination of some executing parts of the composition and rollback at a large number of nodes or redirect the failed service to different mirror sites.

Evolution of business requirement: Business requirements often change introducing new functionality to the services on offer. For instance, an airline decides to implement new rules for booking travel tickets. This kind of evolution to business requirements often calls for the adaptation of existing services. If all the processes of obtaining booking information are carried out concurrently and if one of the processes fails, there should be a mechanism enabling the other process to be rolled back also. So a failure situation may require the termination of some executing parts of the composition and rollback at a large number of nodes.

Each of these examples requires communication between many nodes, most of which are difficult to anticipate as they often depend on the specific service composition at that time. In a context where new compositions may be developed, anticipation would be next to impossible. Error handling is a typical crosscutting concern where implementation requires modification at a large number of places in the code that partially depend on the node where an error occurs and where the corresponding error handlers are executed. It is clear that business requirements are often crosscutting the legacy code if the legacy code has to be adapted (Navarro et al., 2006).

There exists a need for a dynamic workflow system for grid services that can meet users demand at run time, and in real time, to support dynamic applications (Anderson & Ahmed, 2006; Joncheere et al., 2006). AOP could be utilized as the means to simplify the lengthy development cycle for the implementation of grid services, demonstrating the alignment in the fundamental properties of both technologies and suggests a fusion that would offer benefits to the development of grid-based applications. However introducing a dynamic capability to the grid services not only provides a solution to the aforementioned problems but also improves the service availability, agility and reliability. Hence, there is a need for a programming methodology which can work well in the dynamic environment that grid computing offers. The requirement is to develop an architecture that would implement dynamic weaving of crosscutting concerns at both the service and the client side of the grid application allowing the grid services to support dynamic applications.

A number of self-adaptation technologies are very limited in terms of their dynamism. Technologies like GrADS can guarantee a performance of the service to certain extent by employing continuous monitoring but does not allow injecting new requirements into the application at runtime (Vadiyar & Dongaral, 2005; YarKhan & Dongarra, 2005). Dynamism in Rudder is limited to the adaptation policies and workflow of the services that is submitted before the service is composed making it semi-static (Li & Parashar, 2005). SaNS is purely focused on selecting the best suited service available in terms of performance by using the best algorithm, and not on adapting the workflow of the service at runtime (Dongarra & Eijkhout, 2002) grid. It presents adaptation as a way to achieve a specific level of performance by exploits the complete environment but again does not allow dynamic workflow adaptation (Coppola et al., 2004). Afpac needs additional code augmentation on the original code for it to be dynamic at runtime making it semi-static and dependent on the augmented code (Aldinucci et al., 2006; Andre et al., 2005; Buisson et al., 2005). Almost all of the technologies identified here claim to be dynamic with self-adaptation but are more concerned with scheduling the service to give the best performance. There is no support for producing a dynamic service workflow allowing the introduction and removal of new functionalities either at the client or within the service at runtime.

Dynamic AOP Technologies

It is clear that there exists a need for a workflow system for grid services that can support dynamic applications to meet the users' requirements at runtime. To this extent, it is observed that AOP with dynamic and distributed weaving embrace the functionality that is required by grid services to make its workflow dynamic and adaptable. However, choosing an appropriate AOP technology to be used with grid necessitates careful consideration as there are a number of competing technologies which may be adopted.

Java Aspect Component (JAC) provides dynamic and distributed weaving needed in grid environment but for JAC to be fully dynamic, a program needs to embed hooks at each possible joinpoints at compile time (Pawlak et al., 2004); where a joinpoint is a point in execution such as a method call and a pointcut is a predicate to match with that joinpoint (Laddad, 2003). This causes a huge performance loss if there are high numbers of joinpoints that are not identified by pointcuts. Open Terracotta, on the other hand, delivers JVM-level clustering as a runtime infrastructure service using AOP providing both dynamic and distributed weaving (Letizi, 2007). This technology increases

the level of abstraction of AOP implementation by removing all the AOP programming details from the programmer. A potential limitation is that the architecture only supports Java, whereas grids should support the use of any programming language. ReflexD accommodates both distributed and dynamic weaving of aspects to the core components and postulates an AOP kernel to support various AO languages to be used on top of its infrastructure (Tanter, 2004); much desired by grid. However, its complex multi-layered approach has more probability of being incompatible with the multifaceted grid infrastructure.

The provision of modularised crosscutting concerns for services to provide dynamic functionality suggests support for the following issues:

- Remote pointcuts which allow the capture of relationships between execution events occurring on different hosts.
- Groups of hosts which can be referred to in pointcuts and manipulated in an advice.
- The execution of an advice on different hosts in an asynchronous or synchronous way.

Flexible deployment, instantiation and state sharing models for distributed aspects (Navarro et al., 2003).

Aspects with Explicit Distribution (AWED) provides such support through three concepts at the language level; remote pointcuts, distributed advice and distributed aspects (Navarro et al., 2003). This approach overcomes all the issues identified in the aforementioned technologies. The DJAsCo implementation of AWED provides both distributed and dynamic weaving of aspect to the core service. Unlike JAC, it can be extended to provide highly efficient advice execution. DJAsCo performance is able to compete with statically compiled aspect language such as AspectJ, while still preserving its dynamic features (De Fraine et al., 2005). Unlike ReflexD, it has got a very simple non-layered architecture which is easier to integrate with grid architecture. Unlike Terracotta and ReflexD, this system is much matured and has been implemented successfully in MOSAIC project to provide dynamic web service management in WSML (Foster et al., 2002b).

Three types of dynamic weaving are supported in DJAsCo; the pre-processor approach where the components are processed beforehand to insert traps at all possible join points; run-time trap insertion approach where traps are inserted and removed on-demand depending on the available aspects; and run-time weaver approach in which the weaver physically weaves, unweaves and re-weaves aspects in target classes entirely at runtime.

DJAsCo implements three key architectural ideas; aspect beans, connectors and the connector registry. Aspect beans define the crosscutting functionality and contain at least one hook to define when the program should be interrupted and what functionality should be executed when interrupted. Connectors are used to put aspect beans into a concrete context. Connectors are used to bind components/services with aspect beans. The connector registry serves as the main addressing point for all DJAsCo entities and contains a database of connectors and instantiated aspects. JAsCo run-time infrastructure is based on a central connector registry that manages the registered connectors and aspects at runtime (Navarro et al., 2003). Whenever a connector is loaded into or removed from the system at run-time, the connector registry is notified and its database of registered connectors and aspects is automatically updated. Whenever a joinpoint is triggered, its execution is deferred to the connector registry, which looks up all connectors that are registered for that particular joinpoint. The connector on its turn dispatches to the applicable aspects.

Every connector registry is responsible for the locally intercepted joinpoints and its locally deployed aspects. In order to allow aspect execution on remote joinpoints, the intercepted joinpoints need to be sent to the other hosts. Likewise, in order to allow aspect execution on remote hosts,

the aspects need to be distributed as well (Navarro et al., 2003). Remote joinpoints can be located and transmitted to remote hosts, aspects are distributed to those hosts to which they are applicable and dynamic weaving supports synchronous advice execution.

Proposed Solution: An Architecture for Dynamic Applications

The proposed grid architecture enables integration or removal of functionalities at runtime which are not anticipated at deployment time. This approach is based on the notion that Java Grid Service applications are in many ways very similar to the non-grid DJAsCo applications. As DJAsCo uses byte-code manipulation to weave its aspects into Java programs, the existing implementation of DJAsCo can be extended to implement aspect-oriented functionality to grid application with minor modifications.

This architecture makes use of the DJAsCo runtime architecture to enable the connector registry to intercept both the client- and the service side of the grid application. Like DJAsCo, whenever a connector is loaded or removed from the system at runtime the connector registry is notified and its database of registered connectors and aspects is automatically updated. Figure 3 illustrates the overall architecture of DJAsCo-G using DJAsCo aspect beans and connectors. This is an extension of the work of Navarro et al. (Navarro et al., 2003).

As illustrated in Figure 3; Grid service 1, Connector 1, Aspect1 and Aspect2 are deployed at Host X; Grid Service 2, Connector2, Connector 3, Aspect 3 and Aspect 4 are deployed at Host Y. The shaded part of the figure highlights the additional functionality needed by the grid service architecture to add the functionality of AWED for enabling dynamic grid workflow. Grid Service 1 and Grid Service 2 are JAsCo enabled services for which the joinpoint shadows are equipped with traps. As a result, whenever a joinpoint is triggered, its execution is deferred to the

Figure 3. DJasCo-G architecture

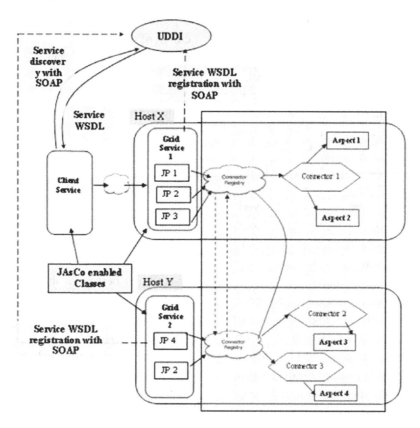

connector registry, which looks up all registered connectors for that particular joinpoint. In order to allow distributed advice execution, these connector registries allow joinpoint information to be distributed to all interested hosts making it possible to intercept all joinpoints; local and remote. The connector on its turn dispatches to the application aspects.

In this example, the client uses Grid Service 1 which has three joinpoints. For joinpoints JP1 and JP2, the execution is deferred to the connector registry which finds the relevant connector in the same host (Host X). However, for the joinpoint JP3, the connector registry on Host X communicates with connector registry at Host Y and executes Advice on aspect 3 in Host Y. After the execution of the advice, the flow of control is passed back to the grid service where the joinpoint was realised.

At runtime, the architecture also relies on components to allow dynamic installation of traps only at those joinpoint shadows that are subject to aspect application, and to support just-in-time compilation for aspects (Navarro et al., 2003). The same architecture can be repeated at the client side as well but is not shown in the figure.

Issue 2: Matchmaking

Once the concept of dynamic service construction using aspects as resources in the grid can be achieved, then the issues of discovery and matchmaking become a significant issue. Resource discovery and service discovery is an important issue for grid computing in answering the questions of how a service requester finds the required resources/services and also how a service provider makes potential service requesters aware of the computing resources it can offer (Ludwig & Reyhani, 2005). In order for a grid to achieve the coordination of distributed resources amongst a dynamic set of individuals and organizations, and to achieve a common collaborative goal, resource discovery and service discovery is a key concept. The problem of service discovery in a grid environment arises through the heterogeneity, distribution and sharing of the resources in different Virtual Organisations (VOs) (Ludwig & Reyhani, 2005). One of the ways for these key concepts of matchmaking to be achieved is through the process of discovery. Matchmaking, a process of evaluation of the degree of similarity between two objects, can be regarded as a common operation in many areas of discovery.

Matchmaking enables both the requesters and providers to dynamically exchange information in a more effective means than most of the traditional methods. Kuokka & Harada (1995) identify that matchmaking has been widely used in various applications and fields where information changes rapidly, such as product development and crisis management. They also believe that dynamic interoperation of such services is critical for coherent operation of the overall system. Matchmaking considers the relationship between two services- an advertisement and the request. Advertisements represent the description of existing services while the request indicates the desired vision of service requirements. Service matchmaking problem is the problem of relationship between these two services. As simple as it sounds, the mission of matchmaking is either to answer whether the advertised service satisfies the request or match the request with one of advertised services (Wang, Li & Fan, 2006).

In an open organization, service providers advertise their capabilities with a matchmaker, which stores all advertisements. To query a service provider for a service, a requester first formulates a meta-query, termed a request, to ask the matchmaker for agents that could respond to it. In terms of the dynamic AOP service implementation, the

service provider would offer a pool of available aspects which may be woven together to form a coherent service. Upon receiving a set of relevant providers, the requester chooses one or more with which to interact and queries them directly. In other words, after the initial discovery of potentially useful providers, requesters and providers interact directly without any further involvement on the matchmaker's part (Sycara et al., 2004).

Metadata and Ontology

Metadata is data which describes the structure and meaning of some other data. Ontology on the other hand is traditionally defined as the science or study of being (Gruber, 1992). It originated from a simple idea of two or more parties having to seek for a common understanding of something in order to ensure that there is a high degree of correlation and similarity between the details of their respective descriptions and definitions. This implies that shared understanding requires shared definitions (Ludwig & Reyhani, 2005).

Corcho et al. (2006) has stated that the Grid vision, of sharing diverse resources in a flexible, coordinated and secure manner through dynamic formation and disbanding of virtual communities, strongly depends on metadata. They believe that currently metadata is used in an ad-hoc fashion and most of it is buried in the grid middleware code libraries and database schemas. The authors also claim that this ad-hoc expression and use of metadata causes a chronic dependency on human intervention during the grid operation of grid machinery, leading to systems which are brittle when faced with frequent syntactic changes in resource coordination and sharing protocols (Corcho et al., 2006). This strongly supports the original notion in this chapter that building automatically adaptive grid with agile services requires a change in the architecture and mechanisms for service development and deployment.

In order to effectively and efficiently use the meta-data and address the issue, a number of semantic-based description frameworks have been put forward. Resource Description Framework (RDF) is a family of W3C specification originally designed as a metadata model. As the need for common data models and data exchange standards intensified, there was a need for fast integration of different data sources as well as to bridge semantic differences (Miller, 1998). With the introduction of notions of ontology, OWL was derived from DAML+OIL and is aimed to be the standardized and broadly accepted ontology language of the Semantic Web (Li & Baker, 2005). OWL is a mark-up language for describing ontological data about a given resource based on the principles of RDF. OWL not only provides structural and content information but also methods for describing the links between topics and subjects, and how the subjects relate (i.e. whether a subject is a subclass of a larger topic, and whether it has a direct or indirect relationship) (Brown, 2005). OWL-S uses OWL as the ontology language to semantically describe Web

Services in terms of their inputs, outputs, preconditions and (possibly conditional) effects, and of their process model (Martin et al., 2004). It allows web service properties and capabilities to be described and discovered, to interoperate,

and be composed in an unambiguous, computer-interpretable form.

OWL-S is organised into three modules as illustrated in Figure 4 (Sycara et al., 2004).

A profile describes Web service capabilities, as well as any additional features that help describe the service; i.e. for advertising and discovering services. This includes input, output, preconditions and effects.

A process model describes the Web service provider's activity, which is how the requester can derive information about service invocation; i.e. gives a detailed description of a service's operation.

A grounding describes how the abstract information exchanges explained in the process model are mapped to the actual messages that providers and requesters exchange; provides details on how to interoperate with a service, via messages.

The OWL-S profile not only describes the functional properties (capabilities) of a service such as its inputs, outputs, pre-conditions, and effects (IOPEs), but also non-functional features including service name, service category, point of contact and aspects related to the quality of a service (Li et al., 2006). Additionally, the latest version of OWL-S has *service classification* and

Figure 4. Top level of the service ontology OWL-S

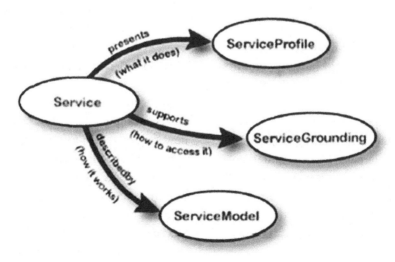

service product properties added to OWL-S Profile specification. The *service classification* property is used to represent the categories to which web services belong. Meanwhile, *Service Product* is used to describe the products produced by web services. Similar to service classification properties, service product properties use semantic concepts to represent their products hence, these are also matched on semantically (Srinivasan et al., 2006).

There have been numerous attempts to solve matchmaking problem in grid. The key approaches that shall be considered here are the boolean approach, the constraint-satisfaction approach and the semantic approach.

Boolean Approach

A common approach for discovery and allocation of resources in grid system is based on Condor (Litzkow et al., 1988). Condor is a widely used approach which relies on a 3-value logic and Classified Advertisement (ClassAd) language. Condor is based on the following phases.

1. Providers of computing resources submit advertisements describing their capabilities and declaring constraints and preferences for jobs that they are willing to run.
2. Consumers submit advertisements describing their jobs and the desired execution environment in terms of constraints and preferences.
3. A matchmaker process matches the resource and consumer request advertisements (Andreozzi, 2006).

Both resource and request advertisements can express requirements and ranking expressions concerning the counterpart. These requirements are Boolean expressions involving constants or ClassAd attributes of the counterpart under evaluation while the rank consists in defining an arithmetic expression synthesising values used

for sorting the services satisfying the constraints (Andreozzi, 2006).

Constraint-Satisfaction Approach

In 2004, Liu and Foster (2004) proposed a novel prototype Redline, a language and matchmaking process that reinterprets the selection of resources as a constraint-satisfaction problem. This extended the ClassAd approach, used by Condor, by enabling resources to be expressed with adaptable and negotiable properties and deals with resource selection operations that involve multiple resources or requests (Andreozzi, 2006).

The Redline language claimed to support four types of matching which were as follows:

Bilateral matching: i.e. given a request and a resource, it check if they match each other.

Gang-matching: i.e. given a request for multiple resources that describes the required properties for every resource and their relationship, and a set of resources, check if these resources satisfy the request.

Congruence matching: i.e. given a set of requests and a resource, a match succeeds if there is a congruence amongst these requests and this congruence matches the resource.

Set matching: i.e. given a request for a set of resources with particular aggregated properties and a set of resources, a match succeeds if this resource set has the required aggregated properties (Lui & Foster, 2004).

Semantic Based Approach

Traditionally, methods for such discovery included name and keyword matching however; most of the new methods seem to be based on ontologies. Semantic enhanced services discovery have mainly been targeted for the Web but efforts have recently been moved on to the grid (Li et al., 2006). One of the more recent proposals in the context of the Semantic Grid is a matchmaking framework based on three selection stages which are context, semantic and registry selection (Ludwig & Reyhani, 2005). It proposes a three step discovery process consisting of (1) application context selection where the request is matched within the appropriate application context, (2) semantic selection, where the request is matched semantically and (3) registry selection, where a lookup is performed (Ludwig & Reyhani, 2005). This approach allows the separate capture of application and grid services semantics and supports application developers and grid services developers in registering application and services semantics separately. For the discovery process, this separation allows a classification of the application semantics in order to find service descriptions in the grid services ontology (Andreozzi, 2006).

Current Grid Matchmaking

The current the service discovery process is primarily based on keyword or type matching i.e. on string and integer comparison. This use of flat attributes not only results in lack of expressiveness while describing a service and service capabilities, but also brings in shortcomings such as when number of these flat attributes grows it can also become unmanageable. UDDI and Globus MDS are two current examples of matchmaking services which use symmetric flat attribute-based matching. UDDI has been used in the web community for business service discovery while MDS has been used in the field of grid computing for node discovery. Both UDDI and MDS support simple query languages and are based on the principle where the values of attributes advertised by nodes are compared with those required by jobs. In these systems, for the comparison to be meaningful and effective, the node providers and consumers have to agree upon attribute names and values. The exact matching and coordination between providers and consumers make such system inflexible and difficult to extend to new characteristics or concepts (Zhang & Song, 2004).

Moreover in a heterogeneous, distributed multi-institutional environment such as the one promised through grid computing it is often difficult to enforce the syntax and semantics. Therefore, flat attribute-based matchmaking such as MDS and UDDI do not offer expressive description facilities, nor provide sophisticated matchmaking capabilities. Hence, it can easily be devised that the existing matchmaking system lacks the ability of inexact matching. In grid environments where so many different implementations of services arc available, that might vary in name and functionality, there is desirable for a more powerful matchmaking process. Semantic Matchmaking is one of the approaches for matchmaking services on the basis of the capabilities that they provide. In order for service advertisements and service requests to successfully compare whether a request matches an advertisement, semantic matchmaking solution requires two properties. These two properties are: a language to express the capabilities of services; and the specification of a matching algorithm. Ontology is used as a language in grid services context for service requester and service provider to share a common understanding of what capabilities the service offers and how they can be put into use. For grid services where service discovery is a significant issue, the need to share a common ontology becomes very important (Ludwig & Reyhani, 2005).

In order to address this problem, instead of these symmetric flat attributes in our proposed system we use ontologies to declaratively describe resources and services using an expressive ontology language. Instead of exact syntax matching, we perform semantic matching by using semantic web service ontology, OWL-S. As a result, the loose coupling between requester and providers descriptions removes the tight coordination requirement between providers and consumers. However, this use of semantic web technologies such as OWL-S has had its share of criticism. It is said that the classical OWL-S matching algorithm cannot tolerate uncertain properties in matching advertised services with service requests and cannot deal with missing (uncertain) properties. These critics argues that one challenging work in service discovery is that service matchmaking should be able to tolerate uncertain properties because in a large-scale heterogeneous system such as the grid, service publishers and requestors may use their predefined properties to describe services, e.g. in the form of OWL-S (Li et al., 2006).

OWL-S/UDDI Matchmaker

OWL-S/UDDI matchmaker is a concept which aims to take advantage of UDDI's proliferation in Web Service technology as well as OWL-S's explicit capability representation (Srinivasan, 2006). Due to UDDI's lack of power to perform full search, it requires a search mechanism which is capable of taking not only the taxonomy information into account but also the inputs and outputs of services to produce more precise results. Hence, the search mechanism resulting from the combination of the semantic base matching and the capability search is far more effective than the current search mechanism. As OWL-S provides both semantic matching capability and capability base searching, it is a perfect candidate (Srinivasan, 2006).

In order take advantage of the semantic matching and achieve symbiosis between OWL-S and UDDI, OWL-S Profile information needs to be embedded inside UDDI data structure and the UDDI registry need to be augmented with an OWL-S matchmaking component for processing OWL-S profile information. In this architecture, the matchmaker component is tightly coupled with the UDDI registry i.e. the matchmaker component relies on the UDDI registry's ports (*publish* and *inquiry*) for its operations. On receiving an advertisement through the *publish* port the UDDI component, the OWL-S/UDDI matchmaker processes it like any other UDDI advertisement. If the advertisement contains OWL-S Profile information, it forwards the advertisement to the matchmaking component. Here, the matchmaker component classifies the advertisement based on the semantic information present in the advertisement (Srinivasan, 2006).

A client can use the UDDI's inquiry port to access the search functionality provided by the UDDI registry, however these searches neither use the semantic information present in the advertisement nor the capability description provided by the OWL-S Profile information. Hence in order to address this problem, UDDI registry is extended by adding a capability port. As a result, UDDI API is also extended to access the capability search functionality of the OWL-S/UDDI matchmaker (Srinivasan, 2006). The addition of a capability port implies that a search could be made based on the capability descriptions of a service. The queries received through the capability port are processed by the matchmaker component; hence the queries are semantically matched based on the OWL-S Profile information.

A Semantic Service Discovery Framework

The following is a description of a proposed service discovery framework for grid environment which relies on ontologies. Based on ontology description, it enables semantic matchmaking and is based on the earlier concept of OWL-S/UDDI matchmaker, and one proposed by Ludwig and Reyhani (2005).

In a matchmaking process, an advertisement is said to match a request, when the advertisement which describes a service that is sufficiently similar to the service requested (Paolucci et al., 2002). Nevertheless, this definition is thought to be too restrictive, as providers and requesters have no prior agreement on how a service is represented and also have different objectives. Hence, a restrictive criterion on matching is therefore bound to fail to recognize similarities between advertisements and requests (Ludwig and Reyhani, 2005). As a result, it is necessary to perform flexible matches, those that recognise the degree of similarity between advertisements and requests in order to provide a softer definition of "sufficiently similar". This degree of flexibility, selected by requesters, has a huge impact on the overall performance of the matchmaker. For example, if they allow little flexibility, they reduce the likelihood of finding services that match their requirements, which means, they minimize the false positives, while increasing the false negatives. On the other hand, by increasing the flexibility of a match, they achieve the opposite effect, that is, they reduce the false negatives at the expense of an increase of false positives (Ludwig and Reyhani, 2005). The matching engine should satisfy the following criteria (Paolucci et al., 2002):

- Support flexible semantic matching between advertisements and requests.
- Minimize false positives and false negatives.
- Encourage providers and requesters to be precise with their descriptions at the cost of either not being matched or being matched inappropriately.
- Do not burden the requester with excessive delays that would prevent its effectiveness.

In the recommended framework, the semantic matching is based on OWL-S ontologies and the advertisements and requests refer to OWL-S concepts and the associated semantics. By using OWL-S, the matching process can perform implications on the subsumption hierarchy leading to the recognition of semantic matches despite their syntactical differences and difference in modelling abstractions between advertisements and requests. The use of OWL-S also supports accuracy, which means that no matching is recognized when the relation between the advertisement and the request does not derive from the OWL-S ontologies used by the registry (Ludwig and Reyhani, 2005).

Being based on shared ontology ensures that the terms have clear and consistent semantics such

that a match is not missed or found based on an incorrect interpretation of the request. Hence, use of these defined ontologies ensures the support for flexible semantic matchmaking. At the same time, minimising false positives and false negatives is achieved with a two/three stage selection stage. The selection stages are as follows:

1. Select advertisements in the application database that can be matched with the request in the same or similar application domain based on application ontology.
2. Semantic Matching/Registry Matching based on the OWL-S/UDDI matchmaker; a registry look up is also performed.
3. Performance Query which acts as a filter to list the result based on their previous performance history.

Like most other matchmakers, OWL-S/UDDI can only find the agents in the registry that claim to offer services closest to the service requested based on capabilities. Due to inadequate capability description and availability of numerous similar agents, if a same task is delegated to different agents with same or similar capabilities, the quality of service (QoS) may vary from agent to agent. Some agents may provide very good service demonstrating high standard whilst some may only show a average level. The matchmaker is further extended by adding the historical performances of the service provider agents to address this drawback. Most of the current matchmaking algorithms are only based on advertised capabilities of provider agents. However, as the performance of service providers has a significant outcome on the successful matchmaking and middle-agents, the initial matchmaking framework is extended where a provider agent can be picked based on past history and performance. Simulation results cleared showed that the agent's historical records have a strong impact on the outcome of matchmaking. The agent's historical records are to be stored in a Performance Database, and consist of

3-tuples with a form as [*nth time service, evaluation, domain*]. The first parameter in the 3-tuple is the ordinal of the service provided, the second is the satisfactory degree returned by the agent received the service, and third is the application domain. The third, the domain knowledge, which is expressed by domain ontology, is optional. It provides a dictionary for the domain knowledge concepts in the machine-understandable form. OWL is used to describe the domain knowledge ontologies. At this stage this is kept as an optional in a view for extending it to a separate database for querying, storing/updating etc.

Proposed Matchmaking Solution

This recommended matchmaking framework consists of service requester (i.e. grid applications), service provides (grid services) and a service discovery matchmaker. The framework consists of number of components which makes up the matchmaker. Instead of describing the individual components separately, these components are described based on the functionalities that they provide. Each pair of request and advertisement goes through a series of matchmaking modules. In the first matching module, a matched is performed depending on the defined application ontology. This is achieved by using a parser to extract and match data from the application ontology. Once the application match is performed, based on these matched results further matching is performed based grid service ontologies and registry matching of the OWL-S/UDDI matchmaker to compute a semantic match. Finally, for semantically matched result, using the performance database, its past history is presented to the requester (grid services).

Registration

Figure 5 shows the first few steps for the service registration process. First, the service providers need to register their services for the matchmaking process. This is done by publishing its WSDL which is then converted using a WSDL2OWL-S converter to get an OWL-S description. The OWL-S description describes the grid services semantically which can be queried using any of the available inference engine. It consists of its service semantics; contact details etc and would be used to register its service semantics in OWL-S/UDDI matchmaker registry and grid service ontology. The Service semantics comprises of a service name, a service description, service attributes (input/output) and metadata information.

Request Processing

The interactions of a service request and the matchmaking process is shown in Figure 6. The process of matchmaking starts with the grid application sending out a request to the matchmaking module in the service discovery matchmaker (Step 1). Once the request is received in the matchmaking module, the request goes through a series of matchmaking modules. In the first matching module, the request goes through the application context matching module. Here, the request is matched within the appropriate context of the application ontology. This means depending on the service request, which came from one of the applications, the appropriate context ontology is chosen and the first match is performed (Ludwig and Reyhani, 2005).

Additional parameters are attached to the request and forwarded to the semantic/registry matching module (2). Semantic matchmaking allows the service request to be matched using the semantics (metadata) of services. Here, also registry look up is performed. For the matched result, the Performance Database is querying to check the past performance of the provider. This set of services is sent back to the grid application (4) to be used by the grid application to call the grid service (5).

Figure 5. The grid service registration process

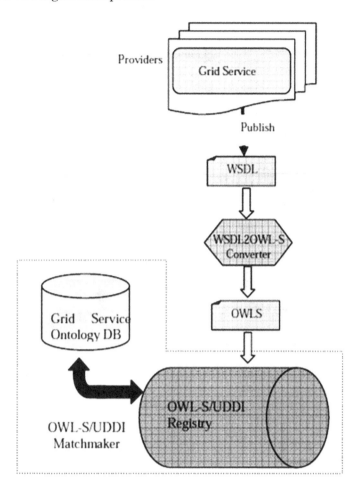

FUTURE RESEARCH DIRECTIONS

The recent emergence of Cloud Computing as a distributed architecture for business and enterprise computing offers an environment with a number of beneficial opportunities for end users, and also raises issues regarding its adoption. Cloud computing could vastly change the implementation, usage and management of computing systems both in the public and private sector. The proposed benefits of the technology would offer reduced overheads by removing procurement and charging by usage, ultimately delivering computing as a utility (Armbrust et al., 2009). An additional feature is the extensibility of the cloud; enabling allocated resources to expand and contract dependant on the requirements for usage (Wheeler, 2008). The gain lies not only with the efficient allocation of resources, but also a green utilization of resources by maximizing the usage of a resource by dynamic reallocation to a job.

In terms of the challenges facing cloud Computing, two of the most significant are security and privacy (Mather et al., 2009). The architectural model requires the end users of the cloud to upload their applications and/or data to data centres usually managed by third parties. Until these challenges are addressed there exists a significant barrier to the widespread adoption of cloud as the computing model for the future.

Figure 6. Grid matchmaking

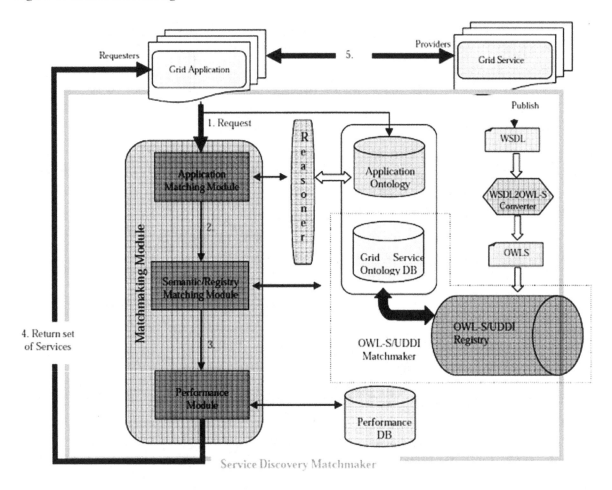

However, both of these challenges can conceivably be identified as cross-cutting concerns. From the definition earlier in the chapter, neither is related to the core functionality of the services that have been implemented yet both are required across a number of the services which may be on offer. Indeed, this notion can easily be extended such that invocations of a service may require changing levels of privacy, for example, dependent on the invoker and the location from which the request is being made.

Given the conceptual similarities between cloud computing and grid computing (Myerson, 2009), the future work on this project will consider the viability of implementing an AOP driven programming model to cloud services in order to leverage the demand-driven nature of a computing cloud.

CONCLUSION

Over the past decade, the field of teleworking has changed considerably. A move to support teleworking adopting service-oriented architectures, such as Web Services, can simplify the development of such systems and leverage existing standards, such as security mechanisms. However, there remain challenges to overcome technical limitations of existing platforms. A solution to these limitations is promised in the emergence of grid computing as an architecture on which service-based applications can be developed.

A means of simplifying the lengthy development cycle for the implementation of grid services has been presented using AOP. The development of Aspect-Oriented Grid Programming (AOGP) has been based on clearly defined benefits demonstrating that an alignment in the fundamental properties of both technologies suggests a fusion would offer benefits to the development of grid-based applications. We are in need of a programming methodology that can work well in the type of dynamic environment grid computing offers. A major property of AOP is that it separates the system-level requirements from other code. The modularity of a system design is increased when compared to a more conventional OOP methodology. In increasing modularity, a cleaner structure for programming grid-based applications has been identified, simplifying development and maintenance. Furthermore, we have seen through experimentation that AOGP is a successful and workable solution.

Implementing this programming architecture, however, does require further modeling in order to be supported within a service-oriented architecture. The flexibility of grid technology to accommodate coordinated resource sharing and problem solving in dynamic, multi-institutional virtual organizations is challenged by its discovery and matchmaking mechanisms. When allied with the discovery that many implementations of dynamic grid architectures do not incorporate the features which would support a fully dynamic framework which enables adaptable grid services to be created, then the flexibility of the architecture may be brought into question. In this chapter, a framework is proposed which expands a model for dynamic Aspect-oriented Programming to support dynamic grid services. Extensions to existing dynamic weaving platforms and discovery/matchmaking implementations offer a solid model on which dynamic services may be constructed. In

terms of remote working, this architectural model facilitates the flexibility to support the differing and evolving needs of those users operating at geographically diverse locations.

REFERENCES

W3C (2004). OWL-S: Semantic markup for Web services. Retrieved on October 14, 2010, from http://www.w3c.org/ Submission/ OWL-S/#1

Abbas, A. (2004). *Grid computing: A practical guide to technology and applications*. Hingham, MA: Charles River Media.

Aldinucci, M., Danelutto, M., & Vanneschi, M. (2006). Autonomic QoS in ASSIST grid-aware components. In *Proceedings of Intl. Euromicro PDP 2006: Parallel Distributed and Network-Based Processing*. Montbeliard, France: IEEE.

Anderson, M., & Ahmed, L. (2006). An aspect-oriented approach to developing a teleworking grid. In *Proceedings of IEEE International Conference on E-business Engineering (ICEBE'06)* (pp. 461-465). IEEE.

Andre, F., Buisson, J., & Pazat, J. L. (2005). Dynamic adaptation of parallel codes: Toward self-adaptable components for the grid. In *Proceedings of Workshop on Component Models and Systems for Grid Applications*. (pp.145-156). Berlin_Heidelberg: Springer.

Andreozzi, S. (2006). *On the quality-based evaluation and selection of grid services*. Unpublished doctoral dissertation, University of Colona, Mira Anteo Zamboni, Bologna, Italy.

Armbrust, M., Fox, A., Griffith, R., Joseph, A. D., Katz, R. H., & Konwinski, A. ...Zaharia, M. (2009). *Above the clouds: A Berkeley view of cloud computing* (Technical Report No. UCB/EECS-2009-28)., Berkeley, CA: University of California.

Braun, I., & Schill, A. (2002) *Building a universal teleworking environment using Web services.* Retrieved on July 25, 2010, from http://www. rn.inf.tu-dresden.de/ scripts_ lsrn/ veroeffent_ print/ IKS2002.pdf

Brown, M. C. (2005). *What is the semantic grid.* Retrieved March 27, 2010, from http://www-128.ibm.com/ developerworks/ grid/ library/ gr-semgrid/

Buisson, J., André, F., & Pazat, J. L. (2005). Dynamic adaptation for grid computing. In P. M. A. Sloot, A. G. Hoekstra, T. Priol, A. Reinefeld, & M. Bubak (Eds.), *Advances in Grid Computing - European Grid Conference* (*EGC 2005*), Amsterdam, The Netherlands, February 14-16, 2005 (Vol. 3470, pp. 538–547). Berlin-Heidelberg, Germany: Springer-Verlag.

Chitchyan, R., & Sommerville, I. (2004). Comparing dynamic AO systems. In *Proceedings of the 2004 Dynamic Aspects Workshop*, Lancaster, England. Retrieved on December, 2010, from http://www.comp.lancs.ac.uk/ computing/ aose/ papers/ DAW2004_ chitchyan.pdf

Coppola, M., Aldinucci, M., Danelutto, M., Vanneschi, M., & Zoccolo, C. (2004*) Assist as a research framework for high-performance grid programming environments* (Technical Report TR-04-09). Italy: Università di Pisa, Dipartimento di Informatica.

Corcho, O., Alper, P., Kotsiopoulos, I., & Missier, P. (2006). An overview of S-OGSA: A reference semantic grid architecture. *Journal of Web Semantics, 2*(4), 102–115. doi:10.1016/j.websem.2006.03.001

Coulouris, G., Dollimore, J., & Kindberg, T. (2005). *Distributed systems: Concepts and design.* New York, NY: Addison-Wesley.

Dangelmaier, W., Kress, S., & Wenski, R. (1997) Telework under the co-ordination of a distributed workflow management system. In *Proceedings of the International ACM SIGGROUP Conference on Supporting Group Work: The Integration Challenge* (pp. 128-137). New York, NY, USA: ACM.

De Fraine, B., Vanderperren, W., Suvée, D., & Brichau, J. (2005) Jumping aspects revisited. In R. E. Filman, M. Haupt, & R. Hirschfeld (Eds.), *Dynamic aspects workshop* (pp.77–86). Retrieved from http://aosd.net/ 2005/ workshops/ daw/ DeFraine Vanderperren SuveeBrichau.pdf

Dongarra, J., & Eijkhout, V. (2002). Self-adapting numerical software for next generation application. *International Journal of High Performance Computing Applications, 17*, 2–7.

Flanagan, D. (1999). *Java in a Netshell* (3rd ed.). Sebastapol, CA: O'Reilly.

Foster, I., Kesselman, C., Nick, J., & Tuecke, S. (2002a). *The physiology of the grid: An open grid services architecture or distributed systems integration.* Presented at the Open Grid Service Infrastructure WG, GGF.

Foster, I., Kesselman, C., Nick, J., & Tuecke, S. (2002b). Grid services for distributed systems integration. *Journal of Computer, 35*(6), 37–46. doi:10.1109/MC.2002.1009167

Globus Alliance. (2005). *Globus Toolkit 4.0.1 stable release notes.* Retrieved March, 2010, from http://www.globus.org/ toolkit/ releasenotes/ 4.0.1/

Gruber, T. (1992). *What is ontology?* Retrieved February 20, 2010, from http://www-ksl.stanford.edu/kst/what-is-an-ontology.html

Joncheere, N., Vanderperren, W., & Van Der Straeten, R. (2006). Requirements for a workflow system for grid service composition. In *Proceedings of the 2nd International Workshop on Grid and Peer-to-Peer Based Workflows (GPWW 2006)* (pp. 365-374). Vienna, Austria: LNCS Springer-Verlag.

Joseph, J., & Fellenstein, C. (2004). *Grid computing*. Upper Saddle River, NJ: Prentice Hall Publishers, Inc.

Kiselev, I. (2002). *Aspect-oriented programming with aspectJ*. Indianapolis, USA: SAMS Publishers.

Kuokka, D., & Harada, L. (1995). Matchmaking for information agents. In *Proceedings of the 14th International Joint Conference on Artificial Intelligence* (pp. 672-678). San Francisco, CA: Morgan Kaufmann Publishers Inc.

Laddad, R. (2003). *AspectJ in action: Practical aspect-oriented programming*. Greenwich, CT: Manning Publications Co.

Letizi, O. (2007). *An introduction to open terracotta*. Retrieved on December, 2010, from http:// www.infoq.com/ articles/ open- terracotta- intro

Li, M., & Baker, M. (2005). *The grid: Core technologies*. Wiley Publications. doi:10.1002/0470094192

Li, M., Yu, B., Huang, C., & Song, Y. H. (2006). *Service matchmaking with rough sets.* Presented at the 2nd International Conference on Semantics, Knowledge and Grid.

Li, Z., & Parashar, M. (2005). Rudder: An agent-based infrastructure for autonomic composition of grid applications. *International Journal of Multi-agent and Grid System*, *1*(4), 183–195.

Litzkow, M., Livny, M., & Mutka., M. W. (1988). Condor - A hunter of idle workstations. In *Proceedings of the 8th International Conference on Distributed Computing Systems (ICDCS 1988)* (pp. 104-111). San Jose, CA, USA: IEEE Computer Society.

Liu, C., & Foster, I. (2004). A constraint language approach to matchmaking. In: *Proceedings of the International workshop on Research Issues on Data Engineering (RIDE 2004)* (pp. 7-14). Boston. IEEE Computer Society.

Ludwig, S. A., & Reyhani, S. M. S. (2005). Semantic approach to service discovery in a grid environment. *Journal of Web Semantics*, *4*(1), 1–13. doi:10.1016/j.websem.2005.04.001

Martin, D., Paolucci, M., McIlraith, S., Burstein, M., McDermott, D., & McGuinness, D. … Sycara, K. (2004). Bringing semantics to Web services: The OWL-S approach. In *Proceedings of the 1st International Workshop on Semantic Web Services and Web Process Composition (SWSWPC 2004)* (pp. 26-42). Berlin-Heidelberg, Germany: Springer.

Mather, T., Kumaraswamy, S., & Latif, S. (2009). *Cloud security and privacy: An enterprise perspective on risks and compliance*. Sebastapol, CA: O'Reilly.

Miller, E. (1998). An *introduction to the resource description framework*. Online Computer Library Center, Inc., Office of Research, Dublin. Retrieved on May 25, 2010, from http://www.dlib.org/ dlib/ may98/ miller/ 05miller.html

Myerson, J. (2009). *Cloud computing versus grid computing*. Retrieved February 2, 2010, from http://www.ibm.com/ developerworks/ web/ library/ wa- cloudgrid/

Navarro, L. D. B., Sudholt, M., Vanderperren, W., & Verheecke, B. (2006). Modularization of distributed Web services using Aspects With Explicit Distribution (AWED). In *Proceedings of OTM Conferences* (pp. 1449-1466).

Paolucci, M., Kawamura, T., Payne, T., & Sycara, S. (2002). Semantic matching of Web service capabilities. In *Proceedings of the International Semantic Web Conference* (pp 333–347). Berlin-Heidelberg, Germany: Springer-Verlag.

Pawlak, R., Seinturier, L., Duchien, L., Florin, G., Legond-Aubry, F., & Martelli, L. (2004). JAC: An aspect-based distributed dynamic framework. *Software, Practice & Experience*, *34*(12), 1119–1148. doi:10.1002/spe.605

Scholtz, J., Chidamber, S., Glass, R., Goerner, A., Rosson, M. B., Stark, M., & Vessey, I. (1993). Object oriented programming: The promise and the reality. *Journal of Systems and Software, 23,* 199–204. doi:10.1016/0164-1212(93)90084-B

Sotomayor, B. (2005). *The Globus Toolkit 4 programmer's tutorial.* Retrieved April 23, 2010, from http://gdp.globus.org/gt4-tutorial/

Sotomayor, B., & Childers, L. (2006). *Globus 4 Toolkit: Programming java services.* San Francisco, CA: Morgan Kaufmann.

Srinivasan, N., Paolucci, M., & Sycara, K. (2006). Semantic Web service discovery in the OWL-S IDE. In *Proceedings of the 39th Annual Hawaii International Conference on System Sciences,* Hawaii, USA (pp. 109). Washington, DC., USA: IEEE Compurer Society.

Sugawara, K., Yu, Y., Ragsdale, B., Hara, H., & KinoShita, T. (2003). Posters: Design of an agent-based middleware for job matchmaking in teleworking community. In *Proceedings of the 2nd International Joint Conference on Autonomous Agents and Multi-agent Systems* (pp.1128-1129). New York, NY: ACM.

Sycara, K., Paolucci, M., Soudry, J., & Srinivasan, N. (2004). Dynamic discovery and coordination of agent-based semantic Web services. *Internet Computing, 8*(3), 66–73. doi:10.1109/MIC.2004.1297276

Tanter, E. (2004). *From metaobject protocols to versatile kernels for aspect-oriented programming.* Unpublished doctoral thesis, École des Mines de Nantes, Université de Nantes, University of Chile.

Vadhiyar, S. S., & Dongarra, J. (2005). Self adaptivity in grid computing. *Concurrency and Computation, 17*(2-4), 235–257. doi:10.1002/cpe.927

Wang, H., Li, Z., & Fan, L. (2006). An unabridged method concerning capability matchmaking of Web services. In *Proceedings of the 2006 IEEE/WIC/ACM International Conference on Web Intelligence* (pp. 662-665). Washington, DC., USA: IEEE Computer Society.

Wheeler, B. (2008). E-Research is a fad: Scholarship 2.0, Cyberinfrastructure, and IT governance. In R. N. Katz (Ed.), *The tower and the cloud.* EDUCAUSE. Retrieved on April 21, 2010, from http://net.educause.edu/ ir/ library/ pdf/ PUB7202k.pdf

YarKhan, A., & Dongarra, J. (2005). Biological sequence alignment on the computational grid using the GrADS framework. *Future Generation Computer Systems, 21*(6), 980–986. doi:10.1016/j.future.2005.02.002

Zhang, Y., & Song, W. (2004). Semantic description and matching of grid services capabilities. Retrieved on May 26, 2010, from http://www.all-hands.org.uk/ 2004/ proceedings/ papers/205.pdf

ADDITIONAL READING

Clark, S. D., & Olfman, L. (2000). Testing the simplified decision model of telework: A quasi-experimental study. In *Proceedings of the 2000 ACM SIGCPR conference on Computer Personnel Research* (pp.102-110). New York, NY: ACM.

Foster, I., & Kesselman, C. (2004). *The grid: Blueprint for a new computing infrastructure* (2nd ed.). Amsterdam, Netherlands: Morgan Kaufmann.

Foster, I., Kesselman, C., Tsudik, G., & Tuecke, S. (1998). A security architecture for computational grids. In *Proceedings of the 5th ACM Conference on Computers and Security* (pp 83-91). New York, NY: ACM.

Gosling, J., Joy, B., Steele, G., & Bracha, G. (2000). *The java language specification* (2nd ed.). Boston, MA: Addison-Wesley.

Grantham, C. E. (1996). Working in a virtual place: A case study of distributed work. In *Proceedings of the 1996 ACM SIGCPR/SIGMIS Conference on Computer Personnel Research* (pp. 68-84). New York, NY: ACM.

Li, W., Zhao, S., Sun, H., & Zhang, X. (2006). Ontology-based QoS driven GIS grid service discovery. In *Proceedings of the 2ⁿᵈ International Conference on Semantics, Knowledge, and Grid* (p. 49). Washington, DC., USA: IEEE Computer Society.

Marks, E. A., & Lozano, B. (2010). *Executive's guide to cloud computing*. Hoboken, NJ, USA: John Wiley & Sons.

Rittinghouse, J. W., & Ransome, J. F. (2009). *Cloud computing: Implementation, management and security*. USA: CRC Press.

Schmidt, B. L. (2000). Issues in teamwork: You can go home again: Successful telecommuting for the technical communicator. In *Proceedings of IEEE Professional Communication Society International Professional Communication Conference* & in *Proceedings of the 18ᵗʰ Annual ACM International Conference on Computer Documentation: Technology & Teamwork* (pp. 25-37). NJ, USA: IEEE Educational Activities Department Piscataway.

Siebenlist, F., Nagaratnam, N., Welch, V., & Neuman, C. (2004). Security for virtual organizations: Federating trust and policy domains. In Foster, I., & Kesselman, C. (Eds.), *The grid 2: Blueprint for a new infrastructure*. Amsterdam, Netherlands: Morgan Kaufmann.

Suvée, D. (2002). *JAsCo: A general-purpose aspect-oriented component language for java*. Unpublished masters thesis, Vrije Universiteit Brussel, Brussels, Belgium.

Velte, T., Velte, A., & Elsenpeter, R. (2010). *Cloud computing: A practical approach*. New York, NY: McGraw-Hill.

Verheecke, B., & Cibran, M. (2004). *Dynamic aspects for Web service management*. Paper presented at the Dynamic Aspect Workshop at the 3ʳᵈ International Conference on Aspect Oriented Software Development (AOSD 2004), Lancaster, UK.

Chapter 14
Enhancing the Grid with Multi-Agent and Semantic Capabilities

Bastian Koller
High Performance Computing Centre Stuttgart, Germany

Giuseppe Laria
Centro di Ricerca in Matematica Pura ed Applicata, Italy

Paul Karaenke
University of Hohenheim, Germany

András Micsik
MTA SZTAKI, Hungary

Henar Muñoz Frutos
Telefónica Investigación y Desarrollo, Spain

Angelo Gaeta
Centro di Ricerca in Matematica Pura ed Applicata, Italy

ABSTRACT

Addressing the requirements of academic end users, the Grid paradigm and its underlying technologies was in past developed and evolved neglecting the needs of potential business end users. Nowadays the trend changed towards the use of Grid technologies within electronic business (e-Business) which at the same time requires adapting existing technologies to allow for more flexible, intelligent and reliable support for business stakeholders. The BREIN project was the first one integrating two so far parallel evolving domains into the Grid, namely multi-agent and semantics. By this, the Grid was enhanced to provide the requested capabilities from business end users. This chapter will show the rationale behind the performed developments and the way how BREIN addresses its four main objectives of enabling and/or enhancing: (i) Autonomy and Automation, (ii) Self-Optimization, (iii) Context-Aware Security, (iv) Reduced Complexity of Use with a dedicated focus on the major pillars of the framework, Virtual Organizations (VOs) and Service Level Agreements (SLAs). With that, a generic solution is presented, which can be applied to a variety of distinct application areas.

DOI: 10.4018/978-1-61350-113-9.ch014

INTRODUCTION

This chapter presents the results of the BREIN project (Business objective driven reliable and intelligent Grids for real business, IST-FP6-034556) which aimed at realising flexible, intelligent Virtual Organisation (VO) support, to significantly reduce the complexity of modern day business-to-business collaborations. The project was active from September 2006 to January 2010 with the plan to enhance classical Grid solutions by integrating Multi-agent and Semantic Web concepts to provide a dynamic, standard based environment for e-Business. The main focus was to move away from the Grid approach of handling individual resources, to a framework that allows providing and selling services, whilst those services usually represent a combination of different resource types.

The main objective of this chapter is to present, how an established technology like the Grid can be improved by integrating concepts and technologies originating from other research domains. By integrating multi-agent capabilities into the Grid, the control and adaptation of resources can be enhanced, to guarantee stable, managed execution across service providers. Additionally the integration of Semantic Web concepts provides the basis for increased interoperability and provides intuitive interfaces for policies and reasoning.

To provide best access for the reader, the chapter is structured as follows. First of all, the background of the work in BREIN is presented covering general issues, which led to the BREIN approach, as well as an examination of base concepts and technologies of the project. This created the basis for the four main BREIN objectives of enabling and/or enhancing: (i) autonomy and automation, (ii) self-optimization, (iii) context-aware security, and (iv) reduced complexity of use.

Furthermore the two validation scenarios of BREIN are described to give the reader further insight into the aims of the project before the concrete results and their innovations of the proj-

ect are presented. These scenarios represent two completely distinct application areas, the High-Performance Computing (HPC) domain and the Airport Logistics sector. Finally, a conclusion is drawn on what has been achieved but also on what needs to be done in future to further strengthen the uptake of Grids in e-Business.

BACKGROUND

From a historic viewpoint, the Grid paradigm was introduced within the academic domain as a concept for shared resources in a collaborative manner. Thereby the assumption was taken, that involved entities have the will to share these resources most likely for free (Foster, 2002). With that, the concept of Virtual Organizations (VOs) was born (Foster, 2001), representing a concept to describe and manage organizational shared resources for the purpose of achieving a common goal.

However, with the growing pervasion of all areas of life with information technology, the traditional ways of performing business also changed with a dedicated focus on the electronic area. Therefore new technologies such as Service-Oriented Architecture (SOA) or Cloud Computing were becoming of highest interest for industry. Especially the collaboration with other business players to extend the own portfolio of services is an important factor with respect to competitiveness in the market, which is in particular also a success criteria for Small and Medium Enterprises (SMEs).

The BREIN project was designed at a time, when the Grid evolved towards an industrial use, but existing solutions still showed a lack of capabilities, and, at the same time, were quite too complex to allow a simple deployment of services. Therefore the approach of BREIN started from the base premise to take into account the capabilities and needs of business end users in all developments and to provide a solution, which is easy to use and maintain.

To realize this, the BREIN consortium aimed at enhancing the classical approaches by integrating concepts and technologies from the Multi-agent and Semantics domains, as these domains were identified as best candidates for enabling enhanced capabilities of the Grid. The BREIN project concentrated on four major areas of development, which needed to be covered to result in a solution fostering uptake of Grids in business. Those four areas are:

1. Virtual Organizations as the base concept for a business Grid.
2. Service Level Agreements (SLAs) as the underlying technology to allow for establishment and control of Quality-of-Service (QoS) agreements which are valid for business execution.
3. Multi-agent systems and Grids as underlying technology.
4. Semantics and Grid as underlying technology.

The following sections give a detailed overview of these areas and why they are addressed.

Virtual Organizations

Virtual Organizations (VOs) are a phenomenon in continuous expansion because they allow an efficient exploitation of collaboration among independent parties to solve problems. During the last years, the VO paradigm has been applied in several concrete cases within several areas of scientific research. In this context, the VO concept has been synonymous of resource sharing and researcher collaboration in order to address large scale problems that needed coordinated use of geographically distributed resources otherwise difficult to be collected in a single location.

Though there is a vast interest in the VO paradigm, there is not a wide agreement on a common definition. From the introduction of the VO concept (Moshowitz, 1986), multiple definitions have been coined as to what should be considered

a Virtual Organization. They differ depending on the defining community and, within the same community, on the different perspectives it is possible to focus on (computational infrastructure, communication based collaboration, information sharing, shared working environments, etc.).

In any case, all these definitions share a common understanding that is: A VO is a group of individuals whose members and resources maybe dispersed geographically and institutionally, yet who function as a coherent unit through the use of cyber-infrastructure (Cummings, 2008).

There are some key characteristics distinguishing a VO with respect to a classic organization, they are:

- Space: A VO takes place among geographically distributed participants.
- Time: A VO has a limited life span, until it performs its tasks or actions.
- Configuration: A VO is operated through the use of ICT that allows the management of members, communication, and resource sharing.

It is clear that according to this view, a VO does not have a permanent structure and it is not confined within a well-defined institutional boundary. Moreover, it is well suited to be dynamically created according with specific needs (the VO goals) to be achieved within an established time interval.

It is worth mentioning that the configuration is a key factor because the advance of the enabling technologies has been having a determinant role in the adoption of the VO paradigm. Furthermore it is not possible to identify a single enabling technology. In fact, depending on the character of the VO, we assist to the dominance of a specific technology rather than another of the spectrum of ICT technologies. So at one end of the spectrum, we find the Grid technologies that are being used for collaboration and resource sharing in large scale research projects. Several experiences exist where Grid technologies have allowed the setting up of VOs that played the role of enabler of system-level science (Foster, 2006) in different research areas such as: physics (LHC - Large Hadron Collider); open science research (TeraGrid); earthquake engineering (SCEC); cancer research (caBIG); etc. At the other end of the spectrum, we find the spread of Web 2.0 technologies that are enabling the setting up of "informal" VOs or virtual communities such as the ones formed by Facebook, Twitter, MySpace, LinkedIn, eBay, etc.

The state of practice highlights that the most prominent experience in using and applying the VO paradigm has been done in the fields of scientific research but there is not a wide acceptance in other disciplines, too. This is because it is still quite hard to form and operate a VO and there are still open issues that arise several challenges in the realization of a VO.

The main issue is represented by the lack of basic toolkits that allow to set up a general purpose VO to be customized according to the specific needs of the application domain. Nowadays, to build up a VO can become a complex task and this caused the emergence of several solutions addressed to solve the requirements of the specific problem.

To overcome these problems it is necessary to come with a common understanding of the VO concept (as said multiple VO definitions exist) and questions as: Where are the boundaries of the VO?, Which are the features to be provide in?, Who are the members of?, etc., should be answered following a unified approach. At this purpose, starting from a bottom analysis, it will be possible to understand the commonalities that characterize the different VO based solutions, in order to define general needs that will constitute the basis for the achievement of a common framework which any specific solution can be built on. This is a hard (OGSA, 2004) challenge and, at the first instance, requires finding solutions to the following problems (Cummings, 2008):

- Definition of common structures to be used as building block for designing customized solutions. The term structure here refers to the identification of a key set of topologies (e.g. peer to peer, main contractor, process oriented, etc.) to be combined in order to define the structure of each own VO.
- To define functionalities able to allow an easy and fast formation of VOs that guarantee a key set of features.
- To integrate the VO with collaboration tools that have to span from well-established tools for structured collaboration to Web2.0 based tool for enabling innovative collaborative models.
- To guarantee the parties that they will retain the control on their own resources.
- To allow a flexible mechanism for provision of services within the VO.
- To support the interoperability through the use of standards.
- To introduce clear and effective means to establish contract based relations within the VOs.

Service Level Agreements

With the evolution of the classical academic Grid towards a business solution the demand for representation of contractual relationships increased and led to dedicated research activities. This was especially needed as the concept of Virtual Organizations needed an underlying technology which represents all the relationships between the different VO members. A well-established technology to represent these relationships in terms of contractual frame (involved parties, penalties, benefits, etc), especially also with respect to the agreed Quality-of-Service (QoS) are Service Level Agreements (SLAs), though being rather handled as paper documents then electronic representations so far.

Historically originating from the telecommunications industry, e.g. as defined by the IT

Infrastructure Library (ITIL, 2009) or the Tele-Management Forum in its SLA Management Handbook (TeleManagement Forum, 2005), the concept of SLAs has gained interest of other business domain, so that it was evolved to address not only telecommunication but rather general business needs.

However, this generalization at the same time also led to the problem of too generic specifications of the content and the language used to represent SLAs in electronic format (XML). Several approaches towards these specifications have been made, but all of them are still rather in a semi-mature state than being product-ready. Looking on the state of the art, there are two approaches which can be labelled as most popular due to showing the highest degree of maturity: WS-Agreement (Andrieux, 2007) and WSLA (Keller, 2003).

WSLA, as published by IBM in 2003, provides a specification for the definition and monitoring of SLAs within a Web Service environment. However, this work has not been continued since the initial publication in 2003 and therefore known problems and bugs were not corrected anymore.

WS-Agreement, which is a specification developed within the Grid Resource Allocation Agreement Protocol Working Group (GRAAP-WG) of the Open Grid Forum (OGF), provides the specification of the contents of a SLA, as well as a protocol for establishing agreements on the usage of services between a service provider and a consumer. Version 1.0 of this specification was published in 2007. It defines a high level language and protocol to represent the services of providers, create agreements based on offers and monitor the agreement compliance at runtime. As mentioned before, both specifications are prominent but none of them is immediately applicable in a business environment. Therefore one task for BREIN was to base on the existing bits and to extend them in a way, which addressed the business requirements as needed. Thereby the intention was to: (i) Enhance SLAs with Semantics to allow for more flexible processing of the data as well as simplified definition of terms by the end users, and (ii) Support SLA management with decision mechanisms, taking into account all available information sources within the BREIN framework.

Multi-Agent Systems and Grids

Grid technology is in particular aiming at more flexible and open architectures which improve cross-organizational applications. SOA has originated a remarkable technology stack for Web Services (WS) standards which contribute to systems interoperability. The same cannot be said for multi-agent systems. Both Grid and multi-agent technology are concerned with problem solving by distributed systems, but focus on different approaches and offer divergent capabilities: Grid standards facilitate the building of secure, robust and reliable VOs to solve problems with distributed resources, but lack the capability to react or adapt to undesired conditions, changing requirements and in dynamic environments.

Multi-agent technology, in contrast, offers the capability for flexible and adaptive problem solving behaviour both on single agent and multi-agent level, but lacks reliability, security, and robustness (Foster, 2004). Thus, combining Grid and multi-agent technology could make use of the advantages of both technologies while avoiding their respective drawbacks.

The Web Service Integration Gateway (WSIG) (Greenwood, 2004) is an official Jade plug-in, which provides bidirectional invocation facility, by which Jade agents can call WSs and WS clients can call Jade agent services. The connection of agents and WSs is implemented using elaborate on-the-fly translation between agent messages and SOAP messages. However, WSIG cannot connect agent platforms via SOAP and does not allow transparent wrapping of agent message content into SOAP, thus it fails to support typical e-Business requirements (dynamically changing business partners, secure communication, etc.).

The AgentWeb Gateway (Shafiq, 2005) is a middleware between agent platforms and WS platforms, which provides protocol transformations similar to WSIG. This approach also lacks the flexibility we missed for WSIG, and furthermore the code seems to be unavailable. We evaluated several other approaches for this aspect of our architecture and found that most of them are not available for re-use. Details of our evaluation can be found in (Micsik, 2009).

Semantics and Grids

As commented above, a Virtual Organization involves the existence of different enterprises collaborating and interacting in sharing resources. This multi-dimensional interaction very frequently encounters, among other technical challenges, serious semantic interoperability problems. These problems mainly occur when the participating entities interpret the terms being used during this interaction in a different manner.

Thus, these enterprises can have different conceptualizations for the domain, data, systems and infrastructure, which imply heterogeneity problem to deal with this diversity. Mainly, this heterogeneity can come from different service, resources, SLA and policies definitions due to different domain conceptualizations. The reason is that standards in the definition of services, resources, etc., are either (1) not being adopted by a critical number of enterprises to allow for realizing network externalities or (2) concern low-level technical or syntactical issues only but not semantics, especially of the respective application domains.

After 2005 a number of EU projects started to conceptualize the Grid domain. The only significant result, the Grid Resource Ontology (GRO) (Brooke et al. 2007) contains more than 100 concepts and relationships, and it covers many important aspects of Grids including processes, infrastructure, users, security, infrastructure, tasks and jobs. However, GRO still lacks service model-

ling aspects, and remains disconnected from the domain of services and the business viewpoint (e.g. business processes).

The Semantic OGSA Ontology (S-OGSA) (Corcho et al. 2006) is an interesting core ontology providing the basis for the Semantic Grid; it adds the notion of semantics into the model of Grid via semantic bindings which can establish the necessary links between Grid entities and knowledge entities. The Semantic Grid is an extension of the current Grid in which information and services are given well-defined meaning, better enabling computers and people to work in cooperation. It refers to an approach to Grid computing in which information, computing resources and services are described using the semantic data model. This makes it easier for resources to be discovered and joined up automatically, which helps to bring resources together to create VOs. The descriptions constitute metadata and are typically represented using the technologies of the Semantic Web, such as the Resource Description Framework (RDF).

ENHANCING THE GRID

BREIN Objectives

BREIN had a set of objectives, which were identified to be of utmost importance to be addressed for fostering the uptake of Grid in business. Summarizing, the four main objectives for BREIN were to enable/enhance (i) autonomy and automation, (ii) self-optimization, (iii) context-aware security, and (iv) reduced complexity of use. This all was targeted by integrating two so far in parallel developed technology domains into the GGrid – multi-agents and semantics.

Autonomy and Automation are the key enablers of the desired business flexibility, as adequate mechanisms need not only to pursue the goal of the single business user, but also to take into account the overall collaborative (VO) goal. All of this before but also during the business execution, even with the need of adaptation to environmental changes (fail of resources). This often leads to tradeoffs, which need to be as optimal as possible for all involved parties. Hand in hand with this, is the needed capability of self-optimization. Where in the classical Grid the best effort practice was quite common used for job and service fulfilment, a business Grid will have to deal with several kinds of customers such as high-priority customers (and jobs) and QoS guarantees (e.g., availability).

Another important aspect in a Grid for business is security. Often neglected by academia driven research, missing adequate security mechanisms are the main barrier of uptake of new technologies in industry.

Previous systems often ignored the fact that subtle changes in a user's 'context' must result in different authorizations. This has to be enabled by a proper solution to address real needs in the business world.

Finally the complexity of existing systems in terms of their use by non-experts had to be reduced. Therefore a "plug-and-play" like approach was needed as well as end users needed easy access to the system to define their business goals and policies in an abstract way, but the system being still able to process this input. At the end, a big step forward was taken, showing on one hand the benefits of merging so far parallel developed technological domains and providing a blueprint for business Grids.

Overall BREIN Architecture

All the challenges arising from the identified objectives have been faced and they have found a concrete solution in the design and development of the BREIN core platform. The architecture of the BREIN platform merges core concepts from the Multi-agent technology, Semantic Web technology and Grids. In this way BREIN integrates relevant solutions that each of these technologies can provide with respect to topics that are basic in BREIN: intelligent adaptive behaviour (agents),

flexible integration in heterogeneous environment (Semantic Web technology), optimized use of distributed resources (Grid).

Figure 1 presents the high level view of the BREIN architecture and as it has been broken down in seven Building Blocks (BB). Furthermore, it is explained how each BB takes advantage of the use of the mentioned technological areas.

The building blocks are grouped into: Management, Agent based capabilities, Infrastructure and Security. Each group is characterized by the relevance that the mentioned technological areas have to achieve the related capabilities:

"Management group": semantic technologies have a particular relevance, here. In fact, the building blocks involved in this group provide functionalities such as: recording and maintenance of contacts with business partners, discovery of services, definition of SLAs trough bipartite negotiations, orchestration and execution of "abstract workflow" related to a customer's request.

"Agent based capabilities group": agent technology is directly involved here, and semantics is indirectly relevant as well. In fact, this group focuses on goal driven planning, and adaptation actions to avoid deviations from the plan. These are typical capabilities provided by a Multi-agent system through coordination and reasoning. Furthermore, agent reasoning is significantly enhanced through the use of semantic technologies.

"Infrastructure group": it provides underlying capabilities to be used transparently by the other groups. The term "use" would highlight that this is not a classic layer because others BBs can work also without using this "underlying capabilities". Examples of capability are: messaging, encapsulation, resource management, semantic annotation, reasoning, ontology storage management. Grid technologies are relevant here, in particular, for classic Grid resource management. Of course, semantic technologies are centric because it is here that the semantic capabilities are made available to the other groups through uniform access

Figure 1. Overview of the BREIN Architecture

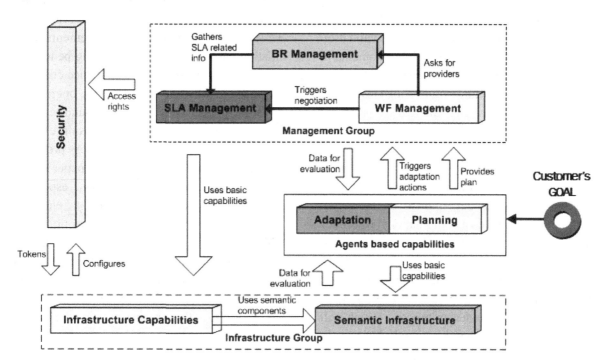

to knowledge base, reasoning component, and ontology storage system.

The security building block supports authentication and authorization capabilities across organizational boundaries. This particularly covers human-supported federation establishment and enactment, VO-centric identity and claims management, and authorization for cross-organizational service invocation.

Figure 1 also illustrates the high-level dynamic behaviour, sketching the basic interactions among the identified groups.

As said, the BREIN architecture is a goal driven architecture, therefore the submission of customers' goal triggers and affects the behaviour of the architecture building blocks. As first step, the Adaptation & Planning BB generates a plan that meets the customer's goal. This plan is submitted to the management group (WF Management) in order to "concretize" it. The concretization process consists of the following steps:

- Identification of external parties that could contribute to the plan execution (BR Management)
- Establishment of business relationship with the identified parties (BR Management)
- Negotiation of SLAs in order to use specific services from these parties and definition of the access rights underpinning such SLA (SLA Management).

The success of the concretization process allows starting the execution of the workflow that "realizes" the plan. The workflow execution implies secure messages exchange with the different parties (supported by the "Infrastructure Capabilities" and Security BB).

Validation through Scenarios

The open and standards based system resulting from the development of the BREIN architecture has been validated in non-trivial scenarios that have been able to validate the features and show the features and capabilities provided by the platform. At the end of the project, the validation has been performed in two different domains in order to demonstrate the generality of the platform as well: the Virtual Engineering Design and the Airport Management. The two scenarios are summarised below:

The Virtual Engineering Design Scenario. New opportunities are arising in the field of Engineering Design, to automate much more of the design process. These are underpinned by the ready availability of low cost computational resources available at marginal costs. If the costs of the automation are high, engineers will continue to rely on the existing 'serial' design process, (look at a design, evaluate it, try a new idea…) rather than automating the design process, which will require much more computational resource. In addition, companies might keep the automation processes in house, buying the required hardware and software, and not outsourcing the process. If Virtual Engineering Design succeeds, it will create new business opportunities for all the stakeholders in the Virtual Organisation. However, even if the costs are low enough, failures in security, in reliability and administration, high transaction costs (thus additional costs for maintaining the transaction) and delays will all compromise the potential new market.

The Visionary Airport Management Scenario. This is based around the desire of Stuttgart Airport to create a new market as a hub for airlines that operate on a point-to-point basis. The new business opportunity is that if the processes described can be automated reliably and securely, there is the potential for Stuttgart Airport to act as a so called 'virtual hub' for different carriers, and for it to be more competitive on a European scale. It will also have new opportunities for the carriers, to enable them to plug into virtual airline networks, but still retaining all the attendant benefits of operating in a point-to-point manner. Again, as the market currently does not exist, all the players

in the virtual hub environment will benefit from the increased throughput in Stuttgart Airport. At the same time, incremental improvements in the existing capability will still give big benefits to Stuttgart Airport, enabling it to reduce costs and increase the reliability of its logistic operations.

Both of these cases are based around activities which are currently not feasible using existing technology. If the traditional business processes were to be used, they would be paper based, with a lot of manual interactions, especially negotiations, between the various stakeholders. This would generate very high transaction costs, which would make the new business uneconomic. Existing middleware does not have the capability to automate either of these cases. The results of the BREIN project validation have demonstrated the feasibility of these scenarios using the BREIN platform that can be considered therefore as an enabling technology, to enable new business opportunities to be created.

In addition, because of their different nature, these two scenarios complement each other to test and evaluate the results from the BREIN project.

The following sections describe in more details the innovations introduced by the BREIN project in order to achieve the planned objectives.

Results and Innovations of BREIN

The BREIN Virtual Organization

Basic to the achievement of the BREIN objectives has been the definition of the BREIN VO concept. As said in the background section it was a challenging task due to the lack of a common definition. . Each of the scenarios, summarized before, involves a number of organisations, the stakeholders, collaborating to exploit the new business opportunities, through a set of business relationships. While there is a common objective to exploit the new business opportunities created, the relationships between the stakeholders can be dynamic and encapsulated within a series of 1-1 and ad-hoc contracts and understandings. Starting from this consideration, BREIN has followed an approach oriented to privilege the simplicity in order to design a VO model as much as generic to be reused in different business sectors and, in the best case, to be used in context different from business as well.

In this respect, the BREIN VO model assumes three basic (and well known) principles:

1. Bipartite Relationships: this is the simplest model a business relationship can be based on (Fujitsu Lab, 2008).
2. Encapsulation: related to the concept of hiding details and separation of concerns introduced since '70s (Parnas, 1972) and that found wider popularity with the introduction of Web Service technologies enabling the Service Oriented architecture approach at the end of 20th century .
3. Orchestration: it is where the Customer of more than one service provider wants the providers to interact. The customer manages this interaction, and thus orchestrates the providers (Terracina et al. 2006).

These principles have led the definition of coordination structure that governs information and material flows as well as the relationships, commitments, responsibilities, and decision making within the BREIN VO.

BREIN is specifically user oriented and as such sees the customer as the main collaboration definition endpoint, in other words the BREIN VO is centric to a main contractor (sometimes called "VO Initiator"), who defines a complex goal to be realised via a (virtual) collaboration. Such a goal definition contains all the collaboration details, i.e. goals, contractual scope, capabilities, requirements and limitations (*Figure 2*). Other VO participants are considered contractors that enter a contractual binding with the main contractor – the concept is identical to customer and Service Provider.

Note that contractual bindings to the main contractor (white arrows) do not imply message flow (red/dark arrows) in the sense of orchestrated transactions. Instead, the interactions may take place according to a predefined choreography across the organisational boundaries, with each organisation being liable to the main contractor.

VOs are initiated with a Service Provider receiving a particular customer need that requires resources beyond its capabilities, and will end with this need being fulfilled by the establishment of collaboration or the collaboration failing in its goal. It is possible to identify the following phases (widely assumed as typical of a VO lifecycle) as of particular relevance to the BREIN VO lifecycle:

*   Identification: during which the service providers and resources are identified that are required to fulfil the respective collaboration's goals.
*   Formation: during which the participants are configured so as to enable cross-enterprise transactions according to the collaboration plan.
*   Operation and Evolution: during which the tasks according to the collaboration plan are executed, i.e., the transactions between participants take place.
*   Dissolution: during which the collaboration is dissolved and each participant is freed from the collaboration requirements.

Putting All Together

Applying the basic BREIN principles (bipartite relationship, encapsulation, orchestration) and using recursively the basic BREIN VO model, it is possible to envisage complex structures that see several basic BREIN VOs to collaborate to achieve an initial customer request.

The underpinning idea is that Service Providers may principally build up their own Virtual Organisation within another VO, i.e. they may use a Virtual Organisation to provide the capabili-

Figure 2. A simple Virtual Organization in the airport context

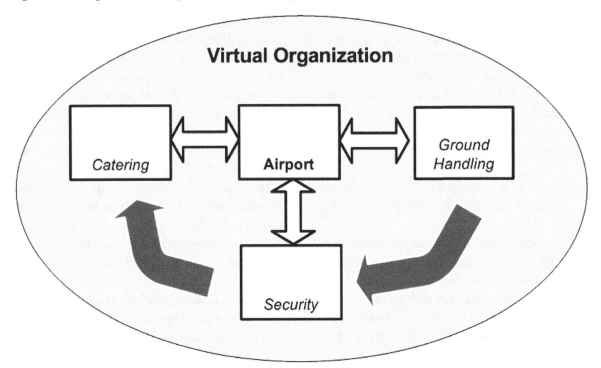

White arrows denote the contractual binding between services, whilst red (dark) arrows depict the (potential) information flow and thus dependencies between services. Here, the airport acts as the main contractor.

ties they expose to other customers, respectively transaction partners. The result is the nested VO structure shown in Figure 3 where each VO follows the basic BREIN VO model.

The subcontracted parties are not necessarily visible to the higher-level VO's main contractor. Figure 3 shows how this model fits with the airport scenario and, more in general, with the supply chain model defined in BREIN. This figure includes several parties involved in the supply chain related to airport management. These parties can form different VOs (e.g. VO1, VO2, and VO3) that have to meet specific goals but there is an implicit relationship between the contracts of the accordingly linked VOs. BREIN foresees to simplify the tasks involved with the goal-driven, intelligent management of this model.

INTEGRATION OF MULTI-AGENT AND SEMANTIC TECHNOLOGIES IN THE GRID

Adaptive Grid Resources

The head body paradigm is used as the leading metaphor for managing resources in the BREIN platform: it implies a conceptual separation of a software agent into two parts – head and body (Haugeneder et al. 1994). The agent's head is used for interactions with other agents being member of the agent society. This includes reasoning about interactions such as participating in cooperative processes for problem solving. The body is encapsulating any other (domain) functionality of an agent. The head body paradigm is used as follows (Figure 4):

Figure 3. A set of three nested VOs

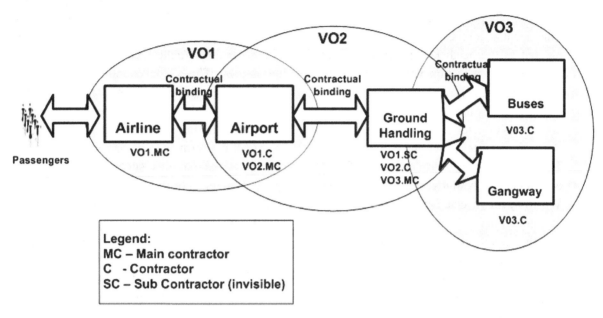

Each Service Provider enacts its own VO as "sub contracted" to the higher VO.

Figure 4. Head body architecture in BREIN

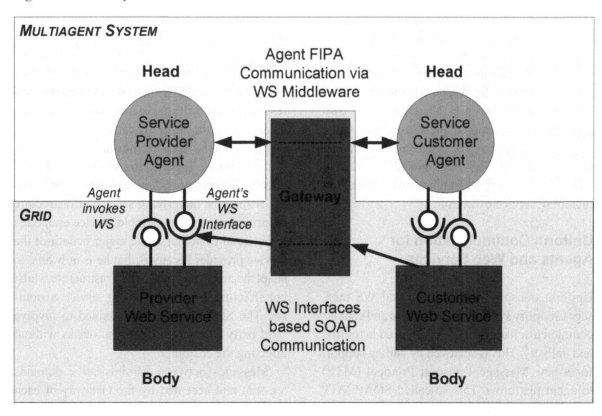

- Web Service resources that are represented by agents are part of the body.
- The agent's core capabilities are implemented in the head; i.e., interactions and especially coordination with other agents in the agent society.
- The agent body has a set of web service operations as effectors, which are able to control some services providing core business.
- The agent has full control over the WS and communicates with it via agent-to-WS and WS-to-agent mechanisms presented later in this section.
- On the conceptual level, agent-to-agent communication takes place using FIPA communication standards.
- On the technical level, agent-to-agent communication is based on Web Service technologies and standards. Therefore, BREIN Software Agents can be part of existing Grid infrastructures and systems.

A WS which is represented by an agent can transparently be invoked by other WSs, respectively clients. The agent can evaluate the invocation requests and can reason if an invocation of the encapsulated WS is in accordance to its own goals. If the invocation request is opposed to the goals, the agent can intercept the invocation and the encapsulated WS is not invoked. In addition, the agent is able to gather monitoring information regarding service execution.

Uniform Communication for Agents and Web Services

Uniform transportation of agent and WS messages simplify system administration and enables common mechanisms to be introduced in routing and delivery. This is achieved by adding support for a new Message Transport Protocol (MTP) to agent platforms. This so-called SOAP MTP add-on (Micsik et al. 2009) is a pluggable driver for sending and receiving SOAP messages and translating them to/from internal agent message format. Each agent platform uses the SOAP MTP add-on configured with a virtual endpoint address, which is mapped to the agent platform address in the Gateway. This virtual endpoint address is also advertised in registries and directories outside the organizational domain, so that external entities will use the virtual address to reach the agent platform.

Agent platforms can be operated in separate organizational domains, such as customers, service providers, or resource providers. Inside each platform the communication between agents is usually not supervised and not restricted. Similarly, agents can access WSs freely inside the domain. However, the communication between agent platforms has to be supervised according to current policies of the embedding domains. In order to allow for a seamless integration of components, a corresponding flexible and adaptive messaging infrastructure, commonly titled as "Enterprise Message Bus", has to be provided.

The Gateway Toolkit provides such a messaging infrastructure by allowing for a "double-blind" virtualization approach. On customer side, the Gateway Toolkit allows to hide the corresponding Service Provider (SP) which allows describing corresponding workflows in a more abstract manner. Additionally, the customer can easily change service providers by adapting the routing information of the Gateway Toolkit infrastructure whilst not affecting the corresponding workflows. The SP can easily hide the underlying service infrastructure by providing virtual, callable service endpoints to potential customers. The major benefit of the service provider hereby is that he is now able to adapt the underlying service infrastructure whilst not affecting the corresponding service customers. The SP is additionally enabled to involve third party SPs for particular sub-tasks without affecting the customer.

Messages between administrative domains are sent and accepted by the Gateway of each domain (Figure 5). In our example the Jade agent platform is used. The Gateway mediates the com-

Figure 5. Inter-organizational agent communication

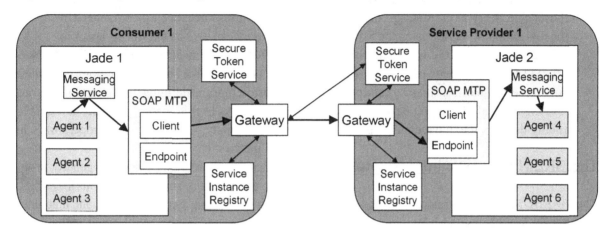

munication between the front end WSs of the two domains. Each front end authenticates itself to their respective Gateway. In the scenario, Jade 1 WS does not need to know the actual endpoint of the Jade 2 WS. Therefore the Gateway allows for the invocation of virtual service endpoints by resolving these virtual to concrete endpoints via the Service Instance Registry (SIR). The SIR also provides additional metadata such as the gateway endpoint that the message has to travel through, as well as the endpoint of the Security Token Service (STS) where tokens affiliated with this service can be requested. Virtual addresses used in SOAP messages can be translated dynamically to appropriate real services.

The STS issues claim-based tokens to authenticated users, respectively agents, and is also involved in the process of establishing federation with the STS in the Jade 2 domain. The consumer-side role of the STS issues tokens that are necessary to pass the security check on the service side. The tokens are generated based on the information that is extracted from the service call message. The service-side role of the security token service acts not as token issuer but as verification instance for security tokens that are attached to the incoming message. It hence has the role of a Policy Decision Point (PDP). In the example of Figure 5, consumer side requests a

service from his own SIR by providing an URN (Uniform Resource Name) and the SIR returns the virtual address along with the endpoints of the gateway and the STS. The provider side SIR will convert the server side virtual endpoint to an actual endpoint where the client request can be satisfied.

The following steps are executed when sending a message to a remote agent platform:

1. The consumer agent addresses the message using the virtual endpoint address of the remote agent on the SP side.
2. The Messaging Service detects that this address belongs to the SOAP MTP, and forwards the message to the SOAP MTP add-on for delivery.
3. The SOAP MTP client prepares the SOAP message, and delivers it to the virtual address of the remote agent, but the outgoing message is actually caught by the local Gateway.
4. The local Gateway identifies the recipient SP using the SIR, and arranges for a security token with the STS of both sides.
5. The message is sent to the Gateway at the service provider side.

6. The SP Gateway checks the access rights for the service, decrypts the message, then finds the real endpoint service using the SIR, and calls the endpoint of the Jade platform.

7. The SOAP MTP of Jade platform 2 reconstructs the original agent message and passes it to the internal Messaging Service, which finally delivers it to the recipient agent.

The BREIN Semantic Infrastructure

The BREIN Semantic Infrastructure underpins the BREIN architecture as it provides a set of capabilities and mechanisms that enhance the capability of the BREIN components to understand and manage metadata. Enriching metadata and providing the mechanisms to support reasoning over the enriched content is the basis for improving semantic interoperability between VO participants. The role of the BREIN Semantic Infrastructure is to provide a unified framework for dealing with semantic metadata at all levels of the BREIN architecture.

Since enterprises have different systems, infrastructure, data (format), domain conceptualization, to deal with this diversity implies a heterogeneity problem. The reason is that respective standards are either (1) not being adopted by a critical number of enterprises to allow for realizing network externalities or (2) concern low-level technical or syntactical issues only but not semantics, especially of the respective application domains. Mainly, the heterogeneity can come from:

Different domain conceptualization: Each enterprise has its own enterprise-specific information, rules and policies to conduct their business. They way how an enterprise conceptualizes the respective domain (i.e., branch of industry) is in general up to the enterprise, and thus greatly contributes to heterogeneity between enterprises.

Different service descriptions: As each provider has its own systems with its data format described in their own way, the service definition can be enterprise-dependent.

Different resource descriptions: The description of the resources or entities managed by service providers can also be enterprise-specific.

Different SLA and policies definition: Service providers like having more control of their infrastructure and defining their own QoS metrics in the SLA. In this matter, in order to achieve user simplicity, we will need interoperability in SLA metrics.

Besides overcoming the heterogeneity problem, semantics also supports the agents in BREIN. Making semantics explicit, formal, and machine-readable is crucial for Multi-agent *t*echnology. The reason is that the BREIN software agents are designed according to the BDI architecture (beliefs, desires, and intentions). It requires that agents can perceive their environment and eventually interact with other agents based on commonly agreed concepts and inter-relations between concepts. BDI agents are able to reason about things such as a service offering and then derive and evaluate alternative answers to such an offering. Therefore, semantics technology in BREIN does not only aim at the heterogeneity problem, but also allow for reasoning.

We can find semantic support for the following functionalities of the BREIN platform:

- Workflow management (concretization of abstract service definitions in abstract workflows, flexible replacement of workflow components, etc.).
- Service Discovery (Service functionality matchmaking based on semantic functionality descriptions)
- Service Selection (Selection of services based on SLA annotated semantically).
- SLA Negotiation (Interoperable SLA format, and semantic assessment of SLA bids and offers).
- Scheduling (Scheduling of jobs using OWL reasoner to find optimal distribution of jobs).

- Outsourcing (Resource interoperability and cooperation over organizational boundaries through a shared conceptualization).
- Planning and Adaptation (Reasoning inside agents to plan service compositions, to detect service execution failures and to adapt scheduled plan according to current status).

The BREIN Semantic Infrastructure supports generic patterns for using semantic technology in various components of the platform, and for various end-user functionalities. We identified the following basic patterns:

Sharing Ontologies: The most fundamental pattern: several components need to use the same core ontologies to establish a common 'lingua franca'.

Semantic annotation of non-semantic structured data: Semantic annotation is a technique to inject references to semantic concepts into structured data while keeping its originally interpretable syntax. Semantic annotations allow us for example to identify parts of XML data with semantic concepts.

Ontology matching (or ontology alignment): It often occurs that parties use different ontologies for the same purpose. Ontology matching is the process of determining correspondences between concepts of different ontologies.

Semantic matchmaking: A semantically described need or goal has to be matched with semantically described object capabilities. Typically, the intersection of potential goals and available capabilities in the solution space has to be computed and analysed in an efficient way.

Reasoning: Reasoning is the way to extract new knowledge, new facts from existing semantic data using logical rules, axioms and techniques such as inference.

Rules: Rules model human thinking, where they are often expressed with an if-then structure. The use of rules creates the possibility for easy customization of reasoning within agents.

Management of Semantic Distributed Index: A distributed semantic index enables semantic matchmaking to be performed across a network of knowledge bases containing different semantic descriptions.

BREIN Ontologies

BREIN applies a modular architecture of Ontologies, where the core Ontologies provide the basic modeling framework. The BREIN core Ontologies are extended for each use-case with domain specific parts required to describe service profiles, resources and properties in the respective domain.

The BREIN core Ontologies act like an upper ontology, presenting high-level concepts of the generic BREIN behaviours. These Ontologies are kept minimal in order to remain domain independent and easily re-usable. The core Ontologies are also split according to different needs of the business side and technology side.

The BREIN Business Ontology is populated with terms needed for processes such as Service Discovery and Negotiation. The aim is to identify the linkage between business related concepts (such as product, market player, etc.) and technical concepts (such as Service Negotiation, Service Discovery, etc.). The Business Ontology will allow clients to describe their business requirements as well as it will allow Service Providers to describe their offers. This enables a "guideline" for existing business scenarios to "virtualize" their business by mapping their concepts to the commonly understood Business Ontology.

The BREIN Technology Ontology describes the technological concepts used in the BREIN framework. The Technology Ontology will allow for example service providers to describe their available resources, the tasks to be executed and their schedules.

The BREIN Business Ontology

Currently, a gap can be observed between business requirements sphere and the actual process implementation sphere of enterprises. Thus, BREIN provides some tools and techniques in order to facilitate the transition from customer requirements (with different terminologies) to execution by means of differentiating the business level which contains customers' requirements from the Information Technology (IT) system level.

The Business Ontology provides a way for describing services and processes as well as Service Level Agreement metrics in a formal way. Basically, a Business Process can be described as a composite process of Business Activities using the Business Ontology. Business Activities can be nested together, until we reach atomic, non-divisible activities called Business Tasks. The Business Ontology uses the S-BPMN ontology developed in SUPER project (Hepp et al. 2007) to describe and annotate business process flows. Moreover, it links the Business Tasks with service description being grounded to services.

The description of these services can be divided into: capabilities descriptions or functional properties which are specified using OWL-S and non-functional properties associating the service with SLA and contract. The SLA can be defined using the QoS ontology, which is a separate part of the BREIN Business Ontology used for describing Quality of Service (QoS) terms. The OWL QoS ontology is created to provide a common understanding of QoS parameters and their semantics between providers and consumers enabling reasoning over QoS properties.

The basic concepts are taken from the quality model defined by OASIS in the Web Services Quality Model (WSQM) specification (Kim & Lee, 2005). WSQM complements existing SLA-related specifications with a general view on quality related roles, processes and attributes. WSQM uses the term Quality Factor for QoS parameters and further categorizes it into sub-factors and

layers concerning the user's view, interoperability and management.

In our ontology, each QoS parameter is associated with a metric characterized by value type (float, integer, boolean, etc.), a value and a measurement unit (e.g. euro, kB, ms). Finally, the QoS parameter can have several statuses depending on if it is requested by a customer, or offered by a provider.

The BREIN Technology Ontology

The BREIN Technology Ontology provides the basis for describing technological concepts and properties of the BREIN platform. This includes the description of Web Services, Grid and non-Grid resources as well as computational components such as computers, disks, operating systems or software agents.

The Technology Ontology is scenario independent, and thus tries to remain on a generic level and to avoid going into too specific details. However, the ontology relies on several other Ontologies:

OWL-S: this is the usual ontology to describe services using OWL (Martin et al. 2007). With OWL-S one can define the capabilities or profile of the service, its process model and its grounding.

OWL-WS: OWL-WS extends the concept of OWL-WS Service to Abstract Process, a kind of Atomic Process without implementation information, and uses the concept of Composite Process for workflow modelling (Beco et al. 2005).

GRO: The Grid Resource Ontology is currently the most comprehensive approach for describing the various resources and activities in a Grid environment (Brooke et al. 2004).

S-OGSA: The Semantic-OGSA defines a model, the capabilities and the mechanisms for the Semantic Grid extending GRO (Corcho et al. 2006).

Finally, the BREIN Business Ontology can also be used together with the Technology Ontology, which creates a full picture of the e-Business environment.

Figure 6. The various aspects covered by the core Ontologies

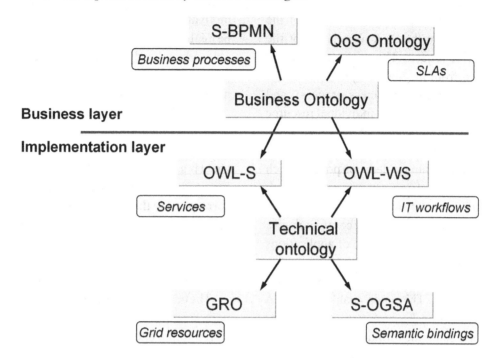

The BREIN Technology Ontology uses OWL-S for the description of processes and services. On top of OWL-S, OWL-WS is used to define abstract processes and describe dynamic workflows. The BREIN QoS ontology is used to define and attach SLA guarantees or QoS values to executable tasks. Finally, the description of computational resources is taken from the Grid Resource Ontology. Due to incompatibilities between GRO and OWL-S, the GRO had to be adapted to the needs of the BREIN Technology Ontology. These changes were provided as a feedback to the maintainers of GRO. S-OGSA connects the resources and services of BREIN with the world of Semantic Web, enabling us to attach semantic descriptions to resources and services.

As a side effect, the BREIN Technology Ontology captures basic relationships between Grid, Multi-agent, Semantics, and Workflow technologies. This aspect is also backed up by the previous effort of creating the BREIN Glossary, where most

useful terms of these overlapping technological areas are collected and defined.

BREIN also provides Ontologies for the description of software licenses, another area lacking advancements in the Grid scene. The BREIN Software License Ontology has been integrated into the inference and rule engines of the BREIN resource allocator, thus enabling to plan also with license availability during job scheduling. The importance of the presented core Ontologies is the domain-independent unification of the business and technical levels of business services, which can be summarized as follows.

In a Business Process each atomic step (Business Task) involves a human or automated task. Automated tasks may be composite, thus one such task may start a whole workflow. An automated task when executed is converted to a service request with SLA definition. These are matched with available services. After a service is selected and negotiated, the service request becomes a job in the internal queue of the service provider. These jobs can be subdivided into subtasks. Each job is then assigned to a resource. The SLA of the job is derived from the SLA negotiated for the original service request. Thus a correspondence is maintained from the bottom (job executed on a resource) to the top (business process), and similarly, there is a link from individual resource SLAs towards the embedding higher level SLAs, contracts and process models. These links enable us to do richer reasoning in decision points, which allows more optimal use of resources on both customer and provider sides.

There are numerous uses of the core Ontologies in the BREIN platform. A group of applications deal with the topic of SLA management: a graphical tool can be used to add semantic annotations to SLA templates. This later enables the SLA Translator tool to translate various SLA definitions into a uniform semantic format, which is used by the service discovery, SLA negotiation and SLA monitoring components.

Similarly, a graphical tool helps to create semantic definitions of workflows and services. These workflows are then executed and converted into semantic descriptions of individual service requests, which become the key input for scheduling and monitoring of resources internally to the service provider. This functionality is implemented using software agents, which consume the semantic descriptions and incorporate them into their local knowledge base.

Agents Using BREIN Ontologies

The Belief-Desire-Intention (BDI) architecture approach (Bratman et al. 1988) is a model for describing rational software agents – agents that reason, based on beliefs, which action to perform to reach given goals. That is, the BDI architecture facilitates goal-driven system behaviour. The model consists of the following concepts: beliefs capture informational attitudes realized as a data structure containing current facts about the world. Desires capture the motivational atti-

tudes realized as goals that represent the concrete motivation; i.e., desires capture a set of goals to be realized. Intentions capture the deliberative attitudes realized by reasoning to select appropriate actions to achieve given goals or to react to particular situations.

Thus, the BDI agents allow reasoning regarding decisions to determine which, possibly conflicting, business goals can be achieved and how the agent is going to achieve these goals. For example, for an agent representing a Grid resource, beliefs correspond to the state, capabilities, and SLAs of the resource; desires represent the business goals of the resource provider, while intentions result from a collection of possible decision mechanisms to select and execute requests to use the resource.

The traditional BDI concept has been integrated with semantics in BREIN: the agent's beliefs, stored in the agent's belief base, are completely based on semantic data. Further, semantic reasoning is applied to derive new knowledge -especially required actions to reach goals- based on the semantic beliefs. Conceptual definitions of SLA parameters, metrics, and economic values as well as resource characteristics are given in an OWL DL ontology. New data arriving to the agents are inserted into the knowledge base, which is automatically enriched using DL reasoning. Agents can then retrieve the results of reasoning via the beliefs. This provides essential support towards the targeted technical interoperability over organizational boundaries, representing real-world business relationships.

We implemented prototype implementations for embedded lightweight semantic core inside BDI agents testing several available software solutions, and found a small but effective extension to our BDI agents.

Enhanced Business Handling with Service Level Agreements

Even though Service Level Agreements have been already mentioned before, this section will pres-

Figure 7. The BREIN SLA concept

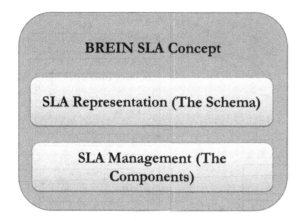

ent the BREIN approach towards SLAs and their management. The BREIN SLA concept foresees a split in two layers (Figure 7). One is addressing the language/schema to define Service Level Agreements and their contents; the other is the (architectural) design of the processing components. Whilst a detailed presentation of the SLA Management components would exceed the limit of this chapter (details can be found in the BREIN Architecture document, cf. Laria et al. 2009), this section will concentrate on the innovations with respect to the representation of SLAs in BREIN.

The basis for the BREIN SLA schema is a merge of WS-Agreement and WSLA (Figure 8). This was a result of previous experience in the TrustCoM project (Wilson, 2007). Thereby WS-Agreement provides the frame and basic structure of the SLA, whilst WSLA is used to describe the respective SLA parameters, metrics and how they are measured.

As stated before, BREINs intention was to integrate Multi-agent and Semantic Web concepts to enhance the support of e-Business end users in setting up and maintaining their business relationships. One of the big problems with SLAs, their definition and management, was that existing solutions performed well, in the case of the involved entities using a common language and by that have a common terminology. But as soon as the entities use different languages the process of finding an agreement (or later executing a service based on the defined terms in the SLA) gets quite difficult, if not impossible.

The SA-SLA Format for Semantic SLAs

BREIN proposes the use of semantic annotations and a new format for semantically annotating SLA descriptions called Semantic Annotations for Service Level Agreement (SA-SLA, Kotsiopoulos, 2008, 2009) to overcome this issue. A semantic annotation is additional information that identifies or defines a concept in a semantic model in order to describe part of that any document element (Lawrence et al. 2005). The annotation mechanism allows for annotating SLA descriptions with pointers to semantic concepts from more expressive Ontologies, coded in formal languages as Web Ontology Language (OWL) or Web Service Modeling Language (WSML), so that SLA-aware components can interpret the content and automate the tasks.

SA-SLA follows the steps of Semantic Annotations for Web Service Description Language (SA-WSDL) (Kopecky et al. 2007) effort, which has become the dominant approach in the area of Semantic Web Services.

Practically, SA-SLA is an extension to the WS-Agreement specification (GRAAP-WG, 2007), with semantic annotations in order to provide the lacking domain vocabulary for WS-Agreement. Elements in a SLA template can be linked with concepts belonging to the BREIN QoS ontology by using the SA-SLA specification. As a result, we have an SLA Template annotated semantically.

The benefit of this annotation approach is that it is backward compatible and protocol independent. This means that there is no enforcement of redevelopment or adaptation of existing SLA management tools. But if preferred, Business Grid infrastructures can benefit from the use of

Figure 8. Merging WS-Agreement and WSLA

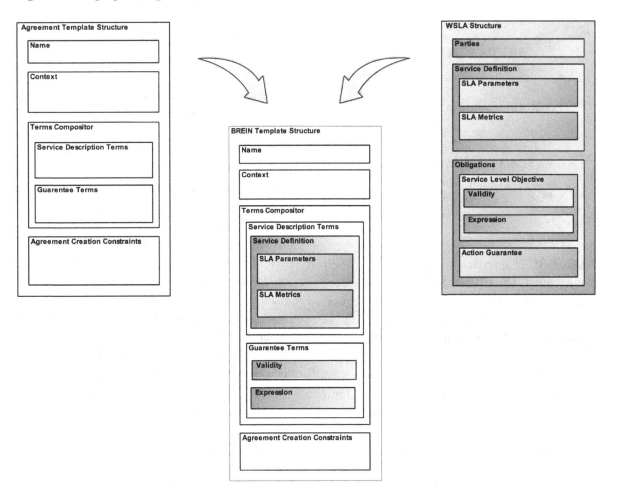

improved SLA Negotiation and later the management of the execution environment of the services.

Adaptive SLA Management

Adaptive SLA management in BREIN addresses SLA negotiation and SLA-based resource management with regards to dependencies between SLAs of different value creation levels. Thus, we apply the Combinatorial Contract Net Protocol (CCNP) (Karaenke, 2010) for multi-tier task allocation which enables a consideration of SLA dependencies over multiple service chain levels.

Further, we utilize the goal-driven approach to represent the different goals of the actors on each level of the service chain. This allows extending the solution space for actions to reach the desired goals. The solution space is represented and supported by a knowledge base, containing semantic descriptions of capabilities, goals, tasks, and offers. Decisions needed to manage the service chain such as matching, ranking, and selecting offers are supported by reasoning on this knowledge base. Further, we utilize the agentification of Grid resources; i.e., Grid resources are represented by agents. This provides the required flexibility of resource management and the utilization of Multi-agent coordination mechanism, especially market-based coordination and Multi-agent negotiation, without central control.

A key aspect is the mapping of real-world service contracts to the technical representation in terms of semantically annotated SLA definitions. This enables the BREIN Software Agents to infer knowledge about necessary actions that have to be performed to provide individually contracted services; i.e., SLA-based resource management. The utilization of explicit semantics further facilitates the interoperability on business level by incorporating domain knowledge in all phases of the service life cycle. The coupling of Grid resources and multi-agent technology allows a seamless utilization of Multi-agent coordination and negotiation approaches for SLA management in SOA.

FUTURE RESEARCH DIRECTIONS

Even though the project has successfully finished and provides an impressive set of achievements (cf. next section), not all (implemented) results can be considered being in a product-ready state yet. Some of the component implementations still miss some planned features and capabilities which may increase their usability to a higher level for commercial entities. This is detailed in the BREIN Evaluation Report (Schubert, 2010). However, in most of the cases, the features should be comparatively easy to realize and were simply not addressed as they were not in the main scope of BREIN.

As the projects main concern was into achieving innovations, integration has been performed where needed, but a fully integrated standalone framework is not available. In terms of future research directions, one main area will be the transfer of the Grid knowledge and concepts not only to business Grids but also to the upcoming trend of cloud computing. Clouds have gained interest by the business stakeholders as this concept is industry driven.

The recently published report on the future of cloud computing (Jeffery, 2010) reports several future research topics, which are:

- Enhanced Scale and Elastic Scalability
- Further developments in Trust, Security and Privacy
- Data Handling
- Programming Models and Resource Control
- Systems Development and Systems Management
- Non-Technically:
- Economical Aspects
- Legalistic Issues

Whilst we avoid now replicating the work of this report (explicit definitions can be found for every topic in the document), some additional, not necessarily Cloud-related future research topics has been found during the developments in BREIN.

Using BREIN ontologies, we can now describe semantically the required QoS parameters for a requested computational job, and if we have the semantically described technical (resource) requirements for a job, we can schedule, monitor and adapt job execution, there is a missing chain between these two requirement sets. Further research is needed to explore the possibilities of reasoning about the resources required for a given SLA, especially in business scenarios, where resource consumption has direct cost effects.

Even though flexibility was introduced by BREIN, a general problem of existing and upcoming solution is that once they are released and new capabilities need to be added (as enhancement or just for the purpose of performing experiments) huge effort is required.

This often leads to the situation where, instead of re-using existing solutions, a new implementation is developed from scratch, especially if it is not the same developer. One future research topic for Grids/Clouds etc is to overcome this issue. Probably, a complete re-thinking has to take place to ensure the continuous evolution towards highly valuable components. Initial concepts had already the idea to integrate the mechanisms and concepts of the Open Model Methodology to allow for abstraction of the capabilities of the system.

A potential approach may be the split of logic and execution base. One could imagine here a plug-in like approach (as described by Koller, 2009, for SLA Management) which allows using a common base implementation whilst changing the logic behind and by that to enable a flexible behaviour of the system. Enabling this would open new opportunities in terms of self-adaptation, as this might allow the system to re-configure itself based on the current context/situation and to increase the competitiveness of its user to a highest degree.

CONCLUSION

To detail the achievements of BREIN with respect to the four main objectives: (i) Autonomy and Automation, (ii) Self-Optimization, (iii) Context-Aware Security, and (iv) Reduced Complexity of Use, we can conclude the following:

Autonomy and Automation

BREIN has enhanced here the state of the art of Grids. The achieved agentification of Grid resources allows for representation of each Grid resource and Service Provider by means of goal-driven software agents. This all is based on the Semantic BDI architecture paradigm. BREIN has embedded decentralized coordination mechanisms within the Framework which makes the use of protocols for resource allocation much more flexible (e.g. with reverse and combinatorial auctions such as the Combinatorial Contract Net Interaction Protocol, CCNP).

In addition resource allocation is enhanced and automated with semantics and virtualization technologies (The Semantically Enhanced Resource Allocator – SERA component as presented in the Architecture document, Laria et al. 2009). In terms of management policies, the BREIN Framework foresees that all Service Level Agreements are offered and negotiated in accordance with the policies of the respective business entity. Thereby policies can be priority driven and may have a high impact on decisions in the system, which may lead to situations where e-Contracts and SLAs are violated on purpose to fulfil another contract.

The Resources themselves can behave in a self-adaptive manner, to ensure fulfilment of SLAs. In case of unexpected events, the BREIN resource management framework adapts the resources automatically and by that enhances the reliability level for the User.

Self-Optimization

The semantic annotations as introduced for service properties allow for enhanced Service Discovery and Selection functionalities. At the same time, these mechanisms enable automated negotiation of Service Level Agreements, which take into account the policies and goals of the respective participants.

For the purpose of self-optimization to avoid violations, the concept of preventive SLAs was added. These preventive SLAs are an adapted version of the SLA with thresholds to enable early detection of upcoming misbehaviour and belong to a set of Risk Management tools for Service Provider and Customer. The BDI paradigm, which was adopted by BREIN, allows for goal-oriented self-optimization through the representation of goals of each software agent and thus actor in the Grid in a formal way (explicitly based on a common conceptualization of the domain, the BREIN Domain Ontologies).

Context-Aware Security

Even though not detailed and discussed in this chapter, the BREIN security addresses a set of challenges of e-Business Security support. BREIN bridges between the high-level security requirements which derive from business objectives and the concrete low level security configuration at the deployment level. BREIN VOs are dynamic and by that need adequate security mechanisms to address cases where e.g. employees of new customers need to be provisioned dynamically with access to a provider's services. Subtle changes in a user context leads automatically to different authorizations. This was often ignored by previous systems but is now addressed by BREIN Security.

Finally BREIN allows for putting own security controls on resources, which are outside of the own organizational boundary, which addresses a more and more increasing need from Customer.

Reduced Complexity of Usage

As several time mentioned, the complexity of previous Grid frameworks was often a reason that hindered the uptake of this technology in business. BREIN developments were performed by trying to balance carefully between the complexity of the solutions themselves and the easy access towards their use. Therefore the complexity of the framework is hidden by extensive automation, e.g. by allowing for automatic creation of virtual machines on demand or resource infrastructure encapsulation (addressing also the upcoming field of Infrastructure as a service, IaaS).

Semantic annotations of Resource, Workflow and Service/SLA descriptions provides the means for enhances specification of terms and to map them more easy within the system. The best example for this, which was also presented in this chapter, is the Semantic Annotated SLA specification. Generally speaking, the integration of Multi-agents and Semantics into the Grid was a big success, showing what may be achieved when leaving the fixed boundaries of the research/ developments path and trying to find complementary concepts and technologies resulting from other domains.

BREIN has successfully validated the "Brain meets brawn" concept, as presented by Foster 2004.

The Framework was designed, partially implemented and validation took place according to the two distinct scenarios ("Virtual Engineering" by ANSYS and "Logistics at the Airport" by the Stuttgart Airport).

The coupling of Grid resources and multi-agent technology allows a seamless utilization of Multi-agent coordination and negotiation approaches for SLA management in the Grid. Using a single message bus for both agents and WSs and exchange of semantic content based on shared ontologies enables advanced inter-organizational interoperability. Heterogeneous Grid and agent environments can use a homogeneous message transport layer which reduces the complexity of system administration. It also enables secure inter-organizational transfer of agent messages between agent platforms, thus facilitating the advantages of both multi-agent and Grid technologies in a single environment. An example for the successful application of all these benefits is SLA negotiation. SLAs can be interpreted and reasoned about inside agents, enabling the use of agent cooperation mechanisms for SLA negotiation. The utilization of explicit semantics further facilitates the semantic interoperability by incorporating domain knowledge in all phases of the service life cycle.

BREIN evolved diverging research with respect to business Grids into a coherent architecture/ concept and managed to keep its development as actual as possible. This led to the very important fact, that BREIN was able to align and validate the framework with the new upcoming Cloud (Infrastructure) Technologies, such as Amazon EC2.

REFERENCES

Andrieux, A., Czajkowski, K., Dan, A., Keahey, K., Ludwig, H., Nakata, T., & Xu, M. (2007). Web Services Agreement specification (WS-Agreement). *Open Grid Forum - Grid Resource Allocation and Agreement Protocol Working Group* (Technical Report GFD.107). Retrieved November 5, 2010, from http://www.ggf.org/documents/ GFD.107.pdf

Beco, S., Cantalupo, B., Giammarino, L., Matskanis, N., & Surridge, M. (2005). OWL-WS: A workflow ontology for dynamic grid service composition. In *Proceedings of the 1ˢᵗ International Conference on E-science and grid Computing* (pp. 148-155). Melbourne, Australia: IEEE Computer Society.

Bratman, M. E., Israel, J., & Pollack, M. E. (1988). Plans and resource-bounded practical reasoning. *Computational Intelligence*, *4*, 349–355. doi:10.1111/j.1467-8640.1988.tb00284.x

Brooke, J., Fellows, D., Garwood, K. L., & Goble, C. A. (2004). Semantic matching of grid resource descriptions. In *Proceedings of the European Across grids Conference* (pp.240-249). Berlin-Heidelberg, Germany: Springer.

caBIG (2010). Retrieved April 15, 2010, from https://cabig.nci.nih.gov

Corcho, O., Alper, P., Kotsiopoulos, I., Missier, P., Bechhofer, S., & Goble, C. (2006). An overview of s-ogsa: A reference semantic grid architecture. *Journal of Web Semantics*, *4*, 102–115. doi:10.1016/j.websem.2006.03.001

Cummings, J., Finholt, T., Foster, I., Kesselman, C., & Lawrence, K. A. (2008). Beyond being there: A blueprint for advancing the design, development, and evaluation of virtual organization. *Final report from workshops on building effective virtual organizations*. Retrieved July 28, 2010, from http://www.ci.uchicago.edu/ events/ VirtOrg2008/ VO_report.pdf

Foster, I., Jennings, N. R., & Kesselman, C. (2004). Brain meets brawn: Why grid and agents need each other. In *Proceedings of the 3ʳᵈ International Conference on Autonomous Agents and Multiagent Systems* (pp. 8-15*)*. New York, USA: IEEE Computer Society.

Foster, I., & Kesselman, C. (2002). *The grid: Blueprint for a new computing infrastructure.*

Foster, I., & Kesselman, C. (2006). Scaling system-level science: Scientific exploration and IT implications. *Computer IEEE Computer Society*, *39*(11), 31–39.

Foster, I., Kesselman, C., & Tuecke, S. (2001). *The anatomy of the grid: Enabling scalable*

GRAAP-WG. (2010). Web Services Agreement specification (WS-Agreement). Retrieved on March 14, 2010, from http://www.ogf.org/ documents/ GFD.107.pdf.

Greenwood, D., & Calisti, M. (2004). Engineering Web service - Agent integration. In *Proceedings of the IEEE International Conference on Systems, Man & Cybernetics* (vol. 2, pp. 1918-1925). Washington, DC., USA: IEEE Computer Society.

gridgridFujitsu Lab, E. (2008). *NextGrid*. Retrieved April 14, 2010 from: http://www.nextgrid. org/ download/ publications/

gridLaria, G., Karaenke, P., Klein, A., Leukel, J., Schuele, M., Kotsiopoulos, I.,Micsik, A. (2010). *Final BREIN Architecture - D4.1.3 V2*. Retrieved August 26, 2010, from http://www.eu-brein.com/ index.php?option= com_ docman&task= doc_ view&gid= 63

Haugeneder, H., & Steiner, D. (1994). Ein mehragentenansatz zur unterstützung kooperativer arbeit . In Hasenkamp, U., Kirn, St., & Syring, M. (Eds.), *CSCW – Computer Supported Cooperative Work* (pp. 203–229). Boston, MA, USA: Addison Wesley.

Hepp, M., & Roman, D. (2007). An ontology framework for semantic business process management. In *Proceedings of Wirtschaftsinformatik 2007*, Karlsruhe, Germany.

ITIL. (2009). *IT infrastructure library*. Retrieved August 3, 2010, from http://www.itil.org

Jeffery, K., Neidecker-Lutz, B., & Schubert, L. (2010). *The future of cloud computing – Opportunities for European cloud computing beyond 2010* (Expert Group Report v1.0).

Karaenke, P., & Kirn, S. (2010). A multi-tier negotiation protocol for logistics service chains. In *Proceedings of the 18ᵗʰ European Conference on Information Systems (ECIS 2010)*, Pretoria, South Africa. Retrieved December 4, 2010, from http://web.up.ac.za/ ecis/ ECIS2010PR/ ECIS2010/ Content/ Papers/ 0068.R1.pdf

Karaenke, P., Micsik, A., & Kirn, S. (2009). Adaptive SLA management along value chains for service individualization, In *International Symposium on Services Science*, Leipzig, Germany (March 2009). Retrieved June 2, 2010, from http://cordis.europa.eu/ fp7/ ict/ ssai/ docs/ cloud- report- final.pdf

Keller, A., & Ludwig, H. (2003). The WSLA framework: Specifying and monitoring service level agreements for Web services. *Journal of Network and Systems Management, 11*(1), 57–81. doi:10.1023/A:1022445108617

Kim, E., & Lee, Y. (2005). OASIS quality model for Web services version 2.0. Retrieved November 23, 2010, from http://www.oasis-open.org/ committees/ download.php/ 15910/ WSQM-ver-2.0.doc

Koller, B. (2009). Towards optimal creation of service level agreements. In *Proceedings of the eChallenges 2009 Conference (eChallenges 2009)*. Istanbul, Turkey. IIMC International Information Management Corporation, ISBN: 978-1-905824-13-7.

Kopecky, J., Vitvar, T., Bournez, C., & Farrell, J. (2007). SAWSDL: Semantic annotations for WSDL and XML schema. *IEEE Internet Computing, 11*(6), 60–67. doi:10.1109/MIC.2007.134

Kotsiopoulos, I., Munoz Frutos, H., Koller, B., Wesner, S., & Brooke, J. (2009). A lightweight semantic bridge between clouds and grids. In *Proceedings of the eChallenges 2009 Conference (eChallenges 2009),* Instanbul, Turkey. IIMC International Information Management Corporation, ISBN: 978-1-905824-13-7.

Kotsiopoulos, I., Soler Jubert, I., Tenschert, A., Benedicto Cirujeda, J., & Koller, B. (2008). Using semantic technologies to improve negotiation of service level agreements. In *Exploiting the Knowledge Economy - Issues, Applications, Case Studies (eChallenges 2008)* (vol. 5, pp. 1045-1052), Stockholm, Sweden. IIMC International Information Management Corporation.

Lawrence, R., & Hyoil, H. (2005). Survey of semantic annotation platforms. In *Proceedings of the 2005 ACM symposium on Applied computing* (pp. 1634-1638). Santa Fe, New Mexico: ACM.

LHC - The Large Hadron Collider. (2010). Retrieved April 15, 2010, from http://lhc.web.cern.ch/lhc/

Martin, D., Burstein, M., McDermott, D., McIlraith, S., Paolucci, M., Sycara, K., & Srinivasan, N. (2007). Bringing semantics to Web services with OWL-S. *Journal of World Wide Web, 10*(3), 243–277. doi:10.1007/s11280-007-0033-x

Micsik, A., Frutos, H. M., Kotsiopoulos, I., & Koller, B. (2009). Semantically supported SLA negotiation. In *Proceedings of the 10ᵗʰ IEEE/ACM International Conference on grid Computing.* Banff, Canada: IEEE Computer Society.

Micsik, A., Pallinger, P., & Klein, A. (2009). Soap based message transport for the jade multiagent platform. In *Proceedings of the 8th International Conference on Autonomous Agents and Multiagent Systems* (pp. 101-104). Industry track, Budapest, Hungary.

Moshowitz, A. (1986). Social dimensions of office automation. *Advances in Computer, 25*, 335–404. doi:10.1016/S0065-2458(08)60477-5

OGSA. (2004). *Towards open gridgrid services architecture*. Retrieved October 10, 2010, from http://www.globus.org/ogsa/

Parnas, D. (1972). On the criteria to be used in decomposing systems into modules. *Communications of the ACM, 15*(12), 1053–1058. doi:10.1145/361598.361623

San Francisco, CA: Morgan Kaufmann Publishers.

SCEC. (2010). *Southern California Earthquake Center*. Retrieved on April 15, 2010, from http://www.scec.org/

Schubert, L., et al. (2010). *BREIN Deliverable D5.6.2 - Evaluation Report*. Retrieved October 12, 2010, http:\\\www.gridsforbusiness.eu

Shafiq, O. M., Ali, A., Ahmad, H. F., & Suguri, H. (2005). AgentWeb gateway - A middleware for dynamic integration of multi agent system and Aeb services framework. In *Proceedings of the 14th IEEE International Workshops on Enabling Technologies: Infrastructure for Collaborative Enterprise* (pp. 267-268). Washington, DC., USA: IEEE Computer Society.

TeleManagement Forum. (2005). SLA management handbook: Concepts and principles (vol. 2). *TM Forum*. Retrieved April 26, 2010, from http://www.tmforum.org/ browse. aspx? linkID= 30755& docID= 11888

TeraGrid. (2010). Retrieved April 15, 2010, from https://www.teragrid.org/

Terracina, A., Beco, S., Kirkham, T., Gallop, J., Johnson, I., Mac Randal, D., & Ritchie, B. (2006). Orchestration and workflow in a mobile grid environment. In *Proceedings of the 5th International Conference on grid and Cooperative Computing Workshops* (pp. 251-258). Washington, DC., USA: IEEE Computer Society.

virtual organizations. (LNCS 2150, pp. 1-4). Berlin-Heidelberg, Germany: Springer.

Wilson, M. D., Schubert, L., & Arenas, A. (2007). *The TrustCoM framework for trust, security and contract management of Web services and the grid V4* (Technical Report). Retrieved October 11, 2010, from http://epubs.cclrc.ac.uk/ work-details?w= 37589

ADDITIONAL READING

Bali, V., Singh Rathore, R., Sirohi, A., & Verma, A. (2009). Information Technology architectures for grid computing and application. In *Proceedings of the 4th International Multi-Conference on Computing in the Global Information Technology* (pp. 52-56). Washington, DC., USA: IEEE Computer Society.

Bird, I., Jones, B., & Kee, K. F. (2009). The organization and management of grid infrastructures. *Computer, 42*(1), 36–46. doi:10.1109/MC.2009.28

Cope, J., & Tufo, H. M. (2008). Adapting grid services for urgent computing environments. In J. Cordeiro, B. Shishkov, A. Ranchordas, & M. Helfert (Eds.), *Proceedings of the 3rd International Conference on Software and Data Technologies (ICSOFT, PL/DPS/KE)* (pp. 135–142). Institute for Systems and Technologies of Information, Control and Communication (INSTICC) Press.

Farrell, J., & Lausen, H. (2007). *Semantic annotations for WSDL and XML schema*. Retrieved on July 10, 2010, from http://www.w3.org/TR/sawsdl

Gruber, T. R. (1995). Towards principles for the design of ontologies used for knowledge sharing? *International Journal of Human-Computer Studies, 43*(5-6), 907–928. doi:10.1006/ijhc.1995.1081

Haller, J., Schubert, L., & Wesner, S. (2006). Private business infrastructures in a VO environment. In P. Cunningham, & M. Cunningham (Eds.), *Exploiting the knowledge economy: Issues, applications, case studies* (vol. 3, pp. 1064-1071). BG Amsterdam, The Netherlands: IOS Press.

Herenger, H., Heek, R., Kuebert, R., & Surridge, M. (2007). Operating virtual organizations using bipartite service level agreements . In Talia, D., Yahyapour, R., & Ziegler, W. (Eds.), *grid middleware and services: Challenges and solutions* (pp. 359–373). US: Springer.

Jacek, K., Tomas, V., Carine, B., & Joel, F. (2007). SAWSDL: Semantic annotations for WSDL and XML schema. *IEEE Internet Computing 1089-7801, 11*(6), 60-67.

Karaenke, P., & Kirn, S. (2007). Service level agreements: An evaluation from a business application perspective. In *Proceedings of eChallenges 2007 Conference*. Netherlands: IEEE Computer Society.

Koch, S., Strecker, S., & Frank, U. (2006). Conceptual modelling as a new entry in the bazaar: The open model approach . In Damiani, E., Fitzgerald, B., Scacchi, W., Scotto, M., & Succi, G. (Eds.), *IFIP International Federation for Information Processing* (*Vol. 203*, pp. 9–20). Berlin, Germany: Springer.

Kopecký, J., Vitvar, T., Bournez, C., & Farrell, J. (2007). SAWSDL: Semantic annotations for WSDL and XML schema. *IEEE Internet Computing, 11*(6), 60–67. doi:10.1109/MIC.2007.134

Kotsiopoulos, I., Soler Juber, S., Tenschert, A., Benedicto Cirujeda, J., & Koller, B. (2008). Using semantic technologies to improve negotiation of service level agreements, *eChallenges '08.*

Kritikos, K., & Plexousakis, D. (2007). A semantic QoS-based Web service discovery algorithm for over-constrained demands. In *Proceedings of the 3rd International Conference on Next Generation Web Services Practices* (pp. 49-54). Washington, DC, USA, IEEE Computer Society.

Ludwig, H., Nakata, T., Waeldrich, O., Wieder, P., & Ziegler, W. (2006). Reliable orchestration of resources using WS-Agreement. In *Proceedings of the 2006 International Conference on High Performance Computing and Communications (HPCC-06)* (LNCS 4208, pp. 753-762). Berlin-Heidelberg, Germany: Springer, 2006.

Micsik, A., & Karaenke, P. (2009). Agent-supported service management and monitoring for flexible interenterprise cooperation. In *Proceedings of the International Conference on Research and Practical Issues of Enterprise Information Systems (CONFENIS 2009)*. Gyor, Hungary.

Mowshowitz, A. (2001). Virtual organization: The new feudalism. *Computer, 34*(4), 110–112. doi:10.1109/MC.2001.917551

Mowshowitz, A. (2002). *Virtual organization: Toward a theory of societal transformation stimulated by information technology*. Quorum Books.

Muñoz Frutos, H., Kotsiopoulos, I., Vaquero Gonzalez, L. M., & Rodero Merino, L. (2009). Enhancing service selection by semantic QoS. In *Proceedings of the 6th European Semantic Web Conference on the Semantic Web: Research and Applications* (pp. 565-577). Berlin: Springer-Verlag.

Oldham, N., Verma, K., Sheth, A., & Hakimpour, F. (2006). Semantic WS-agreement partner selection. In *Proceedings of the 15th International Conference on World Wide Web* (pp. 697-706). New York, NY: ACM.

OWL Working Group. (2010). *Web Ontology Language (OWL)*. Retrieved June 28, 2010, form http://www.w3.org/2004/OWL/, 2004.

Papazoglou, M. P., & Heuvel, W. J. (2007). Service oriented architectures: Approaches, technologies and research issues. *The International Journal on Very Large Data Bases Journal, 16*(3), 389–415. doi:10.1007/s00778-007-0044-3

Rosenschein, J. S., & Zlotkin, G. (1994). *Rules of encounter*. Cambridge, MA: The MIT Press.

Wilson, M., Arenas, A., Chadwick, D., Dimitrakos, T., Doser, J., & Giambiagi, P. ...Tuptuk, N. (2006). The TrustCoM approach to enforcing agreements between interoperating enterprises. In G. Doumeingts, J. Müller, G. Morel, & B. Vallespir(Eds.), *Interoperability for Enterprise Software and Applications Conference* (pp. 365-375). London, UK: Springer.

Wooldridge, M. (2000). *Reasoning about rational agents*. Cambridge, MA: The MIT Press.

Wooldridge, M. (2009). *An introduction to multiagent systems*. Hoboken, NJ: John Wiley & Sons.

KEY TERMS AND DEFINITIONS

Grid: An inter-organizational stateful loosely-coupled Service-Oriented Architecture. grids are typically more focused on the resources backing them up (to which they provide an interface) than a classic SOA.

Multi-Agent System: Consists of agents that jointly solve a given problem by coordinating their individual behaviour. A multi-agent system is being formed by the inter-relations of the agents, not by an explicitly given problem. Thus a multi-agent system is a sub group within the agent society.

Ontology: An ontology is a formal, explicit specification of a shared conceptualization. It describes the concepts and inter-relations between these concepts of a domain of interest.

Quality-of-Service (QoS): In the Grid world, QoS describes a quantifiable, measurable level of a particular aspect of a service offered by a provider, such as service metering and cost, performance metrics (response time, for instance), security attributes, (transactional) integrity, reliability, scalability, and availability. QoS is described in terms, describing the entity that is measured, how it is measured, and the value (minimum, equality or maximum) to be achieved. QoS is formalized as a contractual agreement between customer and provider in an SLA, which is agreed by both parties as the level of service promised by the provider. Sometimes the contract will be terminated successfully, other times a penalty fee will be paid.

Service Level Agreement (SLA): A SLA is a contract between a service provider and a service user or customer that specifies the level of service that is expected during the term of the contract. SLAs might specify availability requirements, response times for routine and ad hoc queries, and response time for problem resolution (network down, machine failure, etc.) (see also OGSA Glossary).

Virtual Organization (VO): BREIN was concerned with business Grids where the formation of virtual organisation is in fact a collaboration between organisations with clearly defined business objectives. The stakeholders of a virtual organisation seek to create new business opportunities through a set of potentially dynamic business relationships which can be represented as a combination of 1-1 and ad-hoc contracts and understandings which clearly define the liability for the offered services.

Web Service (WS): A Web service is a software service offering an interface described in a machine-processable format (specifically WSDL). Requesters interact with the Web service using SOAP messages, typically conveyed using HTTP with an XML serialization. Other message formats and protocols can also be used, but are not standardized.

Chapter 15
Flow–Based Networking Architectures under Mixed Internet and Grid Traffic

César Cárdenas
Tecnológico de Monterrey – Campus Querétaro, México

Maurice Gagnaire
Telecom ParisTech, France

Víctor López
Universidad Autónoma de Madrid, Spain

ABSTRACT

Quality-of-Service (QoS) is a key issue for grid services provisioning. QoS architectures originally developed for the Internet such as DiffServ (DS) have been tested in grid environment. We present in this chapter the investigation on the potentialities of a new innovative Internet QoS architecture known as Flow-Aware Networking (FAN). FAN is a flow-based networking architecture and it appears as the most promising alternative to DS for QoS provisioning in IP networks. DS proceeds to traffic differentiation and QoS provisioning through IP packet marking whereas FAN consists in implicit IP flow differentiation and a flow-based admission control. A grid traffic session may be seen as a succession of parallel TCP flows with voluminous data transfers (e.g. GridFTP). In this chapter, we compare by means of computer simulations the performance of FAN and DS architectures under the mix traffic composed by Internet and grid services.

DOI: 10.4018/978-1-61350-113-9.ch015

INTRODUCTION

Grid networks consist in large-scale distributed hardware and software resources (computing, storage, information, network components, equipment, sensors, etc.) that provide flexible, pervasive, and cost-effective services to the users. The "Grid" term has been adopted in analogy with the power Grid. Furthermore, by sharing distributed resources on-demand, grid networks enable the creation of virtual organizations (utility computing, utility storage, etc.) (Foster & Kesselman, 2003). Grid networks are progressively deployed over IP (Internet Protocol) networks. Several IP access router architectures have been proposed for QoS provisioning in IP-based Grid networks. Some of them are inspired from the DS architecture: GARA (Foster, Roy, & Sander, 2000), NRSE (Bhatti et al., 2003), G-QoSM (Al-Ali et al., 2004), and GNRB (Adami et al., 2006). Nevertheless, none of these proposals has been widely adopted. QoS provisioning for IP-based Grid networks remains today a big challenge because of the distributed nature of physical components and network resources. To solve this problem, several investigations referring to DS have been carried out (Sander et al., 2000), (Foster et al., 2004), (Leigh et al., 2000), (Rio et al., 2003). Moreover, new QoS concepts and architectures have been tested in experimental platforms: Equivalent Differentiated Services (EDS) (Vicat-Blanc, Echantillac, & Goutelle, 2005), programmable networks (Vicat-Blanc & Chanussot, 2004), active networks (Lefevre et al., 2001), DiffServ-IntServ approach (Yang et al., 2003). This work proposes the evaluation of a new promising approach for QoS provisioning in Grid networks called Flow-Aware Networking (FAN) (Oueslati & Roberts, 2005). Whereas DS-based approaches proceed to per-packet traffic control, FAN relies on per-flow traffic control mechanisms. Compared with packet-based router, the FAN architecture offers enhanced performance in terms of packet processing (Park et al., 2006). Our previous work (Cárdenas et al., 2007; Cárdenas et al., 2008; Cárdenas & Gagnaire, 2008; Cárdenas et al., 2009; Cárdenas & Gagnaire, 2009) has shown that the second generation of FAN (2G-FAN) confirms the superiority of FAN over DS under Grid traffic only, even if flow parallelization of Grid sessions tends to reduce this benefit. In this work we extend our previous analysis by introducing Internet traffic and Grid traffic. The traffic load of the Grid services is increased assuming that in future years this kind of traffic will increase. Internet traffic modeled at the flow level can be represented by two types of flows: elastic and streaming. Elastic flows are legacy file transfers and Web traffic while streaming flows are Voice over IP services. Two metrics are adopted: the average transit delay and the average goodput of a Grid session in an IP access router.

This chapter is organized as follows. In following section, we briefly recall the basic characteristics and objectives the DS architecture and its application to the grid environment through several QoS provisioning architectures. Here, we describe the GARA architecture (Foster, Roy, & Sander, 2000) that aims to extend the DS functionalities for the Grid environment and is the most important proposal. The section of Flow-Aware Networking (FAN) Architecture is dedicated to the description of the second generation FAN (2GFAN) architecture. Initially designed for traditional IP networks, we show how the 2GFAN architecture may be adapted to the grid environment. In next section, we compare by means of computer simulations the performance of DS and 2GFAN architectures applied to IP access routers in the context of Grid and Internet traffic. We describe and conclude this chapter in the two final sections.

BACKGROUND

Native IP technology is connectionless and only offers Best Effort (BE) services. Two paradigms have been proposed to improve QoS in IP networks: Integrated Services (IntServ) (Braden et al., 1997) and Differentiated Services (DiffServ) (Blake et al., 1998). IntServ (IS) is based on the concept of flow defined as a packet stream that requires a specified QoS level and it is identified by the vector "IP source address, IP destination address, Protocol, TCP/UDP source port, TCP/UDP destination port."

QoS is reached by the appropriate tuning of different mechanisms: resource reservation, admission control, packet scheduling and buffer management. Both packet scheduling and buffer management act on per-flow basis. The state of the flows must be maintained in the routers and periodically updated by means of a resource reservation signaling system. Since it needs to detect each single flow, the cost and complexity increase with the number of flows, IS lacks of scalability.

DS has been proposed to solve the scalability problems of IS. DS classify an aggregation of the traffic in 64 different classes by means of a label in the DS Code Point (DSCP) field of the IPv4 packet header. Identification is performed at edge nodes. The DSCP specifies a forwarding behavior (Per-Hop Behavior; PHB) within the DS domain. Same DSCP may have different meanings in consecutive domains and negotiations are needed. The class selector PHB offers three forwarding priorities: Expedited Forwarding (EF), Assured Forwarding (AF) and Best Effort (BE). Packets marked with the highest drop precedence are dropped with lower probability than those characterized by the lowest drop precedence. Although DS does not suffer from scalability problems, it is not able to provide the required end-to-end QoS to IP flows (Giordano et al., 2003). To overcome the limitations of IS and DS, the Flow-Aware Networking (FAN) approach (Roberts & Oueslati, 2000) described below has been proposed.

Currently, almost all grid services are being supported by undifferentiated, nondeterministic, best effort IP services. Grid networks must support many large-scale data-intensive applications requiring high-volume and high-performance data communications. In grid networks, network performance is not limited to the support for high-volume data flows. It is also measured by the capacity of the network to control fine-grained applications (Travostino, Mambretti, & Karmous-Edwards, 2006).

Early attempts to integrate grid environments and networks services were primarily focused on Application Programming Interfaces (APIs) that linked the grid services to Layer 3 services. Using this approach, DS-based router interfaces must ensure that applications requirements could be fulfilled by network resources and are controlled by grid services. The combination of Grid services and DS techniques provides capabilities for governing many basic network process elements, including those related to policy-based service determination, priority setting, highly granulated (individual packet) behavior control (through DSCP marking), application classification, flow characteristic specification, service level specification, policy governance for services, resource requests (including those for router resources), dedicated allocation, use monitoring, and fault detection and recovery (Travostino, Mambretti, & Karmous-Edwards, 2006).

Moreover, experiments demonstrated that combining grid services DS (EF), can provide grid applications with significant control over network behavior. These initiatives showed that this control can be implemented not only at network edge point, but also within edge hosts. All these remarks are at the origin of the General-purpose Architecture for Reservation and Allocation (GARA) (Foster, Roy, & Sander, 2000) specifications that are part of the Globus Tool kit (GT). GARA was created to manage admission control, scheduling, and configurations for grid resources, including network resources. GARA has been used in experimental implementations to interlink grid applications with IS and DS-based routers as well as for Layer 3 resource allocation, monitoring, and other functions on local or wide-area networks. GARA is extensible to other network layers and is not specifically oriented to services at a specific layer. GTK is currently being extended to Open Grid Services Architecture (OGSA) which also embraces Web services.

Other efforts to provide network QoS in grid networks are: NRSE (Bhatti et al., 2003), G-QoSM (Al-Ali et al., 2004), and GNRB (Adami et al., 2006). Network Resource Scheduling Entity (NRSE) try to overcome the difficulties of GARA by storing per-flow/per-application state only at the end-host involved in the communication. Service demands can also be online or in advance. Furthermore, NRSE can negotiate automatically a multi-domain reservation by communicating with its counterpart on the remote network, on behalf of its user. A drawback of NRSE is that the API is not clearly defined.

Grid Quality of Service Management (G-QoSM) is a framework to support QoS management under the Open Grid Service Architecture (OGSA). It supports many types of resources. Grid Network-aware Resource Broker (GNRB) is a centralized and enhanced per-domain Grid Resource Broker with the capabilities provided by a Network Resource Manager. GNRB make possible the design and implementation of new mapping/scheduling mechanisms to take into account network and computational resources. GNRB allows requests of network status and can reserve network resources. A problem may arise when the number of administrative domains rises up since the GNRB may become a bottleneck. Also, the administrative domain is very sensitive to GNRB failure. A new concept for QoS provisioning in grid networks based on Virtual Machine approach is in development (Keahey et al., 2005). It provides very fine grain reservations of CPU time, disk and network bandwidth. The main idea is the reservation of resources and the run of the jobs on top of them.

FLOW-AWARE NETWORKING (FAN) ARCHITECTURE

Flow-Aware Networking (FAN) Architecture

As mentioned above, currently, almost all grid services are being supported by undifferentiated, nondeterministic, best effort IP services. In terms of QoS provisioning, IS lacks of scalability. DS has been proposed to solve the scalability problems of IS. Although DS does not suffer from scalability problems, it is not able to provide the required end-to-end QoS to IP flows (Giordano et al., 2003). Most of the traditional QoS provisioning architectures for grid services are based on the DS architecture and modifications. To overcome the limitations of IS and DS, the Flow-Aware Networking (FAN) approach (Roberts & Oueslati, 2000) has been proposed. FAN was previously studied and compared versus DS under grid traffic only (Cárdenas et al., 2007; Cárdenas et al., 2008; Cárdenas and Gagnaire 2008; Cárdenas et al. 2009; Cárdenas and Gagnaire 2009). In this chapter we extend previous work by evaluating and comparing FAN versus DS under mixed Internet and grid traffic.

A first generation (1G) of FAN was proposed in (Roberts & Oueslati, 2000) as a new approach to offer QoS at flow level. A flow can be considered a stream of packets with same header attributes and with a maximum inter-packet space and is classified explicitly (like in DS). Second generation of FAN (2GFAN) performs implicit classification (no packet marking as in DS, no resource reservation as in IS) of flows into either streaming (high-priority) or elastic (low-priority), and defines an admission control mechanism. 2GFAN seeks two objectives: on the one hand, it gives preference to streaming flows on attempts to minimize the delay and loss (signal conservation) they experience but, at the same time, it aims at assuring a minimum throughput rate to elastic flows (throughput conservation).

Figure 1. One FAN routers' interface

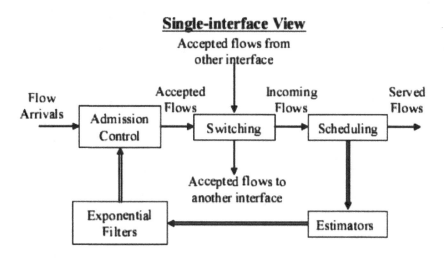

2GFAN simplifies network operations leading to potentially significant costs reductions in the IP backbone because it increases network efficiency. It requires no change to existing protocols and no new protocols, it can be implemented as an individual device connected to each BE router interface. 2GFAN combines two flow-based traffic control mechanisms: Per-flow Fair Queuing (pfFQ) and Per-flow Admission Control (pfAC). pfFQ ensures that link bandwidth is shared equitably between contending flows and pfAC ensures the scheduler performs correctly even in overload by keeping the rate at pfFQ above a minimum threshold. On high capacity links fair queuing is enough to guarantee low packet delay and loss for real-time flows (whose rate is less than the fair rate). An accepted flow is protected during all its transmission time if the time interval between two packets of that flow keeps below a timeout value. To this aim, accepted flows are registered in a list called Protected Flow List (PFL). Figure 1 shows one interface of FAN router.

The queuing in 2GFAN architectures has one priority queue and a secondary queuing system. The admission control is proactive measurement-based and of threshold type. Packets of flows emitting at less than the current rate in pfFQ are

given priority. To accomplish their tasks, 2GFAN uses two estimators: Priority Load (PL) and Fair Rate (FR). PL is the service rate of the priority queue and FR is the service rate a new TCP flow can get when using fair queuing. PL is estimated every several milliseconds (packet timescale) and FR is estimated every several hundred milliseconds (flow timescale). The fair rate measure is equivalent to the available throughput available for a new TCP connection and is estimated using the TCP phantom technique (Afek Mansour, & Ostfeld, 1996). The priority load estimator represents the amount of bytes served by the priority queue during the sampling period. Figure 2 shows the structure of the admission control. Where, C is the link capacity, FRth is the minimal FR or guaranteed rate, and PLth is the maximal PL.

Incoming flows are denied access to the system, when the 2GFAN architecture cannot guarantee a given performance level (delay and fair rate). The complete process is as follows: When a packet arrives at the system, the admission control finds the flow, fn, it belongs to and evaluates whether such fn is in its inner Protected Flow List (PFL). This list stores the IDs of each flow already accepted and transmitted over the IP layer. If

Figure 2. Mathematical structure of the FAN's admission control

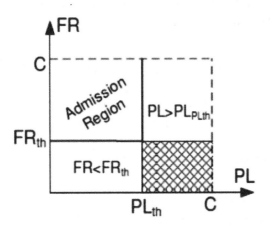

fn∈PFL, then the packet is served. Otherwise, the packet is part of a new flow which must pass through the admission control process. When so, it is tested whether PL<PLth and FR>FRth, that is, whether a given QoS guarantees defined by the PLth and FRth thresholds are maintained or not. If this is the case, the new flow is accepted; otherwise, it is rejected. Although flows already accepted are somehow protected, only those flows which transmit at a lower rate than FRth are treated as streaming flows (high-priority). All the others are considered as elastic flows and receive less preference. This is done in order to avoid flows which abuse from the system resources. Finally, a Priority Fair Queuing (PFQ) policy, as defined by Kortebi, Oueslati, & Roberts (2004) which is based on the Start-time Fair Queuing algorithm (Goyal, Harrick, & Chen, 1996), is used to give preference to streaming over elastic flows. This process is explained in Figure 3.

Basically, PFQ is a PIFO (Push In First Out) queue, which stores packet information (flow identifier, size and memory location) and time stamp, the latter determined by the SFQ algorithm. The PFQ queue is split into two areas delimited by a priority pointer (see Figure 4), whereby streaming flows are temporally stored at the pri-

ority queue area (at the head of the queue), and the elastic flows are stored at the tail of the queue. Preference is given to the priority area since it is served before the non-priority area. Finally, the queue stores elastic and streaming packet count statistics, which are further used to compute the values of PL and FR. In addition, an Active Flow List (AFL) is maintained by the PFQ. This list is similar to the PFL defined above, but it also saves the amount of packets transmitted per flow in the recent past. The flows with the greatest amount of transmitted packets, also known as greatest "backlog," may be discarded under severe congestion conditions. This list may be thought to pose scalability problems. However, as shown in (Kortebi et al., 2005), this is not the case, and 2GFAN scales well.

Some FAN architectures have been tested (Benameur, Oueslati, & Roberts, 2003), (Park et al. 2006), patented (Oueslati & Roberts, 2010), (Roberts, Oueslati, Kortebi, 2006), standardized (ITU-T E.417, 2005) and commercialized (Anagran, 2004). In addition, in (Park et al. 2006) authors compared flow-based and packet-based routers; flow-based approach offers enhanced performance in terms of packet processing. Also, to our knowledge, the only research work on QoS at flow level and related to grid networks but applied to cluster networks is (Sem-Jacobsen et al., 2004). Their results show that flow level bandwidth guarantees are achievable with two of their proposed admission control schemes; they achieved an order of magnitude in jitter and latency in individual flows. All the above show that FAN is a promising approach for provisioning QoS.

Motivations for FAN and DS Comparison under Grid Environment

If a new architectural paradigm (i.e. FAN) has to be explored for grid computing applications, a benchmark about its benefits versus the DiffServ architecture has a positive impact to the

Figure 3. FAN admission control flow diagrams

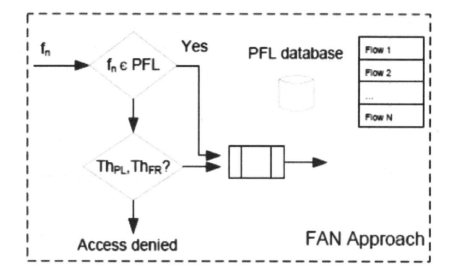

grid networking research community if the new architecture has benefits comparing to DiffServ. Our first motivation is to test if the flow-based approach is an alternative architecture of DS for provisioning QoS in grid networks. Second, we want to evaluate the advantages of flow-based admission control versus DS under grid environment. Moreover, with FAN, admissions decisions become network-aware or bring the network as first-class resource (Travostino, Mambretti, & Karmous-Edwards, 2006). Also, flow admission decisions in FAN are based on real-time measurements of the network performance. Network resources are then allocated according to the current network state. Additionally, the fact that FAN ensures a minimum throughput to elastic flows allows throughout guarantees to accepted GridFTP sessions. Third, In GARA advance reservation is one of the requirements and FAN can use its PFL to facilitate the reservation process. Our last motivation is due to the originality of our approach which has not yet been considered in the literature.

EVALUATION OF THE DIFFSERV AND FAN ARCHITECTURES UNDER INTERNET AND GRID TRAFFIC

Topology

Our first objective is to outline, by means of computer simulations, the benefit of FAN over DiffServ when both architectures are working under Internet and grid traffic. Also, we will study the effect of the variation of a specific grid traffic parameter (e.g. number of parallel TCPs per grid session) in the performance of FAN and DiffServ architectures. Discuss solutions and recommendations in dealing with the issues, controversies, or problems presented in the preceding section. We use event-driven simulations by means of the Network Simulator 2 (NS-2) to perform our evaluation. We use the dumbbell topology in our evaluation. This is the most used topology to evaluate TCP performance. This configuration, depicted in Figure 5, assimilates the IP backbone to an ingress edge router and to a remote egress router. Two types of traffic sources are connected to the ingress router via two optical point-to-point (P2P) optical access networks. The bandwidth ca-

Figure 4. Priority fair queueing system

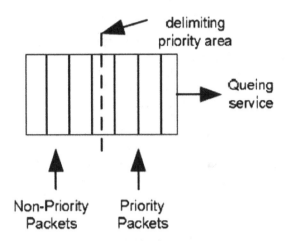

pacity of the optical fiber links is set to 100 Mbps. In choosing a P2P access architecture rather than a PON architecture has been mainly motivated by simplification purposes. Indeed, the impact of the MAC protocol of a PON should have brought an additional complexity. At the opposite, we wanted to describe the best as we could both traffic TCP/IP and grid traffic sources and FAN or DiffServ architectures in our simulation environment.

According to a survey about the real use of grid platforms (http://www.ec-gin.eu/), 73% of all the traffic use one-to-one communication scheme therefore a point-to-point simple dumbbell topology represents a real scenario. Figure 5 depicts our simulation scenario.

As mentioned above, three types of sources are connected to the border router. The capacity of the optical link used between the ingress and the egress routers is set to 200 Mbps. In practice, bit rates of the order of the Gps are achieved in an IP backbone. If an evaluation for 1Gbps is needed we assumed that scalability in simulations can be applied according to Pan et al. (2005).

We limited de facto this capacity to twice the capacity of the access link in order to guarantee acceptable simulation durations and memory space requirements. Propagation delay within the IP backbone has been set to 10 ms. We have

neglected such delays in the access network since 10 ms corresponds to 2000 km whereas an optical access link is of the order of a few tens of kilometers. The size Qc of the buffer used at the ingress router is set to delay bandwidth product of the IP backbone networks. We have then Qc = Delay x C = 10ms x 200Mbps = 2×10^6 bits. By taking a packet size of 1000 Bytes = 8000 bits per packet. Qc = 250 packets.

Internet and Grid Traffic

There is background traffic of Internet type. Internet traffic won't change during all simulations and is composed by single TCP flows representing WEB traffic and single UDP flows representing VoIP traffic. The interested traffic is grid and will be evaluated by increasing the load from it. All traffic sessions/flows (Internet and grid) will arrive following a Poisson process.

Internet traffic at packet level granularity can be approximated by a self-similar process (Crovella & Bestravos, 1997). Nevertheless, designing traffic control mechanisms for this traffic is very complex (e.g. Token Bucket configuration) (Oueslati & Roberts, 2005). By looking the Internet traffic at the granularity of flows is easy to see that the traffic is mostly concentrated on the TCP (elastic) and UDP (streaming). It was shown that traffic control at flow level is appropriate because users perceive QoS at this time-scale (Bonald & Roberts, 2003).

IP traffic may be represented by sessions mutually independent arriving as a stationary Poisson process (Floyd & Paxon, 2001) in the case of a large number of independent demands (Kulkarni, 1996). An Internet session is a set of flows whose originating times are separated by random times called "think times" (Roberts, 2004). This can be modeled as a Kelly network with a processor sharing queue and a infinite server feedback (Kelly, 1994). It has been shown that the output process for this network is Poisson if the input is also a stationary Poisson process. This property is known

Figure 5. IGoFAN experiment topology

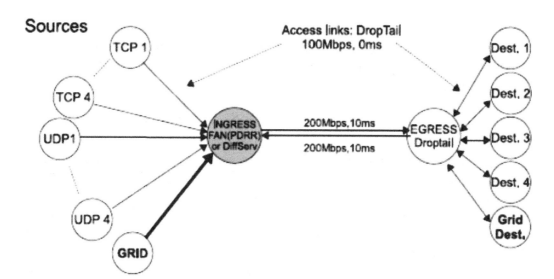

as Poisson-In-Poisson-Out (Chen & Yao, 2001) and justifies that flows, as conceived by FAN architectures, arrive following a Poisson Process.

IP traffic is mainly composed by single TCP flows and single UDP flows. Single TCP flows are of Reno type sending packets of 1000 Bytes with a maximum window size of 20 packets. The size of single TCP flows follows a distribution probability of truncated Pareto with parameter of 1.5 and an average flow size of 25 packets, minimal flow size of 8 packets and maximal flow size of 1000 packets. The Pareto distribution has the heavy-tail property. The heavy-tail property has been observed in Internet traffic measurements (Floyd, 2007). Truncated Pareto converges faster than Pareto non truncated (Masoom & Nadarajah, 2006). UDP flows are of on/off type. The duration of on and off periods follow an exponential distribution with average E[on] = 350ms and E[off] = 650ms. The rate of transmission when on is 64 Kbps. The average transmission rate is 0.35 x 64Kbps = 22.4 Kbps. The average size of UDP packets is 190 Bytes. The average duration of UDP flows is 60 seconds (1 minute).

To the best of our knowledge, no grid traffic modeling has been published at the date of this study (Volker, 2004). In this work, we assume that grid traffic arrivals follow a stationary Poisson process. Also, our model is based in the fact that the most used software platform in grid community is Globus Tool Kit (GTK) and offers a transport service called GridFTP (Madrichenko, 2005). GridFTP has the option of parallel channels where several TCP connections are sent at the same time. GridFTP has reached near to 90% of use over a 30Gbps link in a memory to-memory transfer. When used to a disc-to-disc transfer, the throughput reached was 58.3% in the same link (Travostino, Mambretti, & Karmous-Edwards, 2006). We assume that our grid traffic is composed of GridFTP sessions that arrive following a stationary Poisson process with several intensities according to the average arrival rates limits (Noro, Baba, & Shimojo, 2005). The average GridFTP session size in our experiments follows a truncated exponential distribution with an average size of 10Mbytes, a minimum size of 10Kbytes and maximum size of 1TByte. These values were obtained of an extensive survey executed in the

European Project EC-GIN. This decision of the exponential distribution is based in some traffic models from Internet used in (Oueslati & Roberts, 2006) and since exponential distributions reduce the complexity of simulations to be performed (Floyd & Paxon, 2001).

Altman et al. (2005) showed that a throughput between 90% and 95% can be reached using between 4 and 6 parallel TCP connections, independently of the loss policy (Altman et al., 2006). Based on these results, in our work we assumed that GridFTP sessions are made of 3 or 9 parallel TCP/Reno connections. TCP Reno was adopted in our simulator since it is the most used transport protocol for bulk data transfers by grid computing applications (Bullot, Les Contrell, & Hughes-Jones, 2003). Therefore, every TCP flow within a GridFTP session is of Reno type with maximum window size of 20 packets. Moreover, GridFTP configuration is end-host specific, therefore we decided to keep per-flow loss policy.

In operational networks, every time a GridFTP session arrives to a router, the number of parallel TCP connections might vary. To evaluate the impact of the number of parallel TCPs, we assume its number is equal for all GridFTP sessions during simulation.

We also assume that job sizes are divisible (e.g. partitionable). We decided to apply a policy of equal quantity per-flow within a GridFTP session. Also, we applied a total GridFTP session admission policy instead of partial admission. Furthermore, a single per-flow scheduling policy was applied. In general, grid traffic consists of short and bulk data transfers, which may be very large compared to Internet traffic. Moreover, grid applications have a larger probability of showing some workflow aspects than Internet applications (an important difference between Internet traffic and grid traffic is that grid traffic generated not only for humans but also for machines). In grid environments a set of nodes participates to a common goal and they are expected to remain available for a long

Table 1. Traffic load scenarios

ρ_g	0.15	0.30	0.45	0.60
Single TCP				
Average Size (Bytes)	25000	25000	25000	25000
Flows per second	100	100	100	100
Source	4	4	4	4
TCP Load	**80Mbps**	**80Mbps**	**80Mbps**	**80Mbps**
VoIP				
Average Rate (bps)	22400	22400	22400	22400
Duration	60	60	60	60
Flows pre second	3.72	3.72	3.72	3.72
Sources	4	4	4	4
UDP Load	**20Mbps**	**20Mbps**	**20Mbps**	**20Mbps**
Bulk TCP				
Average Size (Bytes)	10000000	10000000	10000000	10000000
Cloud sessions per second	0.375	0.750	1.125	1.500
Sources	1	1	1	1
Grid Load	**30Mbps**	**60Mbps**	**90Mbps**	**120Mbps**
TOTAL LINK LOAD (Mbps)	**130Mbps**	**160Mbps**	**190Mbps**	**220Mbps**

time. Table 1 shows traffic load scenarios used in our evaluation.

Evaluation Metrics

Since we are interested to measure the QoS provisioned to grid computing applications, the metrics will be the average goodput and the average delay of GridFTP sessions. In grid computing applications, the goodput metric is most important that the throughput since most of the data transferred is used by applications for distributed computing. Distributed computing uses data to solve problems no matter how many packets are rejected the important metric is to have all the job on the destination sites and on time.

The GridFTP session goodput is the sum of individual TCP goodputs. That is the number of bytes per second of the sum of all individual TCP flows without taking into account the bytes on the packet retransmissions. goodput is a subset of throughput consisting only of the useful traffic. The goodput is also known as the Application throughput.

The other metric we will observe in our experiments is the GridFTP session delay which is the time between the first packet of first individual TCP flow belonging to the GridFTP session is sent until the last packet of the last individual TCP flow is also sent. That is the sejourn time of all the TCP flows belonging to the GridFTP session plus the bottleneck link delay in our dumb bell topology.

Operation and Management Policies

In a first step we will study the parallelization effect. We will vary the number of parallel TCP flows within a grid session. Two values will be studied: 3 and 9 parallel TCP flows per GridFTP session. In FAN, the FR threshold was configured with the value of 0.05 and the PL threshold with the value of 0.8.

The estimation period was kept as proposed by Kortebi, Oueslati, & Roberts (2004). We also assumed the same values for PL and FR. The rate of the TCP flows is limited by the access rate. Current access rates are low compared with those of the cores. Even if they provide more FR to TCP flows they will be limited by the access rate. The DS architecture was configured in NS-2 as near as possible to the GARA configuration: we choose 3 physical queues, one per traffic class, and 1 virtual queue per physical queue; standard implementation of DS architecture in NS-2 allows 4 physical queues and 3 virtual queues per physical queue (Pieda et al., 2000).

We choose WRED as queue management protocol. In WRED all probabilities of dropping an out-of-profile packet is based on a single queue length. We choose the queue dedicated to the grid traffic class as a reference to drop packets of all classes. Scheduling is configured as strict priority with different rates for each class (5% of the link capacity for the TCP class, 20% of the link capacity for the UDP class and the rest for the grid class). The Policer (smoother) is the TokenBucket with the Committed Information Rate (CIR) equal to FR estimator of FAN and updated at the same time interval (100ms) and the Committed Burst Size (CBS) of 10 packets (10000 Bytes). RED parameters are fixed at 0.6 and 0.8 of each virtual queue size like in (Altman et al., 2005), and the maximal probability is 0.5. The default queue weight is 0.002.

Simulation Setup

We simulated several times (i.e. 3 to 5) each scenario (column) represented in Table 1 with independent seeds for the random number generator at each simulation run. We follow the recommendation of (Umlauft & Reichl, 2007) to found the independent seeds. We developed a script to test various seeds and found those to ensure independence. Then, we use the "next-substream" utility of NS-2 to found the next independent sub-stream.

Figure 6. Average GridFTP session goodput—IGoFAN—3 vs. 9 parallel TCP flows per GridFTP session

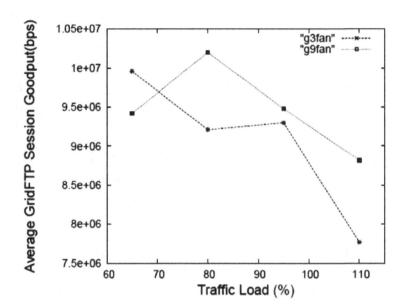

In the TCL we generate the flow random arrivals using the exponential distribution and not the uniform method since it delays a lot the simulations. We created a general script to simulate all the systems' configuration so with another script we run each scenario the number of defined times. This enable the possibility to run continuously several scenarios and got metrics at the same time optimizing the usage of the available computing resources. Metrics were organized in a separated excel sheet and then graphs were printed with another script.

All experiments were run under Linux Ubuntu 2.6.27-7-server with SMP. We had just four cores to run all scenarios needed, each core was composed by a Intel Xeon CPU running at 2.33 GHz with a cache size of 4096 KB. All the experiments were performed with NS-2 version 2.34 released on June 17, 2008.

Parallelization Effect on GridFTP Session over FAN (IGoFAN)

Figure 6 shows the average GridFTP session goodput with 3 and 9 parallel TCP flows per GridFTP

session. The bigger the number of parallel TCP flows per GridFTP session the bigger the goodput. This can be explained as follows, since the average size is divided in equal quantity among all individual TCP flows belonging to a GridFTP session, as the number of TCP flows increase they have less quantity to transfer. Since they interact during the transfer the bigger the number of parallel TCP flows the bigger the probability to have congestion and packet losses and therefore the bigger the goodput.

Figure 7 shows the average GridFTP session delay with 3 and 9 parallel TCP flows per GridFTP session. The bigger the number of parallel TCP flows per GridFTP session the lower their average delay. Since the GridFTP session size is divided equally among all individual parallel TCP flows, the bigger the number of parallel TCP flows the lesser their size. If the size of a TCP flow is small they might be considered as priority flows and they are served quickly than bigger flows. The lesser the number of parallel TCP flows per GridFTP session the bigger their size and they might be considered in second priority and therefore their delay is longer.

Figure 7. Average GridFTP session delay—IGoFAN—3 vs. 9 parallel TCP flows per GridFTP session

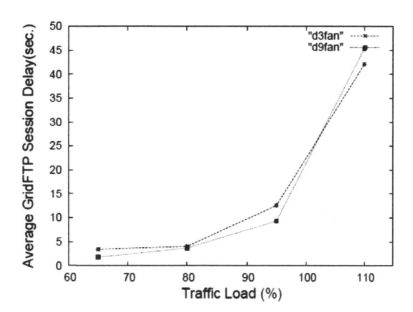

Parallelization Effect on GridFTP Session over FAN vs. DS (IGoFAN vs. IGoDS)

In the following set of results we are interested to compare the performance of FAN versus DS architecture. Therefore we do not compare the DS architecture with different configurations. We compare the FAN versus the DS architectures by varying the number of parallel TCP flows per GridFTP session and the RTT.

Figures 8 and 9 show the average GridFTP session goodput of FAN and DS architectures with 3 and 9 parallel TCP flows per GridFTP session respectively. The lesser the number of parallel TCP flows per GridFTP session the better the goodput provided by the DS architecture. On the contrary, the bigger the number of parallel TCP flows per GridFTP session the better the goodput provided by the FAN architecture. This can be explained as follows. As the number of TCP flows per GridFTP session increase, the lesser the size of individual flows. Those flows received priority in the FAN architecture. Furthermore, if

the number of parallel TCP flows is lower their size is bigger and they are took into account in second priority. In conclusion, FAN outperforms DS when the number of parallel TCP flows per GridFTP session increase.

Figures 10 and 11 show the average GridFTP session delay for FAN and DS architectures with 3 and 9 parallel TCP flows per GridFTP session respectively. The bigger the number of parallel TCP flows the better (lower) the average GridFTP session delay. This was explained as for the goodput results. As the number of TCP flows per GridFTP session increase, the lower the size of individual flows. Those flows are served with priority compared bigger other flows.

FUTURE RESEARCH DIRECTIONS

Currently Cloud computing has gained momentum among the research community. In practical terms, Cloud computing is supported by grid computing. At the level 3 of the ISO/OSI (TCP/IP) there are no significant implications when

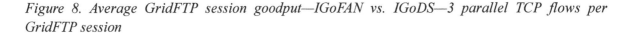

Figure 8. Average GridFTP session goodput—IGoFAN vs. IGoDS—3 parallel TCP flows per GridFTP session

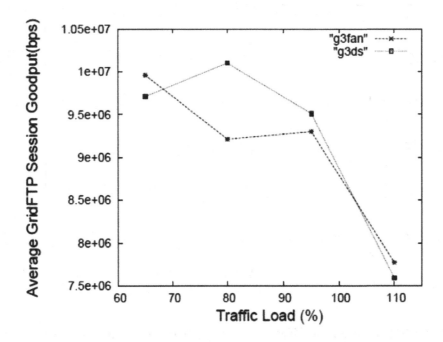

Figure 9. Average GridFTP session goodput—IGoFAN vs. IGoDS—9 parallel TCP flows per GridFTP session

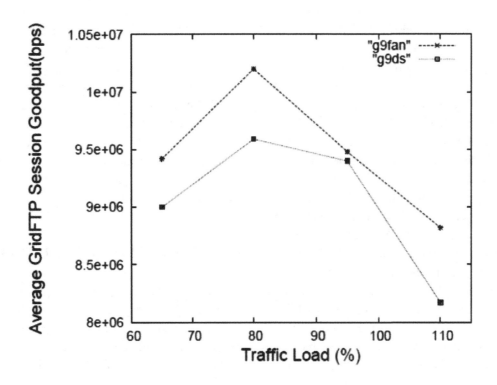

Figure 10. Average GridFTP session delay—ICoFAN vs. ICoDS—3 parallel TCP flows per GridFTP session

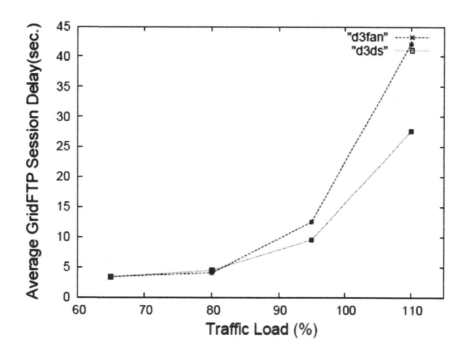

Figure 11. Average GridFTP session delay—ICoFAN vs. ICoDS—9 parallel TCP flows per GridFTP session

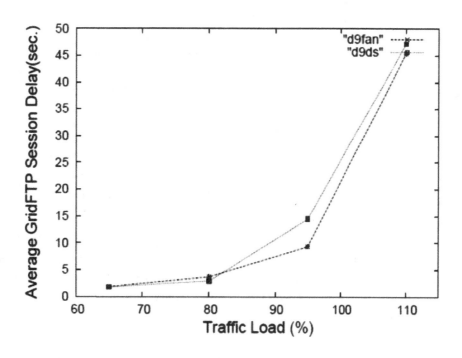

we are talking of big file transfers. The Internet traffic model considered might embrace current use of Cloud computing. When the data centers are located outside a private domain, the name is Cloud computing. In the future Cloud will become the main infrastructure for computing, storage and networking. To have a more realistic evaluation of the FAN versus DS architectures we must include storage and computing algorithms. Moreover, we also must include at least a domain and perhaps multidomain topology. The assumption of stochastic process arrival will be met in the future since the number of users is increasing day after day.

CONCLUSION

In this chapter we presented research on QoS provisioning for Grid Computing. We introduced a state of the art on this issue and their networking foundations. We propose a new promising QoS paradigm as a potential solution to this matter and a performance comparison between this potential networking paradigm (FAN) and the DS architectures. This comparison is justified since most of the current QoS provisioning solutions for grid computing applications at the IP level are based on the DS architecture.

Therefore, if new solutions should be explored a benchmark versus the DS architecture is obligated. In a first step, in this chapter we have explored the impact on FAN performance of the number of parallel TCP flows in the metrics. In a second step, we compared the performance of FAN and DS when the number of parallel TCP flows are modified. In FAN architectures we conclude that the bigger the number of parallel TCP flows per GridFTP session the better (bigger) the goodput. With respect to average GridFTP session delay, we have some evidence to conclude that the bigger the number of parallel TCP flows per GridFTP session the better (lower) the delay.

In conclusion, the bigger the number of parallel TCP flows the better the performance provided to Grid Computing applications in FAN architectures. When comparing FAN and DS architectures, we conclude that the bigger the number of parallel TCP flows per GridFTP session, the better (bigger) the goodput offered to GridFTP sessions by the FAN architecture. Moreover, the bigger the number of parallel TCP flows per GridFTP session the better (lower) the delay offered to GridFTP sessions by the FAN architecture. In conclusion, the bigger the number of parallel TCP flows the better the performance of FAN architecture over DS architecture. If the number of parallel TCP flows is lesser the performance of FAN architecture is lesser also. Therefore, a general conclusion of this chapter is that the bigger the number of parallel TCP flows per GridFTP sessions the better the performance of FAN architectures and the better the superiority of FAN architectures versus DS architecture.

REFERENCES

Adami, D., Giordano, S., Repeti, M., Coppola, M., Laforenza, D., & Tonellotto, N. (2006). Design and implementation of a grid network-aware resource broker. In *Proceedings of the 24ᵗʰ IASTED International Conference on Parallel and Distributed Computing and Networks* (pp. 41-46). ACTA Press Anaheim.

Afek, Y., Mansour, Y., & Ostfeld, Z. (1996). Phantom: A simple and effective flow control scheme. *ACM SIGCOMM Computer Communication Review, 26*(4), 169–182. doi:10.1145/248157.248172

Al-Ali, R., Sohail, S., Ran, O., Hafi, G., Von Laszewski, A., & Amin, K. (2004). Network QoS provision for distributed grid applications. *International Journal of Simulation Systems . Science and Technology, 5*(5), 13–27.

Altman, E., Barman, D., Tuffin, B., & Vojnic, M. (2005). Parallel TCP sockets: Simple model, throughput and validation. In *Proceedings of the 25th IEEE International Conference on Computer Communications* (pp. 1-12). Washington, DC., USA: IEEE Computer Society.

Altman, E., El-Azouzi, R., Ross, D., & Tuffin, B. (2006). Loss strategies for competing AIMD flows. *Journal Computer Networks: The International Journal of Computer and Telecommunications Networking, 50*(11), 1799–1815.

Anagran Product (2004). *Intelligent flow routing for economical delivery of next-generation network services.*

Benameur, N., Oueslati, S., & Roberts, J. (2003). Experimental implementation of implicit admission control. In *Proceedings of the 23rd NMDG Meeting.*

Bhatti, S. N., Sorensen, S., Clark, P., & Crowcroft, J. (2003). Network QoS for grid systems. *International Journal of High Performance Computing Applications, 17*(3), 219–236. doi:10.1177/1094342003173009

Blake, S., Black, D., Carlson, M., Davies, E., Wang, Z., & Weiss, W. (1998). *RFC 2475.* An architecture for Differentiated Services (DiffServ). Retrieved from http://www.ietf.org/rfc/ rfc2475.txt

Bonald, T., & Roberts, J. (2003). Congestion at flow level and the impact of user behaviour. *Computer Networks, 42*(4), 521–536. doi:10.1016/S1389-1286(03)00200-7

Braden, R., Zhang, L., Berson, S., Herzog, S., & Jamin, S. (1997). *RFC 2205.* Resource ReSerVation Protocol (RSVP). Retrieved from http://www.faqs.org/ rfcs/ rfc2205.html

Bullot, H., Les Contrell, R., & Hughes-Jones, R. (2003). Evaluation of advanced TCP stacks on fast long-distance production networks. *Journal of Grid Computing, 1*(4), 345–359. doi:10.1023/B:GRID.0000037555.53402.4f

Cárdenas, C., & Gagnaire, M. (2008). Performance comparison of Flow-Aware Networking (FAN) architectures under GridFTP traffic. In *Proceedings of the 23rd ACM Symposium on Applied Computing* (pp. 2079-2084). New York, NY: ACM.

Cárdenas, C., & Gagnaire, M. (2009). Evaluation of Flow-Aware Networking (FAN) architectures under GridFTP traffic. *Journal of Future Generation of Computer Systems, 25*(8), 895–903. doi:10.1016/j.future.2008.08.002

Cárdenas, C., Gagnaire, M., López, V., & Aracil, J. (2007). Admission control for grid services in IP networks. In *Proceedings of the 1st IEEE Symposium Advanced Networks and Telecommunications Systems* (pp. 1-2). Washington, DC., USA: IEEE Computer Society.

Cárdenas, C., Gagnaire, M., López, V., & Aracil, J. (2008). Performance evaluation of the Flow-Aware Networking (FAN) architecture under grid environment. In: *Proceedings of the 20th IEEE/IFIP Network Operation and Management Symposium* (pp. 481-487). Washington, DC., USA: IEEE Computer Society.

Cárdenas, C., Gagnaire, M., López, V., & Aracil, J. (2009). Admission control for grid services in IP networks. *Journal on Optical Switching and Networking, 6*(1), 20–28. doi:10.1016/j.osn.2008.05.003

Chen, H., & Yao, D. D. (2001). *Fundamentals of Queueing Networks.* Berlin, Germany: Springer.

Crovella, M. E., & Bestravos, A. (1997). Self-similarity in World Wide Web traffic: Evidence and possible causes. *Journal of IEEE/ACM Transaction on Networking, 5*(6), 835-846.

Floyd, S. (2007). Metrics for the evaluation of congestion control mechanisms. *IETF Document*. Retrieved from http://www.rfc-editor.org/rfc/ rfc5166.txt

Floyd, S., & Paxson, V. (2001). Difficulties in simulating the Internet. *Journal of IEEE/ACM Transaction on Networking, 9*(4), 392-403.

Foster, I., Fidler, M., Roy, A., Sander, V., & Winkler, L. (2004). End-to-end quality of service for high-end applications. *Computer Communications, 27*(14), 1375–1388. doi:10.1016/j. comcom.2004.02.014

Foster, I., & Kesselman, C. (2003). *The Grid 2: Blueprint for a new computing infrastructure.* Burlington, MA: Morgan Kaufmann.

Foster, I., Roy, A., & Sander, V. (2000). A quality of service architecture that combines resource reservation and application adaptation. In *Proceedings of the 8th International Workshop on Quality of Service* (pp. 181-188). Washington, DC., USA: IEEE Computer Society.

Giordano, S., Salsano, S., Van den Berghe, S., Ventre, G., & Ginnakopoulos, D. (2003). Advanced QoS provisioning in IP networks: The European premium IP projects. *IEEE Communications Magazine, 41*(1), 30–36. doi:10.1109/ MCOM.2003.1166651

Goyal, P., Harrick, M. V., & Chen, H. (1997). Start-time fair queuing: A scheduling algorithm for integrated services packet switching networks. *IEEE/ACM Transactions on Networking, 5*(5), 690–704. doi:10.1109/90.649569

ITU-T E.417 (2005). *Framework for the network management of IP-Based networks.* Retrieved from http://www.catr.cn/ radar/itut/ 201007/ P020100707520690724694.pdf

Keahey, K., Foster, I., Freeman, I., & Zhang, X. (2005). Virtual workspaces: Achieving quality of service and quality of life in the grid. *Journal of Scientific Programming, 13*(4), 265–276.

Kelly, F. P. (1994). *Reversibility and stochastic networks.* Wiley InterScience.

Kortebi, A., Muscariello, L., Oueslati, S., & Roberts, J. (2005). Evaluating the number of active flows in a scheduler realizing fair statistical bandwidth sharing. *ACM SIGMETRICS Performance Evaluation Review, 33*(1), 217–228. doi:10.1145/1071690.1064237

Kortebi, A., Oueslati, S., & Roberts, R. (2004). Cross-protect: Implicit service differentiation and admission control. In *Proceedings of Workshop on High Performance Switching and Routing* (pp. 56-60). Washington, DC., USA: IEEE Computer Society.

Kulkarni, V. G. (1996). *Modeling and analysis of stochastic systems.* Chapman and Hall/CRC.

Lefevre, L., Pham, C., Primet, P., Tourancheau, B., Gaidioz, B., Gelas, J. P., & Maimour, M. (2001). Active networking support for the grid. In *Proceedings of the IFIP-TC6 3rd International Working Conference on Active Networks* (pp. 16-33). London, UK: Springer-Verlag.

Leigh, J., Yu, O., Verlo, A., Roy, A., Winkler, L., & DeFanti, T. (2000). *Differentiated services experiments between the electronic visualization laboratory and Argonne national laboratory.* EMERGE Report. http://www.evl.uic.edu/cavern /papers/ DiffServ12_12_2K.pdf

Mandrichenko, I., Allcock, W., & Perelmutov, T. (2005). *GFD-47, GridFTP v2 Protocol Description.* Retrieved from http://www.ogf.org/ documents/GFD.47.pdf

Masoom Ali, M., & Nadarajah, S. (2006). A truncated Pareto distribution. *Computer Communications, 30*(1), 1–4. doi:10.1016/j.comcom.2006.07.003

Noro, M., Baba, K., & Shimojo, S. (2005). QoS control method to reduce resource reservation failure in datagrid applications. In *Proceedings of PACRIM. IEEE Pacific Rim Conference on Communications, Computers and signal Processing* (pp. 478-481). Washington, DC., USA: IEEE Computer Society.

Oueslati, S., & Roberts, J. (2005). A new direction for quality-of-service: Flow-aware networking. *Next Generation Internet Networks*, 226-232.

Oueslati, S., & Roberts, J. (2006). Comparing flow-aware and flow-oblivious adaptive routing. In *Proceedings of the 40th Annual Conference on Information Sciences and Systems* (pp. 655-660). Washington, DC., USA: IEEE Computer Society.

Oueslati, S., & Roberts, J. (2010). Method and device for implicit differentiation of QoS in a network. *United States Patent 7646715.*

Pan, R., Prabhakar, B., Psounis, K., & Wischik, D. (2005). Shrink: A method for enabling scalable performance prediction and efficient network simulation. *IEEE/ACM Transactions on Networking, 13*(5), 975–988. doi:10.1109/TNET.2005.857080

Park, J., Jung, M., Chang, S., Choi, S., Young Chung, M., & Jun Ahn, B. (2006). Performance evaluation of the flow-based router using Intel IXP2800 network processors. In *Proceedings of the International Conference on Computational Science and Its Applications (ICCSA)* (LNCS 3981, pp. 77-86). Berlin-Heidelberg, Germany: Springer-Verlag.

Pieda, P., Ethridge, J., Baines, M., & Shallwani, F. (2000). A network simulator differentiated services implementation. *Open IP, Nortel Networks.* Retrieved from http://www-sop.inria.fr/ members/ Eitan.Altman/COURS-NS/ DOC/DSnortel.pdf

Rio, M., Di Donato, A., Saka, F., Pezzi, N., Smith, R., Bhatti, S., & Clarke, P. (2003). Quality of service networking for high performance grid applications. *Journal of Grid Computing, 1*(4), 329–343. doi:10.1023/B:GRID.0000037551.92756.4e

Roberts, J. (2004). A survey on statistical bandwidth sharing. *Computer Networks, 45*(3), 319–332. doi:10.1016/j.comnet.2004.03.010

Roberts, J., & Oueslati, S. (2000). Quality of service by flow aware networking. *Philosophical Transactions of the Royal Society of London Series A, 358*(1773), 2197-2207.

Roberts, J., Oueslati, S., & Kortebi, A. (2006). *Procede et dispositive d'ordonnancement de paquets pour leur routage dans un rseau avec dtermination implicite des paquets traiter en priorité.* WO/2006/051244.

Sander, V., Foster, I., Roy, A., & Winkler, L. (2000). A differentiated services implementation for high-performance TCP flows. *Computer Networks, 34*(6), 915–929. doi:10.1016/S1389-1286(00)00162-6

Sem-Jacobsen, F. O., Reinemo, S. A., Skeie, T., & Lysne, O. (2004). Achieving flow level QoS in cut-through networks through admission control and DiffServ. In [PDPTA]. *Proceedings of International Conference on Parallel and Distributed Processing Techniques and Applications, 3,* 1084–1090.

Travostino, F., Mambretti, J., & Karmous-Edwards, G. (2006). *Grid networks: Enabling grids with advanced communication technology.* Wiley Interscience. doi:10.1002/0470028696

Umlauft, M., & Reichl, P. (2007). Experiences with the ns-2 network simulator explicitly setting seeds considered harmful. In *Proceedings of Wireless Telecommunications Symposium (WTS 2007).* doi: 10.1109/WTS.2007.4563316

Vicat-Blanc Primet, P., & Chanussot, F. (2004). End to end network quality of service in grid environments: *The QoSINUS approach*. Retrieved from http://www.broadnets.org/2004 / workshop-papers/ Gridnets/primet.pdf

Vicat-Blanc Primet, P., Echantillac, F., & Goutelle, M. (2005). Experiments with equivalent differentiated services in a grid context. *Future Generation Computer Systems*, *21*(4), 515–524. doi:10.1016/j.future.2004.10.009

Volker, S. (2004). *GFD-I.037, Networking issues for grid infrastructure*. Retrieved from http://www.ggf.org/ documents/ GWD-I-E/GFD-I.037.pdf

Yang, K., Guo, X., Galis, A., Yang, B., & Liu, D. (2003). Towards efficient resource on-demand in grid computing. *ACM SIGOPS Operating Systems Review*, *37*(2), 37–43. doi:10.1145/769782.769787

About the Contributors

Nikolaos P. Preve received his BS, MS, and his PhD degree from the School of Electrical and Computer Engineering of the National Technical University of Athens (NTUA), Athens, Greece. He is currently working in the field of computer networks research in both national, European and international projects while he is specialized in computer and telecommunication networks. He has been mainly involved as a project leader, and technical manager of several successfully integrated projects both in national and international level. He is also in parallel teaching in the School of Electrical and Computer Engineering at the National Technical University of Athens, Greece, and in the Department of Informatics at the Technological Educational Institute of Athens, Greece. His main research interests are in the fields of wireless networks, mobile and personal communications, parallel and distributed computing, and grid computing.

* * *

Laeeq Ahmed is currently working as Assistant Professor, Department of Computer Science and Information Technology, University of Engineering and Technology, Peshawar. He completed his Masters in Distributed Systems in 2006 from IBITE (School of International Business Information Technology and Enterprise), Liverpool Hope University, UK. He received his Bachelors in Computer Science from Edwardes College Peshawar, Pakistan in 2003. Laeeq Ahmed has been actively involved in teaching and research in the areas of Grid Computing, Distributed Systems, Middleware development and Algorithm design. He has authored and co-authored various research papers in journals of international repute including the IEEE Communications. He has presented his research work in various international conferences including the IEEE ICEBE and the IEEE ICET.

Mark Anderson's research builds on earlier work investigating the overlap between Virtual Organisations and teleworking through focussing on the technical solutions that may be adopted to support virtual communities either in the workplace or as a means of supporting communities of learners in Higher Education. The concept of virtual communities has much in common with the notion of Virtual Organisations that form a central component in the theoretical underpinning of Grid Computing. This work has moved to address the same issues within Cloud Computing, rapidly emerging as the next-generation platform for business computing. The scope of the research has been extended to also examine the generic needs of distance learners to explore the similarities between teleworkers and distance learners in relation to supporting their activities through service-oriented computer.

Giuseppe Andronico was born in Catania (Italy) in January 1965. He graduated in Physics "cum laude" at the University of Catania in 1991 and since 1995 he holds a PhD in Physics from the same university. Since March 2001, he is Technologist at the INFN Sezione di Catania. Since his graduation, his main research activity has been done in the realm of Theoretical Physics. He has been involved in lattice field theory simulations. Since late 1999 he has been interested in Grid Computing participating to several initiatives: European DataGRID, INFN Grid, EGEE, and EGEE-II. In these initiatives he has been involved in developing code, in operations, in training and in dissemination activities. More recently he has been involved in some European funded projects: EELA, EUMEDGRID, EUChinaGRID and EGEE-III.

Antun Balaž graduated from the University of Belgrade in 1997 and holds a PhD degree in physics since 2008. Currently he is an Associate Research Professor at the Institute of Physics Belgrade, and serves as a technical coordinator of Serbian NGI AEGIS. Dr. Balaž was operations (SA1) activity leader in SEE-GRID-2 and SEE-GRID-SCI projects, and Serbia country representative for Grid operations in EGEE-II and EGEE-III. Currently he coordinates Serbian participation in PRACE-1IP, EGI-InSPIRE and HP-SEE projects. Research interests of Dr. Balaž are in devising efficient HPC algorithms for calculation of path integrals and their applications in condensed matter physics, Bose-Einstein condensation and disordered systems, as well as application of Monte Carlo methods, HPC and distributed computing. He has published more than 60 papers in peer-reviewed scientific journals and conference proceedings.

Tiwonge Msulira Banda is Projects Manager at UbuntuNet Alliance for Research and Education Networking. He was born in Nkhata Bay (Malawi) in September, 1981. He graduated in Environmental Science at the University of Malawi in 2005 and has since been involved in the development of research and education networking in Sub-Sahara Africa and following up on issues of infrastructure for research collaboration. He has had interest in grid computing and high performance computing since 2008. He was involved in the EU-funded (FP7) ERINA4Africa project in 2010, which studied Africa's e-Infrastructure potential for boosting research and innovation. He was also involved in the GLOBAL project that developed the Virtual Conference Centre, Globalplaza.org.

Roberto Barbera graduated in Physics "cum laude" at the University of Catania in 1986 and since 1990 he holds a PhD in Physics from the same University. He currently is Associated Professor at the Department of Physics and Astronomy of the Catania University. Since 1997 he is involved in the NA57 Experiment at CERN SPS and in the ALICE Experiment at CERN LHC. Since 1999, he is interested in Grid and High Performance Computing. He is author of about 150 publications (scientific papers and chapters of books) and more than 300 presentations at international workshops and conferences. Since 2002, he is the responsible of the GENIUS Grid portal project and, in 2004; he created the international GILDA Grid infrastructure for training and dissemination that he coordinates since the beginning.

Harold Enrique Castro Barrera graduated in Computer Science at Universidad de los Andes in 1989, he got a DEA (MSc) from the Institut National Polytehcnique de Grenoble (INPG) in France and since 1995 he holds a PhD in Computer Science from INPG also. After working in the European industry, since 2005 he is associate professor at the Computing and Systems Department at Universidad de los Andes. He is the director of the COMIT (Communications and Information Technology) research group which main research focus is distributed systems and networks. He personally leads institutional and national grid initiatives, and his interest areas are: distributed systems, grid and cloud computing, virtualization, data networks and mobile computing.

Bruce Becker obtained his PhD in experimental heavy-ion physics from the University of Cape Town. He is a member of the ALICE experiment and the SA-CERN programme of the Department of Science and Technology which supports the activities in South Africa related to collaboration with CERN. He also holds an honorary research associateship with iThemba Laboratory for Accelerator-Based Science in Cape Town. As coordinator of the South African national grid, his responsibilities have included organising training sessions at participating institutes, building consensus on deployment and organisational issues, promoting and extending the usage of grid services to new scientific communities and encouragement of institutional deployment of grid services at the major universities. His current position is Senior Researcher at the CSIR Meraka Institute, where he continues to coordinate the deployment and integration of research facilities into the national grid, and the national cyberinfrastructure (SANReN and CHPC).

Mario José Villamizar Cano is an Instructor Professor in the Department of Systems and Computing Engineering at Universidad de los Andes, Colombia. He received a Master in Engineering (MSc) in Computer Science from the Universidad de los Andes, in 2010. Since 2008, he has been participating in the COMIT (Communications and Information Technology) research group, specifically in the UnaGrid and UnaCloud institutional grid initiatives, and projects of chemical engineering and bioinformatics related with distributed applications and workflows for HPC infrastructures. His research interests include virtualized cluster environments, desktop grid and volunteer and computing systems, cloud computing infrastructures, distributed storage, parallel applications, and bioinformatics applications and workflows.

César Cárdenas holds a PhD (Summa Cum Laude) in Telecommunications with specialty in networks and computer science from Telecom ParisTech, France; a Master in Satellite Communications from Telecom Paris, Site de Toulouse, France and Summer Session Program from the International Space University hosted at Rice University and NASA JSC. He has studies of Master in Management from the University of Guanajuato and the BSc (with honors) in Electrical Engineering and Communications from Tecnológico de Monterrey Campus Querétaro. Since 1996, he is assistant professor at the Mechatronics Department in Tecnológico de Monterrey Campus Querétaro. Currently, he is the President of the IEEE Querétaro Section. His research interests are future networking and applications architectures, future engineering education, social intelligence design and technology design for social change. Author/co-author of several journals, more than 70 international conferences and national conferences, and 5 book chapters. Participation in more than 100 international, national and local projects.

Subrata Chattopadhyay is Chief Investigator for the GARUDA National Grid Computing Initiative -foundation phase and head of System Engineering and Networking Group at C-DAC, Bangalore. He was involved in setting up the PARAM Padma, Supercomputing facility and the formation of HPC user group and addresses their requirements. He has also contributed to the setting up of high speed communication fabric of GARUDA and looking at the challenges of deploying grid middleware across various platforms of supercomputers. He is also Deputy Technical Manager of the EU-IndiaGrid2 Project.

Gang Chen was the physicist of L3 experiment at CERN from 1991-1994; since 1995-1996, he was post-doc at and member of BESII. In 1996, he joined the AMS (Alpha Magnetic Spectrometer) for the International Space Station. His main jobs were on detector developments and physics simulations. Since 2003, he has been the director of the Computing Centre of the IHEP. He is in charge of the provision of a High Performance Computing infrastructure for BESIII, ARGO-YBJ and LHC projects. He has been a member of International High Energy Physics Computing Coordination Committee (IHEPCCC) since 2005. Starting from 2004, he has been leading a group to build the WLCG site in for LHC experiments.

Leandro N. Ciuffo is a Coordinator in the Directorate of R&D at RNP (Brazil's National Education and Research Network), where he has interacted with scientific communities concerning new approaches to advanced network use. Before joining RNP, he spent three years and a half at INFN Catania, where he was WP Manager in the EELA (FP6) and EELA-2 (FP7) e-Science projects, with responsibilities for dissemination, training and user support activities. Leandro holds a BSc in Computer Science from the Universidade Federal de Juiz de Fora (UFJF) and an MSc in Computing from the Universidade Federal Fluminense (UFF).

Alexandru Costan is a postdoctoral researcher within the KerData team at INRIA Rennes, working on scalable storage in cloud environments. In 2011 he obtained a PhD in Computer Science from the Politehnica University of Bucharest, for a thesis focused on self-adaptive behavior of large-scale distributed systems based on monitoring information. His main research interests include: cloud storage, MapReduce applications and the autonomic behavior of distributed systems.

Manoj Devare received his MSc degree from the University of North Maharashtra, India, and a PhD from Bharati University, India, both in Computer Science. His research deals with Multi-Scale High Performance Computing in Grids and Cloud technologies, and innovative applications of those technologies to scientific problems in such domains as congestion control and Computational Fluid Dynamics. Dr. Manoj was first to coin the concept of Desktop Clouds. Dr Manoj obtained the Best Research Paper Award, at the International Conference ICSCI 2008, Hyderabad, India. He is also a Post Doctorate Fellow at Center of Excellence on HPC, University of Calabria, Italy.

P. S. Dhekne is a former Associate Director Electronics & Instrumentation and currently he is a Raja Ramanna Fellowship at Computer Division, BARC and a Scientific Consultant to Principal Scientific Advisor to Government of India. He is chair of the Grid Committee within the National Knowledge Network Plan. He served as a deputy project manager for EU-IndiaGrid and he was a member of its PMB. He is also Deputy Project Manager of the EU-IndiaGrid2 Project.

Salvatore Distefano received the master's degree in computer science engineering from the University of Catania in October 2001. In 2006, he received the PhD degree on "Advanced Technologies for the Information Engineering" from the University of Messina. His research interests include performance evaluation, parallel and distributed computing, software engineering, and reliability techniques. During his research activity, he participated in the development of the WebSPN and the ArgoPerformance tools. He has been involved in several national and international research projects. At this time, he is a postdoctoral researcher at the University of Messina. He is a student member of the IEEE.

Maurice Gagnaire is Professor at the Networks and Computer Science Department of Telecom-ParisTech in Paris, France. He is coordinator of the Networks, Mobility and Services Group and leads a research team in the field of optical networks. He is a member of two European Networks of Excellence and French representative of European COST 291 on Optical Digital Networks. He has authored/co-authored about 90 technical papers in IEEE or IFIP international journals or conferences. He participated in the writing of two collective books and author of two books. He has chaired the IEEE Globecom 2006 symposium on Optical Networks. He has been appointed at multiple occasions as an expert by the French Ministry of Industry, the Flemish Government of Belgium and the National Science Foundation of the USA. He is a member of the IEEE and of the IFIP WG6.10 on Photonic Networking. He is a graduate from the INT, Evry, received his DEA from the University Paris 6, his PhD from the ENST (1992) and his Habilitation from the University of Versailles (1999), France.

Philippe Gavillet holds a Doctorat ès Sciences Physiques from the University of Paris VI (Orsay). He has been involved in several successive HEP programmes at CERN: Bubble chamber (81cm Orsay, 2m CERN HBC), European Hybrid Spectrometer (EHS), LEP (DELPHI) and LHC (LHCb) experiments, contributing mainly to hadron spectroscopy. As of Latin America related matters, he has been Project Coordinator of the EU Project (CI1*-CT94-0118): "UFRJ-CERN Collaboration in the DELPHI Experiment at LEP and in the R & D Programme for the LHC" (1995-1997) and was recently in charge of the relations between CERN and Brazil. He is currently a member of the Grid Initiatives for e-Science virtual communities facility in Europe and Latin America (GISELA) EC funded project.

Philipp M. Glatz received his BSc and MSc in Telematics specializing in System-on-Chip-Design and Computational Intelligence from Graz University of Technology, Austria, in 2005 and 2007, respectively. As a university assistant with the Institute for Technical Informatics at Graz University of Technology, Austria, he is assigned research and teaching duties. Currently, he is a PhD candidate in electrical and computer engineering. His research interests include wireless sensor networks and power awareness with a focus on network coding, energy harvesting, measurement and integration. He is a member of the Institute of Electrical and Electronics Engineers.

Antonios Gouglidis holds a diploma in Information Technology Engineering from the Technological Educational Institute of Thessaloniki in Greece, and an MSc in Distributed Interactive Systems from Lancaster University in United Kingdom. Currently he is a PhD candidate in the Department of Applied Informatics at the University of Macedonia in Greece, with a research topic on access control in Grid computing systems. He has received awards and scholarships for his academic excellence from the Greek State Scholarships Foundation, the Rotary Foundation and the Onassis Public Benefit Foundation. He has worked in the private sector as a software engineer and is presently employed as a secondary school teacher by the Greek Ministry of Education, Lifelong Learning and Religious Affairs. His research interests include the areas of Information and network security, access control in Grid and Cloud computing systems and digital forensics.

Maria Grammatikou is a Senior Researcher and Coordinator of the Network Management and Optimal Design Laboratory (NETMODE) of NTUA of Greece. She works as a teaching assistant in NTUA. Her research interests include topics on management and optimal design Quality of Service of computer communication networks, security and intrusion detection systems, electronic commerce and Web-based technologies, parallel/distributed systems and communication systems evaluation. She has a PhD in Computer Science from the NTUA of Greece. She has an extensive experience in software systems design & development and she has participated in many European projects. She is a member of the WG7/TC48 Working Group.

Lucio Grandinetti is professor at the Faculty of Engineering, University of Calabria (UNICAL), Italy. At the same university, I currently hold the position of Vice Rector (since 1999) and coordinator of the PhD Degree Program in the area of Managament Science and Engineering. At the above mentioned University, I was Director of the Department of Electronics, Informatics, and Systems for ten years, as well as member of the University Administration Council and President of the Faculty's Management Engineering Degree Course. My scientific background is in Electronic Engineering and Systems Science. I am a graduate of the University of Pisa, Italy and the University of California at Berkeley. I have also been a post-doc fellow at University of Southern California, Los Angeles and Research Fellow at the University of Dundee, Scotland. I have been a member of the IEEE Committee on Parallel Processing, and European Editor of a book series of MIT Press on Advanced Computational Methods and Engineering. Currently I am member of the Editorial Board of four international journals. I am author of many research papers in well-established international journals and Editor or co-Editor of several books on algorithms, software, applications of Parallel Computing, HPC, Grids. Since 1994, I have been part of several Evaluation Panels of European Projects within various ICT and Infosociety Programs; I have also been reviewer of many EU Projects in the above Programs. I have been recipient and scientific leader of many European-Commission-Funded projects since 1993 (e.g. Molecular Dynamics Simulations by MPP Systems, EUROMED, HPC Finance, WADI). I have been recipient and scientific leader of several national projects (CNR progetti finalizzati, Grid.it, PRIN). I am one of the founders of the Consortium SPACI (Southern Partnership for Advanced Computational Infrastructures), a pioneering Grid infrastructure experiment in Italy. Currently I am: Director of the Centre of Excellence on HPC established at the University of Calabria by the Italian government, Co-managing director of a Supercomputing Centre jointly established by the University of Calabria and NEC Corporation, Recipient and scientific leader of some European-Commission-Funded projects (among others, BEINGRID), Project leader of a node of the most important European Grid Infrastructure for e-science named EGEE.

Salma Jalife graduated at the Computer Engineer Faculty of Engineering, UNAM (1981-1985) and obtained her Master Degree in Science with specialty in Telecommunications, University of Colorado at Boulder, USA (1991). She has lectured courses, seminars, conferences on telecom and Information Technologies nationwide and abroad. She has a relevant career at UNAM where she collaborated on the design of the largest Latin American telephone and data network of 1990, with the installation of 13,000 telephone lines. In 1992, she joined the Ministry of Communications and Transportation (SCT) where she became the Chief of Staff of the UnderMinister of Communications and Technological Development, participating in the construction of the Private Network for the Federal Government and the Strategic Communications Plan 1993-2000. Since the creation of the regulatory authority for telecommunications in 1996 she became the General Coordinator for International Affairs. In 2003, she was appointed commissioner of COFETEL and Head of the Engineering and Technology Department. As Mexican representative of the government, she occupied different chairmanships of International working groups on telecommunications and radiospectrum issues at APEC, CITEL(OAS) and ITU. In June 2006 she joined CUDI, where she is currently coordinating projects oriented to the use of NRENs and its applications. She also participates in the International affairs of such NREN. She has been responsible for the creation of the community of interest of Oceanography and has participated in the consolidation of the Grid community at CUDI. She is also an independent international consultant and has worked for the governments of Colombia and Costa Rica in their restructuring of the telecom sector. She published a report on the assessment for the TEL Working Group at APEC in 2009, participated in an ITU consultancy to ANATEL-Brazil on the Mexican telecommunications regulatory environment and during the election years in Mexico she participates as a technical advisor on the Committee for the Mexican Elections PREP at the IFE.

Mandeep Joshi is currently working as a senior developer at Bottomline Techonologies and specializes in application development mainly in the payment industry and document management industry. His research interest lies in the area of programming languages with an acute focus on improving product availability. He did his schooling in Nepal and has a Bachelors Degree from Greenwich University and Masters Degree from Liverpool Hope University. He passed his Masters Degree with a Distinction and received 'MSc Deans Award' for his achievement.

Dimitrios Kalogeras is affiliated with the Institute of Communications & Computer Systems (ICCS), National Technical University of Athens (NTUA). Within NTUA, he is a Senior Researcher at the Network Management & Optimal Design Laboratory (NETMODE), School of Electrical & Computer Engineering. He obtained his Engineering Diploma (1990) and the Doctorate degree (1996), both in Electrical & Computer Engineering from NTUA. His research spans several aspects of advanced network technologies and protocols. He is consulting on planning the new generations of GRNET (the Greek National Research & Education Network) during the last three phases of its network evolution including its latest hybrid optical design and the NTUA Campus Local Area Network. Dr. Kalogeras was involved in several European Research & Technological Development projects, e.g. on IPv6 (6Net) and on Network Security (GEANT2 / GN2 – JRA2). He served in several European Commission technical panels and, for two terms, he was with the Technical Committee of the Trans-European Research & Education Networking (TERENA). He has participated in the evolution of Paneuropean Academic research network since TEN-34 following up within TEN-155, GN, GN-2 and currently with GN3.

Sujan Kansakar was born in Kathmandu, Nepal and graduated from University of Liverpool in 2007, with a Masters (MSc) in Distributed Systems. He also holds a First class Bachelors (Combine Honours) degree from the same university. Sujan is currently working in the private IT sector in the UK as a Professional Service Consultant but still maintains a strong interest in the grid computing research especially in resource discovery, semantic, artificial immune system and intrusion detection. Sujan has received awards and scholarships for his academic excellence from the University of Liverpool for both his Masters and Bachelors degree.

Paul Karaenke is a researcher and PhD candidate in the Department of Information Systems 2 at the University of Hohenheim, Stuttgart, Germany. He received his Diploma in Information Systems from the University of Mannheim, Germany, in 2007. His research interests are in the areas of interaction protocols, multi-agent resource allocation, multi-agent simulation, and service level agreements in service-oriented computing.

Dr.-Ing. Bastian Koller received his diploma degree in computer science from the University of Würzburg in 2004. Later he joined the High Performance Computing Centre Stuttgart, where he worked as research assistant in a variety of national and international projects such as NextGRID, BEinGRID or FinGRID. From 2006 to 2010 he was Technical Manager of the BREIN project which addressed Grids for Business. 2007 he became head of the "Service Management and Business Processes" department of HLRS. In 2011 he received his PhD from the University of Stuttgart for his work on "Enhanced SLA Management in the High Performance Computing Domain".

John Wajanga Aron Kondoro studied BSc (Education) at the University of Dar-Es-Salaam in 1979; he obtained MSc (Physics), University of Florida at Gainesville (USA) in 1983 and PhD (Physics), University of Saarbrucken, Germany in 1990. Professor Kondoro has won several awards, International Atomic Energy Agency) (IAEA) fellowship for training in applications of Nuclear Physics (1981), Fellowship of the Deutscher Akademischer Austauschdienst (DAAD) foundation (1985), Fulbright Fellowship to the USA (1994), Research grant of the Third World Academy of Sciences (TWAS) (1998). Professor Kondoro was appointed on the UbuntuNet Alliance Board in April 2009. He worked at the Department of Physics, University of Dar-Es-Salaam from the position of Tutorial Assistant (1981) to the rank of Associate Professor in Physics in 2000. He is currently working as Principal of the Dar es Salaam Institute of Technology as Principal since 1999 until to-date.

Giuseppe Laria obtained the BS degree in Electronic Engineering at the University of Salerno in 2001. His research activities concern with the study of: Grid technologies and their application in the business world; Commodity Technologies to implement Grid Service and their integration with COTS components; SOA and Next Generation Grid for e-business; SOA for designing of VO management framework. He has been holder for 4 years of a research contract at the University of Salerno working on 'Grid Technologies and Applications'. He is co-author of several scientific papers related to Web and Grid technologies. He has participated and has been participating since 2002 in IST projects (GRASP, AKOGRIMO, eLeGI, BREIN). Currently he is mainly involved in ARISTOTELE (FP7) and Qualipso projects (FP6) as internal project manager and WP leader.

Simon C. Lin is in charge of the Academia Sinica Grid Computing (ASGC) and acting as the committee member of Overview Board, Management Board and Grid Deployment Board of the LHC Computing Grid (LCG) project led by CERN. He is also responsible for the Asia Federation and a member of PMB in EGEE project. His current focus is to build the Grid infrastructure for e-Science in Taiwan and to participate in the Global Grid project in order to support the scientific computing, High Energy Physics and Bio-informatics applications, etc.

Víctor López received the MSc (Hons.) degree in telecommunications engineering from Universidad de Alcalá de Henares, Spain, in 2005 and the PhD (Hons.) degree in computer science and telecommunications engineering from Universidad Autónoma de Madrid (UAM), Madrid, Spain, in 2009. The results of his PhD thesis were awarded with the national COIT prize 2009 of the Telefónica

Foundation in networks and telecommunications systems. In 2004, he joined Telefónica I+D as a Researcher, where he was involved in next generation networks for metro, core, and access. He was involved with several European Union projects (NOBEL, MUSE, MUPBED. In 2006, he joined the High-Performance Computing and Networking Research Group (UAM) as a Researcher in the ePhoton/One+ Network of Excellence. Currently, he is an Assistant Professor at UAM, where he is involved in optical metro-core European projects BONE and MAINS. His research interests include the analysis and characterization of services, design, and performance evaluation of traffic monitoring equipment, and the integration of Internet services over optical networks, mainly Optical Burst Switching (OBS) solutions and multilayer architectures.

Vasilis Maglaris was born in Athens in 1952 and is the founder and director of the Network Management and Optimal Design Laboratory at NTUA since 1989. He received the Diploma in Mechanical & Electrical Engineering from NTUA, Greece in 1974, the MSc in Electrical Engineering from the Polytechnic Institute of Brooklyn, New York in 1975 and the PhD degree in Electrical Engineering & Computer Science from Columbia University, New York in 1979. In 1989, he joined the faculty of the Electrical & Computer Engineering Department of the NTUA, where he is Professor of Computer Science. He served as the Chairman of the Board of the Greek Research & Technology Network – GRNET, the National Research & Education Network (NREN) of Greece from its inception in September 1998 until June 2004. Since October 2004, he has been the Chairman of the National Research & Education Networks Policy Committee (NREN PC).

Bernard Marie Marechal graduated in Physics in 1964 at the University of Grenoble (France). Since 1969 he holds a Doctorat ès-Sciences Physiques from the University of Paris. He worked at CERN (1965 to 1969), at the Centro Brasileiro de Pesquisas Físicas - Brazil (1969-1970), at CERN (1971 to 1974), at the Universidade de Brasília - Brazil and, from October 1976 onward, at the Federal University of Rio de Janeiro - UFRJ - Brazil, where he created and coordinated the Laboratório de Física Aplicada and the Laboratório de Física de Partículas Elementares. He has been Vice-Director and Director of the Physics Institute of the UFRJ. He coordinated several international projects under the agreement between CNRS/FRANCE and CNPq/BRAZIL. He was the EELA Deputy Project Coordinator, then Project coordinator of EELA-2 and currently he is the Project Coordinator of GISELA (all EC funded Projects).

Alberto Masoni, research director at INFN, where he worked since 1988, obtained a degree in Physics in 1984 and was the former Project Manager of the EU-IndiaGrid Project. He has been involved in the management of large computing projects, such as the Project Committee for the INFN Computing Regional Centre, the phase-2 costing Committee for the CERN Computing centre, the LHC Computing Grid Project where he was first member of the management board and is now member of the Grid Deployment Board. Since its constitution he has been a member of the Executive Board of INFN-Grid Special Project which manages and coordinates the INFN participation to national and international grid projects. He was the Scientific Director of the Cybersar project a 14 M-euro National Objective Project of the Italian Ministry of University and Research (www.cybersar.it) awarded as Project of Excellence by the Italian Ministry of University and Research Authority. He is also a member of the Italian Grid Initiative Executive Board and Project Manager of the EU-IndiaGrid2 project.

Ludek Matyska is a full professor at Masaryk University (MU) as well as a senior researcher at CESNET. Since 1994, he has been a head of the Supercomputing Center at MU and also a vice director of the Institute of Computer Science there. He works for CESNET since 1998, serving as principal co-investigator of its research programmes. He chairs the national grid infrastructure and has been involved in many national (e.g. METACentrum, Distributed Data Storage (DiDaS), MediGRID) and international projects (e.g. GridLab, CoreGRID, DataGrid, EGEE, EGEE II and the EGI_DS, EGI InSPIRE, EMI), either as principal investigator or as a head of the CESNET or MU team. Ludek Matyska will be principal investigator and will bring into the eSCAPE project his long term experience in Grid setup and operation, middleware development and training, as well as wide managerial experience.

Ioannis Mavridis is Assistant Professor of Information Systems Security at the Department of Applied Informatics of University of Macedonia, Greece. He holds a Diploma in Computer Engineering and Informatics from the University of Patras, Greece and a Doctor's degree in Mobile Computing Security from the Aristotle University of Thessaloniki, Greece. He is a member of Working Group 11.3 on Database Security of International Federation for Information Processing (IFIP). He has participated in several research projects working on the area of IT security. His research interests include the areas of computer and network security, Information Assurance and Security, cyber security, access control in collaborative, mobile, pervasive and grid systems, Semantic Web and security ontologies.

Redouane Merrouch is the head of the Moroccan National and Academic Network (MARWAN). He has also the responsibility of the National Grid Computing Infrastructure in Morocco (MaGrid). He has a PhD in Physics from the Caen University. His main interest and activity is in computer networking for R&D community.

András Micsik is a senior researcher at MTA SZTAKI (Computer and Automation Research Institute of the Hungarian Academy of Sciences) and holds a PhD in Informatics at ELTE University in Budapest. He was active in the digital libraries field in all DELOS projects starting from 1995. His main interests are (semantic) interoperability and collaborative work support. He contributed to several international research projects in the topics of sharing metadata vocabularies, collaborative rating and filtering, peer-to-peer repository networks, etc. Recently he worked on the application of Semantic Web technologies in service-oriented architectures, including the topics of agents and Semantic Web in business Grids, and rule-based pro-active collaboration support. He has more than 40 scientific publications. He is regular member of the program committee of the ECDL and ICADL conference series.

Yannis Mitsos received his Diploma in Electrical and Computer Engineering from the Democritus University of Thrace in 1999. His Diploma thesis was focused on the implementation of control algorithms using digital signal processor interworking with FPGAs. Since 2003, he holds a PhD degree from the Electrical & Computer Engineering Department of the National Technical University of Athens (NTUA). His PhD thesis explores the performance analysis of distributed functionality in high-performance network processors. Since 2005 he works for GRNET focusing on the deployment of regional infrastructure projects in SEE. Currently he is head of GRNET NOC.

Athanasios Moralis holds an Engineering Degree from the National Technical University of Athens -NTUA (2000). He is currently a researcher at the Network Management & Optimal Design Laboratory (NETMODE), School of Electrical & Computer Engineering, NTUA. Since his graduation, he was involved in several National & European projects focused on Security and Grid Computing. Other research interests include, BPMS, Intrusion Detection Systems and P2P computing.

Kai Nan is currently serving as Associate Researcher in Computer Network Information Center (CNIC), Chinese Academy of Sciences (CAS). He has worked for CNIC since 1999. At present he is the Director of Collaboration Environment Research Center, which is a department dedicated to research and development for Collaboration Technology and e-Science Applications under CNIC. His research interests include data grid, collaborative computing and e-Science applications. Nan has served as technical lead on many projects funded by the Ministry of Science and Technology, China and the National Science Foundation of China. Currently he is responsible for the System Platform for Scientific Database of CAS, a key project of the CAS 10th five-year Informatisation Program, and co-lead of Scientific Data Grid, a project of the 863 Program.

Suhaimi Napis is a Director at InfoComm Development Centre (iDEC) and a Director of E-Research of MYREN. Suhaimi Napis is involved in GRID and Bioinformatics Roadmap for Malaysia and involved in Asia Pacific Advanced Network for 10 years and currently the Director of Natural Resource Area.

Salwa Nassar is Head of the HPC team of the Egyptian National Authority of Remote Sensing & Space Sciences. She is also Head of the Computer & Systems Department and the Grid & HPC technologies group of the Egyptian Electronics Research Institute.

Francis Xavier Ochieng works as a Lecturer and Research Fellow at the Institute of Energy and Environmental Technology (IEET) of the Jomo Kenyatta University of Agriculture and Technology (JKUAT). His main areas of expertise are the Technical, economical, Numerical Modelling and simulation of renewable energy systems and resources. He has over 12 years experience in this field and is moving into the utilisation of grid computing in Numerical modelling and simulation of Renewable energy systems and resources. He holds a BSc (Appropriate Technology) from Kenyatta University in Kenya, an MSc (Renewable Energy) from University of Oldenburg, Germany and is currently finishing his PhD (Wind Energy) in a sandwich programme between JKUAT and University of Oldenburg. His work experience spans both local and international firms like German Wind Energy Institute (DEWI) in Germany, Pico Energy (UK), Action Aid International – Regional office for Africa, Practical Action Eastern Africa, GTZ and ADRA Somalia among others. In addition, he runs his own consultancy firms (www.energiekonsult.com) which deals not only with renewable Energy systems, resource assessment, Numerical and grid computing, but also is involved in a lot of related research and consultancies.

Marco Paganoni graduated in Physics "cum laude" at the University of Milan in 1990 and since 1994 he holds a PhD in Physics from the same university. He is currently Associated Professor at the Department of Physics of the University of Milano-Bicocca. He has contributed to the construction of the electromagnetic calorimeters and the exploitation of the physics potentials of both DELPHI and CMS experiments at CERN. Since 2004, he is coordinating the INFN effort for the CMS computing, based on the Grid paradigm. He has lead the EUAsiaGrid project, funded in the frame of the European Commission VII Framework Program and aimed at promoting the uptake of e-Infrastructures in the Asia-Pacific region. He is co-author of more than 300 publications in the domains of Particle Physics and ICT.

Florin Pop is Assistant Professor of the Computer Science and Engineering Department of the University Politehnica of Bucharest (UPB). His research interests are oriented to: Scheduling in Distributes Systems, Predictive Systems, Intelligent Optimization Techniques, Electronic Services and Standards, and Communication Protocols. He received his PhD in Computer Science in 2008 with "Magna cum laude" distinction. He has received an IBM PhD Assistantship in 2006 (top ranked 1st in CEMA out from 17 awarded students) and a PhD Excellency grant from Oracle in 2006-2008. He is member of RoGrid consortium and participates in several research projects (national and international), in collaboration with other universities and research centers from Romania and from abroad.

Vassiliki Pouli is a research assistant at the Computer Science Division of the Electrical & Computer Engineering Department of NTUA (NETMODE laboratory). She received the diploma in electrical and computer engineering at the National Technical University of Athens in 2005. Since 2005, she has been a teaching assistant in the course "Network Management and Intelligent Networks" of the last semester of the Department of Electrical and Computer Engineering, National Technical University of Athens. She has been involved in numerous European research projects (e.g. GRIDCC, HELLASGRID, ARGUGRID, GN2 / 3, EGEE) conducting research to resolve various issues concerning the design and development of architectures, ensuring quality of service applications and security of systems. Her main research interests are in networking, security, service level agreements, trust and negotiation of agents.

Ognjen Prnjat works at the Greek Research and Technology Network, coordinating European Commission-funded HP-SEE (High-Performance Computing Infrastructure for South East Europe's Research Communities), and SEERAEI (South East European Research Area for eInfrastructures) projects. He was previously coordinator of SEE-GRID series of projects, which dealt with setting up Grid infrastructure in the region; and for 6 years the Regional Operations Centre manager for "Enabling Grids for e-Science in Europe" project. In these roles, he is responsible for organizing various aspects of scientific computing in the region, and its sustainability and integration in pan-European eScience trends. With SEERA-EI, his work branches into programme management and policy work in eInfrastructures. Previously Ognjen was in University College London, where as a Research Fellow he led technical and project management aspects of a number of EC ACTS/IST and UK EPSRC projects in diverse fields of computing and telecoms; as well as teaching at MSc level. He holds Bachelor of Eng. Degree in Electronics and Electrical Eng. from University of Surrey; and MSc and PhD in telecommunications from University College London, UK.

Antonio Puliafito is a full professor of computer engineering at the University of Messina, Italy. His interests include parallel and distributed systems, networking, wireless, and GRID computing. He was a referee for the European Community for the projects of the 4th, 5th, 6th, and 7th Framework Program. He has contributed to the development of the software tools WebSPN, MAP, and ArgoPerformance. He is a coauthor (with R. Sahner and K.S. Trivedi) of the text Performance and Reliability Analysis of Computer Systems: An Example-Based Approach Using the SHARPE Software Package (Kluwer

Academic Publishers). He is the vice president of Consorzio Cometa, which is currently managing the Sicilian grid infrastructure. He is a member of the IEEE and the IEEE Computer Society.

Depei Qian is professor at the Beihang University, director of Sino-German Joint Software Institute. Since 1996 he has been involved in the activities of the expert group for the National High-tech Research & Development Program (the 863 program). He was the chief scientist for the 863 key project on high performance computer and core software. Currently, he is the chief scientist of the 863 key project on high productivity computer and Grid service environment. He has been working on computer architecture and computer networks for many years. His current research interests include high performance computer architecture and implementation technology, grid computing, distributed systems, network management and network performance measurement. He has published more than 100 papers in journals and conferences.

Sijin Qian is a collaborator at European Organization for Nuclear Research (CERN) (Switzerland). Since 1994, he is involved in the software development, the detector construction and the physics analysis of CMS experiment on LHC at CERN. In the years 2006-2008, he acts as the PKU group leader and in charge of the Activity-5.1 (Project dissemination activity) in the EUChinaGRID project; he also organized the construction and operation of CN-Beijing-PKU Tier-3 Grid site in PKU.

Mario Reale graduated in High Energy Physics in 1992 at the second university of Rome, Tor Vergata. He then got a PhD in High Energy Physics from the University of Wuppertal, Germany, discussing a thesis on the fragmentation of heavy and light quarks into hadrons in hadronic Z decays, within the framework of the DELPHI experiment at LEP, CERN, Geneva, Switzerland. He worked for 4 years in industry, both in Rome and Turin, Italy, as a control and software engineer. (CRF, Orbassano (TO), Etnoteam Spa (Rome). He joined the DataGRID project in September 2001, working for the CNAF centre of INFN, working in WorkPackage 8 (High Energy Physics Applications) as an experiment-independent tester. He also joined the Integration Team and led the INFN DataGrid testing team. He then joined the EGEE project working at CERN (2004-2006). From 2006 till today he has been working at the Italian Academic and Research network (GARR, Rome), on the task in charge of ensuring and testing the IPv6 compliance of the gLite EGEE middleware, and he is currently technical coordinator of the EUMEDGRID-Support project.

Mohamed El-Refaey is one of the cloud computing thought-leaders. He has over 11 years of experience in leadership positions with established public companies and startups, with high profile and diverse experience in software design and development in e-commerce, BPM, EAI, Web 2.0, Banking applications, financial market, Java and J2EE, HIPAA, SOX, BPEL, SOA, Linux Server Security hardening and cloud security, and late four years with the focus on virtualization technology and cloud computing. He promotes for Cloud Computing topics nationally in conferences, focus groups, and research activities, and internationally in technical papers, books contribution, and international groups working in the field. He holds an MSc degree in computer science, in performance evaluation and workload characterization in the cloud and virtualized environment. He has been awarded in recognition of innovation and thought leadership while working as an IT Specialist at EDS (HP now). He worked in several positions in software architecture, research and development; He has a very good hands-on experience in implementing private cloud systems, with many success stories in reducing the cost and improving the manageability of his company's internal and production systems. He is also a co-author in the Wiley book about cloud, Cloud Computing, Principals and Paradigm. He is also leading the Cloud Security Alliance, Egypt Chapter activities. Mohamed can be found working in his current start-up EgyptCloud Technologies, where he orchestrates the vision of cloud computing products and services.

Bhaskar Prasad Rimal is Cloud Computing researcher and Cloud advocate. He received BEng (IT) from Pokhara University, Nepal and his MSc (Information Systems) from Kookmin University, Korea under Korean Government fellowship. His research interests are in the area of Distributed Systems. In particular, his research emphasizes practical and theoretical aspects of scheduling and resource management problems in Cloud Computing and Grid Computing. He is the author and co-author of more than 10 scientific publications.

Edgar Eduardo Rosales Rosero is a solution architect consultant in the Research Center of the School of Engineering at Universidad de los Andes, Colombia. He received a Masters in Engineering (MSc) in Computer Science from the Universidad de los Andes, in 2010. Since 2008, he has been participating in the COMIT (Communications and Information Technology) research group, as research assistant. Particularly, he worked in the analysis, design, testing and implementation of the UnaCloud project through his master thesis. He is also developing a technology infrastructure project for a governmental institution. His research interests include cluster, grid and cloud computing especially in terms of opportunistic models, virtualization, desktop grids and volunteer computing systems.

Federico Ruggieri is an INFN Senior Physicist and Director of Research. He spent most of his professional life working on On-Line and Off-line Computing Systems for High Energy Physics experiments at CERN and at Frascati, INFN National Laboratory. He promoted the first GRID project approved and funded by the European Commission: DataGRID. He played an important role in the development of the Networks for Research in Italy and GARR the National Research and Academic Network. From 2006 to 2008, he led two projects co-funded by the European Commission VI Framework Program EUChinaGRID and EUMEDGRID and he is presently the coordinator of EUMEDGRID-Support project. Since 2005, he has been a professor of Data Acquisition and Control of Experiments in the Laurea Magistrale in Physics of the University of Roma TRE. Dr. Ruggieri has a list of more than 340 articles and publications in the domains of Physics, Data Acquisition and ICT.

Marco Scarpa received the degree in computer engineering in 1994 from the University of Catania, Italy, and the PhD degree in computer science in 2000 from the University of Turin, Italy. He is currently an associate professor in performance evaluation at Messina University. He coordinated the development of the software package WebSPN, a tool to solve stochastic Petri nets with nonexponentially distributed firing time transitions. His interests include performance and reliability modeling of distributed and real-time systems, phase type distributions, distributed systems, and software performance evaluation techniques. He has been involved in several research projects.

Cevat Şener received his BS, MS and PhD degrees in Computer Engineering at the Middle East Technical University (METU). After working in the industry, he moved to the same department as a research assistant where he has continued his career as an instructor. He had been a visiting researcher at SZTAKI in Hungary and at Queen Mary and Westfield College in UK. His main areas of interest are high-performance computing, distributed systems and computer networks. Dr. Şener represented METU academically in TR-Grid Initiative. He has supported gridification of various applications from numerous disciplines and also led the User Support Activities WP in the SEE-GRID-SCI FP7 project.

Mehdi Sheikhalishahi is currently a PhD student in Computer Science at the University of Calabria in Italy working on critical trends in Cloud Computing, more specifically Mehdi's PhD thesis is about Energy Efficient computing in Infrastructure-as-a-Service cloud model. In addition, Mehdi's major research interests lies in the fields of promising computing technologies such as High Performance Computing, Grid and Cloud Computing with theoretical consideration.

Dipak Singh is Director in ERNET and he heads network operations. He is responsible for interoperability of Indian Grid GARUDA and European Grid EGEE at the network level. He represented India in the TEIN3 activity and ERNET India in EC funded project 6CHOICE. D. Singh was the former EU-IndiaGrid Network Planning Support Work Package Manager.

Axel Tenschert studied German philology, computer sciences and text technology at the University of Bielefeld. In August 2007 he started working at the High Performance Computing Center of the University of Stuttgart as computer scientist and PhD student. Beside this, he has been involved in various national and European research projects in the area of semantic information management and distributed computing (such as grid computing and cloud computing). Additionally, he is doing research dealing with adapting semantic technologies such as ontology matching to distributed computing environments.

Yousef Torman is working as executive director of the Jordanian Universities Network (JUNet), he worked as a Computer Center Director at Jordan University of Science and Technology. Currently he is responsible for the management of Jordanian National Research and Education Network. He is a member of many national committees and initiatives that focus on research and education. The main focus of Yousef is to promote and encourage the use of technology and networks for research and education, mainly the Higher Education. His role in the project will be in the management and administration of the project, dissemination and promotion, certification and all other administrative issues.

Alex Voss is Lecturer in Software Engineering in the School of Computer Science at the University of St. Andrews. His research interest is to study how people use distributed systems and his recent work has focused on the use of grid and cloud computing technologies in research. He has a PhD in Informatics from Edinburgh University and has worked in the areas of e-Research, Software Engineering, Computer Supported Cooperative Work and Participatory Design. Through his PhD work, he has developed a practical approach to collaborative system development involving IT professionals and domain experts. Working in the setting that the system under development will be used in, developers can switch rapidly between requirements elicitation, development of iterations and testing, often within the same day. Before joining St. Andrews, he worked at the Manchester Hub of the National Centre for e-Social Science, where he studied the uptake and adoption of e-Research technologies. Alex led an e-Science Institute research theme on this topic, managed the JISC-funded Wider Uptake of e-Infrastructure

Services project and was a co-investigator on the JISC-funded e-Infrastructure Use Cases and Service Usage Models project as well as the EU FP7-funded EUAsiaGrid project. He has published over 30 papers in journals and conferences.

Reinhold Weiss received the Dipl.-Ing. and Dr.-Ing. degrees in electrical engineering and the Dr.-Ing.habil. degree in real-time systems from the Technical University of Munich, Germany, in 1968, 1972, and 1979, respectively. In 1981, he was as a visiting scientist with IBM Research Laboratories, San Jose, CA. From 1982 to 1986, he was a professor of computer engineering with the University of Paderborn, Germany. He currently is a professor of electrical engineering and the head of the Institute for Technical Informatics, Graz University of Technology, Austria, and the author or a coauthor of more than 170 publications. He is a member of the International Editorial Board of the US journal Computers and Applications, the Institute of Electrical and Electronics Engineers, the Association for Computing Machinery, Gesellschaft fór Informatik, and the Austrian Association for Electrical Engineering.

David West is a project manager at DANTE and has been responsible since its outset for the EUMEDCONNECT project which provides e-Infrastructure for research and education in the Mediterranean region since 2004. He also leads and manages regional networking programmes in Asia Pacific (TEIN3) and Central Asia (CAREN).

Colin Wright is currently Manager: Cyberinfrastructure, Meraka Institute. He has an MPhil from Imperial College and a PhD from the University of the Witwatersrand, Johannesburg, both in Numerical Analysis. Computing and Computational Science have been the focus of his research career, having published many papers in this discipline. He successfully supervised 17 Masters and 4 PhD students in the areas of Numerical Analysis and Computational Science. Colin Wright was Professor of Computational Science at the University of the Witwatersrand until his retirement in 2009. Besides playing an active academic rôle he also took on academic management positions serving as Head of the School of Computational and Applied Mathematics, Wits and Dean and subsequently Executive Dean of the Faculty of Science. He then took on the position of Head of the School of Computer Science. He has contributed significantly to University and national Cyberinfrastructure strategy formulation and management.

Index

T

U

V

W

X